Child Poverty and Deprivation in the
Industrialized Countries,
1945–1995

Child Poverty and Deprivation in the Industrialized Countries, 1945–1995

Edited by

GIOVANNI ANDREA CORNIA

AND

SHELDON DANZIGER

CLARENDON PRESS · OXFORD
1997

Oxford University Press, Great Clarendon Street, Oxford OX2 6DP
Oxford New York
Athens Auckland Bangkok Bogota Bombay
Buenos Aires Calcutta Cape Town Dar es Salaam
Delhi Florence Hong Kong Istanbul Karachi
Kuala Lumpur Madras Madrid Melbourne
Mexico City Nairobi Paris Singapore
Taipei Tokyo Toronto Warsaw
and associated companies in
Berlin Ibadan

Oxford is a trade mark of Oxford University Press

Published in the United States by
Oxford University Press Inc., New York

British Library Cataloguing in Publication Data
Data available

Library of Congress Cataloging in Publication Data
Child poverty and deprivation in the industrialized countries,
1945–1995 / edited by Giovanni Andrea Cornia and Sheldon Danziger.
Includes bibliographical references (p.   ) and index.
1. Poor children—History—20th century. 2. Poverty—History—20th century.
I. Cornia, Giovanni Andrea. II. Danziger, Sheldon.
HV713.C3826 1997 96-36784
362.7'09172'2—dc20
ISBN 0-19-829075-6

1 3 5 7 9 10 8 6 4 2

Typeset by Best-set Typesetter Ltd., Hong Kong
Printed in Great Britain by
Biddles Ltd, Guildford & King's Lynn.

To our children,
Marco, Jacob, and Anna

ACKNOWLEDGEMENTS

It is only with the generous support, assistance, and involvement of many people that a book of this scope can see the light of day. A particular thanks goes first of all to the authors, who not only gave their time, energy, and ideas to writing the individual chapters, but also rigorously updated their contributions as new data came to hand.

The ongoing interest and support of many colleagues in UNICEF provided vital intellectual sustenance throughout this project. The commitment and dedication to improving children's lives of the late James P. Grant, UNICEF Executive Director, has been and will remain a source of inspiration. Richard Jolly, former UNICEF Deputy Executive Director, also deserves a special word of thanks for his many suggestions when the structure of this book was being developed. Thanks also go to Alexander Zouev, Rudolph Hoffman, John Donahue, Dr Nyi Nyi, Karl Eric Knutsson, and to colleagues in the Geneva UNICEF office for their suggestions and criticisms at various stages of the writing of this book. The Italian, UK, Portugal, and German National Committees for UNICEF also provided valuable assistance and support in gathering information.

Colleagues in other organizations and academic institutions also provided valuable inputs, suggestions, and criticisms during the initial phase of the project. Special thanks are extended to Barbara Boyle Torrey, Szusza Ferge of the Institute of Sociology and Social Policy of Eotvos Lorand University, Budapest, Olga Remenets of the Russian Goskomstat, Sándor Sipos of the World Bank, Peter Townsend of the University of Essex, and Helmut Wintersberger.

All those involved in the production of this book at the UNICEF International Child Development Centre, Florence, Italy, are gratefully acknowledged. Cinzia Iusco-Bruschi provided untiring and efficient secretarial support. Patrizia Faustini, Renato Paniccià, and Enrico Sborgi gathered and elaborated vital documentation. Finally, a special thanks is extended to Anny Bremner who edited the text and prepared it for publication.

None of the people or organizations mentioned, however, is responsible for the views expressed in this book or for any errors that may have remained.

Giovanni Andrea Cornia
Sheldon Danziger

CONTENTS

NOTES ON THE CONTRIBUTORS

ANDREA BOLTHO is Fellow and Tutor in Economics at Magdalen College, University of Oxford. He has also held visiting professorships at the Collège d'Europe, Bruges, the International University of Japan, the Bologna Centre of the Johns Hopkins University, and at the Universities of Venice, Paris, and Turin. In addition to numerous academic articles, his publications include *Foreign Trade Criteria in Socialist Economies* (1971), *Japan—An Economic Survey* (1975), and *The European Economy: Growth and Crisis* (ed.) (1982).

JONATHAN BRADSHAW is Professor of Social Policy at the University of York, England. He is Director of the Institute for Research in the Social Sciences and Associate Director of the Social Policy Research Unit as well as co-ordinator of the EU Observatory on National Family Policies. His main research concerns are poverty and living standards, family policy, and social security policy. Recent publications include *Lone Parent Families in the UK* (1990, with Millar), *Support for Children: A Comparison of Arrangements in Fifteen Countries* (1993, with Ditch *et al.*), and *Social Assistance Schemes in the OECD Countries* (1996, with Eardley *et al.*).

GIOVANNI ANDREA CORNIA is Director of the World Institute for Development Economics Research, Helsinki. Prior to this, he was Director of the Economic and Social Policies Research Programme at the UNICEF ICDC, Florence, Italy. He has held other positions in UNICEF, with UNCTAD, the UNECE, and the Economic Studies Centre of FIAT. He has written extensively on economic and social policies in developing and transitional economies. He has co-authored and co-edited several books, including *From Adjustment to Development in Africa: Conflict, Controversy, Convergence, Consensus?* (1994, with G. K. Helleiner), *Children and the Transition to the Market Economy: Safety Nets and Social Policies in Central and Eastern Europe* (1991, with S. Sipos), and *Adjustment with a Human Face* (1987, with R. Jolly and F. Stewart).

SANDRA KLEIN DANZIGER is Associate Professor of Social Work and Project Director of the Michigan Program on Poverty and Social Welfare Policy at the University of Michigan. Her research interests include the causes and consequences of adolescent pregnancy and parenthood and the effects of welfare programmes on child and family well-being.

SHELDON DANZIGER is Professor of Social Work and Public Policy, Faculty Associate in Population Studies and Director of the Research and Training Program on Poverty, the Underclass and Public Policy at the University of Michigan. He is the co-author of *America Unequal* (1995) and co-editor of *Confronting Poverty: Prescriptions for Change* (1994) and *Uneven Tides: Rising Inequality in America* (1993). Before joining the University of Michigan, he was Director of the Institute for Research on Poverty at the University of Wisconsin.

GASPAR FAJTH is an economist-statistician working on the Economic and Social Policies Programme of the UNICEF International Child Development Centre, Florence, Italy. Prior to joining UNICEF, he was Director of the Department of Standard of Living and Human Resources Statistics of the Hungarian Central Statistical Office. His research interests are in the fields of consumer price statistics, macro- and micro-economic welfare indicators, labour and social assistance issues, and family support policies. He has contributed to several journals and books on these topics.

ALFRED J. KAHN is Professor Emeritus at the Columbia University School of Social Work. He is also Co-director of the Cross-National Studies Research Program. Together with Sheila Kamerman, he has authored and edited numerous books and articles in the fields of comparative child and family policy, child care, parental leave, income transfers, and personal social services. Their most recent publication is *Starting Right: How America Neglects Its Youngest Children and What We Can Do About It* (1995).

SHEILA B. KAMERMAN is Professor at the Columbia University School of Social Work and Co-director of the Cross-National Studies Research Program. She is the co-author and co-editor of many books and articles on comparative child and family policy, child care, parental leave, income transfers, and personal social services. Her most recent publication is *Starting Right: How America Neglects Its Youngest Children and What We Can Do About It* (1995, with Alfred J. Kahn).

SHIGEMI KONO is currently Professor of Demography at Reitaku University, Japan. He previously held the position of Director-General of the National Institute of Population Problems, Ministry of Health and Welfare, Japan, and was Chief of Estimates and Projections Section, Population Division, United Nations, 1967–78. His research lies in the areas of population theories and demography of fertility and ageing. His publications include *The Population of the World* (1986).

Sᴠᴇɴ E. Oʟssᴏɴ Hᴏʀᴛ teaches sociology at Stockholm University, Sweden. He is the author of *Social Policy and the Welfare State in Sweden* (1993) and co-editor of *Scandinavia in a New Europe* (1994, with T. P. Boje).

Mᴀʀᴛʜᴀ N. Oᴢᴀᴡᴀ is the Bettie Bofinger Brown Professor of Social Policy at Washington University, St Louis, Missouri. She has written extensively on social policy, child and family welfare, and social security, including *Women's Life Cycle: Shotoku Hoshou no Nichibei Hikaku* (Women's Life Cycle: A Japan-U.S. Comparison in Income Maintenance) (1992, with S. Kimura and H. Ibe), *Women's Life Cycle and Economic Insecurity: Problems and Proposals* (1989), and *Income Maintenance and Work Incentives: Toward a Synthesis* (1982).

Lᴇᴇ Rᴀɪɴᴡᴀᴛᴇʀ is Research Director of the Luxembourg Income Study and Professor of Sociology, Emeritus, Harvard University. His research has centred on comparative studies of social stratification and social policy: he co-authored *Public/Private Interplay in Social Protection, Income Packaging in the Welfare State*, and the recently published OECD volume on *Income Distribution in OECD Countries*.

Cʜɪᴀʀᴀ Sᴀʀᴀᴄᴇɴᴏ is Professor of Family Sociology at the University of Turin, Italy. In addition to acting as Italian expert in the EU Observatory on Policies to Combat Social Exclusion, she is member of the Italian Poverty Commission. She has published extensively on the family, social policies, and gender, including *Sociologia della famiglia* (1988), *Età e corso della vita* (1986), and *Le politiche contro la povertà in Italia* (1996, with N. Negri).

Mᴀɴᴜᴇʟᴀ Sɪʟᴠᴀ is currently engaged as an economist with CESIS (Centro de Estudios para a Intervenao social) in Lisbon, Portugal. A former Professor of Social Policy at the High School of Economics and Management at the Technical University of Lisbon, she also served on the Consultative Committee of the EEC for the Third Programme against Social Exclusion. She is the author of several studies on poverty, income distribution, economic and social policy, and planning.

Tɪᴍᴏᴛʜʏ M. Sᴍᴇᴇᴅɪɴɢ Is Professor of Economics and Public Administration at the Maxwell School of Citizenship and Public Affairs, Syracuse University, USA, and Director of Maxwells' Center for Policy Research. He is also the Overall Project Director of the Luxembourg Income Study project which he founded in 1983. During 1994–5, he was a Fellow at the Center for Advanced Study in the Behavioral Sciences at Stanford University. Professor Smeeding has written extensively on child poverty and is an active participant in several organizations involved in cross-disciplinary research on vulnerable groups.

JONATHAN STERN is a doctoral candidate in Social Work and Sociology at the University of Michigan.

TATIANA ZIMAKOVA is Project Manager of the Russian NGO Social Sector Support Project of the National Association of Social Workers. She is also affiliated with the Russian Academy of Sciences Institute of International Economic and Political Studies. She has acted as consultant for UNICEF, International Research and Exchange Board (USA), National Association of Social Workers (USA), and various Russian governmental and non-governmental organizations. She has taught social policy at the Academy of Labor and Social Relations (Moscow) and served as People's Deputy of the Moscow City Council, 1982–7.

1

Common Themes, Methodological Approach, and Main Findings

GIOVANNI ANDREA CORNIA AND SHELDON DANZIGER

The living standards and social well-being of children throughout the industrialized world improved remarkably between the end of World War II and the early 1990s. For instance, infant mortality declined over the past fifty years at a dramatically faster pace than during the interwar period, thus saving millions of children's lives. However, child welfare is now at a turning-point, most clearly in Eastern Europe but also—more subtly—in the West. While economic and social progress continues in many domains in many countries, deteriorations in the social fabric and in the social policy scaffolding have emerged. Uncertainties about the future of welfare state programmes that have helped protect children and families from the vicissitudes of the economy in the post-war period raise concerns that the beginning of the twenty-first century may represent an era of retrogression and inequality.

The chapters in this volume carefully review trends in the economy, public policies, and the family in advanced industrial countries—the market economies of the West and the formerly centrally planned, but now transitional, economies of the East. Each chapter analyses how these trends have interacted to affect child poverty, child health, and child well-being. The evidence presented supports a clear warning that, given the current radical changes in the global economic environment and in family structure, any weakening of social policies targeted on children could erode much of the progress of the past forty-five years, especially in the East, but also in the West. At a time when the world is shocked by dramatic crises that threaten the existence of millions of children, such as those of Rwanda, Somalia, and Bosnia, fears of a deterioration in child well-being in advanced economies may appear misplaced. They are not. The possibility of a serious erosion in child well-being is not remote. Indeed, several chapters in this volume document large increases in poverty and declines in well-being over the past decade.

1.1. Scope and Historical Context

This volume, unlike most cross-national studies which analyse only Western democracies (e.g. McFate, Lawson, and Wilson, 1994) or only the formerly centrally planned economies of Central and Eastern Europe (e.g. UNICEF ICDC, 1993, 1994, 1995; Barr, 1994), uses a common framework to analyse data on trends in the welfare of children in industrialized countries of Eastern and Western Europe, Oceania, Japan, and North America. Its primary contributions are as follows.

First, it provides an initial examination of how economic and social policy changes since the fall of the Berlin wall have affected child welfare conditions. The chapters suggest that the collapse of the communist system has already had and will continue to have important 'systemic effects' not only on countries still in the midst of transition to a market economy, but also in Western market economies and many developing countries (Sub-Saharan Africa, in particular). Though the end of communist control was desirable and beneficial in political terms, it has caused a painful recession and social crisis in Eastern Europe (EE) and the countries of the former Soviet Union (FSU) which have lowered living standards, increased inequality, and affected children more negatively than other groups in the population.

In the advanced economies of the West, the overall impact of these events remains unclear as their ramifications are still working themselves through the international economic and political systems. None the less, the collapse of communism has already contributed to major changes—political system changes (as in Italy), recessionary trade shocks (as in countries such as Finland that were heavily dependent on trade with the socialist bloc), frictional unemployment increases associated with reductions in military expenditure (as in California, where large reductions in defence contracting and military personnel occurred), and huge fiscal efforts entailing increased taxes and declining real wages (as in Germany, where huge subsidies had to be channelled to the former GDR and to support large numbers of migrants and economic and political refugees from beyond the former 'iron curtain'). Besides Germany, many other Western European countries have experienced sizeable inflows of legal and illegal migrants from Eastern Europe.

The fall of communism, in addition to these direct economic and political effects, has also undermined public support for governments in general and social policies in particular. Critics of the 'social welfare state' have equated it ideologically with the 'failed socialist state' and have challenged the credibility of policies which rely on the state, rather than the market, to promote social needs. The chapters in this volume do not defend the *status quo*. Indeed, some suggest ways in which the welfare state in some countries might become more market-oriented. None the less, the sharp decline in well-being in the East following the demise of communism demonstrates that market mechanisms cannot, on their own, ensure child welfare. The second main contribution of this volume is to link the analysis of major economic trends—for example, the globalization of the economy, labour-saving technological change—with an analysis of the effects of social policies on families and children. Economic analyses tend to focus primarily on labour market outcomes. Yet the chapters in this volume suggest that labour market changes also increase the demand for social welfare spending, affect governments' range of policy alternatives, contribute to changes in marital stability, and thus both directly and indirectly affect child well-being. For instance, globalization and trade liberalization may reduce wages and employment in high-wage countries and, hence, the government's ability to react to economic shocks. In a closed economy, one might respond to higher unemployment by raising payroll taxes to fund higher unemployment benefits. But in an open economy, such a tax increase would raise prices, further disadvantaging the country's international competitiveness, and causing additional reductions in employment. Falling wages and higher unemployment might also create added strains on marital stability, thereby increasing child poverty. Of course, in low-wage countries, the effects of globalization on child poverty might be quite positive, as increased employment and wages would directly improve children's standard of living, while also raising public revenue available for social programmes.

Third, the chapters confirm that in many industrialized countries long-standing trends in divorce and lone parenthood, fertility, and out-of-wedlock child-bearing are accelerating. Problems of family structure and stability are particularly ominous for child well-being in the transitional economies. Changes in family structure and stability have larger effects on the welfare of children in an environment of slow growth, rising inequality, and reduced social spending than was the case in the post-World War II era when growth was rapid and the welfare state was expanding. The chapters point to a general absence of new approaches—beyond the traditional ones advanced by the conservative right—for addressing family problems. In most countries, progressive forces have not organized a public policy response because they perceive the family as a predominantly private domain. Consequently, family-related problems have reached epidemic proportions in some countries.

Fourth, common problems of child well-being are examined within a consistent methodological framework for both the market and transitional economies. This common framework reveals striking similarities among all industrialized economies in terms of economic performance, changes in family structure, policies promoting social protection, and child welfare outcomes for the first four post-war decades. The major divergence between East and West emerges only after the shift away from communism towards the market.

1.2. Methodology and Hypotheses

1.2.1. *Representative sample of countries*

To explore the hypotheses detailed below, the chapters in this volume analyse the same child welfare indicators across Western and Eastern industrialized countries. We selected seven prototypical countries for our in-depth case-studies: Russia, USA, UK, Portugal, Italy, Sweden, and Japan. This range of countries represents the main areas of the developed world (to reflect differences in cultural approaches), country size (both small and large), income levels (to capture the influence of resource availability on child welfare), prototypes of welfare state (to account for different orientations towards economic and social policies), and child welfare levels (broadly varying poverty rates, infant mortality rates, and educational attainments). For each country, changes in child well-being since the end of World War II are examined in a standard manner.

1.2.2. *Analysis of specific hypotheses and periodization*

The book examines the current and projected evolution of child well-being in a historical context. While child well-being in all advanced economies in 1995 is far superior to what it was in 1945, the chapters distinguish three distinct subperiods in both the East and the West, each with specific hypotheses concerning child well-being.

The first hypothesis is that during the 'golden age' (from the end of World War II until about the first oil price shock of 1973) economic growth was rapid, the welfare state expanded, and the living conditions of children—material and physical—improved dramatically across all income classes and population groups. A sub-hypothesis is that progress in non-economic indicators of child deprivation (such as IMR and educational attainment) was faster than that in income-based indicators during this period. Even though most determinants of child welfare contributed positively, a second sub-hypothesis argues that a primary source of the reduced deprivation was the rapid reconstruction/development of universal health, education, and social security systems by the welfare state (Gordon, 1988) made possible in an economic environment in which the public expected the state to intervene to correct market failures and in which rapid economic growth produced rising government revenues.

The second hypothesis is that this period was followed by an 'era of stagnation' (from the early 1970s until the end of the 1980s) characterized by a slow-down in the rates of economic growth and social spending

growth on children and families, and much slower improvement in indicators of child well-being. A sub-hypothesis is that a divergence in the rate
of welfare progress emerged across countries and by different types of
welfare indicators. The book examines whether 'new forms of poverty
and deprivation' (including early out-of-wedlock child-bearing, youth
unemployment, and drug abuse) have been widespread in the East as well
as the West and whether their influence on child welfare has been as
pernicious as is often claimed. The book also explores the effects of
changes in economic performance on traditional measures of poverty
(those associated with low wages or unemployment), and whether inequalities which had narrowed during the 'golden age' widened (by
country, region, race, gender, and social class).

The third hypothesis is that we are in the midst of a 'post-Cold War era'.
This period, which began at the close of the 1980s, will dramatically affect
child well-being in the former centrally planned economies and, together
with technological change and trade liberalization, is influencing child
well-being in the West in ways that have only been partially documented
and are even less understood. The transition to the market economy has
contributed to a dramatic demographic revolution in the East and has
reshaped the organization of society as well as having obvious effects on
the functioning of the labour market and the level and distribution of
living standards. This appears to be a period of rising instability, with
increased inequality among population groups. In the East, it points to
retrogression, and in the West, retrenchment of the welfare state.

1.2.3. Common set of determinants of child outcomes

Each chapter considers three main factors that have affected child outcomes, positively or negatively, in the industrialized countries of the East
and the West. These include economic changes—the rate of growth of
output, unemployment rates, and the organization of economic institutions; demographic changes—rates of marriage and divorce, fertility,
out-of-wedlock child-bearing, and lone parenthood; and public policy
changes—labour market policies, income maintenance policies, the provision of health and educational services. Although analysis emphasizes
how each of the economic, demographic, and public policy factors influences child outcomes, the authors recognize that these factors are not
independent; i.e. changing rates of economic growth can lead to increased
or decreased expenditure on behalf of children or to increases or decreases
in the percentage of children living in lone-parent families.

1.2.4. Measurement of child welfare

The contributors to this volume include economists, sociologists, social
policy analysts, and poverty researchers; and a multidisciplinary perspec-

tive is applied. Traditionally, economists measure well-being (or welfare, used interchangeably throughout) in one of two ways. The most common approach, following Sen (1985), is the 'income or opulence approach', which equates well-being with an individual's income, consumption, or possession of commodities. Loss of well-being for a society's children is associated with a decline in income or consumption per capita, loss of assets, and greater indebtedness. To measure a child's poverty requires a comparison of the absolute level of one of these indicators with some normative threshold (e.g. the poverty line, the recommended daily intake of nutrients, the 'normal' value of the food share). In this case, loss of welfare is denoted by an increased number of poor, an upward shift in food shares, and so on.

This economic approach, however, can be problematic during periods of rapid structural transformations, such as those examined in this book. First, although there is a substantial correlation between income or consumption and the dimensions of well-being (i.e. life expectancy, good health, nutritional adequacy, literacy), individual differences in income or consumption account for only a small percentage of individual differences in mortality, morbidity, nutrition, literacy, etc. Other factors also influence child well-being—the human capital, health practices, and time use of family members; the size, structure, and stability of the family; and social and environmental conditions (infrastructure, epidemiological protection, and access to 'public goods' such as health, education, child care). Understanding changes in child well-being thus requires a broader approach, even though it is very difficult to measure some of these variables. The chapters herein pay special attention to family structure and stability and, wherever possible, examine these other influences on child well-being.

A second problem with the narrow economic approach is that income declines normally trigger household and collective responses, including the search for greater efficiency in expenditure, shifts in consumption structure, better targeting of public resources, rationing, migration, and so forth (Safilios-Rothschild, 1980; Cornia, 1987), which may protect children from some negative effects of income reductions. Welfare indicators sometimes even improve when household incomes decline. In the UK, for instance, mortality indicators improved more rapidly during World War II (a period of stagnant incomes and limited food supplies) than during the two preceding decades (Sen, 1995). Similarly, during the 'lost decade' of the 1980s in Latin America, IMR, life expectancy at birth, and school enrolment improved steadily even though the absolute number of the poor increased by 60 million (UNICEF ICDC, 1994; Cornia, 1994).

Third, changes in indicators based on household income or consumption may not reflect changes in child well-being because attention is generally not given to intra-household allocation. For example, in some families a decline in income might be reflected in reduced adult, but not child, food consumption. Thus, we examine non-income indicators of child deprivation and well-being, including infant mortality, child health, and school achievement, in addition to child (income) poverty.

Fourth, the meaning of income and other 'opulence indicators' differs between an economy affected by 'shortage-flation' and queuing, as in Eastern Europe and the former Soviet Union, and a market economy where true market prices and greater consumer choice exist. The same real income will yield different child outcomes under such divergent market conditions.

Finally, income is difficult to measure, especially during periods of hyperinflation, radical fluctuations in relative prices, and rapid structural economic changes such as those prevailing in most Eastern European countries. The accuracy of income and consumption statistics in these countries is subject to changing biases (including better sampling frameworks, but also growing underreporting).

For these reasons, complete reliance on economic measures to gauge children's standards of living would fail. The chapters in this volume therefore incorporate a second approach—'capabilities-based welfare indicators'. Such indicators emphasize variations in the capabilities of individuals to function: their ability to have a long and healthy life, to be well-nourished, literate, safe, and so on. This approach focuses not so much on the 'means' (i.e. income, wealth), but the 'ends' (quality and quantity of life), the achievement of which depends not only on control over monetary resources but also on the other family and societal factors mentioned above. The chapters present information on a variety of demographic, health, education, and other outcomes.

In some countries and in some time-periods these two types of indicators provide discordant evaluations of the level and trend in child well-being. They are highly correlated when the determinants of child outcomes are swiftly moving in the same direction. For example, during the 'golden age' when both economic growth and public spending growth were rapid, child poverty and child deprivation indicators improved rapidly. Similarly, during the transition to the market economy in the Eastern countries, drops in the real standard of living were so great that income-based and capabilities-based indicators of child well-being both declined dramatically. In other cases, the indicators moved in opposite directions, thus raising interpretive issues regarding appropriate policy responses.

1.3. Main Findings

In spite of the difficulties involved in gathering comparable data over time and across countries, several broad conclusions emerge from the national case-studies and the cross-national thematic chapters. The findings of the book can be summarized in ten main points.

1.3.1. *Common trends in growth, income distribution, and social policy between 1945 and 1989*

A surprising finding of this book is that, despite different institutional and ideological frameworks, initial conditions, resource endowments, development levels, and policy approaches, the industrialized market economies of the West and the centrally planned economies of the East experienced broadly similar economic, public expenditure, and income distribution trends between 1945 and 1989. Such a high degree of convergence has rarely been observed in economic history.

Andrea Boltho (Chapter 3) documents that national output grew by almost 5 per cent per year in both the East and the West during the 'golden age'. Trends in public expenditure, not surprisingly, paralleled trends in economic growth. In market economies with a fixed tax structure, economic growth produces greater tax revenue. Thus, the rapid growth of the post-war era—as well as expansion in the tax base and moderate increases in tax rates—allowed a rapid expansion of public expenditure in general and social spending in particular. In both East and West, two major macroeconomic events affected child well-being in the years following the oil shock of 1973. First, Boltho describes how, over the 1970s and 1980s, the rate of growth substantially slowed (to 2–3 per cent per annum) and, second, that this slow growth yielded less public revenue at a time when the needs of children required greater public expenditure. Since the early 1970s, increased public spending has tended to be financed by increased public debt. Governments, for the most part, were reluctant to curtail spending or raise taxes at the pace required to match a rapidly rising expenditure. Indeed, in the 1970s, when it was hoped that the slow-down in economic growth would prove transitory, spending was not greatly affected. Only in the 1980s were significant efforts made by governments, especially in the USA and the UK, to cut back the scope of government spending and taxation. Other countries tended to allow aggregate spending to rise, but at a slower rate than previously, and attempted to restrain the growth of taxes as a percentage of GDP.

1.3.2. *Rapid progress followed by slower rates of improvement*

Overall, child well-being improved rapidly between 1945 and 1989. Giovanni Andrea Cornia (Chapter 2) describes these gains over the two subperiods, from 1945 to 1973, and from 1973 to 1989. In relative—but not absolute—terms, progress over the entire 1945–89 period was more rapid than during the preceding 200 years. During the 'golden age', improvements in economic conditions and policy attitudes were much more favourable to child well-being than in either the era of stagnation or the post-Cold War era. Gains were particularly rapid in those countries, such as Russia, Japan, Germany, and Italy, which emerged from World War II quite poor and with large war-related destructions.

Since the early 1970s, the rate of improvement in child welfare in many industrialized countries has slowed. In Eastern Europe and the former Soviet Union this slow-down evolved into stagnation and then into an overt welfare crisis as the transition overturned many earlier welfare achievements. During this period, in countries such as the USA, the UK, Ireland, and most states in Eastern Europe, child poverty rose; in these and many others, class, regional, and race differentials which had narrowed during the 'golden age' have persisted or widened. Several of the case-studies provide indications of increased problems in the areas of environment-related child morbidity (such as asthma), child abuse, emotional disturbances and psychosocial dysadaptation, and social deviance.

In Sweden, Japan, and to a lesser extent Italy, overall progress has continued since the early 1970s, though at a slower pace. In Sweden, comprehensive and active social policies, especially labour market and family policies, have compensated for the economic dislocations associated with globalization and technological change. In Japan, public support for social welfare remains relatively modest by Western European standards. None the less, an egalitarian income distribution, rapid economic growth and very strong intergenerational family ties, social cohesion and social control have ensured ongoing progress in economic indicators of child well-being.

All countries experienced not only similar economic trends and pressures on the public sector, but also similar trends in family structure. Most have experienced rising inequality in labour market incomes, but some, much more than others, have avoided significant increases in child poverty.

1.3.3. *Children have been more affected than any other group, especially the elderly*

Several national case-studies in this volume document that the risks of poverty and other forms of deprivation have grown faster, or have declined more slowly, for children than for other vulnerable groups, such as the elderly. In a number of countries, especially the USA, these risks are even higher for children in single-parent and socially unstable families, for children of the long-term unemployed, those engaged in precarious and low-paying jobs, and migrants, as well as for children living in backward areas and inner cities.

Giovanni Andrea Cornia (in Chapters 2 and 13) provides additional evidence that children suffered disproportionately in Eastern Europe during the 1973–89 period and even more during the transition to the market economy. Between the mid-1970s and the late 1980s, poverty rose faster among children than for any other group in countries as different as Ireland, Poland, and the USA. Chapter 13 illustrates that, contrary to the widespread perception that the aged have been the main victims of the transition in Eastern Europe, children have been most affected (except in the case of mortality, which has increased most severely among middle-aged males). These results are mainly due to the surge in unemployment and its duration, together with shrinking unemployment benefits; the increased number of people working at low wages or who receive remuneration only after long delays; and the better indexation of pensions relative to wages, child allowances, unemployment benefits, and social assistance.

Portugal provides an exception to this general rule. Manuela Silva (Chapter 9) describes dramatic changes in Portugal's experience. Despite very rapid economic growth, it remains one of the poorest countries in the European Community. Portugal differs from the other case-studies in that child poverty is about the same as that for all persons—quite high. This reflects the fact that the social security system that has been so effective in reducing poverty among the elderly in other advanced countries is lacking here.

1.3.4. Growing performance divergence among countries and country reranking

The case-studies and Chapter 2 suggest that during the 'golden age' the rates of progress in child welfare were similar among countries and social groups. Since the mid-1970s, however, rates of improvement have diverged across countries and regions. For most child welfare indicators, this has meant shifts in the ranking of countries and regions. For instance, in 1960, the USA, Czechoslovakia, and Japan ranked tenth, twelfth, and sixteenth respectively for the under-5 mortality rate (U5MR). By 1989, Japan had jumped to first place (gaining fifteen positions), while the USA and Czechoslovakia had respectively fallen to the twentieth and twenty-fifth places (Sipos, 1991).

For different reasons, two countries where stagnation in child well-being has been most evident are the USA and the former Soviet Union. Although there are many causes for these trends, large and sustained military expenditures in periods of slow growth displaced spending that other countries used for social programmes targeted on children.

Sheldon Danziger, Sandra Danziger, and Jonathan Stern (Chapter 7) analyse this retrogression for the USA and examine the American paradox of 'poverty amidst plenty'. The USA emerged from World War II as the richest nation and the one whose children—together with Scandinavian children—fared better than those of any other nation in terms of standard of living, child health, and so on. During the twenty-five years following World War II, economic growth was rapid and widely shared, and though other countries grew faster, American living standards remained at the top. At the same time, the welfare state expanded rapidly. The period since 1973, however, has been a very difficult one for American children. Growth in living standards stalled, marital instability and out-of-wedlock child-bearing soared, the welfare state was trimmed, public expenditures on the defence sector increased during the Reagan years, and income tax became less progressive. As a result, already large gaps between rich and poor children, white and black children, two-parent and one-parent families widened even more.

As in other English-speaking countries, including the UK, Ireland, Canada, and Australia, child poverty and inequality increased in the USA. Poverty among American children is greater than in other Western European countries with similar levels of per capita income. Large numbers of children do not have medical insurance, and living conditions have become harsher in the inner cities. America remained one of the wealthiest nations, but on many indicators of child well-being it lagged well behind its industrial competitors and even some of the emerging nations. For instance, in 1994, infant mortality rate (IMR) was 6.5 per 1,000 in Slovenia (which is still in the midst of transition to the market economy) and 7.9 per 1,000 in the USA where, more than in any other country, people rely on market forces rather than the public sector for their basic health and education needs.

Jonathan Bradshaw (Chapter 8) analyses the effect on children of the UK's long-term slide in its standard of living relative to those of other European nations. The rate of growth in GDP in the UK was much lower than that in the other OECD countries between the early 1950s and the mid-1980s. Only during the 1984–94 decade was its growth rate roughly the same as the OECD average. While the last decade has been brighter in terms of economic growth, it has been a difficult one for children. Child poverty and inequality have increased more in the UK than in most other Western countries, with the exception of the USA, due in part to a retrenchment of the welfare state.

Giovanni Andrea Cornia (Chapter 6) documents the Russian roller-coaster—enormous improvements in most dimensions of child well-being during the reconstruction following World War II, stagnation during the period from the early 1970s to the late 1980s, and then a drastic reduction in living standards as the transition from communism brought precipitous falls in output and living standards and dramatic increases in poverty and mortality. At around 18 per 1,000, IMR in 1994 was no lower than at the end of the 1970s.

Evidence of growing divergence in social indicators was very pronounced after 1989. Overall, the divergence was the greatest between the former socialist countries and the OECD group, but is also surprisingly large within the former. For instance, over 1989–94, the crude death rate (CDR) declined in Central Europe, rose moderately in the Caucasus and South-eastern Europe, and escalated sharply in the Baltic and Slavic Republics of the former Soviet Union. As a result, the standard deviation of the distribution of CDR rose by 40 per cent in only five years. From most perspectives—child welfare, economic performance, social protection, institutional efficiency—the former socialist bloc has splintered into very different components. How far can this process go without causing negative reactions is an open question.

In Japan, Sweden, and Italy social progress has continued more or less unaffected since the early 1970s. Chiara Saraceno (Chapter 10) documents dramatic improvements in child well-being in Italy over the past forty-five years after the country emerged from World War II with high unemployment, poverty, infant mortality, and illiteracy. By the 1990s, Italy's living standard was above that of the UK and its poverty and infant mortality rates were below those of the USA. Publicly funded health care and educational services, from preschool onwards, were widely available. Sven Olsson Hort (Chapter 11) describes the steady evolution of Sweden's 'model welfare state'. There has been no major reversal in basic indicators of child well-being in Sweden. Compared to other countries, Sweden's children have among the lowest infant mortality and income poverty rates, the highest educational attainment, and are provided with the broadest range of public services.

1.3.5. *Growing differentiation among regions, social groups, and age-groups*

Growing cross-country differentiation in recent years has been accompanied by divergent performances within regions, social groups, races, level of education, family types, and age-groups in many countries. For example, in the USA, IMR declined to a record low of 7.9 per 1,000 live births in 1994. At the same time, the ratio of the rate for blacks to that for whites grew from 1.6 in 1950 to 2.2 in 1991. In Italy, despite considerable average progress, north–south differentials in most child indicators persist and might have increased for some, including perinatal mortality and school drop-outs. Inequalities persist in most countries between the living standards of children living in single-parent as compared to married-couple families. Even in Sweden, social class differences in various child outcomes remain, though they are not as glaring as those in other countries.

Differentials appear to have widened also among children of different ages. Infants and younger children have been better protected by the welfare state and have suffered less from labour market and institutional changes than have youth. In most countries, problems of delinquency, early out-of-wedlock births, and drug abuse have increased.

1.3.6. *Different types of indicators show different rates of progress*

In most cases, progress in 'basic capabilities' (child survival and initial development, as measured by IMR, U5MR, primary enrolment rates, and so on) has not been accompanied by gains in 'child socialization' and 'adolescent protection'. In some cases, the forces leading to improvements in one area may induce a worsening in the other. Portugal (Chapter 9) is a case in point, having made impressive gains in many non-income dimensions of child well-being. Its IMR, which in 1950 was about four times the US rate, had by the early 1990s caught up (around 8 per 1,000), primarily because increased public revenue generated by the output and exports 'boom' of the late 1970s and 1980s funded expansions of key social programmes. In contrast, even though illiteracy has been greatly reduced and educational attainment increased, their absolute levels remain respectively high and low relative to other industrialized countries. For example, the school enrolment rate for 16-year-olds has stayed at a low 40 per cent in recent years.

Meanwhile, child labour remains a serious social problem in Portugal. The rise in child labour is due to inefficiencies in the secondary education system and to an expanding underground economy. The export-led boom increased the number of small manufacturing enterprises that employ uninsured and low-paid children. Also, the emergence of the 'consumer society' during the 1980s encouraged many young people to enter the labour market at an early age. Similar examples can be found in the economies in transition. Between 1989 and 1995, despite a severe recession, Hungary, Czech Republic, Slovakia, Slovenia, and Poland showed little regression for basic capabilities indicators. In contrast, adverse changes did occur in child socialization and adolescent protection (pre-primary enrolment rates, births to under-age mothers, youth crime rate, secondary school enrolment, and so on). For instance, the number of youth imprisoned rose sharply in four of these countries, while enrolments in kindergartens fell in three and stagnated in one at a relatively low level (UNICEF ICDC, 1995).

How can these divergences be explained? First, infant mortality reduction and infant health have been a national priority in most countries for decades. Detailed IMR data are regularly collected and widely disseminated, and the cost of IMR reduction, public health, basic education, and so on are modest. In contrast, deterioration in social protection for older children is less visible, and is more difficult and more expensive to reverse. The high 'social cost' in terms of lost future growth and greater public expenditures required for rehabilitation or repression remain 'unperceived'. Data are often incomplete and little publicized. In some cases, such as births to under-age mothers, deteriorations are often regarded as a problem of individual irresponsibility rather than one of a collective nature. In others, including child labour, part of society actually gains from these activities.

1.3.7. The most successful countries face growing child socialization problems

The countries which have achieved very high levels of income per capita, the lowest child poverty rates, and satisfactory levels of adolescent protection tend to have very low, and falling, fertility rates (1.2–1.4) and growing problems of child socialization. In these countries, most children will grow up without siblings. An only child is less likely to have a peer as role model and more likely to be surrounded by adults who focus their attention, care, and expectations on him or her. Failure to develop constructive leisure time activities for these children and the absence of companions of their own age outside the family may lead to relational difficulties and dependence on television. In these countries, child-care services have started to assume the additional role of providing children with the company and stimulus of other children of similar ages (Saraceno, 1992). Therefore, any policy introducing price barriers (in the form of user fees) to the use of these services tends to penalize children's socialization needs.

Martha Ozawa and Shigemi Kono (Chapter 12) show that the Japanese economic miracle—characterized by fast growth and low unemployment—has trickled down to almost all Japanese children. On most dimensions of child well-being, Japan ranks at or near the very top: IMR, child poverty rate, high school completion rate, percentage of children living in two-parent families. This fast progress has, however, been accompanied by a rapid decline in nuptiality and fertility. Ozawa and Kono caution that the hard work and societal discipline which has produced these achievements have created strong social pressures on women and children. Unless the economy and public policy become more responsive to children and families, the marriage and fertility rates will continue to fall and the stresses of childhood will begin to overshadow the relative lack of material deprivation.

Relational problems for children may also arise from the increased number of 'reconstituted families', i.e. families consisting of step-parents and step-siblings. While these new family types are now almost as common as lone-parent families, legislation is not yet prepared to account for the relationships and mutual obligations which arise in such complex arrangements. Other problems in 'reconstituted' families involve more complicated generational and parental relationships which may require new regulation and support interventions.

1.3.8. Demographic changes are a main cause of children's changing conditions

Life-cycle events and changes in family formation and stability, reproductive behaviour, mortality rates among parents, and labour force participation of women—as well as a slow adaptation of social policy to the new needs these changes entail—have emerged as important sources of child deprivation. In most industrialized countries the number of dual-worker families has grown steadily. While this trend reduced poverty (documented, for instance, in the US case-study), it has also posed new difficulties for working mothers, who must combine the demands of the workplace and household with child-care duties. Social policy has only partially responded to this new challenge and has thus negatively affected fertility rates and several components of child welfare. While most nations offer a paid maternity leave of various durations (Chapter 5), the USA still lacks such a measure, although many job contracts include a paid leave.

None the less, except in Scandinavia, child-care services for under-3-year-olds remain scarce and costly. Olsson Hort (Chapter 11) notes that gender relationships have evolved further in Sweden than in most other advanced economies, in part because part-time employment in the public sector is widely available and because of generous state-financed parental child-care leave. The ratios of female to male labour force participation are higher in Sweden than in other countries. By making the workplace 'family friendly' and by providing generous children's allowances and paid leave, Swedish policies seem to have contributed to a 'baby boomlet', which is quite a contrast to the continuing fertility decline in Italy and Japan.

During the last twenty years, in addition to the increase in one-child and dual-worker families, there has been a steady rise in lone-parent families. Historically, the one-parent family is not a new phenomenon. However, the sources of monoparentality have radically shifted: divorce and, increasingly, births to never-married mothers, rather than widowhood, now account for most lone-parent families. While monoparental households tend to be poorer than two-parent households, the living standards of widows and their children are generally better protected by the welfare state than that of divorced or unmarried mothers and their children (MacLean, 1990). A 'complete income package' for unmarried lone mothers and their children, combining labour market or transfer income and a modicum of child-care services, has seldom been developed. While most pronounced in the USA and in continental and Northern Europe, marital instability also appears to be increasing in the Mediterranean countries and in Japan.

1.3.9. *Impact of public social policies on child welfare*

Income transfers, labour market policies, and social policies regarding public health, education, and child care have been quite successful in many countries. The 1973–89 period, however, was characterized by a slow-down in the rate of growth of public expenditure for children, benefit erosion, increasing selectivity, and growing policy biases in favour of other social groups. Sweden's low level of poverty and inequality is due primarily to its activist labour market policies. But in a period of globalization and technological change, these policies have become more expensive. As a result, even Sweden is under pressure to hold down or reduce public spending.

Gaspar Fajth and Tatiana Zimakova (Chapter 5) examine the recent setbacks of social policy evident in most countries of the former Soviet Union. In contrast, the nations of Central Europe, 'where the socialist welfare state was most advanced, have sustained a comprehensive system of social safety nets despite difficult economic conditions. In these countries, social policies appear to have moderated the negative impact of macroeconomic shocks and the inefficiencies inherited from the communist era. During the transition, the share of public social expenditure on GDP rose steadily as a share of both GDP and public expenditure.

Sheila Kamerman and Alfred Kahn (Chapter 4) expand on Boltho's analysis of trends in public expenditure by examining detailed trends in the level and composition of social expenditures for children and their families in the West. They find that although these expenditures rose rapidly in the post-war era and more modestly since the early 1970s, they have not grown as rapidly as did public pensions for the elderly or health care expenditures. Most governments find it difficult to restrain spending on pensions for the elderly, which tend to be indexed to the inflation rate, and for health care, which has grown more rapidly than inflation. As a result, the relative importance of child and family benefits has declined as many countries do not index them for inflation. Family benefits have also fallen as a percentage of disposable family income. For example, in the OECD countries, family benefits for a married, two-child, one average earner family amounted to 15.3 per cent of disposable income in 1975 and 11.4 per cent in 1992.

Kamerman and Kahn also document the wide variation in spending for children and families in Western countries, showing that countries like Germany, the Netherlands, France, and the Nordic countries spend much more than others like Japan and the USA.

1.3.10. *Future prospects are cautiously positive, but clouded by growing uncertainty, especially in Eastern Europe*

In the 1990–4 period, growth was less than 2 per cent in most Western countries, while output fell by about 4 per cent per year in Eastern Europe and by about 10 per cent per year in the countries of the former Soviet Union. Child welfare deteriorated sharply in most areas in most countries of Eastern Europe, while basic trends in the West were basically unaffected.

In spite of these recent disappointments, it is possible that advances in technology and heightened public awareness of the new problems facing children and adolescents may facilitate the search for new solutions in the public and private sectors. In the West, economic growth improved re-markably in 1994–5 and is expected to continue at a moderate, but steady, pace. In addition, there are signs that, with the exception of the Slavic and Caucasus nations of the former Soviet Union, output and welfare indicators are starting to rebound in Central Europe and the Baltic States. Furthermore, the economic and social reforms underway in many coun-tries of Eastern Europe may, if successful, lead to long-run improvements in child well-being.

As this review has argued, however, the potential gains that a 'business as usual' scenario would produce might not be satisfactory for several reasons. First, child welfare in several countries of the former Soviet Union may stagnate at very discouraging levels. The return to steady progress appears problematic and is difficult to visualize because of the dominant trends there—persistent macroeconomic instability, predatory and unjust privatization, demise of the state, chaos in public finances, growing income inequality, and lack of coherent and adequately funded social policies.

In addition, child welfare in Eastern European countries could de-teriorate if the transition to the market continues to be unregulated, particularly in countries where social protection and unemployment com-pensation schemes, and the resources to fund them, are still inadequate. In most of the FSU, the debate about new approaches to the delivery and financing of social services is heavily conditioned by a pervasive 'demise of the state'. This phenomenon has reached unexpected propor-tions as the dismantling of institutions and social norms of the socialist regime has not been accompanied by the development of satisfactory substitutes. The weakening or collapse of the state and its central powers has made the pursuit of any policy, other than 'pure *laissez-faire*', almost impossible.

A second source of instability and concern arises from the crisis of the family: the fall in fertility rates in spite of considerable improvements in material well-being and social services, and the increased number of children in incomplete, poorer, and socially fragile families. This phenomenon seems to be accelerating in the transitional economies.

A third reason for alarm is the erosion, rather than reform, of the welfare state in Western Europe and the continued inability of American society to resolve its chronic problems of unequal access to basic services, underinvestment in public health, child care, education, and social protection (i.e. problems that undermine social solidarity, welfare outcomes, and more importantly for the defendants of the *status quo*, long-term economic growth). In Europe, Britain, and Italy, for instance, the creeping erosion of the welfare state has included the introduction of user fees for many services (in health, education, child care, and so on), even though they have the positive externalities of quasi-public goods, and of a growing trend towards the privatization of some services. Finally, many countries have experienced increasing unemployment and inequality in the distribution of earnings. Together with the adverse changes in family structure and stability, this has contributed to new forms of economic and social marginality.

1.4. Some Tentative Policy Recommendations

Given the broad variations across the industrialized countries of the East and West in economic conditions, the nature of the welfare state, societal norms, and ideological orientations, it would be presumptuous to conclude that a simple set of universal lessons could be applied in all countries to reduce child poverty and deprivation. What is feasible in Sweden may be ideologically impracticable in the USA or economically impossible in Russia. Therefore, the following recommendations, which are elaborated in greater depth in Chapters 13 and 14, seek to provide a generic guide to policy-making in industrialized countries:

1. *Monitoring the well-being of children.* An understanding of how economic, demographic, and policy changes affect child outcomes requires the availability of systematic data for both the determinants and outcomes. Most countries could do a better job in collecting and analysing data on child poverty and deprivation. This is particularly true of information on the 'new deprivations' affecting children, such as child abuse, homelessness, mental health, and social marginalization, where data are difficult to find or interpret. A strong case can be made for close monitor-

ing of child outcomes in 'societies in transition', such as the Eastern European economies, and in Western nations affected by changes in family structure, the effects of which are far from understood.

2. *Labour market policies*. Much of the increased child poverty since the 1970s is due to technological changes that have reduced the demand for less-skilled relative to more-skilled workers and to the increased globalization of the market economies. These changes caused rising unemployment in many high-wage European countries, especially those whose labour market institutions allowed little wage flexibility (for instance, France, Germany, the Netherlands), and increased work at low wages in economies with less labour protection and more wage flexibility (such as the USA). Most children in low-income families have parents who do not expect to earn enough to keep their families out of poverty; their poverty is not simply a problem of insufficient social welfare and income transfers.

The case for legislation increasing the minimum wage has recently been made in a number of countries. In others, such as France, there has long been an active policy to periodically adjust the minimum wage. Similarly, active labour market policies are needed to augment the skills of the long-term unemployed, to encourage employment in the private sector, and to create jobs in co-operatives and other public-private enterprises when structural unemployment is high.

3. *Strengthening social protection systems for children and families*. Remarkable progress has been accomplished in most industrialized countries over the last fifty years in the areas of old-age pensions and unemployment compensation. In contrast, trends in the relative incidence of poverty among children, the elderly, and other groups at risk show how the implementation of child and family policies has been less complete in most market economies. Life-cycle events like divorce, birth or illness of a child, as well as spatial relocation are still associated in many countries with a high risk of falling into poverty. Benefits guarding against these risks, such as paid maternity leave, child allowance, ensured advance child support, and free health care for all children, are either non-existent, means-tested, or grossly insufficient in their amounts.

Action is required in many countries for the formulation of a comprehensive social welfare policy focused on children and families. The necessary resources can to a large extent be obtained from a reordering of public spending priorities, and in a number of countries where recent tax changes have been regressive and income inequality has increased, through higher taxation of the rich. In several of the formerly centrally planned economies, this would require the establishment or redesign of the overall method of taxation.

4. *Free or subsidized public services.* The countries that have achieved the greatest advances over the past fifty years in infant mortality, child health, educational attainment, and other areas have been those which have provided free or subsidized medical, educational, and social services. Some industrialized countries have major gaps in these facilities. In many others, some services for young children and working mothers, such as day-care centres for young children, are still unevenly developed. Their strengthening would contribute to the implementation of a child- and family-focused social policy, and would be particularly beneficial for children living in lone-parent families.

The increasing tendency to cover budgetary shortfalls in social ministries by sharper targeting, user fees (which are said to improve allocative efficiency), and community financing should be carefully evaluated. While 'nominal fees' have often been shown to be welfare enhancing, 'substantial fees' can indeed raise prohibitive price barriers for the poor and near-poor. While targeting can be a useful tool of social policy, its application should be avoided for goods with important externalities. Targeting has been most efficient when done by categorical criteria and not by means-testing. The latter approach often implies high administrative costs and entails large welfare costs because of the exclusion of deserving households (Cornia and Stewart, 1993).

5. *Reinvigorating 'the family' and local communities.* Many social pathologies and emotional problems of adolescents could be prevented with more stable, cohesive, and responsive communities and families. A related objective of social policy should be a non-ideological strengthening of family and community support and transfers. This can be an important first safety net to be complemented by the formal system. In some countries (like Japan or Poland), the law stipulates the obligation to assist given members of the same family before approaching public institutions. During the recent period of adjustment, policy-makers have often assigned private transfers an important (and probably excessive) anti-poverty role, exonerating the state from its obligations. None the less, it would be beneficial to child well-being if better use were made of the positive values and energies of family and community solidarity while maintaining universal coverage of public services.

6. *Family support policies.* In an era of increased divorce and out-of-wedlock child-bearing, there is a greater need for increased private transfers from absent parents (usually fathers) to the custodial parent. In most countries, single-mother families are one of the poorest groups. They would gain both from increased private, as well as public, transfers.

7. *Targeted support for children and adolescents in highly deprived situations.* Many of the policies discussed above should be universal in coverage and in the extent of provision. Even if they were all set in place,

however, some children would still experience acute deprivation. Specific interventions would be necessary in this, it is to be hoped, small number of cases.

1.5. Unanswered or only Partially Answered Questions

Our analysis has documented the significant effects of several factors on child welfare. It has not, however, attempted to specify how market reforms and reforms of the welfare state could be implemented to foster the specific child-related policies which we recommend. We conclude by raising three questions which appear to be most important for informing a public policy that is responsive to the needs of children, with the hope of stimulating further research.

Can rising earnings inequality be moderated through efficient changes in labour market institutions? If so, what are 'efficient' institutional arrangements that are both feasible and desirable?

Can the increase in monoparental families and births to under-age mothers be reversed? This trend negatively affects both the mother and the child. In addition to providing support to children and mothers in these families, there is an urgent need to confront the question of why a growing number of young women, East and West, are giving birth in conditions of inadequate income, unfinished schooling, and weak family structures. This 'life choice' appears to be counterproductive as it reduces the young woman's chances of completing school, finding a job, and getting married.

Can the provision and financing of 'public goods' and the welfare state in general be overhauled? The neoclassical political economy (NPE) has strongly questioned the excessive role of governments, emphasized the inefficiencies of public provision, and reassessed the redistributive potential of the tax-and-transfers system. According to this viewpoint, the role of the state in the provision of public goods has to be carefully circumscribed. Employment-related health insurance and privatization of public and merit goods ought to be promoted, while the government should retain the role of 'residual provider' only for the extremely poor and for areas unreachable by the private sector.

There are strong indications, however, that this approach has resulted in lower utilization of merit goods and welfare levels, increased differentiation in use and standards amongst social groups, insufficient human capital formation, and reduced redistribution. There is thus a need to explore alternatives to the dominant 'welfarist' and 'NPE' paradigms by exploring new models of provision which avoid the usual inefficiencies of public supply and the exclusion and fragmentation typical of the neo-liberal approach. In our view, a promising line of research is that which assigns a greater provisioning role to the non-governmental sector and to the market, but which assigns to the state the role of financing and regulating the modalities (and prices) of provision by these sectors. In this context, it would be useful to explore—in a non-ideological way—the role of private transfers, statutory family transfers, and non-governmental organizations. What is their poverty alleviation impact?

PART I

Child Poverty and Deprivation: From the Golden Age, to Stagnation, to transition

2

Child Poverty and Deprivation in the Industrialized Countries: From the End of World War II to the End of the Cold War Era

GIOVANNI ANDREA CORNIA

2.1. Child Poverty and Deprivation in Historical Perspective: From the Early 1950s to the Mid-1970s

2.1.1. Conditions in industrialized countries in the early 1950s

Not long ago, acute poverty, poor health, and other forms of deprivation were quite common among the children[1] of most industrialized countries,[2] and possibly more common than in several developing countries today. An examination of trends in the infant mortality rate (IMR)—a key indicator of overall child welfare—shows (Table 2.1) that in the early 1950s the IMRs of Southern and Eastern Europe and the USSR were about 30 per cent higher than the rate recorded at the end of the 1980s in Latin America and broadly equivalent to those of South-East Asia or North Africa (United Nations, 1989). During 1950–5, most Western European countries and Japan had infant mortality rates close to 50 per 1,000, almost twice as large as those observed in China at the end of the 1980s. By 1950–5, only North America, Northern Europe, and Australia had attained infant mortality levels below the critical threshold of 30 per 1,000 (Table 2.1).

Information on the post-war incidence of child poverty is much scarcer than on infant mortality. The limited data available confirm the situation highlighted by the IMR analysis. For example, census data from the USA show that in 1949 more than 45 per cent of all children lived in families with incomes insufficient to provide adequate nutrition, housing, transportation, medical care, and the like (Table 2.2). Even in 1959 about a

---

[1] The terms 'child' and 'elderly' refer in this chapter respectively to the under-18 and over-65 populations.

[2] In this chapter the term 'industrialized countries' comprises North America, Western and Eastern Europe, the USSR, Japan, Australia, and New Zealand.

Table 2.1:   Infant Mortality Rate by Country and Region, Selected Years
(per 1,000 live births, five-year averages)

	1950–5	1960–5	1970–5	1975–80	1980–5	1985–90[a]
North America	25	20	17	13	11	9
Canada	36	26	16	12	9	7
USA	28	25	18	14	11	10
Northern Europe	28	21	16	12	10	8
Denmark	28	20	12	9	8	7
Finland	34	19	12	9	6	6
Ireland	41	28	18	15	9	9
Norway	23	17	12	9	8	7
Sweden	20	15	10	8	7	6
UK	28	22	17	14	11	9
Western Europe	44	26	18	13	10	9
Austria	53	32	24	16	12	11
Belgium	45	27	19	13	11	10
France	45	25	16	11	9	8
Germany	48	28	22	15	11	9
Netherlands	24	16	12	10	8	8
Switzerland	29	20	13	10	8	7
Southern Europe	79	52	31	23	18	15
Greece	60	50	34	25	15	17
Italy	60	40	26	18	13	11
Portugal	31	76	45	30	20	15
Spain	62	42	21	16	11	10
Yugoslavia	128	80	45	35	30	25
Eastern Europe	83	44	28	23	19	17
Bulgaria	92	36	26	22	17	16
Czechoslovakia	54	23	21	19	16	15
German Dem. Rep.	58	31	17	13	11	9
Hungary	71	44	34	27	20	20
Poland	95	51	27	23	20	18
Romania	101	60	40	31	26	22
USSR	73	32	26	28	26	24
Japan	51	24	12	9	7	5
Australia and New Zealand						
Australia	24	20	17	12	10	8
New Zealand	26	21	16	14	12	11

[a] The data for 1985–90 were projected on the basis of past trends. They, however, fit, with only minor variations, the real changes in IMR over that period.
Source: United Nations (1989).

quarter of all children in the USA were still living in poverty. Moreover, the situation was probably worse in Europe and Japan, which had structurally weaker resource bases and had suffered severe losses during World War II.

Table 2.2: Poverty Rates in the USA for Selected Census Years and Population Groups[a] (percentages)

Age-group	1949	1959	1969	1979
Children (0–14)	47.6	26.1	15.6	17.1
Elderly men (+65)	55.3	33.2	22.2	10.6
Elderly women (+65)	69.4	38.6	32.1	18.0
All persons	39.8	22.1	14.4	13.1

[a] The data presented were obtained by means of the 1959 fixed poverty line. For the years 1949, 1969, and 1979, the 1959 poverty line was adjusted to take account of inflation.

Source: Derived from Smolensky *et al.* (1988).

These cross-country differences in 'initial welfare conditions' reflect similar disparities in levels of development, standards of living, rural–urban differentials, social security systems, and demographic trends. Already by the mid-1920s, for instance, Sweden had developed a comprehensive school meals system, subsidized housing, day-care centres and kindergartens, and paid maternity leave (Myrdal and Myrdal, 1934; Myrdal, 1941). Meanwhile, most Mediterranean and Eastern European countries still exhibited high fertility and infant mortality rates.

Cross-country variability in child welfare was due also to the differential impact of the war. The USA did not have to address the problems of reconstruction and housing shortages. On the other hand, most countries in Eastern and Western Europe faced the daunting task of reconstruction and—in the case of Italy and Germany—development of new constitutional frameworks. In Eastern Europe, the immediate post-war years were marked by economic transformation under conditions of stress and shortages.

2.1.2. *Rapid improvement over the 1950–75 period*

Despite these differences, the quarter-century between 1950 and 1975 is considered by most social scientists as a 'golden age' of social development. It witnessed spectacular declines in child poverty, infant mortality, and illiteracy. The nutritional status of children improved rapidly in parallel with the fast and steady growth in household incomes, control of major infectious diseases, and the beneficial effects of antibiotics. Progress was facilitated by the increase in coverage of preventive and curative health services. The spread of national health services and similar systems made these facilities, including hospitalization, virtually free of charge in most countries.

Most industrialized countries achieved greater reductions in infant mortality (particularly in post-neonatal mortality) and morbidity than ever before recorded (Table 2.1). Rollet and Bourdelais (1993), for instance, indicate that while infant mortality in France had declined five times (broadly from 300 to 60 per 1,000) between 1750 and 1945, it then declined almost eight times (to 7 per 1,000) over the subsequent forty-five years (see Figure 2.1). During this period, there was an overall convergence in IMR levels. The decline was faster in Japan (75 per cent), Poland, Bulgaria, Finland, and the USSR (around 70 per cent) than in the UK and Greece (around 40 per cent) and the USA (35 per cent) (Table 2.1 and Figure 2.2). Thus, the rapid progress generally realized in the less developed and war-torn countries reduced substantially both the absolute and relative distance separating them from the better-off industrialized countries at the end of World War II.

Similar advances reduced the number of children living in poverty (as indicated, for instance, in Table 2.1 by the sharp drop in the US poverty rate between 1949 and 1969) and improved educational access and quality for most children. In addition, the downward trend in fertility that had been evident for many decades was suddenly reversed in all industrialized countries (except Japan) between the mid-1950s and the early 1960s (Table 2.3). This 'baby boom' increased the size of the child population in the 5–14 age bracket by 43 million between 1950 and 1970. The larger

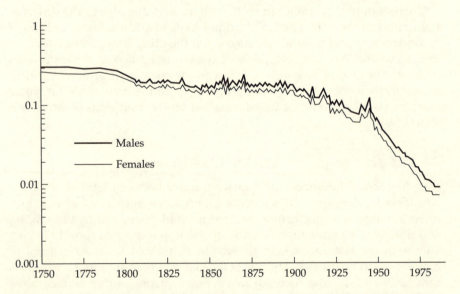

Fig. 2.1 Evolution of Infant Mortality in France, 1750–1987 (semi-logarithmic scale)

Source: Rollet and Bourdelais (1993).

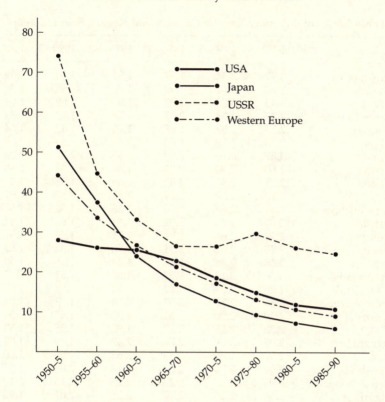

Fig. 2.2 Infant Mortality Rates for Selected Countries and Regions, 1950–1955 to 1985–1990

Source: Based on United Nations (1989).

number of children within families, along with the greater number of couples who were marrying and having at least one child, meant that children suddenly became more 'visible', thereby spurring greater public awareness of their needs and rights.

Even with this considerably expanded child population, secondary school enrolment ratios increased, pupil–teacher ratios declined, and physical infrastructure improved. For example, the secondary school enrolment ratio increased in Italy from 35 to 61 per cent between 1960 and 1970 and in the then German Democratic Republic (GDR) from 39 to 92 per cent over the 1960–70 period (UNESCO, 1987). During the same years, compulsory schooling was extended in most industrialized countries from 5–6 to 9–10 years. In turn, preschool education developed in response to the growing participation of women in the labour force. It also aimed to integrate children living in unsatisfactory socio-economic conditions into the school system at an earlier age. Although most Eastern

Table 2.3:   Total Fertility Rate by Country and Region, Selected Years

	1950–5	1960–5	1970–5	1975–80	1980–5	1985–90
North America	3.47	3.34	1.97	1.91	1.80	1.89
Canada	3.70	3.61	1.97	1.77	1.66	1.70
USA	3.45	3.31	1.97	1.93	1.82	1.92
Northern Europe	2.32	2.78	2.07	1.78	1.79	1.84
Denmark	2.53	2.58	1.96	1.70	1.42	1.54
Finland	2.98	2.58	1.62	1.64	1.69	1.66
Ireland	3.37	3.96	3.80	3.46	2.87	2.28
Norway	2.60	2.90	2.25	1.81	1.69	1.80
Sweden	2.21	2.33	1.89	1.65	1.65	1.91
UK	2.18	2.82	2.04	1.72	1.80	1.81
Western Europe	2.39	2.68	1.94	1.63	1.58	1.58
Austria	2.09	2.78	2.01	1.64	1.61	1.47
Belgium	2.34	2.66	1.94	1.71	1.59	1.57
France	2.73	2.85	2.31	1.86	1.87	1.82
Germany	2.08	2.48	1.62	1.44	1.36	1.40
Netherlands	3.06	3.12	1.97	1.58	1.51	1.55
Switzerland	2.28	2.51	1.82	1.52	1.53	1.53
Southern Europe	2.69	2.72	2.52	2.26	1.82	1.54
Greece	2.29	2.20	2.32	2.32	1.97	1.53
Italy	2.32	2.55	2.27	1.92	1.55	1.33
Portugal	3.05	3.09	2.76	2.42	1.99	1.60
Spain	2.57	2.89	2.89	2.63	1.86	1.60
Yugoslavia	3.69	2.70	2.32	2.20	2.08	1.96
Eastern Europe	2.95	2.33	2.23	2.25	2.13	2.10
Bulgaria	2.50	2.19	2.17	2.25	2.01	1.92
Czechoslovakia	2.89	2.40	2.34	2.36	2.09	2.00
German Dem. Rep.	2.37	2.45	1.71	1.81	1.83	1.70
Hungary	2.72	1.82	2.08	2.11	1.80	1.82
Poland	3.62	2.65	2.25	2.26	2.33	2.15
Romania	2.87	2.01	2.63	2.55	2.22	2.28
USSR	2.82	2.54	2.44	2.34	2.35	2.43
Japan	2.75	2.01	2.07	1.81	1.76	1.68
Australia and New Zealand	3.25	3.37	2.58	2.11	1.94	1.89
Australia	3.18	3.28	2.54	2.09	1.93	1.86
New Zealand	3.54	3.79	2.79	2.20	1.96	2.04

Sources: United Nations (1991, 1993).

European countries developed child-care services in the 1940s and 1950s to an extent unknown in the West (outside of Scandinavia), demand for these services—due to much faster increases in employment rates among married women than in Western countries—far outpaced the supply (Heinen, 1991).

Following the 'baby boom' of the immediate post-war years, the total fertility rate (TFR) started its gradual decline in the majority of the industrialized countries. With the exception of the USSR (where TFR has declined only marginally over the last forty years) and of Southern Europe (where the sharpest decline occurred after 1975), most of the sizeable fertility decrease took place over the 1960–75 period. In the USA, TFR fell from 3.58 around 1950 to 1.95 around 1975; large declines were also observed in Australia, New Zealand, and Japan. Over the same period, fertility fell from 2.3 to 1.9 in Northern Europe, from 2.4 to 1.8 in Western Europe, and from 2.9 to 2.2 in Eastern Europe (United Nations, 1989). Large drops in fertility probably contributed to the rapid IMR decline between 1950 and 1975 as some of the births avoided were high-risk ones, generally with relatively high parity and at close intervals.

Japan represents a special case: following a slow decline in fertility during the first four decades of the twentieth century, a sudden and sharp decline was recorded, precisely when the USA and Western Europe were experiencing the 'baby boom'. TFR more than halved between 1947 and 1957, falling from 4.54 to 2.04 (Japan Institute of Population Problems, 1986; Preston and Kono, 1988).

2.1.3. *Main determinants of improvement in child welfare prior to the mid-1970s*

An exhaustive analysis of the causal factors behind the improvement in child welfare prior to 1975 is beyond the scope of this chapter. Nevertheless, the role of some of the main structural determinants over the 1950–75 period is clear. Changes in the trends of these determinants over the subsequent period (mid-1970s to end-1980s) may underlie the surge in child welfare problems observed in some industrialized countries during this later period (see Section 2.2).

1. *Rapid and widespread growth in household incomes.* The quarter-century from the late 1940s to the early 1970s recorded a brilliant economic performance: output, productivity, investment, and employment all grew steadily, except during the short-lived recession induced by the Korean War of 1950–3. And, central to our analysis, growth in household incomes surpassed any recorded historical experience. High growth rates of GDP and net material product (NMP) per capita (Table 2.4) ensured that average household incomes broadly tripled in Japan and Eastern Europe between 1950 and 1970 and doubled in North America. Even in countries with relatively less exuberant growth, household incomes increased substantially. Between 1949 and 1973, for instance, the median family income (at 1967 prices) in the USA rose from about $US 4,300 to close to $US 9,000 (Danziger and Gottschalk, 1988).

Government economic intervention—in particular, a consistent demand management policy—was a major reason for the post-war growth

Table 2.4: Yearly Growth Rates of Total Output, 1955–1990 (percentages)

	GDP or NMP per capita					
	1955–60	1960–70	1970–5	1975–80	1980–5	1985–90
North America	2.2	3.1	1.7	2.4	1.9	1.8
Western Europe	3.9	3.8	2.9	2.4	1.4	2.9
Eastern Europe	6.9	4.5	7.4	3.0	2.1	−0.1
USSR	9.3	4.8	5.3	3.3	3.6	1.5
Japan	7.7	9.1	2.3	3.1	3.2	4.3
Australia and New Zealand	2.1	3.9	2.3	0.5	1.9	0.7

Sources: Cornia (1990); World Bank (1994).

acceleration. Equally crucial were labour market policies, which contributed to the achievement of virtual 'full employment' in the late 1950s and
early 1960s. Between 1960 and 1967, average unemployment rates were
1.3 per cent in Japan, 2.7 per cent in Western Europe, 1.9 per cent in
Australia, 4.9 per cent in North America, and less than 1 per cent in the
socialist bloc, where different institutional arrangements guaranteed full
absorption of available labour.

Full employment, higher real wages, and the social security schemes
introduced to varying extents by all industrialized countries after the war
led to improvements in the degree of inequality in pre-tax, pre-transfer
income distribution and, even more so, in that for post-tax, post-transfer
incomes. A comprehensive review of income distribution data for the
post-war period (Sawyer, 1976: 26) concludes that

broadly, it would appear that through the 1950s there has been some movement
towards greater equality almost everywhere. In the 1960s and early 1970s, the
same remained true for France, Italy, Japan and the Netherlands. The picture is
unclear in Germany . . . and in the United Kingdom . . . In North America, there
seems to have been a marginal move away from equality.

The same report indicates that in the late 1960s and early 1970s net income
transfers (generally to the bottom two or three deciles of the population)
accounted for 4–5 per cent of national income in most industrial market
economies and for no less than 15 per cent in Sweden in 1972.

2. *The birth of the welfare state.* World War II was an important turning-
point in the history of social security. In several Western countries (but not
in Eastern Europe) social security programmes had already developed
late last century and in the early part of this century (Barr, 1993). However, except for Sweden, coverage was limited and benefits meagre, while
eligibility varied from one programme to another. In addition, the social

assistance measures that had been introduced (as during the Fascist regime in Italy) often restricted freedom of choice, particularly for women (Saraceno, 1992). Moreover, under the strain of the Great Depression of the 1930s, several schemes, including unemployment insurance, were abandoned or replaced by relief assistance. Indeed, at the end of the war, several nations, including Japan, the USA, and Portugal lacked any significant social security policy.

Inspired by pioneering analyses, such as the famous Beveridge Report and Alva and Gunnar Myrdal's *Crisis in the Population Question*, or by the principles of socialist social policy, comprehensive social security systems were developed after the war. New schemes were introduced and earlier ones were consolidated or extended. Patterns varied substantially from country to country, but systems generally included:

- pensions (old-age, invalidity, and survivor),
- health benefits (against sickness and work injury),
- unemployment benefits,
- family allowances (maternity leave, child benefits, and others), and
- public assistance.

In addition, virtually free health care, child care, and education were increasingly provided by national health and education services, with the exception of a few Western countries, including the USA and Portugal. The main difference between the Western and Eastern versions of social security was that unemployment and social assistance were completely absent in the latter countries, though they generally provided additional family benefits (such as birth grants, leave during a child's sickness, child-care leave, and so on) and a myriad of subsidies to young couples.

Social security expenditure grew rapidly over the 1950–75 period, reflecting rapid extension of coverage, demographic factors (such as ageing of the population), or improved real benefits per capita. Figure 2.3 shows that the average percentage of social security expenditure on GDP increased between 1950 and 1975 by 7 points in the USA, 13 in continental Western Europe, and about 8 in the Commonwealth countries. At 11 per cent of NMP, average social security expenditure in Eastern Europe (including the USSR) in 1960 was somewhat higher than elsewhere. During the 1960–75 period, however, it rose more slowly than in most other industrialized countries. Expenditure on pensions and health benefits grew fastest. The contribution of social security expenditure to reducing the incidence of poverty—particularly among the elderly—was remarkable, as for instance in the USA (Table 2.2).

In Eastern Europe, furthermore, the welfare state was complemented by an impressive array of subsidies for basic foods, children's goods, energy,

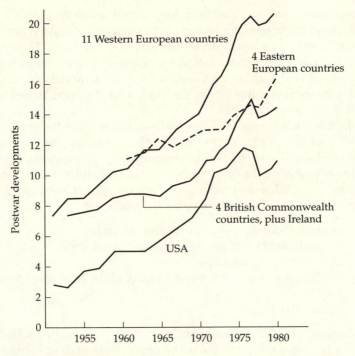

Fig. 2.3 Average Expenditure on Social Security as a Percentage of GDP or NMP for Selected Countries or Country Groupings,[a] 1950–1980

[a]The eleven Western European countries included are Austria, Belgium, Denmark, Finland, France, Germany (Fed. Rep.), Italy, the Netherlands, Norway, Sweden, and Switzerland. The four Commonwealth countries are Australia, Canada, New Zealand, and the United Kingdom. The four Eastern European countries are Czechoslovakia, Hungary, Poland, and the USSR.

Source: Gordon (1988).

transport, and housing, which played a decisive role in helping poor families maintain adequate diets, clothing, acceptable housing conditions, and adequate access to basic drugs. These subsidies absorbed between 10–15 per cent of NMP and often exceeded total government expenditure on health and education combined (Cornia and Sipos, 1991). Though subsidized, housing generally remained in short supply, especially in cities (Sipos, 1991).

3. *Changes in demographic structures and family characteristics*. The family exerts a major influence on child well-being, as a basic unit of society, natural environment for the growth of children, and main place where decisions on health, education, consumption, and leisure are taken. Changes over the 1950–75 period in the number, size, stability, and 'quality' of families in industrialized countries contributed considerably to the

observed reduction in child poverty and mortality as well as to the improvement in enrolment rates and school achievement. Or, at least, the changes in family structure over this period were not extensive enough to exert a negative influence on child well-being, as they did during the following period.

Given the differences in initial conditions described above, it is striking that from the 1950s most industrialized countries exhibited similar trends in marriage, family stability, and reproductive behaviour. First, in most economies, the first twenty years after the war were a 'golden age of marriage' (Segalen, 1981). Never before nor afterwards was the proportion of people marrying so high, especially in the Nordic countries, where in the 1950s and early 1960s only about 5 per cent of all women had never married, as against over 20 per cent before then (Saraceno, 1992). Similar trends were observed in the USA, Japan, and the Southern European countries, where—though still significant—the increase in marriage rates appeared later (ibid.). The picture in the socialist bloc was more complex. While national authorities actively promoted marriage, outlawed consensual union and abortions, and encouraged a 'demographic recovery' by means of a series of legal and welfare measures (see Chapter 6), the emphasis placed on the creation of the new 'socialist man' (Neményi, 1990) made official ideology *vis-à-vis* the family and parental authority rather ambivalent.

Second, the trend towards nuclearization of the family, begun several decades earlier, intensified. This and the trends towards more and younger marriages had the effect of reducing family size. In addition, migration to cities (where available dwellings were smaller) contributed to the growth of nuclear families in countries such as Poland, the USSR, and Yugoslavia where a rural tradition of multigenerational families had been strong. The trend towards nuclearization of the family was less apparent in Japan. In 1955, over one-third of Japanese households were still three-generational (Preston and Kono, 1988).

Third, changes in family stability did not negatively affect child welfare. Research shows that the risks of poverty, early death, school failure, and accident are affected by the structure and stability of the union in which the child grows up (Adamchack, 1979). In this regard, the marriages of the 1950s and early 1960s in Western countries were distinguished by considerable stability. Longer life expectancy was pushing back death, the major cause of family disruption until then. Separation was unusual. Divorce was not even legal in many countries; and where it was legal, it remained a rare occurrence. While modest rises in divorce rates (Table 2.5) and separation rates as well as a decline in remarriage rates were recorded in the first two post-war decades, with the exception of the USSR, the increase in crude divorce rates during this period was a fraction of that recorded over the 1970s and 1980s (Table 2.5 and Figure 2.4).

Table 2.5: Crude Divorce Rate in Selected Countries and Average Annual Change, 1960–1990

	Rates						Average yearly changes			
	1953	1960	1970	1980	1985	1990	1960–70	1970–80	1980–5	1985–90
North America	1.44	1.28	2.41	3.89	3.70	3.82	0.11	0.15	-0.40	0.02
Northern Europe	0.90	0.93	1.46	2.28	2.41	2.14	0.05	0.08	0.03	-0.05
Western Europe	0.82	0.76	0.99	1.64	2.01	1.93[a]	0.02	0.07	0.07	-0.02
Eastern Europe	0.98	1.27	1.36	1.93	2.11	1.76	0.01	0.06	0.04	-0.07
Former USSR	—	1.27	2.68	3.50	3.36	3.39[b]	0.14	0.08	-0.03	0.01
Japan	0.87	0.74	0.93	1.21	1.38	1.27	0.01	0.02	0.03	-0.02
Australia and New Zealand	0.83	0.67	1.05	2.38	2.58	2.60	0.04	0.13	0.04	0.00

[a] 1991 figure. [b] 1989 figure.

Sources: Council of Europe (1993); United Nations, *Demographic Yearbook* (various years).

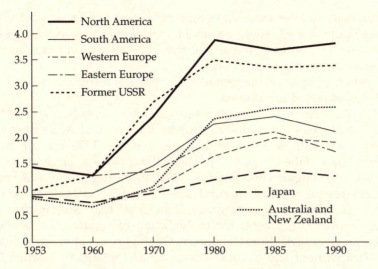

Fig. 2.4 Evolution of the Crude Divorce Rate, 1953–1990

Sources: Based on Council of Europe (1993); United Nations, *Demographic Yearbook* (various years).

Furthermore, births to single mothers increased only modestly or not at all up to 1970.

Lastly, parental education, a proxy of 'quality' of the family and a primary predictor of child survival, school performance, and other child welfare indicators (Caldwell, 1979; Cochrane, 1980), improved steadily throughout the period under examination (UNESCO, 1982 and 1987). Female education was fostered in particular, and the role of women in society was redefined. Partly as a result of increased female labour force participation, greater emphasis was given to gender equality and women's involvement in the family and society.

It is tempting to conclude, therefore, that changes in the structure and stability of the family between the early 1950s and early 1970s, while not always favourable, did not adversely influence child well-being as occurred during the subsequent two decades.

2.1.4. *Unresolved child-related problems in the early to mid-1970s*

By the early 1970s, children's problems in advanced societies seemed to have been broadly solved. Two factors contributed to this belief. First, more than two decades of fast and steady progress had helped reduce the incidence of child poverty as well as of most of its more visible manifestations, such as infant mortality and unequal access to education and child care. Second, an ever more comprehensive state family support system was being developed. These positive factors were reinforced by an optimistic economic outlook, the end of the 'baby boom', and growing concerns over an ageing population.

However, in spite of the remarkable progress recorded, a number of problems remained unresolved.

1. *The persistence of substantial numbers of children in pockets of 'traditional poverty'*. European Community estimates indicate that while the overall poverty ratio had declined to 12.8 per cent by 1975 for the twelve member states of the Community, it was about twice as large in Portugal and Greece (O'Higgins and Jenkins, 1989). In Portugal, one study places the incidence of poverty in rural areas in 1973–4 at 45 per cent (da Costa *et al.*, 1985). The same analysis suggests that poverty was even higher (above 50 per cent) for the children of certain socio-economic groups, such as agricultural labourers. Over 30 per cent of such children were born without any medical assistance, and a large proportion lived without running water (53 per cent), electricity (20 per cent), or a bathroom (33 per cent). About half of these children would not complete four years of elementary education, while only 1–2 per cent would finish secondary or higher education. Large numbers of children would start working in their early teens, while many would be affected by 'hidden monoparentality' as fathers migrated abroad in search of employment. Rural Portugal was not a unique case. There were similar situations in the mid-1970s in large pockets of underdevelopment throughout Southern and Eastern Europe as well as in the Asian Republics of the former USSR, in 'inner city' ghettos of the USA, and in marginal areas of several Western European countries (see Chapters 7 and 10). Hence, even traditional poverty, linked to material deprivation, had not completely disappeared.

2. *The unequal distribution of improvements in child welfare among social classes and regions*. While mortality differentials among countries had diminished, differences in perinatal, infant, and child mortality rates among social groups did not narrow between 1950 and the early 1970s, suggesting firm stability of class differences in mortality.

Infant mortality declined considerably in France for all social groups between 1950 and 1970. However, the differential between unskilled workers and professional classes moved only from 2.76 in 1950 to 2.49 in 1970 (United Nations, 1982). In the USA, the non-white-to-white infant mortality ratio rose markedly between 1950 (1.66) and 1966 (1.88) to decline to 1.70 in 1975 (Children's Defense Fund, 1989). Similarly, the ratio of the percentage of non-white-to-white infants born with low birth weight steadily increased from 1.44 in 1950 to 1.94 in 1975 (ibid.). Even in countries with broader access to basic services, such as the Scandinavian and Eastern European countries, inequalities in child health persisted or even widened. In Denmark, the overall neonatal mortality rate declined between 1970 and 1974 from 11 to 8 per 1,000, but the differential between children born to unskilled workers and those born to self-employed parents increased from 2.6 to 3.3 (Townsend and Davidson, 1982). Similar results were found for Poland. Finally, a comprehensive review of twenty-six studies on social class and infant mortality for Europe and the USA (Antonovsky and Bernstein, 1977) concluded that in the mid-1970s strong class differentials in infant mortality persisted. In 1975, a newborn in an unskilled worker's family in Western Europe and the USA was still, on average, two to three times as likely to die during the first year of life as was a newborn in a professional family (ibid.).

Finally, the fast improvement in living conditions did not bring equal benefits to all areas. In Italy, as shown in Table 10.2, the ratio of perinatal mortality between the areas with the best (North-east) and worst (South) performance increased from 1.37 to 1.50 between 1951 and 1970. Even greater regional imbalances in performance were observed for most social indicators in the former USSR (Riazantzev *et al.*, 1992).

3. *The surfacing of new problems.* Often referred to as 'new poverty', a set of problems, not necessarily associated with material deprivation, became much more acute in the subsequent two decades and were largely the result of the pattern of social and economic development adopted during the three post-war decades. First, the proportion of the population living in cities increased sharply, reaching 60–80 per cent by 1975. Social contacts and community solidarity weakened. Lack of public spaces for playing, meeting, and services (typical of most new peripheries) led to growing problems concerning child socialization and care, loneliness, marginalization, and TV dependence.

The amount and quality of adult–child and child–child interaction diminished, rendering adolescent psychosocial development increasingly problematic. In the Soviet Union, public authorities spoke of 'social orphans', as trends in family structure led to greater nuclearization, monoparentality, and increasing hours of solitude for children left at home alone. The problem of early child socialization was aggravated by the increased female labour force participation in countries still lacking early child-care facilities and still following a traditional division of child-rearing responsibilities. Female labour force participation in 1975 was about 51 per cent in the USSR, 45 per cent in Eastern Europe, and between 32 and 38 per cent in North America and Western Europe (United Nations, 1980). Finally, rapid migration to Western and Northern European countries by citizens from other industrialized or developing countries often led to problems of cultural and social marginalization, as well as to problems of school attendance and academic achievement for migrant children.

2.2. Slow-Down and Polarization in Child Welfare Progress? 1975–1989

2.2.1. Broad tendencies

Trends in child welfare over the 1975–89 period differed substantially from those observed between 1950 and 1975 for at least three reasons. To start with, progress in child welfare slackened in a number of countries. In some, including the Soviet Union and the USA, this slow-down was pronounced. Secondly, differentials in child welfare levels among countries widened. While Japan and Sweden were largely unaffected, the economic dislocations of the second part of the 1970s and 1980s reverberated on child welfare in several European countries. Finally, the 'new poverties', which had begun to surface in the late 1960s, intensified. The dynamics of these phenomena are complex and often assume country-specific characteristics. However, four factors may be seen as central to these processes.

2.2.2. Causes of the welfare slow-down

1. *Slow growth, rising unemployment, and worsening income distribution.* Economic growth slowed down from the early to mid-1970s in all industrialized countries. In market economies, growth of GDP per capita fell sharply from an average of 4 per cent in the 1950s and 1960s to a meagre 1 to 2 per cent over 1980–7 (Table 2.4; see also Table 3.1). In a number of years, particularly 1974–5 and 1980–3, growth in GDP per capita actually turned negative in Italy, the UK, and the Federal Republic of Germany. Only Japan, Norway, and Finland were not affected.

The slow-down in growth in the market economies was accompanied by marked increases in inflation and unemployment, two factors significant in the rise of poverty. Inflation had remained broadly constant at 2–3 per cent per annum during the 1950s and 1960s, but accelerated to 10 per cent (for the OECD as a whole) in the 1977–9 period. In the 1980s, it declined gradually as stringent monetarist policies were put in place. Although successful in combating inflation, these policies provoked two severe recessions (in 1974–5 and 1981–3) which, together with the decline in the labour intensity of production, swelled the ranks of the unemployed. The total number of unemployed in the OECD—which had fluctuated below 10 million during 1950–73—tripled between 1973 and 1982. The subsequent recovery was only able to trim back total unemployment to 25 million in 1990, while the long-term unemployed (especially in the European Union) rose to 40 per cent of the total (OECD, 1995).

The social security systems set in place in the 1950s and 1960s, and further extended in many countries in the 1970s, meant that most unemployed did not fall into poverty. However, as unemployment benefits have limited duration and are not shared equally by all segments of the labour force, such as the young (who have not yet built up entitlements) and part-time workers, unemployment remained a major cause of income loss, growing insecurity, and, for some, poverty. Only a few countries escaped the unemployment explosion, among them Japan where the unemployment rate increased to a modest 2.4 per cent over 1980–5 to drop to 2.1 per cent in 1990. Conversely, the situation was most acute in Western Europe, where unemployment has remained at 11 per cent since 1985 (Chapter 3).

With industrial restructuring and the spread of the low-productivity service sector, the 1975–89 period saw an increase in part-time and low-paying jobs. Although low-paying jobs offer additional employment and earning opportunities—particularly for women and the young—they contribute to rising poverty in one-earner households. In the USA, Canada, and Australia, low pay resulted from declining real wage rates, particularly at the bottom of the wage ladder (OECD, 1995). In the USA, for instance, earnings from full-time, year-round work in 1979 at the minimum hourly wage of $US3.35 were sufficient to lift a family of three above the poverty line. By 1988, the minimum wage had lost about 30 per cent of its purchasing power (Children's Defense Fund, 1989).

These trends in unemployment, insecure, poorly paid, and unregulated informal-sector employment, and the decline in minimum wages outweighed the effect of an overall increase in the number of income-earners in many industrialized economies. Between 1975 and 1989, median household incomes in real terms declined in some countries. In the USA, for instance, the real median family income declined from about $US29,000 a year in 1979 to $US27,700 in 1985, equivalent to the 1969 level (Danziger and Gottschalk, 1988). Similar evidence is available for France, where average wages lost 2 per cent of their purchasing power between 1982 and 1988, Australia (Edgar *et al.*, 1989), and other countries. In contrast, mean household expenditure rose in Japan by 53 per cent over the 1975–85 period (Preston and Kono, 1988).

In marked contrast to 1950–60 trends, income distribution became more unequal in most industrial market economies from the mid-1970s to the end of the 1980s, including the UK, France, the Netherlands, Canada, Australia, the USA, and Japan (see Table 3.10). Only in the case of Portugal does evidence point in the opposite direction. In addition, the wage share in total income fell steadily (OECD, 1995). Generally speaking, the trend towards greater inequality appears to result from many forces, including (i) endogenous changes in earnings distribution and employment patterns; (ii) demographic changes, such as population ageing and the surge in monoparental families; and (iii) policy-driven changes in the macroeconomy (particularly the interest rate), minimum wages, collective bargaining and progressivity, and the extent of the tax and transfer system (ibid.).

With regard to endogenous changes in earnings distribution, two main sets of factors have been identified. In most industrialized market economies, the demand for unskilled labour and employment in manufacturing have fallen substantially over the last two decades, concurrently with the rapid growth in imports of low-skill-intensive manufactured goods from developing countries. In addition, the rise of computers and other labour-saving technologies have drastically changed the distribution of skills, productivity, and earnings. Most analyses, especially those on the USA (see Wood, 1994 for a recent review of the literature), attribute most of the fall in the demand for and earnings of unskilled workers to this latter factor. However, new empirical evidence drawn from a broader set of developed market economies indicates that trade with developing countries has also been a significant factor in the increased earnings disparity.

The 1970s and 1980s also marked a period of growth slow-down in the centrally planned economies of Europe. Between the 1950s and 1980–6, growth in net material product (NMP) per capita fell from 6.9 to 2.2 per cent in Eastern Europe and from 9.3 to 3.6 per cent in the USSR (Table 2.3). Poland, Hungary, and Czechoslovakia, where the decline was most pronounced, recorded drops in NMP per capita for several years. The crisis intensified over the latter part of the 1980s, reaching unmanageable dimensions towards the end of the decade. By 1989, growth had turned negative in most of the region. By then, radical economic reforms (see Chapter 13) had become unavoidable.

As discussed in detail in Chapter 3, economic performance in the centrally planned economies of Europe started to deteriorate when the supply of labour (from rural areas, the incorporation of women in the labour force, and population growth) dwindled and the system concurrently failed to generate the increased technological innovation and microeconomic efficiency needed to compensate for this supply stagnation. Although these difficulties were recognized, policies did little to resolve the growing inefficiencies and tensions. Hungary was the only country to adopt a few timid reforms in the 1970s. Even modest reform attempts were brutally repressed in Czechoslovakia in 1968.

The economic growth slow-down provoked a different welfare impact in the centrally planned economies. Loss of employment was not an issue. However, with growth slackening—and an intensification of effort in the areas of capital accumulation and defence—expenditures for a variety of social purposes were gradually drained (see Chapters 5 and 6). Those waiting to profit from the extension of public services and social benefits or in line for better housing (such as the populations of secondary cities or remote rural areas) were most severely affected (Riazantzev *et al.*, 1992).

In some centrally planned economies (such as Hungary and the USSR), the distribution of earnings deteriorated moderately between the mid-1970s and the late 1980s (see Table 3.12). In addition, household budget survey data suggest that the distribution of household disposable incomes worsened sharply in Poland and moderately in Hungary (Riazantzev *et al.*, 1992), while apparently improving in the USSR (Braithwaite and Heleniak, 1989). However, as these household data do not take into account the influence of the spread of dual distribution systems, growing regional differences in the supply of consumer goods, and rising shortages, they most likely seriously underestimate the extent of the inequality increase. With stable administered prices, open inflation was not an issue until the late 1980s. The growth in 'suppressed inflation' associated with slow growth in material production led to increasing *de facto* rationing of basic goods. Some people and some areas were affected more than others: queuing required more time, and those without access to privileged distribution networks or with little time were hardest hit. Married women and single mothers with full-time jobs on top of household and child-care responsibilities had to put in much longer work-days, exceeding their own previous levels as well as those of most men.

2. *Growing instability, erosion of the traditional family, and the rise in monoparental families.* In all industrialized countries—regardless of political regime—changes in family structure underway since the 1950s accelerated sharply in the 1970s and 1980s. Though with important variations from one country to another, the traditional family became less common and other types of family structures, such as one-parent families, 'reconstructed families', and unmarried cohabiting couples became more frequent.

Marriage rates declined sharply, particularly from the early 1970s, in practically all industrialized countries (Table 2.6). At the same time, there was an increase in consensual unions, particularly in Northern Europe. In Sweden, the share of unmarried cohabiting couples rose from 1 to 15 per cent of the total between 1970 and 1979 (Trost, 1985). Even more startling, this share increased among women in the 20–4 age bracket from 29 to 44 per cent in only six years (United Nations, 1988). This phenomenon was almost as pronounced in France, the Federal Republic of Germany, and the USA, but much more modest in Southern and Eastern Europe. Cohabitation became accepted not only among the young, but also as an alternative choice involving all ages and including parenthood.

Consensual unions contributed to a major increase in out-of-wedlock births, representing, in 1980, 42 per cent of all births in Sweden, 38 per cent in Denmark, and over 20 per cent in the German Democratic Republic (Wynnyczuk, 1986). In most cases, however, children of consensual unions were not as likely to suffer major material or psychological deprivations as those of never-wed women, particularly where family

Table 2.6: Marriage Rates by Main Country Groupings, 1970–1990

	1970	1975	1980	1985	1988	1989	1990
North America	9.55	9.25	9.20	8.70	8.45	8.50	8.45
Northern Europe	7.45	6.55	5.83	5.45	5.97	6.75	5.38
Western Europe	7.72	6.67	6.18	5.72	5.83	6.05	6.23[a]
Southern Europe	8.16	8.50	6.64	6.14	5.96	6.28	6.06
Eastern Europe	8.37	9.16	7.98	7.37	7.18	7.20	7.30[a]
Former USSR	9.70	10.70	10.30	9.80	9.40	9.40	9.20
Japan	10.40[b]	8.40	6.60	6.10	5.80	5.80	5.80
Australia and New Zealand	9.25[b]	7.75	7.40	7.45	7.10	6.95	6.90

[a] From 1990, GDR is included in the Western Europe grouping. [b] 1971.

Sources: Council of Europe (1993); United Nations (1995).

legislation had been adapted to this new social reality. Yet, cohabitation was usually less stable than marriage and children born to cohabiting couples were more likely to experience a family break-up and to have lived in several types of households before reaching adulthood (Saraceno, 1992).

The most serious cause of concern for policy-makers during this period was the unrelenting rise in monoparentality. The incidence of single parenthood depends upon trends in divorce/separation, remarriage, risk of widowhood, and births to single mothers.

As noted earlier, divorce rates peaked immediately after the war and then rose only moderately until the early 1970s. During this decade, however, rates accelerated sharply (Table 2.5), resulting, it is claimed, at least in part from women's increased labour force participation rate which provided them with the financial autonomy to end unsatisfactory marriages (Saraceno, 1992). Remarriage rates also declined, while improved adult health conditions clearly reduced the risk of widowhood. Finally, as shown in Table 2.7, the share of out-of-wedlock births in total births, which had declined in most countries until the mid-1960s (or mid-1970s in Southern Europe), started to rise rapidly again from that point.

The net result of these four trends was a substantial rise in single-parent families. Table 2.8 documents the sources of this increase in the USA. There were (and remain) significant racial differences in the USA regarding the likelihood of children living in lone-parent households and the number of years they spend in such households. The Panel Study on Income Dynamics (Duncan and Rodgers, 1990) found that 22 per cent of black children spend all of their first fifteen years in one-parent households, compared to less than 2 per cent of white children. According to OECD (1990), lone-parent families represent 10–15 per cent of all families with dependent children in member countries, with the exception of

Table 2.7:   Share of Out-of-Wedlock Births in the Total by Main Country Groupings, 1970–1990

	1970	1975	1980	1985	1988	1990
North America	10.2	14.2[a]	16.2	20.5[b]	23.6	26.0
Northern Europe	8.8	14.5	19.5	26.5	31.1	33.3
Western Europe	5.6	6.2	8.3	12.1	14.0	17.3[c,d]
Southern Europe	4.1	4.2	4.2	5.4	8.0	8.7
Eastern Europe	7.0	7.3	9.0	11.7	12.3	8.8[d]
Former USSR	8.2	8.2	8.8	9.1	10.2	11.2
Japan	0.9	0.8	0.8	1.0	1.0	1.0
Australia and New Zealand	11.3	13.3	16.3	20.2	—	—

[a]Excluding Canada. [b]Figure for Canada refers to 1986. [c]Excluding Belgium. [d]For 1990, GDR is included in the Western Europe grouping.

Sources: Council of Europe (1993); United Nations, *Demographic Yearbook* (various years). *Eurosocial Reports* (1990); Bruce (1995); US Bureau of the Census (1990*a* and 1992*a*).

Table 2.8:   Children 0–18 Years Living with One Parent, USA, Selected Years

	1970	1982	1985	1986	% Change 1970–86
Child lives with mother, who is:[a]					
Divorced	2.3	5.1	5.3	5.4	135
Separated	2.3	3.1	3.0	2.9	26
Never married	0.5	2.8	3.5	3.6	620
Widowed	1.4	1.1	0.9	0.9	−36
Total children living with mother only[a]	7.5	12.5	13.1	13.2	76
Child lives with father, who is:[b]					
Divorced	177	658	750	796	350
Separated	152	255	329	289	90
Never married	30	114	260	318	960
Widowed	254	144	162	145	−43
Total children living with father only[c]	748	1,189	1,554	1,579	111

[a]Number in millions. [b]Number in thousands. [c]Includes children in 'married, spouse-absent' families, not separately shown.

Source: Cherlin (1988).

Ireland, Japan, and Spain, where the share is less than 10 per cent. However, the proportion of families experiencing a lone-parent 'phase' has grown everywhere.

Outside the USA, the incidence of monoparental families rose as swiftly. By the mid-late 1980s, of all families with children, 17 per cent were one-parent families in Sweden, 15 per cent in Canada, around 14 per cent in Denmark and the UK, approximately 13 per cent in France and Germany, from 10 to 12 per cent in Belgium, Luxembourg, Czechoslovakia, and the Netherlands, between 5 and 10 per cent in Ireland, Italy, Portugal, and Spain, about 7 per cent in Japan, and less than 5 per cent in Greece (US Bureau of the Census, 1990b; Kiernan and Wicks, 1990; Kroupová, 1988). These data, however, must be interpreted with caution, since both the children's ages and the definition of 'lone parent' differ (Saraceno, 1992).

Similarly, national sources show the following broad percentages of children were living in single-parent households around 1985—Australia, Czechoslovakia, France, and Italy: 9–10 per cent; Canada, Germany, Ireland, Poland, Sweden, and the UK: 10–13 per cent; Norway, 19 per cent; and the USA, a staggeringly high 26 per cent. Again, Japan was an exception with a low 4.8 per cent.

Paternal mortality was still an important, though declining, cause of monoparentality in most countries. Finally, children in Canada, Great Britain, Sweden, and the USA were more likely to be affected by high out-of-wedlock births than those in France, Germany, and especially Italy, Portugal, and Spain. None the less, the trends were similar in all the industrialized world.

This extensive discussion of trends in monoparentality is justified by the severe material and psychosocial deprivation it can cause for children. Three separate risks can be identified (Garfinkel and McLanahan, 1986). First, there is a much higher risk of falling into poverty, with all the attendant implications of inadequate nutrition and other material deprivations. This risk is greatly accentuated because discrimination against women in the labour market renders the earning power of the primary breadwinner (the mother) both relatively low and lower than that of men; the contribution of other family members—especially the non-custodial father—is low; and in most countries, public transfers to mother-only families, with the exception of widows, are still quite meagre. Children in these families are also more likely to be poor in adulthood and (in the case of daughters of single mothers) to be on welfare themselves.

Secondly, there is increased risk in lone-parent families of inadequate parental guidance, supervision, and parent–child interaction, resulting in higher probabilities of injury, insufficient stimulation, and reduced educational achievement. In addition, with limited resources and income insecurity, there is evidence that single mothers may have lower educational aspirations for their children than do married mothers. Research on cognitive ability, for instance, shows that children in one-parent families scored lower than children in two-parent families and had substantially higher chances of dropping out of school, committing delinquent acts, and engaging in drug and alcohol use.

Finally, there is a stronger likelihood of emotional and psychological maladaptation in these children due to identity problems caused by the absence of a parent. A panel study of children born out of wedlock in Czechoslovakia shows these children's greater need for emotional and social support (Dunovsky, quoted in Wynnyczuk, 1986). In addition, research on the effect of family formation behaviour shows that daughters who grow up in single-parent families are less likely to marry, more likely to divorce, and more likely to become heads of single-parent families themselves (McLanahan and Sandefur, 1994).

3. *The relative neglect of social policy towards children and adolescents.* Over the fifteen years from 1973 to 1989, social security systems were strengthened in both industrial market economies and centrally planned economies. Pension coverage was broadened and existing programmes were improved or consolidated. Overall, social expenditure as a proportion of GDP expanded in many industrial market economies until 1980–1, at which point major efforts were undertaken to contain public expenditure and budget deficits (see Chapter 4). While government consumption expenditure (which includes health and education outlays) was stabilized or even reduced, social security transfers continued to grow, partly for reasons beyond the control of governments (ageing of the population or persistently high unemployment rates, for instance). As major exceptions to this trend, most Scandinavian countries started to reduce the proportion of social security transfers, although from extremely high levels (20–5 per cent of GDP).

By the end of the 1980s, the main elements of family policies included (see also Fajth, 1994 on this and McFate *et al.*, 1995):

- *Maternity (or paternity) leave,* with an average duration of six months and with cash benefits of around 80–100 per cent of the mother's salary (or, exceptionally, of the father's, if he is taking the leave). In the USA, however, at the end of the 1980s, guaranteed maternity leave existed only in a few states, and its duration was generally reduced to about twelve weeks (a general scheme was introduced in 1993 but is still unpaid; see Chapter 7). In all countries of Eastern Europe and the USSR, an *ad hoc child birth grant* (between a quarter and a half of an average monthly salary) was also made available.
- *Child-care leave,* generally granted in most Eastern European countries to mothers of children up to 3 years of age, providing a

proportion (around 50 per cent) of the mother's salary. *Leare for child's sickness* (generally up to sixty days a year at about 50–90 per cent of the salary) was also available in these countries.

- A public, often universal, *child benefit*, aimed at partially offsetting the cost of raising a child. In some countries, however, the child allowance was conceived as a selective antipoverty transfer or pronatalist tool. The USA and Japan were the only industrialized countries which had not introduced a child allowance by the late 1980s. Amounts varied enormously, from close to zero in Spain, to about 3 per cent of the average manufacturing wage (for a family with two children) in Canada, Poland, and Ireland, to around 10 per cent in Austria, Belgium, Sweden, and Czechoslovakia, and to 20.5 per cent in Hungary, a country that developed a strong social policy after the repression of 1956 (see Chapters 4 and 5). In the USA, the Aid to Families with Dependent Children (AFDC) provides means-tested cash payments for caretakers of needy children, if they have been deprived of parental support.
- *Child support (alimony) payments*, introduced in some Western and Eastern European countries (all of Scandinavia, France, and Poland, among others). This benefit is advanced to the custodial parent by a government agency when child support payments owed by the absent parent are not paid, paid irregularly, or are too low. The same agency assumes responsibility for the collection of child support from the absent parent. This benefit still lacks general application.
- The universal provision of free or highly subsidized *preschool education, health care, and compulsory education for nine to eleven years* for all children.

Although most countries—with the exception of the USA, Japan, and Australia—shared the same broad approach to family policy, the actual value of amounts transferred varied considerably (see Chapters 4 and 5). In the early 1980s, the overall value of cash transfers represented 95 per cent of the earned income of an employed single mother in Sweden, 60 per cent in France, about 30 per cent in the UK and Federal Republic of Germany, and 20 per cent in Pennsylvania (USA) (Kahn and Kamerman, 1983). In Eastern Europe, the priority accorded to social expenditure, child and family benefits, and social services made them, with few exceptions (the USSR, for instance), comprehensive, fairly generous, and widely available. The child allowance was particularly important and absorbed a greater share of national income than in most OECD countries. For this reason, Hungary and Czechoslovakia have been singled out—together with Sweden, Norway, and France—as the countries with 'an explicit and comprehensive family policy' (Gordon, 1988: 22). The generosity and comprehensiveness of child benefits were particularly important for families with more than two children or with multiple risks (single parenthood, disabilities, and so on). For such families, child benefits accounted for between one-third and one-half of total income, and effectively protected them from severe deprivation (Zimakova, 1993; Cornia and Sipos, 1991).

In the Central European countries with explicit family policies, such as Czechoslovakia and Hungary, the value of overall transfers in favour of children reached 5.3 and 6.4 per cent, respectively, of GDP (Chapter 4; Gordon, 1988). Even these generous transfers were unable, however, to prevent the fall into poverty of a substantial number of children (Szalai, 1992). A much weaker social policy had, meanwhile, taken shape in the former USSR and other less developed Eastern European countries.

Child-care services were well developed in this region. Enrolment in crèches and kindergartens was higher than in most OECD and developing countries. At the end of the 1980s, for instance, enrolment in preschool education for 3–6-year-olds stood at 97 per cent in Czechoslovakia and 87 per cent in Hungary. While this was, in part, due to the high employment rates for women, it positively affected children, whose proper development depends on adequate interaction with other children and appropriate forms of stimulation.

These positive features of social policy were, however, obscured by explicit or hidden problems. First, with slow growth since the mid-1970s, benefits did not increase or even contracted. Second, effectiveness of social policy was sharply reduced by overcentralization, lack of incentives, and paternalism. Furthermore, an excessive role of the state in child socialization contributed to the weakening of the family's role in the upbringing of children. Third, in spite of proclaimed universal access to public services, substantial differences existed for health care, education, housing, and recreation.

As noted, social policy—and particularly the tax and transfer system—can be assessed in terms of their ability to remove children from poverty (Table 2.9). The impact of public transfers appears highest in Sweden and Norway (which rely on universal benefits) and lowest in Australia and the USA (where means-tested programmes are more common). It also appears that, with the exception of Sweden and Norway, the impact of public transfers in reducing the incidence of poverty is somewhat lower among single-parent families which, even after transfers, continue to experience much higher poverty rates than the average (see Figures 14.1 and 14.2).

Increasingly, benefits and social services to families became means-tested, leaving more and more people cut off from benefits or having to pay user fees for 'public goods'. More of the social security burden thus fell on families, kinship networks, and communities, just when needs

Table 2.9:   Role of Public Transfers in Removing Various Types of Families
from Poverty, Selected Countries, around 1980–81

Country	Percentage of poor families		Overall poverty reduction rate
	Pre-tax/ pre-transfer	Post-tax/ post-transfer	
(a)Families with children			
Australia	17.6	15.0	14.8
Canada	13.6	8.6	36.8
Germany, F.R.	7.9	6.9	12.7
Norway	12.1	6.4	47.1
Sweden	10.4	4.4	57.7
Switzerland	4.4	4.1	6.8
UK	14.1	8.5	39.7
USA	16.6	13.8	16.9
(b)Single-parent families			
Australia	67.6	61.4	9.2
Canada	48.0	35.3	26.5
Germany, F.R.	37.2	31.9	14.2
Norway	35.2	17.6	50.0
Sweden	33.1	7.5	77.3
Switzerland	14.5	11.9	17.9
UK	53.1	36.8	30.7
USA	49.3	42.9	13.0
(c)Elderly families			
Australia	72.2	23.8	67.0
Canada	56.8	5.9	89.6
Germany, F.R.	80.6	17.1	78.8
Norway	76.6	19.6	74.4
Sweden	87.9	2.6	97.0
Switzerland	59.8	7.3	87.8
UK	77.6	40.9	47.3
USA	59.0	18.7	68.3

Source: Adapted from Smeeding *et al.* (1988), table 5.11.

were swelling because of economic and labour market conditions and
changes in family structure and instability. Table 2.9 highlights an important feature of this shift in social policy in industrial market economies:
poverty reduction rates are much higher in most cases for the elderly than
for both one- and two-parent families. This is due to the relative back-
wardness of social policies for the family. Indeed, with the possible exception of some countries in Northern and Eastern Europe, most family
allowances: (i) continually lagged behind inflation, average wages, and
other transfers; (ii) were rarely universal in nature; and (iii) have only
slowly and incompletely adjusted to the emergence of profound changes

in the social fabric and the rising numbers of children with specific needs, such as the children of migrants.

Child benefits were indexed to inflation in only about one-fourth of the market economies, but they changed less in most socialist countries of Europe where open inflation was not an issue. There were many examples of declines, though at times temporary, in the real value of child benefits in countries as different as Italy (Artoni and Ranci Ortigosa, 1989), the USSR (Likhanov, 1987; see also Chapter 6), Portugal (da Costa *et al.*, 1985), and the USA (Palmer *et al.*, 1988), while in others the decline in the value of child benefits was relative to the value of transfers to other social groups such as the elderly (Table 2.10).

As the social support needs of children and the elderly are very different, it does not make much sense to compare the ratios of Table 2.10 in any particular year. More interesting are trends over time. They reveal that the ratio remained broadly constant in three cases, declined in five, and increased moderately in the Federal Republic of Germany and substantially in the UK. This means that although a broadly adequate policy to protect the elderly from poverty was developed over the last few decades, the formulation and resources for a comprehensive family policy were still not in place. This is all the more surprising in view of the radical changes in family structure and stability. As a result, a number of new family types requiring policy support have emerged, among which are:

- *More dual-worker families*. In all industrialized countries the number of families in which both parents work grew steadily during this period (Jallinoja, 1989). While this trend had a positive impact on child poverty, it also created new difficulties for working mothers, who had to juggle the demands of jobs and house-

Table 2.10: Per capita Family Benefits as a Percentage of per capita Old-Age Benefits, Selected Countries and Years, 1960–1984

	1960	1970	1975	1980	1984
Australia	8.5	5.6	3.7	7.9	10.3
Canada	11.3	6.0	10.1	5.7	5.0
France	28.0	16.2	15.4	14.4	13.5
Germany, F.R.	1.4	2.3	7.4	8.1	6.4
Italy	18.1	9.3	8.7	5.3	4.5
Japan	0.0	21.6	17.7	13.9	11.9
Netherlands	9.8	10.7	8.7	9.7	10.3
Sweden	15.8	13.4	14.8	12.2	10.1
UK	7.8	9.8	7.3	18.0	21.1
USA	1.4	3.2	3.6	3.3	3.0

Source: Varley (1986).

hold and child-care duties. However, except in Scandinavia, child-care services for under-3-year-olds remained scarce and costly. Kindergartens and primary school services were better catered for in terms of cost and quantity, but the organizational arrangements often remained insufficiently responsive to the needs of families.

- *Fewer children per family.* In the 1980s, more and more children grew up without siblings. An only child is more likely to be the focus of closer attention, care, and expectations of his or her parents, but has fewer opportunities for child companions. Thus, child-care services started to assume the role of providing company and peer stimulus for children (Saraceno, 1992). Policies introducing price barriers to these services tended to penalize the socialization needs of children growing up in these circumstances.

- *An increasing number of one-parent families.* While the living standards of widows and their children were generally better protected than those of divorced or unmarried mothers and their children (MacLean, 1990), and while divorced mothers could, at least in principle, count on the alimony provided by their former husbands, unmarried lone mothers were at highest risk as they generally had to rely only on themselves, their relatives, or public welfare. For these women and their children, a 'complete package' combining labour market or transfer income and a modicum of child-care services has seldom been developed.

- *More 'reconstituted' families.* Families consisting of step-parents and step-siblings gradually became almost as common as lone-parent families. However, legislation did not develop as fast to account for the relationships and mutual obligations which arise in such complex families. Problems in 'reconstituted' families, involving complicated generational and parental relationships, may require new regulation and support interventions.

4. *Weakening of community linkages.* Erosion of community solidarity and 'civil society' also negatively influenced child and, particularly, youth welfare over the 1975–89 period. Community solidarity inevitably weakened with rural-to-urban migration. This undermined extended family, kinship systems, and traditional social networks. Straining to adjust to city life, rural families experienced cultural conflicts and insecurity, social disorganization, and loss of control (Chapters 9 and 10).

Changes in living arrangements were another factor in the weakening of social relations. Children living in small high-rise apartments, for instance, often experience social isolation and alienation. They may have limited social experiences and motor activity during their early years and it is more difficult for them to play outdoors or with other children. A Japanese study found that children in high-rise housing show a delayed independence in fundamental daily practices compared with other children (Oda *et al.*, 1989).

Limited nurturing of 'civil society' by a public policy increasingly intent on promoting the virtues of individualism might also have been a relevant factor in the erosion of a sense of community. To sustain progress towards social goals, state institutions need to be supported by a vibrant civil society comprising churches, trade unions, sport and leisure clubs, boy scout groups, neighbourhood associations, and other community organizations. These 'social intermediaries' exert a positive social control, and serve as a useful complementary mechanism for the delivery of child care, youth socialization, and social assistance services. While it is difficult to prove conclusively that the institutions of civil society weakened during the 1970s and 1980s, this might be suggested by the growing socialization problems faced by youth (see below).

2.2.3. *Evidence on child poverty and deprivation over the mid-1970s to the late 1980s*

1. *Overall poverty.* With the exception of the USA, data on the incidence of poverty have never been abundant. For the 1975–89 period, however, more information has become available. In addition, international comparability has improved. This allows a tentative picture to be drawn of overall and child poverty around 1990 and of its changes over the last ten to fifteen years. It should be noted, however, that problems of data availability (particularly for Eastern Europe) and comparability temper the robustness and general applicability of conclusions.

Overall poverty increased in most countries of Western and Southern Europe, the USA, Hungary, Poland, Yugoslavia, and probably Australia. In contrast, in Japan, Sweden, Belgium, possibly Czechoslovakia and Norway, poverty has continued to fall; lack of information on the USSR, several of the Eastern European countries, and New Zealand precludes any specific conclusions.

In 1989 the Commission of the European Communities estimated the incidence of relative poverty for the twelve-member Community for the 1975–85 period (O'Higgins and Jenkins, 1989). People were considered to be in poverty if they lived in households with an adjusted disposable income of less than 50 per cent of the average adjusted disposable income. The study calculated that the poor rose from 38 to 44 million. Most of the increase occurred between 1980 and 1985 and concerned all countries in the Community, with the exception of Luxembourg and Greece where the poverty level remained stable, and of Belgium and France where poverty declined. The largest increase was found in the UK.

The composition of the poor changed markedly over 1975–85, with similar trends in the twelve countries. The number of elderly living in poverty declined sharply, while levels increased rapidly among the unemployed, those employed in precarious jobs, migrants, and single parents. Independent studies using comparable methodologies came to similar conclusions for Germany (Hauser and Semerau, 1989), Italy (Commissione di Studio Istituita presso la Presidenza del Consiglio dei Ministri, 1985), Ireland (Callan *et al.*, 1989), and the UK (Bradshaw, 1990).

Poverty estimates for the USA, Canada, and Japan were obtained by means of absolute poverty lines kept constant over time in real terms. In Japan, the percentage of persons living in households with a monthly expenditure of less than 100,000 yen declined from 25 to 9.5 per cent between 1975 and 1985 (Preston and Kono, 1988). In the USA, in contrast, the overall poverty ratio, which had been in continuous decline until 1979, rose sharply until 1983, before decreasing only marginally over the following years (Smolensky *et al.*, 1988). Despite a growth slow-down in Canada, poverty declined substantially between 1970 and 1979, and modestly over 1979–86 (Hanratty and Blank, 1992). The contraction in poverty during the first period was largely due to increases in median family incomes, while in the subsequent period poverty fell because—unlike in the USA—fairly generous income transfers were maintained and expanded.

Comprehensive poverty data for this period for the countries of Eastern Europe and the USSR are unobtainable, as 'poverty analysis' was explicitly discouraged until recently. Data for Czechoslovakia show that the proportion of families with children living below a minimum social level of consumption declined from 11.4 to 8.2 per cent of the total between 1975 and 1985 (Kovarik, 1988). In addition, the number of the poor (i.e. people with incomes below $US 50 a month in constant prices) increased sharply in Yugoslavia (from 17.5 to 24.8 per cent); rose modestly until 1983 in Hungary, and subsequently returned to its 1978 level; and literally exploded in Poland (from 9.2 to 22.7 per cent), particularly during the period of martial law (Milanovic, 1991). Poverty data in the USSR were published for the first time in 1988: 14.5 per cent of the population, or around 41 million people, were found to be living below the poverty line. Questionable data reliability, however, means that caution should be used when utilizing these statistics in international comparisons (Ellman, 1990).

Thus, after more than two decades of steady progress in all industrialized countries, poverty started to rise again from the mid-1970s in about two-thirds of the countries for which data are available, albeit with different characteristics and among different social groups.

2. *Child poverty.* As may be expected, the rise of poverty—or its slower decline—did not spare young children and adolescents. Quite the contrary. The changes described in the previous section (rising unemploy-

ment, unstable jobs, income inequality, family instability, and weak social policy) resulted in a more than proportional increase in child poverty in the Western market economies (Table 2.11).

These data indicate that between the early 1970s and late 1980s-early 1990s, child poverty increased markedly in the USA and the UK, and modestly (from very low levels) in Germany, the Netherlands, and Norway. Child poverty stagnated at a high level in Australia and at a low level in France, while modest declines were recorded in Canada, Belgium, Finland, and Sweden. While making use of different types of poverty lines, other analyses confirm the trends in Table 2.11 for Germany, the USA, Canada, and Sweden (Hauser and Semerau, 1989; Smeeding *et al.*, 1988; Wolfson, 1989; and Erikson and Fritzell, 1988).

Evidence relative to countries not included in Table 2.11 allows us to complete the picture. These estimates have generally been obtained by means of absolute poverty lines and provide robust estimates of child poverty within each country, but are not strictly comparable across countries. They suggest that between the mid-1970s and the mid-1980s, child poverty rose in Ireland (15.7 to 26 per cent; Callan *et al.*, 1989) and Hungary (17.1 to 20 per cent; Szalai, 1989), but declined rapidly in Japan (25.3 to 10.9 per cent; Preston and Kono, 1988) and Czechoslovakia (11.4 to 8.2 per cent; Kovarik, 1988). In the latter two countries, however, this decline faltered in the 1980s. Finally, though no direct estimates of child poverty are available for Poland and Yugoslavia, the increases in overall poverty in these two countries have certainly been accompanied by at least a proportional rise in the number of poor children (see Milanovic, 1991).

These data tend to suggest that the improvements in child poverty of the 'golden age' were reversed or slowed down. Indeed, child poverty rates increased in nine of the seventeen countries for which trend data between 1970 and 1990 are available, stagnated in two, and decreased in six. The rise was most pronounced in the USA, Ireland, the UK, Poland, and Yugoslavia. In most of these countries, the most rapid increases were recorded during the 1980s. As a result, at the end of the 1980s, child poverty in industrialized countries ranged widely, between 3 and 26 per cent.

Two distinct clusters can be singled out. A *'high child poverty cluster'* of countries which experienced an increase (or stagnation at high level) in child poverty during this period (with rates between 10 and 26 per cent). This group includes the English-language countries (the USA, Ireland, UK, Canada, Australia), possibly Italy and the centrally planned economies (with the exception of Czechoslovakia). It also takes in the less prosperous nations of Southern Europe, where poverty might have declined but not rapidly enough to reduce the number of children living below an acceptable income threshold. For instance, child poverty was between 25 and 30 per cent for Spain (Equipo de Investigacion

Table 2.11: Changes in Child Poverty Rates in Selected Market Economies, 1967–1991

Nation	Years	Period 1 <1971	Period 2 1972–5	Period 3 1978–81	Period 4 1982–5	Period 5 1986–8	Period 6 1990+
USA	1969,74,79,86,91	13.2	17.9	18.5	—	22.9	21.5
Australia	1981,85,90	—	—	14.0	14.0	—	14.1
Canada	1971,75,81,87,91	15.2	13.1	13.8	—	13.7	13.5
Belgium	1985,88	—	—	—	3.4	3.1	—
France	1979,84	—	—	6.4	6.5	—	—
Germany	1973,78,83	—	3.9	3.0	4.3	—	—
Netherlands	1983,87	—	—	—	2.5	4.1	—
UK	1969,74,79,86	5.2	6.7	8.5	—	9.9	—
Finland	1987,91	—	—	—	—	2.9	2.5
Norway	1979,86	—	—	3.8	—	3.8	4.6
Sweden	1967,75,81,87	5.7	1.9	3.9	—	3.0	2.7

Notes: Measure—percentage of children living in families with disposable cash incomes less than 50 per cent of the adjusted median disposable income for all families. Nations for which we have only one point estimate and no trend estimate: Ireland (1987) 12.6 per cent; Italy (1986) 10.8 per cent; Luxembourg (1985) 4.0 per cent; Switzerland (1982) 3.3 per cent.

Source: Computed by Timothy Smeeding on Luxembourg Income Study Database.

Sociologica, 1984) and Portugal (da Costa *et al.*, 1985; Silva and da Costa, 1989). The *'low child poverty cluster'* of countries which were able during this period to maintain or improve progress made during the 'golden age' (with rates ranging between 2 and 7 per cent) includes the Western and Northern European countries and Japan. As noted in the above discussion

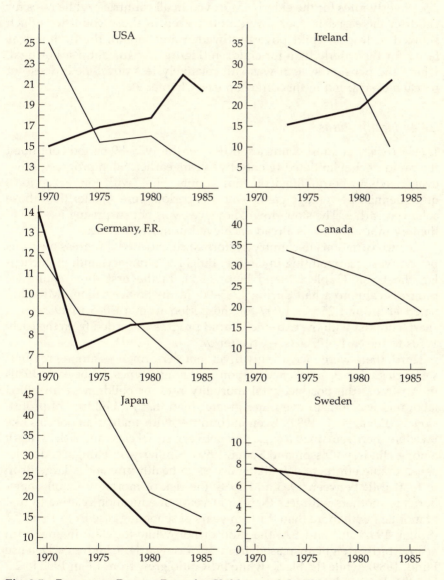

Fig. 2.5 Percentage Poverty Rates for Children and the Elderly in Selected Countries, 1970–1985

and throughout this book, these countries broadly maintained full employment and low income inequality, or sustained generous transfer policies in favour of the unemployed and children.

Before concluding this section, it is worth emphasizing one of the most pronounced phenomena of the 1975–89 period, i.e. the divergent paths of poverty rates between children and the elderly. As may be seen in Figure 2.5, poverty rates for the elderly improved in all countries, while rates for children increased in four. In addition, even in those countries which showed a drop in child poverty (Sweden and Japan), the decline was faster for the elderly than for children (Figure 2.5). In contrast, Portugal, where the pension system was still relatively less developed, does not reveal a clear trend in this direction (see Chapter 9).

2.2.4. Health status

1. *IMR trends.* In most countries, IMR over the 1975–89 period continued the rapid decline initiated twenty-five years earlier. Such progress, however, needs to be qualified on four counts. First, with few exceptions, quinquennial percentage gains over this period were smaller than those achieved earlier. The slow-down, however, was not surprising in view of the low mortality levels already achieved in most countries.

Second, variations in country performance widened. Progress over this period was disappointing in Greece, Bulgaria, Hungary, and, in particular, the USSR (Table 2.1 and Figure 2.2). In the first three countries, progress came to a halt during 1985–90. In the Soviet Union, IMR stagnated at around 25 per 1,000 for the period from 1970–5 to 1985–90, a sharp contrast with the extremely rapid progress recorded from the early 1950s to the early 1970s (see Chapter 6).

Third, there were increasingly divergent performances among regions, social classes, race, level of education, and family types. In the early 1980s in Australia, the post-neonatal mortality rate for children of unskilled labourers was four to five times greater than that for children of professionals (Edgar *et al.*, 1989). Even in countries with egalitarian policies like Sweden, there remained a close link between social class and risk of death among children (Olsson and Spånt, 1991). Similarly, in Hungary, despite considerable efforts at equalizing access to health care and a large drop in total IMR between 1965 and 1988, the risk of mortality among newborns to mothers with less than eight years of education relative to that of mothers with more than thirteen years of schooling rose from 1.6 to 3.1 (Szalai, 1992). In the USA, the ratio of non-white-to-white infants born at low birth weight increased from 1975 onwards (Children's Defense Fund, 1989), while the black–white IMR ratio grew from 1.6 in 1950 to 2.2 in 1991. Regional disparities in health also persisted or worsened. In the USSR, IMR ranged from 11 per 1,000 in Latvia and Lithuania to 53 in

Turkmmenistan in 1988 (Riatzantsev *et al.*, 1992). Despite considerable progress in child health, in Italy, north–south differentials in perinatal mortality widened during the period under consideration (Chapter 10).

Fourth, considerable 'excess infant mortality' still existed in 1989 in most industrialized countries, excepting Scandinavia and Japan. Considerable improvements in medical technology had lowered the 'biological minimum' to about 4–5 per 1,000 live births. This was largely due to the improved chance of survival of low-birth-weight infants and to a reduction in mortality from other endogenous causes. In addition, medical advances allowed identification of high-risk pregnancies and their termination if necessary. If a rate of 5 per 1,000 had been reached by 1989 in all industrialized countries, about 184,000 infant deaths would have been avoided each year.

2. *New child morbidity*. The incidence of communicable diseases, acute respiratory infections, and diseases of the digestive tract decreased radically in all countries, as evidenced by the reduction in post-neonatal and child mortality. There was, however, a growth in 'new child morbidity', an umbrella term that includes environment-related ailments, psychological and behavioural problems, developmental dysfunctions, dyslexia, and accidents. It appears that new morbidity was more prevalent in this period among boys and in children from families characterized by low education levels, unstable employment, financial difficulties, and maximal exposure to environmental stress (noise, pollution, overcrowding, and low hygienic standards).

Food poisoning increased, as did food intolerance, allergies, and asthma. During the 1980s, for instance, the number of allergy cases among children grew on average by 10 per cent in Czechoslovakia (Struk, 1990). Similar developments occurred in Poland (Duch, 1993). In the USA, the number of children hospitalized for asthma increased by 225 per cent between 1970 and 1987 (*Newsweek*, 22 May 1989). Poor quality of the air affected children in industrial and mining areas, such as the Polish coal district of Silesia. In Hungary, asthmatic diseases rose five times during the 1980s (Orosz, 1990), while Yugoslavia witnessed an analogous trend. Incidence of tumours among children in heavily polluted areas of Poland, Czechoslovakia, and the USSR was reported to have increased by between 43 and 200 per cent (ZG TPD, 1990; Struk, 1990; Shcherbak, 1991, cited in Sipos, 1991).

Second, the emotional well-being and mental health of children and adolescents became more problematic. The suicide rate among adolescents increased in the USA, Norway, Canada, the UK, and Sweden (until the late 1970s) and in the 1980s in France. No consistent trend was detectable in West Germany, while there was a decline in Italy and Czechoslovakia (Cherlin, 1988; Consiglio Nazionale dei Minori, 1988; Kovarik, 1988; Palmer *et al.*, 1989; Hultén and Wasserman, 1992). In Britain, the most pronounced increase in suicide rates between 1941 and 1950 and 1971 and 1980 was for 15–19-year-old boys and for 10–14-year-old girls (Hultén and Wasserman, 1992). A study of Swedish suicide trends between 1974 and 1986 found that the rate was particularly high for males over 15 years and that, after road accidents and cancer, suicide was the most common cause of death for boys and young men (ibid.). Youth who took their own lives were found to have suffered from loneliness, depression, lack of adult support, and inability to live up to their own or others' expectations (see Chapter 12). Another review which examined the suicide rate for the 15–24 age-group in eleven Western market economies between 1980 and 1986 points to consistent and large increases (ranging between 10 and 250 per cent) in every one of the countries analysed (Barba Navaretti and Galleani D'Agliano, 1992).

Survey data on the use by young people of mental health services show that the number of consultations for emotional, mental, and behavioural problems has risen significantly since the late 1960s. In the USA, the increase was found to concern primarily the children of broken families. Although the growing availability of facilities and personnel providing psychological support may have facilitated increasing recourse to such services, it is believed that the increase can rather be traced to changing family patterns, the breakdown of traditionally stabilizing institutions, loneliness, the loss of a sense of purpose and sense of community, and—in several countries—the growing pressure to compete for limited educational opportunities (Cherlin, 1988; and Chapters 11 and 12).

Third, despite a sharp decline in the overall accident rate and a growing tendency for resulting injuries to be less serious, accidents were still the most frequent cause of child mortality and morbidity in countries as different as Sweden and Italy (Ekblad, 1993; Chapter 10). In Sweden, accident victims accounted for an estimated 10 per cent of utilization of care services by children. The 13–15 age-group was the most accident-prone. Traffic accidents represented the largest danger, particularly as inadequate play facilities and open areas meant that children were often forced to play on the streets.

2.2.5. *Social protection and social deviance*

The issue of physical and sexual abuse of children came to the fore in the 1980s, though it is difficult to judge to what extent this is due to a greater awareness of an existing problem or to a dramatic growth in its prevalence. An increasing number of cases were reported in the USA (Children's Defense Fund, 1989), the UK (Bradshaw, 1989), and in Italy (Saraceno, 1990), among others. Increased public awareness was certainly in part responsible for the growing number of abuse cases brought to the attention of service agencies. However, two reasons add credibility to the hypothesis that child abuse was on the rise. First, several studies have shown that unemployment and economic stringency tend to increase family violence. In addition, homelessness—another growing phenomenon in the UK (Bradshaw, 1989), the USA (Children's Defense Fund, 1989), Australia (Edgar *et al.*, 1989), and other countries with increased reporting of child abuse cases—put children at increased risk of abuse. Second, the actual number of prosecutions for cases of abuse and neglect increased, for instance, in the USA and the UK.

Over the 1970s and 1980s, the social behaviour and attitudes of young people changed profoundly. Theft and violence, use of illicit drugs, and early sexual activity outside marriage increased. In the USA, these three phenomena appear to have expanded until the early 1980s, when they broadly levelled off (Cherlin, 1988). In other countries, the picture is quite different. Teenage pregnancies exhibited a heterogeneous trend. They decreased in North America and all of the Nordic and North European countries, with Ireland registering a marked decrease, while there was an upward trend in all of the Southern and Eastern European nations, except the German Democratic Republic and Italy. Japan also recorded a relatively significant rise, although the percentage of teenagers among all pregnant women in Japan remained the lowest in the world.

Following a fairly rapid increase throughout the 'golden age', juvenile delinquency continued to climb until the early 1980s in practically all Western countries. Since then, the increase has flattened out in the USA, West Germany, Sweden, the UK, and Italy (Table 2.12) as well as in Austria and Switzerland. While various sources confirm that the juvenile crime rate remained at about the same level in the USA, the decline in Italy, Ireland, and the UK was partly due to the growing use of cautions and community services rather than sentences (Consiglio Nazionale dei Minori, 1988; Ghiolla Phadraig, 1990; Bradshaw, 1989). In at least another eight countries, including Japan (where adult crime rates have been shifting downwards since the end of the World War), the increase continued or accelerated until the end of the 1980s (Table 2.12; Barba Navaretti and Galleani D'Agliano, 1992). In addition, juvenile crime rates rose steadily for all Eastern European countries for which data could be compiled (Sipos, 1991).

Available analyses indicate that serious and repeated juvenile crime tended to remain confined to areas of marginality, but that many more children committed damage to public property, shoplifted, exerted violence against persons, and stole. The increase in crime was found to be particularly rapid in the latter part of the 1980s, especially among institutionalized children, children with low educational levels, school drop-

Table 2.12:   Juvenile[a] Offences[b] in Selected Countries (per 100,000 inhabitants)

	1977	1980	1985	1988
USA	1,213.2	1,251.4	890.3	911.9
Japan	352.1	473.4	590.8	643.6
France	553.0	745.3	728.0	672.0
West Germany	1,188.8	1,326.5	1,043.2	931.9
England and Wales	1,878.6	1,746.9	1,741.9	1,619.1
Scotland	99.3	225.0	46.7	—
Northern Ireland	619.3	912.3	417.3	326.4
Hungary	—	109.7	171.1	183.5
Italy	—	—	117.4	134.9[c]
Netherlands	893.3	1,027.4[d]	1,352.6	1,354.8
Spain	5.7	147.1	557.0	832.9
Sweden	—	—	1,449.9	1,514.7

[a] Definition of 'juvenile' differs for individual countries: USA, 0–18; Japan, 14–19; France, 13–18; West Germany, 0–17; England and Wales, 10–16; Scotland, 8–15; Northern Ireland, 10–17; Hungary, 14–18; Italy, 14–18; Netherlands, 12–18; Spain, 0–16 until 1987, 0–20 thereafter; Sweden, 15–17. [b] Computed as the number of total crime per 100,000 inhabitants multiplied by the rate of juvenile offenders on total offenders. [c] 1981 figure. [d] 1986 figure.

Source: International Criminal Police Organization (1990).

outs, children with weak family bonds, and—in countries such as Italy, Germany, the Netherlands, Sweden, and Switzerland—among immigrant children (Barba Navaretti and Galleani D'Agliano, 1992).

This period also signalled increasing involvement of children and adolescents in substance abuse, though it is almost impossible to form a quantitative picture of the phenomenon. Official statistics show a relatively low, and at times declining, rate of drug use in countries such as Italy and the UK. Indirect evidence, however, suggests the contrary. In the UK, the number of deaths attributed to the toxic effect of solvent abuse trebled between 1980 and 1986 (Bradshaw, 1989). In the post-industrial city of Milan in Italy, the number of minors put in institutions for drug use doubled in only two years. In addition, there is evidence that dependence on hard drugs is increasing rapidly, while it is stagnating or decreasing for light drugs (Cherlin, 1988). There are also indications that the age of initiation into substance use has declined. Children as young as 8 and 9 years of age have been reported to consume cocaine in inner-city areas of New York and Washington, DC. In the centrally planned economies of Europe, drug abuse remained relatively less common than in most Western countries, though the problem of alcoholism grew more steeply. In Hungary, for instance, the number of children at risk of becoming alcoholic increased 2.5 times between 1971 and 1987.

2.3. Conclusion

The foregoing analysis has shown that many—perhaps most—income- and capabilities-based child welfare indicators improved in industrialized countries during the period going from the mid-1970s to the end of the 1980s. Yet, a number of disturbing indications emerged over this period in the areas of family stability, child poverty, 'new child morbidity', and in the field of adolescent socialization, deviance, and protection. In addition, unlike during the 'golden age', differential achievements (by region, social class, race, level of education, and so on) appear to have persisted or widened, despite often considerable average improvements. The long-run impact of this growing differentiation in child welfare is very worrying, but far from understood.

As the reader can see in Chapters 13 and 14, the unsatisfactory trends in child welfare identified over the 1973–89 period in several of the countries under study appear with hindsight to be the harbinger of the even more alarming changes occurring during the post-communist era. These disturbing trends were the result of a more general polarization and marginalization of society. But they were also the outcome of a social policy which has been—almost universally—biased against children and youth, paying only scant attention to the drastic changes which had occurred in family structure and social fabric. A consistent response to child welfare problems for the future will therefore require not only measures in the field of employment and incomes, but also in those of family allowances, services for children, and policies which strengthen the family and the community.

3

Growth, Public Expenditure, and Household Welfare in the Industrialized Countries

ANDREA BOLTHO

3.1. Introduction

This chapter surveys some of the major macroeconomic and policy trends in the industrialized countries of the East and West that may have had a bearing on household welfare and child poverty during the fifteen or twenty years from the oil shock of 1973 to the end of the 1980s or early 1990s. In many ways, this is an apt period for analysis. In the East, it covers the end of the central planning era to 1989. In the West, it stretches over three business cycles going from the peak of 1973 to that of 1989–91. Subsequent developments are largely eschewed since systemic changes and output collapses in one area and a deep recession in the other introduce strong elements of non-comparability with earlier trends. Though a recovery is now taking place in both East and West, it is not sufficiently established (and far too few comparable data are, as yet, available) for it to be included in this discussion.

Any survey of macroeconomic events over such a time-span could examine many topics and numerous countries. To keep the task manageable, the chapter limits itself to an investigation of three areas in which major changes seem to have occurred that, directly and indirectly, are bound to have affected child welfare:

- the pronounced deceleration in overall growth that has been observed in the industrialized market and centrally planned economies from the mid-1970s onward;
- the changes that took place over the same period in both East and West in public expenditure and taxation as a result of the shortfall in growth and of new attitudes and approaches to economic policy;
- the modifications in household-income distribution consequent upon both lower growth and changes in public spending and tax policies.

Many thanks are due to Giovanni Andrea Cornia and Andrew Glyn, both of whom made numerous and very useful comments on an earlier draft.

Space constraints also dictate limitations on country coverage. On the Western side, the analysis includes the seven major economies (the USA, Japan, Canada, Germany, France, Italy, and the UK), as well as some of the smaller European countries (particularly Austria, the Netherlands, Spain, and Sweden). On the Eastern side, an attempt is made to cover the former Soviet Union and some of the smaller economies (especially Bulgaria, Czechoslovakia, the ex-German Democratic Republic, Hungary, and Poland). The frequent lack of reliable data, however, precludes as detailed an examination as that presented for the countries of the Organisation of Economic Co-operation and Development (OECD).

The next three sections look in turn at the issues of growth, public expenditure, and household incomes. Each section examines the experience of the market economies, then that of the centrally planned countries, and ends with some comparative comments. The concluding section presents a summary of the main arguments, underlines some parallels and differences between East and West, briefly surveys the recessions of the early 1990s, and provides a few pointers for the future.

3.2. Growth

That a slow-down in growth occurred throughout the industrialized world in the last two decades is well known. Before the 1970s, growth had been exceptionally rapid and relatively smooth in both East and West. While only few industrialized countries had ever grown at much more than 3 per cent per annum for a prolonged period in the years preceding World War II, virtually none grew by less than 4 per cent annually between the early 1950s and the early 1970s. This 'golden age' came to an abrupt end sometime in the mid-1970s. Evidence for the deceleration is shown in Table 3.1. The top part presents the familiar story for the OECD area—two sharp and sudden breaks in trend took place after 1973 and 1979, following the oil shocks of those two years. The data also show the recovery in economic activity of the late 1980s, a recovery which was no doubt related to the 'counter' oil shock of 1986.

The lower part provides tentative Western estimates on a GDP basis for Eastern Europe. While the figures are clearly subject to error, they are much more reliable than the official statistics on net material product (NMP). These have always been thought by Western experts to be upward biased, and recent revelations in Eastern Europe about the extent of earlier statistical misreporting have fully confirmed such doubts (Zoteev, 1991). As they stand, the data show a pronounced slow-down, which is not much more gradual than in the West. Moreover, in contrast to the OECD growth revival of the late 1980s, the performance of the centrally planned economies deteriorated further in the closing years of the decade.

Table 3.1:   Growth Rates of GDP, 1950–1994 (average annual percentage changes)

	1953–73	1973–9	1979–84	1984–90	1990–4
USA	3.4	2.5	1.8	2.8	2.2
Japan	9.3	3.6	3.5	4.6	1.5
Canada	4.7	4.2	2.3	3.3	0.3
France	5.3	2.8	1.5	3.0	0.8
Germany	5.4	2.4	1.0	3.1	2.3[a]
Italy	5.3	3.7	1.7	3.0	0.7
UK	3.0	1.5	0.8	3.4	1.4
Austria	5.4	2.9	1.4	2.9	1.8
Belgium	4.3	2.2	1.5	2.6	1.2
Denmark	4.1	1.9	1.7	1.9	2.0
Finland	5.1	2.3	3.3	3.4	−2.1
Netherlands	4.8	2.7	0.7	3.0	1.6
Spain	6.1[b]	2.3	1.3	4.2	1.0
Sweden	4.0	1.8	1.7	2.2	−0.7
Switzerland	4.4	−0.4	1.5	3.0	0.2
Western Europe	4.7	2.5	1.4	3.3	1.2
Total OECD Area	4.3	2.7	2.0	3.2	1.7

	1950–73	1973–82	1982–9	1989–94
Soviet Union	5.0	2.1	2.4	−12.4[c]
Bulgaria	6.1	2.4	0.8	−6.7
Czechoslovakia	3.8	1.8	1.6	−4.3
GDR	4.6	2.6	2.5[d]	—
Hungary	4.0	1.9	0.3	−3.4
Poland	4.8	0.5	2.0	−2.4
Romania	5.9	3.7	1.4	−6.6
Yugoslavia	5.7	5.0	1.0	—
Eastern Europe	5.0	2.8	1.6	−4.0
Eastern Europe and Soviet Union	5.0	2.3	2.1	−9.5

[a] All Germany. [b] 1954–73. [c] Russia from 1992. [d] 1982–8.

Sources: OECD, *National Accounts* (various issues) and *Economic Outlook*, June 1995: Maddison (1989); IMF, *World Economic Outlook* (various issues).

3.2.1. The OECD countries

As already mentioned, the deceleration which set in after 1973 was sudden, sharp, and pervasive. Every OECD country shared in the negative experience of stagflation in 1974–5 and 1980–2. Thereafter, recovery occurred in 1983–6, gathered speed in the late 1980s, but then gave way to a recession in the early 1990s which was particularly sharp in Western Europe and Japan. North America and Western Europe have since picked up again, but the Japanese economy was, at the time of writing, still in the grips of a prolonged bout of stagnation.

The immediate causes of the two earlier breaks in trend were the two oil shocks. The direct impact of these shocks on consuming countries was both inflationary and deflationary: inflationary because of the upward push given to the price of an essential commodity, and deflationary because of the fall in demand that was generated by the shift in world income towards the low-spending economies of the Organization of Petroleum Exporting Countries (OPEC). As a result, both the aggregate demand and supply schedules for the industrialized countries shifted inwards in a way which led to a combination of higher prices and lower quantities (Bruno, 1984). And these effects were superimposed on fragile economies, many of which were suffering from high inflation, and some of which were slowing down in the wake of an earlier tightening of policies.

Yet, these direct effects of the oil shocks cannot provide the full reason for a medium-term deceleration which very nearly halved the OECD area's growth rate over two decades. Most explanations for this trend worsening in performance point to the operation of a number of additional and interrelated demand and supply factors that contributed to further inward shifts of the aggregate demand and supply schedules over the medium run (Bruno, 1984).

On the supply side, an important feature of the shock in the mid-1970s was the reluctance of wage-earners to bear the inevitable brunt of the deterioration in the terms of trade. Thus, real wage targets in most countries remained geared to earlier trends of income growth. Yet, the room available for such growth had been sharply curtailed not only by the deterioration in the terms of trade, but also by a medium-run deceleration in productivity growth, itself largely caused by the shock (Bruno and Sachs, 1985). In such circumstances, wage resistance exacerbated inflation and shifted the adjustment on to profits. The drop in profits led, in turn, to a sharp decline in investment. And the demand-side slump was intensified by the switch to restrictive policies, designed to curtail inflation, that took place in some countries after 1974 and in virtually all after 1979 (Boltho, 1984).

A widespread, though not universal, consequence in Europe of such developments was a sharp increase in unemployment. Before 1973, most of the OECD countries had achieved an unprecedented state of virtual full employment. Earlier agricultural economies had traditionally experienced underemployment on the land; more recent industrialized societies had suffered from the cyclical unemployment generated by business cycles. By the 1960s, Western Europe, Japan, and North America had been broadly able to eliminate both these phenomena.

Unfortunately, the achievement was short-lived. By the early 1990s,

Table 3.2:   Unemployment in Selected OECD Countries,[a] 1960–1994
(per cent of the labour force)

	1960	1973	1979	1990	1994
USA	5.4	4.8	5.8	5.4	6.0
Japan	1.7	1.3	2.1	2.1	2.9
Canada	6.4	5.5	7.4	8.1	10.3
France	1.1	2.6	5.8	8.9	12.5
Germany	1.0	1.0	3.2	4.8	6.9[b]
Italy	5.5	6.2	7.6	10.3	10.2[c]
UK	1.3	2.2	5.0	6.9	9.6
Austria	2.4	1.0	1.8	3.2	4.4
Belgium	3.3	2.3	8.2	7.2	9.7
Denmark	1.9	0.9	6.2	9.6	12.1
Finland	1.4	2.3	5.9	3.4	18.2
Netherlands	0.7	2.2	5.4	7.5	7.2
Spain	2.4	2.5	8.4	15.9	23.8
Sweden	1.7	2.5	2.1	1.5	8.0
Average (unweighted)	2.6	2.7	5.4	6.8	10.1

[a] Figures are not strictly comparable across countries. [b] West Germany. [c] 1993.

Sources: OECD, *Historical Statistics* (various issues); *Economic Outlook*, June 1995.

unemployment in most Western European countries had risen to rates not previously recorded in the post-war period (Table 3.2), and by the mid-1990s may have reached levels comparable to those of the Great Depression (Boltho, 1993). In addition, this unemployment carried with it two particularly unwelcome aspects: a sharp jump in the number of spells and a concentration on marginal segments of the labour force. Long-term unemployment is much more prevalent today than in earlier decades; so, too, is youth unemployment, which, in Southern Europe in particular, affects as much as 30–40 per cent of the relevant age-groups.

Japan and the USA were less severely hit by rises in unemployment. There, the growth deceleration was mainly reflected in a productivity slow-down which limited the erstwhile rapid expansion of real wages. In the USA in particular, this slow-down was associated with a substantial increase in the number of relatively low-paying and part-time jobs.

Much controversy surrounds the respective roles of demand and supply factors in explaining the worsening performance. Supply forces probably dominated the experience of the later 1970s. Thus, the climb in unemployment between 1975 and 1979 'should be attributed to the fact that real wages remained above market-clearing levels in most economies' (Bruno and Sachs, 1985, p. 171). This explanation, however, broke down in the 1980s, when profitability was restored to levels close to, or even above, those recorded in the early 1970s. It was then the continuing, indeed reinforced, tightness of policies which was primarily responsible for the semi-stagnation of much of the decade (Sachs, 1983; Bruno, 1986). And tight policies, particularly following German unification, were clearly responsible for Europe's recession of the early 1990s.

While the two oil shocks, as well as labour market and economic policy reactions, can throw a good deal of light on the reasons for the slow-down in growth, they may not tell the whole story. Arguably, some longer-run forces, stemming paradoxically from earlier successes, may also have been at work (Boltho, 1982*b*). Most of these forces had to do with the exhaustion of the favourable conditions which had propelled growth in the previous two decades, particularly in Western Europe and Japan. According to some, the growth tempo was bound to falter because of the gradual saturation of household demand for durables, the production of which had acted as an engine of growth (Mazier *et al.*, 1984). Others lay more stress on the shrinking technological gap between the USA and the rest of the OECD area, or on the dwindling scope for transferring labour from agriculture to industry (Lindbeck, 1983).

Yet, the most important single factor that would have almost inevitably made for deceleration is to be found in the already-mentioned great success of the 1960s—the attainment of virtual full employment. This, together 'with a diminished supply elasticity of agricultural or foreign workers to the urban sectors of the European economies, was bound to lead, in conditions in which the growth tempo had not slackened, to a strengthening of labour power and to a shift in income distribution away from capital' (Boltho, 1982*b*, p. 24). The strengthening of labour is illustrated, for instance, by growing unionization, by the strikes of the late 1960s in all the major European economies, and by the spread of legislation in the early 1970s, inspired by trade unions, to protect employment (Bernabè, 1982). The shift of income away from profits is well documented in OECD publications (Hill, 1979).

These trends were more pronounced in Europe and Japan than in North America. Yet, a worsening in the growth climate had also occurred in the USA in the wake of the over-expansionary stance of the late 1960s that had been partly induced by the Vietnam conflict. The inflationary consequences of such policies strongly contributed to the breakdown in the early 1970s of the international monetary system created at Bretton Woods. Already well before the oil shocks, wage-push and simultaneous reflation in many countries had set the world on a path of accelerating inflation. The shocks acted as detonators, but the underlying deterioration in performance had made some slow-down inevitable.

3.2.2. *Eastern Europe*

Eastern Europe's growth experience exhibited both similarities with and differences from that of the developed market economies. At the aggregate level, the extent of the break in the 1970s and 1980s seems almost identical, particularly if the Soviet Union is excluded from the data shown in Table 3.1. The timing of the slow-down, however, differed. While the OECD countries saw their growth interrupted very suddenly, the deceleration in most of the centrally planned economies occurred more gradually, usually in the second half of the 1970s and, again, in the second half of the 1980s.

A less pronounced reaction to the oil shocks should have been expected given the institutional framework of these economies (Portes, 1980). Many of the factors which were so disruptive in the West were either absent or muted in the East. Thus, in principle, the centrally planned economies should not have been affected by short-term inflationary or deflationary impulses, since domestic prices were rigidly controlled and planners could ensure that aggregate demand was always set at (or even above) full-employment levels. Given the lack of these initial unfavourable effects, there should have been little need for the aggressive wage bargaining and restrictive policy reactions which occurred in the OECD area.

It is true that the impact of the changes in the terms of trade on domestic absorption could not be avoided. However, for two Eastern countries (Poland and the Soviet Union), the changes were actually positive, given the significant level of net energy exports. Elsewhere, the unfavourable effects should have been felt more gradually than in the West, thanks to the practice of applying a five-year moving average of world prices to transactions among the countries of the Council for Mutual Economic Assistance (CMEA). Finally, borrowing on world capital markets became much easier in the 1970s. This should have allowed continued imports of raw materials, investment goods, or technology, thus facilitating, at least initially, the maintenance of rapid growth.

Despite all this, performance worsened sharply. Though most of the five-year plans for the second half of the 1970s incorporated a slow-down, actual performance usually fell short even of such less ambitious targets. While the immediate impact of the shocks was modest, their longer-term influences turned out to be severe. In several countries, for instance, the terms of trade deterioration were eventually larger than those incurred in Western Europe. Greater dependence on imported energy was one reason. Another seems to have been an inability to raise prices on exports to the market economies given that the Western European downturn (and protectionism) were limiting demand for CMEA goods. By the 1980s, these problems were being compounded by the debt crisis, which forced most countries of the area into various degrees of austerity.

Yet, however serious these problems, it is unlikely that, on their own, the oil shocks and attendant difficulties could have explained a halving, or worse, of the growth rate. Hence, even more than for the market economies, explanations for deceleration must also be sought in other forces, either at work during the period, or stemming from earlier successes.

At a proximate level, the step-up in investment in the earlier years of that decade must have led to more bottlenecks and unfinished projects than usual (Marer, 1981), as well as to a later slackening in the investment effort (Alton, 1981). More generally, incremental capital–output ratios rose everywhere, in the wake of lengthening 'gestation' periods, falling capacity-utilization rates and an ageing capital stock (Benini, 1990). And the sharpest case of slow-down (Poland) owes much to the planners' loss of control over investment and incomes in the mid-1970s, a period of accelerating but ultimately unsustainable growth (Fallenbuchl, 1981).

Yet, as in Western Europe, some of the slow-down was inevitable, since it reflected the exhaustion of the permissive supply conditions which had fuelled earlier growth. Indeed, the importance of this factor is probably greater for the planned than for the market economies, because the former relied much more on continuously rising labour and capital inputs for their growth rates. As labour reserves in agriculture dwindled, as population growth slowed down, as participation rates rose to record levels, and as political constraints made it increasingly difficult to sacrifice consumption in favour of investment, some slow-down in the pattern of so-called 'extensive' growth seemed bound to occur.

This inevitability was reinforced by the 'systemic' difficulties hampering productivity growth. Thus, rigid central planning, or even half-hearted attempts at reform, were increasingly unable to speed up the rate of innovation. In the relatively simple economies of the 1950s and 1960s, the centralized command structure had been able to deliver significant gains in living standards. When the scale and sophistication of the economies grew, the well-known informational and incentive difficulties of central planning swelled exponentially. As complexity rose, the cumbersome planning machinery could no longer keep pace.

Many of these difficulties were well known. Yet little was done to improve matters. Hungary hesitated on the brink of a market economy for nearly two decades; the Soviet Union and Czechoslovakia, if anything, recentralized their economies after some timid reforms in the late 1960s; the GDR, let alone Romania, stuck to a Stalinist model throughout.

3.2.3. An overview

The preceding discussion has suggested that some slow-down in growth was inevitable in both the market and the centrally planned economies. Structural changes were at work weakening some of the factors which had propelled Europe and Japan, particularly the gradual dwindling of ample supplies of underemployed labour in the countryside. Many Western countries were also exhausting the supply of abundant American technology as their industries approached best-practice levels, and some of this effect may have been at work in Eastern Europe too.

Yet, such forces can explain neither the suddenness nor the severity of the crisis. Suddenness in the West came from two oil-price shocks. In the East, the shocks' direct and indirect effects were less severe, at least in the 1970s, thanks to the (partial) insulation provided by central planning and to massive external borrowing. Other special factors, however, differing from country to country, brought about sudden interruptions in the growth process.

Severity, on the other hand, was rooted in both 'systemic' problems and policy responses. In the West, the systemic feature which most influenced the period was the persistence of high inflation. Generated when the power of trade unions was rising on the wave of continuing growth and full employment, this inflation was given further impetus by the spiral in commodity prices and was only broken after years of slow expansion and soaring unemployment. Something similar may also have been at work in the East. Just as continuous full employment in the market economies had meant that dismissals ceased 'to play their role as a disciplinary measure' (Kalecki, 1971, p. 140), so too, at least in the Soviet Union, labour shortages had 'reduced the manager's ability to discipline workers or his willing-ness to discharge loafers' (Levine, 1982, p. 165). In one case, the main consequence was higher inflation; in the other, slackening productivity growth. More importantly, however, mounting Eastern problems were directly linked to the shrinking capacity of the planning system to cope with the demands of an increasingly sophisticated economy.

Arguably, in neither case did policies help ease the problems. Indeed, they may have worsened them—in one case, because of too much activ-ism; in the other, because of too much inertia. In the West, the sharp monetary and fiscal squeezes of the 1980s (and early 1990s) appear to have been an over-reaction which exacerbated unemployment without doing much to reduce inflation (Beckerman and Jenkinson, 1986). In the East, on the other hand, the policy mistake was to cling far too long to outdated planning methods. Reform attempts were few, piecemeal, and timid. By creating uncertainty, they may well have contributed to the generation of further inefficiencies.

3.3. Public Expenditure and Taxation

An important characteristic of the 'golden age' had been a large expansion of the public sector, particularly marked throughout Europe, but also in evidence in North America and Japan. In the centrally planned economies, the increase came from a conscious attempt to raise welfare by directly supplying more social services. In the OECD area, it reflected a combination of buoyant tax revenues, generated by rapid growth, and a relatively high income elasticity of demand for non-defence public goods, traditional 'merit goods, and for a new form of 'semi-merit' good that could be called 'security' (Boltho, 1982a). Thus, transfer payments to households were one of the fastest growing items in government spending.

One of the major consequences of slower growth in the last fifteen to twenty years has been a deceleration in public expenditure growth. But the slow-down was perhaps milder than might have been expected. Thus, the evidence (Table 3.3) shows that in all the economies examined here the shares of total public expenditure in GDP, or those of public consumption in NMP, were higher at the end of the 1980s than they had been either just before the first oil shock, or in the late 1970s. Indeed, some increases were remarkable. Italy, Japan, and Spain, for instance, recorded rises in the ratio of public expenditure to GDP since 1973 that are a multiple of those

Table 3.3:   Trends in Public Expenditure, 1960–1994 (percentages)

	1960	1973	1979	1991	1994
Public spending in per cent of GDP					
USA	25.5	28.9	29.9	34.0	33.5
Japan	17.5	22.4	31.1	31.4	35.8
Canada	27.4	33.9	37.3	46.0	47.4
France	34.6	38.3	45.0	50.5	54.9
Germany	32.4	41.5	47.2	47.9[a]	49.0[a]
Italy	27.5	34.6	41.6	53.5	53.9
UK	31.0	38.8	40.9	40.7	42.9
Austria	35.7	41.3	48.2	49.6	51.5
Netherlands	32.0	43.5	53.3	54.6	54.4
Spain	18.7[b]	23.0	30.1	43.5	45.6
Sweden	31.0	44.7	60.0	61.3	68.8
Western Europe	30.5	37.2	43.9	48.9	51.0
Total OECD Area	26.5	31.1	35.9	40.2	41.5

	1960	1973	1980	1989
Public consumption in per cent of NMP				
Soviet Union	7.4	8.9	10.5	11.8
Bulgaria	3.3	3.6	3.8	5.9
Czechoslovakia	17.8	19.1	20.2	26.0
GDR	13.1	15.0	15.8	15.7
Hungary	—	9.0	10.6	11.4
Poland	7.7	10.2	12.4	7.5
Romania	—	—	6.8	4.4
Eastern Europe[c]	11.4	12.7	13.9	14.1
Eastern Europe and Soviet Union	8.2	9.7	11.3	12.3

[a] All Germany. [b] 1964. [c] Excluding Romania.

Sources: OECD, *Historical Statistics, 1960–1988,* and *Economic Outlook,* June 1995; Vienna Institute for Comparative Economic Studies, *Comecon Data* (various years).

achieved between 1960 and 1973. And in Eastern Europe, if the figures are to be believed, Czechoslovakia registered an even more impressive performance, despite the fact that it had by far the highest initial share of public consumption in NMP.

3.3.1. *The OECD countries*

That the deceleration in public expenditure growth was lower than the deceleration in output growth is perhaps most surprising for the West. Here, public expenditure should have been affected not only by the consequences of a less buoyant economy, but also by important changes in the conduct of policies. At a macroeconomic level, the fight against inflation led to greater fiscal stringency almost everywhere; at a microeconomic level, a widespread concern with the alleged disincentive and misallocation effects of excessive government spending and taxation generated strong pressures in favour of cuts in the expenditure flows.

It seems clear from the data that these pressures were operative only, if at all, in the 1980s and early 1990s. Between 1973 and 1979, in merely six years, the GDP share of public expenditure in the OECD area rose by virtually the same amount by which it had risen in the preceding thirteen years. Developments in the 1980s, on the other hand, were more subdued. Indeed, in a few countries, such as Germany, Sweden, and Britain, the share of expenditure in GDP actually declined in the latter part of the decade, while in most others it tended to stabilize. Recession in the early 1990s, as well as the costs of German unification, have, however, led to renewed and often sharp increases to record highs in Europe as well as in Japan.

Such aggregate developments were influenced by a host of factors in addition to the policy stance (such as cyclical swings in activity, and relative price movements). More importantly, in the present context, they reveal very little about those items of expenditure that most impinge on household welfare—particularly social security transfers and expenditure on merit goods. Evidence for these is shown in Table 3.4. Taking transfers first, the overall impression seems to confirm what was seen for the aggregate share—the relatively rapid growth of the late 1970s gave way to a marked slow-down during the 1980s.

Care must be taken in interpreting these trends, however, at least in the European context. A significant share of the recorded increases merely reflected automatic effects. Thus, one major item of transfer expenditure, unemployment benefits, soared in the 1980s in the wake of the sharp rise in the number of jobless. A very rough adjustment for this factor would suggest that perhaps one quarter of the 2.2 percentage-point increase in the GDP share between 1979 and 1991, shown in Table 3.4, may have been due to increases in unemployment compensation pay-

Table 3.4: Indicators of Public Expenditure in Selected OECD Countries, 1960–1991 (in per cent of constant price GDP)

	1960	1973	1979	1991
Public transfers to households[a]				
USA	4.6	8.1	9.2	11.2
Japan	4.7	6.0	10.8	11.6
Canada	7.3	9.0	10.1	14.3
France	9.4	13.3	17.5	20.8
Germany	10.4	12.1	15.4	14.2
Italy	8.6	12.9	14.1	20.3
UK	5.6	7.6	9.7	12.2
Austria	9.6	12.5	15.8	16.6
Netherlands	(6.7)	18.7	24.8	24.6
Spain	2.6	8.2	12.7	14.6
Sweden	7.1	11.9	18.0	21.7
Average (unweighted)	7.0	10.9	14.4	16.6
Public current expenditure on merit goods[b]				
USA	5.3	7.0	6.7	6.5[c]
Japan	—	5.1	5.5	4.3
France	—	—	10.9[d]	10.4[c]
Germany	—	10.8	11.9	11.6[c]
Italy	—	9.3	8.7	9.5[c]
UK	9.3	10.3	11.1	10.7
Austria	11.5[e]	10.5	11.9	12.3[c]
Netherlands	6.1	6.2	6.4	5.4[c]
Sweden	5.9[f]	14.8	17.6	17.3[c]
Average (unweighted)[g]	—	9.2	10.0	9.7

[a] Social security benefits and social assistance grants deflated by the private consumption expenditure deflator. [b] Final consumption expenditure on education, health, social security and welfare, and housing and community amenities, deflated by the government consumption expenditure deflator. [c] 1989. [d] 1983. [e] 1964. [f] 1963. [g] Excluding France.

Source: OECD, *National Accounts of OECD Countries* (various issues).

ments (as against less than 10 per cent in 1973–9). As a consequence, other transfer payments rose only rather moderately (for instance, in Austria and Spain), or even fell as a share of GDP (for instance, in Germany and the Netherlands).

It is important to note that a shift seems to have occurred within these transfers between the early 1970s and the mid-1980s in the relative importance of pensions and family benefits. The share of the former continued to rise quite rapidly, reflecting in part population ageing, while the share of the latter fell almost everywhere (Varley, 1986). On a real per capita basis, child benefits dropped sharply in Spain over the period and remained almost stagnant in Italy, Sweden, and the USA (ibid.). Of the countries examined here, only Germany and the UK showed a substantial rise, but in Britain, at least, this probably gave way to declines towards the end of the decade.

The conclusions for current expenditure on education, health care, welfare, and housing are similar. Following relatively rapid increases between 1973 and 1979, spending growth was sharply curtailed in the 1980s in most of the countries for which data are available (especially in the Netherlands). Only Austria and Italy were able to stand against the general trend.

The overall impression is unmistakable. In the 1980s, the growth of transfer payments to households and of expenditure on merit goods decelerated quite sharply. In the 1960s, these programmes had been boosted by expansions in entitlements, by improvements in per capita benefits, and by demographic forces (OECD, 1976a, 1976b, 1977). By the 1980s and early 1990s, with demographic trends still requiring higher expenditure in most cases and unemployment raising one particular transfer component, the search for economies meant that policy-makers had to opt for restrictions on benefits and for no further extensions in coverage. Indeed, in some countries, encouragement was given to the privatization of a number of government services and to the voluntary withdrawal of citizens from the public provision of merit goods, trends that seem to have continued in the first half of the 1990s.

While the growth of public expenditure slowed down, this was much less true for taxation. Total tax revenues, as a per cent of GDP, rose as rapidly in the 1980s as they had in the 1970s. This was an inevitable consequence of the priority given to the fight against budget deficits, at least outside the USA (Table 3.5). The phenomenon was particularly marked in the relatively low-tax countries (Italy, Japan, and Spain), but tax pressures rose even in such very highly taxed economies as France and Sweden.

In this area, too, aggregate developments masked a trend which had important (and unfavourable) consequences for household welfare—changes in the weight of various kinds of taxes in the total tax take. The most notable shift, in some countries at least, was a switch away from (broadly progressive) income taxes to (inevitably regressive) indirect taxes (OECD, 1989). The share of the latter in GDP had gradually decreased in the 1960s and 1970s, largely as a result of the lowering of tariff barriers. This pattern was reversed almost everywhere in the 1980s, as domestic sales of goods and services became subject to higher tax rates.

A better overall impression of the possible regressive impact of trends in taxation may be gained by considering not only indirect taxes, but also

Table 3.5: Total Tax Revenues in Selected OECD Countries, 1965–1991 (in per cent of current price GDP)

	1965	1973	1979	1991
USA	25.8	28.6	28.8	29.8
Japan	18.3	22.5	24.4	30.9
Canada	25.4	30.8	30.6	37.3
France	34.5	35.0	40.2	44.2
Germany	31.6	36.3	37.8	39.2
Italy	25.5	24.4	26.6	39.7
UK	30.4	31.3	32.6	36.0
Austria	34.7	37.1	41.0	42.1
Netherlands	33.2	41.8	44.0	47.0
Spain	14.3	18.7	23.3	34.7
Sweden	35.2	41.4	49.2	53.2
Average (unweighted)	28.1	31.6	34.4	39.5

Source: OECD, *Revenue Statistics of OECD Member Countries, 1965–92*.

Table 3.6: Indirect Taxes and Social Security Contributions in Selected OECD Countries, 1965–1991 (in per cent of current price GDP)

	1965	1973	1979	1991
USA	9.9	11.6	12.2	13.9
Japan	8.8	8.9	11.5	13.5
Canada	11.9	13.0	13.3	15.9
France	25.0	25.7	29.8	31.4
Germany	18.9	21.8	23.1	25.8
Italy	18.8	18.2	18.3	24.2
UK	14.7	14.0	14.4	18.2
Austria	21.6	23.0	25.6	26.7
Netherlands	19.7	26.2	28.7	29.3
Spain	9.8	14.0	16.7	22.1
Sweden	15.3	18.7	25.2	29.0
Average (unweighted)	15.9	17.7	19.9	22.7

Sources: OECD, *Revenue Statistics of OECD Member Countries* (various issues).

social security contributions, the progressiveness of which is usually very limited. Table 3.6 shows a fairly mixed picture. Italy and Spain, in particular, but also Japan and France, actually reduced the importance of regressive taxation relative to income taxes. At the other end of the spectrum,

Germany, the UK, and the USA swung massively in the opposite direction, while Austria and Sweden did so in a more moderate manner.

A further important change common to many OECD countries was a retreat from progressiveness in income-tax schedules. Between 1975 and 1988–9, twenty-one OECD countries cut their top marginal rate of income tax, and twelve raised their lowest marginal rate (OECD, 1989), generating a much more compressed tax structure. In some countries, the shifts were very pronounced, with the UK and the USA leading the way (top marginal rates declined from 83 to 40 per cent and from 70 to 28/33 per cent, respectively). Fairly sharp downward changes also occurred in Canada, Italy, and Japan.

In summary, despite continuing increases in public expenditure, the combined effects of shifts in spending away from some major social programmes and in tax policy towards a broadly regressive position meant that in the 1980s and early 1990s most OECD countries turned their backs on, or at least severely eroded, the concept of a generous welfare state that had been current during the 1960s. This was most evident in Britain and the USA, but even Germany, Sweden, and the Netherlands were affected. Elsewhere, the impact may have been less severe, but no economy went against the tide.

3.3.2. Eastern Europe

Eastern European developments in the public expenditure area, before the fall of communism, are more difficult to document because of the imperfect nature of the available data. Table 3.3 showed that the share of public consumption in NMP had risen throughout the area both before and after the slow-down of the mid-1970s. Hence, on the surface at least, it would appear that, as in the market economies, the worsening overall economic performance was not fully reflected in the growth of collective consumption.

Table 3.7:   Public Non-defence Expenditure
in Selected Eastern European Countries, 1965–1988
(in per cent of constant price GNP)

	1965	1975	1980	1988
Bulgaria	10.3	9.8	11.9	12.4
Czechoslovakia	9.6	9.4	9.9	10.2
GDR	12.5	11.2	11.3	12.6
Hungary	8.1	7.9	8.5	10.1
Poland	10.1	7.4	8.2	10.0
Average (unweighted)	10.1	9.1	10.0	11.1

Sources: Alton (1981, 1989).

This impression is reinforced by the data assembled in Table 3.7, which presents tentative Western estimates of the GNP share of government consumption (excluding defence) for the smaller Eastern European economies. While in the decade to 1975 this share had declined (largely because of the buoyancy of output growth), the subsequent period saw a widespread, if modest, recovery. Yet, as in the case of the Western economies, such aggregate data may not throw much light on how household welfare fared during the period. Piecemeal evidence on budgetary expenditure on social welfare items suggests rising shares in NMP between the mid-1970s and the late 1980s for the GDR, Hungary, and the Soviet Union, but declines in Poland and Romania. None of this provides a very complete picture. A better impression can probably be gleaned from more indirect indicators of performance in three main areas—housing, health care, and education.

In the housing field, any negative effects from the economic slow-down appear to have occurred with a relatively long lag. During most of the

Table 3.8: Indicators of Housing Activity in Selected Eastern European Countries, 1961–1989

	1961–70	1971–5	1976–80	1981–9
Dwellings constructed per 1,000 inhabitants				
Soviet Union	9.9	9.0	7.8	7.5
Bulgaria	5.4	5.6	8.0	7.0
Czechoslovakia	6.2	8.4	8.6	5.9
GDR	4.2	4.7	6.7	6.4
Hungary	6.0	8.4	8.5	6.2
Poland	5.5	6.8	7.5	5.0
Romania	—	—	7.7	5.7[a]
Average (unweighted)[b]	6.2	7.2	7.9	6.3
	1965–70	1970–80	1980–7
Growth of investment in residential construction[c]				
Soviet Union		6.9	3.0	6.8
Bulgaria		10.8	7.9	3.2
Czechoslovakia		11.4	2.6	−1.6
GDR		13.1	9.0	2.0
Hungary		11.0	4.5	−2.8
Poland		7.6	7.1	−2.0
Average (unweighted)		10.1	5.7	0.9

[a] 1981–8. [b] Excluding Romania. [c] Average annual percentage changes

Sources: United Nations Economic Commission for Europe (UNECE), *Economic Survey of Europe* (various issues).

1970s, residential construction was buoyant and the rate of dwellings completion per 1,000 of the population reached record levels everywhere outside the Soviet Union. Developments in the 1980s, however, were radically different. Completion rates declined quite sharply and the growth of investment slumped, with only the Soviet Union going against the trend (Table 3.8). Slower population growth and reduced rural–urban migration explain part of the investment drop. However, the chronic shortages in, and the poor quality of, much of the housing stock suggest that needs remained significant.

The available quantitative indicators for the health sector, on the other hand, point to continuing advances—labour inputs rose through the 1970s and 1980s in all countries, bar Hungary, while investment (outside Czechoslovakia and East Germany) either grew or remained constant (UNECE, 1990). Increases from 1975 onward were also recorded in the number of doctors and hospital beds per population, with the exception of the reasonably well-supplied GDR (ibid.). On the expenditure side, Western estimates of the resources devoted to this sector suggest that the share of GNP spent on health, after recording broad stability between 1965 and 1975, rose from 3.1 to 3.7 per cent in the following decade to 1985 in the five smaller Eastern European economies considered here (Eberstadt, 1989).

Yet, such relatively flattering data mask a deterioration in the population's health standards. It has been known for some time that in the Soviet Union, for instance, life expectancy at birth had been declining, in contrast to experience almost everywhere else. A similar, if less pronounced, trend was also evident in other Eastern European countries (Eberstadt, 1989). Trends in infant mortality were equally worrying. Through the 1980s, the Soviet Union showed a worsening performance, while the improvements recorded elsewhere in Eastern Europe fell short of those achieved in the more advanced countries of Western Europe (ibid.).

While some of the reasons for these developments may lie in inappropriate dietary patterns or in a greater use of tobacco, part of the blame can almost certainly be ascribed to the health care system, and in particular to 'the mismatch (between the) labor-extensive, low-costs approach of the Soviet health model and the actual needs of the local population' (Eberstadt, 1989, p. 108). Lower economic growth from the mid-1970s on, while not directly responsible for a deterioration that has clearly earlier and deeper roots, must also have contributed.

Education probably suffered least from the economic slow-down. Though investment growth decelerated in the 1980s, labour inputs continued to increase, as did some of the physical indicators of performance. Thus, all the countries in the area increased the number of children in preschool education. Secondary education enrolment ratios also grew between 1980 and 1989 in Hungary, Poland, and Romania (UNICEF ICDC, 1993). And while some countries experienced a drop in the total number of people receiving education, this trend reflected changing demographic pressures rather than the slackening of an effort that had always distinguished the socialist economies.

3.3.3. An overview

Statistical problems and institutional differences render comparative judgements in this area very difficult. In the West, many social services are only partly provided by government and are financed by tax systems that can be more or less progressive. In the East, all social services were directly supplied by the state and their financing was ensured by a general budget in which a mildly progressive system of household taxation played only a relatively minor role.

These differences notwithstanding, the marked and very similar slow-downs in economic growth in both areas inevitably had restrictive effects on the expansion of public spending and, in particular, on a number of items directly linked to household welfare. In the West, while unemployment transfer payments soared, the growth of expenditure on health and education was curtailed, at times sharply. In the East, it was mainly investment in housing that suffered, though some cut-backs also took place in health and education. Interestingly, in both areas the negative effects on public expenditure for merit goods were somewhat lagged. The initial impact of the recession was concentrated on investment or on material consumption. But by the same token, it is likely that any overall economic recovery (already in place in the West, only timidly beginning in the East), will take time in restoring spending on health care, education, housing, and transfers to households to the levels they might have reached in the absence of the sharp deceleration in growth.

3.4. Household Incomes

Household incomes grew more rapidly than total output in the 1950s and 1960s. In addition, thanks to the achievement of full employment, to the decline in the agricultural sector, and to the expansion of the welfare state, income inequalities were also reduced, at least in Western Europe. Thus, 'despite a surprisingly stable pre-tax earnings structure, the distribution of post-tax income has none the less changed towards greater equality in those European countries for which reasonably reliable data are available. Fairly pronounced changes have taken place in Italy, the UK and the Netherlands; more modest ones in France and Germany' (Sawyer, 1982, pp. 216–7). Broadly similar conclusions hold for Japan, though not for the two 'superpowers', where changes seem to have been rather small. In the USA between 1947 and 1972, the lowest five deciles and the top decile lost ground to middle-income families (Sawyer, 1976); meanwhile, there was a remarkable stability in Soviet distribution statistics between 1960 and 1975 (Braithwaite and Heleniak, 1989).

This picture changed after the mid-1970s. Slower growth in virtually every industrialized country, terms-of-trade deteriorations in most, and more restrictive fiscal policies as well as rising unemployment, at least in the market economies, were bound to have negative effects on real disposable household incomes. In so far as in the West the worsening in performance was felt to be due, in part at least, to a shift away from profits, while in the East it may have arisen from outdated planning methods, policies to restore profitability, or reforms intended to strengthen market forces, were, similarly, bound to worsen income distribution.

Table 3.9: From GDP to Household Disposable Income[a] in Selected OECD Countries (average annual percentage changes)

Eleven-country average	1960–73	1973–9	1979–91
(a) Levels of grow rates			
Real GDP	5.3	2.8	2.4
Primary household income[b]	5.5	3.0	2.0
Primary household income[c]	5.9	3.0	1.8
Disposable household income	5.4	3.1	1.7
	1960–73 to 1973–9		1973–9 to 1979–91
(b) Changes in growth rates			
Deceleration in real disposable household income	−2.3		−1.4
due to:			
Growth deceleration	−2.5		−0.4
Income distrib. effect	0.0		−0.6
Relative price effect	−0.4		−0.2
Policy effect	0.6		−0.2

[a] Primary household income is here defined as employee compensation and entrepreneurial income; it therefore excludes property income. Disposable household income is equal to this definition of primary income, plus social security benefits and social assistance grants and minus direct taxes and social security contributions. [b] Deflated by GDP deflator. [c] Deflated by private consumption expenditure deflator.

Sources: OECD, *National Accounts of OECD Countries* (various issues).

3.4.1. *The OECD countries*

In Western countries, the slow-down in the growth of household income was very sharp, particularly if attention is focused on income from employment and self-employment (excluding, therefore, dividend, interest, and rents). The aggregate data presented in Table 3.9 suggest that, contrary to trends in the 1960s and 1970s, growth in this category of household income between the late 1970s and the early 1990s was below that of total output and had on average fallen to little more than 1.5 per cent per annum.

The proximate reasons for this marked deceleration are shown in Panel B of the table, which decomposes the overall slow-down in the growth of real disposable income into four main 'effects'. The first, the deceleration in output growth, is self-explanatory. The second, called the 'income distribution effect', measures the difference between the growth rates of total output and of primary household income (excluding income from property), both deflated by the GDP deflator. It thus provides some idea of the shift away from labour and towards capital income. The third, or 'relative price effect', measures the impact on real household income of differences in the behaviour of the GDP and of the private consumption deflators (hence it is influenced by shifts in the terms of trade). The fourth, or 'policy effect', measures the impact of taxes and transfers in modifying the growth of primary real household incomes.

By far the main reason for the slow-down in the 1970s was the abrupt fall in the OECD's growth rate. Indeed, had income not continued to shift massively away from profits, household welfare would have suffered a good deal more. The worsening in the terms of trade also added to the squeeze on personal incomes, while tax and social security policies made a significant countervailing contribution. In the 1980s, on the other hand, the further slow-down had only a relatively small impact, with the bulk of the deceleration in household receipts now accounted for by a very large movement in income distribution away from labour income and towards profits. In addition, relative price shifts continued moving against households, if to a lesser extent than earlier. Finally, policies also made a small negative contribution.

These, of course, are only average trends which hide a great deal of diverging country experience. In some economies (Britain, Japan, Spain), output growth accelerated in the 1980s. In others (in particular, Italy and again Britain), the terms of trade improved. Nor was the policy stance invariably restrictive—household disposable income grew faster than primary income in, for instance, the USA, France, Spain, and Sweden. Yet, the income distribution shift towards profits was nearly universal (the exceptions—Canada, Britain, and the USA—are entirely due to the cycli-

Table 3.10: Income Distribution Trends in Selected OECD Countries[a]
(percentage of household disposable income going to the highest
and lowest quintiles)

		Mid-1970s	Late 1970s	Mid-1980s	Late 1980s
USA	Highest	42.8	39.9	41.9	—
	Lowest	4.5	5.3	4.7	—
	Ratio	9.5	7.5	8.9	—
Japan	Highest	37.8	38.0	37.9	39.2
	Lowest	8.3	8.8	8.0	7.8
	Ratio	4.6	4.3	4.7	5.0
France[b]	Highest	43.6	42.4	43.0	—
	Lowest	5.3	6.1	5.9	—
	Ratio	8.2	7.0	7.3	—
Germany[c]	Highest	44.8	38.1	39.1	39.0
	Lowest	6.9	7.2	7.1	7.5
	Ratio	6.5	5.3	5.5	5.2
Italy	Highest	46.4	40.4	42.2	—
	Lowest	5.2	7.4	6.9	—
	Ratio	8.9	5.5	6.1	—
UK	Highest	36.0	36.0	38.0	41.0
	Lowest	9.7	9.4	9.2	7.6
	Ratio	3.7	3.8	4.1	5.4
Netherlands	Highest	37.1	37.0	38.3	36.9
	Lowest	8.5	8.1	6.9	8.2
	Ratio	4.4	4.6	5.6	4.5
Sweden	Highest	31.4	30.2	30.9	—
	Lowest	10.7	11.2	11.1	—
	Ratio	2.9	2.7	2.8	—

[a] Figures are not comparable across countries. [b] Primary income, 1984 prices. [c] Net income.

Sources: World Bank, *World Development Report* (various issues); Canceill and Villeneuve (1990); Colombino (1991); CSO, *Economic Trends*, May 1993; Euler (1988); Hertel (1992); Olsson and Spånt (1991).

cal effects of the 1990–1 recessions which, predictably, depressed profits more than labour incomes).

While such aggregate trends can easily be illustrated, thanks to the availability of internationally comparable data, the same is not true of issues of income distribution. In this area, the information available is scanty, often dated, seldom consistent across time and hardly ever across space. The discussion below is therefore inevitably more tentative. In particular, it makes no attempts at inter-country comparisons.

Some of the available evidence on trends in household income distribution is presented in summary form in Table 3.10. The broad impression for the 1970s is that (post-tax) income differentials narrowed. This seems to have occurred in Italy, Germany, and the USA, and was probably also the case in Japan, France, and Sweden. At the time, welfare states were still being expanded, taxation remained broadly progressive, and unemployment had not yet risen very sharply.

The 1980s saw a sharp movement in the opposite direction. This was most pronounced in the UK and the USA, the two countries at the forefront in spurning the more egalitarian principles of earlier decades, particularly in their newly found preference for regressive tax policies. But rising unemployment, the spread of part-time and low-paid jobs, income shifts from wages to profits, as well as more restrictive fiscal policies, also led to greater income differentials elsewhere. Even Sweden recorded some worsening in more recent years, despite its long-run trend towards equality (Olsson and Spånt, 1991).

Table 3.11: From GDP to Real per capita Incomes in Selected Eastern European Countries (average annual percentage changes)

	Levels		Changes
	1965–73	1973–88	1965–73 to 1973–88
Soviet Union			
Real GDP per capita	3.5	1.3	−2.2
Real income per capita	5.4	2.9	−2.5
Bulgaria			
Real GDP per capita	4.0	1.5	−2.5
Real income per capita	6.2	3.1	−3.1
Czechoslovakia			
Real GDP per capita	3.1	1.3	−1.8
Real income per capita	6.0	2.0	−4.0
GDR			
Real GDP per capita	3.1	2.6	−0.5
Real income per capita	4.8	4.7	−0.1
Hungary			
Real GDP per capita	3.0	1.2	−1.8
Real income per capita	5.4	1.6	−3.8
Poland			
Real GDP per capita	4.5	0.3	−4.2
Real income per capita	6.5	1.7	−4.8
Average (unweighted)			
Real GDP per capita	3.5	1.4	−2.1
Real income per capita	5.7	2.7	−3.0

Sources: Maddison (1989); OECD, *Economic Outlook*, June 1992; UNECE, *Economic Survey of Europe* (various issues).

3.4.2. *Eastern Europe*

Not unlike Western countries, the centrally planned economies of Eastern Europe also experienced a slow-down in the growth of real household income greater than that in total output after the mid-1970s. Since the accounting categories are not the same, a decomposition similar to that of Table 3.9 is not possible for Eastern Europe. The simpler picture shown in Table 3.11 links Western estimates of GDP growth to Eastern estimates of the growth in real per capita incomes. It should be noted that the latter are not strictly comparable with the former and may exaggerate any rise in economic welfare in so far as inflation (open and repressed) has usually been underestimated.

Yet, data imperfections are unlikely to mask the broad trends that were at work. The overall impression conveyed by the table is not very different from that gleaned earlier for the OECD economies. While the growth of output on a per capita basis slowed down by some 2 percentage points in the area as a whole between the pre-1973 and the post-1973 periods, the deceleration in per capita real income growth was of 3 percentage points. The need to maintain (or even step up) defence expenditure and capital formation must have meant that the curb on absorption required to pay for worsening terms of trade had to come primarily from cuts in private consumption.

The most severe squeezes in living standards in absolute and relative (to GDP) terms were imposed in Poland, followed by Czechoslovakia and Hungary. Real incomes in the GDR, on the other hand, appear to have weathered the slow-down almost unscathed, but the accuracy of East German data is more suspect than that of most other countries in Eastern Europe.

Assessments of what happened to the distribution of these more slowly growing incomes are fraught with even greater difficulties than in the West. Not only is information on household income distribution scanty, but, even more so than in the West, the data can be very unreliable as indicators of welfare. In economies in which the supply of many consumer products was often insufficient to meet demand, so that rationing became a standard allocating mechanism 'money income ceases to be the sole determinant of capacity to acquire goods; to a degree, fortitude in searching out supplies and standing in queues, and plain luck, become consequential' (Bergson, 1984, p. 1058). And the difficulties of drawing strong conclusions from the data are compounded by the existence of special privileges to some members of society, in the form, for instance, of access to restricted shops or privileged allocation of housing and particularly desirable services, such as foreign travel.

Cross-country comparisons, very hazardous at the best of times even in the OECD area, are thus virtually impossible in this instance. Trends over

Table 3.12:   Income Distribution Trends in Selected East European Countries

	Mid-1970s	Early 1980s	Late 1980s
Earnings[a]			
Soviet Union	—	3.0	3.2
Czechoslovakia	2.6	2.4	—
Hungary	2.6	2.6	3.1
Poland	3.1	2.5	2.8
Household incomes[b]			
Hungary			
Highest	32.3	32.3	34.7
Lowest	10.8	11.3	10.5
Ratio	3.0	2.9	3.3
Poland			
Highest	36.9	—	39.2
Lowest	9.0	—	6.5
Ratio	4.1	—	6.0
Memorandum item:			
Soviet Union (ratio of top to bottom decile)	4.2	4.2	3.4

[a] Ratio of top to bottom decile. [b] Percentage of household income going to the highest and lowest quintiles.

Sources: Atkinson and Micklewright (1990); Braithwaite and Heleniak (1989).

time, however, may be less open to distortions. Some of the available evidence is shown in Table 3.12. The general impression is that differentials narrowed somewhat between the late 1970s and the early 1980s, only to open up again in more recent years. And piecemeal evidence suggests that poverty may also have increased in the 1980s, at least in Hungary and Poland (Cornia, 1990). Indeed, the movement towards increasing inequality may be underestimated by the data. Anecdotal evidence suggests that the 'black economy' and moonlighting by workers had spread in the 1980s in a number of Eastern economies. Equally, increasing supply difficulties through the decade must have made access to special shops an even greater privilege than earlier.

3.4.3. An overview

As for growth and public expenditure, East and West exhibited a number of common trends in household incomes from the early 1970s, despite significant institutional differences. Thus, in both sets of economies the growth of absorption had to be curtailed by more than that of output, and real household incomes, in turn, suffered more than did absorption.

The parallel also held for income differentials. As overall income grew more slowly, its distribution changed in less equitable ways in both areas. During the 1970s, often under the impact of earlier policies and trends, the movement towards equalization had continued in many countries. The opposite seems to have been the case in the 1980s and probably also in the early 1990s. Almost everywhere, the data show widening differentials. In the West, much of this was the result of deliberate policies designed to restore incentives. In the East, the aim was less clearly stated, but, where economic reforms were pursued, widening differentials were accepted as an inevitable component of 'marketization'.

3.5. Conclusions

One of the recurring themes of the foregoing account of major economic developments in the industrialized countries of East and West has been the surprising presence of many parallels through time. Despite vastly different institutional structures, the market and the centrally planned economies experienced broadly similar macroeconomic, public expenditure, and income distribution trends both in the boom years of the 1950s and 1960s and in the crisis years that followed 1973.

Output growth rates had been unprecedented in both sets of countries after World War II. The absorption of surplus rural labour by industry and the ample availability of new technologies were some of the common reasons for this success. Yet, policies also played a part. In the West, their role was indirect—belief in the power of demand management and other policies to stabilize output and raise growth may well have contributed to the high investment of the period. In the East, planning turned out to be relatively efficient in mobilizing resources in what were still backward economies. In both areas, governments wanted high growth and, on the whole, achieved it.

Similar, too, were the social welfare aims of the period. Full employment was considered a priority in both areas; the opportunities for collective consumption were greatly enlarged in market and socialist economies alike; and income distribution became more equal under the combined influence of autonomous trends (for instance, urbanization or rising female participation rates) and policies (including tax and transfer programmes in the West, compression of wage differentials in the East, and much better access to education everywhere).

The oil shocks of the 1970s interrupted this progress. In the fifteen to twenty years since 1973, growth was roughly halved, the expansion of collective consumption was cut back, and income differentials widened again under the influence of both market forces (for example, increasing unemployment in the West, the diffusion of 'submerged' economies in the East) and policies (for instance, decreasing tax progressiveness in the market economies, the beginnings of reforms in the planned ones). Arguably, however, the oil shocks were no more than detonators that precipitated and amplified a situation that was unsustainable. This would seem most obvious in the case of the East where the weaknesses of central planning were becoming increasingly apparent. A slow-down in growth would have come even in the absence of other disturbances. Western problems appeared less obvious at the beginning of the 1970s. Yet, the gradual acceleration of inflation in the 1960s bode ill for sustained growth. And according to many observers, the welfare state had also been gradually sapping dynamism and flexibility.

The slow-down in growth eventually prompted a radical reorientation of policies. In the West, this occurred through the 1980s and has continued in the early 1990s. In many countries, full employment was sacrificed to the fight against inflation, public spending growth was cut, reforms diminished the progressiveness of the tax system, and income distribution worsened. Eastern policies to the late 1980s were more timid, but here too the consequences of slow growth, the needs of defence, and the start of market-oriented reforms led to cuts in public consumption and to larger income differentials.

In both sets of countries, household welfare was bound to suffer. Some of this was made inevitable by macroeconomic and systemic trends. Arguably, however, policies worsened the situation, particularly in the West, which shifted sharply towards a newly found faith in market forces. The indifference to rising unemployment or poverty levels, the cuts in some basic welfare provisions, and the almost deliberate encouragement to greater inequality that characterized the policies of some countries, strongly suggest that the shift away from the 1960s went too far. The policy switch in the East was less deliberate. Here, the major mistake lay in the initial reluctance to contemplate reforms, a reluctance which made future surgery more indispensable and painful.

Prospects are, as always, clouded by political uncertainty, particularly in Eastern Europe. Barring major new shocks, however, the outlook for the OECD economies would seem mildly optimistic. The supply side has been boosted by ongoing technological progress and (possibly) by some market-inspired reforms. And demand could be more buoyant now that the policy-makers are somewhat less concerned with inflation. There are few signs, however, that the 1980s' obsession with cutting back state intervention is giving way to a more balanced attitude. High budget deficits and rising debt levels in many countries will, in particular, continue to restrict public spending.

Fiscal stringency, in turn, is likely to clash with rising needs. Almost everywhere, falling public investment has led to a worsening infrastructure. In many countries, ageing populations will require a growing income share to be devoted to health care and pension payments. And unemployment will probably remain high, at least in Europe, where it is most entrenched. Rising welfare costs and additional demands on social safety nets seem inevitable; yet, in the present climate of opinion, they are unlikely to be met.

The short-term picture for household welfare in the East is, if anything, grimmer. The postponement of reform for the best part of two decades has made painful shocks inevitable. Three of the ostensible achievements of the socialist economies—full employment, price stability, and relative income equality—have been jettisoned as efficiency, price rationality, and incentives are being restored. It is, of course, true that the earlier system delivered a state of full employment that masked massive underemployment, an absence of inflation that hid substantial repressed inflation, and a compression of income differentials that ignored the privileges of the *nomenklatura*. For most of the population, the loss of these semi-achievements is, none the less, very painful and living standards have fallen sharply.

Over the longer term, however, the combination of reform and educated labour forces should result in a substantially improved performance. Allied with reasonable growth in the West, this could result in a much better overall picture by the end of the century. Household welfare could then benefit, if the resources that faster growth provided were to be directed to those areas of public expenditure that were neglected, at times even grossly, from the mid-1970s to the early 1990s. Seen in a broader historical perspective, the recent difficult period may then appear as merely a brief hiatus in the rising prosperity of the industrialized world.

4

Investing in Children: Government Expenditures for Children and their Families in Western Industrialized Countries

SHEILA B. KAMERMAN AND ALFRED J. KAHN

4.1. Scope and Questions

The trends and patterns in governmental social expenditures (societal inputs)[1] and related programme choices designed to improve the well-being of children in advanced industrialized countries between 1960 and the early 1990s form the focus of this chapter. The major stress is on the years following 1975, when economic growth slowed in these countries. While it has been said that child well-being improved between the 1950s and the early 1970s, but has deteriorated since then, this chapter does not assess child well-being *per se*, but rather examines trends that have occurred in child-related government social expenditures within and across these countries.

The Organisation for Economic Co-operation and Development (OECD) has reported that overall social (social protection or social welfare) expenditures, including income transfers and health, education, and other social service outlays, advanced in real terms and as a share of GDP during the 1960s and first half of the 1970s, but fell thereafter through the early 1990s. The question here is whether the same pattern holds for public social expenditures for children and their families.

The specific questions addressed for the period from the mid-1970s to the early 1990s are:

- Did social expenditures for children increase or decrease?
- Was there a relative increase or decrease in proportion to GDP and other social welfare expenditures (for example, those for the elderly)?
- Did expenditures increase or decrease in some child- and family-related fields but not in others?

[1] We refer variously to 'social protection', 'social expenditure', 'social security and welfare', as per usage in OECD, EU, etc. and meaning about the same thing.

- Did expenditures increase or decrease in some countries but not in others?
- How did these developments compare with prior years, particularly the 1960–75 period, often referred to as the 'golden age' of social policy?
- Can some or part of any shifts be explained by demographic changes, economic decline (or growth), alterations in benefits and benefit levels, or variations in country policy orientations?

Social expenditures for children and their families as discussed here cover government expenditures on education and health care and on a general category called 'family benefits'. Clearly, education expenditures are targeted largely on children. Health expenditures for children are seldom disaggregated from health expenditures generally. The heart of our discussion is thus the 'family benefits' category: cash transfers and tax benefits granted for children and their families. These benefits vary considerably among countries in absolute value, which raises important questions: What is or should be the function of family benefits, and at what level should they be provided? What would constitute an adequate standard?

Government expenditures for children and their families climbed throughout most of these years, but never kept up with the growth in public investment in pensions for the elderly or health care generally, either before or after 1975. Education expenditures swelled dramatically in the 1960s, but shrank as a portion of social expenditures and GDP after 1975. In real dollar terms, per child family benefit expenditures continued to rise throughout both time-periods, but dropped further and further behind pensions and health expenditures, and contributed less to disposable family income. This chapter argues that the modest value of cash family benefits in many countries and their decreasing significance in most are largely the result of political choices and decisions. Demographic changes, although important, do not account for the full reduction in family benefits as a share of social expenditures. A re-examination of the function(s) of family benefits and the development of more goal-oriented family policy strategies are strongly recommended.

4.2. Limitations and Caveats

Efforts to compare social expenditures for children and their families over time and cross-nationally are constrained (and potentially skewed) by data gaps, definitional inconsistencies, and incompatibilities in data classification (Barbier, 1990). For example, social expenditures are often classified according to function (income transfers, health, education) rather than by population or age-group (children, the aged). The composition of reported data varies as well (in some countries, education expenditures are part of social expenditures, in others they are not). Moreover, it is often impossible to disaggregate expenditures for children (or even for families with children) from overall social expenditures.

Likewise, data on tax expenditures and benefits for children and their families are often not available. In addition, national social expenditure data rarely include private social expenditures or occupational benefits; yet these, too, may affect child well-being and vary across countries. For example, in the USA in 1991, public social expenditures were 20.5 per cent of GDP, while private social expenditures constituted an additional 13.3 per cent. Comparable data, however, are not available for the other OECD countries.

Finally, expenditures may be classified differently from country to country (for example, child care as an education expenditure, a health expenditure, or a personal social service expenditure; government child support or maintenance as a social insurance benefit, a special family benefit, or social assistance). The OECD definitions of what each country includes in its data on 'family' benefits are largely used in this discussion. Given these caveats, some comparisons can none the less be made.

This chapter draws extensively on the OECD database and, to a lesser extent, on European Economic Community (EEC) now the European Union (EU) social protection accounts data.[2] For programme details, patterns, and trends, it relies primarily on the research of the authors and their colleagues in various countries.

4.3. The 'Golden Age' of Social Policy: 1960–1975

From about 1950 to the first oil shock of 1973 an unprecedented economic surge in Western industrialized countries was accompanied by an extensive rise in the role of government, especially in the scope of social policies. Countries dramatically increased their level of social protection and access to pensions, health care, and education services (OECD, 1985, 1988a). Excluding Portugal and Spain, for which data are not available for this period, average social expenditures as a share of GDP among the OECD countries climbed from 12.3 to 21.9 per cent (Table 4.1). The growth in expenditures as a proportion of GDP ranged from below 50 per cent in Austria and New Zealand to well over 100 per cent in the Netherlands and Norway and to almost 300 per cent in Denmark (Table 4.1). The annual

---

[2] The OECD social expenditure database was changed in 1996 to make it more compatible with the European Union social protection accounts data, and includes some different definitions of family benefits. (OECD Labour Market and Social Policy Occasional Papers, No. 17, *Social Expenditures Statistics of OECD Member Countries*. Provisional version, 1996.) This chapter uses the database in effect in prior years.

Table 4.1: Government Social Expenditure as a Percentage of GDP, 1960–1990

Country	1960	1975	1980	1985	1990
Australia	9.5	17.6	17.3	18.4	17.7
Austria	17.4	23.4	26.0	28.8	29.9
Belgium	—	28.7	33.9	35.8	30.6
Canada	11.2	20.1	19.5	22.6	25.5
Denmark	9.0	27.1	35.1	33.9	33.9
Finland	14.9	21.9	22.9	22.8	33.8
France	14.4	26.3	30.9	34.2	31.9
Germany	17.1	27.8	26.6	25.8	27.5
Greece	—	10.0	12.6	19.5	—
Ireland	11.3	22.0	23.8	25.6	25.2
Italy	13.7	20.6	23.7	26.7	—
Japan	7.6	13.7	16.1	16.2	15.3
Netherlands	12.8	29.3	31.8	30.7	34.4
New Zealand	12.7	19.0	22.4	19.8	—
Norway	11.0	23.2	24.2	23.5	35.5
Portugal	—	—	17.3	—	20.8
Spain	—	—	15.6	—	23.8
Sweden	15.6	27.4	33.2	32.0[a]	39.6
Switzerland	8.2	19.0	19.1	20.5[a]	—
UK	2.4	19.6	20.0	20.9	27.6
USA	9.9	18.7	18.0	18.2	20.1
OECD Average[b]	12.3	21.9	23.3	24.6	27.9

[a] 1984 figure. [b] The OECD average figures are the unweighted averages, excluding Portugal and Spain, for all years and Belgium and Greece for 1960.

Sources: OECD (1988*a*) for 1960–85 data; OECD (1994), table 16 and Education Expenditures from *OECD in Figures, 1994*; (1990/1 Education Expenditures), for 1990 data.

average gain in social expenditures in real terms between 1960 and 1975 was 6.5 per cent in reporting countries (Table 4.2).

Social expenditures as a portion of total government spending rose nearly 23 per cent, from 47.7 per cent in 1960 to 58.6 per cent in 1975. Given the importance of social spending in total government expenditures, it is not surprising that high government expenditure countries (Denmark, Germany, the Netherlands, and Sweden) and low government spenders (Japan and Switzerland) occupied similar positions in social spending.

While a swell in expenditures for children and their families was part of a general upturn in social expenditures during these years, it also reflected emerging special attention to children. It has been suggested that economic growth, demographic changes, and a desire to invest in human capital accounted for this advance. In any case, one may ask if the expansion in expenditures for children and their families paralleled that in social expenditure and the growth in economies generally.

Table 4.2: Growth of Real Social Expenditure
(per cent per year[a])

Country	1960–75	1975–85
Australia	8.1	2.9
Austria	3.5	3.9
Belgium	—	3.6
Canada	7.6	3.0
Denmark	8.8	5.1
Finland	5.6	2.8
France	7.3	4.4
Germany	4.8	1.4
Greece	—	7.9
Ireland	7.3	4.3
Italy	5.5	3.4
Japan	8.5	5.7
Netherlands	6.4	3.1
New Zealand	4.0	1.5
Norway	8.3	10.6
Sweden	5.9	1.7
Switzerland	8.1	2.6
UK	3.9	2.0
USA	6.5	2.4
OECD Average	. 6.5[b]	3.4

[a] Expenditures in constant prices were obtained by deflating current price data by the GDP deflator.
[b] Belgium and Greece are not included in the average.
Source: OECD (1988*a*).

Family benefits in the OECD database include primarily child and family allowances, but also public assistance benefits such as the means-tested Aid to Families with Dependent Children (AFDC) in the USA, Supplementary Benefits (Income Support) in the UK, and certain special family-related income and housing allowance benefits in other countries. Except for child or family allowances, there is little consistency across countries.

Maternity and parenting benefits are not included by OECD, but instead come under sickness benefits in most countries or as part of unemployment benefits in Austria and Canada, for example. Since these data are not disaggregated, only trends in family benefits excluding maternity and parenting benefits can be reported here. Trends in both family and maternity-parenting benefits are included in EEC data referred to briefly, below, in context.

In real dollars, annual family benefits increased on average by about two-thirds between 1960 and 1973, from $220 per child under 15 per year

Table 4.3: Family Transfers at 1980 Prices and PPS US Dollars per Child under Age 15, 1960–1984

Country	1960	1973	1984	Annual growth rates	
				1960–73	1973–84
Australia	184	166	511	−0.8	10.9
Austria	295	522	1,012	4.5	6.5
Belgium	—	—	—	—	—
Canada	228	208	318	−0.7	3.8
Denmark	145	762	1,012	13.6	2.6
Finland	151	164	383	0.6	8.1
France	657	878	1,305	2.3	3.7
Germany	61	128	528	5.9	15.1
Greece	—	41	77	10.7	6.1
Ireland	106	206	217[a]	5.3	0.9
Italy	393	367	423	−0.5	1.3
Japan	0	366	562	—	4.0
Netherlands	215	618	914	8.5	3.6
New Zealand	345	452	603	2.1	2.7
Norway	122	414	684	9.9	4.9
Sweden	408	806	808	5.4	0.1
Switzerland	30	95	177	9.2	5.8
UK	137	230	855	4.1	12.8
USA	45	220	232	13.0	0.5
OECD Total	220	369	590	5.3	5.2

[a] 1983 figure.

Source: Data from Varley (1986).

to $369 in 1980 dollars (Table 4.3). France was the most generous country, providing $657 per child in 1960 and $878 in 1973. Other generous countries included Sweden, Denmark, and the Netherlands. The least generous in 1973 were Greece, Switzerland, and Germany.

Between 1960 and 1975, expenditures on family benefits gained almost 20 per cent as a portion of GDP, climbing from 2.2 to 2.6 per cent (Table 4.4). Denmark, France, Japan, Netherlands, New Zealand, and Sweden spent significantly more. Australia, Greece, Switzerland, UK, and the USA allocated less.

In contrast, expenditures on the major social programmes increased far more during this period (Tables 4.5, 4.6, 4.7). Health expenditures (some of which were targeted at children) grew by 70 per cent, from 4 to 6.8 per cent of GDP; pension expenditures jumped by 65 per cent, from 4.3 to 7.1 per cent of GDP, and education expenditures surged by almost 70 per cent, from 3.4 to 5.7 per cent of GDP. Although family benefit expenditures relative to GDP increased, their rate of growth was more modest than that of the major social programmes.

Table 4.4: Family Benefit Expenditure as a Share in GDP, 1960–1990

Country	1960	1975	1980	1984	1990
Australia	2.1	1.0	2.5	2.8	—
Austria	2.2	2.8	3.6	3.2	2.8
Belgium	—	—	—	—	—
Canada	2.6	2.8	1.4	1.3	1.0
Denmark	1.1	4.3	4.3	4.0	5.1
Finland	3.7	2.0	2.2	1.9	4.3
France	4.7	4.6	4.5	4.8	4.5
Germany	0.4	2.2	1.9	1.3	1.3
Greece	—	0.4	0.6	0.6	—
Ireland	2.4	2.7	2.0	—	2.8
Italy	4.0	2.7	1.7	1.4	—
Japan	0.0	4.2	3.9	3.1	2.4
Netherlands	2.0	3.0	3.2	2.6	2.0
New Zealand	3.9	4.9	4.7	3.6	—
Norway	1.6	2.3	2.4	2.4	3.6
Sweden	2.8	3.1	3.1	2.2	2.7
Switzerland	0.3	0.5	0.6	0.6	—
UK	1.4	1.8	3.4	3.5	4.5
USA	0.4	1.2	1.0	0.8	0.9
OECD Average	2.2	2.6	2.6	2.4	2.9

Sources: Based on Varley (1986). Table 6 data as a per cent of table 1 (Social Expenditure as a per cent of GDP) from OECD (1988*a*). 1990 figures based on OECD National Income Accounts data as a per cent of table 1, 1990 GDP data.

As a proportion of public social expenditures generally, family benefits declined dramatically between 1960 and 1973, falling an average of more than 3 per cent each year. Denmark, Greece, Germany, and the USA were the only countries in which the share of such benefits advanced: Germany through the broadening of its family allowance benefit and the USA through the expansion in AFDC, its means-tested public assistance benefit for single mothers and their children. In contrast, Canada, Finland, and Italy experienced especially large reductions: 7.9, 8.9, and 7.7 per cent, respectively.

Of particular importance in assessing social expenditures are the growth patterns in the major social programmes, and how they compare with developments in family benefits. For all OECD countries, between 1960 and 1975 education as a component of total social spending dropped from 28 to 25 per cent, health care climbed from 19.6 to 22.5 per cent, and pensions remained at around 31 per cent. In contrast, the portion accounted for by family benefits plummeted by 30 per cent, from 17.3 per cent to 12.2 per cent. The only countries directing a greater part of social

Table 4.5:   Health Expenditure Share in GDP, 1960–1990

Country	Total expenditure on health					Public expenditure on health				
	1960	1975	1980	1985	1990	1960	1975	1980	1985	1990
Australia	4.6	5.7	6.6	6.8	8.2	2.4	3.6	4.1	4.9	5.6
Austria	4.4	7.3	7.9	8.2	8.3	2.9	5.1	5.4	5.3	5.6
Belgium	3.4	5.8	6.6	7.1	7.6	2.1	4.6	5.3	5.5	6.8
Canada	5.5	7.3	7.4	8.4	9.5	2.4	5.6	5.5	6.4	6.9
Denmark	3.6	6.5	6.8	6.1	6.3	3.2	5.9	5.8	5.2	5.2
Finland	4.2	6.2	6.3	7.3	7.8	2.3	4.9	5.0	5.6	6.3
France	4.2	6.7	7.4	8.4	8.9	2.4	5.3	6.0	6.8	6.6
Germany	4.7	7.8	7.9	8.2	8.3	3.2	6.3	6.3	6.4	6.0
Greece	2.9	4.0	4.2	4.2	5.4	1.7	2.5	3.6	4.1	4.1
Iceland	5.9	—	6.9	7.8	—	2.3	6.5	5.7	6.4	—
Ireland	4.0	7.7	8.5	8.0	7.0	3.0	6.3	8.0	6.9	5.2
Italy	3.9	6.7	6.8	6.7	8.1	3.2	5.8	5.6	5.4	6.3
Japan	3.0	5.6	6.6	6.6	6.8	1.8	4.1	4.6	4.8	4.8
Netherlands	3.9	7.7	8.2	8.3	8.0	1.3	5.9	6.5	6.5	5.7
New Zealand	4.4	6.4	7.2	5.5	7.3	3.6	5.3	6.0	4.4	6.0
Norway	3.3	6.7	6.6	6.4	7.5	2.6	6.4	6.5	6.2	7.1
Portugal	—	6.4	5.9	5.7	6.7	0.9	3.8	4.3	4.0	4.1
Spain	2.3	5.1	5.9	6.0	6.6	1.2	3.6	4.3	4.3	5.3
Sweden	4.7	8.0	9.5	9.4	8.6	3.4	7.2	8.8	8.5	6.9
Switzerland	3.3	7.1	7.2	7.9	7.8	2.0	4.7	4.7	5.4	5.3
UK	3.9	5.5	5.8	6.1	6.2	3.3	5.0	5.2	5.2	5.2
USA	5.2	8.4	9.2	10.7	12.4	1.3	3.6	3.9	4.4	5.2
OECD Average	4.0	6.8	7.1	7.3	7.8	2.4	5.1	5.5	5.6	5.7

Sources: OECD (1988*a*), table 13; OECD (1994), table 2, for 1990 data.

expenditure towards children than the average were Canada, Denmark, France, Italy, Japan, and New Zealand.

An OECD analysis (*OECD Observer*, 1984) suggests that only a modest portion of total growth in expenditures was directed towards coping with demographic shifts; more important were enhanced coverage and rising real benefits. In short, social expenditures increased more rapidly between 1960 and 1975 than both the rate of economic growth and the rate of growth of total public expenditures. Expenditures for children and their families expanded primarily due to rising health and education expenditures. Family benefits gained, but their growth was not as rapid. Indeed, despite the increased numbers of children throughout the 1960s, child-specific expenditures other than those in education did not increase rapidly, and family benefits as a portion of overall social expenditures fell. The declining child poverty during these years was due more to economic growth and rising wages.

Table 4.6: Public Pension Expenditure as a Share in GDP[a], 1960–1990

Country	1960	1975	1980	1985	1990
Australia	3.3	4.5	4.9	4.9[b]	—
Austria	9.6	12.5	13.5	14.5	14.5
Belgium	—	10.5	11.9	10.3	—
Canada	2.8	3.7	4.4	5.4	6.0
Denmark	4.6	7.8	9.1	8.5	9.6
Finland	3.8	6.1	6.5	7.1[b]	6.3
France	6.0	10.1	11.5	12.7	12.7
Germany	9.7	12.6	12.1	11.8	10.8
Greece	—	4.8	5.8	10.7	11.3
Ireland	2.5	4.2	4.5	5.4	4.5
Italy	5.5	10.4	12.0	15.6	14.2
Japan	1.3	2.6	4.4	5.3	5.7
Netherlands	4.0	8.9	11.0	10.5	11.3
New Zealand	4.3	5.3	7.6	8.1	7.6
Norway	3.1	8.0	7.9	8.0	9.9
Portugal	—	4.1	6.1	7.2	—
Spain	—	4.3	7.3	8.6[b]	—
Sweden	4.4	7.7	10.9	11.2	11.3
Switzerland	2.3	7.7	8.0	8.1	7.8
UK	4.0	6.0	6.3	6.7	6.4
USA	4.1	6.7	6.9	7.2	7.0
OECD Average[c]	4.3	7.1	8.2	8.9	9.2

[a] These data indicate the relationship between current public expenditure on pensions and GDP in current values. Public pensions include both transfers through social programmes and pension payments to retired government employees. [b] 1984 figures. [c] The OECD average is the unweighted average of the available data for these 21 OECD countries.

Sources: OECD (1988*a*), table 7.0; OECD (1994) for 1990 data.

4.4. The Tough Years: 1975–1990

4.4.1. Social expenditures during the decline in economic growth

The years after 1975 witnessed a fall in economic growth (marked by the 1973–4 and 1979–80 oil shocks and high inflation), recessions in the early and late 1980s, a slow-down in growth rates of social expenditures generally, and a plateauing or even a drop in certain social expenditures for children. It is not clear whether the expansion in preschool and child-care services and in new categorical child benefits (maternity-parenting benefits, child support and maintenance benefits) in some countries offset the declines in other areas (child and family allowances, for example). It is also unclear whether the changes in tax benefits and in the patterns of family income distribution in some countries have exacerbated or medi-

Table 4.7:   Education Expenditure Share in GDP, 1960–1990

OECD Country List	1960	1975	1980	1985/6	1990/1
Australia	2.8	6.1	5.8	4.7	4.7
Austria	2.0	3.5	3.8	6.0	5.4
Belgium	—	—	—	5.4	5.4
Canada	3.0	6.3	6.0	6.6	6.7
Denmark	—	8.1	7.7[a]	7.2	6.1
Finland	6.6	6.6	6.2	5.2	6.7
France	—	5.8	5.7	5.0	5.4
Germany	2.4	5.4	5.1	4.3	4.0
Greece	1.6	1.9	2.4	2.8	—
Ireland	3.0	6.1	6.5	5.9	5.5
Italy	3.7	5.0	5.6	—	—
Japan	4.0	4.9	5.0	5.1	3.7
Netherlands	4.5	7.5	7.2	6.6	5.6
New Zealand	2.7	4.5	4.2	4.9	—
Norway	3.8	6.7	6.3	6.2	6.8
Sweden	4.6	5.6	6.5	7.5	6.5
Switzerland	3.0	5.6	5.5[a]	4.8	5.4
UK	3.6	6.8	5.6	5.0	5.3
USA	3.6	6.3	5.7	4.8	5.5
OECD Total	3.4	5.7	5.6	5.4	5.5

[a] 1979.

Sources: OECD (1985), annexe, for 1960 and 1975 data; *OECD in Figures, 1990* for 1985/6 data; *OECD in Figures, 1994* for 1990/1 data.

ated the negative effects of the trends in social expenditures for children. Finally, although family benefit expenditures continued to rise on a per-child basis even in the 1980s, the rate of increase and the extent of the rise varied more widely across countries than it had earlier.

In the OECD, the average share of social expenditures in GDP climbed 27.4 per cent between 1975 and 1990, from 21.9 per cent to 27.9 per cent—a significant increase but not the dramatic 78 per cent gain of the earlier fifteen-year period (see Table 4.1). The growth rate ranged from a high of 54.8 per cent in Finland and 53 per cent in Norway (both near the average in 1975) and 45 per cent in Sweden (already a leader throughout 1960–75) to a small decline in Germany. The big spenders were Austria (changing from a laggard to a leader), Belgium, France, Netherlands, and the four Nordic countries (Denmark, Finland, Norway, and Sweden), while the laggards were Australia, Japan, Portugal, and the USA.

The real growth in social expenditures averaged 3.4 per cent between 1975 and 1985, almost a 50 per cent decline from the earlier period (Table 4.2). Countries exhibiting higher growth rates included Austria, Denmark, France, Japan (starting from a lower base), and Norway. Slow growth countries were Germany, New Zealand, Sweden, Switzerland, the UK, and the USA.

A comparison of the income elasticities of the growth in social expenditure in relation to GDP in the 'golden years' (1960–73) and the 'tough years' (1973–90) suggests little difference through the early 1980s. Social expenditure growth outpaced economic growth between 1973 and 1984 as it did in the earlier period, and paralleled the patterns of government spending generally. In the late 1980s, however, growth was more constrained and social spending just kept pace. The OECD average rose slightly from 1.28 during 1960–73 to 1.37 during 1973–84, but then declined to 1.07 between 1985 and 1991 (Table 4.8). Moreover, there was substantially less variability after 1973. This suggests that the slower growth in expenditures had more to do with sluggish economic growth than with changes in social policies.

In terms of real growth, only those countries which had previously been below or close to the average (Australia, Japan, New Zealand, and Spain) showed a significant jump beyond the rate of GDP growth between 1973

Table 4.8: Elasticities of Government Social Security and Welfare Transfers in Relation to GDP, 1960–1991

Country	1960–73	1973–84	1985–91
Australia	1.05	1.41	—
Austria	1.13	1.27	1.06
Canada	1.19	1.33	1.22
Denmark	1.48	1.36	1.15
Finland	1.22	1.25	1.32
France	1.14	1.31	0.98
Germany	1.07	1.28	0.93[a]
Greece	1.25	1.39	1.01[a]
Ireland	1.27	1.35	0.90
Italy	1.24	1.22	1.05
Japan	1.33	1.87	1.00
Netherlands	1.49	1.51	0.97
New Zealand	0.95	1.31	1.11
Norway	1.73	1.11	1.39
Portugal	1.25	1.38	—
Spain	1.09	1.39	1.05
Sweden	1.43	1.33	1.13
Switzerland	1.71	1.82	1.00
UK	1.27	1.39	0.96
USA	1.39	1.18	1.06
OECD Average	1.28	1.37	1.07

[a] 1990.

Source: Varley (1986), table 3. The 1985–91 calculations are from OECD National Accounts database.

and 1984; and only Finland and Norway showed any large increase beyond the GDP growth rate in the late 1980s. Average OECD social expenditures, which had risen from about 48 to 59 per cent of government expenditures during the earlier period, rose only slightly to just under 62 per cent between 1975 and 1990.

Expenditures for pensions and health care as a proportion of GDP increased significantly, but at a much slower rate between 1975 and 1990 (Tables 4.5 and 4.6). Education expenditures fell slightly from 5.7 to 5.5 per cent (Table 4.7). And family benefits rose slightly, from 2.6 to 2.9 per cent, largely at the end of the 1980s (Table 4.4).

As a proportion of social expenditures, health expenditures rose slightly over the 1960–86 period (from 22.5 per cent to 23.7 per cent) and pensions advanced significantly (from 30.3 per cent to 36 per cent). Education continued to lose ground with respect to other benefits (primarily because of the diminishing size of child cohorts), from 25 per cent to 22.2 per cent. And the portion of social expenditures allocated to family benefits dropped still further, from 12.2 to 9.8 in 1986 and 9.7 in 1990.

The family benefit pattern, however, varied across countries. In the Netherlands, family benefit expenditures were high and continued to rise until 1980 before beginning to decline; in Sweden, they declined through 1984, recovering somewhat by 1990. In Denmark, they continued to rise until 1982, then declined only to go up again each year between 1987 and 1990. In contrast, in Greece (and Spain and Portugal, not in these tables) family benefits were very low, about 15 per cent of the OECD average. Eurostat data for the countries in the EU show that real family benefits continued to rise between the early 1980s and the early 1990s in Denmark, France, and Luxembourg, among the high spenders, and in Ireland, Italy, and the UK among the low spenders.

Average per child expenditures in 1980 real dollars increased between 1973 and 1984, from $369 to $590, a jump of 60 per cent, not much lower than that of the earlier period (Table 4.3). France remained the leader, furnishing $1,305 per child, and both Denmark and Austria provided around $1,012. Slightly behind these three were the Netherlands, the UK, and Sweden. Greece, Switzerland, Ireland, and the USA were the laggards. The rate of growth in benefits, about 5.2 per cent per year on average, was similar to that of the previous period. Illustrating the variability in trends and patterns during these years, however, the level of per child benefits in thirteen countries climbed until the mid-1980s; in seven others the peak occurred in the 1970s, while in five of these a new peak was attained in the late 1980s.

An assessment of the trends in family benefits shows that what is meaningful is apparently *not* that family benefits declined in real value per child (indeed they went up substantially over 1975–90), but rather that they continued to drop as a portion of social expenditures generally, and that their rate of growth as a proportion of GDP fell relative to both the earlier period and the rate of growth in pensions and health expenditures. *Family benefits, modest to begin with and usually not inflation-indexed, did not keep up with the trends in other major social programmes, particularly the benefits for the elderly. They did not keep pace as a portion of GDP or as a portion of social expenditures. As a result, the economic well-being of children remained largely dependent on the earnings and incomes of parents, and far less dependent on government income transfers.*

An analysis of the EEC social protection statistics, which do not cover education and which include fewer countries than the OECD accounts, confirms the OECD data trends. The only difference is the smaller amount of variability.

Table 4.9: Cash Transfers to Married Couples with Two Children, 1972–1990 (as a percentage of gross earnings—average production worker (APW))

Country	1975	1985	1990	1975–85	1985–90
Australia	0.9	3.2	7.9[a]	2.3	4.7
Austria	8.9	15.4	17.4[a]	6.5	2.0
Belgium	13.3	11.9	16.2[a]	−1.4	4.3
Canada	4.7	3.2	10.3[a]	−1.5	7.1
Denmark	4.7	4.0	5.6	−0.7	1.6
Finland	4.1	6.2	6.6	2.1	0.4
France[b,c]	11.7	7.5	7.0	−4.2	−0.5
Germany	6.2	4.8	4.4	−1.4	−0.4
Ireland	2.4	3.2	3.2	0.8	0.0
Italy	10.7	9.7[d]	10.6[a]	−1.0	0.9
Japan	0.0	0.0	—	—	—
Luxembourg	6.1	10.7	11.3	4.6	0.6
Netherlands	6.7	8.1	7.3	1.4	−0.8
New Zealand	5.0	9.3	2.5[a]	4.3	−6.8
Norway	4.3	8.0	12.2	3.7	4.2
Sweden	6.7	7.7	9.9	1.0	2.2
Switzerland	3.8[e]	6.1	6.0	2.3	−0.1
UK	2.5[e]	8.4	6.1	5.9	−2.3
USA	0.0	0.0	0.0	0.0	0.0
OECD Average	6.0	7.5	8.5	1.5	1.1

[a] Includes tax benefits where OECD country data include them. [b] For the purpose of the table, children are defined as between the ages of 5 and 12. For France, the cash benefits for younger children are far more generous. [c] Housing allowances for families with children are also provided, but are not included in these data. [d] 1984 figure. [e] Taxable benefit.

Sources: 1972, 1975 data are from OECD (1978), table 8; 1982, 1985 data are from *OECD Observer*, 127 (March 1984), and 145 (April/May 1987).

4.4.2. Family benefits and family income

We now examine changes in the ratio of family benefits to the average gross earnings of a production worker. OECD analysts have periodically examined the impact of policy on the economic situation of a hypothetical worker, in this case a married person with two children between the ages of 5 and 12. Cash transfers as a percentage of gross earnings increased from 6.0 to 8.5 per cent between 1975 and 1990 (Table 4.9). The countries showing the greatest jumps were Australia, Canada, and the UK, where family benefits as a percentage of gross earnings more than doubled from a very low base, and Austria and Luxembourg, where the package almost doubled but from a 1975 base already above the OECD average. In contrast, France, Germany, and New Zealand registered declines in the relative value of family benefits. None the less, France remains among the more generous countries given the presence of other family benefits not shown in Table 4.9, such as special benefits for under-3-year-olds and, as in Sweden, housing allowances for families with children. (Housing allowances are included in the OECD family benefits list for Sweden but not for France; see Kahn and Kamerman (1983) on the importance of housing allowances for family income.) In 1975, Germany's family benefits were about the OECD average, but by 1990 they were only about half the average. Japan and the USA provided no universal family benefits during these years.

Table 4.10: Real Wages in Industry in the EEC, Japan, Sweden, and the USA, 1978–1990 (1980 = 100)

Country	1978	1985	1990	Growth/Decline	
				1978–85	1985–90
Belgium	95.2	95.4	103.3	0.2	7.9
Denmark	102.8	97.5	106.2	−5.3	8.7
France	96.9	106.8	108.7	9.9	1.9
Germany	97.4	100.8	114.9	3.4	14.1
Ireland	99.0	102.4	112.3	3.4	9.9
Italy	100.7	106.5[a]	—	5.8	—
Luxembourg	100.0	92.6	112.4	−7.4	19.8
Netherlands	100.3	97.2	106.2	−3.1	9.0
UK	99.5	109.2	105.8	9.7	−3.4
EUROPE 9	99.1	100.9	106.6	1.8	9.3
Japan	98.0	107.5	113.1	9.5	5.6
Sweden	101.6	95.6	115.7	−6.0	20.1
USA	107.2	100.2	95.3	−7.0	−4.9

[a] 1984 figure.

Sources: European Union (1990 and 1994).

Table 4.11: The Share of Family Benefits (Taxes and Transfers) in Disposable Income, for a Married, Two-Child, One Average Worker Family, Selected Years

Country	1975	1987	1992
Australia	13.6	7.4	9.8
Austria	22.9	18.6	20.2
Belgium	21.1	19.9	28.0
Canada	12.4	12.3	15.9
Denmark	15.6	12.5	19.1
Finland	21.5	11.7	8.8
France	23.4	14.2	7.9
Germany	15.9	14.5	6.2
Ireland	17.6	13.6	3.8
Italy	12.5	11.3[a]	7.8
Japan	5.9	5.8	—
Luxembourg	26.3	23.4	10.8
Netherlands	15.8	10.4	10.7
New Zealand	9.8	8.9	2.0
Norway	14.7	16.5	14.7
Sweden	16.9	11.4	12.7
Switzerland	10.5	11.3	6.7
UK	14.4	11.5	7.4
USA	13.5	6.7	—
OECD Total	15.3	13.0	11.4

[a] 1986 figure.

Sources: 1972, 1975 data are from OECD (1978*b*), 1972–76, table 9; 1984 data are from OECD (1986), table 4; 1987 data are from *OECD in Figures, 1990* and OECD (1993).

These patterns are affected by trends in real wages, but family benefits and wages are not explicitly linked by policy (Table 4.10). The UK, whose family benefit package increased the most between 1975 and 1985 in relation to gross earnings, also had rapid growth in real wages during these years. However, its family benefit package continued to rise between 1985 and 1990, while wages decreased. In contrast, in Denmark and Germany, while family benefits declined in the early 1980s (or late 1970s), wages also decreased; but when the package expanded in the late 1980s, wages rose too. Different again is the situation for France where real wages increased while the family benefit package shrank somewhat, and for Japan which did not supplement wages at all with family benefits for children in the age-group specified in the OECD analysis.

Unlike the post-World War II period when real wages rose rapidly in all countries, real wage growth was negative between 1978 and 1985 in five of the twelve countries shown in Table 4.10 and was slow in most other countries. However, in the late 1980s real wages rose in all countries, except the UK and the USA. The OECD examines the impact on disposable income of family benefits (cash transfers *and* tax benefits) as well as income taxes and social insurance contributions (Table 4.11). Thus defined, the value of family benefits, as a proportion of disposable income fell from 15.3 to 11.4 per cent between 1975 and 1992. Despite the continued expansion in the real value of family benefits, the effects of higher tax rates, lower tax benefits, or higher wages diminished their contribution to family economic well-being. The countries offering large benefits in relation to disposable income in the early 1990s were Austria, Belgium, and Denmark; Canada, Norway, and Sweden were only a little behind; Japan and the USA, once again, lagged.

This analysis underscores the importance of trends with regard to wages. If wages had increased over the last two decades, the pattern of declining family benefits would have had a lesser impact. Indeed, in some countries, rising wages did help compensate for falling family benefits. In some countries where real wages fell, higher family benefits offset some of the loss. In still others with diminishing real wages, however, often only the economic contributions of working wives counterbalanced a parallel drop in the contribution of family benefits to disposable family income. In the USA, the lack of family benefits and the decline in the value of child (dependent) tax exemptions exacerbated a simultaneous decline in the value of real wages.

To sum up, as a portion of GDP, social expenditures rose dramatically between 1960 and 1975, but only at about one-third that rate in the following fifteen years. Although family benefits gained as a portion of GDP between 1960 and 1975, the growth rate was far lower than that of social expenditures generally and was even more modest after 1975. In addition, while family benefits expanded in absolute terms and in real value, they generally declined as a portion of social expenditures from 1960 on. Even where supplemented by maternity and parenting benefits, family benefits expenditures never kept pace with the surge in expenditures for pensions and health care.

Noteworthy, however, is the fact that the real values of family benefits were sustained after 1975; indeed, the value of these benefits increased as much between 1975 and 1985 as in the earlier period. Family benefits also increased in relation to gross earnings after 1975, but declined as a portion of disposable income. The increase was apparently not sufficient, however, to compensate for flagging child tax benefits or for higher income and payroll taxes on disposable income. On the other hand, in some countries, real benefits fell in value proportionately as real earnings and disposable income went up.

Finally, to summarize briefly for 1985 to the early 1990s:

- Government expenditures as a share of GDP did not change, but social expenditures rose significantly as a share of government expenditures.
- Within social expenditures, education expenditures remained stable, pension expenditures grew modestly, and health expenditures grew more significantly.
- Family benefits claimed a larger share of GDP than in recent decades, but continued to decline as a segment of total social expenditures despite a real increase on a per-child basis.
- Transfers to 'traditional' one-earner families grew modestly, although benefits became less significant as a percentage of family income.

4.5. Contributory and Compensating Factors

4.5.1. Demography

Since 1960 the portion of the population under age 15 has declined, while the elderly portion has increased. The share of children in the population

Table 4.12: Percentage of Population Under 15 in OECD Countries, 1960–1992

Country	1960	1975	1988	1992	1960–75	1975–88	1988–92
Australia	30.6	28.1	22.3	22.0	−2.4	−5.9	−0.1
Austria	22.1	23.6	17.5	17.5	1.5	−6.1	0.0
Belgium	23.5	22.2	18.2	18.2	−1.3	−4.0	−0.1
Canada	33.6	26.6	21.1	20.7	−7.0	−5.5	−0.4
Denmark	25.2	22.1	17.5	17.0	−3.1	−4.6	−0.5
Finland	30.4	21.8	19.3	19.2	−8.6	−2.5	−0.1
France	26.4	24.1	20.4	20.0	−2.3	−3.7	−0.4
Germany	21.3	21.7	14.6	15.5	0.4	−7.1	0.9
Ireland	31.1	30.3	28.2	26.8	−0.8	−2.1	−1.4
Italy	25.0	23.9	15.0	15.7	−1.1	−8.9	−0.7
Japan	30.2	24.5	19.7	17.3	−5.7	−4.8	−2.4
Luxembourg	21.4	20.9	17.1	17.7	−0.5	−3.8	0.6
Netherlands	30.0	25.1	18.4	18.3	−4.9	−6.7	−0.1
New Zealand	32.9	30.0	23.4	23.1	−2.9	−6.6	−0.3
Norway	25.9	24.5	19.1	19.1	−1.4	−5.4	0.0
Sweden	22.0	20.7	17.8	19.0	−1.3	−2.9	1.2
Switzerland	23.5	22.5	16.9	16.8	−1.0	−5.4	−0.1
UK	23.1	23.8	18.9	19.2	0.7	−4.9	0.3
USA	31.1	25.1	21.6	21.9	−6.0	−3.5	0.3
OECD Average	26.8	24.3	19.3	19.2	−2.5	−5.0	−0.2

Sources: OECD (1979), for 1960 and 1975 data; *OECD in Figures*, 1990, 1991, 1992, 1993, and 1994 edns.

is largest in Australia, Ireland, and New Zealand, and smallest in Germany and Italy (Table 4.12). Children as a percentage of the population decreased from 26.8 per cent in 1960 to 19.2 per cent in 1992. In contrast, the percentage of the total population aged 65 and over rose over the same period from 10.5 to 14.1 per cent.

None the less, the OECD accounting framework attributes most social expenditures growth in the major sectors (pensions, health, education) to more extensive coverage and higher real benefit levels. Demographic shifts were responsible for only a small portion of the growth, about 20 per cent (*OECD Observer*, 1984).

There is no consistent link between demographic change and family benefit expenditure trends. Decline in the number of children may lead some countries to spread the same level of expenditure over a smaller group (augmenting individual benefits), encourage others to raise spending in the hope of raising fertility, or permit still others to reduce spending. All that can be said is that overall, between 1960 and 1990, family benefit shares of social expenditure dropped about 10 per cent more than the rate of child population decline, while the pension share of social expenditures jumped by almost 40 per cent more than the increase in the aged share of the population.

If spending on family benefits had been sustained or paralleled the trends in pension expenditures in proportion to demographic shifts, social protection for children would have been far more extensive. At the same time, other changes added to the needs of children and were only partially addressed by governments in these countries (Kamerman and Kahn, 1989; Sorrentino, 1990). Between 1970 and 1992, divorce rates more than doubled in Belgium, Canada, Finland, France, Netherlands, Norway, Sweden, and the UK, and almost doubled in Denmark and Germany. The increase was a relatively lower 50 per cent in the USA, but at about 21 (per 1,000 married women) in 1990, the USA had the highest divorce rate of the OECD countries, followed at a great distance by the UK, Canada, Denmark, and Sweden.

Out-of-wedlock births mounted dramatically in many countries. Rates of single parenthood (overwhelmingly female) doubled between 1970 and the end of the 1980s. The highest rates were in the USA and the Scandinavian countries, with Canada, Germany, the Netherlands, and the UK not too far behind. Because women earn less than men, the climb in mother-only families has exacerbated the economic situation of children, and placed new demands on social policies.

More women, especially married women with children, have entered the labour force in response to the rising financial costs of rearing children, the failure of husbands' wages to keep pace with inflation, the declining value of family benefits, their increased opportunities, and the rise in the opportunity costs for women remaining at home. The labour force participation rates for women in the prime child-bearing years (25–

34) surged dramatically; participation of women with children aged three and older is now taken for granted in most industrialized countries.

In the face of economic need, families tried to raise their living standards through reliance on the labour market. In most countries, adequate family benefits were not an available alternative. Whether they should be is a topic for policy debate.

4.5.2. *Policy and programme developments*

The demographic and social changes highlighted above have had major implications for social policy, and appropriate policy responses have emerged in some countries. Every OECD country, except the USA, provides a family allowance or child tax credit. These were first instituted in some countries (Belgium, France, Italy, Netherlands) during the 1930s or even earlier (New Zealand in 1926). Most countries adopted family allowances following World War II, making them a relatively recent policy. Most countries also revised their family allowance laws in the late 1960s as part of the social reforms of those years (see Kamerman and Kahn, 1978, 1983; Gordon, 1988; Bradshaw *et al.*, 1993, offers a more recent report).

Maternity benefits were created initially in the late nineteenth century and were well established in Europe by World War I. The 1960s and 1970s saw a significant extension in the duration of these benefits, while the 1970s and 1980s witnessed an expansion of the proportion of women (and men in some countries) using the benefits. The new parenting and child-rearing policies provide for extended job-protected and paid leaves following the end of the basic maternity-parenting leave, and apply until the youngest child is somewhere between one and a half and 3 years old (Kamerman and Kahn, 1991). While serving a small subgroup among families with children, the leave and related benefits can be important. For example, the benefits which support a post-childbirth leave of two to three years in Austria (Badelt, 1991) form a very small part of social expenditures but supplement a family's income by as much as 20 per cent.

For the most part, housing assistance is not included as family benefits in social expenditure data, though they are often substantial. Kahn and Kamerman (1983) found that housing allowances in 1980 supplemented the disposable earned income of a Swedish family consisting of one average earner, a spouse, and two children by 17 per cent, and a similar French family by 6 per cent. Single-parent families and those with lower earnings benefited considerably more.

Advanced maintenance (guaranteed child support) payments are included in family benefits for Denmark and Sweden, but not for Austria, Finland, Germany, or Norway. In 1980, these payments supplemented by almost 50 per cent the net earnings (after taxes) of single Swedish mothers who earned half the average wage. As a result, these families were better off economically in Sweden than in any of seven other industrialized countries. These benefits now exist in all the Nordic countries, in Austria and France, and to a limited extent in Germany (Kahn and Kamerman, 1988).

Social assistance, the means-tested cash benefits provided to the poor, is included in family benefits for some (not all) countries in the OECD database. This raises the issue of the role of social assistance as a vehicle for family benefits.

Child-care services have expanded enormously in many countries since 1975. These expenditures are counted as educational spending in some countries, but defined as personal social services in others (and thus not included at all). Child-care services are important to children and occur on a large scale. For most countries, expenditures for personal social services for troubled children and their families are also not included in these data.

In some countries there have been specific programmatic responses to recent changes in the family and to other child- and family-related problems. These have taken the form of cash benefits (such as advanced maintenance), new or extended parenting leave and benefits, special help for single mothers, and child welfare and child protection programmes. Most involve subgroups of families and modest numbers at any time. Significantly larger expenditures have been made for child care. Although family benefits are important, the main improvements in family economic well-being since 1975 have come from increased family labour market efforts rather than from increased benefits. The emerging reliance of mothers on the labour market is of particular significance as men's real earnings have stagnated in many countries.

4.5.3. Poverty

Family benefits serve a diversity of purposes; in some countries they represent a response to poverty. Certainly, generous benefits help prevent or alleviate poverty. But both benefits and poverty reflect a country's wealth as well as its attitudes towards income disparity and public policy. In short, poverty may be considered as an independent or dependent variable.

Drawing upon the material discussed earlier and adding child poverty data from the Luxembourg Income Study from the early 1990s (Rainwater and Smeeding, 1995) it is possible to explore these relationships (Table 4.13). We note the inclusion of the UK for completeness, although its poverty rate is for 1986, and the omission of France, for which the most recent poverty rate is for 1984 (below). We observe immediately the high correlation between country ranks for child poverty and country ranks for family benefit share in social expenditures. England is the outlyer: a considerable family benefit effort, proportionately, but still high child

Table 4.13: Poverty and Family Benefit Expenditures, and per capita GDP

Country and year of poverty calculation	Child Poverty		Family Benefit Share in Social Expenditures (1990)[b]		Family Benefit Share of GDP[c]		GDP Per Capita (1990)[d]		Effects of Government Policy[e]			
	% of children poor[a]	Rank (Lowest = 1)	%	Rank (Highest = 1)	%	Rank (Highest = 1)	Dollars	Rank (Highest = 1)	Pre-Gov't Poverty %	Pre-Gov't Poverty Rank	Rank Change	Rate Change
Australia (1990)	14.0	11	—	—	—	—	15,951	9	19.6	9	−2	−5.6
Canada (1991)	13.5	10	4.0	9	1.0	8	19,120	2	22.5	10	0	−9.0
Belgium (1992)	3.8	4	—	—	—	—	16,405	7	16.2	7	+3	−12.4
Denmark (1992)	3.3	3	14.9	2	5.1	1	16,765	4	16.0	6	+3	−12.7
Finland (1991)	2.5	1	12.6	3	4.3	3	16,453	6	11.5	2.5	+1.5	−9.0
F.R. Germany (1989)	6.8	7	4.8	7	1.3	7	18,291	3	9.0	1	−6	−2.2
Italy (1991)	9.6	8	3.9	10	—	—	16,021	8	11.5	2.5	−5.5	−1.9
Netherlands (1991)	6.2	6	6.0	6	2.0	6	15,766	11	13.7	5	−1	−7.5
Norway (1991)	4.6	5	10.1	4	3.6	4	15,921	10	12.9	4	−1	−8.3
Sweden (1992)	2.7	2	6.7	5	2.7	5	16,687	5	19.1	8	+6	−16.4
UK (1986)	9.9	9	16.3	1	4.5	2	15,720	12	29.6	12	+3	−19.7
USA (1991)	21.5	12	4.3	8	0.9	9	21,499	1	25.9	11	−1	−4.4

Sources: [a] Rainwater and Smeeding (1995), table 2. Poverty is defined as percentage of children living in households with adjusted disposable incomes less than 50 per cent of median adjusted disposable income for all persons. Income includes all transfers and tax benefits. [b] Table 5. [c] Table 9. [d] *OECD in Figures*, 1992 edn.: 24–5. Per capita at current prices, in dollars, using purchasing power parities. [e] Rainwater and Smeeding (1995), table A-2.

poverty. Among these countries, the UK is one of the poorest, as measured by per capita GDP.

The same pattern holds if one examines child poverty rank and the rank for family benefits as a share of GDP.

It will also be noted that the low child poverty countries are also among the six highest ranked countries for social expenditures as a percentage of GDP; here the rank order correlation is less precise, however, since—as noted—pensions and health care are larger components than are family benefits in social expenditures.

These results do not occur automatically because of country wealth. The six low child poverty countries among the twelve include Belgium, Norway, Netherlands, which rank 7, 10, 11 in per capita GDP. The USA, Canada, Germany, which rank respectively 1, 2, 3 on per capita GDP, and 12, 10, and 7 on child poverty. Finland, with the lowest child poverty rate, and Sweden, which follows it, rank 6 and 5 on per capita GDP.

Our final columns in Table 4.13, compared to the first column, show high effort in reducing poverty from the pre-transfer child poverty rates in such countries as the UK and Canada. These countries, nonetheless, still have relatively high rates, but we also note high effort in some countries that do achieve low rates.

What of France? Using 1984 data, this is among the countries with an enormous child poverty rate drop from pre-transfer (25.4 per cent) to post-transfer (6.5 per cent). In the mid-1980s, France was *a* or *the* leading country in family benefit shares in social expenditures, family benefit share of GDP and per child family transfers.

The recent conclusion of Rainwater and Smeeding (1995: 17) serves to summarize:

> These findings [on the extent to which government programmes reduce poverty] correlate well with overall cash expenditures on the nonaged as a percent of GDP . . . Low transfer countries (e.g. Australia, Italy, the USA) produce lesser reductions in child poverty than do high transfer countries (e.g. Scandinavia, Northern Europe). Nations that have managed to produce a downward trend in child poverty are either those that spend a lot (e.g. Sweden) or those whose spending has increased through the 1980s (e.g. Canada).

These exploratory observations suggest that if poverty is the outcome variable of interest, the critical issue may be *either* per capita GDP *or* the family benefit effort.

4.6. At the Country Level

4.6.1. *Sweden and the other Nordic countries*

By almost all criteria, Sweden has been a leading country in government social and family expenditures. Sweden has increased investment in the well-being of its elderly population and maintained its generosity towards children, albeit at a lower level, in recent years.

Sweden is high in child expenditures and low in child poverty; it is also one of the highest wage countries. Family benefit generosity is thus not due to wage failures. Similarly, Swedish women are more likely to work than elsewhere (89.4 per cent of women aged 25–34 were in the labour force in 1988) and mothers participate at a remarkably high rate (85 per cent in 1988). Moreover, the manufacturing wage rates for Swedish women are 90 per cent of those for men, unusual for any country. Sweden's family allowances, parental benefits, and other children's services accounted for 12.5 per cent of all social expenditures in 1989 (compared with the OECD figure of 6.7 per cent) and 4.3 per cent of GDP (compared with the smaller OECD figure of 2.9 per cent). For 1990, child and family cash benefits claimed 7 per cent of social expenditures for a total of 14.5 per cent (compared with 6.7 per cent in Table 4.1) and 5.1 per cent of GDP.

Whatever the pressures later in the 1990s, Sweden showed no major policy shifts with regard to family benefits in the early 1990s. The higher unemployment rates and declining GDP created economic concerns which generated discussion of non-wage labour costs and social policy generally. However, as of the close of 1994, the cut-backs seem very modest to 'outsiders', and affected sickness benefits, parental insurance, unemployment insurance (at the margin), and delayed implementation of a child-care guarantee for children over 18 months of age.

As the 1990s began, Sweden's cash transfers as a percentage of gross earnings and as a percentage of disposable income for a married one-earner family with two children were slightly higher in 1990 than the OECD norm (Tables 4.9 and 4.11). What Sweden accomplished for social programmes in the 1985–92 period reflected the assignment of a larger share of economic growth to social expenditures than many other countries (Table 4.8), something it had not done in the earlier periods.

The ongoing work of the Nordic Social-Statistical Committee permits a more complete review for Denmark, Norway, Sweden, and Finland (see Table 4.14). Between 1978 and 1990, these countries (excluding Finland) increased expenditures on family benefits as a percentage of social expenditures and as a percentage of GDP. Except for Denmark, these data generally show higher country family benefit expenditures as a percentage of GDP than reported by the OECD database (Table 4.4). The major discrepancy arises through the inclusion of expenditures for services, particularly child care (Table 4.14). The expenditure total for services under family benefits in Denmark and Sweden is larger than the cash benefit total. The reported increases in social expenditures hold if one converts from 1978 to 1990 prices and whether the analysis is per capita or aggregate. The trend is firm.

Table 4.14:   Expenditures for Family Benefits in Nordic Countries, 1978–1990 (in percentages of total social expenditures and as a percentage of GDP)[a]

	Denmark	Finland	Norway	Sweden
Family benefits as a percentage of social expenditures				
1978	10.7	12.6	8.6	12.5
1981	10.6	13.3	12.3	11.5
1984	10.2	14.5	11.5	11.8
1987	11.9	14.6	11.6	12.1
1990	11.9	13.8	11.9	14.5
Family benefits as a percentage of gross domestic product				
1978	2.8	2.8	1.9	3.9
1981	3.2	2.9	2.7	3.9
1984	2.9	3.1	2.5	3.9
1987	3.3	3.8	3.1	4.2
1990	3.5	3.5	3.5	5.1
1990 family benefits in millions of kronor or Finmarks				
TOTAL	28,243	18,587	22,864	68,370
Cash benefits (total)	12,761	11,182	15,387	33,342
Maternity	3,963	3,254	2,484	12,520
Child allowance and other	8,799	7,928	12,903	20,822
Services (total)	15,482	7,404	7,477	35,028
Child care	10,065	5,727	3,727	29,254
Other	5,417	1,677	3,750	5,774
Currency units per $US (1990)	6.189	3.824	6.250	5.919

Sources: Adapted from tables 8.1.1 and 8.2.1 in Knudsen (1990). 1990 data from *Social Security in Nordic Countries*, tables 3.1.7 and Appendix; tables 1a, 1b, 1d, 1e. Tax expenditures, moderately significant, not shown for Finland and Norway. The 1987 totals were 2,852 and 1,950 respectively.

What does this investment bring? These are the only countries with guaranteed child-care space for the over-3s (Denmark, Finland, Sweden) and the under-3s (Finland) or children from the age of 18 months (Sweden); high-quality group-care facilities and family day-care services; they have the most flexible options for working parents, including subsidies for extended parental leaves for at-home care of infants and toddlers, and partially reimbursed non-relative in-home care (Finland); benefits to stay home to care for a sick child, to visit day care or school; guarantee of parents' right to a shorter work day when children are young (Sweden, Denmark, and Finland); excellent records on all child health indicators; virtually no child poverty as known in the USA, Canada, Australia, and most of the rest of Europe.

4.6.2. France

For three decades, France has been the highest spender on family benefits, both in relation to GDP and in actual dollar equivalents. However, family benefits did not keep pace with wages or family income. Compared to single persons, conditions for families with children have generally deteriorated. When the guaranteed minimum income programme for the poor was initiated in the late 1980s, officials were startled to discover that families with children constituted 37 per cent of beneficiaries even though the programme had targeted the single and the childless.

None the less, France has done significantly better by children and their families than most other countries. How has this been accomplished?

Family policy has a long tradition in French social policy. Family benefits were established after World War II in a commitment to social solidarity (to compensate families for the costs of rearing children) and pronatalism (to increase the birth-rate). 'Social justice', the redistribution of income to low-income families with children, became an additional goal in the 1960s and remains so today. Support for the role of women in paid employment as well as within the family, by easing the tension between work and family life, emerged as a fourth goal in the late 1970s.

French policy has targeted these goals through a package of cash benefits, some of which are universal, some selective as to category of need, and some income-tested; these benefits have been supplemented by a family-unit-based tax system. Since 1945, when family allowances were established, the benefits have increased in number, become more categorical and more income-tested, and now cover children up to age 18, regardless of the employment status of parents. They do not, however, provide for coverage of a first child.

The benefits are significant, especially for single mothers, low-income families with three or more children, and to a lesser extent all families with young children. Although political consensus is gone, the continued interest of both the left and right in family benefits has made it possible for these benefits to provide an important income protection.

Between 1975 and the early 1990s, however, cash transfer and tax benefits for a husband/wife, one-earner family with two children declined as a portion of average gross earnings from 11.7 per cent to 7.0 per cent (Table 4.9), and fell dramatically as a portion of disposable income from 23.4 to 7.9 per cent (Table 4.11).

Some programmes continued to expand. Family and maternity benefit expenditures increased by about one-third in real francs between 1985 and 1992, despite a slight decline in the number of families with two or more children, and the numbers of children (CNAF, 1993). Moreover, while expenditures for the universal family allowance for second and subsequent children dropped slightly in real terms and the real value of an allowance to a family with two children declined by 1.7 per cent, other family expenditures increased. New categorical benefits have been introduced for young children and for child care. In addition, the basic family allowance has been extended to cover youths up to age 22 (1994), a new Guaranteed Minimum Income programme for families with three or more children was introduced (1988) as well as a Guaranteed Minimum Income for low-income individuals and families (RMI) (1988). Expenditures on lone-parent family benefits have risen slightly (along with the numbers of these families). And expenditures on housing allowances have increased by more than one-third, with beneficiaries remaining constant. Tax benefits for families with children also increased during these years.

Finally, while the numbers of under-3 children with working mothers increased by 22 per cent between 1982 and 1990, the numbers of 2-year-olds in the *maternelle* rose by 25 per cent, the numbers of 0–3-year-olds in subsidized crèches increased by 55 per cent, and children cared for by a partly subsidized licensed family day-care mother (child-minder) rose by 22 per cent (*Recherches et Prévisions*, 1994).

Some of the recent increase in spending reflects government's response to the high unemployment rate in France, leading to increased use of income-tested family benefits. Continued changes in family structure also play a role.

4.6.3. Germany

Germany's family policy is somewhat different from that of Sweden or France (*Sozialbericht*, 1990). In marked contrast to France with its multi-categorical strategies to support options, or the Nordic premiss of the two-worker family, Germany's more conservative government encourages 'family work', whether this work is carried out by an employed or at-home mother. The government and the constitutional court have stressed the right to child-conditioned cash benefits, tax concessions, and service expenditures to reduce the burden of child-rearing for families.

Germany's social expenditures as a percentage of both total government expenditures and of GDP have been higher than the OECD average since the 1970s (in 1990, following the burdens of reunification, Germany was at the OECD average on these items), but its spending on family benefits has been below the OECD norms throughout. In 1990, its family benefits as a share of GDP were in a class with the low-ranking USA and Canada (Table 4.4). By contrast, it was a leader in total health expenditures and pensions, partly because of its ageing population.

Since the mid-1980s, there have been significant increases in income-conditioned child allowances and child-conditioned tax concessions, major growth in the child-rearing grant to at-home parents, more pension concessions for at-home child-rearing, and some state-level increases in child-care expenditures. As these are reflected in the German social budget, the expenditure level reaches about 3.5 per cent of GDP, with tax concessions exceeding direct cash benefits. And, with an especially large shrinkage of the under-15 cohort, the per child benefit was among the highest in the EU both for 1980 and 1990.

4.6.4. United States of America

The USA has consistently ranked among the low government spenders on social programmes. (The importance of voluntary sector expenditures must be acknowledged, but without comparable data for other countries the analysis here has to be limited to public expenditures.) The USA provides no family allowance; its cash family benefits are the means-tested public assistance benefits provided under the AFDC programme. Both direct cash payments and tax benefits to children and their families declined in real value in the 1970s and 1980s. Legislation enacted in 1990 and 1993 made a small but significant difference, but legislation proposed in 1995 may do worse than reverse this. Only Australia and Japan spend a smaller share of GDP on social programmes and compare with the USA in the small portion of disposable income constituted by family tax and transfer benefits.

Why has the USA been so penurious? While the Europeans were improving and upgrading their programmes in the 1960s and early 1970s, the USA tackled the unfinished business of its welfare state, moving on other social policies (for example, establishing health care programmes and improving pensions and assistance for the elderly). While the Europeans stressed solidarity and redistribution, the USA dealt with civil rights, racial prejudice, and poverty. And while the USA focused on poverty, the UK, the country most similar in its social policy, concentrated on child poverty in particular.

There is little concern in the USA with the level of support provided for children, either the poor or more affluent. Family benefits are viewed as appropriate primarily for the poor or the dependent, and should be kept low to avoid alleged moral hazards such as work disincentives and encouragement for out-of-wedlock births. However, since the mid-1980s, wages in low-earner families have been supplemented through the tax system (the Earned Income Tax Credit—EITC), a transfer not counted as family benefits. Only in 1993 did the USA enact a parental leave policy, and it was limited to unpaid leave. Real wages have declined steadily since 1975, in contrast to most other OECD countries. Moreover, it was the only country, other than Britain, where average real wages declined between 1985 and 1990.

Using US data sources, rather than the OECD series, child and family expenditures rose between 1984 and 1990 by about 25 per cent (National Committee on Children, 1991; Garfinkel, 1995; Kamerman and Kahn, 1995). Most of the growth was due to increased EITC expenditures, food stamps, child care, and health care expenditures. However, Garfinkel's data, compared to similar series for the Nordic countries, UK, or Germany, continue to show the USA as a laggard, particularly given its per capita wealth (Garfinkel, 1995).

4.6.5. Japan

Japan has one of the most rapidly declining child populations and the most rapidly growing elderly population. Despite its high per capita GDP, Japan ranked slightly below average in real expenditures per child in the mid-1980s (above Germany and twice as generous as the USA). Its social policies, developed largely since World War II, contain a large component of means-tested, assistance-like benefits and emphasize the role of the private sector in providing social protection, either through the occupational welfare system or through the informal sector.

Like the USA, Japan provides no universal child or family allowance, but established a means-tested child benefit in 1971. Initially, the benefit covered third and subsequent children until secondary school age; in 1984, it was extended to second children, but was limited to those below the age of school entry. Eligibility was recently restructured to target children under the age of 3. In addition, Japan introduced a child-rearing allowance in 1961, similar to the AFDC programme in the USA, which is targeted on poor single mothers (or children in poor families with a disabled head of household) and provides public assistance to poor families (and other poor).

Japan also has a national health insurance benefit. It offers some personal social service provision for children and families, child-care services including preschool education (largely for 4-year-olds), an extensive occupational welfare system, and some significant child-related benefits and services paid for at the local level which do not show up in the OECD database.

In constant (1985) yen, social expenditures more than doubled between 1975 and 1988, health expenditures doubled, and pensions rose by 71 per cent. In contrast, child benefits had an erratic history. They increased dramatically between 1960 and 1975, while the child share of the population decreased by 19 per cent. Between 1975 and 1988, child benefits declined by about 36 per cent, while the child share of the population declined an additional 18 per cent. In the latter period, however, public assistance expenditures, child-care and preschool services as well as personal social service expenditures increased, suggesting some possible substitution effects.

As Japan confronted its current and projected birth-rate (1.45 in 1992), child and family benefits re-emerged on the national agenda and new legislation was enacted in the early 1990s. Family allowance benefit levels for all children up to age 3 were doubled, although eligibility is still income-tested. In 1991, an unpaid but job-protected leave for up to one year after childbirth was granted to working mothers and fathers. However, in about two-thirds of large firms, no applications for leave were received in the year following passage of the bill.

The Japanese have recently increased their commitment to children and family benefit expenditures are expected to increase as a result, though it is not yet clear how significant this will be.

4.6.6. Summary

Our brief comments on these five countries illustrate our conclusions. First, child and family expenditures in each country are not included in the existing databases, but do exist in the countries' own expenditure reports. These 'invisible family benefit expenditures' are most significant in Sweden and France, already leading countries in generosity towards children, as well as in Germany. Second, in all the countries, but most dramatically in Sweden, some growth in service expenditures paralleled a decline in cash family benefits and these appear to be a substitute for the cash benefits. This is especially true with regard to child-care services. Third, while lower fertility rates and smaller child cohorts seem to have generated support for more generous child benefits in some countries, in others the growth in female labour force participation rates may have generated new needs for policy responses. In still others, the combination of both trends led to more extensive support across the political spectrum. Fifth, some intimations of the importance of history, culture, and politics may be seen. Those countries with explicit family policies approached expenditures for children as an investment in the future; others viewed children as a consumption good, focusing support more narrowly on reducing poverty among the poorest. Political commitment made a difference, especially during the years when resources were more constrained and pressures from politically powerful groups increased.

4.7. Conclusions

Family benefits have not done well, relatively. Although they continued to grow in real terms through both the 'golden' and the 'tough' years, they continued to decline as a portion of social expenditures throughout both periods. Family benefits, in particular family allowances, have declined over time in most countries as a portion of disposable family income.

It appears that the family benefits turning-point was probably not the mid-1970s, but might have been the 1960s, when pension and health expenditures first began to rise dramatically. Instead of a sudden downward turn in family benefit expenditures, the change might have been a steady but gradual decline in social expenditure shares over the last thirty years. Or it might have been due to a shift in the types of public expenditures on children, emerging most visibly in the 1980s. In contrast, pensions grew as a portion of GDP and social expenditures, especially in the latter years, and were increasingly linked to wages and often to prices as well. Family benefits are obviously not to children as pensions are to the elderly. 'Family benefits' as a concept is not well established. Family or child allowances are at the heart of this system, yet even this benefit is not fully 'mature'. The value of a family/child allowance in relation to gross wages, for example, varies enormously, from 17.4 per cent of wages in Austria in 1990 to 2.5 per cent in New Zealand. And their significance and impact cannot be assessed without comparable data on child tax benefits as well.

In some countries, family allowances began as pronatalist policies, provided only to third and subsequent children. In most countries, they sought to fill the gap between market wages and family need. In several countries, in the late 1970s and early 1980s, child/family allowances were viewed as an 'antipoverty' measure and targeted on children in low-income families. However, the child poverty outcomes in Table 4.13 reveal that their impact in reducing poverty is typically very limited. Nevertheless, countries that put together a diversified and generous package of family benefits (family allowances, housing allowances, advanced maintenance benefits, maternity/parenting benefits) can reduce child poverty and appreciably raise family income.

Countries that provide only a modest family allowance or use a social assistance strategy that targets poor children only are unlikely to achieve the goal of adequacy. Social assistance is the least effective strategy since countries are not willing to provide assistance at a level comparable to modest wages.

Family allowances could never provide primary economic support. The combination of wages and family allowances was intended together to constitute a family wage. By design, therefore, an adequate income standard for children requires jobs and adequate wages for parents. And in the late twentieth century, in many countries, at least one-and-a-half average wages are needed to support that standard; one wage alone is not enough, especially if it is the mother's. An effective social policy model must encompass both labour market and family policies (Kamerman and Kahn, 1988, 1989).

A recent study in eight European countries (Ploug and Kvist, 1994) found that unemployment, economic pressures, problems of financing, and devaluations have led to reductions in social benefits. However, this trend has not affected family benefits. Moreover, almost all cash benefit improvements have focused on family benefits: family allowances (UK, France); parental leave and leave to care for sick children (Denmark, Norway); a variety of tax and benefit improvements for families with children and extension of pension credit for at-home care of a child (Germany).

Countries vary in their family benefit efforts, and while wealth, demography, and economic changes explain some differences, more is going on. The trend analysis and particularly our country 'cases' suggest that much of the variance beyond the variables discussed is in the realm of political choice: countries decide what they want to do and either find the political will to do it or decide that the political effort would be excessive. If the new and growing needs of children and their families in industrialized countries are to be met, this issue of political choice must be underscored in analyses of child and family expenditures and, more importantly, must be effectively addressed so that political effort may be transformed into political will.

5

Family Policies in Central and Eastern Europe: From Socialism to the Market

GASPAR FAJTH AND TATIANA ZIMAKOVA

5.1. Introduction

With the collapse of the totalitarian regimes of Central and Eastern Europe (CEE), the social policies developed over several decades throughout the region suddenly appeared to lose all relevance. During the first phase of the region's economic and political transformation, starting around 1989, it was held that only minor social progress had been achieved during the socialist period. In a series of elections in the region—from those of early 1993 in Lithuania to the early 1995 vote in Bulgaria—the original reformer, rightist governments fell from power, with the exception of the Czech Republic and Russia. Interestingly, these were the two countries where the gains and losses of the transition have been the greatest. Between these two poles, reformist ex-communists were voted back into power in the hope that they would maintain both reforms and social measures. But governments have little room to manœuvre with the present economic crisis, and there is little evidence of such reforms. Yet there is an urgent need to develop meaningful and sustainable social policy under the present conditions. From the remnants of the socialist welfare state, family support policies may provide constructive and forward-looking arrangements.

5.2. Social Transfers during the Socialist Period

5.2.1. The development of the socialist welfare state

The socialist welfare systems across Central and Eastern Europe resembled to some extent the welfare states of market economies. Two of the five pillars of social security—health and old age/invalidity insurance—had similarly broad profiles (Ferge, 1991), though expenditures tended to be relatively smaller in the East. However, guaranteed employment and comprehensive family support policies were more widespread.

The rapid growth of the socialist welfare state had a strong political component. Services provided through 'public consumption funds' were considered essential for economic growth and to ensure popular support for regimes. A well-educated, healthy, motivated, and reliable workforce, for instance, was crucial for the forced industrial programmes (Lane, 1990). Broad access to basic health and education services, combined with political and administrative pressure to enforce high take-up, led to rapid achievements, as reflected in welfare indicators. Between the early 1950s and the mid-1960s, infant mortality fell by 56 per cent in the USSR and by 41 per cent in Central and Eastern Europe (UNICEF ICDC, 1994). Even greater reductions were accomplished in illiteracy, child labour, and chronic undernutrition along with poverty-related diseases such as tuberculosis.

Social spending from 'public consumption funds' increased more rapidly than did wages, raising real living standards and per capita income (Table 5.1). These funds provided cash benefits and free or reduced-cost services (widespread subsidies on goods meant further welfare gains) through the social security system as well as other kinds of agencies. Public consumption funds embraced:

- pensions and family benefits, including old-age, invalid, survivor, and social pensions; benefits for the disabled and disaster victims; burial-cost allowances; pregnancy, childbirth, and

Table 5.1: Cumulated and Average Annual Growth of Real Income and Public Consumption Funds, 1961–88 (percentages)

	1961–70		1971–80		1981–8	
	Cumulated	Annual	Cumulated	Annual	Cumulated	Annual
Growth in real per capita household income						
Bulgaria	168	5.3	149	4.1	132	3.6
Hungary	159	4.8	135	3.1	111	1.4
GDR	140	3.5	163	5.0	141	4.4
Romania	163	5.0	179	6.0	—	—
USSR	159	4.8	146	3.9	114	1.5
Czechoslovakia[a]	147	4.0	129	2.6	132	3.6
Growth in public consumption funds						
Bulgaria	282	10.9	228	8.6	144	4.7
Hungary	213	7.9	295	11.4	125	2.9
GDR	160	4.8	198	7.1	147	5.0
Romania	237	9.0	190	6.6	—	—
USSR	207	7.6	167	5.3	139	4.2
Czechoslovakia	193	6.8	162	5.0	144	4.7

[a] Personal consumption per capita.

Sources: Zimakova (1993). Calculated on the basis of SEV (1981, 1989).

parental care benefits; allowances for single mothers and large families;
- student stipends for secondary and higher education institutions and for vocational training;
- free health services, social security, and subsidized recreation and tourism;
- free education, culture and art expenditures, including day-care centres, schools, and orphanages; secondary vocational and higher education programmes; libraries, museums, and clubs;
- housing maintenance not covered by rent;
- other benefits, including lump-sum cash benefits not incorporated in wages and salaries, enterprise-run cafeterias, and so on.

The doubling of real incomes gave rise to major shifts. Overall, consumption reached acceptable levels across all social classes, and essential material requirements were largely provided for, including a reasonable—in some cases excessive—per capita food intake.

Table 5.2: Social Security Expenditure[a] in Selected Countries and Regions, 1965–83 (percentages of GDP)

	1965	1970	1975	1980	1983
Comparison of individual CEE countries with neighbouring market economies					
Bulgaria	10.0	13.7	16.0	12.2	12.6
• Greece	9.2	10.8	10.8	12.2	17.6
Czechoslovakia	18.0	18.0	17.2	18.9	20.9
Hungary	10.9	11.0	14.9	18.3	18.7
East Germany	12.7	12.3	14.3	15.8	14.7
• West Germany	16.6	17.1	23.7	24.0	24.3
• Austria	17.7	18.5	20.2	22.5	24.2
USSR	11.6	11.9	13.6	14.0	13.8
• Finland	10.5	12.5	15.7	18.0	20.6
Comparison among different regions					
Eastern Europe	12.3	12.9	14.6	15.2	15.2
Western Europe	16.1	17.1	23.0	25.3	27.2
Northern Europe	11.6	14.7	19.5	22.9	24.6
Southern Europe	10.1	11.1	13.8	13.8	16.2
Canada	9.4	11.8	14.2	13.7	16.5
USA	7.0	9.5	13.1	12.6	13.8
Japan	5.1	5.3	7.6	10.8	12.0

[a]Social security expenditures are taken to include medical care, sickness, invalidity, employment injury, unemployment, old age and survivors, family and maternity benefits, and public assistance.

Source: ILO (1988).

However, social expenditure growth slowed from the 1970s, and the regimes were increasingly unable to catch up with the economic development and welfare levels of capitalist economies. Table 5.2 shows that, despite similar structures and functions of social transfers, substantial differences existed among the Central and Eastern European countries, especially in the USSR, where social transfers, including family support benefits, were less articulated.

Prior to the late 1960s in-kind benefits made up the bulk (55–70 per cent) of social expenditures (except in Czechoslovakia); important changes in the structure of social spending were implemented thereafter. Cash benefits increased in importance, as the pension system was extended to all population groups. Entitlements to family/child benefits and maternity leave were expanded, and initiatives like parental and child-care leave were adopted in many countries.

The socialist welfare state bore strongly on the welfare of children, partly through family support benefits and partly through specific health, recreation, and educational services aiming to improve maternal and child well-being and to encourage families to raise children.

Maternity and child health services was one of the first areas to achieve considerable progress. In most countries, free services were part of a comprehensive system of health and social insurance. Access was gained through state employment and co-operative sectors or, for the few self-employed, through membership in state-controlled associations. In some countries, such as Hungary and the GDR, free health services were *de jure* universal and provided from the mid-1970s on the basis of citizenship, although health services showed both regional and occupational inequalities. Maternal and child health coverage reached high levels across the region: almost 100 per cent of deliveries were attended by trained personnel; immunization rates stood at 95–100 per cent for tuberculosis, 85–100 per cent for measles, diphtheria, tetanus, pertussis, and polio; and attendance rates for pregnancy consultation services were close to 100 per cent by the 1980s. Summer camps, sporting and recreation facilities for children or families with children were widely available.

Free compulsory education covered primary school in all countries and secondary education in some. Private schools were excluded on political and equity grounds. Almost all children attended public education; repetitions and drop-outs were rare. In addition, school meals, after-school care and special courses in languages, music, and gymnastics were also often free or nearly so. Several other subsidies, including those for books and equipment, kept schooling costs to a minimum. Vocational training, as part of secondary education, was widely supported by state enterprises, which also offered on-the-job training and grants.

5.2.2. *Family support policy as a social contract and an extension of economic policy*

If the socialist welfare state provided a social contract between the regime and the people (Bialer, 1980; Lapidus, 1983; Hausloher, 1987; Adam, 1991; Wegren, 1991), generous family support provisions provided a social contract between the state and working mothers. In contrast to many industrialized countries where female employment increased rapidly in the 1970s, women's employment was high in socialist countries in the 1950s and was almost as high as men's by the mid-1970s. Women's work was not only encouraged, it was expected (Deacon, 1992).

Socialist economic policies relied on the extensive and centralized use of capital. Low consumption and high investment ratios were necessary to catch up with the industrialized nations and to offset low efficiency of investments and high military spending (Zimakova, 1993). The state used income policies to hold wages at low levels. Indeed, a smaller share of national income went to earnings in Central and Eastern Europe than in the West.

Family benefits, therefore, had two functions: to promote female employment through child-care assistance and to adjust wages for family size and compensate for temporary wage losses. Comprehensive and relatively generous transfer schemes and services were needed because wage levels were so low.

Paid maternity leave, provided through social security funds, was available to employed mothers before and after delivery of a child for four to seven months. Women were entitled to 50–100 per cent of their salary, often depending on their employment record or on birth order. Paid leave for employed parents to care for a sick child (up to 9–14 years of age) at home was available in most countries. Entitlement was either limited by days per year (usually sixty), or by illness (one to three weeks). In Romania, unlimited leave was available, but only until children reached age 3, and the allowance was set at 50–100 per cent of the wage, depending on length of service.

Either parent could take an extended parental leave and return to their job (and last wage). In most countries, paid leave was available when children were under 1–2 years of age, after which an additional year's leave without or with partial pay could be taken. Romanians, however, were offered only non-paid leave for under-3-year-olds. Eligibility for paid leave was attached to a minimum (often six months) employment record, although in a few countries parents who had not been employed could receive a minimum allowance, the benefit was usually equal to the minimum wage. Allowances, provided by the employer, were paid from social security funds (except in Czechoslovakia).

This complex system of paid leave developed gradually over the last decades of socialism. However, a considerable proportion of mothers (especially highly educated women working in responsible jobs) did not take full advantage of the system, and many parents chose to rely on nurseries, if available.

Nurseries offering child care for infants under age 3 operated under the supervision of the health administration, which often reflected the kinds of facilities, staff, and practices. Employer-run units generally offered better services. Most nurseries and kindergartens, however, were not located in the workplace. The share of enterprise-run units was 8 per cent in Hungary, 15 per cent in Russia, and 27 and 20 per cent respectively in the Czech Republic and Slovakia.

The number and capacity of nurseries grew until the end of the 1970s, though overcrowding remained a problem. In most countries, congestion eased in the 1980s, as parents increasingly took extended maternity and parental leave. In Czechoslovakia and the USSR, on the other hand, the number of children in nurseries rose until the late 1980s. Poorer and less well-educated parents tended to use nurseries more than those who could afford to stay at home. The nursery system covered only a minority of children, ranging from 8–9 per cent in Poland to 30–40 per cent in the USSR at the end of the 1980s, and large urban–rural differentials existed.

Kindergartens offered full-day preschool education for 3–6-year-old children of employed women. Administered under the supervision of education ministries, kindergartens provided day care, child socialization, and development functions. There was rapid expansion in the 1970s and 1980s, easing overcrowding, improving coverage rates and decreasing urban–rural differences. Around 70–85 per cent of the relevant child population was covered by public or semi-public (state enterprise-run) kindergartens by the end of the 1980s.

Despite political statements to the contrary, the state was not obliged to provide either nursery or kindergarten care for children of working parents; coverage depended on capacities. Fees were usually based on family income, but were very low as no adjustment had been made for several decades. State enterprise-run units were also available for children on a residence basis, but priority was given to the children of parents employed by the firms providing the facility. Although some kindergartens served children of non-working mothers, working parents received preferential treatment.

Monthly child or family allowances helped compensate families for the additional costs of child-raising and also encouraged fertility. The benefit, paid from social security funds, ranged between 3–20 per cent of the average wage, with eligibility tied to a full-time employment record. In many countries, the family allowance was targeted at lower-income families through differential benefit levels (Bulgaria and Poland until 1989), eligibility (USSR), or both (Romania). Allowances were generally higher for larger families and for single-parent households (except in Czechoslovakia). The incidence of family allowances was strongly progressive.

Tax allowances and tax credits, on the other hand, did not play a significant role in family support, except in Czechoslovakia, where childless persons paid higher wage taxes.

Subsidies or controlled prices on goods also reduced the burden of child-rearing. While most food products were subsidized, child-related items such as milk and milk products often enjoyed the highest subsidies. Other items, including children's clothes, furniture, books, and toys, were also heavily subsidized.

Total family assistance amounted to 5–7 per cent of GDP in the better-off socialist countries, about half that in Poland, and only 2 per cent in the USSR (see Table 5.3).

In addition to child-related subsidies, comprehensive subsidies for food, rent, heating, and clothing were available to all families. Such indirect transfers were huge throughout the region, reaching 7–8 per cent of GDP in the Central European countries around 1989 (Chu and Schwartz, 1994; UNICEF ICDC, 1994). In absolute terms, high-income households and households without children benefited more from such subsidies. However, the lower the family's income and/or the larger the number of children, the higher was their share of transfers (Kupa and Fajth, 1990). Taking into account all subsidies, the share in the GDP of total income support for families with children (as shown in Table 5.3) could be considerably adjusted upwards (by about 2 per cent in Hungary, for example). While the socialist countries were spending on average 3 percentage points less than OECD countries on the social sector, they were allocating on average 1.3 percentage points more on cash family assistance benefits (Rutkowska, 1991). Family support was emphasized in Central and Eastern Europe, even relative to spending for health care or social security for the elderly.

5.2.3. Achievements and failures of socialist social policies

Accomplishments of the socialist welfare state were in three main areas: impressive improvements in basic public health and material welfare following World War II; high levels of economic security and low levels of extreme poverty; and generous family support with high female employment rates. Its weaknesses, increasingly felt from the 1970s, related to consumer welfare, unfavourable health trends due to unhealthy lifestyles and environmental degradation, as well as inadequate responses to specific needs and problems.

Paid child-related leave in Central and Eastern Europe was generous and could have served as a model for market economies. Parental leave, for example, originated as a social policy innovation of Hungary's 1967–8

Table 5.3: Family Support and Total Cash Transfers, In-kind Benefits, and Subsidies, in Three Central European Countries and the Soviet Union, 1989 (percentages of GDP)

	Czecho-slovakia	Hungary	Poland	USSR
Family support measures				
Cash transfers	3.1	4.4	2.3	2.0
Family allowance	2.2	3.0	2.0	—
Maternity leave	0.3	0.2	0.1	—
Parental leave	0.2	0.6	0.1	—
Sick child leave	0.2	0.1	0.0	—
Grants and other	0.2	0.5	0.1	—
Indirect transfers	1.1	0.9	0.0	—
Transport, etc.[a]	0.2	0.2	0.0	—
Housing investment 'bonuses'	—	0.7	—	—
Income tax relief	0.9	0.0	—	—
Benefits in-kind[b]	1.1	1.1	0.7	—
Nurseries	0.1	0.2	0.1	—
Preschools	0.4	0.6	0.6	—
School meals	0.3	0.2	—	—
Other	0.3	0.2	—	—
Total	5.3	6.4	3.1	—
Total transfers, benefits, and subsidies				
Total cash and in-kind transfers	29.3	25.5	17.2	20.2
Cash benefits	13.1	14.8	9.4	10.1
Health care benefits	4.4	3.5	3.4	3.0
Education benefits	4.2	4.7	3.7	5.1
Consumer and housing subsidies	—	8.0	5.2	1.3
Memorandum item: GDP	100.0	100.0	100.0	100.0

[a] Includes only those subsidies which could be separated and identified as child-related. [b] For Czechoslovakia and Poland, only public expenditures; for Hungary, also the 'social' expenditures of enterprises.

Sources: Cornia and Sipos (1991); KSH (1991); TRANSMONEE Database. USSR data on education also include expenditure on culture and art; they were calculated from National Economy of the USSR in 1990, Moscow, 1991.

economic reform and gradually spread both east and west. Regular family allowances were also relatively generous and were *proportionally* larger in Central and Eastern Europe than in market economies: for one-earner households in the West, family benefits supplemented net earnings in the mid-1980s by amounts ranging from 3.7 per cent in Canada to 20.3 per cent in Austria (Kamerman and Kahn, 1988), while in 1989 in Central and Eastern European countries such supplements ranged from 19.6 per cent in Romania to 41 per cent in Hungary (Milanovic, 1992).

However, results were mixed in many areas. For example, even though low income inequality and large food subsidies allowed calorie intake levels similar to those in richer market economies (Brooks *et al.*, 1991), the nutritional quality of the food was poor (Cornia, 1994). Although kindergarten enrolment rates among 3–5-year-olds were high (Gordon, 1988), the quality of child-care services was often poor, especially in south-eastern countries and the USSR. In 1989, the majority of parents in the USSR (58 per cent) were not satisfied with the quality of preschool institutions. The percentage of dissatisfied parents was even higher in Estonia (79 per cent), and in Lithuania and Azerbaijan (75 per cent) (Goskomstat, 1990*a*).

Systematic underinvestment in the health care system prevented it from responding to new problems. Thirty-five per cent of hospitals in the former USSR, for instance, did not possess electrocardiograph machines; and of those that did, 65 per cent lacked the appropriate paper (Feshbach and Friendly, 1991). Health facilities in rural areas often had to do without the most rudimentary requirements, such as hot water (UNICEF ICDC, 1994). Although contraceptive use in CEE countries was estimated to be higher than 70 per cent by the end of the 1980s (except in Romania), modern forms of contraception were still not widely available (except in Hungary). Abortion policies oscillated between an almost total ban in Romania and liberal access in most other countries, resulting in its use as a major form of birth control. The Soviet Union, for instance, had the world's highest abortion rate at the end of the 1980s: 181 per 1,000 women in the 15–44 age-group.

Economic security, moreover, was increasingly undermined by a lack of work incentives and an uncompetitive economic environment. The consumer market offered mainly low-quality goods and services produced and rendered by state-owned enterprises. Imbalances on the market brought 'consumer security' into question; even basic goods and services could disappear or were chronically missing.

Finally, the emphasis on full employment and the strong role played by the state in child socialization reduced the social, cultural, and educational functions of the family. The tendency to place children from problem families in state institutions, rather than to resolve the problems through social support to the family itself, further weakened the family's role. This situation contributed to the erosion and growing instability of the nuclear family, to the weakening of solidarity between generations, and to the undervaluation of citizens in post-productive age.

5.3. Challenges and Constraints of Family Policies during the Transition

5.3.1. *Drives for changes*

Since 1989 political turmoil and far-reaching economic transformations have drastically changed life in Eastern Europe. At first, transition

brought inflation and rising poverty, though income differentials remained small. But poverty intensified during the second period (from
1993), despite an easing of the macroeconomic crisis (UNICEF ICDC,
1995). Income inequality grew and societies were increasingly divided
between winners and losers.

Macroeconomic stabilization hit 'public consumption funds' mainly
through inflation shocks during 1989–91, which were fuelled by the removal of price subsidies. The abandonment of price controls produced
considerable pressure for policies to compensate families.

Massive drops in production and the transformation of socialist enterprises entailed sharp rises in unemployment (with the exception of the
Czech Republic) around 1990–2, affecting women more than men everywhere but Hungary and Slovakia. Real wages plummeted, which, together with rising unemployment, caused poverty rates to surge. The
overwhelming social crisis was reflected in a large deterioration in demographic, health, and welfare indicators (UNICEF ICDC, 1994).

Since 1993 signs of both recovery and a deepening crisis have accelerated the growth in income inequality both within and between countries.
Joblessness remained high in Central and South-eastern Europe and mass
long-term unemployment emerged. In Russia, Belarus, Ukraine, and
Moldova, where open unemployment was previously avoided, more restrictive monetary policies and the erosion of non-paid employment policies have more recently led to higher levels of unemployment. While real
wage decline stopped, wage inequality increased in Central Europe, and
monopolistic wage patterns became decisive in countries of the former
USSR. Influential economic and financial lobbies have increasingly sought
to lower state redistribution levels and to raise investment ratios.

5.3.2. *Changes in family support policies*

Increased cash family support acted as a 'shock absorber' during the first
phase of transition. Around 1989–91 separate or additional child allowances partially compensated for price increases in most countries, and
parental leave provisions were strengthened, reflecting fears of looming
unemployment and to offset cut-backs in preschools.

Even though real income and employment losses remained large (and
in many countries the stabilization is not complete), these efforts were
mostly discontinued after 1992. At the same time, the fragile growth since
1993 has contributed to efforts to reduce public expenditure, even by
slashing entitlements and transforming a comprehensive system into a
'residual, targeted regime'.

Public expenditure on cash family support has plunged in real terms
since 1989 (Table 5.4), despite intentions to compensate for inflation and
structural transformations. This reflects changes in governments' views
on family support policies and transformations in the labour market and

Table 5.4: Changes in the Real Value and Importance of Selected Public Expenditures Compared to GDP, 1989–1993

	GDP	All public expenditures	Pensions	Family benefits[a]	Aid[b]	Health care	Education
Changes in GDP shares, 1989–93							
Albania	—	—	0.2	−0.4	6.1	0.9	0.8
Bulgaria	—	—	0.8	−1.0	0.9	1.5	0.5
Czech Republic[c]	—	—	−0.1	0.3	0.1	4.6	0.7
Hungary[c]	—	—	2.5	0.7	2.4[d]	1.2	0.9
Poland[c]	—	—	8.2	0.1	2.2	2.1	1.4
Romania	—	—	0.7	−1.7	0.3[e]	0.4	1.4
Russia[c]	—	—	—	—	0.2	−0.2	−1.3
Slovakia	—	—	1.8	−0.8	1.2	−0.3	−0.3
Ukraine	—	—	2.7	0.9	—	0.7	1.0
Changes in real value of expenditures, 1989–93[f]							
Albania	−36.0	−12.2	−33.7	−70.0	x40	−14.0	−20.5
Bulgaria	−30.4	12.0	−24.0	−56.2	500.0	2.0	−22.6
Czech Republic[c]	−21.6	−5.9	−21.8	−13.7	50.0	53.0	−8.2
Hungary[c]	−20.7	2.1	2.8	−4.9	x20	5.7	−4.3
Poland[c]	−13.8	—	30.5[g]	−14.0	x18	41.0	15.2
Romania	−32.3	−1.2	−24.8	−73.7	200.0[e]	−21.8	8.6
Russia[c]	−38.5	—	—	—	180.0	−35.5	−49.4
Slovakia	−26.1	−0.3	−9.0	−48.8	250.0	−30.8	−30.2
Ukraine	−39.6	—	—	—	—	−21.1	−23.1
Share of expenditure in GDP, 1989 (%)							
Nine-country average	—	53.9[h]	7.0[i]	2.7[h]	0.2[j]	3.4	4.1

[a] Cash expenditures. [b] Includes expenditures on unemployment compensation and social assistance. Increases are sometimes shown by a multiplier ('x'): 'x40' means that expenditures rose by a factor of 40. The jump in expenditures under this item is explained by the fact that 1989 expenditures were often close to zero. [c] Data refer to 1989–92, except for GDP which refers to 1989–93. [d] Preliminary estimates for 1989–92. [e] Estimates for 1989–91. [f] Real value data have been produced by using the GDP deflator, which may lead to results which are very different from those achieved using another deflator, such as the CPI. [g] Estimates achieved by deflating pension payments by the CPI. [h] Six-country average. [i] Eight-country average. [j] Three-country average.

Source: Fajth (1994).

demographics. While the immediate justification for erosion in family benefits is the severe economic crisis, shifts in the economic paradigm were even more important. First, the drop in family benefit expenditure is larger than would be induced by the shrinkage in production. Second, although the share of public expenditure in GDP dropped in most transition economies, social spending in general did not: other transfers (pensions, social assistance, and especially unemployment compensation) received more favourable treatment, even though some brought heavier burdens on public budgets.

The reductions in the labour force and sweeping demographic changes have also lowered public expenditure (as reflected in Table 5.4). Spending on family allowances, maternity, and child care dropped due to shrinkage in eligible populations: between 1989 and 1994, young child cohorts decreased by 10–25 per cent, and occasionally even by a third; female employment dropped by similar amounts due to increasing labour market passivity (in addition to growing unemployment queues).

1. *Family allowances.* Family allowance schemes seemed the appropriate tool to cushion the negative effects of the transition on children, particularly as the removal of price subsidies and the subsequent inflation necessitated broader compensation regimes.

In Hungary, family allowances became completely universal in 1990. In the Czech and Slovak Republic, they remained work-related, but separate price compensations introduced in 1991 were available to all citizens. Social security was kept as a framework for family benefits in Bulgaria and Poland at the beginning of the transition, but former barriers to high wage earners were lifted to cushion the effects of price shocks and for administrative simplicity. In Romania, a similar move was part of the popular 'euphoria' measures of 1990.

In the Soviet Union in 1991, price compensation for children, set according to age, was only available to families with per capita incomes less than four times the minimum wage. A comprehensive family allowance was introduced in January 1994 in Russia, replacing separate price compensations and social-assistance-type family benefits. At the same time, several other republics introduced family allowances for children up to ages 16–18. Due to the expansion of eligibility, family allowance coverage grew during the first years of the transition. However, in most countries entitlement remained linked to social security contributions or employment, resulting in an erosion in coverage. In more recent years, eligibility has been narrowed.

Table 5.5 presents the numbers of 0–18-year-old children receiving family allowances in selected countries. It illustrates the initial improvements in absolute coverage and the losses thereafter.

The fact that the benefit remained social-insurance-based has led to reduced coverage even when and where no overt changes in entitlement

Table 5.5: Coverage of 0–18-Year-Olds by Family Allowances and Child-related Price Compensation Payments[a] in Selected Countries, 1989–1994

	1989	1990	1991	1992	1993	1994
Czech. Republic	99.5	99.4	97.1	92.1	92.0[b]	—[c]
Slovakia	92.4	92.0	89.5	93.8	91.3[c]	—[d]
Hungary	84.3	91.1	93.1	93.1	92.4	91.3
Bulgaria						
social insurance[e]	76.7	80.3	81.0	69.9	65.0	65.9
social assistance[f]	—	—	1.7	3.0	7.0	8.5
together	76.7	80.3	82.7	72.9	72.0	74.4
Romania[g]	63.8	71.0	66.3	65.0	—	—
Belarus	—	—	0.3	93.9	56.2	—
Russia[h]	—	—	—	26.7[i]	23.8[i]	23.2[j]
Ukraine	—	—	—	55.0	—	68.0

[a] Recipient children as a percentage of all 0–18-year-olds irrespective of the actual eligibility criteria existing in countries. [b] Only family allowances; since mid-1993 state compensation benefits (fixed-sum compensation replacing certain price subsidies) have been means-tested in the Czech Republic. [c] Both the state compensation benefit and the allowance have been means-tested. [d] In 1994, price compensations were discontinued. A parallel benefit regime was adopted for family incomes below thresholds of two times and 1.5 times the poverty line, with benefit values differentiated by the age of the child. [e] Includes also price compensation from 1990. [f] Until 1994 included only price compensation. [g] Recipient children as a percentage of all 0–16-year-olds. [h] Estimate includes 1½–6-year-olds and children of single mothers benefiting from allowances in April. [i] Considering price compensation, the coverage rates were about 90 per cent over 1992–3; results from the 1993–4 household surveys as quoted in Avraamova (1994). [j] January.

Sources: Fajth (1994); TRANSMONEE Database.

were made, due to the rapidly shrinking employment ratios. Only Bulgaria partially offset these effects by complementing social-insurance-based benefits with a municipal-level benefit for the non-insured. This scheme was introduced in 1986 to provide maternity and parental leave benefits for uninsured mothers. From 1991 this channel has been used to deliver monthly price compensation payments for each child (from 1994 also basic family allowances). In the absence of a universal or complementary social assistance regime, this erosion can be quite substantial. In Russia, where overt unemployment only recently appeared, hundreds of thousands of underemployed or only formally employed workers remained in state enterprises so that they could retain their right to social benefits. None the less, with rising numbers working outside the formal sector or unemployed, erosion of access set in after 1993.

Most often, however, even where coverage rates improved, large deterioration in the value of family transfers occurred, especially given the drastic subsidy cuts. The real value of per-child family allowances is now lower in every country than prior to the transition. Cash supplements tended to only partially offset the subsidy cuts and proved totally inadequate with subsequent price increases. The attrition of child benefits has been greater than the drop in real wages in all countries (Table 5.6).

In Hungary, consumer price subsidies were partially transferred and added to cash benefits (family allowances and pensions), while wage adjustments were at the discretion of employers. Against 'market-induced' price movements, none the less, only pensions were indexed, and family allowances were left to erode.

In Poland, following considerable cuts after 1989, the family allowance was set at 8 per cent of the average wage between 1990 and 1992. However, because of 'overshooting' inflation and late benefit adjustments, by 1994 benefits were worth less than 4 per cent of the average wage. In other countries, compensation schemes instituted as a result of subsidy cuts and soaring prices were separate from the family allowance. In the Czech Republic, Slovakia, and Bulgaria, flat-rate separate compensation protected against inflation in 1990, and the ratio between allowances plus compensation and wages became more favourable after the first price shocks. This temporary move presumably reflected a recognition that children had been more affected than other groups by the removal of subsidies. New benefit regimes combining compensation and allowances were introduced in 1993 in Slovakia and 1994 in the Czech Republic, but by then their joint real value had declined by 15–35 per cent.

In some high-inflation countries, such as Bulgaria, *ad hoc* price compensation surpassed the family allowance in importance, becoming the *de facto* family allowance. However, its value has fallen rapidly in recent years relative to wages, which have also been plummeting. In Albania, where no family allowance system existed before the transition, a monthly adult benefit and child allowance were introduced in August 1992 to compensate for consumer price increases (GOA and UNICEF, 1993). A bread allowance was added in June 1993, bringing the total allowance to about 20 per cent of the unemployment compensation and around 10 per cent of the average urban wage.

In most countries of the former USSR, benefit values have been pegged to the minimum wage. However, because of downward pressure on minimum wages (Vaughan-Whitehead, 1993), the family allowance has lost most of its value. As the minimum wage plunged in Ukraine, for example, the benefit for families with children was raised from 50 to 90 per cent of the minimum wage, and a bread allowance was added. In Russia too, price compensation for children became more important than traditional family allowances. The new unified system of January 1994 attempted to restore the relative value of price compensation and family allowances,

Table 5.6: Level of Family Allowance[a] and Related Price Compensations
in Real Terms (1989 = 100) and in Comparison to the Average Wage
in Selected Countries, 1989–1994

Benefit	1989	1990	1991	1992	1993	1994
Czech Republic						
In real terms	100.0	91.0	58.1	52.3	43.3[b]	41.2–59.3[c]
with compensation	100.0	110.6	92.6	87.7	80.1[b]	74.8–94.9[d]
% average wage[e]	10.4	9.8	8.3	7.0	5.6[b]	4.9–7.1[c]
with compensation	—	11.9	13.2	11.7	9.4[b]	8.1–10.3[d]
Slovakia						
In real terms	100.0	90.7	56.2	51.2	44.4	40.1–87.5[f]
with compensation	100.0	101.6	85.9	77.4	67.1	36.2–78.8[f]
% average wage	10.5	9.9	8.3	7.2	6.2	5.4–11.8[f]
with compensation	—	12.1	13.2	12.1	10.4	5.4–11.8[f]
Hungary						
In real terms	100.0	98.1	87.7	78.3	73.4	61.8
% average wage[g]	20.5	21.8	19.9	18.1	17.0	14.6
Poland						
In real terms	100.0	165.1	185.8	183.3	135.5	102.0
% average wage	2.6	5.8	6.5	6.7	5.4	4.0
Bulgaria						
In real terms	100.0	80.8	18.4	10.3	6.6	3.5
with compensation	100.0	87.6	82.3	59.5	57.9	39.9[h]
% average wage	12.8	9.8	3.7	1.8	1.1	0.8
with compensation	—	10.7	16.6	10.5	10.1	7.4[h]
Romania[i]						
In real terms	100.0	97.5	58.0	40.8	26.1	20.9
% average wage	10.5	9.7	7.2	5.8	4.8	4.2

[a]'Family allowance' here is the average monthly per-child benefit going to a couple (or the most typical group of recipients) with two children. The figures for the benefit 'in real terms' have been deflated using the average CPI. [b]Data refer to benefits paid for January–October in that year. [c]Since November 1993, a new allowance regime has been introduced which differentiates allowances by age. [d]From October 1993, only families with income less than twice the poverty line (minimum living standard—MLS) were eligible for the price compensation (state compensation benefit), which on average was about two-fifths of the benefits. In October 1994, it was raised from 220 to 320 Crowns for children in families with incomes less than 1.5 times the MLS, which has not been included in the above calculation. [e]Wages refer to gross wages. [f]In 1993, a 16,500 Crown upper income threshold was introduced. In 1994, price compensations were discontinued. A parallel benefit regime was adopted for family incomes below thresholds set at two times and 1.5 times the poverty line (MLS), with benefit values differentiated by the age of the child. [g]For gross wage, the ration was 15.9 per cent in 1989. [h]From 1994, families receiving price compensations for children through social assistance channels became entitled to the family allowance as well. [i]Calculated from the average value of all allowances and including compensations.

Sources: Fajth (1994); TRANSMONEE Database.

Table 5.7:   Family Allowance in Russia, 1992–1994
(percentages of the average monthly wage)

Allowance for	1992		1993		1994
	January	December	June	September	January
Under-1½-year-olds	14.2	6.2	8.6	1.5	10.1
1½–6-year-olds	10.7	5.0	2.9	1.2	10.1
6–16-year-olds	5.9	2.8	1.4	0.6	6.0
Children of single mothers	11.9	5.6	3.2	1.4	9.1

Source: Nell and Stewart (1994).

which had dwindled during the two previous years of bold reform (Table 5.7).

After 1992, the rapid decline in the real value of family benefits highlighted the need to target benefits to the poor. Only Romania introduced universal eligibility, though compulsory school attendance was a condition, from 1993. While this was an appropriate response to declining primary enrolment rates resulting from increased child labour in rural areas, its effectiveness is limited by the diminished benefit value. In the Czech Republic and Slovakia, the 'shock absorbing' goal has been replaced by that of equalizing and ameliorating family wages of the working poor. In the Czech Republic, the price compensation benefit was withdrawn from about 20 per cent of families with children in January 1993. The new family allowance regime introduced in 1994 was restricted to families with incomes less than twice the official poverty line. Slovakia followed a similar path: in September 1994, families with incomes more than double the relevant poverty line lost eligibility and those with incomes 1.5–2 times the poverty line now receive reduced benefits. About 88 per cent of children remain covered (Wolekowa, 1995). From July 1995 the Czech government intends to further tighten eligibility, thus excluding about one-third of all children (Hirsl *et al.*, 1995).

In Hungary, where pressures to reduce public expenditure mounted as public debt increased, restrictions on eligibility to the poor (those earning around 70 per cent of the average wage) provoked fierce debate. The compromise solution accepted by Parliament in 1995 maintained universal rights for families with three or more children (10–11 per cent of all families with children) and withheld benefits from about 20 per cent of children (TARKI, 1995).

Means-testing in the sense of income (wage) conditioning has gained ground again in Poland and in several post-Soviet republics. For instance, an average per capita income threshold of 1.5 times the minimum wage replaced unconditional entitlement in Azerbaijan. In Poland, a per capita income threshold (50 per cent of the average wage) replaced social insurance entitlement. In countries of the former USSR, social insurance determined entitlement (and in the more industrialized parts, children of the registered unemployed also receive entitlements), and several additional municipal benefits (for bread, school uniforms, recreation, etc.) have been provided on means-testing rather than work-related conditions.

Frequent attempts to achieve better targeting have been made by replacing differentiation in benefit values by family size or birth order with differentiation by the child's age (or with flat benefit regimes), and/or by household income level. Benefit schemes that aim to equalize wages horizontally tend to allow for rising parental expenditures for older children (as it is obvious that adolescents eat more then younger children, need more new clothing, require additional educational expenses, and so on). The new systems in Slovakia and the Czech Republic clearly follow this path: they offer higher benefits for older children, while at the same time distinguishing two broad income groups (those in or close to poverty and those above poverty levels but still relatively poor). In the USSR, on the contrary, more generous allowances have always been provided for small children; indeed, adolescents received no cash allowances at all (unless they were disabled or children of single mothers). This preferential treatment has largely been retained in the new benefit regimes of successor Slavic states (see Table 5.7).

Finally, several countries have employed flat-rate benefits presumably for administrative simplicity and/or to cushion inflation shocks. This occurred in Poland between 1990 and 1993 (claiming 8 per cent of the average wage) and in Azerbaijan since 1993 (with benefits set at 30 per cent of the minimum wage) and in most cases where price compensation became *de facto* family allowances.

2. *Maternity and sick-child benefits.* Maternity leave, sick-child leave, and birth grants have a great direct impact on the health of the newborn, young children, and mothers. For this reason, and because of a drop in demand for female labour, maternity leave was left unchanged or even occasionally lengthened around 1990, and no reductions have since been introduced (Table 5.8). However, increasingly flexible entitlement periods in many countries indicate that labour market considerations predominate. For instance, in addition to the expansion of paid maternity leave from 112 to 126 days in the USSR in 1990 and to 140 days in Russia in 1992, limitations on pre- and post-delivery division (56 + 56 days) were removed. As the value of the maternal benefit is usually tied to the individual wage, it is more easily protected from inflation than family allowances. Nevertheless, the real value can fall during periods of high inflation or significant price shocks, as the long-term benefit is fixed to the pre-leave wage.

Table 5.8: Features of Maternity Leave Benefits, 1989–1993

	Duration	Value	Eligibility	Changes since 1989
Bulgaria	120–180 days in two parts depending on number of children	100% of last wage	linked to employment	—
Czech Republic	28 weeks	90% of last wage	270 days of health insurance eligibility in last two years	cut in the replacement rate from 90% to 67%
Hungary	4 weeks before and 20 weeks after delivery	65–100% of last wage depending on length of employment	180 days of employment in last two years	—
Poland	16 weeks for first child; 18 for second or following child	100% of last wage	linked to employment	—
Romania	112 days	50–85% of last wage depending on employment record; uniformly 94% for third or following child	linked to full-time employment	—
Russia	56 + 56 days	100% of last wage	linked to employment	1992: 140 days 1993: extended to unemployed if laid off during pregnancy
Slovakia	28 weeks	90% of last wage	270 days of health insurance eligibility in last two years	—
Ukraine	112–126 days	50–100% of last wage depending on length of employment	linked to employment	1991: 140 days

Sources: Zimakova (1993); TRANSMONEE Database.

Maternity benefits now provide considerably less support than in the past to women and their families. The gap between the potentially eligible and those covered has widened in all countries where such estimates can be made. It is estimated at about 15 per cent in the Czech Republic, 22 per cent in Hungary, and 41 per cent in Poland. Since it is unlikely that so many young women would choose to withdraw from the labour force, the main cause of this trend is probably to be found in a rise in active or passive unemployment among women, an increase in pregnancy among women who are too young to enter the labour market, and a decline in take-up rates among the eligible for fear of competition on the labour market. In Bulgaria, larger numbers of women claiming benefits than seem to be eligible suggests that they are staying more frequently or for longer periods on maternity leave than they are entitled to. One-time birth grants have been maintained in all countries, and the real value of the grant has remained relatively stable despite inflation. Several countries provide the grant only to expectant mothers who have had a check-up; this has contributed to the nearly 100 per cent check-up rate among pregnant women in these countries. No such health incentive policy has been introduced yet in Romania or in some countries of the former USSR, despite increases in foetal deaths and infant mortality.

The sick-child leave benefit has on the other hand been overtly trimmed in many cases. In the Czech Republic, for instance, the earnings replacement rate of the benefit was cut in 1993 from 90 to 67 per cent. The benefit remains unchanged in Poland and Romania, though only parents of under-3-year-olds are eligible in Romania. In Bulgaria, the replacement rate has been reduced from 100 per cent to 70–90 per cent for over-9-year-olds. Changes in labour markets and in the workplace environment, as well as the shifting of the provision to employers (for instance, in Hungary), have had negative effects on take-up rates.

3. *Assistance for toddlers.* Take-up of nursery care has declined in a few countries, such as Hungary. In others, including Czechoslovakia and Russia, nurseries were favoured until the end of the 1980s when a sudden policy shift occurred. In Poland, nursery places were halved between 1989 and 1992 (Balcerzak-Paradowska and Kolaczek, 1994). Large-scale closures of nurseries in all countries have led to plunging enrolment rates (Table 5.9). In a few cases, such as Hungary in 1993, the number of places, and therefore enrolment rates, stabilized. However, in most countries the downward trend is still continuing.

Parental leave schemes aim to ensure that the caregiving parent does not have to return to work immediately after the expiry of the maternity benefit. These were generally made more attractive throughout the region to ease excess labour market supply and to compensate for the divestiture of the mostly employer-based nursery facilities. In Russia, 'nursing' leave was extended from six to eighteen months in 1991, and the amount of the

Table 5.9: Children in Nurseries and Parents on Parental Leave, 1989–1993

	1989	1990	1991	1992	1993
% of 0–2-year-olds in nurseries					
Azerbaijan	19.0	18.0	17.0	16.0	16.0
Bulgaria	12.8	11.8	11.8	11.5	10.8
Czech Rep.	13.8	8.1	4.0[a]	3.5[a]	—
Hungary	8.1	7.5	6.7	6.4	6.7
Poland	8.5	8.0	6.7	5.4	—
Romania	4.4	4.3	4.2	4.3	3.9
Russia	34.7	28.6	24.3	—	—
Slovakia	12.8	9.3	—	—	—
Ukraine	28.3	22.4	18.8	15.8	14.5
Parents on parental leave per 100 0–2-year-olds					
Azerbaijan	—	—	—	—	—
Bulgaria	34.0	33.0	32.0	—	—
Czech Rep.	50.0[a]	51.0	72.9	75.0[a]	—
Hungary	65.8	68.1	70.5	70.6	70.0
Poland	41.4	36.9	31.3	26.3	—
Romania	—	—	—	—	—
Russia	—	—	—	—	—
Slovakia	34.0[a]	41.0[a]	49.0[a]	42.0[a]	25.0[a]
Ukraine	—	—	—	—	—

[a] Estimated.

Source: TRANSMONEE Database.

benefit was raised from 40 per cent of the minimum wage to between 45 and 60 per cent. The 'child-care' leave, a six-month unpaid leave until 1991, was extended to cover parents of $1^1/_2$–3-year-old children, and a small paid benefit was added, which increased in May 1994 to 50 per cent of the minimum wage. Belarus, Ukraine, and several other CIS countries took similar steps. In Romania, where no paid leave had been provided before 1989, a leave incorporating a cash benefit of 65 per cent of the pre-leave wage was introduced in 1990 for parents employed full time. The leave was available until the child's first birthday. It appears likely that most eligible women took advantage of the leave.

Parental leave take-up rates increased in the Czech Republic and Slovakia after 1990, when the maximum paid leave was extended from two to three years, the benefit value was increased 1.5 times, and a price compensation benefit was added (Table 5.9). Increasing recourse to parental leave was also influenced by the closing down of many nurseries. The benefit value was adjusted several times and pegged to the adult subsistence minimum; the social insurance basis of eligibility was strengthened.

The value of the parental leave benefit remains rather low in most countries, leading to a drop in family income and often to temporary poverty. Consequently, in a few countries parents are now permitted to work within certain limits while in receipt of the benefit. In the Czech Republic, for instance, mothers can work up to two hours per day and earn up to about 30 per cent of the average monthly wage.

In Hungary two parental leave benefits have existed since 1986. The 'child-care fee' provided a generous social security benefit: 75 per cent of the relevant wage for a maximum of two years (from 1988). The other, 'child-care aid', paid from general state revenues, provided a minimum payment for an additional year or for a total of three years for unemployed parents; in this way, parental leave was universally accessible. However, a radical transformation of these programmes was proposed in March 1995, with benefits no longer universal and providing less than the minimum wage. Poland, increasingly targeting the poor, cut the income threshold for eligibility from 25 to 18 per cent of the average per capita income of households in 1992, and the value of the benefit itself was reduced from 25 per cent of the pre-leave wage to a flat 21 per cent of the average wage.

4. *Support for pre-primary and primary education.* Economic difficulties and privatization of enterprises, declining female employment rates, and public budget austerity all contributed to a drop in kindergarten places and enrolments of 3–6-year-old children. Enrolments declined by as much as 10–25 percentage points, despite declining child cohorts. The two exceptions to date are Hungary and Azerbaijan (see Table 13.4). In Hungary, many kindergartens were transferred from state enterprises to municipalities during the socialist era, and since 1989 this transfer has been completed. In Azerbaijan, on the other hand, enterprise-run facilities have not yet been closed. However, in 1989 most kindergartens were publicly owned, although the central government financing usually did not keep pace with inflation. Consequently, municipalities, which have administrative responsibility, either lack the financial resources to take over kindergartens or must limit enrolments.

Around 1990, most countries began boosting kindergarten fees. In Poland, the fees rose from one-quarter to more than a third of the average wage between 1989 and 1991. They were then cut back and made dependent on family income. However, a new flat-rate fee was introduced in 1995. In Romania, fees doubled in 1990. The almost immediate drop in enrolments, however, challenged this approach. In 1991, fees were frozen or increases were limited everywhere, but continuing financial problems kept this issue on the agenda. In Bulgaria, for example, fees doubled in 1993. A regulation introduced in Russia in 1992 limited user fees to 20 per cent of costs and 10 per cent for families with three or more children.

The substantial drop in enrolments is a disturbing trend, given the important role of kindergartens in social development and school preparation. In Ukraine, 181,800 unmet requests for enrolment were recorded in

1990. This figure fell to 52,900 in 1993 (Libanova and Paliy, 1995), signalling not an improvement in supply but a growing sense of futility. In the Czech Republic, increasing educational problems among children entering compulsory education have been reported (Hirsl, 1995).

Private kindergartens, which may be better able to provide high-quality services, tend to be accessible only to children of higher-income families. Children in poorer households may thus be excluded if public kindergartens are privatized. On the other hand, student transfers to private kindergartens could free up municipal services. However, private initiatives have remained sporadic to date.

Even compulsory education now places a greater burden on parents. Public income-assistance schemes for education have been cut back or discontinued for families, and even public education often has a price now. For primary education in Russia, the estimated per-child costs to families increased from 1 to 3 per cent of the average wage between 1989 and 1991. In Poland, where families had already been covering 20 per cent of overall expenditures and 100 per cent of boarding and book expenses in 1989, the corresponding costs to families rose from 3 to 4 per cent of the average wage. However, in Poland, as well as in other Central European countries, parent committees have managed to supply public schools with fresh resources by creating foundations, seeking sponsors, and undertaking business projects.

There are also additional 'hidden' costs in education. Extra-curricular courses increasingly charge flat fees, regardless of income level. This can lead to a sort of 'shadow' education system, as the 'extra' services gain importance at the expense of the basic ones.

5.4. The Adequacy of Current Family Support Approaches

5.4.1. *Coverage: Social security entitlements and universalism*

Social security frameworks inherited from the former regimes are frequently considered outdated for family support policies, as they tend to provide broad and unconditional entitlements (Libanova and Paliy, 1995) or because they should deliver only contributory benefits (Barr, 1994; Lazutka and Sniukstiene, 1995). Eroding coverage rates, however, raise doubts as to whether social security or work-related support is adequate for family benefits, given the loss of employment guarantees. The problem resides less in the decline in access and more with the question of which population groups are affected. Wherever social-insurance-based schemes have been in place, there is evidence that coverage has been eroded for low-income groups.

In Hungary, where the allowance was universal, the incidence of per-child benefit was flat across income groups, indicating equal access. In contrast, in Poland, where the allowance was supplied through social insurance, the actual per-child benefit received rose with the parents' income (Fajth, 1994). This could only reflect the exclusion of low-income families from social insurance, as the benefit itself was actually the same for each user.

5.4.2. *Shrinking benefit values: A false escape*

Maternity benefits should be large enough to prevent a significant drop in family incomes. Thus, the pre-leave wage of the mother is the benchmark. In a policy perspective, full-salary benefits indicate an emphasis on health concerns, while lower benefits at sick-pay rates reflect work incentive considerations. The case of Bulgaria suggests that scaling back from 100 per cent replacement rates might be needed in some countries to avoid situations of abuse. However, with stricter administrative controls, low abuse rates could be achieved at 90 per cent rates (like those in the Czech Republic until 1993) or even 100 per cent (Hungary).

Sharply falling birth-rates have reduced public outlays on maternity benefits, without cuts or erosions in entitlement. The incidence of low birth weight, a highly sensitive indicator of the nutritional and health status of mothers, has edged up in Belarus, Bulgaria, Romania, Moldova, and somewhat more moderately, but still significantly, in Russia, and even in the Czech Republic (and in Slovakia until 1991, the last year for which data are available) (UNICEF ICDC, 1994; Cornia and Paniccià, 1995). The share of complicated pregnancies (below age 20 or above 35) has increased as well. Cut-backs in maternity benefits and stricter eligibility requirements for maternity and sick-child leave may have undesirable consequences for maternal health and nutrition. Furthermore, they may yield only small savings and even lead to rising public expenditures for curative child and maternal health.

Parental leave benefit replaces income and eases pressure on the labour market for the relatively young and inexperienced and for women. Its value should either be set as a percentage of the individual wage (a social insurance-type approach, as in Hungary) or as a flat rate, providing a sum equal to the minimum wage. It should not be lower than the unemployment benefit as this could lead to reliance on unemployment compensation to bridge the gap between maternity leave and kindergarten. However, parental leave schemes have generally provided between 55 and 66 per cent of unemployment compensation in effect around 1993, for periods two to six times longer (Fajth, 1994).

The present low levels of family allowances reflect a lack of political will to index benefits. The minimum wage, used mainly in countries of the former USSR, has been an ineffective yardstick because it too was not properly indexed. Official poverty line thresholds, such as those applied in the Czech Republic and Slovakia ('minimum subsistence level') may fare somewhat better from this perspective, especially if they are employed systematically. But poverty lines also have not been adjusted regularly and often become arbitrary: for instance, the current Czech poverty line (representing less than 35 per cent of per capita consumption) is considered by many observers to be too low (Hirsl *et al.*, 1995). Ideally, benefits should be set as a proportion of the average wage. The case of Poland, however, shows that this solution may only partially help prevent benefits lagging too far behind sinking real wages, and cannot guarantee improvement, in the absence of political will, when real wages start to climb. Arrangements set in absolute (nominal) terms rather than relative terms tend, on the other hand, to open the door for attrition through inflation.

The traditional yardstick for family allowance schemes is that they at least cover the child's food costs. In Central and Eastern Europe, child food costs amounted to about 15–20 per cent of the national average wage and 10–15 per cent for families living near the poverty threshold prior to the transition (Zafír, 1991; Sipos, 1992). As real wages have fallen considerably, the share of food costs must have increased (even though consumption was adjusted). Consequently, a minimum 15 per cent threshold is to be recommended now. If this cannot be guaranteed (due to macroeconomic problems), it is better to target (or to sharpen the targeting) than to allow benefit values to sink below this threshold. At present, family allowances are below 15 per cent of average wages everywhere in the region (with the exception of Hungary); and in most countries they are also below the 10 per cent threshold (see Table 5.6), even where targeting has excluded better-off families.

5.4.3. *Targeting benefits on the poor*

As has been widely recognized, despite broad transfer systems, poverty in Central and Eastern Europe under socialism was always concentrated in households of pensioners and large families, due to compressed wage distribution, full employment, and low savings rates. With the transition to democratic and market conditions, children remain the most vulnerable group. Their chances of growing up in a poor family are even higher now than in the past; even more so for children in larger families. Family benefits, therefore, could be used even more efficiently as anti-poverty tools under present conditions.

Figure 5.1 shows the distribution of social expenditures across population deciles by income in Poland. Family benefits appear to be much more concentrated on the poor segments of the population than are pensions. It would appear that they act more as a pro-poor measure than as social assistance, and provide almost as much help to the poor as do unemploy-

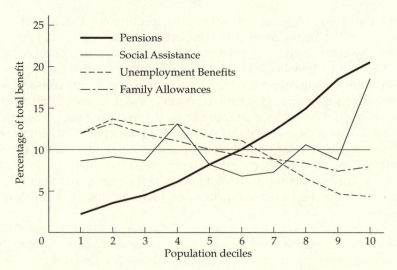

Fig. 5.1   Incidence of Main Per Capita Income Transfers by Decile in Poland, 1993
Sources: Fajth (1994). Author's calculations from TRANSMONEE Database.

ment benefits. However, the pro-poor character of family allowances can, and indeed should, be strengthened.

Child poverty has increased considerably in the region, firstly in absolute terms: at present about 40–60 per cent of children live in families earning below the 1989 poverty levels, compared with 5–20 per cent at the beginning of the transition (UNICEF ICDC, 1994). Longitudinal investigations have revealed large entry and exit rates for poverty in Hungary. Apart from young children, who tend to remain in poverty, less then one-quarter of the poor stayed poor over 1992–4 (Andorka, 1994). If this observation is representative for the region, and considering the sluggish labour turnover and persistent nature of unemployment (Boeri, 1994), poverty may very often be due to early life-cycle periods and changes in the demographic composition of households, primarily due to births. This would underscore the importance of family supports as a *per se* well-targeted benefit. The region is also characterized by a relatively shallow poverty gap (Cornia, 1994) which, again, points to the potential power of family allowances to keep poor households out of poverty by means of relatively small additional incomes. Targeting, however, is used increasingly both in Central Europe and in many countries of the former USSR to means-test family benefits, primarily by employing family income as the criterion of eligibility. Efficient targeting presupposes the removal of a family's support benefits from the social insurance system. Universal systems (which ensure access on citizenship or residence grounds) reach poor children more effectively than do social insurance systems, which

Table 5.10: Eligibility and Take-up Rates by Family Size of an Experimental One-time Income-tested Family Allowance Compensation in Hungary, September 1994

	All	Share among entitled families with children	Actual user
Families with 3 and more children	10.3	18.3	12.2
Families with 2 children	38.5	46.2	42.1
Families with 1 child[a]	51.2	35.3	45.7
TOTAL	100.0	100.0	100.0

[a] Including those families which remained with one child.
Source: TARKI (1995).

tend to miss the non-employed. Social assistance offers a similarly defective approach: it should correct irregular, and not systematic, individual income problems. It also has low take-up rates due to social stigma. Results of an experiment in Hungary in 1994 show that while families with three or more children are vastly over-represented among the poor, they are under-represented among those who actually take up a non-automatic income-tested complement to family allowances (Table 5.10). The use of income as a condition may also lead to misuses because of the large share of uncontrolled income in the region, while deterring some of the truly needy. In Poland, for instance, parental leave has been tied to very low income thresholds. According to the Polish Household Budget Survey, only 3 per cent of the population were living below the eligibility threshold in 1992. Still, about one-quarter of households with small children were receiving the benefit (Table 5.9).

There are several indirect ways of reaching populations in need without using income tests directly. Families with three or more children, incomplete families, and families with children headed by inactive or unemployed persons tend to be among the poor. While such households constitute a minority of all families with children, their needs are straightforward and easily controllable.

Poverty investigations, moreover, point to the age of the child as a relatively effective indicator of low family income. Most people marry and have children at an early age (24–6 years on average) in Central and Eastern Europe (a pattern that interestingly has not changed so far despite drops in nuptiality and fertility). For young people, wages and lifetime earnings tend still to be low. Benefit regimes that give preference to young children over their older peers, or to bigger families over one-child families, may act against horizontal equity considerations, but promote vertical equity and lessen absolute poverty.

5.4.4. Health, early child development, and education goals

Children may be hurt by nursery closures, particularly if parents are unable to remain at home to care for them or cannot make proper alternative arrangements. However, nurseries are not the ideal place for infants. In most instances, one-to-one care provided by parents or other adult family members, such as grandparents, is preferable. Moreover, quality supervision of institutions can be problematic. Prior to the transition, for example, many nurseries suffered from neglect or overcrowding and provided low-quality care. Health considerations still stop many parents from relying on these institutions.

Declining nursery enrolments in many countries are due partly to declining demand (UNICEF ICDC, 1993). Between 1989 and 1993, for instance, fertility dropped by about 10 per cent and female employment rates shrank from 82 per cent (for Czechoslovakia) to 70 per cent and 62 per cent, respectively, in the Czech Republic and Slovakia. In Bulgaria, the female employment rate plummeted from 93 to 66 per cent. At least in Central and South-eastern Europe, formal-sector female employment rates have slid back to levels similar to those in the market economies of Western and Southern Europe. Countries of the former USSR are heading in the same direction. This situation points again to the importance of parental leave schemes.

Young children over the age of 2 increasingly need contact with their peers. The spread of the one-child family model makes kindergartens crucial for child socialization and cognitive development. None the less, the goal of 100 per cent kindergarten enrolment rates seems to have been abandoned. Lower female employment rates appear to have had a minimal effect on declining kindergarten enrolments; inadequate promotion, closures, and/or higher fees are the principal reasons. Finally, there is also evidence that the efficiency and equity of compulsory education systems may be eroding due to deteriorating support.

5.5 Conclusions

The welfare state developed over the last decades of socialism was built on the premiss of full employment, and social benefits were thus tied to work. Family support policies within this system of guaranteed employment—at low wages—served several functions: they fostered high female labour force participation rates, promoted pro-natalist goals, and ensured acceptable levels of consumption across all social strata. Indeed, significant progress was made in several welfare indicators during this period. At the same time, however, full-time, industrial-type employment for both men and women, together with the strong role assumed by the state in child socialization, hastened the erosion of the traditional family and family values. The emphasis on employment also led to a weakened sense of solidarity between generations and the undervaluation of elderly citizens.

With the transition to the market economy, this welfare framework became increasingly inadequate. While employment or social-security-based benefit regimes made sense when employment was guaranteed, prices were centrally controlled and subsidies were available, they became meaningless when unemployment increased, prices soared, and poverty spread. New demands, fuelled by sweeping economic, demographic, and social changes, required new family support responses. Yet governments have wavered between attempts to maintain outdated benefit regimes and pressures to look backwards to early industrial times or towards a residual welfare model, alien not only to the socialist past but also to the traditions of Central and Eastern Europe.

By oscillating between the past and the future, between outdated models and revolutionary approaches, governments have frequently failed to respond to the mounting poverty and hardship suffered by the populations, particularly the children. Shrinking maternity and parental leave coverage, increasing exclusions and insignificant values of child and family allowances, eroding child-care services, and rising barriers and inequality in access to early child education will certainly not help economic recovery. More meaningful and sustainable approaches are urgently needed.

The problem of inadequate access is acute for kindergarten enrolment and for all cash-benefit regimes that are still linked to social insurance entitlement. To prevent unwanted exclusions, family support programmes should preferably be universal and, if targeting is required, use categorical conditions rather than personal income declarations. Even well-targeted systems prove to be inadequate, however, if the allowances are insufficient to lift families with children out of poverty and hardship, which is the case of most family allowances in the region at present.

It is not easy to improve targeting, and current changes sometimes have unwanted side-effects. The removal of pronatalist policies, for example on family allowances, could increase poverty. The needs of children should not be separated from the family context: while teenagers may have higher consumption needs, family income also tends to be higher by this time. This consideration stands in sharp contrast with recent changes in allowance regimes in many countries.

Targeting could also be improved by revaluating preferences of the different kinds of family support. There is evidence that maternity, parental, and sick-child leave benefits, even though linked to wages, tend to favour lower-income families with young children and are more pro-poor than family allowances. This suggests that leave benefits, and parental leave in particular, may be efficient tools for assisting the needy; and a rise in the presently low benefit levels could improve aggregated targeting of family benefits. This could be carried out relatively easily as, with declining fertility rates and the shrinking child population, maternity leave, sick-child leave, and birth grants are coming to represent a smaller burden on public budgets.

Finally, the objectives of the various family support benefits should be better defined in the context of the multifaceted changes currently occurring in Central and Eastern Europe. Kindergarten enrolment, for example, should not be as directly affected by labour market or fiscal restructuring concerns as it presently is. For maternity benefits, health considerations should continue to override fiscal or labour market concerns. While goals in maternal and child health, early child development, and equal opportunities for women should be maintained when reshaping the structure of leave benefits, the reduction of child poverty should receive high priority and be decisive in planning family allowances. It should be these concerns, and not the masked interests of other louder pressure groups decrying fiscal hardship, that drive reforms.

PART II

National
Case-Studies

6

Child Poverty and Deprivation in Russia: Improvement, Standstill, and Retrogression

GIOVANNI ANDREA CORNIA

6.1. Introduction

Over the last fifty years, the welfare of Russian children has fluctuated considerably. During the decades of 'extensive growth' of the 1950s and 1960s, impressive improvements were attained in the fields of nutrition, health care, and education. Indeed, in many areas, including infant mortality reduction, the progress achieved was among the most rapid recorded for the entire industrialized world.

This positive trend gradually slowed to a halt, and in some cases was even reversed, during the following twenty years of slow growth, unfavourable changes in family structure and stability, gradual weakening of social policies and institutions, and erosion of social consensus.

Though desirable and indeed unavoidable, the political and economic reforms initiated in the late 1980s and early 1990s are exacerbating problems inherited from the socialist era. The result has been a literal explosion in mortality rates (including, to some extent, those for infants and adolescents), an unprecedented population crisis, and an incapacitating erosion of the health, education, and child-care systems. Furthermore, acute problems of social protection of children have become apparent. Indeed, from almost every perspective, with the exception of mortality, children are the population group most negatively affected by the transition to the market economy. At the time of writing, as the slide in living conditions has not yet stabilized and social policy continues to suffer from design, funding, and, even more so, implementation problems, the future of Russian children appears to be clouded by persistent difficulties.

The author would like to thank Sheldon Danziger for comments on an earlier draft of this chapter and Robert Zimmermann and Anny Bremner for the collection of information and the editing of the chapter.

6.2. The Golden Age, 1950–1971

Despite the massive destruction inflicted on the country during World War II, pre-war levels of industrial and agricultural production had been recovered by 1950. Even the most critical estimates indicate that economic growth between 1950 and 1971 was significant, close to twice that of the subsequent period. Between 1950 and 1965, national income increased at an average annual rate of 8.9 per cent and per capita real incomes at almost 7 per cent (UNECE, 1967). In 1965, a reform was undertaken to reverse the economic slow-down of the early 1960s, when national income had advanced by 'only' 6.5 per cent each year.

Economic growth permitted substantial improvements in human welfare and a boost in social expenditure (Table 6.1). The rise in public social spending after World War II also reflects the government's effort to compensate for the enormous population losses suffered during the first half of this century. (Conservative estimates place the population losses during World War II at 25 million people (Ellman, 1994).) Public policy thus concentrated on restoring appropriate levels of health, nutrition, overall welfare, skills, and social stability.

Numerous legislative and economic measures sought to consolidate the family as a social unit and create more favourable conditions for childbearing. For example, decrees implemented during the 1950s and 1960s reestablished the distinctions between unregistered unions and civil marriage and between 'legitimate' and out-of-wedlock children that had been abolished after the revolution. Divorce was made more complicated and expensive. An effective alimony mechanism in support of children was created. Unmarried and childless adults were subject to 'punitive' taxes, while parents with many children received progressive subsidies (depending on the number of children) and were the first to obtain scarce public housing (Riatzansev *et al.*, 1992). At the same time, abortions

Table 6.1: Government Social Expenditures in the USSR, 1940–1989 (in percentage of total government expenditure)

	1940	1960	1970	1980	1985	1989
Total social expenditures	23.5	34.1	36.2	33.5	32.5	35.1
Of which:						
Education and science	12.9	14.1	16.0	13.6	12.8	—
Health care	5.2	6.6	6.1	5.0	4.6	6.4
Social security	1.8	8.9	8.2	8.1	8.2	—
Lone mothers[a]	0.7	0.7	0.3	0.1	0.2	—

[a] Public transfers to lone mothers and to families with many children.
Sources: Zimakova (1991).

were forbidden, except when the mother's life was in danger. Other child and family policies were particularly well developed and typically included generous maternity leave and benefits, childbirth grants, childcare leave, child nursing benefits, and almost universal child allowances (see Chapter 5).

Despite rapid urbanization and rising female labour force participation, the traditional multi-generation family remained prevalent during this period and the divorce rate only began to show signs of increasing around 1965. In general, this facilitated the care of children and, unlike the previous period, cushioned them against the calamities of 'Stalinist modernization'. Moreover, the priority accorded to social expenditure enabled the creation of an extensive education and public health system. In addition, the population benefited from large consumer subsidies on food, housing, and other essential goods which, while distorting the price structure and draining precious budgetary resources, raised household welfare.

Thus, despite a sizeable baby boom (which pushed up the crude birthrate to 2.63 per cent in the early 1950s), the number of infant deaths per 1,000 live births shrank from 182 in 1940 to 81 in 1950 and 23 in 1971, representing the most rapid progress among all industrialized countries. Interestingly, the decline in the infant mortality rate (IMR) in Russia followed a peculiar trend. Unlike the situation in Czarist Russia where, as elsewhere at such levels of development, IMRs in rural areas had been higher than those in urban areas, a reverse situation held until 1953. This shows that 'socialist primitive accumulation' was carried out largely at the expense of human welfare in urban areas. This trend was reversed in the second half of the 1950s, and rural–urban IMR differentials once more mirrored the conventional pattern until 1971.

Noticeable progress was achieved at this time in reducing the most visible symptoms of child poverty. Indeed, Russia boasted low income inequality and absolute poverty rates, even when the privileges of the *nomenklatura*, the differential access of social groups to the 'official', 'preferential', and 'parallel' markets, and the opportunity cost of queuing were taken into account. However, in terms of relative deprivation (as gauged by the lack of high-quality social services, lack of nutritious diets, housing shortages, and so on), child poverty remained fairly common. In the meantime, new social problems, arising mainly from the inadequate 'socialization' of children, had begun to surface.

6.3. The Prolonged Stagnation of 1971–1989

Only minimal improvements in child welfare were attained during the 1970s and 1980s, as exemplified by the quasi-stagnation of IMR which dropped only slightly from 23.0 to 17.8 per 1,000 live births between 1971

and 1989. Yet even these sobering statistics do not fully reflect the erosion
of child welfare during this period.

6.3.1. Determinants of the stagnation in child welfare

1. *Sluggish growth and worsening income distribution.* From the early 1970s,
the USSR experienced a gradual deterioration in economic performance,
which lowered the average annual GDP growth from the 5 per cent
recorded for the 1950–71 period to 2.1 per cent over 1973–82, and then
down to 1.9 per cent between 1982 and 1988 (see Chapter 3).

During the 1950s and 1960s, central planning achieved significant 'extensive growth'. Performance started to falter, however, when the extensive supply of labour began to dwindle and when it became necessary
to increase the rate of innovation, technological progress, and micro-
economic efficiency in order to sustain output growth. While some slow-
down in growth was unavoidable, this deceleration was mainly the result
of the rapidly mounting technological, information, and incentive difficulties faced by 'Soviet-type economies' as the scale and sophistication of the
economy increased.

With the Gini coefficient edging down from 28.2 to 25.1, official
data indicate a decline in income inequality between 1970 and 1986
(Braithwaite and Heleniak, 1989). However, income distribution most
likely deteriorated, as such statistics disregarded the influence of the
spread of dual distribution systems, growing regional differences in the
supply of consumer goods, and rising shortages, i.e. factors that had a
large (though poorly documented) disequalizing impact on the distribution of private consumption (ibid.; Kornai, 1986). By and large, growing
differences in the distribution of 'real' private consumption emerged between Moscow and other important cities, the supply centres along the
Baikal–Amur railroad on the one hand and the rural areas and remote
cities on the other (Riazantsev *et al.*, 1992).

2. *The rise of military expenditure.* Though government social expenditure and private consumption continued to grow in absolute terms after
1970, their shares fell between 1970 and 1985, especially those of family
allowances and health care. Despite accounting problems, it is generally
accepted that military spending was a significant factor in the social
expenditure squeeze over this period. With a markedly lower national
income, a steep drop in the GDP growth rate, and accelerating military
expenditure in the USA, the USSR had to concentrate a mounting share of
total resources on military R&D and expenditure to maintain military
balance with NATO. Military build-up therefore took a greater toll on
non-military investment, private consumption, and social expenditure in
the USSR than among her competitors (Feshbach, 1989). By 1989, the
military sector absorbed an amount of national resources similar to those

Table 6.2:   Comparison of Social and Military Expenditures
in the USSR, 1989

	% of NMP[a]	% of GDP	% of Government budget
Military expenditures			
Narrow (official)	11.0	8.4	16.2
Broad[b]	22.8	16.2	31.1
Total social expenditure[c]	25.8	18.4	35.1

[a] Net material product. [b] Includes outlays for servicing military hardware, for basic and applied military research, training for defence industry workers, military training in civilian institutions, for secret military development funds, and so on. [c] Includes education and science, heath care, social security, and programmes for lone mothers.

Source: Zimakova (1991).

of the entire 'social sector' (Table 6.2). In turn, the inefficiency and isolation of the military complex did not generate the positive technological spillovers on the civilian sector that were observed in the Western bloc.

3. *Decline in health care quality and access.* Limited improvements in the health status of children and mothers in the 1980s may also be closely linked to the inferior quality of health care services. With insufficient attention given to maintenance and modernization, this period witnessed a gradual erosion in the health care infrastructure, as suggested by the decline in budget share allocated to health care between 1960 and 1985 (Table 6.1).

By the late 1980s, nearly a quarter of all maternity wards and one-third of paediatric hospitals did not have hot water; the number without sewerage ranged between one-tenth and one-fourth and one-third had 2–2.5 times less floor space per bed than the recommended amount and serious infrastructure deficiencies were recorded even in specialized wards (Riazantsev *et al.*, 1992). Inadequate resource allocation and poor project management hampered the construction of new maternity and paediatric clinics. Between 1986 and 1988, only 22 per cent of the planned new maternity beds and 27 per cent of the planned new paediatric beds became available for use (ibid.).

4. *Demographic factors.* A main determinant of poverty in Russia has traditionally been the relatively large number of dependent children per employed family member. This ratio declined on average from 0.785 in 1970 to 0.656 in 1979, but it rose again to 0.731 between 1979 and 1987. This rise, together with the stagnation in family allowances, contributed to the slow or negative growth of private consumption of part of the population.

Of the 6.3 per cent of all families living below the 75-rouble poverty line in 1989, some 60 per cent were young and had a substantially higher share of children than was found in the total (Braithwaite and Heleniak, 1989). Generally, families with more than one child per economically active adult could be classified as poor. Moreover, data on income according to the age of wage-earners showed that the average Soviet couple could support more than one child without crossing the poverty line only after the age of 40. In any case, most young couples entered the ranks of the poor at the birth of a first child because of the mother's temporary inability to work and the inadequacy of maternity transfers (Shatalin *et al.*, 1990; Zimakova, 1991).

5. *The erosion of the family*. Notable changes in family formation and stability were recorded during these two decades. While the crude marriage rate declined imperceptibly, the crude divorce rate jumped from 1.5 per 1,000 around 1960 to 3.0 in 1970, and then up to over 4.0 throughout the 1980s (Table 6.3). Children no longer constituted a major obstacle to divorce: more than 80 per cent of all divorced couples in 1989 had children, and about 480,000 children and adolescents—or 1.2 per cent of the population aged 0–18—were separated from one of their parents due to divorce in that year alone. The rise in incomplete families was due also to the surge in the number and proportion of children born out of wedlock (Table 6.3).

Funding and design problems in social policies contributed to the weakening of the family. To start with, the rise in female labour force participation in the 1970s was not accompanied by a corresponding increase in the supply of child-care services. In addition, the volume of social transfers to lone mothers and large families declined, precisely when the number of incomplete families was on the rise.

Quite independently of financial factors, a number of systemic biases in family policy contributed to reducing their relevance and effectiveness. Paternalism and lack of popular participation engendered a strong dependence and cynicism among the population, while the weakening of family cohesion brought about by a combination of ill-conceived and forced 'child socialization' and unfavourable economic conditions provoked serious and long-term repercussions for Soviet society (Gukova, 1988).

6.3.2. *Changes in the welfare of children*

As a result of changes in the above factors, improvements in child welfare started to flag from the beginning of the 1970s.

1. *Stagnant infant mortality rate and declining life expectancy at birth (LEB)*. As noted, between 1970 and 1989, IMR declined only marginally, particularly in rural areas, and only after a small increase in the first half

Table 6.3: Family Formation, Stability, and Reproductive Behaviour: Russia, 1960–1994

	1960	1970	1980	1985	1989	1990	1991	1992	1993	1994
Crude marriage rate[a]	12.5	10.1	10.6	9.7	9.4	8.9	8.6	7.1	7.5	7.3
Crude divorce rate[a]	1.5	3.0	4.2	4.0	4.0	3.8	4.0	4.3	4.5	4.6
Children in divorces[b]	n.a.	277.6	444.9	502.4	479.1	466.1	522.2	569.1	593.8	680.0[c]
Crude birth-rate[a]	23.2	14.6	16.0	16.7	14.6	13.4	12.1	10.7	9.4	9.4
Total fertility rate	2.63[d]	1.97[e]	1.87	2.05	2.01	1.89	1.73	1.55	1.39	1.42[c]
Births to unmarried women[f]	13.1[g]	10.6[h]	10.8	12.0	13.5	14.6	16.0	17.2	18.2	19.0[c]
Births to women under 20[i]	4.1	9.2	8.7	9.1	11.8	13.9	15.4	16.5	17.7	18.0[c]
Abortion rate[i]	186.5[j]	253.4	204.6	187.5	204.9	206.3	201.0	216.4	235.2	260.0[c]

[a] Per 1,000 population. [b] In 1,000s. [c] Estimate. [d] 1958–9. [e] 1969–70. [f] As per cent of total births. [g] 1960–4. [h] 1970–4. [i] Per 100 live births. [j] 1961.

Sources: UNICEF ICDC (1993, 1994, 1995); Personal communication of Olga Remenets of the Russian Goskomstat.

Table 6.4: The Welfare of Children and Adolescents: Russia, 1970–1994

	1970	1980	1985	1989	1990	1991	1992	1993	1994
Infant mortality rate[a]	23.0	22.0	20.8	17.8	17.4	17.8	18.0	19.9	18.7
Under-5 mortality rate[b]	28.8	28.0	26.0	22.0	21.4	21.9	22.1	24.3	25.0[c]
Age 5–19 mortality rate[d]	0.8	0.75	0.68	0.69	0.69	0.74	0.76	0.83	0.90[c]
Preschool enrolment rate[e]	49.0	64.9	68.3	69.3	66.4	63.9	56.8	57.4	55.5[c]
First-level enrolment rate[f]	—	76.1	77.4	81.9	82.6	82.3	81.4	79.4	80.4[c]
Second-level enrolment rate[g]	—	95.6	98.9	96.3	95.3	93.6	92.3	91.4	91.8[c]
New adoptions[h]	—	—	—	12.3	12.8	13.0	13.9	15.3	—
Children w/foster parents[h]	—	—	—	125	128	131	136	146	—
Children in institutions[i]	—	—	—	122	113	103	100	104	—
14–18-year-olds sentenced[h]	—	—	—	62.4	79.3	85.0	91.0	104.9	111.4

[a] Per 1,000 live births. [b] Per 1,000 live births. [c] Estimate. [d] Per 1,000 relevant population. [e] Percentage of relevant population; the figures for 1980 and 1985 are gross enrolment rates. [f] Percentage of population aged 6–9 years; the figures for 1980 and 1985 are gross enrolment rates. [g] Percentage of population aged 10–16 according to UNESCO methodology. [h] In 1,000s. [i] This variable is the total number of orphans, social orphans, children with disabilities and children in conflict with the law.

Sources: UNICEF ICDC (1993, 1994); Personal communication of Olga Remenets of the Russian Goskomstat.

of the 1970s (Table 6.4). The poor performance of IMR would be even more evident if consideration was given to a number of classification problems which *de facto* reduced IMR by as much as 15 per cent in relation to those countries which adopted the World Health Organization (WHO) classification standards (Davis and Feshbach, 1980; Anderson and Silver, 1986).

The slow decline in IMR in Russia resulted from two conflicting trends. While post-neonatal deaths due to digestive, respiratory, and infectious diseases continued to descend, there was almost as large an increase in neonatal deaths due to perinatal causes and congenital anomalies. Indeed, by the mid-1960s it had become apparent that further progress in IMR would not be possible without the introduction of 'intensive' and relatively costly approaches and equipment in the areas of neonatology and perinatology. However, efforts in these fields were not successful due to inadequate financing and promotion (MZO, 1990).

The IMR stagnation was symptomatic of a broader health crisis which has developed in Russia (and in most of the socialist bloc) since the late 1960s. Indeed, LEB exhibited a similar pattern to that of IMR, though the deteriorations began somewhat earlier (Table 6.5). By 1987, however, it had regained its pre-1965 peak, largely as a result of the anti-alcohol campaign implemented during the Gorbachev era (Tarschys, 1993).

2. *Child morbidity.* The stagnation of the economy, health system, and social structure as well as the worsening environmental pollution of the 1970s and 1980s clearly had a detrimental effect on the general health status of children. To start with, the number of young children with chronic diseases and the victims of accidents soared. Children treated for injuries or toxic poisoning rose from 33.5 per 1,000 in 1970 to 39.4 in 1989. Meanwhile, child deaths due to the same factors shot up from 26,000 to 39,000 during the same period (MZO, 1990).

The health of schoolchildren was no brighter. In 1989, about 16 per cent of all 6-year-olds were not healthy enough to begin school, and over 30 per cent of this age-group were functionally immature. In addition, 53 per cent of all school-aged children had some health problem, and these tended to worsen sharply for pupils of older age-groups (Riazantsev *et al.*, 1992).

The lack of proper hygiene in many schools, the growing pressure to do well as pupils advanced, and insufficient exercise were likely to have contributed to this situation. For instance, the high incidence of acute intestinal diseases among children and preschoolers was due to the inadequate water supply and poor water quality. On the positive side, the incidence of preventible infectious diseases, such as diphtheria, poliomyelitis, whooping cough, and measles, was reduced to marginal levels as mass-scale vaccination was sustained.

Table 6.5:   Adult Mortality in Russia, 1960–1994

	1960	1965	1970	1980	1985	1989	1990	1991	1992	1993	1994
Life expectancy at birth[a]											
Men	63.0[b]	64.3[c]	63.2[d]	61.5	63.8	64.2	63.8	63.5	62.0	58.9	58.2
Women	71.5[b]	73.4[c]	73.6[d]	73.0	74.0	74.5	74.3	74.3	73.8	71.9	71.4
Crude death-rate[e]	7.4	7.6	8.7	11.0	11.3	10.7	11.2	11.4	12.2	14.5	15.6
Maternal mortality rate[f]	129.2	125.6	105.6	68.0	54.0	49.0	47.4	52.4	50.8	51.6	52.0[g]
Young adult mortality rate[h]	2.6	—	2.9	3.0	2.0	1.8	2.0	2.1	2.5	3.0	3.2[g]
Middle-aged adult mortality rate[i]	7.2	—	8.0	9.9	10.4	9.1	9.4	9.5	10.7	13.6	14.0[g]
Elderly adult mortality rate[j]	42.6	—	45.2	50.8	53.4	47.7	48.8	48.6	49.9	56.6	60.1

[a] In years. [b] 1958–9. [c] 1965–6. [d] 1970–1. [e] Per 1,000 births. [f] Per 100,000 live births. [g] Estimate. [h] Per 1,000 population aged 20–39. [i] Per 1,000 population aged 40–59. [j] Per 1,000 population aged 60+.

Sources: UNICEF ICDC (1993, 1994). Personal communication of Olga Remenets of the Russian Goskomstat for 1994 estimates.

3. *Nutrition*. Despite historically high levels of food intake, some nutrition-related problems were prevalent during this period. Firstly, low-income families—which generally include a larger than average share of children—consumed greater quantities of animal fats, potatoes, sugar, salt, bread, and alcohol but up to 50 per cent less fruit and vegetables, good-quality meat, and fish than high-income families (UNICEF ICDC, 1993). This unbalanced diet led to an abnormally high incidence of nutrition-related health problems among low-income groups, including a high prevalence of hypertension, heart diseases, obesity, and micronutrient deficiencies (vitamins, iron, zinc, calcium, and iodine). At greatest risk of inadequate micronutrient intake were school-aged children, pregnant women, women of child-bearing age, and the elderly. Inadequate micronutrient intake among children led to anaemia, goitre, poor vision, rickets, and other ailments.

Secondly, fewer women breastfed and for shorter periods. Little was done to reverse this trend, despite earlier evidence of higher mortality among bottle-fed children (Merkov, 1965). The production and distribution of milk substitutes for formula feeding were inadequate, and the frequency of nutritional diseases and vitamin deficiencies increased.

4. *Child care and education.* Preschool enrolment rates for 3–6-year-olds rose from 49 per cent to 69 per cent between 1970 and 1989 (Table 6.4). Despite this quantitative expansion, made essential by the rapid increase in activity rates among women, overcrowding increased, the quality of services deteriorated, and close to 2 million children remained on the waiting lists throughout most of the 1980s.

Enrolments in primary (6–9 years) and 'presecondary' (10–14 years) school showed remarkable improvement in the 1970s, resulting however in serious overcrowding throughout the system (UNESCO, 1990). The share of pupils in second and third school shifts slowly shrank from 29 per cent in 1970–1 to 17 per cent in 1980–1. It then began to rise again, reaching 22 per cent in 1989–90, signalling that the infrastructure had been expanding at a pace slower than the rate of growth of the school population (FiS, 1989; Goskomstat, 1990*b*; SDF, 1990).

5. *Delinquency among adolescents.* In the idealistic vision of communism, crime was seen as a remnant of capitalism that would vanish with the rise of true socialism. Yet, between 1970 and 1989, juvenile delinquency steadily escalated, jumping for instance by 10 per cent between 1987 and 1988 and by a further 20 per cent between 1988 and 1989 alone (SDF, 1990), reflecting all too clearly the severe social dislocation encumbering Russian society.

Crime rose most rapidly among 14–15-year-olds. In the 1960s, less than 15 per cent of juvenile crimes involved children under 16; in the 1970s, the share rose above 20 per cent, and in 1989 almost a third of juvenile offenders belonged to this age-group. More and more frequently,

11–13-year-olds were also found among the young delinquents (Gerbeev, 1989).

This crime spiral resulted in increased institutionalization of adolescents. In 1988 alone, almost 13,000 children were placed in custody because of criminal offences, despite the fact that the prevalence of criminality among institutionalized children was 7–10 times higher than among the general child population.

6.4. The Transition Crisis of 1989–1994

In spite of the great hopes pinned on a rapid transition to the market economy, ten years after *perestroika* was launched and three and a half years after the adoption of the 'Gaidar Plan', it is now glaringly evident that the market reforms introduced since 1990 and 1991 have come up against enormous, unexpected, and, at times, untreatable economic problems.

6.4.1. *Determinants of the continuing decline in child welfare*

As noted, the deterioration in welfare indicators began around 1987. However, this trend has substantially accelerated during the reform period.

1. *Sharp economic recession, falls in household incomes, and growing inequality.* The recession, which began in 1990, intensified in 1991 and touched its lowest point in 1992. The fall in GDP decelerated marginally in 1993 and continued in 1994, though it is expected to improve slightly (–7.0) in 1995 (Table 6.6). The combined decline of GDP over the 1989–94 period is estimated at 48 per cent. While figures may overestimate the extent of the recession because of under-registration of output in the expanding informal sector, this GDP drop is unparalleled in European economic history of this century.

Unavoidably, these steep falls in output have been accompanied by a sharp contraction in wages and household incomes. After an initial increase in 1990, the index of real wages plunged by about 53 percentage points in 1992 alone, broadly stabilized in 1993, and fell further in 1994 (Table 6.6).

Growing problems of late payment of wages means, however, that in 1993 and 1994 their real drop was even more severe. By November 1993, wage arrears accounted for 21 per cent of the monthly wage bill (Nell and Stewart, 1994), and the problem worsened in 1994.

The decline in real wages has been accompanied by a whirlwind increase in wage dispersion. Real wages in the 'strong sectors' (transport, oil extraction, some manufacturing sectors, and banking), stopped declining

Table 6.6: Main Economic Changes in Russia, 1980–1994

	1980	1985	1989	1990	1991	1992	1993	1994
GDP growth rate[a]		2.5[b]	1.6	-2.0	-12.9	-18.5	-12.0	-15.0
State budget deficit/GDP ratio[c]		—	—	-1.3	-2.9	-3.0	-4.9	-9.9
Annual inflation rate[d]		1.0	1.5	5.4	98.2	1,627	974.1	320
Employment rate[e]	85.1	86.7	87.1	87.1	85.5	83.7	82.2	80.5[f]
Registered unemployment rate[c]		—	—	—	0.1	0.8	1.0	1.7
Unemployment rate (ILO concept)[g]		—	—	—	—	3.0	5.3	6.8
Index of real wages[h]		—	—	100	112	57	54	43
Minimum wage/average wage[i]	40.1	35.2	26.6	23.1	15.1	5.6	10.3	5.8
Average pension/average wage[j]	33.3	36.7	33.5	33.7	33.8	25.8	33.6	34.4
Minimum pension/average wage[k]	25.9[l]	22.6[l]	22.4[l]	23.1	28.1	18.4	19.3	18.8
Wage earners w/wages <50% average wage[c]		—	11.9[m]	12.3[m]	20.3[n]	28.3[m]	43.9[f,m]	—

[a] Per cent yearly change. [b] Refers to net material product in 1985–8. [c] In percentages. Given the difficulty in computing the budget deficit/GDP ratios, the figures should be viewed with caution. [d] Average inflation rate computed on retail prices for the USSR as a whole; 1.0 refers to 1980–5; measured from December to December. [e] Percentage of the working-age population, excluding those on parental leave. [f] As percentage of the labour force. [g] Persons aged 16 years and over without a job (or earnings) who are actively seeking a job and are willing to adapt in order to take up a job. [h] Estimated by deflating nominal wage changes by the consumer or retail trade price index. 1990 = 100, December. [i] 1991–4, December. [j] The ratio of the average monthly 'own right' old-age pension to the average wage, including compensation. [k] Including compensation for price increases from 1992 onwards. [l] Figures for workers/collective farmers are 16.1 (1980), 15.1 (1985) and 24.0 (1989). [m] December. [n] September.

Sources: UNICEF ICDC (1993, 1994).

in 1993, and often increased in 1994. In contrast, wages in agriculture and public social services (health, education, child care, social assistance) continued their downward trail. For instance, wages in the health sector fell from 80 per cent of the national average before the liberalization to 60 per cent in 1993. In addition, the minimum wage has been allowed to fall precipitously (Table 6.6). As a result, 44 per cent of all workers earned below 50 per cent of the average wage in 1993 (Nell and Stewart, 1994), the lowest ratio of all countries in transition for which information is regularly compiled (UNICEF ICDC, 1994).

The fall in income per capita is also linked to the surge in joblessness (Remenets, 1995; Table 6.6). While registered unemployment rose marginally, the actual number of unemployed is far greater. Many laid-off workers do not register at unemployment offices because of the high 'transaction cost' involved and the low value of the benefits. In addition, an important share of the labour force is employed at zero hours and wages (though some workers receive non-cash benefits, such as child-care services and subsidized meals) because of the tax benefits available to firms. The excess wage tax, calculated on the average wage paid by a firm, provides a substantial incentive to companies to keep unneeded workers on extremely low (or zero) salaries, rather than laying them off (Shapiro and Roxburgh, 1994).

Finally, the negative trend in average incomes has been influenced by the volume and incidence of transfers. Overall transfers for pensions, unemployment compensation, and child allowances have remained broadly constant as a share of the national income and have therefore not compensated for falling wages and growing inequality.

While pensions broadly declined in line with wages (Table 6.6), child allowances and other child-related income transfers—which until recently were linked to the minimum wage—fell steadily from the beginning of the transition until January 1994 (Table 6.7). A new system was introduced in January 1994, which increased the child allowance to about 6–10 per cent

Table 6.7:   Child Benefit as a Percentage of Average Monthly Wage

	Child <1.5	1.5–6 years	6–16 years	6–16 single mother
January 1992	14.2	10.7	5.9	11.9
August 1992	8.5	6.8	3.8	7.7
December 1992	6.2	5.0	2.8	5.6
June 1993	8.6	2.9	1.4	3.2
September 1993	1.5	1.2	0.6	1.4
January 1994	10.1	7.1	6.0	9.1

Note: A new system of benefits was introduced in January 1994.

Source: Institute for Socio-Economic Studies of the Population, from Goskomstat.

Table 6.8:   Distribution of Nominal Incomes among Pentiles of Population
(percentages)

Income pentiles	1991	Mar. 1992	Sept. 1992	Mar. 1993	Sept. 1993	Mar. 1994 (forecast)
I (lower)	9.4	8.5	7.2	7.6	7.0	6.4
II	14.0	13.4	12.3	12.3	11.6	11.3
III	17.9	18.2	17.0	16.8	16.0	16.1
IV	22.8	22.4	23.2	22.8	22.0	22.8
V (higher)	35.9	37.5	40.3	40.5	43.4	43.4
(top 5%)	12.7	—	—	15.9	18.9	17.7
Gini co-efficient	0.256	0.278	0.319	0.316	0.344	0.354

Source: Institute for Socio-Economic Studies of the Population, from Goskomstat, cited in Nell and Stewart (1994).

of the average wage. However, even with this new system, in early 1994 the child allowance–average wage ratio was still about 30 per cent lower than its pre-January 1992 value, while the real value of the allowance was only about 40 per cent of its pre-January 1992 level.

As a result of all these trends, overall income inequality has rapidly widened. While the Gini coefficient broadly stagnated over 1986–91, it had increased sharply by March 1994 (Table 6.8) and for 1994 as a whole it is estimated to have reached 0.40 (Remenets, 1995), i.e. a substantially higher level than in most OECD countries (see Chapter 3). In March 1994, the wealthiest 5 per cent of the population controlled the same share of income as the bottom 40 per cent. As recent income surveys are being affected by growing underreporting of income, it is likely that inequality has risen even more.

2. *Public expenditure crisis, changes in social policy, and deterioration of social services.* The transition to the market economy has been accompanied by a public finance crisis, rendering the implementation of a meaningful public expenditure and social protection policy either impossible or inherently inflationary.

Assessing the recent fiscal changes in Russia is by no means an easy task. First, hyperinflation makes annual estimates of GDP, tax revenue, and public expenditures both difficult and unreliable. Second, trends towards decentralization of public social expenditure and taxation mean that consolidated tax and expenditure accounts must be constructed. This, however, is a very difficult undertaking. Third, it is practically impossible to measure the decline in expenditures by ministries and enterprises in the social services following the decentralization of these services to local governments.

Contrary to other economies in transition, where widening government deficits also resulted from fast-rising expenditures on social safety nets, the main cause of the fiscal deficit in Russia was a sharp fall in tax revenues. This was due to the depth and duration of the recession, the inadequacy of the old taxation system, the slow implementation of a badly needed tax reform, and, most of all, poor tax administration, growing evasion, and intensifying conflicts between central and local government (Wallich, 1992). During the first quarter of 1992, actual tax collection, at 26.8 per cent of GDP, was less than half the projected level, mainly because of large shortfalls in the collection of foreign trade taxes, VAT, and alcohol excise (ibid.). Similar tendencies were observed in subsequent years, including the first quarter of 1995.

Within this context, the *share* of public expenditure allocated to health, education, child care, and other social services increased since cuts predominantly affected consumer subsidies and the defence sector (Table 6.9). However, because of the fall in the public expenditure–GDP ratio and in GDP itself, the index of *real public social expenditure* on health declined sharply. In 1993, health expenditure, for instance, was 56 per cent of its 1989 level (UNICEF ICDC, 1994).

The pattern of expenditure cuts has aggravated the problems induced by the decline in expenditure. The adjustment has so far taken place mainly through a sharp fall in the construction of new facilities and purchase of equipment. Second, there has been a radical reduction in purchases of current inputs, including drugs, vaccines, heating fuel, meals for patients, sanitary equipment, and so on. Though also suffering a large drop, the wage bill dropped less than proportionally.

The most adverse impact (including on perinatal mortality) was caused by the large decline in the purchase of new equipment and drugs, which compounded the chronic shortages and obsolescence inherited from the past.

Similar considerations apply in other areas: the lack of teaching equipment has reduced the relevance of public education and worsened the drop-out problem; the closure of student hostels has damaged the educational opportunities of students from peripheral areas; the inadequate heating and supply of hot water in institutions for children and the elderly have aggravated the incidence of certain diseases and exacerbated sanitation problems.

Changes in health policies have involved a shift in responsibility towards local authorities, an opening of doors to private providers, and the introduction of medical insurance and unregulated user fees. However, 'expenditure decentralization' has exacerbated inequality in health care among the members of the Federations and the various *oblasts* (whose resources vary greatly). Health insurance excludes the young and unemployed who do not have a history of contributions but are probably in greatest need. User fees have raised considerable price barriers for those unable to pay even for the most basic treatments.

Table 6.9: Health Budget Expenditure in the Russian Federation, 1992–1993

	1989 Total	1991 Total	1992			1993[a]		
			Total	Federal	Local	Total	Federal	Local
Health expend., in bl current roubles	—	24.4	341.2	67.4	273.8	1,407.9	355.1	1,052.8
wages	—	—	128.5	30.6	97.9	593.1	114.9	478.2
social insurance contribution	—	—	48.8	11.6	37.2	225.3	43.7	181.7
material expenses	—	—	163.9	25.2	138.7	463.1	70.1	392.9
fund for the intro. of medical insurance	—	—	—	—	—	126.4	126.4	0
Health share of total state budget	5.1	5.4	6.2	1.7	16.8	8.3	3	20.3
Health share of GDP	3.6	3.5	2.3	—	—	3.1	—	—
Index of real public health expenditure per capita[b]	—	—	11.6	2.3	9.3	12.2	3.1	9.1

[a]Projected. [b]Calculated using a deflator equal to the average of the GDP deflator and the deflator of medical services and health inputs.

Sources: Davies (1993); UNICEF ICDC (1994).

3. *Further erosion of the family.* Conceivably, the most dramatic indication of the painful process of transition is provided by the abrupt and radical changes recorded in family formation, stability, and reproductive behaviour.

First, the crude marriage rate fell by 30 per cent between 1989 and 1994 (Table 6.3), mainly because of the problems of securing adequate employment among new entrants to the labour force, negative expectations about the future, and the sharply rising cost of housing and rentals faced by potential brides and grooms (Cornia with Paniccià, 1995).

In turn, the crude divorce rate climbed by about 15 per cent and involved a growing number of children. Their well-being is therefore seriously affected by emotional problems and limited financial support. Indeed, only 4 per cent of divorced fathers contribute to the upbringing of children of their former marriages and in 32 per cent of divorce cases the children involved never see their fathers again.

The crude birth-rate and the total fertility rate have also fallen in an unprecedented manner (Table 6.3). The fertility plunge was accompanied by a parallel increase in the proportion of out-of-wedlock births (Table 6.3), which is likely to be the harbinger of substantial increases in child abandonment, institutionalization, poverty, and psychological maladjustment. As a result of this trend and the increase in divorce rates and mortality among middle-aged males, 13 per cent of all families are now lone-parent families (Avraamova, 1994). Finally, the percentage of first births in the total has risen sharply, from 46 per cent in 1989 to almost 60 per cent in 1993, suggesting that the number of one-child families will continue to rise in the future.

4. *The collapse of the state and weakness of civil society.* Economic hardship, budgetary cuts, and increased psychosocial stress created conditions for falls in living standards, violent behaviour, non-compliance with regulations, and illegal actions. However, the recent massive loss of social welfare in Russia could not have occurred without a simultaneous collapse of the regulatory, inspection, and repressive apparatuses of the state.

There are obvious difficulties in documenting the symptoms of this collapse. However, anecdotes abound, all of which point to the rebounding effects of moving from an overregulated to an underregulated society. Once excessively repressive, police controls have swung to being too few and too lax. With large salary falls and the ideological vacuum accompanying the transition, cases of police inefficiency, corruption, and even infiltration by criminal organizations have multiplied. Similar considerations apply to the judiciary and to state agencies responsible for social services, work and air safety, traffic control, first aid, food hygiene inspection and quality control, tax collection, and so on.

Meanwhile, the 'social intermediaries' (trade unions, associations, non-governmental organizations, and other civil society bodies) have also been severely weakened. With large rises in masked unemployment, trade unions have been unable to maintain a sense of concern on work safety issues. Similarly, budgetary restrictions and political changes have contributed to the dismantling of youth associations, an important factor in the considerable upswing in adolescent mortality and juvenile crime rates.

6.4.2. *Changes in the welfare of children*

Though necessary and welcomed, *perestroika* and market reforms in Russia have imposed huge welfare costs on the entire population, and on children in particular.

1. *Sharply rising child poverty.* Estimates of the incidence of poverty and extreme poverty over the 1989–93 period based on a variety of thresholds are presented in Table 6.10. These estimates do not always coincide because different poverty lines and income surveys are sometimes used or because the surveys refer to different months of the same year. Despite these differences, it is clear that poverty and extreme poverty rose sharply in early 1992 and fluctuated around these levels over the two subsequent years. The decline in extreme poverty to around 3 per cent between March 1992 and December 1993 (Table 6.10) is largely a statistical illusion due to the lowering of the extreme poverty threshold.

Table 6.10: Incidence of Poverty According to the Various Poverty Lines in Russia, 1991–1994 (percentages)

Poverty lines	1991	1992		1993		1994 (forecast)
		March	Dec.	March	Dec.	
Physiological	1.0	19.0	4.8	7.4	2.8	3.6
% of 1989 average wage	(20)	(17)	(15)	(15)	(11)	(13)
Survival	11.7	57.0	28.2	38.4	36.2	40.2
% of 1989 average wage	(37)	(30)	(29)	(29)	(34)	(38)
Ministry of Labour[a]	—	25.7[b]	27.0[c]	35.0	27.0	—
% of 1989 average wage	—	—	—	(22)	(23)	—
Used in this chapter[d]	—	—	—	—	—	—
Poverty	14.0	50.1[e]	55.9	53.4	44.3	—
% of 1989 average wage	(40)	(40)	(40)	(49)	(40)	—
Extreme poverty	2.5	23.0[f]	31.3	26.1	20.5	—
% of 1989 average wage	(24)	(24)	(24)	(24)	(24)	—

[a] Computed by Ministry of Labour and Social Statistics. [b] Refers to 1992 Q1. [c] Refers to 1992 Q4. [d] Derived from Nell and Stewart (1994) and MONEE Database. [e] Refers to August. [f] Refers to 1992 Q2.

Source: UNICEF ICDC (1994).

The spread of poverty has struck huge blows to the 'old poor', namely members of large and single-parent families, people with severe disabilities, minority groups, and the elderly subsisting on minimum pensions. The transition has also created a category of 'new poor', i.e. working-age people and their dependents, youth in search of first employment, unemployed workers or workers at low or zero hours, minimum-wage workers, and low-paid social sector employees. To these should be added the growing numbers of people in single-parent families, migrants, and refugees.

Contrary to the widespread view that the aged have been the main victims of the transition, most analyses unambiguously indicate that poverty has risen significantly faster among children and working-age adults than for pensioners. For instance, in 1993 a striking 47.5 per cent of families with two children and 60.9 per cent with three or more lived in poverty (increasing from 38.1 and 60.3 per cent respectively in 1992). For lone-parent households, the risk of poverty in 1993 was considerably higher at 62.1 and 72.3 per cent respectively (jumping from 53.8 and 68.4 per cent respectively in 1992) (Russian Longitudinal Monitoring Survey, 1993). Other data show almost 50 per cent of children living below the poverty level, against a national average of 37 per cent (Russian Economic Trends, 1993).

Four main factors underlie this unexpected development: the surge of unemployment (broadly defined); the sharp increase in the number of people on very low wages or whose wages are paid only after long delays; better indexation of pensions relative to public sector wages, child allowances, and unemployment benefits; and the faster than average increase in the cost of raising children (Remenets, 1995). User fees were introduced for many child-related services. In addition, the manufacture of 'children's goods' (baby carriages, clothes, and so on) dropped by almost 50 per cent between 1991 and 1992 and by even more in 1993, with sharp repercussions on prices (Avraamova, 1994).

A child now represents a real burden on the well-being of a family. Despite a steep decline in consumption of children's items, 77 per cent of families now spend at least half of their resources on their children (Kornyak, 1994). Today, only those families with one child and both parents working full-time are able to provide for his or her healthy development.

2. *A sharp increase in overall mortality and a more contained but significant rise in IMR.* The most startling sign of the Russian 'transition crisis' is the sharp rise in the crude death-rate. The jump, from 10.7 per 1,000 in 1989 to 15.6 in 1994, significantly 'outclassed' trends witnessed in other transitional economies not affected by war or famine (Table 6.5). This increase was most pronounced over the 1992–4 period and among men of working age. Diseases of the heart and circulatory systems and external causes

(including alcohol poisoning, homicide, suicide, and accidents) were responsible for over 70 per cent of the total increase in mortality (UNICEF ICDC, 1994). As a result, male life expectancy at birth fell steadily from 64.2 years in 1989 to 58.2 in 1994—a value lower than the retirement age and 10–14 years lower than those observed in Western Europe. Meanwhile, female life expectancy dropped from 74.5 to 71.4, making it five to eight years below Western equivalents (Table 6.5).

'Social stress' is the main cause of the spiralling number of deaths among middle-aged adults. Past analyses undertaken in the USA, Canada, Britain, and Finland have demonstrated that the most prevalent sources of stress are family breakdown, death of relatives, job insecurity and unemployment, depression, poverty, and migration (Eyer and Sterling, 1977; Beale and Nethercott, 1985, 1989; Moser *et al.*, 1986, 1987; Smith, 1992; Anda *et al.*, 1993; Kalimo and Vuori, 1993). The risk of death among people affected by these factors was found to be between 1.5 and four times higher than for the control group. All of these stressors have worsened markedly during the past four years in Russia: marriage rates fell, divorce rates mounted, and poverty rates and unemployment shot up. In addition, large domestic migrations—often under unfavourable conditions—have been reported following the disintegration of the former Soviet Union.

This barrage of 'paternal mortality' has affected child welfare, with substantially increased risks of orphanhood, institutionalization, poverty, lower school achievement, and difficult socialization. In addition, Russian infants and adolescents have been directly affected by a significant increase in mortality. As shown in Table 6.4, until 1992 IMR did not show any significant variation from its 1989 level. However, it jumped to 19.9 (per 1,000 live births) in 1993, though it declined in 1994.

While congenital- and perinatal-related deaths rose slowly in the 1980s, the last five years have seen an abrupt degeneration (Figure 6.1). This unwelcome change suggests a worsening of the situation in the field of perinatal care as well as mounting problems in pregnancy screening and the management of conditions requiring more sophisticated interventions, such as prematurity and congenital anomalies.

Surprisingly, a surge in deaths due to respiratory, digestive, and infectious diseases has also contributed to the rise in IMR. This reflects a severe weakening of even basic maternal and child health programmes, including child immunization.

While the 5–15 age-group exhibits generally favourable variations in death-rates over time, a small but quite generalized increase in mortality due to accidents and suicide has been recorded for the 15–19 age-group (particularly boys) indirectly confirming the extent of erosion of the family and youth institutions as well as a breakdown in law and order.

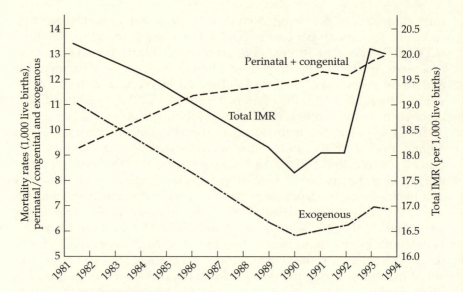

Fig. 6.1   Changes in Infant Mortality Due to Congenital and Perinatal Causes and to Exogenous Causes, Russia, 1989–1993
Source: Nell and Stewart (1994).

3. *Rising disease and disability incidence among infants and children.* The number of children and adolescents suffering various illnesses, allergies, and invalidity accelerated distinctly with the inception of the reform process. Indeed, the past four years have witnessed a resurgence of several 'poverty diseases', including infectious, parasitic, and sexually transmitted diseases (UNICEF ICDC, 1994).

The situation is particularly worrying with regard to measles, whooping cough, tuberculosis, and diphtheria, the incidence of which reached epidemic proportions in 1994 (Table 6.11). In addition, whereas in 1989 one in every eight infants was born with a disease or fell ill while still in maternity hospital, this proportion rose to one in five children in 1992 and had reached one in four by 1993.

The spread of infectious diseases among children is tied to the erosion of immunization coverage for DTP, the effects of civil strife, migration, growing homelessness, reduced compliance with prophylactic norms, and suspicions about the public health system's ability to provide adequate services.

Between 1985 and 1993, the number of under-16-year-olds with disabilities (mainly psychoneurological or related to eyesight or hearing loss) increased by a factor of four, reaching 342,700 (Kornyak, 1994). Medical care for disabled children costs three times more on average than 'normal' medical care, and many families with disabled children are becoming impoverished. Fathers fail to endure the burden of a disabled child in one out of every three cases and leave their families.

4. *Changes in the nutritional status of children.* Since 1991 more and more families have been forced to reduce their consumption of high-quality foods, such as dairy products, meat, fish, and vegetables. Consumption differentials by income level are widening and 40 per cent of young families are said to be spending a shocking 80 per cent of their incomes on food. In addition, school feeding programmes are deteriorating and now provide mainly carbohydrates and few proteins and micronutrients (Avraamova, 1994).

Anthropometric data suggest, however, only a moderate deterioration in the nutritional status of children. The Russian Longitudinal Monitoring Study (1993) estimates that the prevalence of moderate and acute wasting (weight-for-height) among 0–6-year-old children in July–October 1992 (when many families were already impoverished) had reached 3.4 per cent, i.e. a fairly high value by international standards. Data from Round 3 (July–September 1993) of the same survey indicate that while wasting had declined marginally to 2.9 per cent, stunting (i.e. height-for-age) had shot up over the same period from 9 to 11.1 per cent (and from 7.5 to 11.4 per cent for the 0–2 age-group). Another 1992 review of nutritional conditions shows that 3 per cent of children in Moscow had low weight-for-height, but it did not reveal any significant variation from prior levels (Health Policy Report, 1993).

Finally, a survey on the nutritional status of children under age 2 conducted in Moscow, Ekaterinenburg, and St Petersburg in 1993 suggests a marked deterioration in dietary intake and nutritional status

Table 6.11: Incidence of Selected Illnesses in the Russian Federation (per 100,000 people)

	1980	1985	1990	1991	1992	1993	1994 Q1-2
Severe intestinal infections	675.0	722.0	534.0	547.0	464.0	515.0	—
Diphtheria	0.2	0.8	0.8	1.3	2.6	10.3	12.1
Whooping cough	4.9	28.8	16.9	20.8	16.2	26.4	23.7
Measles	14.5	13.0	12.4	13.8	12.5	50.1	—
Viral hepatitis	255.0	227.0	227.0	192.0	136.0	132.0	86.0
Meningitis	7.3	8.4	4.5	4.0	3.5	3.6	3.5
Syphilis	23.0	9.8	5.3	7.2	13.4	34.3	45.7
Gonorrhoea	196.6	148.1	128.0	128.6	169.6	237.4	—
Tuberculosis	47.4	45.2	34.2	34.0	35.8	44.7	30.6
Total illnesses	—	—	651.2	667.5	615.6	1,089.4	—

Source: Nell and Stewart (1994).

(CARE-USA, 1993). A high number of mothers indicated, for instance, that they frequently or occasionally could not adequately feed their small children and that food consumption had worsened in 35–40 per cent of families, particularly for meat, milk, vegetables, and fresh fruit. As a result, 25 per cent of children's diets did not contain the recommended protein allowance, 20–30 per cent had deficiencies in the vitamin B group, 30 per cent in vitamin A, 40 per cent in food fibre, and 41–48 per cent in ascorbic acid.

5. *A widespread decline in child care and enrolments in preprimary and secondary education.* Though the cognitive and psychosocial benefits of preschool education have long been recognized in Russia, the preschool enrolment rate (for the 3–6 age-group) fell from 69.3 to 55.5 per cent between 1989 and 1994 (Table 6.4). This decline is cause for concern as 'family substitutes' can only be of limited relevance for peer interaction and school preparation. The crèche enrolment rate contracted even more sharply, from 53 per cent in 1989 to 32 per cent in 1993. In this case, the shift from service- to family-based care is not, in itself, a source of preoccupation if it is accompanied by adequate parental leave.

While the new policy on preschool education aims at transferring many of these services to local authorities, their decentralization has been characterized by financial chaos and by the closure of kindergartens managed by state enterprises. Moreover, local authorities have closed some of their kindergartens, despite increases in user fees and radical cost-saving efforts. A survey of twenty-five territories of the Russian Federation, for instance, shows that between 2 and 10 per cent of the preschool facilities run by local authorities were closed during the 1991–3 period alone (UNICEF ICDC, 1993).

Demand factors, however, have played an even more crucial role. Indeed, the new fees for school meals, heating, and so on represent a substantial proportion of the average wage and have thus triggered an abrupt contraction in the demand for kindergarten services. In addition, the escalation of female unemployment and the desire to reduce what was perceived as an excessive role of the state in child socialization contributed to the weakened demand.

With regard to compulsory education, even though the basic principle of free provision of primary and secondary education has not been abandoned, a tightening of budgetary resources has resulted in fewer facilities, lower subsidies, higher fees for books, meals, and teaching materials, and a deterioration in the quality of education. No major changes, however, have been observed in primary enrolment rates.

At the same time, new legislation has deprived adolescents of certain educational rights. Only nine years of schooling are now mandatory. There have also been reductions in the number of places in the ninth through eleventh years, the number of student stipends granted, and the number of places available in student hostels, and the cost of meals in school canteens has spiralled. These changes have limited the educational prospects of many students and contributed to the drop in secondary enrolment rates from 96.3 to 91.4 per cent between 1989 and 1993 (UNICEF ICDC, 1994).

6. *An increasingly difficult socialization and growing crime rates among youth*. The overall crime rate climbed by nearly 70 per cent between 1989 and 1992 (UNICEF ICDC, 1994). Most of this increase concerns crimes against property, is motivated by material gain, and can be related to the deteriorating economic situation, the perception of growing income inequality, the erosion of law and order, and the increase in alcohol consumption.

One of the most alarming features of this 'crime wave' is the rapid 'juvenization' and 'feminization' of delinquency. The number of 14–17-year-olds involved in crimes rose from 153,000 in 1990 to 204,000 in 1993, while that of 14–18-year-old youths sentenced almost doubled between 1989 and 1993 (Table 6.4).

The growth in youth crime can basically be traced to the erosion of those 'institutions', i.e. the family, school, work, and youth associations, entrusted with the socialization of adolescents. Budgetary problems have contributed to the dismantling of the extensive network of youth associations developed during the socialist period. In addition, the contraction in enrolment rates and the rise in drop-out rates in secondary schools as well as the increasing difficulties in securing a job have contributed to pushing an increasing number of adolescents on to the street. Youth are increasingly seeking some income from any kind of activity. Often, crime offers the most practical means of realizing unmet aspirations.

7. *Abandonment, adoption, and institutionalization of children*. While child protection policies in Russia have traditionally relied upon state institutions, the transition has heightened the risk of child abandonment and institutionalization. In 1993, almost 80,000 children were deprived of parental care and placed under state care (Kornyak, 1994). Around 1 per cent of all newborns were abandoned by their mothers during the first hours of their lives in maternity homes, mainly for reasons relating to the indigence of parents or illness within the family (ibid.).

Yet changes in legislation during the transition have, if partially, corrected some of these structural problems. Indeed, between 1989 and 1992, the number of children below 18 in institutions declined from 2.9 to 2.4 per cent of the relevant age group (UNICEF ICDC, 1994).

Several conflicting trends may be at work here. Many attribute this phenomenon to the contraction in births rather than to a reduction in 'risk factors' behind child abandonment. If anything, these factors—poverty, divorce, orphanhood, and births to unmarried mothers—have all worsened.

An increase in the number of adoptions and foster families also played a role (Table 6.4), signalling that improvements are feasible, even in difficult times. The easing of legislation is likely to have facilitated the demands for adoption and fostering. Indeed, evidence suggests that the demand for adoptions of small and healthy babies often exceeds the supply of children whose parents have fully relinquished their parental rights.

6.5. What Can Be Done?

Even a modest improvement in the predicament of Russian children requires arresting the output downslide of the last four years, curbing inflation, and halting the disintegration of the state. To achieve this, urgent measures are needed (not discussed here for reasons of space) to control inflation by non-recessionary methods, restructure industry 'at a human pace', continue privatization, vastly improve tax collection, and strengthen the state. It would thus be naïve to claim that the plight of Russian children can be stabilized by means of child and family policies alone. Yet, social policies like those illustrated below can substantially contain further deterioration and speed up recovery-induced welfare improvements (see also Chapter 14).

6.5.1. Policies to support family incomes

At present, many workers with dependent children are trapped in inefficient enterprises, employed at zero hours, officially unemployed, self-excluded from the labour force, or employed in the informal sector where—given widespread market failures—real incomes are often below the poverty line and growth is hampered by institutional bottlenecks.

Severe organizational and tax collection problems do not allow sufficient scope for introducing even a limited 'minimum income guarantee' package. Instead, this objective may be achieved through a judicious mix of policies promoting employment and self-employment, improved wage regulation, and targeted income transfers.

1. *Greater labour absorption through the promotion of self-employment and the creation of new firms.* This objective can be achieved through institutional and legal interventions aimed at removing 'barriers to entry' and obstacles preventing the efficient functioning of factor markets (for land, labour, industrial assets, credit, and know-how). In addition, better access to training, physical infrastructure, and industrial services will also be crucial for promoting employment in the small-producer sector.

2. *Wage policy.* While excess labour in the public administration must be gradually reduced, wages in sectors such as health, education, and social

welfare must be better linked to the average wage. In addition, the minimum wage should be raised to a meaningful level (a third to a quarter of the average), while wage arrears should be liquidated. Also, in the longer term, it would be desirable to adjust approaches to wage negotiation so as to contain rising wage disparities among sectors with similar productivity.

3. *Passive and active labour market policies.* Unemployment compensation should be tied to average wages and granted under clearer conditions than at present. Active labour market policies dealing with the entry or reintegration into the workforce of young people and workers who have been laid off should be implemented on a preferential basis through professional training, public work programmes, and the strengthening of administrations managing these schemes. These are preferable to other income transfer programmes because they contribute to the accumulation of human capital and to a much-needed refurbishing of deteriorating clinics, schools, and water and sanitation systems. Furthermore, they are less affected by the 'adverse selection' problems associated with other income transfer programmes.

4. *Income transfers.* Due to their low value in recent years, child allowances have had an insignificant effect on containing rising child poverty. They should therefore be increased so as to cover a fixed share of child-rearing costs (or about 15–20 per cent of the average wage). Should budgetary considerations impose the targeting of this allowance only on poor children, the focus should be on children in families headed by single mothers, families with two or more children, handicapped children or parents, unemployed heads, or families cumulating multiple deprivation. In addition, its value should be raised from the third child, as the risk of child poverty increases more than proportionally in larger families.

6.5.2. Service availability and financing

The following measures ought to be considered.

1. *The universal and free provision of key basic services should be fully preserved.* While this policy has been retained in principle, the key inputs needed for the functioning of services (life-saving drugs and books in schools, for instance) should also be provided free of charge. In addition, the federal government should consider taking responsibility for the financing of key child welfare services, such as basic health, primary and secondary education, and child care.

2. *Service reorganization and reallocation of public expenditure.* Within each sector, efficiency improvements can be achieved through better staff deployment, rationalization of procedures, the introduction of 'nominal user fees' (up to 5–10 per cent of service costs), inhibiting irrational use, and greater competition among public, private, and voluntary providers for

state-financed services. There are also ample opportunities for reassigning resources towards more progressive and efficient programmes or input types. In the health sector, for instance, a gradual reduction in personnel levels would allow the purchase of more inputs and equipment or wage rises. Finally, part of expenditure absorbed by military and production subsidies should be reallocated to health care, education and training, water utilities, and social safety nets.

3. *User fees*. Because of its negative welfare impact, the practice of unloading a growing share of social service costs on beneficiaries should be tightly regulated. While 'substantive user fees' might be suitable for high-income services (university education, non-life-saving surgery, nurseries, and so on), they should be excluded for basic services. For these activities, even 'nominal user fees' must be strictly regulated.

6.5.3. Legislation for the protection of children and youth

A containment of the social fall-out of the transition calls for further improvement of legal provisions on child protection, adoption, fostering, and child support, while backing of the enterprise and NGO sectors in the fields of apprenticeship programmes and youth associations should be strengthened to check the recent wave of youth crime, child abuse, and accidental deaths.

6.5.4. A radical improvement in tax collection

Greater resources will be needed for the financing of even a moderate (and non-inflationary) poverty alleviation and social protection policy. Low yields, large tax evasion, institutional conflicts between the federation and its constituents, and limited progressivity of the present tax system have greatly reduced the poverty alleviation potential of tax-and-transfer policies. It is thus essential to raise the tax–GDP ratio by several points, while the tax load should be distributed more equitably, evasion combated, and administration strengthened.

7

The American Paradox: High Income and High Child Poverty

SHELDON DANZIGER, SANDRA K. DANZIGER,
AND JONATHAN STERN

7.1. Introduction

Recent demographic, economic, and public policy trends indicate that high poverty rates for American children are a persistent feature of the nation's economic and social landscape. In 1992, the official poverty rates were 21.9 per cent for all children, and about 40 per cent for all black and Hispanic children and white non-Hispanic children living in mother-only families.[1] In contrast, the poverty rate for white children living in two-parent families was 10 per cent, and for elderly persons, 12.9 per cent. For most white children, poverty lasts only a few years, but many minority children experience severe disadvantage throughout their entire childhood.

In any year about three-quarters of America's 15 million poor children under the age of 18 live in families that receive some government income maintenance benefits. About one-quarter, falling through all safety-net programmes, receive nothing. Other countries provide much more generous benefits to poor children. Blank and Hanratty (1993) estimate that if the USA adopted the Canadian system of social benefits, child poverty could be reduced by more than half.

In the early 1960s, when the overall poverty rate was about 20 per cent, President Johnson declared War on Poverty. The planners of this initiative assumed that active government policies implemented in a growing, full-employment economy would reduce the official measure of poverty to virtually zero by 1980 (Lampman, 1971). Child poverty did indeed de-

Maria Cancian, Giovanni Andrea Cornia, David Dickinson, Lorraine Klerman, Jodi Sandfort, and Robert Wood provided valuable comments on earlier drafts of this chapter.

[1] The official US poverty line provides a set of income cut-offs which vary by family size. In 1992, the poverty line for a family of four was $14,335, about 39% of the median income of all families and 32% of the median for a family of four. The official poverty lines, used for more than thirty years, are adjusted annually for price increases, but do not vary with real income. Thus, in 1967, the poverty line for a family of four was about 43% of the median for all families.

cline, from 23 per cent in 1964 to 14.4 per cent in 1973, as both social spending and the economy boomed. Since that time, however, it has increased.

While the 1970s was a decade of growth in social welfare spending, it was also a period of disappointing economic performance. Productivity and economic growth slowed, family income stagnated, and prices and unemployment rose. The fact that poverty remained virtually constant during the 1970s indicates that antipoverty policies were successful in offsetting the increased economic adversity (Danziger and Gottschalk, 1985, 1995).

However, the official perspective of the early 1980s, evident in social spending cuts undertaken by President Reagan, was quite different. Antipoverty programmes themselves were blamed for the failure of poverty to fall during the 1970s as it had during the previous two decades (Murray, 1984).

According to President Reagan:

With the coming of the Great Society, Government began eating away at the underpinnings of the private enterprise system. The big taxers and big spenders in the Congress had started a binge that would slowly change the nature of our society and, even worse, it threatened the character of our people. . . . By the time the full weight of Great Society programmes was felt, economic progress for America's poor had come to a tragic halt. (Remarks before the National Black Republican Council, 15 September, 1982)

In 1964, the famous War on Poverty was declared. And a funny thing happened. Poverty, as measured by dependency, stopped shrinking and then actually began to grow worse. I guess you could say, 'Poverty won the War'. Poverty won, in part, because, instead of helping the poor, Government programmes ruptured the bonds holding poor families together. (Radio address, 15 February, 1986)

The 'Reagan Experiment' assumed that if government spending was reduced, productivity and economic growth would increase and prices, unemployment, and poverty would fall. The evidence from this experiment is now in. Poverty did fall somewhat during the 1982–9 economic recovery. However, the 1989 rates of 12.8 per cent for all persons and 19.6 per cent for children remained above those of 1979, the previous business-cycle peak. Poverty increased again in the early 1990s due to recession and fell only slightly as the economy recovered.

Between the late 1980s and 1994, some progressive policy changes were initiated. The Tax Reform Act of 1986, the Family Support Act of 1988 (a welfare and child support reform bill), and further tax changes in 1990 and 1993 targeted substantial additional resources to poor families with children. When President Clinton was elected in 1992, there seemed to be further support for an expansion of policies targeted on poor children. President Clinton did expand spending in some programmes in his first two years in office, but his proposal for universal health insurance was defeated in 1994. By 1995, the Republican Congressional majority had proposed much larger reductions in social welfare spending than those of the Reagan years.

Government has thus done little to combat rising child poverty. And, although the economy has grown modestly since the late 1970s, income inequality has dramatically increased. Between 1973 and 1992, the inflation-adjusted, family size-adjusted income of the poorest one-fifth of families with children fell by 26 per cent, while that of the richest one-fifth increased by 20 per cent. By 1992, the adjusted income of the richest quintile of families with children was ten times larger than that of the bottom quintile; in 1973, this ratio was 6.5 (US House of Representatives 1994: 1,196).

America's high child poverty rate will only fall significantly if an expanded antipoverty initiative is put into place. To undertake such a programme, Americans would have to believe three propositions: first, that government programmes can effectively resolve social problems; second, that poverty is caused primarily by structural economic barriers and not primarily by pathological behaviour; and third, that spending taxpayers' money to reduce child poverty represents a sound investment in the productivity of the next generation. All of these propositions were invoked for the War on Poverty in 1964. Yet, three decades later, none would be endorsed by a majority of legislators.

Thirty years ago poverty was attributed primarily to lack of skills. Because the least skilled had difficulty finding jobs and earning enough to support their families, policies were needed to raise the educational level of poor children and to increase family incomes. Policy-oriented discussions now emphasize personal responsibility and downplay government's obligation to ensure a minimum standard of living. For example, an informal commission (Novak *et al.*, 1987: 99) concluded that:

For such persons, low income is in a sense the least of their problems; a failure to take responsibility for themselves and for their actions is at the core. It would seem to be futile to treat the symptom, low income, rather than the fundamental need, a sense of self.

The Republicans who took control of Congress in 1995 are sympathetic to this view. Their Personal Responsibility Act seeks to increase work effort and promote two-parent families by reducing antipoverty spending. Their primary goal is to eliminate the federal budget deficit and to finance tax cuts for the non-poor.

It is too soon to know whether the proposed drastic reduction in social spending will become law. It is clear, however, that momentum towards expansion of the welfare state has been derailed. Thus, America's high child poverty rate and its negative consequences for children are likely to persist into the next century.

7.2. Economic Factors

7.2.1. Trends in family incomes and poverty

Trends in family incomes and poverty since the early 1970s stand in sharp contrast to the quarter-century economic boom following World War II. Real median family income grew by about 40 per cent between 1949 and 1959 and by another 40 per cent between 1959 and 1969 (Table 7.1). Poverty for all persons dropped by about 10 percentage points during each decade.

During this era the 'American dream' was fulfilled for most families. The real incomes of the rich, the poor, and the middle class all doubled between the late 1940s and the early 1970s. If some benefited more than others, they tended to be those who had started at a greater disadvantage, such as racial and ethnic minorities and the less educated.

The period after 1973 has been one of stagnation. Real median family income in 1992 was only about 2 per cent above the 1969 level, and poverty was higher. Furthermore, unemployment has been high for much of the past two decades (Table 7.1). This disappointing macroeconomic performance refuted two key expectations of the War on Poverty planners. They thought that poverty could be alleviated against a background of steady economic growth because the business cycle could be controlled.

Table 7.1: Family Incomes, Poverty, and Unemployment Rates, Selected Years, 1949–1992

Year	Median family income (1992 $) (1)	Official poverty rate, all persons (%) (2)	Unemployment rate (%) (3)	Cash transfers per household (1992 $) (4)
1949	18,282	34.3[a]	5.9	1,085
1954	21,747	27.3[a]	5.5	1,380
1959	26,069	22.4	5.5	2,186
1964	29,707	19.0	5.2	2,686
1969	36,062	12.1	3.5	3,214
1974	36,718	11.2	5.6	4,236
1979	37,853	11.7	5.8	4,727
1984	35,694	14.4	7.5	4,556
1989	38,710	12.8	5.3	4,659
1992	36,812	14.5	7.4	4,491

[a] Estimate based on unpublished tabulations from March Current Population Surveys by Gordon Fischer, US Department of Health and Human Services.

Sources: *Current Population Reports*, Series P-60, for cols. 1 and 2; US Council of Economic Advisers (1995) for col. 3; Danziger and Gottschalk (1985) and authors' tabulations from the March Current Population Survey, for col. 4.

This was a reasonable assumption at the time, as median family income growth was positive each year from 1958 to 1969. They also believed that economic growth together with low unemployment rates, anti-discrimination policies, and education and training programmes, would raise all incomes at about the same rate. At best, income growth for the poor would exceed the average rate.

Instead, since the early 1970s, economic growth has been slow and income inequality has increased both within and between most socio-economic groups. The gaps in living standards have widened between the rich and the poor, between the rich and the middle class, and between the most-skilled and least-skilled workers.

7.2.2. Trends in male earnings

A major contributor to rising child poverty has been the increasing percentage of men who do not earn enough to support a family of four persons at the poverty line (about $14,000 in 1992). Some of these 'low earners' do not work at all; others work only sporadically during the year; still others work full time, full year, but at a low wage rate.

Table 7.2 shows the percentage of men aged 25–54 in each of five education categories whose earnings were below the poverty line for a family of four for 1949–89.[2] For each of the three race/ethnic groups, education is negatively correlated with low earnings. The data for the post-1969 period do not show the kind of economic progress that Americans in the post-World War II era came to expect. Between 1949 and 1969, the rate of low earnings declined dramatically for all education and all race/ethnic groups and large declines occurred in each educational category.

Most of this drop was due to rapid real earnings growth throughout the distribution, as mean real earnings for these men more than doubled between 1949 and 1969. As a result, the official US poverty line, which is fixed in real terms, fell as a percentage of this mean from 107 to 46 per cent. The incidence of low earnings fell further because inequality decreased slightly: those at the bottom experienced more rapid increases in earnings than did those at the top (Danziger and Gottschalk, 1993, and 1995).

In 1989, however, mean real earnings for these men were virtually the same as they had been two decades earlier. As a result, the incidence of low earnings (with education held constant) increased sharply because earnings inequality increased. The increases in low earnings were particularly dramatic for less educated men, as the college premium—the ratio of the earnings of college graduates to those of high school graduates—

---

[2] The official poverty rates (see Table 7.1) are lower than the rates of low earnings in Table 7.2 because they are based on total family income and thus include income from other sources and because they reflect actual family size.

Table 7.2: Men, Aged 25–54, with Low Earnings[a], by Educational Attainment, 1949–1989

Years of school	Men with low earnings by completed years of schooling (%)					
	0–8	9–11	12	13–15	16+	All men
White, Non-Hispanic						
1949	53.2	37.8	30.0	31.0	24.5	40.1
1959	34.4	17.7	13.2	13.1	10.6	19.6
1969	24.5	12.7	8.3	9.7	7.9	11.8
1979	35.9	24.0	14.9	14.8	10.7	16.4
1989	54.8	38.1	21.9	17.4	10.6	20.2
Black, Non-Hispanic						
1949	85.0	70.4	63.4	66.4	52.8	79.7
1959	65.0	45.9	36.7	29.5	18.2	53.5
1969	46.0	32.3	20.0	18.0	16.4	32.0
1979	55.5	45.6	32.7	28.7	18.7	36.9
1989	69.5	60.4	43.2	31.5	17.5	41.8
Hispanic						
1949	76.0	53.2	46.4	—[b]	—[b]	67.8
1959	57.2	24.6	22.7	23.4	—[b]	43.9
1969	37.7	18.4	16.4	18.4	12.2	26.3
1979	43.8	32.8	24.5	22.4	19.3	31.4
1989	60.2	50.5	35.2	26.9	18.0	38.1

[a] A man is classified as having low earnings if his earned income from wages, salaries, and self-employment is below the poverty line for a family of four: $2,417, $2,955, $3,714, $7,355, and $12,674 in each of the five years. [b] Cell size below 75 men.

Source: Computations by authors from Public Use Microdata Samples of the Decennial Censuses of 1950–90.

widened substantially. Between 1969 and 1989, the low earnings rates for high school graduates (12 years of completed schooling) increased by 13.6, 23.2, and 18.8 percentage points for the three race/ethnic groups, much greater than the increase for the college-educated. The rate for high school graduates in 1989 was almost as high as that of men with eight or fewer years of school in 1969.

In sum, over the past two decades a smaller proportion of men earned enough to support their families on their own. Children's well-being did not decline as rapidly, however, as the increasing earnings of wives and declining family size (as discussed below) cushioned the decline in male earnings. None the less, the experience of slow economic growth and the absence of poverty reduction for such a long time ran counter to American expectations of rising living standards and contributed to voter dissatisfaction with government programmes and policies.

7.2.3. Trends in the contribution of women to family incomes

For the past several decades, women in general, and mothers in particular, have increasingly participated in the labour force. In 1950, about one-fifth of married women with children were working; in 1992, the figure was about two-thirds. Weeks worked per year and mean real wages of married women have also increased, while male earnings stagnated. By the early 1990s, the earnings of wives accounted for about one-quarter of family income, roughly double their contribution two decades earlier (Cancian *et al.*, 1993*a*).

The antipoverty impact of women's earnings has also increased over time. In 1973, the poverty rate for children living in married-couple families was 7.2 per cent; it rose by about 1 percentage point to 8.2 per cent in 1989. However, poverty would have risen by an additional 3 percentage points had wives not increased their contribution to family income (Danziger and Danziger, 1993: 67).

7.2.4. Trends in government income transfers

The 1980s were also difficult for families dependent on government transfers. As with family income and male earnings, the recent trend in government support differs from that in the decades following World War II. Cash transfers per household (for all households) doubled between 1949 and 1959 and almost doubled again by 1974 (Table 7.1). After 1974, most transfer growth was in social security and other benefits targeting the elderly, and not in public assistance (welfare) programmes for children. Between fiscal years 1978 and 1987, federal expenditures targeted on children declined by 4 per cent in real terms, while those for the elderly increased by 52 per cent (US House of Representatives 1990*a*: 1,065–6). Spending on welfare, housing, food stamps, and Medicaid for those who are neither aged nor disabled made up only 11.9 per cent of total social welfare expenditures in 1980, compared to the 66 per cent for the elderly (Ellwood and Summers, 1986). The elderly thus experienced large declines in poverty and increases in income that were much more favourable over 1969–92 than the trends shown in Table 7.1 for all persons.

Welfare receipt among poor children increased rapidly with the War on Poverty. While less than 15 per cent of poor children in 1960 received welfare benefits, this increased to 50 per cent in 1969, and peaked at about 80 per cent in 1973. Welfare receipt then fell to about 50 per cent in 1982, before rising to 63 per cent in 1992 (US House of Representatives 1985: 212; 1994: 399). In contrast, almost all other industrialized countries provide a child allowance for all children and more generous income-tested transfers to a greater percentage of poor children (Smeeding, 1992).

A smaller percentage of poor children were removed from poverty by government benefits in the mid-1990s than in the early 1970s. Economic changes increased the number of poor children, and programme changes left fewer eligible to receive benefits: state governments allowed cash welfare benefits to be eroded by inflation in the late 1970s, and rule changes and budget cuts in the early 1980s made it more difficult for the unemployed to receive unemployment insurance (UI) and more difficult for welfare recipients to combine earnings and cash assistance.

Eligibility for unemployment insurance in the USA is based on one's work history, and receipt is time-limited, typically twenty-six weeks. Therefore, some of the unemployed are not eligible because of insufficient work history or have been unemployed for more than twenty-six weeks. In a typical year over 1955–93, about 45 per cent of the unemployed received benefits, a much lower rate than in Western Europe.

The political economy of UI changed dramatically during the Reagan era. In response to a severe recession in the mid-1970s, Congress instituted a programme of extended benefits. As a result, the number of unemployed receiving benefits shot up to about 75 per cent in 1975 (Figure 7.1). The recession of the early 1980s was more severe, but the Reagan Administration restricted the UI programme and benefit receipt fell to the historical low of 30 per cent. In response to the recession of the early 1990s, Congress once again instituted a temporary extension of benefits, so that about 50 per cent of the unemployed received benefits.

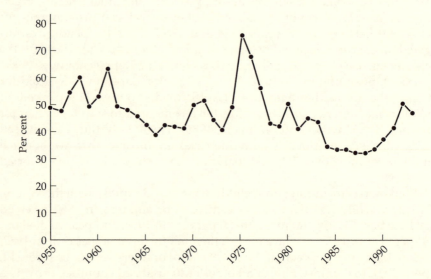

Fig. 7.1 Unemployed Workers Covered by Unemployment Insurance, 1955–1993
Source: Nichols and Shapiro (1995).

Table 7.3: Poverty Rates and the Antipoverty Impact of Cash Transfers for Persons Living in Families with Children, Selected Years, 1967–1992 (percentages)

	Pre-transfer poverty	Pre-welfare poverty	Official poverty	Per cent of pre-transfer poor persons removed from poverty by:	
				Cash social insurance	Cash public assistance
	(1)	(2)	(3)	(4)[a]	(5)[b]
Non-elderly male head					
1967	11.5	10.3	10.0	10.4	2.6
1969	9.1	8.0	7.5	12.1	5.5
1974	9.8	8.0	7.4	18.4	6.1
1979	9.6	7.8	7.2	18.8	6.3
1984	12.3	10.3	9.7	16.5	5.2
1989	10.7	9.4	8.9	11.9	5.3
1992	12.5	10.6	10.0	14.8	5.4
Non-elderly female head					
1967	58.8	52.4	49.1	10.9	5.6
1969	61.0	54.4	48.5	10.8	9.7
1974	59.6	53.1	46.5	10.9	11.1
1979	53.5	48.6	43.3	9.2	9.9
1984	55.6	51.4	47.9	7.5	6.3
1989	52.0	49.1	46.8	5.5	4.4
1992	56.1	53.1	49.9	5.4	5.5

[a] Cash social insurance transfers include social security, railroad retirement, unemployment compensation, government employee pensions, and veterans' pensions and compensation. Defined as ((col. 2 − col. 1)/column 1 × 100). [b] Cash public assistance includes aid to families with dependent children, supplemental security income, and general assistance. Defined as ((column 3 − column 2)/column 1 × 100). The total antipoverty effect of cash transfers is the sum of cols. 4 and 5.

Source: Computations by authors from March Current Population Survey computer tapes.

Table 7.3 shows the trends in poverty and the antipoverty impacts of major cash income transfer programmes. The antipoverty impacts are measured by the percentage of all pre-transfer poor persons that are removed from poverty by these programmes. The calculations are sequential, so that all social insurance benefits are first added to pre-transfer incomes, yielding the pre-welfare poverty rate in column 2. Welfare transfers are then added, yielding the official poverty rate in column 3. Poverty rates are almost five times higher for persons in female-headed than in male-headed families. None the less, the poverty trends are similar: declines from the late 1960s to the late 1970s, and increases thereafter.

The 1992 rate was virtually identical to the 1967 rate for each type of family.

Cash social insurance transfers removed a greater percentage of the pre-transfer poor from poverty in all years than did public assistance transfers because more of the pre-transfer poor received them and because the average social insurance benefit was higher. Column 5 of Table 7.3 shows that the decline since the 1970s in the antipoverty effect of cash public assistance (welfare) for female-headed families with children has been very large. Thus, even if a progressive reform of welfare and child support policies could be enacted (discussed below), the antipoverty effect of the American welfare state would likely remain one of the least effective among industrialized countries (Smeeding, 1992; McFate, Smeeding, and Rainwater, 1995).

Since the late 1960s, male-headed families have received higher amounts than female-headed families (Figure 7.2). This result follows for several reasons. First, the typical social insurance benefit is based on a fixed percentage of past earnings. Thus, average benefits for men exceed those for women because men's average wages are higher. Second, women are more likely to receive welfare benefits, which are not conditioned on previous labour force experience, and are less generous than

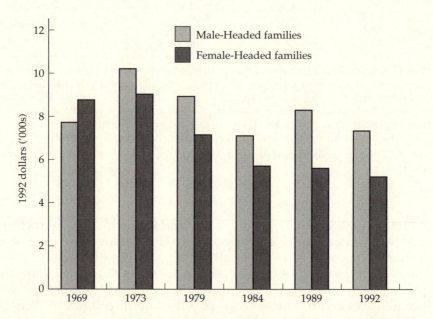

Fig. 7.2 Families with Children: Mean Cash Transfers Pre-Transfer Poor Recipients (1992 $)

Source: Computations by authors from Current Population Survey Computer tapes.

social insurance benefits.[3] Figure 7.2 also shows a dramatic decline in the average cash benefit (in constant 1992 dollars) received by poor families from all programmes after 1973. For male-headed families, the decline was from about $10,000 to about $7,500 in 1992; for those headed by females, from about $9,000 to about $5,000.

After 1973, rising unemployment, declining male earnings, and stagnating family incomes raised poverty by more than social spending could reduce it. Families with children received diminished cash transfers and were most affected by the changing labour market conditions—stagnant wages, rising inequality of earnings, higher relative unemployment rates for the young and least skilled (Smolensky *et al.*, 1988).

7.2.5. *Trends in personal income taxes*

Low-income families have also been treated poorly by the tax system. The trend in the post-tax position of the poor was even worse than pre-tax trends due to increasing personal taxes during 1975–86. In 1975, a four-person family with earnings equal to the poverty line paid 1.3 per cent of its earnings in personal taxes; by 1986, 10.4 per cent.

The Tax Reform Act of 1986 did eliminate federal income taxes for most poor families with children; it also lowered all marginal tax rates and broadened the tax base by reducing tax preferences. Additional changes beneficial to working poor families were passed in 1990 and 1993. By 1996, a family of four with earnings at the poverty line will have after-tax income that is 8.6 per cent higher than its earnings. This will represent a shift of about 20 per cent of earnings between 1986 and 1996.[4]

Despite these pro-poor changes, the federal tax system was less progressive in 1990 than in the mid-1970s for two main reasons (see Pechman, 1990 and US House of Representatives, 1990*b* for a detailed discussion). First, social security (payroll) taxes have risen relative to income taxes. While income tax is mildly progressive, the social security tax is mostly proportional with respect to earnings but regressive with respect to family income. Second, the income taxes of the very rich have been cut much more than have those of other taxpayers. In 1981, wealthy taxpayers faced a marginal tax rate of 50 per cent on earnings and 70 per cent on property income; in 1994, their marginal rate was 36 per cent on all income sources

[3] For example, maximum monthly unemployment benefits in 1994 for a married worker with two children who earned $9.00 per hour, somewhat less than the average wage, ranged from $568 per month in the lowest-benefit state to $1,360 per month in the highest (US House of Representatives 1994: 286–7). On the other hand, cash welfare (Aid to Families with Dependent Children) benefits for a family of four in 1994 were $435 in the median state and ranged from only $144 to $792 per month (excluding Alaska and Hawaii, ibid.: 368–9).

[4] In 1995, the Republican Congress proposed scaling back the Earned Income Tax Credit as part of its plan to reduce the budget deficit and cut taxes for middle- and upper-income families. If this were to become law, some of the gains of the poor via the income tax would be scaled back.

(the very few taxpayers with annual income above $250,000 were subject to a 39.6 per cent rate). The effective tax rate paid by the richest 5 per cent of families fell by about one-fifth and that of the richest 1 per cent by more than one-third between the early 1970s and late 1980s (Pechman, 1990).

7.3. Family Structure, Family Size, and Child Poverty

Children's economic well-being has also been negatively affected by changes in family structure. The rising percentage of children living in mother-only families and the shift from ever-married to never-married single mothers tend to increase child poverty, as illustrated by Table 7.4.

Several trends stand out. First, for every race/ethnic and family structure group shown, the poverty rate fell rapidly between 1949 and 1969. Second, while overall child poverty was about the same in 1979 as in 1969, the rates fell somewhat for almost every married couple and single-mother group. Third, poverty increased for all children and for almost all the demographic groups during the 1980s, despite the 1983–9 economic recovery. Fourth, there are large differences in poverty rates when children are classified by the race, as well as by the gender, of the heads of their families.

In 1989, about 6 per cent of white non-Hispanic children living in two-parent families were poor, a rate substantially lower than that of all persons or all elderly persons. The highest poverty rates were those for children living in single-mother families, which remained as high as the

Table 7.4: Trends in Poverty among Children by Family Type (percentages)

Race/ethnicity and family structure	Poverty rate				
	1949	1959	1969	1979	1989
All children[a]	47.6	26.1	15.6	15.5	17.7
White, Non-Hispanic families	41.2	18.8	10.4	9.9	10.9
Married-couple families	39.3	16.9	7.7	6.5	6.4
Mother-only families	73.1	57.7	44.0	36.3	39.6
Black, Non-Hispanic families	87.0	63.3	41.1	37.1	39.7
Married-couple families	85.7	57.9	29.0	18.2	15.2
Mother-only families	93.4	84.4	67.9	62.1	64.6
Hispanic families	73.0	53.3	33.3	29.6	32.5
Married-couple families	71.6	51.3	28.8	20.6	23.4
Mother-only families	92.4	74.3	64.3	65.9	62.7

[a] For 1949–69, 0–14-year-old children are included; for 1979 and 1989, 0–18-year-old children are included.

Source: Computations by authors from the Public Use Microdata Samples of the 1950, 1960, 1970, 1980, and 1990 Decennial Censuses.

rate for all children in the late 1940s! The poverty rate in the early 1990s for all children was as high as that in the late 1960s.

The disaggregation in Table 7.4 describes trends, but it does not identify their determinants. The data are consistent with divergent interpretations. The stability in the poverty rate for all black children, for example, obscures drops in poverty for each family type. In an accounting sense, the stability in the overall rate is due to the increased *percentage* of black children living in mother-only families. Poverty-increasing demographic changes appear to have offset poverty-reducing economic change.

These facts do not suggest a unique policy response. On the one hand, the increase in mother-only families might have been caused by adverse economic conditions which might have increased marriage avoidance and divorce among black males and reduced their ability to support their children (Wilson, 1987, 1995). In this case, demographic and economic trends are not independent. Policy responses should then attempt to reduce male joblessness and raise earnings (ibid.).

In contrast, other analysts attribute rising out-of-wedlock child-bearing and single motherhood to moral and behavioural deficiencies and male irresponsibility. According to this view, jobs are available, but 'the jobless are shielded from a need to urgently seek work by government benefits, or by the earnings of other family members' (Mead, 1988, 1992). Indeed, the decline in child poverty among black children in two-parent families reflects declining labour market discrimination and shows that, if parents were to stay married and remain in the labour force, then the poverty problem would be much less important. Child poverty is thus attributed not to economic difficulties, but to attitudinal and family problems. Remedies include moral suasion, a reduction of welfare, and the enforcement of work and child support obligations (Novak *et al.*, 1987).

Of course, few scholars believe that either of these polar views can fully explain the observed trends in child poverty and living arrangements. A less extreme variation of each could account for part of the changes. However, the interrelationships among labour market conditions, government programme regulations, and individual decisions regarding work behaviour, welfare recipiency, marriage, and child-bearing are very complex.

Given this caveat, we report the results of one study which attempted to measure the effects of demographic factors on child poverty (Gottschalk and Danziger, 1993). Table 7.5 shows the distribution of children by family structure and size in 1968 and 1992. Over this period, the percentage of both black and white children living with two parents declined and there was a large drop in the number of children per family for both races and types of families.

Table 7.6 shows the child poverty rate for children using the family classification of Table 7.5. In each year, child poverty in two-parent fam-

Table 7.5: Distribution of Children by Family Type and Number of Children per Family (percentages)

Family structure/no. of children per family	Black women		White women	
	1968	1992	1968	1992
Husband–wife family	67.8	41.3	93.1	83.8
One	6.4	7.9	12.3	17.0
Two	11.6	14.7	24.9	37.3
Three	11.9	11.1	23.3	19.9
Four or more	37.9	7.7	32.6	9.7
Mother-only family	32.3	58.7	7.1	16.2
One	2.7	11.4	1.3	5.3
Two	4.7	16.3	1.8	6.8
Three	5.2	13.8	1.5	2.9
Four or more	19.7	17.1	2.5	1.2
All children[a]	100.0	100.0	100.0	100.0
Weighted number, millions	8.3	9.6	57.6	43.4

[a] Totals may not sum to 100.0 because of rounding. Each child in a family in which a woman under the age of 55 is a spouse or family head is counted once. The data are weighted to reflect only that population, among black and white non-Hispanics.

Source: Computations by authors from March 1969 and March 1993 Current Population Survey computer tapes.

Table 7.6: Poverty Rate for Children, by Family Type and Number of Children per Family (percentages)

Family structure/no. of children per family[a]	Black women		White women	
	1968	1992	1968	1992
Husband–wife family				
One	8.4	10.2	3.1	3.4
Two	12.9	12.8	3.6	5.1
Three	18.9	19.4	5.5	10.7
Four or more	38.0	35.8	13.2	15.2
Mother-only family				
One	43.3	41.8	21.6	32.9
Two	54.2	57.4	29.1	37.1
Three	66.1	72.9	47.1	59.8
Four or more	82.6	92.7	61.9	83.2
All children	42.1	47.6	9.9	13.1

[a] Each child in a family in which a woman under the age of 55 is a spouse or family head is counted once. The data are weighted to reflect only that population, among black and white non-Hispanics.

Sources: Computations by authors from March 1969 and March 1993 Current Population Survey computer tapes.

ilies is much lower than in single-mother families. A husband-wife family with four or more children is less likely to be poor than a mother-only family with only one child. Thus, the shift in family structure away from married-couple families was poverty-increasing, while the reduction in the number of children per family was poverty-decreasing. The small changes in poverty for all children (Table 7.6) were thus due to the large, but offsetting, impacts of several demographic and economic changes. By far, the major poverty-increasing factor was the increase in mother-only families. However, poverty-reducing declines in the number of children per woman and increased education almost exactly offset the single-parent effect. If single parenthood and income inequality had not increased, child poverty would have been much lower. However, without the decline in family size and increased educational attainment of women, child poverty rates today would be substantially higher.

7.4. The Consequences of Poverty

Figure 7.3 shows how changes in the economy and public policies have contributed to increased poverty. The increased economic hardship and changes in social norms regarding marriage, non-marital sex, and child-bearing are also shown as having independent effects on family structure (Jencks, 1992). Poverty and economic hardship and the rise in mother-only families then affect a variety of child outcomes, which, in turn, influence the well-being of the next generation.

Child problems among the poor tend to be associated with familial as well as economic hardships. In the figure, the increase in mother-only families is shown as both the cause and the consequence of poverty and economic hardship (Garfinkel and McLanahan, 1986; Ellwood and Crane, 1990). In turn, family composition and family income have independent effects on children's outcomes.

The highlighted box in Figure 7.3 denotes those domains in which deficits are more likely among the poor (Huston, 1991 and Children's Defense Fund, 1994). By many measures (as discussed below) and across several stages of childhood, poor children are at greater risk. Economically disadvantaged children are more likely to suffer from congenital problems, reduced access to medical care, inadequate parental attention, and to live in environments that are hazardous to their safety and their cognitive and physical development (Schorr, 1988; Children's Defense Fund, 1994).

Marital disruption or living with a single parent is associated with developmental, emotional, and academic difficulties (Cherlin *et al.*, 1991), though it is not easy to determine the process by which they affect children (McLanahan and Sandefur, 1994). For our purposes, it is sufficient to

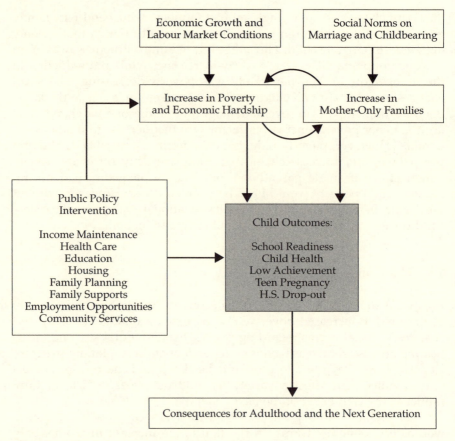

Fig. 7.3   Poverty and Outcomes: The Cycle of Risk

note that children from poor families and from single-mother families are more vulnerable as they develop.

Vulnerability that begins early, in turn, affects adolescent outcomes. While growing up in an affluent, two-parent family does not grant a child immunity from teenage pregnancy, juvenile delinquency, substance abuse, and high school drop-out, these problems are much more common among the disadvantaged.

The chances of being poor as an adult are over three times greater for children who experience poverty compared to those who were never poor (Hill *et al.*, 1985; Corcoran, 1995). Their reduced earnings capacity, skill level, and employment opportunities undermine their own chances of providing a secure future for their children. Furthermore, those whose early misfortunes are confounded by high school drop-out and/or teen-age pregnancy are more likely to become poor adults, less likely to marry, and more likely to rely on welfare, and to have children who also drop out of school or become parents as teens (for instance, Furstenberg *et al.*, 1987).

7.4.1. How poverty affects children

Parker *et al.* (1988) use the term 'double jeopardy' to describe the process by which poor children suffer a higher incidence of these adverse health and developmental outcomes. Poor children are more likely to be exposed to negative risk factors, and, the effects of these risks tend to be greatest for poor children. The most significant risk factors are the following:

1. *Stress.* The poor encounter more frequent stressful events, including housing problems, financial difficulties, and the death of a relative or friend, and more chronic family stress. Stress is particularly high among poor women with young children (Parker *et al.*, 1988; McLoyd *et al.*, 1994). Poverty tends to erode the ability to handle new problems. Because of this, the poor are more likely to have mental health problems after experiencing negative life events (McLoyd, 1990).

Increased stress interferes with a mother's ability to respond appropriately to her infant. Children from highly stressed environments are at an increased risk of developmental and behavioural problems, including poor performance on developmental and IQ tests, impaired early language development, poorer emotional adjustment, and greater school problems (Bee *et al.*, 1986).

2. *Inadequate social support.* Poor homes are typically associated with isolation from society, inadequate social support networks, and social isolation (Cochrane and Brassard, 1979). Some poor families move often and may have few community attachments.

Social support has both indirect and direct effects on children. Stressed parents with emotional support and friendships, material assistance, and help with child care tend to parent better. A good social network for the parent gives the young child contact with a larger world. A well-supported and connected household provides cognitive and social stimulation and greater emotional support.

3. *Maternal depression and mental-emotional illness.* Maternal depression and socio-economic status are also correlated (poor adults have more mental problems than do the non-poor). Maternal depression has been linked to adverse child outcomes, such as lower birth weights, more accidents, failure to thrive, more surgical procedures, sleep problems, childhood depression, attention deficit disorder, socially isolating behaviour at school, and withdrawn and defiant behaviour in adolescence (Parker *et al.*, 1988).

We now examine in greater detail how poor children fare relative to non-poor children for selected childhood outcomes.

7.4.2. *Infant mortality and low birth weight*

Although the infant mortality rate (IMR) has been declining for decades (Table 7.7), the US rate has not fallen as rapidly as in other developed countries (see Chapter 1 of this volume). The periods of rapid decline were the 1940s and 1970s. The IMR continued to fall in the 1980s, but at a slower pace. In the 1950–5 period, the USA IMR ranked sixth among twenty industrialized nations, but by the late 1980s it ranked last (10.6) far behind Japan (5.2), Finland (5.8), and Sweden (5.8), nations which in the early 1950s had IMRs 1.5 to 2.5 times higher than the USA (Rosenbaum, 1989).

The IMR for black Americans declined from 72.9 in 1940 to 17.6 in 1991, but their rate has usually been about twice that of whites (Table 7.7). There is also great variation in IMR across states and metropolitan areas. The IMR for whites in some states, about 7.0 in Massachusetts and Minnesota, compares quite favourably with that of industrialized countries with the lowest rates. Similarly, the highest metropolitan area IMRs for blacks, about 25.0 in Washington, DC, Detroit, and Philadelphia, are as high as those in some developing countries. These large variations by race and across geographic areas reflect wide disparities in income, access to medical care, and other aspects of the social environment.

Change in the IMR over time depends on economic conditions, but also on access to health care. Social programmes designed to improve maternal and child health were responsible for a substantial portion of the post-World War II declines (Starfield, 1988), especially improvements in after-birth care, nutrition, and housing conditions. There was a downturn

Table 7.7:   Infant Mortality Rates, by Race,[a] 1940–1991 (deaths prior to the age of one per 1,000 live births)

Year	Black	White	Total	Ratio Black to White
1940	72.9	43.2	47.0	1.69
1950	43.9	26.8	29.2	1.64
1960	44.3	22.9	26.0	1.93
1965	41.7	21.5	24.7	1.94
1970	32.6	17.8	20.0	1.83
1975	26.2	14.2	16.1	1.85
1980	21.4	11.0	12.5	1.95
1985	18.2	9.3	10.6	1.96
1990	18.0	7.6	9.2	2.37
1991	17.6	7.3	8.9	2.41

[a] As of 1989, race for live births is tabulated by race of mother; for prior years, by race of child.

Source: National Center for Health Statistics, *Advance Report of Final Mortality Statistics, 1991, Monthly Vital Statistics Report*, 42/2, US Dept. of Health and Human Services, Hyattsville, Maryland, 1993.

Table 7.8:   Births to Women Obtaining Late or No Prenatal Care
(percentage of all births)

Risk factors	1975			1990		
	White	Black	All	White	Black	All
Selected ages:						
Under 15	21.1	18.8	19.8	20.9	19.9	20.3
15–19	10.6	13.9	11.7	10.6	14.6	11.9
20–24	5.8	10.2	6.8	6.9	12.0	8.0
Marital status:						
Married	3.9	7.5	4.4	3.2	5.8	3.5
Unmarried	18.9	13.6	16.2	11.7	14.1	12.8
Completed schooling:						
0–8 years	13.6	14.4	14.4	16.2	17.3	16.0
9–11	8.6	10.2	10.2	10.6	16.7	12.2
12	3.2	4.2	4.2	4.3	10.7	5.6
Over 12	1.6	2.1	2.1	1.6	5.5	2.2
All births	4.9	10.4	6.1	4.9	11.3	6.1

Source: National Center for Health Statistics as reported in US House of Representatives (1993), 1153.

in IMRs after 1965, when Medicaid greatly expanded access of the poor to prenatal and other medical services. The post-1973 downturn can be attributed to the increased availability of legalized abortion, including confidential access for adolescents.

The mid-1980s were characterized by relative stagnation in IMRs, despite economic recovery, in part because poverty remained higher than in the 1970s and in part because of continuing inadequacies in access to medical services. For example, in 1983, only 75 per cent of pregnant white women and 50 per cent of pregnant black women had the minimum nine prenatal visits recommended by medical experts (Collins, 1989). Table 7.8 shows the percentage of babies born to mothers who obtain no care or receive care only during the last trimester of pregnancy. Wide disparities were present in both 1975 and 1990 across those factors which are correlated with poverty—race, age of mother, marital status, and education.

Low birth weight (LBW), a major contributor to infant death, could be reduced by better prenatal care. Seventy-five per cent of all neonatal mortality is associated with LBW, whereas most post-neonatal deaths occur among babies of normal birth weight. While neonatal death-rates are most sensitive to technological changes, death-rates among infants later in the first year of life are more responsive to the social environment and to access to medical services. In fact, some portion of the drop in infant mortality that began in the late 1960s may have been due to a fall in

LBW incidence. This was a period of great technological progress in the treatment of LBW infants: survival rates increased and severe disability among survivors was reduced (Collins, 1989). The incidence of LBW has remained fairly stable over the past fifteen years. Low maternal education, unemployment, lack of health insurance, and poverty are important correlates (Stein *et al.*, 1987; Wise *et al.*, 1985).

7.4.3. Child health and development

Child health, like IMR, shows long-run improvements for all children, but persisting disadvantages for the poor. The incidence of preventable diseases, injuries, hospitalization, malnutrition, and lead poisoning have all declined over the past fifty years (Klerman, 1991). However, the USA lags behind other industrialized nations with regard to these child health indicators. It ranks fifth to seventh (depending on the particular age and gender group) among seven advanced nations on child death-rates due to accidents or injuries, and fourth or fifth on child deaths from medical causes (Starfield, 1994).

On most indicators, poor children fare worse than non-poor children. For example, low-income children are more than three times as likely to die from all causes as other children (Children's Defense Fund, 1994). Disparities were particularly large for deaths due to motor-vehicle, fire, and drowning accidents, homicide, perinatal conditions, infectious and parasitic diseases. Income status was not a significant factor in child deaths from cancers or suicide (ibid., 66). National surveys document that poor children are more likely to suffer from asthma and bronchitis, inadequate nutrition, physical growth retardation, mental and emotional problems, cognitive and intellectual delays, and limitations of daily activities due to chronic conditions (Klerman, 1991). Poor preschool-aged children were more likely to have a deficient intake of ten of sixteen nutrients. These deficiencies are correlated with physical and cognitive developmental delays (Cook and Martin, 1995).

Poor children experience a larger incidence of reported child abuse and neglect as well as higher rates of hospitalization (Klerman, 1991). In a 1991 national survey, poor children were absent from school 6.4 days compared to 4.9 days for non-poor children; 64 per cent of the former were reported to be in excellent or very good health compared with 87 per cent of the latter (Starfield, 1994, table 4).

Korenman *et al.* (1995) found large differences in socio-emotional and cognitive development between children who grew up in long-term poverty and those who grew up in the middle class.[5] Poor children scored 5.3

---

[5] In addition to controlling for economic status, other controls included mother's cognitive test score, marital status, education, smoking or drinking behaviour during pregnancy, and other socio-economic variables.

points lower on a vocabulary test, 5.9 points lower on a mathematics test, and 6.0 points lower on a reading test. These are large differences—about 15 per cent of the mean scores of this national sample of children. Similar results were found in a longitudinal study of IQ among low birth weight babies (Duncan *et al.*, 1994).

7.4.4. School achievement and attainment

Poor children are more likely to have low grades, poor attendance, negative attitudes towards school, and higher drop-out rates. Wolfe (1990) concludes that poor children are three times more likely to drop out of high school than are prosperous children, and that each year a child is poor reduces her probability of graduation by nearly 1 per cent.

Although poor children complete fewer years of schooling, successive generations across the income spectrum have completed more years of education than their parents (Mare, 1995). Differences in educational attainment between men and women, among race and ethnic groups, and across income classes have narrowed substantially over the past fifty years. In fact, women in the most recent cohorts have equalled or surpassed men in college attendance and graduation (ibid.). For people born in the 1960s, college attendance rates vary from less than 20 per cent for foreign-born Hispanics to 70 per cent for native-born Asian-Americans. About one-half of whites and one-third of blacks attend college at some time (ibid.)

Between the late 1960s and early 1990s, the percentage of 18–24-year-olds who were not enrolled and had not completed high school fell from about 19 to 14 per cent (US House of Representatives, 1993). Table 7.9 shows that poor children are more than twice as likely as middle-class children to drop out and more than ten times as likely as children of the rich.

Hill and Sandfort (1995) reviewed fourteen studies of the effects of parental income on numerous educational outcomes—completed years of

Table 7.9: 16–24-Year-Olds, Not in School and Not High School Graduates, October 1992 (percentages)

	Poorest quintile	Middle three quintiles	Wealthiest quintile	All youth
All Youth	24.6	10.1	2.3	11.0
White	19.0	7.9	1.9	7.7
Black	24.0	9.6	0.8	13.7
Hispanic	44.7	25.2	9.6	29.4

Source: Children's Defense Fund (1994), 81.

schooling, grade point average, receipt of special education, high school graduation, college entry, and so on. In thirteen studies, parents' education and income were positively related to the child's achievement.

7.4.5. Adolescent child-bearing

The daughters of the poor are more likely than those of the non-poor to become young single parents, thereby reproducing child poverty in the next generation. Teen parents are less likely to marry and to complete high school, less likely to have good employment prospects, and more likely to have long spells of poverty and welfare dependency than women who delay child-bearing into their twenties (Furstenberg, 1995; Maynard, 1995).

Adolescent child-bearing is much more common in the USA than in other industrialized countries. Part of this differential is attributable to the higher US poverty rates and explains part of the racial differentials in early child-bearing. Some of the differential is attributable to inadequacies in the family planning system; in particular, to the fact that teenagers have less access to contraceptives than teens in countries with national health insurance systems. Around 1990, the US adolescent birth-rate, 62 per 1,000, was twice that of the next highest country (Table 7.10). The rank orderings, incidentally, are similar to the rank orderings of the child poverty rate. The English-speaking nations, USA, UK, Canada, and Australia, have much higher rates than Northern and Western Europe.

The birth-rate to unmarried 15–19-year-old women doubled from 22 to 45 per 1,000 between 1970 and 1991. The rates were much lower, but the pace of increase was higher, for white than black single women: the rate

Table 7.10: Adolescent Birth-Rates[a] (births per 1,000 women, 15–19 years of age)

USA, Total	62	Norway	17
Whites	43	Sweden	13
Blacks	118	Spain	13
Hispanics	107	Italy	10
UK	33	France	9
Canada	26	Denmark	9
Austria	23	Netherlands	8
Australia	22	Japan	4

[a] All data are for 1991, except Canada, Australia, and Denmark (1990), Spain (1989), and Italy (1988).

Sources: Child Trends, Inc., *Facts at a Glance*, Jan. 1994 and Feb. 1995.

for whites tripled from 11 to 32 per 1,000; that for blacks increased from 97 to 113 per 1,000.

Early sexual activity and teen pregnancies have increased for all income classes and racial and ethnic groups. Yet, early child-bearing is more common among poor adolescents and girls living in poor neighbour-hoods (S. K. Danziger, 1995). Like the double jeopardy of poverty for child health, teenage childbirth is influenced by both family processes and structural or environmental factors, such as lack of parental supervision, inadequate educational environments, poor future employment pros-pects, and limited access to reproductive health services.

7.5. Reducing Poverty in America

7.5.1. *The goals of an antipoverty agenda*

If America is to reduce child poverty to the level achieved by most Western industrialized nations, it must implement a comprehensive antipoverty agenda. Sawhill (1988) suggests that such an agenda should be built on the assumption that, first, parents must take greater responsi-bility for children through increased work by single-mother families and increased child support by absent fathers and, second, the public sector must offer greater employment and educational opportunities so that the poor will be able to transform their efforts into higher incomes.

The War on Poverty was based on the belief that both the initial endow-ments brought to the market by the disadvantaged and how those endow-ments were compensated were adversely affected by labour market imperfections. We believe these assumptions are still correct thirty years later, despite the fact that they are now out of political favour.

Social solidarity is a concept that is mostly unknown in America. In-stead, two decades of slow growth and rising inequality have reinforced the individualistic belief that anyone who works hard can get ahead and that those who do not are personally responsible for their plight. Most Americans believe that the falling wages of less educated workers and the slow growth in the living standards of the middle class are unconnected to the economic problems of the working poor, the unemployed, and welfare recipients. The problems of the former are blamed on a government that 'taxes *us* too much' and the problems of the latter are blamed on a govern-ment that 'gives *them* too much'. The politics of the day support tax cuts for the rich and the middle class and spending cuts for the working poor and welfare recipients. If we are correct, however, that the American dream has withered for millions of families because of structural changes in the labour market, then the current attack on the welfare state will only exacerbate poverty and inequality.

In this section, we look beyond current politics and advocate policies for the longer-run that would both raise the endowments that children will bring to the labour market in the coming decades and—at the same time—raise the current incomes of poor families to offset immediate hardship. Because there is relatively little, however, that government can do to raise the productivity of today's least skilled mature workers, it is necessary to focus on income supplementation policies. Consider, for example, a 45-year-old without a high school diploma who works full time at a wage which is too low to raise his/her family above the poverty line in a job which does not provide health insurance. Wage supplements, subsidized medical care, and early education for his/her children may increase the educational attainment of the next generation, even if nothing is done to raise the earnings of the family head directly.

According to Murnane (1988):

> [T]he roots of the low achievement of many American children lie in the circumstances of poverty in which they live. Consequently, educational policy changes not accompanied by policies that significantly reduce the poverty will have only modest influences on their academic achievements.

In other words, direct service strategies should raise the health and attainment and, hence, productivity of the young, while policies that alleviate poverty would make it easier for the children to remain in school and benefit more from education and training programmes, and thus reduce the poverty of subsequent generations.

7.5.2. Income supplements

Policies to supplement earnings for the working poor and to provide work opportunities for the non-working poor would offset some of the economic hardship being generated by the labour market. The poor have not rejected the labour market; rather, employers have rejected many less skilled, less experienced workers who are willing to work, even for low wages. The public sector should ensure that every family has at least one full-time worker earning the minimum wage. These families would then be able to escape poverty via additional income supplements that subsidize their access to child care and medical care.

Additional income supplements would build on the recent expansion of the Earned Income Tax Credit (EITC), a refundable tax credit targeted on low-income families with children that has become the largest income supplementation programme for the working poor. The EITC has been politically popular because it assists only those who work; it helps two-parent as well as single-parent families; and it raises the employee's take-home pay without increasing labour costs. The EITC was introduced in 1975 and expanded in 1986, 1990, and 1993. By 1996, for every dollar earned by the poorest families, the EITC will provide an additional 40 cents up to a maximum of $3,560 (more than 20 per cent of the poverty line for a family of four). The credit is reduced as incomes approach the poverty line and is phased out at about twice the poverty line.

The Dependent Care Credit (DCC) in the federal income tax allows working single parents and couples to partially offset work-related child-care costs. Because the credit is not refundable and because the Tax Reform Act of 1986 eliminated the income tax liability of many of the poor, only a minimal percentage of this tax relief is received by poor and low-income families. On the other hand, higher-income taxpayers receive credits of up to $960. Given the high cost of child care, and the fact that it consumes a substantial proportion of the earnings of many low-income families, the maximum subsidy rate (now 30 per cent) should be raised for the poorest families and the DCC should be made refundable. Subsidizing child care for the working poor is much more popular than government provision of day care because it minimizes government intervention in parental choices.

While federal taxation of the poor has been reduced in the last decade, a family of four at the poverty line is exempt from taxation in only ten of the forty states with a broad-based personal income tax (Gold, 1987). State tax relief for the poor remains an important priority. States could expand assistance to the working poor by adopting earned income credits in their own income taxes, as six states have done in the early 1990s.

Additional income supplements are necessary for mother-only families. The Child Support Assurance System (Garfinkel 1988, 1992) would target all children in single-parent families and would reduce poverty and welfare dependency through increased parental support. Uniform child support awards would be financed by a percentage-of-income tax on the absent parent. If this amount is less than a fixed minimum level because the absent parent's income is too low, the support payment would be supplemented up to the minimum by government funds.

These income supplementation measures would reduce poverty for those whose incomes are already close to the poverty line. More attention also needs to be focused on raising the wages of those whose earned income remains low. The ratio of the minimum wage to the average wage is much lower in the USA than in other industrialized countries which have legislated minima, or than the ratio of customary entry level wages to average wages in countries without legal minimum wages. The US minimum wage is not indexed to inflation; rather, it is dependent on periodic legislative adjustments. From 1950 to 1980, Congress typically increased the minimum wage at least every five years. However, during the eight Reagan Administration years, it remained at its 1981 level ($3.35 per hour) until it was increased to $3.80 (or 38 per cent of average earnings) in 1990 and $4.25 in 1991. To restore the minimum wage to its real

1978 level would require an increase to about $6.00 per hour in 1995. President Clinton proposed an increase to $5.15 (in two steps) early in 1995, but the issue was not considered by the Republican majority in Congress.

7.5.3. Employment opportunities

More attention must also be focused on bringing the non-working poor into the labour market. In the mid-1980s, many state-level experiments with welfare-to-work programmes were put into place. Most provide increased training, employment, and social services to long-term non-working welfare recipients (Gueron and Pauly, 1991). Once recipients are working, it is hoped that they can escape poverty through a combination of increased child support and access to transitional child care, health care, employment, and training services, as well as the other income supplements discussed here.

Most of the working poor, however, do not receive welfare, which is restricted primarily to mother-only families. Given the public's preference for work relative to cash assistance, the demand for low-skilled workers should be increased by establishing a low-wage job-of-last-resort open to all poor adults.

Public service employment (PSE) was eliminated by the Reagan Administration and remains politically unpopular. Two major complaints with the programme in the 1970s were that it was expensive and that PSE workers merely replaced other public employees. We think that a PSE programme for low-skilled workers can avoid these problems. Costs could be held down by providing low-wage jobs that might pay 10–15 per cent below the minimum wage so as to encourage movement into available minimum-wage private-sector jobs. Displacement of other workers could be minimized by requiring that PSE workers be employed in areas where services are not currently provided. These jobs would provide the safety net for poor persons who want to work, but are left behind by the private labour market.

7.5.4. Direct services

Direct service policies intervene in the cycle of risk to offset the negative consequences associated with child poverty. A number of interventions have improved child health, cognitive development, and educational outcomes. These measures may focus on families, children, or community institutions and have often produced promising results, though government funding restrictions have prevented their adoption on a wider scale.

Indeed, public health injury prevention initiatives reduce child deaths from environmental hazards (Klerman, 1991); federal nutrition programmes improve pregnancy and birth outcomes and child health; programmes promoting access to prenatal care for teen mothers and poor women reduce the incidence of low birth weight and increase participation in nutrition and other service programmes (Seitz and Apfel, 1994). Early interventions with at-risk infants reduce developmental problems and improve cognitive development (Brooks-Gunn *et al.*, 1995); and early educational interventions with disadvantaged children increase IQ scores and academic achievement, with effects lasting into early adolescence (Campbell and Ramey, 1994).

Four key areas for expansion of direct service programmes are needed and, according to recent research, would improve child outcomes substantially:

1. *Prenatal care.* Many poor pregnant women, especially adolescents, receive inadequate prenatal care, either in terms of quality or the number of visits. Lack of health insurance is a major barrier, as are provider shortages in some geographic areas or provider unwillingness to serve the disadvantaged (Institute of Medicine, 1988). The Children's Defense Fund (Hughes *et al.*, 1989) estimates that each dollar spent on providing prenatal care to pregnant women saves up to nine dollars over the lifetime of a child. Thus, extending medical coverage to all poor and near-poor pregnant women and children would produce substantial public savings in the future.

2. *Child health.* Enacted in 1965, Medicaid is a joint federal–state public health insurance programme which reimburses health care professionals for services provided to eligible poor families and their children. All pregnancies and all children born after October 1983 whose families are below the official poverty line are eligible for Medicaid; coverage, however, varies substantially across states. Medicaid has had a positive effect on child health. In the 1960s, poor children were less likely to see a doctor and had a lower frequency of hospitalization than non-poor children, but their average length of stay was longer, suggesting that they were more in need of care. After Medicaid was instituted, the hospitalization rates and number of doctor visits for poor children became similar to those of non-poor children (Starfield, 1985).

Various factors mitigate Medicaid's effect on children's health. States differ in criteria for eligibility, services covered, reimbursement rates for physicians, and so on. One survey found that over 60 per cent of physicians in ten cities did not accept Medicaid patients because the fees paid were below their regular fees (Children's Defense Fund, 1994). Wolfe (1994) advocates basic universal health care for all pregnant women and all children (under age 19) as the first step toward national health care in the USA.

3. *Nutrition.* The Special Supplemental Food Program for Women, Infants and Children (WIC) provides cash grants to state governments to

supply food packets and vouchers to the poor. It also offers nutrition education and counselling in conjunction with health care to pregnant and breastfeeding mothers and to children up to age 5 in low-income families determined to be at special nutritional risk. The WIC programme, begun in 1972, was designed to be both preventive and therapeutic and to help reduce the number of low birth weight and unhealthy infants and young children.

The programme has been effective—the birth weights of children born to WIC recipients are 30 to 50 grams higher than those of children born to non-participating mothers, and teenage WIC recipients are less likely to bear LBW infants (Chelimsky, 1984; Klerman, 1991). The Children's Defense Fund reports that every dollar spent on WIC's preventive component decreases short-term hospital costs by three dollars. Despite the programme's effectiveness, WIC reached less than two-thirds of eligible women and children in the early 1990s (Carnegie Corporation, 1994). The gaps in WIC coverage are attributed to an absence in some areas of the health resources needed to meet legislative requirements and underfunding.

4. *Early childhood education.* Two federal programmes seek to reduce poverty's negative impact on educational achievement by improving the school-readiness and cognitive functioning of poor children: Head Start and Chapter 1 of the Education Consolidation and Improvement Act of 1981. In 1994, about 700,000 3- and 4-year-olds participated in Head Start at a cost of $3.3 billion dollars; in 1991, Chapter 1 supported instructional services to 5 million school-aged children at a cost of $6.1 billion (Murnane, 1994).

Head Start is designed to reduce later school failure by providing comprehensive education, health care, nutrition, and social services. Children attend preschool classes typically on a half-day schedule; active parent participation is encouraged. Health services include dental, nutrition, and mental health screenings. Head Start centres serve meals and offer or co-ordinate social services for the entire family. Chapter 1 funds compensatory education for disadvantaged children living in areas with high poverty rates. The local school districts decide which services they will provide.

While it has been difficult to assess the long-term effects of Head Start and Chapter 1, many analysts advocate an expansion to all eligible children, approximately twice the number served in the early 1990s (Barnett, 1993; Currie and Thomas, 1994; Murnane, 1994).

7.6. Summary

The income supplementation, employment, and direct service programme expansions that we advocate would be expensive and come at a time when the majority in Congress is intent on cutting back the scope of the welfare state. Yet, the research suggests that such spending cuts will merely raise the future costs associated with child poverty. Our proposals could be financed in part through higher taxes on the non-poor, whose marginal tax rates are well below those in other industrialized countries and well below what they were during the long economic boom following World War II.

The poor have benefited relatively little from economic recovery because of changes in the structure of the economy that have adversely affected their incomes and because of inattention to their plight. Adoption of the policies proposed here could reduce the child poverty rate; maintenance of the *status quo* will subject another generation of children to lives of hardship and unrealized potential.

8

Child Welfare in the United Kingdom: Rising Poverty, Falling Priorities for Children

JONATHAN BRADSHAW

8.1. Introduction

The well-being of children is not only an indication of a society's moral worth; children are human capital, the most important resource for a society's future. This was recognized by the person in charge of the government of Britain in the 1980s:

[C]hildren must come first because children are our most sacred trust. They also hold the key to our future in a very practical sense . . . We need to do all we can to ensure that children enjoy their childhood against a background of secure and loving family life. That way, they can develop their full potential, grow up into responsible adults and become, in their turn, good parents. (Margaret Thatcher, George Thomas Society, Inaugural Lecture, 17 January 1990.)

Perhaps an ominous indication that children in the UK have not come first lies in the difficulties in tracing recent trends in the well-being of poor children. Although the UK has an excellent database on living standards, social conditions, and social attitudes, children have not been the primary focus of attention in data collection and analysis.

The consequences for children of increasing poverty, cuts in benefits and services, and the impact of demographic changes have yet to be observed. The manner in which material, emotional, and social processes affect children in adolescence and influence their adult lives as parents, in employment, and in old age is not well understood. Human beings are robust. But children are also vulnerable, and that vulnerability provides ample reason to focus on the questions raised by child poverty and deprivation, even if the answers can only be tentative.

The author is extremely grateful to Majella Kilkey for her assistance in revising an earlier version of this chapter.

8.2. Child Poverty from the 1940s to the 1980s

Britain emerged from World War II with a national consensus to establish a 'welfare state' which would attack Beveridge's five giants: want, disease, ignorance, squalor, and idleness. A spate of legislation in the 1940s introduced a national social security scheme, a health service free at the point of demand, and a national education service for children aged 5–15. At the same time, Keynsian economic policies contributed to high employment. This period brought unprecedented improvements in living standards. If a series existed which traced trends consistently over the last forty-five years it would show falling poverty and reduced inequalities (Goodman and Webb, 1994). General improvements in living standards and health and welfare services led to rapid improvements in the status of children (Halsey, 1988).

Consensus on the value of the welfare state began to break down from the mid-1960s. The ideas of critics from the right found expression in the 1979 election of a Conservative Government led by Margaret Thatcher. What have been the consequences for children?

8.3. Child Poverty since 1980

Since 1977 there has been an unprecedented surge in income inequality and poverty in the UK. While average incomes have risen (by 36 per cent between 1979 and 1991–2), inequalities have increased, more children live in families with low relative incomes, and many are worse off in real terms than they were in 1979.

Before rehearsing the evidence, terms must be defined carefully as there is no official definition of poverty in the UK. Indeed in 1989, John Moore, then Secretary of State for Social Security, declared the 'end of the line for poverty', claiming that living standards had improved so much since the early 1900s and the pre-war period that poverty no longer had real meaning and that 'individuals and organisations concerned with poverty were merely pursuing the political goal of equality' (Speech, 11 May 1989).

It is this author's view that poverty can only be understood in relative terms, as a degree of deprivation of normal patterns of living which is morally unacceptable. Poverty is a form of social exclusion. It is potentially harmful for the health and well-being of individuals and eventually for society as a whole.

A heated debate is currently under way on the validity of poverty statistics. Poverty is most commonly measured indirectly. For many years the main indirect measure was a government series 'Statistics on Low Income Families' (not poverty!), for which estimates were derived from the Family Expenditure Survey. This series was produced annually from

Table 8.1: Percentage of Children in the UK in Low Income Families, 1979–1989

	1979	1981	1983	1985	1987	1989
Income at/or below SB/IS level						
% of all children	12.4	18.1	22.5	23.9	25.7	25.8
Income at/or below 140% SB/IS level						
% of all children	21.4	33.0	38.5	36.5	37.2	35.4

Note: 1979–87 based on the supplementary benefit scales, 1989 figures based on the income support scales, so the latter are not strictly comparable.
Source: Social Security Committee (1992).

1974 until 1979, and then biannually until 1985. The statistics related family incomes to the national scale of social assistance benefits ('supplementary benefit') for the unemployed. This supplementary benefit (SB) is effectively the minimum safety net decided upon by Parliament that people without other resources should receive. It is also an 'equivalent' standard which takes into account variations in family composition.

The proportion of children living in families with incomes at or below 140 per cent of the SB standard increased between 1979 and 1989 by 47 per cent (Table 8.1) to 35.4 per cent of all children. The proportion of children in families with incomes at or below the SB standard increased by 84 per cent over this period to 25.8 per cent.

The justification for setting the poverty standard above the supplementary benefit level is that families dependent on that benefit have, as a result of disregarded earnings and savings and additional payments, incomes above that level. However, the government challenged the Low Income Families series, not least because if benefit levels were improved in real terms, this had the disconcerting effect of increasing the number of people defined as poor. Despite much criticism (Social Services Committee, 1988*a*), the government discontinued the series after 1985. The Institute of Fiscal Studies (1990) has produced tables for 1987 and 1989, though comparability has been undermined by the replacement in 1988 of supplementary benefits by income support which has different scales of benefit.

A new series giving the proportion of 'Households Below Average Income' has been published for the 1979 to 1991–2 period. The latest report by the Department of Social Security (DSS, 1994) shows the following:

- While average real incomes rose by 36 per cent between 1979 and 1991–2, the income (after housing costs) of the bottom decile (10 per cent) fell by 17 per cent (or 9 per cent if the self-employed are excluded).

- The proportion of individuals living in families with incomes (all after housing costs) below 50 per cent of the contemporary average increased from 9 to 25 per cent between 1979 and 1991–2. The proportion of couples with children living below this threshold increased from 8 to 24 per cent and the proportion of lone parents shot up from 19 to 59 per cent.
- This increase in low incomes has particularly affected children. Table 8.2 shows that the proportion of children living in families with incomes below 50 per cent of the average increased from 10 to 32 per cent during this period. In contrast, the proportion of individuals in families with a head or spouse over the age of 60 has increased from 20 to 36 per cent.
- These relative measures of low income relate family income to a proportion of the rising contemporary average. However, the proportion of people with incomes below 50 per cent of the average held constant in real terms since 1979 has also increased from 9 to 11 per cent. The proportion of children living below this threshold increased from 10 to 15 per cent.

These semi-official series indicate rising economic hardships for families with children. There has also been a surge in the dispersion of income since 1977. The Central Statistical Office data analysis (1994*a*) compares the distribution of shares of original income (income from earnings, rents, dividends, and interest) and the distribution of shares of post-tax income (after the impact of social security benefits and direct and indirect taxation). The results for 1979 and 1992 are summarized in Table 8.3. The original income of the bottom two quintiles fell from 12.4 to 8.1 per cent during this period, while the share of the top quintile rose from 43 to 50 per cent. The share of post-tax income of the bottom quintile fell from 9.5 to 6.5 per cent and that of the top quintile increased from 37 to 44 per cent. Gini coefficients for both original income and post-tax income have risen and families with children have been greatly affected: in 1979, 21.0 per cent of children were in the bottom quintile; by 1991–2, the proportion had increased to 26.8 per cent.

Jenkins and Cowell (1994) concluded that economic growth has benefited the rich substantially more than the poor—27 per cent of income

Table 8.2: Children in Households below Average Income, 1979–1991/92 (income below 50% of the contemporary average after housing costs)

	1979	1981	1983	1985	1987	1988–9	1991–2
% of all children	10	18	17	20	26	25	32

Sources: Department of Social Security (1994) and reports for earlier years.

Table 8.3: Changes in Equivalized Quintile Incomes Shares (percentage shares of total income, 1979–92)

	Lowest				Highest	Gini co-efficient
	1st	2nd	3rd	4th	5th	
Original income						
1979	2.4	10	18	27	43	44
1992	2.1	6	15	26	50	52
Post-tax income						
1979	9.5	13	18	23	37	29
1992	6.5	11	16	23	44	38

Source: CSO (1994*a*), table 1, appendix 2.

growth in the 1980s went to the richest 5 per cent and 60 per cent went to the richest 20 per cent. While the real incomes of the very poorest group fell, those of the middle- and high-income groups rose.

Direct measures of poverty and inequality are less available. One exception is the Thames Television Breadline Surveys carried out in 1983 and 1990. These surveys defined poverty as the lack of one or more items that 50 per cent of the population consider necessities. In 1990, 20 per cent of people lacked three or more necessities, 11 per cent could not afford five or more, and 6 per cent lacked seven items. In general, the proportion of the population lacking particular necessities tended to fall between the surveys, but those which showed least improvement or an increase were families with children. There was no improvement in the proportion of such families unable to afford toys or leisure equipment, celebrations on special occasions, presents for families or friends, a hobby or leisure activity. In addition, there was an increase in the proportion of families who could not afford separate bedrooms for children over 10 of different sexes, a weekly outing for children, or fortnightly visits by children's friends for a snack. Those most likely to lack necessities were families with children dependent on income support (mainly families with an unemployed head and lone-parent families).

The Family Budget Unit explored what low-income families could afford (Bradshaw, 1993). They drew up a low-cost budget which could sustain a modern minimum living standard and found that the benefits paid to families dependent on income support were below this level. It was particularly inadequate for families with children. Their estimate of the minimum costs of a child were 61 per cent higher than the child benefit and 41 per cent higher than the scales of income support for a child (Oldfield and Yu, 1993). This work contributes to a body of evidence (Brown, 1994) that families with children on income support are bearing the greatest brunt of the increased poverty.

Table 8.4: Children in Families on Family Income Supplement or Supplementary Benefit to 1988 and Family Credit or Income Support after 1988 ('000s)

	FIS/Family Credit	SB/Income Support	Total
1979	184	955	1,139
1982	306	1,793	2,099
1985	415	—	415
1988	438	2,195	2,633
1991	736	2,497	3,233
1993	993	3,207	4,200

Sources: DSS (various).

Table 8.4, based on administrative statistics, shows the number of children dependent on supplementary benefits/income support (with sick, disabled, unemployed, or lone parents) or on family income supplement/ family credit (parents with low earnings). The total number of children on these benefits has fluctuated, but the trend has been inexorably upwards—increasing from 8 to 33 per cent of all children between 1979 and 1993.

The amount payable for all normal expenditures in May 1994 for a couple with two children under 11 was £120 plus weekly housing costs. One study of the living standards of families on income support (Bradshaw and Holmes, 1989) wrote:

The lives of these families, and perhaps most seriously the lives of the children in them, are marked by the unrelieved struggle to manage with dreary diets and drab clothing. They also suffer what amounts to cultural imprisonment in their homes in our society in which getting out with money to spend on recreation and leisure is normal at every other income level.

8.4. The Causes of Child Poverty and Deprivation since the Early 1980s

Although there is still debate about the causes and consequences of these trends, it is clear that three interacting factors contributed to the sharp increase in the prevalence of child poverty and deprivation.

8.4.1. *Economic trends*

The UK economy suffered from endemic long-term weaknesses for many years, even before the 1980s, including low levels of investment and productivity, frequent trade disputes, a higher inflation rate than that of its competitors, a trade imbalance, and slow economic growth. Most importantly, labour demand has not kept pace with supply, resulting in very high levels of unemployment. While the government's determination to control inflation has exacerbated the unemployment situation, socio-demographic and technological factors, and competitive pressures arising from the globalization of the economy have also contributed.

Employment shrank by more than 5 per cent between 1979 and 1983, and then began to rise. It peaked in 1990 at a level only 2 per cent above that of 1979, even though the potential labour force had grown by 7 per cent over this period.

Unemployment rose from 6.3 per cent in July 1980 to 11.9 per cent in July 1986 (Department of Employment count). Although labour demand picked up after 1983, unemployment remained very high as more married women and the baby-boom generation entered the job market. It began to fall in 1986, due mainly to declining numbers of young people entering the labour force (15–24-year-olds declined by 1.1 million between 1981 and 1988). By July 1990, unemployment had fallen to 6.1 per cent, but rose again thereafter to almost 11 per cent in January 1993 (DE count). In May 1994, unemployment dropped to 9.3 per cent, although unofficial estimates place this figure closer to 12.8 per cent (Unemployment Unit). Female unemployment has been less affected: 5.0 per cent in May 1994 compared with the male rate of 12.7 per cent. Young people aged 16–17 have been hardest hit; latest figures (International Labour Organisation definition) suggest that up to 17 per cent are unemployed.

Long-term unemployment has increased steadily, even during periods of declining unemployment. In 1991, 21 per cent of the unemployed had been out of work for more than one year; by April 1994, this had risen to 38 per cent. Men have been more subject to long-term unemployment than women. In April 1994, 41 per cent of unemployed men had been claiming for more than one year compared to 28 per cent of women.

Full-time male employment declined by 8 per cent between 1983 and 1994, while male part-time work increased by 80 per cent. At the same time, the number of women in full-time employment increased by 12 per cent and the number of women in part-time work by 33 per cent. The proportion of married women with children in both full-time and part-time work has increased since 1977.

Table 8.5 examines the labour force participation of mothers. Employment rates were substantially lower among mothers of the very young, particularly among lone mothers. It also shows that the proportion of employed married mothers with dependent children increased by more than one-fifth between 1977 and 1992, especially among those with a youngest child under 5. The employment rates for lone mothers, however, declined, largely due to falling participation rates of lone mothers with very young children. Therefore, while married mothers with children

Table 8.5: Married Women and Lone Mothers with Dependent Children: Percentages Working Full-time and Part-time by Age of Youngest Dependent Child, 1977–1992

Age of youngest dependent child and working status of mother	1977–9	1981–3	1985–7	1989–91	1990–2
Married women with dependent children					
Under 5 years					
Full-time	5	6	9	14	14
Part-time	22	19	25	32	33
All working	27	25	34	46	47
Five years and over					
Full-time	21	20	22	27	27
Part-time	45	44	46	47	47
All working	66	64	68	74	74
All ages					
Full-time	15	14	17	21	21
Part-time	37	35	37	40	41
All working	52	49	54	62	63
Lone mothers					
Under 5 years					
Full-time	13	7	9	8	8
Part-time	13	11	11	14	14
All working	26	18	20	23	22
5 years and over					
Full-time	26	25	23	27	26
Part-time	29	29	33	32	32
All working	56	54	55	60	59
All ages					
Full-time	22	19	18	18	17
Part-time	24	23	24	24	24
All working	47	42	42	43	42

Source: General Household Surveys.

under 5 increasingly entered the labour market, lone mothers with young children retreated somewhat from paid employment.

In general, employment has become much more episodic, temporary, and short term. There has been a shift for both men and particularly women from manufacturing to service jobs and part-time employment has grown. The largest part of the increased employment of married mothers with young children related to their entry into part-time jobs. The reverse was the case for married mothers with older children. Instead, while lone mothers with a youngest child under 5 showed little growth in part-time participation rates, those with a youngest child aged 5 or over made the greatest gains in terms of part-time employment.

The living standards of families were also strongly affected during the 1980s by rising earning differentials. Salaries increased more quickly than did wages, and those of skilled workers rose more rapidly than those of the unskilled. There is no minimum wage in Britain; low pay is endemic and has expanded. Between 1979 and 1993, the number of employees with gross weekly earnings below the Council of Europe's 'decency threshold' increased from 7.8 million to 9.8 million. For full-time workers the increase was from 28.3 to 37.0 per cent of all full-time employees (Low Pay Unit, 1994).

Following equal pay legislation in the 1970s, the gender disparity in earnings narrowed. Differentials remained stable for most of the 1980s, with women's earnings at 67 per cent of men's, and then began to narrow so that by 1993 the proportion reached 79 per cent. The earnings of young people also fell further behind those of adults: between 1979 and 1993, young people's earnings as a proportion of adult earnings fell from 61 to 50 per cent for 18–20-year-olds and from 42 to 34 per cent for 16–17-year-olds (Low Pay Unit, 1994).

8.4.2. *Demographic changes*

The family as we have known it in Britain since the turn of the century is undergoing profound changes. In common with most industrialized countries, the fertility rate has been below replacement level since 1977 and, at 1.80 in 1992 is relatively high compared with most other European countries. It has also been fairly stable for some time.

Until the 1960s, marriage had never been more popular. Whereas only 70 per cent of women born in 1900 married, 92 per cent of those born in 1946 married, and they were marrying earlier. However, marriage is now on the wane. The England and Wales first marriage rates for men have more than halved, dropping from 82.3 (per 1,000 persons 16 and over) in 1971 to 37.2 in 1992. In addition, the age of first marriage is rising. While in the early 1970s a pregnant young woman opted for marriage, this is now her third choice, after abortion and out-of-wedlock birth.

Remarriages account for a growing proportion of all marriages; over a third of the total involves a previously married partner. While the remarriage rate has always been higher for men than women, it declined from 227.3 persons per 1,000 divorced men in 1971 to 64.6 in 1992.

Consensual unions between partners of the opposite sex have rapidly become very common. Of those women marrying in the late 1960s, only 6 per cent had cohabited. By the late 1970s, the figure had jumped to 33 per cent, and for those marrying between 1985 and 1988 it was 58 per cent. In addition, by the late 1980s about 70 per cent of women had cohabited between marriages. Childless cohabiting couples share many similarities with childless married couples. However, cohabiting couples with children tend to be more disadvantaged than their married counterparts (Kiernan and Estaugh, 1993).

Divorce climbed from 2.3 per 1,000 married men in 1961 to 13.7 in 1992. Four in ten marriages now end in divorce, and the chances are much higher for younger marriages, recent marriages among the previously divorced, and for marriages following cohabitation. One consequence, however, of changing family forms is that divorce is less useful as an indicator of family breakdown as no record exists of breakdowns in co-habiting relationships. A better indicator is the number of lone-parent families (see below).

The decline in marriage and accompanying increases in cohabitation have also been associated with a rapid rise in out-of-wedlock births. Of all conceptions in 1990, 43 per cent occurred outside marriage and a third of these resulted in legal abortions. The proportion of births outside marriage has shot up from 6 per cent of all births in 1961 to 31.2 per cent in 1992, with increases for all ages of mothers. In 1991, the number of single lone parents overtook the number of divorced lone parents for the first time. Teenage conceptions are also relatively high in the UK, having risen from 57.1 per 1,000 women under 20 in 1981 to 65.3 in 1991. None the less, over three-quarters of out-of-wedlock births were registered in the name of both parents and three-quarters of these were living at the same address. Thus, over half of out-of-wedlock births appear to be to stable cohabiting couples.

The number of lone-parent families more than doubled between 1971 and 1991. With 19 per cent of all families with children headed by one parent, the UK has the highest proportion of lone-parent families in the European Community. For the majority of these women, lone parenthood is a temporary episode—over half of divorced women remarry within five years. Nevertheless, in addition to the personal and emotional crisis of a relationship breakdown, lone parenthood usually means a period of poverty and dependence on social security, and for many that dependency lasts a long time (Bradshaw and Millar, 1991).

The cumulative result of these trends is a huge increase in families with complex forms. Eight per cent of all families with children are step-families (Haskey, 1994). About the same number of children are members of part-time step-families when they visit for weekends or holidays. As children usually live with their mother after a separation or divorce, there are seven times more full-time stepfathers than stepmothers.

The most common cause for concern about these trends relates to their consequences for children. By the time they are 16, one in four children will have experienced the divorce of their parents, others are born to single parents, or experience the disruption of their non-married parents' relationship. However, a recent review of the research on the impact of family disruption on children (Burghes, 1994) concludes that detrimental consequences for the most part are small. There is no doubt that poverty is much more likely for lone parents (Millar, 1989). Maintenance (alimony) from former partners is received by less than one-third of lone parents, and payments are low and irregular. And, as has been noted, the proportion of employed lone mothers has declined. During the 1980s, the proportion of lone parents dependent on social security increased.

8.4.3. Social and fiscal policies

The third main explanation for the recent increase in poverty and inequality lies in the social and fiscal policies pursued by successive Conservative governments. These governments sought to cut public expenditure in order to cut taxation, but have failed in both of these aspirations: with public expenditure as a proportion of GDP at 45 per cent in 1994, it is higher than it was in 1979–80. While there have been substantial cuts in the taxation of the better off, direct and indirect tax is on average higher today than it was in 1978. Several factors contributed to the failure to reduce public expenditure: the massive costs of providing benefits for the unemployed, the prematurely retired, and the sick and disabled; the increased demands of an ageing population; and the recent sharp increase in the real level of rents and, therefore, housing benefits. Nevertheless, the government might have achieved these cuts if there had not been such a high level of public support for *increased* welfare spending even at the cost of increased taxation. Commitment to welfare state spending has increased since 1979: the proportion of the population favouring cuts in taxation, even if it meant cuts in services, fell to only 3 per cent in 1991 (Jowell *et al.*, 1992).

However, some policy changes have contributed to the rise in poverty and inequality. There has been a shift from direct taxation of income and capital to indirect taxation of consumption, such as VAT on domestic fuel. Income tax rates have been cut, particularly for higher rate tax-payers, though increases in national insurance contributions have partly offset these cuts. Most personal tax allowances have been raised in line with prices, but they have not kept pace with increased earnings. Families thus start paying taxes at lower relative levels of earnings, even at levels where they are considered poor enough to receive housing benefit and family credit, which are designed to relieve poverty. The proportion of higher incomes taken in taxes has fallen, while this proportion has risen for lower incomes. The shift to indirect taxes has made the system less progressive.

The social security system has become a more important vehicle for redistribution and exchange. There have been a host of changes to the benefit system since 1979, the most significant of which was the 1980 decision to break the link between benefits and earnings. Since 1980, most benefits have been uprated by prices only. Thus, as real earnings have grown, the living standards of those dependent on benefits have declined relative to those of the average worker. The value of the single person's pension in relation to earnings fell from 23.2 to 17.7 per cent between 1979 and 1993. If this pension had risen as fast as earnings since 1979, it would now be roughly one-third higher. If benefits continue to be uprated only for prices and if real earnings continue to increase, by 2050 the basic pension will amount to only about 7 per cent of average earnings. Such a decline in the relative living standards of pensioners would jeopardize the financial base of the state pension scheme and destabilize the intergenerational contract. The social security system reinforces social cohesion and helps to protect the vulnerable. Diminishing its value will inevitably undermine social solidarity.

A further change has been the drift from reliance on contributory benefits to selective and income-related benefits. These are not claimed by all those entitled to them and, in combination with the tax system, create poverty traps as benefits fall when earnings rise. The recent increase in real housing costs has tended to undermine the government's attempts to reduce the impact of this poverty trap.

A number of other important incremental changes to the social security system, designed to save public expenditure, have had a significant cumulative effect on families. The unemployed have endured the abolition of an earnings-related unemployment benefit and child additions to the benefit, and stricter rules regarding linked periods of unemployment. This has recently culminated in the proposal to replace the unemployment benefit by a Job Seekers' Allowance. There has been a simultaneous massive increase in the numbers of unemployed dependent on income support. Lone parents are worse off under income support, but other groups have also suffered, particularly as a result of the replacement of discretionary additions by the cash-limited and mainly loan-based Social Fund as well as the introduction of water charges and VAT. One of the most dramatic changes in the income support scheme was the ending of entitlements altogether for 16–18-year-olds. The idea was that young people should stay on at school or enter the Youth Training Scheme (YTS), with places guaranteed for all who needed them. However, YTS has not delivered either the quality or the quantity of training required and young people have had to fall back on their families. Although a hardship scheme was eventually established to provide an income for young people without parental support, it has proved cumbersome and ineffective. The outcome has been a huge increase in youth homelessness. The recent rise in youth crime is also partly related to this negative development.

The impact of social policies on services and their effects on families are difficult to assess. Of all the social programmes, housing has suffered the largest expenditure cuts. The house-building programme was emasculated, rents rose sharply, council houses were sold, mortgage debts and repossessions increased. The growth in homelessness has exposed thousands of children to the acute deprivation of bed-and-breakfast accommodation (see below).

The number of under-5 children in full-time nursery education has remained constant, and the proportion of young children enrolled in schools has risen consistently; more than two-fifths of all 3-year-olds were enrolled in 1993 compared with less than a third in 1984; the figure for 4-year-olds was almost 90 per cent compared to 77 per cent in 1984 (Central Statistical Office, 1990). Most of these attend part time.

Associated with the rising labour participation rates for married women, there has been a significant increase in day-care services provided by child 'minders' (despite some anxiety about the quality). In 1990, relatives, friends, or neighbours provided child care for almost two-thirds of employed mothers with a youngest child under 5 (Holtermann and Clarke, 1992). Privately provided child care is the next most important form of care—the number of places in private nurseries doubled between 1984 and 1989 (Moss and Melhuish, 1991). Overall, the proportion of under-5 children in some form of day care increased from 14 per cent in 1976 to 20.1 per cent in 1990 (Kumar, 1993).

Thanks mainly to demographic changes between 1979 and 1989, the average class size in primary schools declined from 23.1 to 22.0 and in secondary schools from 16.7 to 15.3 (Hansard 20 March 1990: col. 518). More recently, class sizes appear to have increased: in 1991–2, the English average was 27 for primary schools and 21 for secondary schools (Central Statistical Office, 1994a). The proportion of 16–18-year-olds staying on beyond compulsory schooling rose from 27 per cent in 1976 to 36 per cent in 1990, although it is still low in comparison with other countries (Central Statistical Office, 1994c: tables 3.12 and 3.13).

The impact of constraints on education expenditure has varied from area to area and across segments of the education system. The school meals service deteriorated in the 1980s largely because of the abolition of price maintenance and the nutritional standard of meals. Between 1979 and 1993, the proportion of pupils taking meals in maintained schools in England dropped from 64 to 43 per cent, and between 1987 and 1988 the number declined by 31 per cent. Currently, around 16 per cent of children in maintained schools receive free school meals (CPAG, 1989; Central Statistical Office, 1994b).

Student grants in tertiary education were cut by 13 per cent between 1978–9 and 1987–8, and an additional 30 per cent cut is to be implemented over the 1994–7 period. The earnings of teaching staff in schools and universities have also been held down, with consequences for morale and problems in teacher supply. Expenditures per pupil in real terms on school books and equipment fell by 0.8 per cent for primary schools and

24.2 per cent for secondary schools between 1978–9 and 1987–8 (Hansard, 8 May 1989). Capital spending fell by 27 per cent between 1981 and 1988 in line with the diminishing school population. Capital spending per pupil in real terms rose by 16 per cent between 1979 and 1989.

Overall expenditure on health care has risen in real terms and as a proportion of GNP, but there has been a heated debate on whether this growth has kept pace with the needs of an ageing population and advances in medical technology (Social Services Committee, 1989).

It is not possible to assess how well maternity and child health and welfare services have fared in the competition for resources *within* health care and personal social services. Prenatal diagnoses of congenital abnormalities and abortions of damaged foetuses have led to a sharp decline in the birth of disabled children. On the other hand, advances in surgical and medical interventions have enabled more damaged children to remain alive longer. Vaccination coverage has gradually but continuously increased, but is still not universal. In 1991–2, for instance, the proportions of unvaccinated children were: diphtheria, 6 per cent; whooping cough, 12 per cent; polio, 6 per cent; tetanus, 6 per cent; and measles, mumps, and rubella, 9 per cent. Large regional differences in immunization rates also persist (Central Statistical Office, 1994*b*).

8.5. The Impact of Recent Trends on Children's Well-being

What has been the impact of these trends on the well-being of children? Poverty is associated with most problems in society, including sickness, premature death, debt, deprivation, crime, relationship breakdown, loneliness, drabness, and neglect. But it is very difficult to separate cause and effect and to conclude that a given increase in poverty or inequality is associated with a given change in outcomes for poor people. The data are often not available over time, are not up to date, or have not yet been published. Many of the potential impacts are long term, and it may be too early to assess the consequences of the last ten years on the well-being of children. Indications of outcome can be considered under two broad headings: physical and behavioural.

8.5.1. The physical impact

1. *Infant mortality*. Table 8.6 presents data on the mortality rates of children in the UK for selected years since 1961. All of these vital statistics show a continuing decline during the 1980s, though the reduction in IMR was much slower than in previous decades (Social Services Committee, 1988*b*). It is arguable that improvements in infant mortality become harder beyond a certain level. The downward trend has been due to better

Table 8.6:   Vital Statistics in the UK (rates per 1,000)

Year	Infant mortality	Neonatal mortality	Perinatal mortality
1961	22.1	15.8	32.7
1966	19.6	13.2	26.7
1971	17.9	12.0	22.6
1976	14.5	9.9	18.0
1981	11.2	6.7	12.0
1986	9.5	5.3	9.6
1991	7.4	4.4	8.1
1993	6.3	4.2	9.0

Source: *Population Trends*, 80 (1995).

intensive care for babies at risk, the changing composition of the population, and fewer babies being born in large families and to younger mothers. None the less, the rates have edged down more slowly in the UK than in some other countries.

There has been considerable debate over whether differentials in infant mortality among social classes in Britain have diminished (Townsend and Davidson, 1982; Illsley and Le Grand, 1987; Carr Hill 1988; Davey-Smith *et al.*, 1990; Phillimore *et al.*, 1994). Nevertheless, IMRs for the bottom class are double those for the top class (Kumar, 1993). The differentials in perinatal mortality rates were maintained between 1975 and 1990 and post-neonatal mortality rates have remained static since the mid-1970s (Rodrigues and Botting, 1989). However, class differentials have narrowed as the rates for the manual classes have continued to fall, while those for other classes have levelled off.

There are large local differences in low birth weight and infant deaths, which are closely related to indicators of social deprivation (Townsend *et al.*, 1988). Although infant mortality has decreased, causes of death related to socio-economic factors have not improved as much. Inner-city areas have low immunization levels and poor housing, high risks of gastroenteritis among babies, and serious problems of tuberculosis among the Asian community. AIDS also poses new threats associated with deprivation. The Office of Population Censuses and Surveys (OPCS, 1988) has concluded that 'Causes of death which can be regarded as "preventable" . . . cause infant deaths in Social Class V at about three times the rate for Social Class I.'

There is also a link between infant mortality, low birth weight, and ethnic origin. In 1990, for instance, the mortality rate among infants of women born in Pakistan was 14.2 per 1,000, compared with 7.5 among infants of women born in the UK (Kumar, 1993).

2. *Childhood deaths.* There has also been a continuing downward trend

in childhood deaths (Table 8.7). For older children and young adults, accidents are now the single largest cause of death, and motor accidents account for the majority of deaths among children above the age of 4 (Woodroffe *et al.*, 1993). Accidents are more common among lower socio-economic groups.

In 1985, suicide accounted for 9 per cent of child deaths. Suicide rates for children aged 10–14 declined from 1.7 per million in the 1940s to 1.3 per million in the 1980s (McClure, 1988). An increase in the rate for females was offset by a decline in the male rate. However, in a local area study (Lowy *et al.*, 1990), it was found that the suicide rate for 15–34-year-olds increased each year between 1975 and 1987, although this may reflect a shift in the willingness of coroners to record verdicts of suicide. Over the 1987–90 period in England and Wales, suicide accounted for 12 per cent of injury deaths in the 15–19 age-group (Woodroffe *et al.*, 1993).

3. *Child morbidity.* No reliable national data exist on trends in the prevalence of handicapping conditions. The number of abortions due to foetal abnormality fell over the last decade, mainly due to a decline in rubella during pregnancy, and advances in the prevention and prenatal diagnosis of congenital abnormalities affecting the incidence of some conditions, including spina bifida, rubella syndrome, and possibly Down's syndrome. However, the main feature of child morbidity has been the increasing prevalence of chronically ill and disabled children, particularly due to improved treatment and advances in surgical management which have helped to keep disabled children alive longer.

The 1989 nationally representative survey of the prevalence of disability among children (Bone and Meltzer, 1989) found a rate of 32 per 1,000 children. The rising numbers of children surviving with chronic illnesses or disabilities are likely to be deprived in relation to their peers because of the increased cost to their families of caring for them (Baldwin, 1985).

Table 8.7: Childhood Deaths in England and Wales, 1971–1992
(rates per 1,000 by age)

	Males				Females			
	1–4	5–9	10–14	15–19	1–4	5–9	10–14	15–19
1971	0.76	0.44	0.37	0.90	0.63	0.29	0.24	0.39
1976	0.65	0.34	0.31	0.88	0.46	0.24	0.21	0.35
1981	0.53	0.27	0.29	0.82	0.46	0.19	0.19	0.32
1986	0.44	0.19	0.26	0.71	0.39	0.16	0.17	0.28
1991	0.40	0.21	0.23	0.69	0.33	0.16	0.15	0.28
1992	0.34	0.18	0.20	0.61	0.29	0.14	0.13	0.29

Source: *Population Trends*, 77, table 13.

Between 1972 and 1991, there was an increase in the proportion of boys and girls reported by their parents as having long-standing illnesses—from 4 to 17 per cent for 5–15-year-old girls and from 6 to 15 per cent for boys of the same age-group. Demands made on health care services by children during this period also increased.

Admissions of children and young adults (under 19) to hospitals and units for the mentally ill rose from 385 to 417 per 100,000 between 1976 and 1986. Admissions to hospitals for the mentally retarded rose from 30.2 to 84.8 per 100,000 over the same period (D.o.H., 1989*b*). However, admission statistics are an unreliable indicator of psychiatric morbidity.

Although immunization coverage increased during the 1980s, reaching 94 per cent for diphtheria and tetanus (Central Statistical Office, 1994*b*), there were epidemics of whooping cough in 1982, 1986, and 1990 and of measles in 1982–3, 1985–6, and 1988–9. Infectious diseases make up 10 per cent of all deaths. Notification rates of meningitis in all age-groups under 15 have been increasing, especially since 1984. Meningococcal meningitis (accounting for 40 per cent of all cases) has risen particularly sharply among younger children. AIDS poses a new threat to child health and survival through child sexual abuse, infection *in utero* and, among adolescents, through intravenous drug use. By the end of July 1992, 403 children under 15 years in the UK had been diagnosed as HIV positive and 47 of these had died (Woodroffe *et al.*, 1993).

Between 1973 and 1983, children's dental health improved, particularly among younger children, though half of the children entering school still showed signs of dental decay (NCB, 1987). Research (Carmichael *et al.*, 1989) has established that the prevalence of dental decay relates to social class. Fluoridation of the water supply was shown to reduce class differentials and was most effective for children in Social Classes IV and V, the two bottom classes and the ones with the highest incidence of dental decay.

4. *Nutrition*. There is considerable concern that children's nutrition deteriorated during the 1980s due to the abolition of price maintenance and nutritional standards for school meals (Whitehead, 1988); in 1993, 43 per cent of children attending maintained schools in England were taking school dinners. One study found that school meals contain between 30–43 per cent of the average daily energy intake, but it also showed that older children, particularly girls, who rely on the food served at non-school outlets have the poorest diets (D.o.H., 1989*a*). The main sources of energy in the diets of schoolchildren are bread, chips, milk, biscuits, meat products, cakes, and puddings. Higher consumption of chips occurs among lower social classes, children of unemployed fathers, and families on benefit. Three-quarters of all children have excessive fat intakes. Iron, riboflavin, and calcium intakes among girls are below recommended levels, and Scottish primary schoolchildren are low on vitamin C and B

carotene. Lobstein (1988) estimated the expenditure on food for families on benefit and found that their diets were 'grossly inadequate', with serious deficiencies in the intake of iron, zinc, magnesium, vitamin C, and folic acid (see also Bradshaw and Morgan, 1987; Bradshaw and Holmes, 1989). Leather (1992) found that a 'modest but adequate' diet would consume 59 per cent of the income of a couple with two children on income support compared with an average of 12 per cent of income that all households spend on food.

The National Study of Health and Growth (NSHG) has surveyed children aged $4^1/_2$ to $11^1/_2$ in England and Scotland since 1972. The surveys indicate a trend towards taller children for the 1972–9 period, but this trend slowed or stopped altogether between 1979 and 1986 (D.o.H., 1990). Carr Hill (1986) found no evidence that the secular trend in growth is continuing at the present time. The survey of schoolchildren's diets (D.o.H., 1989a) shows that children are significantly shorter in families on benefits or in which the father is unemployed. No discernible diminution was found in the height differentials among children aged 20–4 in the various social classes between 1940 and 1980. The 1983 NSHG considered children from ethnic minorities and inner cities. Afro-Caribbean children were generally the tallest, while inner-city whites and the children of all other ethnic minority groups were generally shorter than the 1982 sample (D.o.H., 1990; see also Central Statistical Office, 1994b).

5. *Racial disadvantage.* In 1991, ethnic minorities represented 9.3 per cent of the population aged 0–15 years (Central Statistical Office, 1994c). The largest ethnic groups, representing over half of the total, are from India, Pakistan, and the Caribbean; almost three-quarters live in metropolitan counties, concentrated in inner-city areas in poor and overcrowded housing. Infant mortality is much higher among certain ethnic groups than it is in the rest of the population, and ethnic groups have their own special health problems, such as sicklecell anaemia and thalassaemia.

Black children experience disadvantage and deprivation in Britain through racism and discrimination. Their parents are more likely to be unemployed or low paid; their housing is likely to be overcrowded and lacking amenities, and access to public services, even access to schools in some areas, is more difficult. Afro-Caribbean children and those of mixed parentage are also at higher risk of being admitted to local authority care than are white or Asian children (Rowe *et al.*, 1989), partly due to the disproportionately high number of black women in prison (NACRO, 1989). While growing up, black children also face additional adjustments in managing the transition from or maintenance of their ethnic culture.

6. *Homelessness and housing conditions.* Although official statistics do not show the full extent of the crisis of homelessness, this problem has increased during the last fifteen years (Table 8.8). Seventy-nine per cent of homeless households in priority need in 1988 included dependent chil-

Table 8.8:   Homeless Households Involving
Children, 1981–1988

	England and Wales	Great Britain
1981	57,000	—
1985	73,000	—
1986	—	87,360
1987	83,000	92,352
1988	—	96,854

Sources: NCH (1988, 1990).

dren or pregnant women (Central Statistical Office, 1990*c*). This proportion was maintained into 1990, when 121,000 such households were recorded for Britain (Kumar, 1993). If the rate of increase in homeless
households has been sustained until the present, this will mean that the
number has doubled since 1981. In London, black households are three or
four times more likely to become statutorily homeless than are white
households.

House price inflation and high interest rates have exacerbated the crisis
in homelessness; repossessions by building societies increased from 4,900
in 1981 to 68,500 in 1992 (Central Statistical Office, 1994*c*). The use of bed-
and-breakfast accommodation to house homeless families with children
has rapidly increased (ibid.), and concern has been expressed at the impact of this type of accommodation on health, development, safety, education, and diet. Family homelessness can also lead to children being
placed in care.

There has also been a dramatic increase in the number of young homeless people aged 16 to 19 who are forced to live on the streets of large
cities. The problem has been exacerbated not only by the shortage in
housing and hostels, but also by changes in social security rules that have
removed entitlement for 16–17-year-olds and reduced it for other young
people (Craig and Glendinning, 1990). One-third of homeless young
people are thought to be living in London; however, the problem is also
growing in provincial areas.

Housing conditions for families with children have also deteriorated. In
1991, 6 per cent of households with children lived in unfit accommodation; in 1992, 11 per cent were in overcrowded accommodation. However,
the situation varied by type of accommodation: privately rented housing,
21 per cent; local authority housing, 18 per cent; owner-occupied housing,
7 per cent (Central Statistical Office, 1994*b*).

Poor families with children are likely to live in public housing in urban
areas. A survey of a random sample of 579 families with children in
Glasgow, Edinburgh, and London found that one-third of dwellings were

damp and almost half contained mould growth, conditions which have adverse effects on symptomatic health, particularly among children (Platt *et al.*, 1988).

7. *Child abuse and protection.* The issue of physical and sexual child abuse came to the fore in the 1980s. Whether this was due to heightened awareness of an existing problem or to growth in prevalence is impossible to decipher (Creighton, 1988; La Fontaine, 1990). The number of children admitted to care each year in England and Wales fell by one-fifth between 1981 and 1991. The total number in care declined from around 90,000 to 55,000 between 1981 and 1992. By 1992, there were 4.3 children per 1,000 being cared for by local authorities in England. A similar rate was recorded for Wales (4.2), but a somewhat higher figure was found for Northern Ireland (5.4) (Central Statistical Office, 1994*a*, 1994*b*). The decline in the number of children in care is set to continue as a result of the Children Act 1989, which encourages local authorities to work with families to help keep them together. Over time, the proportion of those in care in residential children's homes has declined, and the proportion boarded out in foster homes has increased. In 1992, 58 per cent of the children in care in England were boarded out (Central Statistical Office, 1994*b*).

8.5.2. *The impact on behaviour*

1. *Educational attainment.* The educational attainment of both boys and girls increased between 1975–6 and 1990. The overall increase in boys attaining at least one higher grade GCE Ordinary level was from 49 to 62 per cent over this period; the increase for girls was from 57 to 72 per cent. None the less, concern has been expressed over educational performance in Britain relative to that in other countries. Sir Claus Moser has noted that only 35 per cent of British 16–18-year-olds were in full-time education, whereas the figures for the USA, Japan, and Sweden were 79, 77, and 76 per cent, respectively (*Independent*, 21 August 1990). Differences in examination performance are seen among ethnic groups (Inner London Education Authority, 1990).

2. *Teenage conceptions.* Whether teenage conceptions are related to poverty and deprivation is highly debatable. Nevertheless, teenage mothers and their children are at high risk of deprivation. The rate of conception for girls under 20 years of age in England and Wales rose from 57.9 to 65.3 per 1,000 between 1977 and 1991 (Table 8.9). The tendency for conception to result in legal abortion has become more common. In 1976, there were 4.4 legal abortions per 1,000 women under the age of 16, and 16.9 per 1,000 women in the 16–19 age-group; by 1990 the corresponding figures were 5.9 and 25.9, and the provisional rates for 1992 were 5.2 and 21.1 (*Population Trends*, 77). The younger the teenager, the more likely she is to opt for an abortion. Currently, less than half of conceptions among 15–16-year-

Table 8.9:   Rates of Conception among Teenagers
in England and Wales, Selected Years
(by age, per 1,000)

Age	1977	1986	1991
Under 14	0.9	0.9	1.3
14	4.9	5.7	6.6
15	17.2	18.5	19.9
16	39.1	41.9	43.4
17	59.1	64.8	65.5
18	78.6	83.6	84.9
19	94.7	93.5	96.0
Total under 20	57.9	62.3	65.3

Sources: Birth Statistics (various).

olds lead to births, while the proportion for women aged 19 is 69 per cent
(Woodroffe *et al.*, 1993).

3. *Child labour.* The UK accounts for one-third of Europe's working
children (Low Pay Unit, 1994). According to one study, some 2 million
children are employed, many in jobs which would normally be carried out
by adults. Much of children's employment is illegal because they are
either under-age or because the jobs or the hours are unsuitable for children. An earlier survey (MacLennan *et al.*, 1985) revealed a relationship
between the unemployment of parents and the likelihood of children
working.

4. *Drug abuse and drinking.* The 1992 British Crime Survey found that 3
per cent of 12–13-year-olds and 14 per cent of 14–15-year-olds admitted to
having taken a drug. The most commonly taken illegal drug among children was cannabis, tried by almost one in ten 14–15-year-olds. These
findings may be conservative estimates since higher levels have been
disclosed in other self-report surveys (MacLennan *et al.*, 1985).

Solvent abuse has been a growing problem among children—1 per cent
of 12–13-year-olds and 3 per cent of 14–15-year-olds had used solvents
(MacLennan *et al.*, 1985). The annual number of deaths associated with
abuse of volatile substances rose from 17 to 134 during the 1978–88 period
(Anderson *et al.*, 1990). In 1990, drug use was the classified cause of 4 per
cent of all deaths among 15–19-year-olds (Woodroffe *et al.*, 1993).

A high proportion of teenagers consume alcohol. In 1992, 57 per cent of
children aged between 11 and 15 drank alcohol—13 per cent did so at least
once a week, 16 per cent once or twice a month, and 28 per cent a few
times a year. Older children are more likely to drink and boys are more
likely than girls to drink occasionally or regularly.

5. *Juvenile crime.* Criminal statistics are notoriously influenced by the
behaviour of the police and the courts. Over time, offences are reclassified,

police recording methods are changed, and detection rates vary. All of these factors undermine the reliability of crime statistics.

Young blacks are particularly vulnerable to discrimination in the criminal justice system. In Willis's 1983 study, young black males were roughly ten times more likely to be stopped by police than were others, while Landau and Nathan (1983) discovered that white juveniles had a much greater chance of being cautioned (as opposed to charged) than was the case for black juveniles.

In England and Wales, the number of juveniles aged 10–16 sentenced or cautioned for indictable offences dropped by 27 per cent between 1979 and 1988. Part of this decline can be accounted for by the decrease in the 10–16 years population group; it is also partly due to an increase in alternative methods such as informal unrecorded warnings by the police. Since 1988, however, crimes committed by juveniles have increased: in 1992, 140,000 children aged 10 to 16 were sentenced or cautioned for indictable offences (Central Statistical Office, 1994b). Delinquency has been associated with long-term unemployment, family discord, and poverty (Tarling, 1982; Graham, 1989), all of which have increased since 1980.

The type of offences committed by juveniles changed very little during this last decade and a half: over two-thirds involved theft or the handling of stolen property. In the 14–16 age range, the percentage of males sentenced to custody remained constant at 11 per cent, while that of females rose slightly, from 1 to 2 per cent.

8.6. Conclusions

During the 1980s, children bore the brunt of the changes in economic conditions, demographic structure, and social policies. Financial poverty doubled during this period, with the result that more children were living in low-income families. Inequalities also became more widespread, and there is no evidence that improvements in the living standards of the wealthier 'trickled down' to the poor.

Conclusions on the effects on children of this increase in child poverty and deprivation can only be tentative. An array of outcomes has been considered, and the conclusions are somewhat mixed.

Since the early 1980s, some indicators have improved despite the increase in poverty. Some indicators, such as infant mortality, show improvement, though at a slower rate. And some outcomes have worsened. The quality of life in economically deprived neighbourhoods in the inner cities has degenerated and poverty has become more spatially concentrated there. These areas are more prone to poor health, crime, drug abuse, depression, and other social problems.

This overall picture conceals great variations in outcome. The inequalities in children's lives have increased. While the lives of children in two-parent, two-earner families living in the south of England in owner-occupied housing and relying on good public services have improved, the standard of living of children in unemployed or lone-parent families living in inner cities in rented accommodation and assisted by deteriorating health, education, and social services has worsened. Black children and families are especially disadvantaged on many fronts.

Wilkinson (1994) argues that inequality (rather than the actual material living standard) has a profound effect on well-being and health by influencing psychosocial welfare. Relative deprivation is linked with stress, low self-esteem, and a sense of failure and inadequacy, depression, inactivity, unhealthy and compensatory eating. Rising unemployment, homelessness, house repossession, crime, and poverty affects not only those involved but touches the sense of security and well-being of us all.

There is a danger that any policy recommendations following on from this review will appear facile. However, a key determinant in the well-being of children is the state of the economy and the access of parents to decently remunerated employment. A child-centred economic policy would assign priority to the reduction of unemployment. Children living in lone-parent families are the victims of ambivalence in policy on the role of women in the labour market. Social policies make it very difficult for lone parents to work in the UK. Lone parents need to be encouraged and enabled to work after their youngest child has reached a certain age. But for this to happen, radical reform of social policy is needed on three fronts—child care, training, and social security. The living standards of children would also be improved by policies which make it easier for families (women) to combine work and child-care responsibilities. In addition, the incomes of families with children need to be enhanced through a statutory minimum wage, improvements in child benefits, and substantial real increases in the level of income support and housing benefit paid to families with children.

For these policies to be enacted, the political climate must be driven by a commitment to collective ideals, including fairness, social justice, the community, and family support. It will involve increasing the level of taxation of those who are better off and have access to the labour market.

Perhaps the most important conclusion to be drawn from this analysis is that a better mechanism must be developed to monitor the state of children in the UK. The impact of social and economic change on children is important enough to warrant an 'Annual Report on the State of Children in the UK'. Finally, and perhaps most obviously, in order to monitor the lives of children properly and to formulate effective social policies, we need to know more about what children themselves think and feel.

9

Child Welfare in Portugal Amid Fast Growth and Weak Social Policy

MANUELA SILVA

9.1. Introduction

This chapter examines the characteristics and dimensions of child poverty in Portugal (excluding the Azores and Madeira) and the impact of economic growth and social policy on the well-being of children during the past four decades. While focusing on children and child poverty, attention is also given to the family. Indeed, in most cases, the economic and social deprivation suffered by children is a reflection of the impoverishment of families. Moreover, the chapter relates fluctuations in child welfare not so much to individual actions, but rather to economic and social policies and institutional changes.

Despite the profound economic and social transformations of the past forty years in Portugal, research on their impact on children has been scarce. Though limited by paucity of data, this chapter therefore pioneers the field. Three sub-periods are studied, each characterized by substantially different approaches to economic and social policy.

9.2. The Plight of Children during the Dictatorship, 1950–1974

9.2.1. Economic growth and social development

With the introduction of the first Medium-Term Development Plan (1953–8), 1953 is a logical reference point for an analysis of economic performance. Economic growth accelerated and was sustained throughout 1953–74 (Table 9.1). Investment rates were high, and productivity was closely in line with the expansion of production. Employment growth rates, however, remained rather low. Real wages climbed considerably, though political factors tended to influence the rate.

The author wishes to thank Ana Cardoso, José Centeio, Clara Gonçalves, Alfredo Bruto da Costa, Maria Leonor Vasconcelos, Maria Luisa Sequeira, Natália Lima de Faria, Eliana Gersão, Maria Justina Imperatori, Figueiredo Lopes, Laborinho Lúcio, José Pereirinha, Heloísa Perista, Maria Manuel Portugal, Maria Anita Quintela de Brito, Maria do Rosário Giraldes, Maria Violante Vieira, and the Portuguese Committee for UNICEF. She is also grateful to the editors of this volume for their extensive editing of an earlier version.

Table 9.1: Selected Macroeconomic Indicators, 1950–1993

Year	GDP overall growth	Inflation[a]	Real wages	Unemployment[b]	Employment	Private consumption	Public consumption	Investment
1953–8	3.5	1.1	3.1	—	-0.1	—	—	—
1959–64	6.0	2.0	7.3	—	0.6	—	—	—
1965–7	6.2	5.1	5.5	—	0.2	—	—	—
1968–73	7.8	7.4	5.8	—	1.6	—	—	—
1980	4.1	16.6	6.7	7.9	—	3.4	3.7	13.6
1985	3.3	19.3	2.3	8.5	-0.5	0.8	6.4	—
1986	4.3	11.7	6.7	8.4	0.2	5.5	7.3	—
1987	4.3	9.4	2.4	7.0	2.6	6.0	2.3	—
1988	4.0	9.7	-0.7	5.7	2.6	6.8	7.3	12.6
1989	5.5	—	1.5	5.0	2.0	2.8	3.1	4.8
1990	4.2	14.5	3.0	4.7	2.3	5.0	1.9	7.5
1991	2.2	14.0	1.9	9.1	3.0	5.2	3.2	2.2
1992	1.5	13.0	4.4	4.1	0.9	4.7	1.5	4.9
1993	-1.0	6.5	0.1	5.5	-2.0	0.3	0.3	5.0

[a] Excluding housing rents. [b] In the narrow sense of those who are unemployed but actively seeking work.

Source: Compiled by the author from official statistics.

There were also profound changes in the country's economic structure, with a shift away from agriculture towards industry. By 1974, the share of industry in GDP had peaked and was starting to contract. None the less, in 1970 agricultural employment remained high compared to other developed countries, and industrial employment was still expanding.

In the 1950s, the country followed an inward-oriented industrialization strategy, developing basic industries catering to the domestic market. A radical change occurred in 1959 when Portugal joined the European Free Trade Association. The 1960s were dominated by the development of a labour-intensive, export-oriented industry. However, by the end of the 1960s, low wage competition from the newly industrializing countries and serious bottlenecks in industry led to a policy shift towards development of the chemical, shipbuilding, and repair industries, modernization of traditional branches of industry, and the adoption of more advanced technologies. The contribution of exports to GDP climbed substantially during this period, rising from an average 17.2 per cent for 1959–64 to 22.5 per cent for 1970–4. Similarly, by the end of the 1960s foreign capital was playing an expanding role: its proportion of gross domestic investment mounted from 0.2 per cent in 1960 to 4.7 per cent in 1973.

However, the social costs of these economic strategies were high, as testified by policies of wage repression, unfavourable agricultural prices (which stifled the farm sector), and low public social service expenditures. The reaction to this 'unbalanced growth' was striking: more than 1.7 million people, 20 per cent of the population, left the country between 1950 and 1973. There was also a mass exodus from villages to industrial areas, mainly Lisbon and Setúbal, which contributed to the formation of large pockets of urban poverty.

This massive internal and external migration wrought serious damage, including large tracts of land left uncultivated, disintegration of family life, abandonment of villages and small towns (children and the elderly were often the only remaining residents), and a rapid ageing of the population. The share of economically 'inactive' people in the overall population represented 14.2 per cent in 1960, but had reached 20.7 per cent by 1970.

On the other hand, migration fostered significant remittances of foreign currency (the average share in family income rose to 14 per cent by 1973), improved the well-being of the resident population (including better nutrition, clothing, and housing), and assisted the development of human resources. For example, the children of emigrants frequently had access to better education systems abroad. Furthermore, migration encouraged more progressive attitudes towards economic growth and the rights of women in rural areas.

Portugal's unbalanced growth pattern also resulted in a gaping discrepancy between the economic and social dimensions of development. Although overall living conditions did improve, the social achievements after more than two decades of sustained economic growth were extremely unsatisfactory. Poverty and inequality persisted: the Gini coefficient stagnated at a very high level (dropping only from 0.451 in 1967–8 to 0.443 in 1973–4 (0.380 in 1980–1) (Pereirinha, 1988). In 1973, 31.4 per cent of all families were living on incomes below an absolute income level that could guarantee the satisfaction of minimum basic needs (Silva, 1982). Seven per cent of all families were surviving on incomes of less than half the minimum subsistence level, and 18.3 per cent had incomes below two-thirds of this level (ibid.). The incidence of poverty was particularly high among rural labourers, unskilled workers, and the economically inactive.

Physical indicators of 'well-being' point to similar conclusions (Silva, 1982). In 1973, the per capita protein intake was below the minimum recommended allowance for around 30 per cent of the population. According to the 1970 census, housing conditions for 29.4 per cent of all families did not meet minimum requirements for water, electricity, sanitary facilities, and density of occupation.

9.2.2. Demographic factors

Population growth has been positive since 1950, except for the migration-dominated 1960s (Table 9.2). However, the number of children and young people and their proportion in the overall population had been declining (Table 9.2).

The last four decades have witnessed marked demographic changes. Following a stagnation in the 1950s, the birth-rate decreased drastically from 23.9 to 16.2 per 1,000 between 1960 and 1980, presumably as a consequence of social changes relating to modernization and emigration. The fertility rate declined slowly, exhibiting a certain 'traditional' stability. No dramatic changes in the age structure of child-bearing women were recorded, at least until 1974 (Figure 9.1). There was, however, a more notable drop in the fertility rate for the 25–49 age-group, though the greatest change occurred only after the revolution.

The trend of small but steady changes during the 1950s and 1960s was also reflected in family size. The number of births to families with two or more children dropped from 45 to 40 per cent between 1960 and 1970. However, during the next ten years, coinciding with the revolution and the end of the dictatorship, the decline reached almost 18 percentage points. Death-rates also showed a small decline, though more substantial before 1974 (Table 9.3), mainly due to decreasing mortality among the younger age-groups.

These demographic changes, however, cannot be understood properly without reference to migration. While emigration has long coloured the

Table 9.2: Principle Demographic Indicators,[a] Continent, 1950–1993

	1950	1960	1970	1980	1985	1990	1991	1992	1993
Total population[b]	7,922	8,293	8,123	9,337[c]	9,506	9,381	9,369	9,373	9,393
Share of 0–18 age-group in total population	38.3	37.2	36.3	33.9[c]	29.8	26.6	25.9	25.3	24.8
Crude birth-rate[d]	23.7	23.9	20.0	16.2	12.8	11.6	11.6	11.5	11.4
Crude death-rate[d]	12.1	10.6	10.3	9.7	9.7	10.4	10.0	10.2	10.7
Natural population growth rate[d]	11.6	13.3	9.7	6.5	3.1	1.2	1.1	1.3	0.7
Migration rate[d]	—	-25.3	-16.4	4.3	-0.6	-3.1	-2.4	-0.1	1.5
Effective population growth rate[e]	—	-12.0	-6.7	10.8	2.5	-1.9	-1.3	1.2	-0.8
Out-of-wedlock live births[f]	—	9.5	7.3	9.2	12.3	14.9	15.8	16.3	17.2
First births[g]	—	33.7	35.2	45.5	47.9	52.3	52.7	52.9	53.8
Fertility rate[h]	—	85.9	78.8	63.8[c]	65.7	47.0	45.8	43.2	44.2
Marriage rate[d]	—	7.8	9.0	7.4	6.8	7.2	7.3	7.0	6.9
Average age at first marriage[d]	—	26.9	26.6	25.1	—	—	—	—	—
Divorce rate[d]	—	0.1	0.1	0.6	0.9	0.9	1.0	1.2	1.2
Life expectancy at 1 year of age									
Males	—	56.4	61.2	64.2	—	—	70.4	71.0	70.9
Females	—	61.6	66.9	70.8	—	—	77.6	78.2	78.0

[a] Some calculations may not sum exactly due to rounding. [b] In 1,000s. [c] 1981; Carrilho, M.J., et al. (1993). [d] Per 1,000 people. [e] Sum of the natural population growth rate and migration rate. [f] Per 100 live births. [h] Per 1,000 women in the 15–49 age-group; 1992–3 data compiled by the author.

Source: Cónim and Carrilho (1989).

Table 9.3: Mortality Rates among Under-5-Year-Old Children, 1955–1993 (rounded averages)

Selected indicators	1955-7	1965-7	1975-7	1980	1986	1990	1991	1992	1993
Infant mortality rate	86.2	63.0	33.9	24.3	15.8	10.9	10.8	8.8	8.4
1–4 year mortality rate	99.4	42.8	19.1	12.9	9.2	6.9	7.3	7.0	6.8
Late foetal mortality rate[a]	—	—	14.6	11.6	9.0	6.7	6.5	6.1	6.1
Perinatal mortality rate	—	39.4	30.0	23.8	17.8	12.4	12.1	10.5	10.1
Neonatal mortality rate	29.2	25.6	20.4	15.5	10.8	6.9	6.9	5.7	5.3
Post-neonatal mortality rate[b]	56.9	37.4	13.5	8.6	5.0	6.8	6.9	5.7	3.1
Death by major causes[c]									
Tumours	99.0[d]	109.6[e]	127.7[f]	145.6	168.6	188.1	189.4	193.8	195.5
Diseases of the circulatory system	308.5[d]	328.8[e]	407.3[f]	413.5	447.5	461.8	471.3	448.5	469.1
Diseases of the respiratory system	113.9[d]	128.6[e]	93.7[f]	70.9	72.9	75.8	72.9	68.4	78.9
Diseases of the digestive system	40.7[d]	48.8[e]	60.3[f]	47.6	50.1	46.8	50.2	49.1	50.4
Accidents, poisoning, and violent deaths	65.5[d]	75.1[e]	115.3[f]	106.2	110.9	105.3	109.9	103.8	93.7

[a] Over 28 weeks. [b] 28 days to 1 year. [c] Per 10,000 under-5-year-olds (Portugal—total). [d] 1965. [e] 1970. [f] 1975.

Source: Compiled by the author from official data. INE (1992).

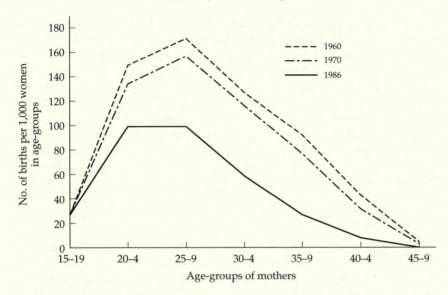

Fig. 9.1   Age-specific Fertility Patterns, Selected Years (per 1,000 women in the age-group)
Source: Cónim and Carrilho (1989).

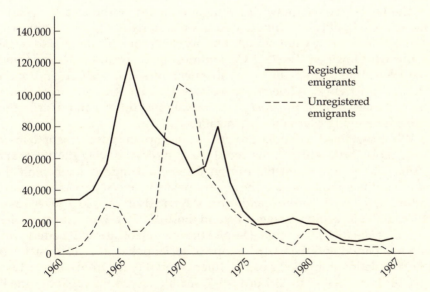

Fig. 9.2   Emigration from Portugal, 1960–1987 (total number of emigrants)
Source: Cónim and Carrilho (1989).

demographic make-up of the country, the 1960s witnessed a historic high point. Between the mid-1960s and the beginning of the 1970s, well over 100,000 individuals were emigrating each year towards the industrialized countries of Western Europe (Figure 9.2). Emigration had far-reaching economic and social implications for children. For many, it meant temporary or even permanent separation from one or both parents. In addition, children uprooted to foreign countries or to new urban environments had to face the challenge and trauma of a new culture, language, and ways of life. An inverse trend developed after the revolution, with half a million Portuguese flocking back from the colonies and an appreciable inflow of foreign migrants.

9.2.3. Social policy and social assistance

Public welfare services have existed in Portugal since the fifteenth century, when Queen Leonor promoted the creation of *Misericórdias* (houses of mercy) to assist the poor and vulnerable. In contrast, social services aimed specifically at children first appeared only in 1882. An 1891 decree required factories employing more than fifty female workers to establish a kindergarten for their children. During the First Republic (1910–26), considerable efforts were undertaken in child welfare, mainly in education and child protection.

The fascist regime, however, obliterated many of these early achievements. The quality of primary education was reduced, public nurseries and kindergartens were closed, and teachers' qualifications and social status were lowered. The 1933 Constitution, in force until 1974, prohibited the government from direct involvement in social welfare and social insurance activities. While public social welfare bodies were created, their function was limited to supervising private institutions and distributing subsidies among charitable organizations.

While sustained economic growth did prompt the government to intervene more forthrightly in the social welfare sector during the 1960s and 1970s, the accomplishments during this period lagged far behind the needs of the population and the government's financial possibilities. Education and health care expenditures stagnated at very low levels until 1974, and increasingly dragged behind those of other European countries.

1. *Child health and survival.* Despite the inequitable growth pattern during this period and the narrow scope of social policy, the health status of the population improved steadily. Infant mortality fell from 86.2 per 1,000 live births in 1955–7 to 33.9 in 1975–7, mainly due to the rapid decline in post-neonatal mortality. An even more radical improvement was evident in the mortality rate among 1–4-year-olds, declining from 99.4 in 1955–7 to 19.1 in 1975–7 (Table 9.3 and Figure 9.3). These gains were achieved despite the extremely low vaccination rate of 10.3 per cent for under-3-

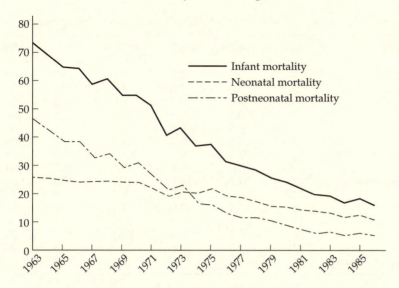

Fig. 9.3 Infant, Neonatal and Post-neonatal Mortality Rates, 1960–1986 (per 1,000 live births)

Source: Compiled by the author from official data.

Table 9.4: Illiteracy and Educational Level of the Population, 1950–1991 (rounded percentages)

	1950	1960	1970	1981	1991
Illiteracy rate	40.3	36.2	39.7	31.2	12.0
Literacy w/o a school-leaving certificate	41.4	28.2	5.3	1.3	—
Primary school graduates[a]	15.8	31.6	47.6	47.0	65.0
Secondary school graduates[a]	1.9	3.2	6.2	17.1	21.5
Graduates from higher education	0.6	0.8	1.3	3.4	8.0

[a] Frequency.

Source: Compiled by the author from census data.

year-olds in 1974. Only 6.5 per cent of under-1-year-olds were immunized against tuberculosis BCG. Furthermore, family planning was ignored or even discouraged.

2. *Education.* Generally poor educational levels and high illiteracy represent two of the major failures of the fascist regime in Portugal. Before the revolution, little effort was made to eliminate illiteracy, which remained virtually unchanged at an appallingly high 40 per cent between 1950 and 1970 (Table 9.4). In 1950, over 80 per cent of the population had not gone

Table 9.5: Gross School Enrolment Rates by Age, 1960–1986 (percentages)

School	Age	1960–1	1965–6	1970–1	1975–6	1985–6
Preprimary	3–4	0.6	1.2	2.1	6.3	23.9
	5	1.6	2.8	4.1	10.4	32.8
Primary	6	18.8	35.1	23.5	51.8	107.1
	7	100.5	104.8	99.5	94.9	105.9
	8	100.5	102.4	100.6	96.6	108.1
	9	100.1	99.2	101.1	97.8	104.9
Preparatory	10	99.6	100.7	109.5	101.9	96.6
	11	72.6	73.8	99.8	93.7	102.2
Secondary	12	54.7	56.4	90.1	87.5	94.4
	13	26.8	29.8	74.8	70.9	82.1
	14	17.9	23.0	31.4	51.0	66.2
	15	18.1	22.5	30.0	43.1	44.8
	16	16.3	20.1	25.3	37.3	39.8
	17	13.3	17.6	21.9	32.8	37.3
'Supplementary'	18	11.1	15.2	20.3	29.3	32.7

Source: Compiled by the author from official data.

beyond the four years of primary school. Although primary education coverage was nearly universal by the end of the regime (Table 9.5), only an insignificant proportion completed secondary or higher education. Poor economic and social conditions and the inadequate education system were the major causes of high drop-out rates.

The dictatorial regime spent very little on education, both in absolute terms and relative to other European countries. In 1960, education expenditure amounted to 1.41 per cent of GDP, compared with 2.05 per cent in France and 2.62 per cent in Sweden. By 1973, these expenditures had risen to 3.34 and 4.84 per cent in France and Sweden respectively, while in Portugal it was still a low 1.77 per cent. Attempts in 1973 to implement some reforms were blunted by political and financing problems, partly due to government outlays for its colonial wars. The situation was particularly critical in preprimary education and specialized education for disabled children. In the early 1970s, only 3 per cent of all under-6-year-olds attended preprimary schools and public kindergartens were not available in most municipalities.

9.3. Revolution, Democracy, Economic Crisis, and Child Welfare: 1974–1985

9.3.1. *A radical shift in social policy*

The revolution which overthrew the dictatorship in April 1974 embodied three main goals: development, democracy, and decolonization. Vast new prospects for economic and social modernization were opened up, greater attention was given to social questions, and significant efforts were made to find solutions to the country's problems. The new 1976 Constitution embodied a fresh approach to social welfare and security, embodying the following principles:

- the right to social security for all;
- a unified and decentralized system, co-ordinated and subsidized by the government in co-operation with unions and other labour groups;
- the participation of private non-profit institutions, regulated by law and subject to governmental financial supervision;
- protection for all in case of illness, old age, disability, death of a spouse or parents, unemployment, and all situations which jeopardize the means of subsistence or the capacity to work;
- the right of orphans and abandoned children to the special protection of society and the government;
- protection of the economic, social, and cultural rights of young people, especially young workers.

A comprehensive social security law was, however, delayed by two major recessions. Finally passed in 1984, the law reinforced the constitutional principles of universality, unity, equality, efficiency, decentralization, protection, solidarity, and participation.

Portugal's social security system comprises two main schemes: a general scheme based on employer and employee contributions, and a government-financed non-contributory scheme covering disadvantaged individuals not otherwise included in the general scheme. Important provisions in favour of children and their families were also introduced. Law 4/84 of 5 April 1984 included the following special measures: ninety days of maternity leave, as well as paternity leave in specific situations; sixty days of leave for adoption of under-3-year-old children; special protection for pregnant women and a breastfeeding subsidy; free health care for under-1-year-olds; special leaves, totalling thirty days per year, to care for an ill or injured child; special subsidies for a disabled child, and the right of a parent to work part time to look after a disabled child or children under 12 years of age; family allowances. This law also established that the government, in co-operation with other public bodies, trade unions, and business organizations, was to create a network of social institutions and services to protect children and their families.

Although quite generous in principle, this law has not been implemented in a consistent fashion. None the less, public expenditure on social security increased from 3.6 per cent of GDP in 1970 to 7.4 per cent in 1974 and 8.6 per cent in 1981, when the second major recession of the post-revolutionary era set in. Even though more restrictive economic policies were implemented then, social security transfers were not retrenched and spending continued to fluctuate around the 1981 level.

Following the 1974 revolution, public policy began to reflect more fully the principle of 'equal opportunity' and to respond to rising demands for a more highly trained workforce (*Plano a Médio Prazo: 1977–80*, 1977). Services and activities, mostly established through the Ministry of Education, aimed to facilitate access to the school system, especially for disadvantaged children, while improving health, nutrition, and social conditions (IASE, 1989).

The school milk programme is one such example. Introduced at the primary school level through pilot projects in 1972–3, it was extended throughout the country in 1975–6. In that year, approximately 50 per cent of the targeted school population (around 500,000 children) benefited from the scheme. Expansion was quite rapid, and the coverage rate, including pupils in preschools and special education programmes, was as high as 99.6 per cent by 1980–1. This programme contributed to an increase in milk consumption from 7.6 million litres in 1975–6 to 22.6 million litres five years later. Cuts in public expenditure have since reduced coverage a little since then to a still high 96.6 per cent in 1987–8.

Similarly, a subsidized school meal programme was initiated, but with less success. By 1987–8 only about 1 per cent of preprimary and primary schoolchildren had access to school cafeterias. Greater progress was made for 'preparatory' and secondary school meals, though coverage was still below 80 per cent in 1987–8. Other social assistance measures within the education system were also instituted, including routine health monitoring and pedagogical evaluations, school accident prevention and insurance, transportation, and special education. While some progress was recorded, levels once again fluctuated due to restrictive policies, especially during the first half of the 1980s.

9.3.2. *Economic crisis, stabilization policy, and social impact*

Portugal suffered two economic crises within twelve years. The first, largely a consequence of the 1973 oil price shock, was worsened by the internal turbulence of 1974–5 and by other domestic factors. Since the mid-1970s, for instance, urban poverty has been aggravated by the immigration of African workers and their families, mainly from Cape Verde. Concentrated in large urban areas, the fertility and birth-rates and average family size of this disadvantaged group are typically higher than the average, reflecting a pattern more commonly found among the poor.

In addition, in 1975–6, in less than one year, more than 500,000 Portuguese, 17 per cent of whom were under 14 years of age, returned from the former colonies. This dramatic influx worsened housing shortages and placed a huge and lasting strain on public services. On the other hand, 'reverse' migration after 1970 from other Western European countries had a positive impact. Returning Portuguese typically brought savings with them, which they usually invested in their villages and towns of origin, contributing thus to the country's modernization and helping to mend the social fabric ripped by emigration.

The impact of the second recession, from 1980 to 1984, was particularly severe. Growth, real wages, investments, and private consumption plummeted; the deficit on the current account soared; the external debt skyrocketed and inflation increased (Table 9.1). The Portuguese government was forced to adopt shock-therapy adjustment policies of the type favoured by the International Monetary Fund. Economic targets were set without due consideration of social costs and the impact of measures on the most vulnerable groups, including poor children, was ignored. Deep budget cuts were imposed on education and social welfare expenditures; even the school milk programme was slashed for a short time.

The economic crisis did not affect all economic sectors or social strata equally. Export-oriented industries, for instance, benefited from the devaluation of the exchange rate. Yet, the real incomes of certain groups, particularly those already receiving low wages or pensions, were sharply reduced. The hardest hit were the unemployed and the economically inactive whose benefits were not indexed. Inflation acted as a powerful lever in the redistribution of income, and income inequality thus intensified. In regions with a high concentration of struggling industries, the incidence of severe poverty increased dramatically and small children were among those who suffered the most.

The general public was not immediately sensitive to the magnitude of the problems, but eventually played an important role in pressuring the government to change its approach. For instance, in the region of Setúbal, the Catholic Church actively pressed the regional and local authorities to implement emergency measures.

The reaction of the economic system to the restrictive policies took various forms. A sizeable underground economy, accounting for an estimated 20 per cent of the economy, emerged. Remittances of Portuguese workers abroad, representing 8 per cent of the national income in 1974 and almost 20 per cent in 1981, helped to soften the fall in incomes. Finally, the traditional family structure provided some support for the unemployed, disadvantaged pensioners, and young people seeking their first job.

No specific and comprehensive analyses exist on the effects of the economic crisis and subsequent adjustment on children. However, empirical data show, for example, that school attendance dropped and children's educational performance deteriorated, especially in the worst-hit areas. In addition, the incidence of infectious diseases such as tuberculosis mounted, larger numbers of infants were left unattended while their parents were at work, and child labour became more widespread. Finally, while IMR continued its steady decline, the proportion of mothers under

15 years of age among the total jumped from 3.1 per cent in 1975–7 to 9.2 per cent in 1985–7. Though this may reflect more accurate monitoring, it is none the less cause for concern.

9.3.3. *Changes in the welfare of children*

1. *Child Health*. Child health has improved considerably since 1974 as a result of the combined effect of rising standards of living and more effective public health services. IMR, for instance, decreased from 33.9 to 15.8 per 1,000 live births between 1975–7 and 1986. The under-5 mortality rate followed a similar pattern, falling from 19.1 to 9.2 per 1,000 over the same period (Table 9.3). A further factor contributing to improvements in child health status may be the extended immunization coverage witnessed since the mid-1970s.

On the negative side, deliberate efforts have been made since 1980 to reduce the scope of the national health service (NHS). Child health services, which come under this overall umbrella, have suffered as a consequence. While the public health expenditure–GDP ratio increased from 6.3 to 7.2 between 1975 and 1985, the percentage of total public expenditures allocated to health spending dropped from 16.5 to 10.4 per cent over the same period. The effects of health cuts may be concretely seen, for instance, in the reduced number of beds available in hospitals, which fell from 52,300 in 1975 to 39,300 in 1985. There was also a 30 per cent drop in the number of health centres constructed or extended during this period.

2. *Education*. The 'Three Ds' programme (Development, Democratization, and Decolonization), initiated after the revolution, aimed to render education accessible to all children without regard to family income or geographical location. Preschool education became a public sector responsibility, and municipalities were offered incentives to create kindergartens. As a result, preschool enrolments rose from 45,000 in 1975 to about 110–113,000 between 1983–5 and 121,000 in 1986–7. In addition, considerable expansion in public expenditure on education and on the numerous child welfare programmes delivered through the school system, as described earlier, resulted in sharply rising primary, preparatory, and secondary enrolment rates.

A special programme to improve disadvantaged children's educational chances was instituted. The programme usually included help in buying books and other learning aids and, in certain circumstances, financial support for food and accommodation. However, it reached less than 8 per cent of preprimary pupils and only about 12–14 per cent of primary schoolchildren. A higher proportion of preparatory and secondary school students benefited from this means-tested programme. By 1987–8, coverage was about 21 and 8 per cent for preparatory and secondary school students respectively. Only families with an extremely low per capita income qualified for this economically insubstantial subsidy.

3. *Juvenile delinquency*. It is difficult to draw an accurate picture of juvenile delinquency and criminality during this period. Moreover, evidence on links between these phenomena and increased poverty is scarce. None the less, the percentage of court cases involving minors for misdemeanours or felonies has dropped or stagnated in recent decades, particularly during the 1974–86 period (Table 9.6). At the same time, relative to the mid-1970s, cases of 'social maladjustment' among minors have increased, especially in urban areas. Likewise, the courts are intervening more frequently to protect child victims of abuse, abandonment, or neglect. It should be noted, however, that there has been a dramatic shift away from institutionalization to parental custody for children in conflict with the law, with a levelling off in the early 1980s.

While available statistics are not always reliable, it would appear that there was a clear upward trend in offences motivated by economic hardship over the 1974–86 period, including by disadvantaged young people. With the exception of robbery and drug-related crimes, juvenile crime rates have however largely stabilized.

4. *Child neglect and child abuse*. With a large share of cases of neglect, abuse, and abandonment not reported to the authorities, information on child abuse has traditionally been limited. The 1979 International Year of the Child started to break this conspiracy of silence, which, as the data in Table 9.6 indicate, appears to conceal a growing problem of child abuse. Considerably improved preventive legal measures have been instituted, but they are still largely inadequate and greater co-operation with the social assistance system is still needed.

In the early 1980s, about 30,000 children were treated in hospital emergency rooms each year for all ailments. One survey (Amaro, 1986) concluded that at least 1.7 per cent of these children were treated as a result

Table 9.6:   Cases before Juvenile Court by Type of Crime, 1964–1987
(per 1,000 youth)

	1964	1970	1976	1980	1985	1987
Abuse	3.6	—	—	—	6.9	12.3
Family maladjustment	1.4	0.4	2.1	3.9	3.8	2.5
Social maladjustment	2.4	0.5	0.9	3.8	6.9	4.7
Begging, vagrancy, prostitution	10.7	13.5	8.7	10.7	9.4	11.1
Misdemeanours	66.7	80.1	84.0	73.9	65.3	61.5
Felonies	14.8	5.2	4.1	7.5	6.7	5.6

Source: Compiled from official statistics.

of neglect or abuse and that an average 6.84 children per 1,000 families were neglected or abused in some way. Physical abuse affected 1.32 children per 1,000 families (ibid.).

The most important reasons underlying child neglect and abuse were (and likely remain) excessive alcohol consumption (85 per cent of cases), unemployment, inadequate housing, illiteracy, low income, and social status of the parents (Amaro, 1986). Among the parents of abused children, 54.1 per cent are illiterate; 33.5 per cent have no formal education, and 20.6 per cent have not completed primary school.

5. *Child labour*. In the past, even children under 10 years of age worked on farms and in shops, and were commonly allotted duties at home such as fetching water and babysitting. However, children were often encouraged with their schoolwork, particularly if their parents were aware of the importance of education, and their intellectual development was not neglected.

With growing industrialization, the face of child labour has changed. Children started working in small enterprises where managers all too often made no distinction between their capabilities and those of older workers. Children were (and often still are) paid low wages, piece rates, or in kind, and invariably had no, or only a fixed term, contract. They were usually not insured, even though, as indicated by the high incidence of accidents, they were often required to perform dangerous tasks. Most working children dropped out of school, though some attended evening classes.

The legal age of employment in Portugal has long been fifteen years, as for compulsory education. However, this norm has been applied inconsistently and child labour has maintained its high levels or even surged over the last two decades, especially in certain geographic areas and economic sectors. Official data, in contrast, point to a steady decline in child labour. The official employment survey published by the National Statistical Institute acknowledges that 48,600 (or 5.2 per cent) of the 10–14 age-group were pursuing some type of economic activity in 1988 and that 4.4 per cent had more or less full-time jobs, representing a considerable improvement on the 7–8 per cent recorded during earlier years. However, these figures obviously represent underestimates, since the illegal nature of child labour makes reporting spotty.

An unpublished study, for instance, estimated that, at 7 per cent, the employment rate among 10–14-year-olds for 1984–7 was about 3 points higher than official values. Another unpublished survey carried out by the Trade Unions of the Textile and Shoe Industry in 1988 identified 228 enterprises employing children. A textile company in Porto, for instance, was found to pay 13-year-olds only 1,000 escudos per month for the first three months and then 6,500 escudos—around one-fifth of the legal minimum wage—in following months.

The causes of child labour are complex and not easy to identify, but seem to be related to the expansion of the underground economy which accompanied the Portuguese economic boom in the late 1970s, and particularly after 1984. Large numbers of manufacturing enterprises, without stable structures or significant financial resources, employ clandestine workers at wages below the legal minimum. Generally unregistered, these labour-intensive and export-oriented enterprises, with scandalous impunity, employ children under 15 years of age. Children cost less, are more malleable to the demands of owners, and can be more readily laid off if business is slack. Indeed, for many unscrupulous entrepreneurs, child workers represent the edge they need to face the competition of larger and technologically more advanced companies. Children are also used as unskilled labour in construction, retailing, and restaurants. They are found in the formal economy as well, both as illegal employees or as 'subcontractors' doing piece work at home, frequently in very unhealthy conditions. In either case, the normal development of the child is jeopardized.

Secondly, child labour persists because in many cases the children's incomes are essential for the well-being of the family. This is especially true for large families, families with only one working adult or in which two adults are working at very low wages, and for families whose main breadwinner is ill or unemployed. In addition, the emergence of the 'consumer society' during the 1980s encouraged young people to seek an independent income and they were thus enticed to enter the labour market at an early age.

The inefficiency of the school system must also bear part of the responsibility for the child labour problem. As noted, failure and drop-out rates are very high and insufficient effort has been made to keep disadvantaged children in the education system. For many of these families, school activities represent a waste of time. All too often parents are the first to encourage their children to enter the labour market. Finally, child labour is also the result of a mentality which envisages the workplace as the school of virtue and the ladder to a useful adult life. Most Portuguese parents of today had to work hard when they were young, and they unconsciously want the same for their offspring.

The social costs of child labour are high. The physical, intellectual, and social development of children is endangered by the long hours and poor working conditions. Second, child labour or any other unregulated labour force creates unfair competition for adult workers and leads to an unjust advantage for those enterprises which resort to it. Finally, it constitutes an impoverishment of the nation's human capital since, by working, children are deprived of the chance to acquire skills.

The complacency of the authorities toward child labour is therefore difficult to fathom. Current child labour laws are inadequate for several reasons (Damião, 1988): they do not ensure sufficient flexibility among economic activity, school, and family; they are too 'soft' on illegal business practices; and they do not guarantee that proper business practices will prevail. The elimination of child labour will require a comprehensive social and economic policy approach. Legal solutions are not enough, though better legislation is certainly needed. In addition, the participation and advocacy of non-governmental organizations can play an important role in promoting and protecting the rights of children.

9.4. Trends in Child Welfare: 1986 and Beyond

In 1986 Portugal entered the then European Economic Community (now the European Union). Although economic growth had already resumed in 1985, EEC entry marked a five-year boom during which GDP steadily expanded, the current account deficit disappeared, the external debt started to decline, investments (including direct foreign investment) took a rapid upturn, and real wages and private consumption advanced. From 1985–6, macroeconomic indicators showed substantial improvement in all major areas, except unemployment which continued to climb (see Table 9.1).

Membership of the European Economic Community apparently created an entirely new foundation for economic and social development in Portugal. It also brought certain advantages in the field of social welfare, namely through financial resources provided by various EEC funds. Yet, there is no reason to be jubilant as these gains may prove to be temporary. Economic growth has not been accompanied by an adequate social policy and, indeed, progress in social welfare and especially in child welfare has been far from satisfactory.

The Portuguese economy is highly dependent upon the external environment. For instance, the restrictive monetary policies followed by some EEC countries, especially Germany, over 1992–4 contributed greatly to weak economic growth and swelling unemployment (Table 9.1).

Social policy in recent years has been inspired by a liberal ideology and determined by the so-called economic policy requirements. Public budget cuts have been severe, though none the less unable to keep public deficit under desirable limits. Meanwhile, there has been a lack of innovative social action to compensate benefit reductions arising from public expenditure constraints. The outcome is a continuous degradation of the quantity and quality of services provided by the public social sectors. In a country like Portugal, where the level of development of the welfare state was always very low, this situation is particularly serious.

9.4.1. Family structure

Recent child welfare trends have also been influenced by changes in the demographic structure and in the stability and reproductive behaviour of families. According to the 1991 census, 57 per cent of all families included under-15-year-olds and 3 per cent of these families were headed by a single parent. These data, however, grossly underestimate the phenomenon due to the statistical criteria employed and assumptions made about families. A survey on low-income families, for instance, placed the number of children in lone-parent families at around 15 per cent: 2.3 per cent with the father and 12.4 per cent with the mother (Silva and Costa, 1989). The study also found that children in poor one-parent families typically only rarely see the non-custodial parent. The 1991 census also recorded more than 1,000 under-15-year-olds living alone or in institutions. Also noteworthy, 42 per cent of children in this age-group lived in households with three adults, normally two parents and a relative, though more frequently in rural areas (Table 9.7).

In Portugal, as elsewhere, a dramatic process of transformation in the family is under way. Sweeping changes in attitudes and practices regarding, among others, sexuality, religion, and division of labour in the home, have made society ill-equipped to cope with the consequences of these radical changes. Women's participation in the labour force has increased, due both to economic factors which have encouraged the spread of two-wage-earner families and to growing recognition of women's right to social and economic independence. Out-of-wedlock births now constitute a significant percentage of the total and recent statistics show a definite upward trend. Although still lower than the European Union average, this percentage is the highest among Southern European countries (Table 9.2). The divorce rate, though starting from a very low level, has climbed.

Table 9.7: Under-15-Year-Olds according to the Composition of their Households, 1991 (in totals and percentages)

	No.	%
One adult male with one or more under-15-year-olds	5,702	—
One adult female with one or more under-15-year-olds	75,426	3
Two adults with one under-15-year-old	355,248	14
Two adults with two under-15-year-olds	579,020	23
Two adults with three under-15-year-olds	240,984	10
Two adults with four or more under-15-year-olds	208,298	8
Three or more adults and one or more under-15-year-olds	1,002,893	42
Others (including under-15-year-olds alone or in institutions)	1,286	—
Total	2,468,857	100

Source: Compiled by the author from census data.

Although these factors are at work in both rural and urban areas, their impact has been stronger in the cities.

9.4.2. *Changes in the welfare of children and families*

1. *The incidence of poverty and living conditions of the poor.* For several years Portugal has exhibited the highest incidence of absolute and relative poverty among countries of the European Economic Community (Costa *et al.*, 1985; Teekens, 1989). Despite rapid growth, between 1980 and 1989–90 (the year of the latest available budget survey), 'absolute' poverty declined only marginally, from 25.2 per cent to 22.3 per cent of all households and from 25.5 to 21.1 per cent of all people (INE, 1990; Costa, 1992).

Alternative estimates for poverty incidence were obtained from the same budget survey data by using 'relative' poverty lines equal to 40 and 50 per cent of both the mean and the median expenditure per adult equivalent unit. For 1989–90, 13 and 22 per cent of families had incomes below 40 and 50 per cent of the mean respectively, while 13 and 7 per cent were below 40 and 50 per cent of the median respectively. The poverty rates obtained with 50 per cent of the mean are very similar to those determined with the 'absolute' poverty line.

Unlike in many other countries, the incidence of poverty among children follows the general pattern: around 21 per cent of children are below the above-mentioned poverty line of 50 per cent of the mean average expenditure per adult equivalent unity. With average levels of expenditure notoriously low in Portugal compared with those of other European countries, the thresholds for the standard poverty lines used herein are therefore relatively restrictive.

In the early 1990s, poverty remains an acute social problem in Portugal. While more recent estimates of poverty rates are not available, there is no reason to believe that the situation has improved. Indeed, for some specific population groups, economic conditions may have worsened during 1992–4 because of the negative trends in unemployment, real wages, real value of social security transfers, and access to urban housing. The groups most severely affected are elderly people living alone on low pensions; families whose breadwinners have little or no education; female-headed households; families with three or more children; families with only one income earner or with two low-income earners.

A glance at consumption patterns and other indicators reveals the main features of poverty in Portugal. Material poverty in rural areas is more severe than in urban centres. While the food share accounts for 41 per cent of the average household expenditure, the figures for the rural and urban poor are 57.4 and 54.1 per cent respectively. The rural poor are also more severely disadvantaged in their access to utilities, sanitation, household

Table 9.8: Indicators of Comfort for Poor and Non-Poor Families, 1990

Indicators	Total	Poor		Non-poor	
		Urban	Rural	Urban	Rural
Houses without					
Electricity	2.3	3.6	9.2	0.3	1.3
Water	11.1	14.7	31.1	3.5	10.3
Bathroom	9.9	13.2	31.5	2.3	8.4
Television	11.5	15.5	32.7	4.2	9.9
Washing-machine	46.9	63.3	85.5	23.8	51.2
Sewing-machine	11.2	14.1	33.2	2.7	10.7
Telephone	58.5	71.2	92.4	34.0	66.6
Refrigerator	11.0	17.5	32.4	2.8	9.5
Radio	15.4	24.1	31.1	9.6	13.4

Source: INE, Family Budget Survey 1989–90. Calculations computed by Leonor Vasconcelos.

appliances, and, more importantly from a child perspective, health care and education (Table 9.8).

About a quarter of the poor are below 18 years of age. Table 9.8 clearly illustrates the concrete deprivations suffered by these children and their families. Children shoulder the brunt of poverty through inadequate diets, health care, education, housing, hygiene, and family and social integration. They are also more likely to remain disadvantaged throughout their lives, which in itself tends to perpetuate poverty. Among the respondents to a sample survey conducted in poor urban areas (Silva and Costa, 1989), 79 per cent stated that their parents had also been poor.

Among the key parental determinants of child poverty are the poor health and nutrition of the mother; inadequate care during pregnancy and delivery; poor working conditions, excessive workloads and emotional stress during pregnancy; and low educational levels. Perhaps the most important determinant of child poverty is education, the most significant vehicle of social mobility. Parental illiteracy or low educational levels, inadequate housing, malnutrition and hunger, child labour, and early participation in domestic duties all spell 'failure' in education. Poor children are thus more likely to be held back and eventually drop out of primary school.

A 1985 country-wide survey on low-income families (Costa *et al.*, 1985) showed that 21 per cent of the poor children in the sample left school without completing first grade and were thus officially illiterate. In addition, 61 per cent of children did not continue beyond primary school level. Of those attending school, 68 per cent had been held back a year at least once. Disadvantaged children who left school at an early age generally entered the labour force almost immediately: 32 per cent of surveyed people in poor families began to work before the age of 10, 37 per cent between the ages of 10 and 12, and 91 per cent before 15 years of age. By the same token, 46 per cent of 12–24-year-olds who had dropped out of school were unemployed at the time of the survey.

The effects of child poverty are also evident in problems of child supervision and socialization. Parents' long working hours and the insufficient space typical of poor housing very often force children to spend their 'free' time in the streets. They are thus exposed to many dangers, including accidents, sexual abuse, drug addiction and trafficking, and criminality.

Existing social and child welfare services are ill equipped to cope with this situation. For example, a 1990 survey of families in a poor neighbourhood of Lisbon found that 56 per cent of all under-6-year-olds did not have access to kindergartens and that 68 per cent of primary schoolchildren were left unsupervised after classes (Silva, 1993). The lack of social services is particularly detrimental for poor children whose families are unable to provide an environment which fosters adequate physical, psychological, and mental development.

In Lisbon and other urban centres new forms of poverty and marginalization have been observed. While not yet fully understood, this 'new' poverty is increasingly evident and cuts across conventional social strata. The homeless, vagrants, and 'professional' beggars have become distinct segments of the urban poor.

2. *Child health and health care*. Improvements in child health have been more or less constant in recent decades (Table 9.3). This is also true for the post-1986 period, although the main health indicators continue to show a considerable gap in relation to European averages. However, the significance of these improvements is open to interpretation. The remarkable decline in IMR since 1976 and through to the early 1990s may be due to large (though not complete) advances in the coverage and quality of child-related public health care services. Improved overall economic and social conditions have obviously also had an impact. None the less, it must not be forgotten that these indicators measure average values which inevitably hide large variations among social groups, between different regions, and even within individual areas.

Considerable problems continue to burden the health care system and are at least partly responsible for the sizeable variations in child well-being. Many health centres, particularly in urban areas, are stretched beyond their limits due to insufficient staffing, especially for qualified personnel. In addition, some health services are hindered by efficiency problems. Little progress has been made to date in integrated maternal and child health care initiatives and efforts to foster public awareness on health issues have also been limited. The urban poor, especially mothers and children, do not benefit adequately from the national health care network. Lack of education and very low incomes constitute strong impediments to access to health services. Among the impoverished, often migrant families, which represent 10 per cent of the Lisbon population, birth-rates and IMR are much higher than the average (Costa and Pimenta, 1991).

Finally, only limited progress in family planning among low-income families may be a further factor slowing improvements in the well-being of poor children. Family planning programmes, with private sector support, first appeared only in the late 1960s. The public health care system took up the initiative in 1976, when special units were supposed to be set up in all public health centres. None the less, 1979 data show that only 240 units were available for a population of 2,359,000 women in the 15–49 age-group (Abecassis, 1979). A number of barriers, including lack of public awareness as well as prejudice or religious reservations, hampered the spread of information and the use of reliable family planning methods. Only a small portion of the female population knew that family planning services were available, and those who did know tended to be among the more highly educated.

3. *Child labour and child protection.* Although the problem of accuracy in calculating the extent of child labour remains, there are some indications that the phenomenon has intensified rather than subsided in the early 1990s. As shown in Table 9.9, estimates using the Family Budget Survey, 1989–90 reveal that 8.6 per cent of children between the ages of 11 and 14 were part of the labour force (employed and unemployed), but this proportion almost doubled to 16 per cent for poor children (Table 9.9). Reports from several labour inspections claim that about 30,000 children were involved in the labour market in 1993.

Table 9.9: Children and Work, 1989–1990 (percentages)

	Total		Poor		Non-poor	
	11–14	15–17	11–14	15–17	11–14	15–17
Students	87.1	58.0	76.5	35.1	90.3	62.8
Workers	5.4	32.2	10.7	40.4	3.8	28.9
Unemployed	3.2	4.8	5.3	15.8	2.6	4.6
Other	4.3	5.0	7.5	8.7	4.3	3.7
Total	100.0	100.0	100.0	100.0	100.0	100.0

Note: Poverty line = 50 per cent of average expenditure per adult equivalent unit (OECD scale).

Source: INE, Family Budget Survey, 1989–90. Calculations computed by Leonor Vasconcelos.

The latest report published by the national Observatory on policies to combat social exclusion encapsulates the problem. It views children's work as a mechanism which generates social exclusion. It violates the basic rights of citizens and, because it threatens children's schooling, has negative consequences on their future integration in the labour market (CISEP, 1994).

Significant steps have been taken in recent years to increase child protection: namely, a system of family shelters (*acolhimento familiar*) was created in 1992 to provide short-term foster care for children of families in need; official protection committees (*Comissões de Protecção*) were set up in 1991 with the aim of protecting children under 12 years of age; and, finally, a support project for children and families was established in 1992, which co-ordinates the activities of the ministries of justice, employment, health, and social security in relation to children at risk.

4. *Child care*. Portugal's integration in the European Economic Community has highlighted what was already well known: the population is generally poorly educated and the schooling system is unable to meet the challenge of improving the skills of new generations. In the late 1980s, major responsibility for preprimary and primary education was passed over to municipalities. Financial resources are allocated by the central government, but the municipalities are in charge of school maintenance, transport of children, and the more social aspects of the education system, such as meal provision and subsidies to needy students. However, there remain some problems to be ironed out in this division of responsibilities.

Preschool education, a main determinant of success in later schooling, is still embryonic. Only 35.6 per cent of 3–6-year-olds were enrolled in public kindergartens in the late 1980s–early 1990s. Moreover, there are substantial geographic variations, ranging from about 70 per cent coverage in the Guarda region to only 27 per cent in Braga and Porto. The fact that two-thirds of all children do not have the benefit of preschool education may explain the low success rates at the primary school level; it is also a clear indicator of the inequalities faced by the children of disadvantaged families.

Coverage is also inadequate for the growing number of dual-worker families. In December 1987, more than 21,000 children were on waiting lists for various public day-care institutions and services (Table 9.10). An even larger number of parents, however, seek other solutions without even bothering to apply to public institutions. Children are looked after by relatives, generally grandparents. Others are placed with individual carers, usually women with no formal professional training and often working from homes lacking appropriate facilities. More affluent families place their children in for-profit private nurseries, where monthly fees may exceed ten times the public per-child family allowance.

Table 9.10: Public Day-care and Free-time Facilities (December 1987)

	Places available	Places filled	Filled/ available places	Waiting list	Waiting list/places filled
'Mini' nurseries	112	101	90.2	50	49.5
Nurseries	4,256	3,948	92.8	963	49.5
Kindergartens	32,834	29,988	91.3	4,882	16.3
Nursery-kindergartens	58,327	53,215	91.2	11,253	21.1
'Homes'	7,082	6,584	93.0	574	8.7
Special education	5,374	5,078	94.5	816	16.1
'Free-time' facilities	38,149	33,404	87.6	2,945	8.8

Source: Compiled by the author from social security data.

9.5. Conclusion and Recommendations

While discussing the general focus of policy action during the 1982–4 recession, Jolly and Cornia (1984) stated that, 'in all that has been written . . . the preoccupations have been overwhelmingly and narrowly economic'. This is especially true in the case of Portugal's two recessions of the first half of the 1980s and the 1990s. During these crises, little attention was paid to their impact on children's well-being. Their plight was either totally ignored or was viewed strictly in relation to service availability. And indeed, this has been the case generally in Portugal's recent history.

The two decades of fast economic growth before 1974 were not accompanied by parallel achievements in social welfare. The important advances achieved in child welfare were not evenly distributed and large pockets of poverty persisted. The pre-revolutionary era taught a clear lesson: while economic growth is essential to the improvement of child well-being, policies specifically designed to enhance child and family welfare are also required.

The 1974 revolution was inspired by three main goals: development, democracy, and decolonization. However, the economic crisis of 1974–6 and the swing towards more conservative government administrations after 1977 slowed the process initiated in 1974. In addition, problems of social marginalization were exacerbated by the considerable immigration from the former colonies.

In the mid-late 1980s, progress accelerated in child welfare indicators. However, economic restructuring combined with the difficulties of adjusting to the international economic order and to membership of the European Economic Community have been accompanied by an upturn in social marginalization. In urban and rural areas, large numbers of children still endure situations of 'old' poverty. 'New' problems among children have also surfaced with increasing instability in the family, inadequate housing, parents' long working hours, low family incomes, and socialization difficulties, especially drug dependence.

The social security system was (and still is) not adequately equipped to confront the complex of problems surrounding these changes. Successive governments have been reluctant to acknowledge the depth and persistence of poverty and have acted only in the most dramatic cases. However, poverty in Portugal is not a cyclical short-term problem. Rather, it is structurally tied to the country's whole process of economic growth.

Portuguese children are still not assured of the benefits of economic growth, nor are they protected from the risks of misdirected development. Indeed, there are reasons to fear that child poverty and social deviance may increase in the near future. Despite the fact that children are considered to have constitutional rights, families are still expected to bear complete responsibility for the development and socialization of their children.

In order to bring about effective change in the welfare of Portuguese children, much more needs to be done. The well-being of children, the nation's future adults, must be awarded priority attention and priority action. The relationship between family income and cost of living and the creation of conditions of income security for all families is a first and vital requisite for child well-being. Primary policy focus should be on wage levels, the minimum wage, unemployment, and the elimination of exploitative working conditions. Secondly, considerable restructuring of the social security system is needed to take greater account of the changes in family structure and their effects on children. In this regard, the family allowance system should be substantially strengthened.

Social services in general, and for children in particular, must be considerably improved in order to ensure child well-being. To this end, greater financial resources, commitment, and initiatives are needed. For instance, concerted efforts to guarantee equal opportunities for children in education are indispensable. This will require the allocation of additional resources to meet the special needs of disadvantaged children.

The issue of social protection for children in need calls for priority attention. Comprehensive, targeted interventions must be undertaken in favour of children and young people living in difficult circumstances, including in the areas of nutrition, school drop-out, social deviance, and drug abuse. More generally, efforts are needed to improve the inadequate housing of large segments of the population. Particularly in the larger cities, the housing problem represents a key factor in present and future poverty, especially for migrants.

Most importantly, a child welfare monitoring system is essential for the development of effective and equitable social policies for children. So too, increased empirical research into the conditions of children's lives is indispensable to improved social policies. On the other side of the coin, public awareness campaigns are needed to enhance community participation and solidarity, which in itself can go a long way towards improving the situation of children.

Finally, the United Nations Convention on the Rights of the Child, ratified by Portugal in 1990, has opened the way to an important and fresh approach to the problems facing the country's children. However, strengthened efforts and commitment are needed for implementation of the provisions of the Convention. To this important end, a national ombudsman for children could make a significant contribution to increasing awareness and understanding of children's special problems and could act constructively to promote and safeguard the rights of children.

10

Growth, Regional Imbalance, and Child Well-Being: Italy over the Last Four Decades

CHIARA SARACENO

10.1. Introduction

During the last forty years, profound economic, social, and political changes have greatly affected the situation of children in Italy. Though available data are far from satisfactory, there has clearly been a marked strengthening of social and political concern for child well-being during this period. Since child deprivation is closely tied, however, to the social and legal definition attached to it, as well as to its social and statistical visibility, caution must be exercised when analysing data collected over long periods. The rise in child abuse, for instance, may be due to increased incidence, to improved reporting methods, or to a revised definition. The reverse is true for child labour, which, due to stiffer sanctions introduced in 1961, may be more liable to under-reporting.

10.2. From the 1950s to the Mid-1970s

Following World War II and until the mid-1950s, Italy was a largely rural and war-devastated country, suffering significant unemployment, high illiteracy, and substantial internal and external migration. Extremely low standards of living prevailed: on average, 45 per cent of family income was spent on food (decreasing to 40 per cent in 1971 and 38 per cent in 1979) (D'Apice, 1981); over 84 per cent of families had no household appliances; even in major cities such as Milan, many households got by without electricity, running water, or sanitary facilities. In 1957, the monthly income of the average blue-collar worker family was insufficient to satisfy minimum necessities. And even in 1958, 62 per cent of white-collar families, 94 per cent of blue-collar families, and 99 per cent of rural families did not have a washing-machine, a refrigerator, or a television.

Between 1959 and 1963, often referred to as Italy's 'economic miracle', all economic aggregate indicators improved dramatically. GNP, per capita income, and aggregate consumption increased respectively at rates of 6.5, 5.8, and 6 per cent per year. At the same time, however, income and consumption differentials by social group and by geographical location (urban and rural as well as regional differences) worsened. These inequalities were reinforced by labour market and wage policies; for instance, industrialization in the South was encouraged by a legalized geographical wage differential (eliminated only in 1969) that gave employees of the same company higher wages in the North than in the South. Moreover, the availability of jobs with social security benefits varied widely by geographical area. Workers in protected jobs in less prosperous areas faced greater demands for support and assistance from family networks. In addition, as families in the South had more dependent children, their standard of living was lower. Finally, more women in industrialized regions worked, whereas high male unemployment rates and competition between adult men and adolescents in the informal economy made it more difficult for southern women to find employment.

These differences strongly influenced the living standards of families and the well-being of children. Although food expenditure absorbed such a large share of poor families' budgets that little was left for leisure or even health and hygiene, it was often not sufficient to provide an adequate diet. White-collar families consumed 25 per cent more beef, about 40 per cent more fresh fish, fruit, and milk, and 20 per cent more cheese than their blue-collar counterparts. Moreover, as blue-collar families were generally larger, the number of children with poor diets, despite growing consumption, was higher than suggested by a family-based comparison. Similar regional differentials existed: in 1963–4, average consumption of animal proteins was 40 per cent higher in the North.

10.2.1. Birth and survival

The 1950s to the mid-1970s witnessed rising marriage rates, reaching 8.2 per 1,000 in 1963 and stabilizing thereafter at around 7.4. There was also a substantial decrease in fertility rates. An apparent trend inversion in the mid-1960s was due to changes in marriage rates and in the age of mothers bearing a first child (Table 10.1). As a result, the absolute number of 0–19-year-old children increased from 16.3 to 17.2 million between 1958 and 1978, while their share in the total population dropped from about 33 to 28.1 per cent (CNR/IRP, 1988).

During the same period, the infant mortality rate (IMR) decreased substantially from 42.3 per 1,000 live births in 1961–2 to 28.2 in 1970–2. Though regional differentials persisted, declines were recorded for all geographical areas (Table 10.2). This improvement was largely due to

Table 10.1: Total Fertility Rate by Geographical Area

Year	North-west	North-east	North-centre	Centre	South	Islands	Italy
1951	1.7	2.1	—	2.0	3.3	3.2	2.4
1956	1.7	1.9	—	2.0	3.0	3.0	2.3
1961	1.9	2.2	—	2.1	3.3	3.1	2.4
1966	2.3	2.4	—	2.3	3.3	3.1	2.7
1971	2.1	2.1	—	2.1	2.9	2.8	2.4
1976	1.8	1.8	—	1.9	2.7	2.5	2.1
1980	—	—	1.4	—	2.2	—	1.7
1985	—	—	1.2	—	1.8	—	1.4
1988	—	—	1.1	—	1.6	—	1.3
1991	—	—	1.1	—	1.1	—	1.3
1992[a]	—	—	—	—	—	—	1.2
1993[a]	—	—	—	—	—	—	1.2
1994[b]	—	—	—	—	—	—	1.2

[a] Preliminary. [b] Estimate.

Sources: ISTAT, various years; Sonnino (1989), 33.

Table 10.2: Infant and Perinatal Mortality by Geographical Area

Year	North-west	North-east	Centre	South	Islands	Italy
Infant mortality						
1951	56.3	47.0	49.7	84.5	77.8	66.6
1960[a]	36.1	31.6	32.0	55.2	46.5	42.3
1970[b]	24.9	21.8	22.5	36.3	32.8	28.2
1980	12.4	12.0	12.2	16.5[c]	—[c]	14.4
1985	8.4	7.9	9.0	12.9[c]	—[c]	10.3
1991	7.4	6.1	8.7	9.7[c]	—[c]	8.3
1992[d]	7.5	6.1	8.7	9.2[c]	—[c]	8.3
1993[d]	6.6	5.4	6.9	8.5[c]	—[c]	7.3
1994[e]	5.1	5.4	6.7	7.9[c]	—[c]	6.7
Perinatal mortality						
1951	43.9	41.4	47.8	56.8	50.6	49.6
1960	36.3	33.9	38.2	49.6	45.1	41.9
1970	28.1	25.2	28.7	37.9	34.0	31.2
1980	16.1	14.6	15.6	19.9[c]	—[c]	17.5
1985	12.6	11.6	12.9	15.7[c]	—[c]	13.2
1991	5.2	7.4	9.5	11.8[c]	—[c]	10.5

[a] 1960–2. [b] 1970–2. [c] South and islands. [d] Preliminary. [e] Estimate.

Sources: *La Population de l'Italie*. Cicred Series. World Population Year (1974); ISTAT, *Annuari di Statistiche Sanitarie*; Mattioli (1988a).

better nutrition among pregnant women, the spread of maternal and child health services, increased hospital births, and the growing use of sterilized formula. Furthermore, prolonging compulsory schooling to the age of 14 in 1962 reduced the number of higher-risk births to young mothers (Pinnelli, 1989).

Death-rates for all age-groups fell during this period, as hygienic and overall health conditions improved. Though no major progress was detected for congenital malformations and respiratory diseases, infant, child, and adolescent deaths due to infectious, parasitic, and intestinal diseases decreased markedly.

Trends in morbidity are less clear. Poliomyelitis and diphtheria almost disappeared between 1960 and 1970, with a spectacular improvement in the South and the Islands where cases of poliomyelitis dropped from 2,353 to 36 over this period. In contrast, the incidence of gastroenteritis, meningitis, and pertussis remained fairly stable, indicating that medical progress had reduced the lethal effects of infectious diseases rather than their incidence among children.

10.2.2. *Child-care services and the needs of mothers*

During this period, paid maternity leave was gradually extended to various categories of working women. By 1977, compulsory leave of two months before and three months after childbirth was provided to all formal-sector female wage-earners, including part-time and seasonal workers. An optional additional period was granted, at reduced pay, with seniority and job maintenance guaranteed (Ballestrero, 1979). Full-time home-makers, self-employed, professional, and rural mothers, and mothers working in the informal sector (a large portion of all working women throughout the 1970s) were, however, not covered.

Child-care services were also expanded during this period. Up to 1971 enterprises employing forty or more women were obliged to organize or contribute to day-care services for the 0–2 age-group. Women working in small enterprises, however, received no such assistance. Financial and organizational responsibility for child-care services shifted to local governments in 1971, with the state's support. The goal of 5 per cent child-care coverage for the 0–2 age-group within five years set by the new law, however, was reached in only in a few urban areas of the Centre-North. By the beginning of the 1980s, southern Sicily still did not have a public child-care centre.

In 1968, the state assumed responsibility for the creation of kindergartens for 3–5-year-old children, which previously had been the sole responsibility of local authorities and not-for-profit agencies. Increased availability of places resulted in steadily rising enrolments, reaching 70

Table 10.3:　Kindergarten Enrolment Rates by Geographical Area, 1971–1991

Year	North-west	North-east	Centre	South	Islands	Italy
1971–2	61.3	65.2	56.3	59.5	52.0	59.4
1975–6	71.2	74.6	71.0	71.6	57.9	70.1
1981–2	82.6	86.7	86.4	81.6	70.8	81.9
1985–6	88.6	92.1	93.3	87.4	76.5	87.7
1990–1	96.8	96.8	97.9	87.9	87.9	92.7

Sources: Schizzerotto (1990); ISTAT.

per cent by the mid-1970s. The gap between the Centre-North and the South narrowed, though the Islands still trailed (Table 10.3).

10.2.3. Schooling

Extension of compulsory education to 14 years and the unification of the middle school in 1962 helped raise school enrolments and reduce class and gender differences. School attendance rose steadily during this period. None the less, in 1971, 5.2 per cent of the population above the age of 14 was illiterate, rising to more than 10 per cent in the South.

Repetition rates, however, were high (Schizzerotto, 1975; Gattullo, 1976; Besozzi, 1983). In 1975–6, the failure rate for first graders was still 4.5 per cent, though it was somewhat lower for higher grades. Failures were also evident in the first year of middle school (8.1 per cent in 1975–6). In addition, many children dropped out of secondary school at the legal working age of 15 or even earlier. In 1976, 15 per cent of children dropped out of compulsory secondary school and this percentage doubles if elementary school drop-outs are included.

The quality of learning was influenced by the unequal distribution of teachers, facilities, and equipment. Throughout the 1960s and 1970s, a shift system operated in many schools, particularly in working-class districts in northern industrial towns. Classes were large—often 35–40 children—though by the early 1970s numbers had been halved, except in the South. Moreover, rural children often attended one-room schools, with a single teacher responsible for all grades.

More than 60 per cent of youths still lacked high school diplomas in the mid-1970s (Fiorini, 1981). The majority not only went to work early, but entered the labour market with few skills. While social class remained a key predictor of educational levels, the proportion of working-class youths completing high school and attending university nearly doubled between 1953–4 and 1972–3, with high school completion jumping from 17 to 30 per cent, and university enrolment from 13 to 25 per cent (Gattullo, 1989).

10.2.4. Child labour

The legal age of employment was raised to 15 years in 1961, though in 1967 it was reduced to 14 for jobs in agriculture and family businesses (when compatible with compulsory school attendance). The 1967 law also determined appropriate jobs for 15–18-year-olds, including work hours, medical supervision, and apprenticeship contracts and classes.

Large numbers of under-15-year-olds worked during the 1950s and even into the 1960s in agriculture, shops, small workshops, and family businesses. A 1971 study by the Ministry of Labour estimated that there were about 130,000 child workers, with a prevalence of girls in the Centre-North and boys in the South. A 1973 inquiry in northern Lombardy found that children accounted for 1 per cent of the region's total work-force. Finally, a 1975 Censis study estimated that 106,000 children were working, the majority of them illegally. Only 51,000 worked while attending school.

From 1959 to 1976, activity rates for the 14–19 age-group more than halved for both sexes, reflecting the impact of longer schooling (Table 10.4). However, these 'official' activity rates must be viewed with caution, as many studies conducted over this period found children working more or less full time in the informal economy (Paci, 1981). Many high school students had some kind of job in the informal economy, either to add to the family income or to satisfy new needs fostered by the expanding consumer society (Ricolfi and Sciolla, 1980).

An almost threefold increase in workplace accidents involving adolescents was recorded between 1950 and 1960, though the increase for all ages was substantially less than 100 per cent (Berlinguer *et al.*, 1978). Thereafter, accidents involving this age-group decreased, though they remained well above the 1950 level despite the decreased activity rates. The 'economic miracle' of the late 1950s thus involved exploitation of young workers, who, due to lack of training and experience, were most at risk of accidents.

Table 10.4: Activity Rates by Sex for the 14–19-Year Age-Group, 1959–1976

Year	Males	Females
1959	69.2	47.6
1964	54.0	37.3
1969	41.3	30.9
1974	30.6	22.8
1976	28.1	21.7

Sources: ISTAT, *Rilevazioni delle forze di lavoro in Italia, vecchia e nuova serie*; Abburrà (1989).

10.2.5. Children in institutions

Between 1951 and 1960, about 193,000 healthy children, including children of migrant families, lived in institutions either because they had no parents or because their parents could not care for them. In addition, 9,000 children in the 0–6 age-group were in orphanages. Institutionalizing a child was often perceived as a means not only of relieving the family budget, but of improving the child's educational chances. Foster homes were rare and mostly limited to the rural tradition of hosting an orphan for payment.

In the late 1960s and 1970s, welfare policy shifted to encouraging families to keep their children and offering support to foster homes. A 1967 adoption law made the 'child's interest' the primary criterion in adoption and stressed a child's right to be raised in a family. None the less, the number of children in institutions decreased substantially only after 1970.

10.3. The 1960s and 1970s: A Golden Age of Child Rights?

An unprecedented concern for children's needs and society's responsibility towards them emerged during the late 1960s and 1970s, as reflected by the introduction of several laws, including the 1967 adoption law; the 1975 family law, which emphasized parental responsibility and eliminated the distinction between illegitimate and legitimate children; regulations on the right of handicapped children to attend kindergarten and normal compulsory education; a 1977 law extending parental leave to working fathers; and norms further restricting child labour.

This new focus, however, highlighted gaps which had not been filled and which threatened to broaden: first, the North–South gap had only been partially and unsystematically narrowed. As many child-related services were mandated to local authorities, differences in local resources and traditions led to considerable inequalities. In addition, economic growth in the most industrialized areas created new risks for children, including pollution-related health problems, traffic accidents, and violence.

Moreover, inadequate attention was given to the situation of children within the family. Thus, little was known and nothing was done about the large numbers of under-3-year-olds who did not attend nursery schools. Only those schoolchildren and adolescents manifesting deviant behaviour usually received attention. Furthermore, family allowances, paid to all wage workers, did not keep up with inflation; this was also the case of tax credits for dependent children. The fascist, pro-natalist origin of these measures, combined with fears that they would encourage fertility, contributed to this disregard and eventually led to a reduction in family allowances and income support measures to a degree unknown in most other European countries. Moreover, in the increasing competition for public resources, adolescents probably suffered the most.

Finally, changes in the family that were partly acknowledged in legislation of this period (divorce was made legal in 1970, and the Family Law of 1975 guaranteed greater equality between husband and wife) revealed new problem areas in the institutional and family framework for children.

10.4. From the Late 1970s to the Early 1990s

10.4.1. Changes in the social and economic environment

Over the last two decades, the political and economic landscape has become much less favourable to public welfare initiatives. At the beginning of this period, public policy continued to enhance government involvement in many social areas. However, the mid-1980s were dominated by debate on the crisis of the welfare state. In addition, the continued rise in the public debt prompted cuts in transfers to local governments, which particularly affected social services. Thus, social policies were, and are, shaped through the annual budget (which determines local government resources, user fees in the health sector, and so forth). This phenomenon became clearer in the 1990s, particularly with the pressure of mounting debt and the requirements of the Maastricht Treaty.

1. *Slower and unstable growth and rising income inequality.* GDP growth slowed considerably during the early 1970s, and, by the end of the decade, economic recession and restructuring in all main industrial branches heightened job insecurity among working-class and lower middle-class families.

While strong social protection mechanisms meant that 1930s-type mass unemployment did not occur, only workers in protected jobs were cushioned by unemployment insurance and other benefits. However, inequalities also rose within the protected sector as recent migrant, unskilled, very young or middle-aged, and female workers were at greater risk of temporary or long-term unemployment. Though even the Centre-North was affected, unemployment increased most sharply in the South and the Islands where, despite considerable public intervention until the end of the 1980s, it became and remains a serious structural problem, particularly among the young and women (Accornero and Carmignani, 1986; Pugliese, 1989, 1993). Indeed, this state support was strongly criticized for merely providing subsidies rather than fostering development (Trigilia, 1992).

Female employment, on the rise since the mid-1960s, nevertheless continued to expand throughout the recession period. This was the case for most age-groups, particularly for those with larger proportions of women raising families.

The generalized fall in incomes was compounded by growing income inequality. While inequality had been reduced to minimum levels between 1977 and 1982 through automatic wage indexation, its elimination resulted in a reversal thereafter (Rossi, 1992, 1994). By 1991, households belonging to the three lowest deciles received 8 per cent of total incomes, while those of the top two deciles accounted for more than 37 per cent.

In addition, regional inequality rose: by 1985, the average income of Centre-North families was 24.7 per cent higher than in the South and the Islands. Since households are on average larger in the South, the gap in income per capita exceeded by far that in income per family. Thus, while in 1985 the gap in average family income between Piedmont and Sicily was 31.1 per cent, the average per capita income gap was 60.4 per cent (Moriani, 1988). In 1992, average expenditure in the Centre-North was 37 per cent higher than in the South on a per-family basis, but 58.4 per cent higher in per capita terms (Freguja, 1994).

The incidence of poverty among families rose steadily throughout the 1980s, going from 8.3 per cent in 1980 to 14.4 per cent in 1989. After the sharp decline in 1990, when it dropped to 11.7, it stabilized somewhat and stood at 10.4 per cent in 1995 (Table 10.5). At the same time, the incidence of poverty increased for larger families (with five or more members), while it decreased for single-person households (mostly elderly). As a consequence, the relative risk of poverty for children increased (Commissione Povertà, 1996a, 1996b).

In 1995 the incidence of poverty among children under 14 was about 15 per cent in the country as a whole, but over 26 per cent in the South. Thus, not only is it more likely that poor children are found in the South and the Islands, but the chances of growing up poor is greater for children there than in the Centre-North.

During the 1980s, spending on family allowances and tax credits for children declined sharply (Artoni and Ranci Ortigosa, 1989). While tax credits for family dependants were extended to all taxpayers, they were not indexed to the cost of living and remained much higher for a spouse (757,000 lira in 1993) than for children (174,000 lira). Only lone parents were entitled to a tax credit of 757,000 lira for the first child.

Furthermore, starting in 1983, family allowances became progressively means-tested, making them an antipoverty subsidy rather than a contribution to child-rearing costs. Since 1987, family allowances have been paid only to families of wage-earners and pensioners below certain income thresholds adjusted for family size. For instance, in 1995 a family of four with a yearly income of 38,860,000 lira received a monthly allowance of 140,000 lira. Families just above the income threshold *de facto* suffer

Table 10.5: Poverty Incidence According to Family Size, by Geographical Area,[a] 1980–1994

No of components	North-west			North-east			Centre			South			Italy		
	1980	1989	1994	1980	1989	1994	1980	1989	1994	1980	1989	1994	1980	1989	1994
1	11.0	9.8	5.2	13.2	14.3	5.1	5.5	9.8	7.0	16.1	27.0	16.8	11.9	15.6	8.7
2	5.0	8.6	5.3	5.7	9.9	4.8	5.7	12.3	8.9	17.6	30.4	20.0	8.9	16.0	10.2
3	1.5	6.1	2.2	0.9	3.7	2.5	2.5	5.4	4.2	8.5	21.1	16.6	3.4	9.9	6.7
4	2.4	6.8	3.1	1.9	3.6	3.6	3.7	7.7	5.1	12.9	21.3	17.8	6.0	12.2	9.1
5 or more	5.8	10.6	9.4	4.7	10.9	8.9	6.2	15.2	10.2	23.0	31.0	32.7	13.8	22.5	21.6
Total	4.7	8.1	4.4	4.5	8.2	4.4	4.5	9.3	6.8	16.0	26.0	20.6	8.3	14.4	10.2

[a] Estimated on the basis of the annual ISTAT household expenditure survey. The poverty line is equal to the average value of per capita consumption for each year. An equivalence scale is used to compensate for differences in family size.

Source: Commissione povertà, 1996.

an economic loss, particularly hard for dual-income families, since no consideration is given to their higher expenses and organizational difficulties. This threshold is, however, raised for lone-parent families and families with a disabled or invalid member. As family allowances are employment-based, poor households of the self-employed and the long-term unemployed have no coverage at all.

While 15.7 million allowances were paid in 1981, this figure had dropped to only 3 million by 1989 (Cazzola, 1994). In 1993, 15,687 billion lira was paid out by wage workers and employers in contributions for these allowances, but only 5,284 billion, or one-third, was redistributed to families.

Finally, it should be noted that there is no national vital minimum for poor families and individuals. Although all regions have their own welfare assistance legislation, criteria for eligibility vary widely. There is no nationally guaranteed minimum income for non-elderly individuals and families.

10.4.2. Changes in the family

Children's well-being during this period was also influenced by major changes in family structure and stability. The sharp decline in the birth-rate reduced the absolute number of children (from over 12 million during 1960–81 to 9.4 million in 1990) and this, combined with increased life expectancy, has reduced their share in the overall population and their social visibility. During the second half of the 1980s, the nationwide fertility rate was 1.3: 1.1 in the Centre-North, 1.7 in the South, and 1.6 in the Islands (Sonnino, 1989, table 1). In the early 1990s, it neared 1.2, with some regions recording below 1.0.

One- and two-child families became common, at least in the Centre-North regions. Less than one-third of all families with under-17-year-olds now have three or more children. Thus child-care services and extracurricular school activities need to better address not only health care and educational requirements, but also children's socialization needs.

Although the activity rate among mothers has traditionally been lower in Italy than in other industrialized countries, it steadily rose as their earnings became an indispensable cushion not only against inflation and job insecurity of the main breadwinner (Negri *et al.*, 1986), but also against greater family instability. In 1991, 43 per cent of mothers of children under 17 were employed, mostly in full-time jobs. In the same year, 52 per cent of all 0–5-year-olds lived in dual-worker families in the North, 44.7 per cent in the Centre, 27.7 per cent in the South, and 19 per cent in the Islands. These percentages, however, decreased for the 6–10 age bracket and even more for the 11–13 group (ISTAT, 1994), indicating that more younger mothers were working and that mothers of two or more children encountered greater difficulties in combining family tasks and paid work.

With low rates of separation and divorce, lone-parent families have traditionally been less common in Italy than in other Western countries. However, the number of legal separations almost tripled between 1975 (19,132) and 1992 (45,754). The same was true of divorces: 10,618 in 1975, 15,650 in 1987, and 25,996 in 1992. Given the lengthy legal procedure required for separation and divorce, the average age of divorcing spouses was fairly high (43 for men and 40 for women in 1991), and the children of disrupted families were usually older. In the great majority of cases, custody of children was awarded to the mother, reaching 90 per cent in 1987 and stabilizing thereafter.

The number of lone-parent families with children under 18 increased by 11.6 per cent between 1983 and 1990, reaching more than half a million. According to the 1991 census, 7.4 per cent of 0–14-year-olds and 10.3 per cent of 15–19-year-olds lived in one-parent families. Lone fathers with children under 18 constituted 1.3 per cent of all nuclear households, while lone mothers accounted for 2.8 per cent (Bagatta, 1994).

While the current Family Law explicitly acknowledges the contribution of homemaking to family well-being, it somewhat paradoxically views alimony not as reimbursement for the homemaking spouse, but as a minimum subsistence allowance for spouses without any means of support. Thus in Milan, for instance, separation cases involving alimony for the female spouse fell from 53 per cent in 1968 to 24 per cent in 1974 and down to 18 per cent in 1987. Child support payments (about 350,000 lira in the early 1990s, often irrespective of the child's age) have usually been inadequate to meet basic needs. Furthermore, allowances are often not granted because the father cannot be found. Even if granted, they are very often never paid, or paid late, or only in part. It is not surprising then that separation and divorce is still more closely associated with the higher- and better educated classes, and that increased marital separation among lower-income groups is closely linked to the wife's economic independence (Barbagli, 1990).

The emotional and economic impact of divorce on children remains a controversial issue. Legislation and social policy in Italy not only do little to encourage parents to stay together or to separate in the least disruptive fashion, but existing laws and procedures make family break-up exceedingly troublesome. On the one hand, the non-custodial parent has almost no rights over the children. A survey conducted in the late 1980s showed that within two years of separation, 20 per cent of fathers were virtually estranged from their children. The figure was higher among the less educated, among fathers who had not participated directly in child-care activities during marriage, and in the South (Barbagli and Saraceno, 1993).

On the other hand, legal procedures for custody, alimony, and child allowances are based on antiquated notions concerning the place of women in the family and society.

10.4.3. Birth and survival

In 1978, a national health system was established. In the mid-1980s, user charges for prescriptions, laboratory tests, and specialist examinations were introduced, primarily to contain public expenditure. Their welfare impact, however, was ignored. The 1993 budget law means-tested all health services according to family income and size, exempting only the elderly on the minimum pension and the certified poor. There is evidence that the use of preventive health services for children (such as dental care) declined as a result (Saraceno and Negri 1993, 1994a). Greater concern for children was shown in 1994, with all children under 10 (and the over-60s) receiving public health services free of charge. The 1995 budget limited exemptions to under-6-year-olds and to the over-65s, if their annual family income does not exceed 70 million lira, irrespective of family size.

Inequalities in access to and quality of health care services persisted, though available data reveal little about trends in class differentials in health service usage and morbidity (Artoni and Ranci Ortigosa, 1989).

IMR continued to decrease steadily into the 1990s (Table 10.2) and other indicators of infant survival also improved. The still-birth-rate was more than halved (from 16.6 to 6.2 per 1,000 live births) and the neonatal and post-neonatal mortality rates respectively declined from 20.5 to 7.5 and from 8.5 to 2.0.

However, regional IMR differentials lingered (Table 10.2) due to disparities in income, environmental conditions, and social services, including low-quality drinking-water and the uneven quality of and access to health services, which are particularly underutilized by pregnant women (Pinnelli, 1989). In 1985, there were thirteen family clinics per 100,000 inhabitants in the North, nine in the Centre, but only five in the South and three in the Islands, all the more striking given the higher fertility rate in the South. As a consequence, despite improved education for girls, IMR was not reduced accordingly in areas where health services remained inadequate (Table 10.6; see also Saraceno and Negri, 1994b).

At the same time, some disturbing trends in child survival, often linked to environmental problems such as pollution and health hazards in the workplace, have appeared, as suggested for instance by a rise in under-weight births in the most highly industrialized areas of the North in the mid-late 1980s (Vittori et al., 1987; Pinnelli, 1989).

Mortality rates for the 0–15 age-group also declined dramatically: from 14 per 1,000 males and 12 per 1,000 females in 1960–2 to 5.3 and 4 respectively in 1979–83 (Lori and Pagnanelli, 1988). Smaller reductions were

Table 10.6: Infant Mortality by Mother's Education and Region, 1987–1988 (per 1,000 live births)

	University	High school	Middle school	Elem. school	Total
North	4.3	6.8	8.3	11.0	7.9
Centre	8.6	7.2	10.6	12.3	9.4
South	9.6	8.6	9.9	14.7	10.9
Italy	7.1	7.6	9.4	13.8	9.5

Source: Consiglio Sanitario Nazionale (1993).

recorded for the older age brackets, but the gap between males and females increasingly widened, due also to the greater tendency for males to engage in at-risk behaviour and activities (Caselli and Egidi, 1989). Although figures after 1978 show a decline, traffic deaths still accounted in 1985 for half of all accidental deaths among 5–14-year-olds and 67 per cent among 15–17-year-olds.

Drug abuse is another area of growing risk for youth. Adolescents are estimated to account for 6 per cent of identified drug abusers, the majority of whom tend to be in the 19–25 age-group (with an upward trend in age). The adolescent share of drug-related deaths declined from 7.8 per cent in 1984 to 1.9 in the first semester of 1993, according to a report by the Prime Minister's Office. However, the phenomenon might be under-represented among under-20-year-olds (Sgritta, 1992). A change in patterns of drug consumption might have raised the age at which dependency may become visible and serious pathologies arise. The state has made a substantial financial effort in this field, with a 50 per cent increase in public health services addressed to drug-dependent people during 1984–90. Yet, 30 per cent (65 per cent in the South) of all local health facilities still do not provide drug-related services. The private, not-for-profit sector, variously with public financing, is active in this service field, though often with problems of overall supervision and monitoring of methods and outcomes.

10.4.4. Child care and education

Provision of preschool services rose steadily, as did the percentage of children attending nursery schools and kindergartens (Tables 10.3 and 10.7). However, cuts in public expenditure, limitations on new hiring, and the transfer to families of a higher share of the costs put greater pressure on local governments and families. Preschool services, although 'to be provided upon individual demand', are not compulsory and user fees are applied, particularly in nursery schools. For under-3-year-olds, nursery school attendance is particularly low in the South (Table 10.7). In contrast,

Table 10.7:   The Percentage of Young Children
Attending Nursery Schools by Geographical Area,
1976–1990

Year	North	Centre	South-Islands	Italy
1976	3.2	2.6	1.0	2.1
1979	5.1	3.4	1.1	3.1
1983	8.5	6.5	1.5	5.0
1986	9.0	6.9	1.8	5.2
1990	11.0	7.5	2.0	6.1

Source: Compiled on the basis of ISTAT data.

as much as 30 per cent of all children may be enrolled in some cities in the
Centre-North. Fees are determined according to family incomes. Nevertheless, poor families, mothers who work odd hours, and disadvantaged
groups are often excluded.

Kindergartens, on the other hand, have long been free of charge for all,
though recently some local governments have introduced an income-
based fee. In addition, the number of public kindergartens increased and
a more balanced national distribution was achieved, thanks to state intervention, particularly in the South. As a result, the enrolment rate rose
from about 70 per cent in the mid-1970s to almost 93 per cent in the early
1990s (Table 10.3). However, some qualitative differences remain in terms
of duration, availability of hot meals, and so on (Schizzerotto, 1989).

10.4.5. Schooling

By 1983 school enrolment had reached 95 per cent among 6–13-year-olds.
However, efforts in the late 1960s to reduce the impact of social differences on educational attainment had lost momentum and had even been
partially reversed. Selectivity and marginalization were common once
more in schools, even in compulsory education, though more so in higher
grades. In 1979–80, only 642 children per 1,000 enrolled completed compulsory schooling without repeating. Repetition rates have since declined
slowly (Table 10.8), though large North–South differences persist. In
1985–6, for instance, 17 per cent on the Islands and 13.1 per cent in the
South repeated the first year of middle school, compared to the national
figure of 11.6 per cent. In 1991–2 the gap narrowed, with 11 per cent
repetition in the South and Islands compared to 9.4 per cent for all students. A similar gap exists in the drop-out rate in compulsory schooling.
In 1983–4, the drop-out rate among first- and second-year middle-
schoolers in the South and the Islands was about double the respective
national averages of 3.8 and 4.2 per cent. By 1990–1, however, the gap had
been reduced sharply.

Table 10.8:   Repetition Rates, 1981–1992

	Elementary school					Middle school
	First	Second	Third	Fourth	Fifth	First
1981–2	2.0	1.5	1.1	1.1	1.3	13.1
1983–4	1.8	1.3	0.9	0.9	1.2	13.0
1985–6	1.5	—	—	—	—	11.6
1991–2	1.1	0.7	0.5	0.4	0.5	9.4

Sources: Based on Bentivegna (1988) and ISTAT.

Table 10.9:   The School 'Wastage' Rate[a], 1975–1992 (percentages)

	Failure rate A			Drop-out rate B		Tension rate (A + B)	
	Elementary	Middle	High	Middle	High	Middle	High
1975–6	3.0	5.6	5.6	4.2	8.1	9.8	13.7
1980–1	1.2	8.8	8.0	4.1	10.7	12.9	18.7
1985–6	1.0	7.9	8.4	3.0	8.8	10.9	17.2
1991–2	0.6	6.2	14.7	—	—	—	—

[a] The drop-out rate is no longer calculated by ISTAT.
Sources: Corrado (1989); ISTAT.

School abandonment—a phenomenon concentrated in the South—may be caused by the family's inability to support their children at school and by inadequate support of teachers and the school system to pupils with learning difficulties and/or living in disadvantaged social circumstances. Table 10.9 synthesizes 'wastage' rate trends over the last twenty years.

In the 1985–6 school year, attendance in shifts still involved 13.7 and 10.4 per cent of primary-school pupils and 5.3 and 3.5 per cent of middle-schoolers in the Islands and the South respectively, though it had been virtually eliminated in the rest of Italy. In 1992, 3.5 and 11.9 per cent of children were still attending primary and middle school in shifts in the South, none in the Centre-North. A Censis survey (1993) judged 68 per cent of schools in the South inadequate on the basis of various indicators, compared to a strikingly lower 8.5 per cent in the north-west.

Not only are children with inadequate schooling disadvantaged on the labour market, they are also at greater risk of involvement in delinquent activities, as confirmed by the fact that a substantial proportion of children in juvenile detention centres are illiterate and/or have not completed compulsory schooling.

Table 10.10:   Middle School Graduates Entering High School, 1981–1991
(percentages)

	North	Centre	South	Islands	Italy
1981–2	65.4	80.3	73.8	74.3	71.4
1983–4	72.3	86.4	77.1	77.2	77.0
1985–6	75.1	90.1	74.1	77.2	77.8
1990–1	99.9	107.1	94.1	98.4	99.3

Sources: Bentivegna (1988); ISTAT.

Enrolments in non-compulsory high school increased during the period, as indicated in Table 10.10. By the early 1990s, 80 per cent of all students who completed middle school enrolled in secondary school (a highly diversified system in Italy). However, abandonment and failure remain very common at this level: the drop-out rate is around 25 per cent for the first two years (up to 40 per cent in 'professional' high schools, mainly attended by children from families with modest economic means). Yet only at the beginning of the 1990s did the Ministry of Education allocate funds aimed directly at disadvantaged children both at the compulsory and high-school levels. High drop-out rates might be interpreted as the school's failure to integrate its students and as an indicator of mistrust among adolescents in the school's ability to prepare them for the labour market. Indeed, only 'professional' high schools have undergone a substantial reform in recent years, involving collaboration between schools, local governments, enterprises, and professional associations.

Some progress has been made in reducing gender discrimination (Schizzerotto, 1988). While school enrolment rates among girls equalled or surpassed those for boys in the mid-1980s (Franchi *et al.*, 1987; Dei, 1988), differences persisted in gender balance in the various types of secondary school. Girls are still more likely to enrol in 'professional' high schools which basically train students for clerical careers, while boys are more likely to attend technical high schools. And girls and boys with similar school diplomas may still not have equal opportunities in the labour market.

An emerging problem concerns immigrant children. Although all school-aged foreign children are accepted in compulsory schools, if they are not legal residents they may not obtain school diplomas and may not be able to enrol in high school. No special programmes have been introduced to help these children with language difficulties and to reduce problems of marginalization.

10.4.5. Children and teenagers in the labour market

Local area studies (CREL, 1980; Tagliaferri *et al.*, 1980), media inquiries (Baglivo, 1980), reports on accidents in the workplace, and school drop-out statistics all attest to the persistence of child labour during this period, at least on an intermittent, seasonal, or part-time basis. In areas of the South, between 20 and 50 per cent of 10–14-year-old children work, at least on an occasional basis. In addition, a 1988–9 survey by the national institute of statistics (ISTAT) found that 13 and 10 per cent of 6–10-year-old boys and girls respectively helped their parents occasionally (likely in farm activities and family-owned businesses) and between 2 and 3 per cent helped relatives and others. In the 11–13 age bracket, the percentage increased to 23.4 per cent for boys and 25.6 per cent for girls.

Children work as street vendors, on farms, in construction, for small-shop owners and craftsmen, and throughout the informal economy. An illness caused by glues, for instance, led to the discovery of children working in the leather industry in Naples. As under-14-year-old children are not prosecutable, they are frequently employed as drug pushers. In recent years, immigrant children have formed an increasingly large proportion of child workers.

During this period, the participation rate of teenagers in the formal labour market decreased steadily in all geographical areas: for 14–19-year-old males it fell from 33.6 per cent in 1977 to 27.6 in 1986 and to 25 per cent in 1991 (the last figure refers to the 14–19 age-group); over the same period, the female rate fell from 29.6 to 24.8 and then to 22.4 per cent. Though the rise in school enrolment was a contributing factor, some adolescents were neither enrolled in school nor working in the formal labour market.

For youth, the probability of finding work in the formal labour market is inversely related to educational level. Youth unemployment, along with overall unemployment, increased between the late 1970s and mid-1980s (Table 10.11). Between 1986 and 1991, a decrease was recorded only in the North. A recent study on unemployment (Pugliese, 1993) found that young people in the South with no or very low education levels are highly disadvantaged with regard to job opportunities and quality of work. Most of these youth belong to poor or economically unstable families and are at great risk of poverty themselves. Young women are worse off: only 35 per cent of 14–19-year-old girls actively seeking work were employed in the South in 1991, compared to 49.6 per cent of boys and 73.3 per cent of girls in the North.

Since 1983 a training and work scheme has sought to address the problem of unemployment among adolescents. This initiative was designed to encourage employers to hire 15–29-year-olds for definite

Table 10.11: 14–17-Year-Olds in the Labour Market, 1977–1991 (percentages)

	North-west		North-east		Centre		South and Islands	
	Employed	Unemployed	Employed	Unemployed	Employed	Unemployed	Employed	Unemployed
1977	77.0	23.0	75.5	24.5	61.2	38.8	56.1	43.9
1979	66.9	33.1	75.6	24.4	68.3	31.7	54.5	45.5
1981	66.3	33.7	72.7	27.3	46.8	53.2	53.8	46.2
1983	56.1	43.9	62.5	37.5	56.9	43.1	48.6	51.4
1986	57.1	42.9	61.7	38.3	58.0	42.0	45.5	55.5
1991[a]	76.7	23.3	82.5	17.5	61.0	39.0	42.0	58.0

[a] For 1991, data refer to the 14–19 age-bracket.

Sources: Mattioli (1988b); ISTAT, *Rilevazione delle forze di lavoro, media 1991.*

periods of time (a maximum of 24 months) with the incentive of lower social security costs. Employers are not obliged to keep the young employees on after this period. It has, however, favoured the 19–29 age-group and those with a secondary school diploma (Mattioli, 1988*b*). Adolescents can now be more easily employed under apprenticeship contracts, though these have not been designed to create jobs.

Although leaving school early represents a risk for entry into the labour market, remaining in school is not perceived as an advantage by many (Censis, 1985; GIOC, 1986). Schools offer little support or motivation to those who would most benefit. Moreover, only low-skilled jobs rarely involving on-the-job training or skill upgrading are usually available to adolescents.

10.4.6. Children in institutions

Increasing attention has been focused on child abuse and sexual violence against children. Private non-profit associations have been set up, including a nationwide hot-line service. Legal, psychiatric, and other forms of assistance have also been established for abused children and their families.

The controversial issue of the boundaries separating responsibilities of the state, the community, and the family has recently been spotlighted for debate. The majority of abused or abandoned children brought to the attention of social workers and the courts come from marginalized families. Thus, the focus on these children may conceal an attempt to exert control over such families. On the other hand, if the strong tradition of family privacy is rigidly respected, then society's most helpless members can be exposed to serious violence. Under Italian law, for instance, incest is punishable only if it occurs openly; that is, if it causes scandal. Public morality is thus better protected than the (usually female) child.

Decreases in the number of abandoned children, including newborns, and children in institutions suggest that there is increased attention to children's well-being. Foster care is now more readily used. Indeed, a new adoption law favours either foster families or small family-like communities over institutions for children who still have families, though the law is implemented very differently at local and regional levels (Sgritta, 1988). The number of children in institutions fell by half between 1975 and 1983, not only due to the drop in fertility rates but also to a reduction in the number of children in orphanages relative to those receiving alternative forms of care. Furthermore, the percentage of illegitimate children in institutions diminished from 68.6 per cent in 1971 to 45 per cent in 1981. A trend reversal seems to have taken place since 1990 due to the increased institutionalization of immigrant children with no family and/or exploited by relatives or others.

In 1978, 48.3 per cent of all children in institutions were in the South and the Islands; this figure rose to 52 per cent in 1983 (Mattioli, 1988*a*) and up to 64 per cent in 1990, indicating that institutionalization remains culturally more legitimate in the South and that fostering has little support there among public authorities (Sgritta, 1988).

Severely disabled children, including children with AIDS, remain the most likely to be institutionalized, though various measures have been developed to support these children and their families, including indemnities and insertion in public schools with support teachers. There were 8,800 disabled children in institutions in 1981 and 4,900 in 1993, over half of whom were in the South.

Greater attention was also focused during the 1980s on institutional mechanisms for the incarceration of minors (Palomba, 1984; Faccioli, 1988). None the less, little research has examined the social environment and background of the children and adolescents involved. Therefore, recourse must be made to data produced by the institutions themselves; such data, however, may tell us as much about how these institutions define deviant behaviour as they do about the children.

The data appear to indicate an absence of clear trends. The number of minors reported for deviant behaviour fell from 23,950 in 1975 to 20,130 in 1985, but increased to 25,240 in 1992. The largest increase was for offences against property (thefts amount to over 40 per cent of all offences), but homicides and personal injuries also rose. The percentage of juveniles sentenced also increased, from 16 per cent of all those brought to trial in 1976 to 19.5 per cent in 1985. However, the likelihood of serving a sentence decreased. During 1981–2, in fact, there was a substantial drop in the number of under-18-year-olds entering penal institutions, from 6,470 to 1,450. Between 1986 and 1991, the number of under-14-year-olds involved in criminal activities increased more than five times, indicating a lowering of the starting age for delinquent behaviour (ISTAT, 1993).

A significant geographic redistribution occurred both in the reporting of deviant behaviour and in sentencing. Minors in the South are now more likely to be found guilty of deviant behaviour and punished. There is also a higher likelihood for children in the South to be involved in serious offences such as homicide and extorsion.

The vast majority of minors in prison come from the most disadvantaged groups in society. They also tend to be illiterate and/or foreign-born. Indeed, deviant behaviour is even less evident among children of white-collar families than it is among adults. None the less, this should not lead to the conclusion that poor, marginalized, or foreign-born children are more prone to deviant behaviour; it may indicate that such minors are more likely to be the focus of the attention of authorities and are less likely to be treated leniently by the judicial system.

Finally, girls form a minority among imprisoned youth, although their percentages have risen rapidly over the past few years, more than doubling from 6.5 per cent of all imprisoned minors in 1985 to 13.9 per cent in 1987. A large percentage of these girls are gypsies and other foreign-born juveniles; indeed, they make up a higher proportion among girls in detention centres than in the overall imprisoned youth population.

10.5. Child Welfare in the Political and Social Debate of the Early 1990s

Child welfare indicators improved generally throughout the 1980s and early 1990s. However, old problems remain and, in some cases, have become more serious, while new ones are emerging: persistent regional differentials in survival chances; a concentration of child poverty in large households and in the South; emerging risks of poverty linked to gender divisions of labour within the family combined with marital instability; and the increasing presence of immigrant children whose rights are unclear and inadequately protected.

Most importantly, concern for children seems to remain on the sidelines in public debate and policy-making. At the same time, the ideological merging of separate issues relating to abortion, marital instability, low fertility, increased numbers of working mothers, and the problems of social integration posed by immigration does not help in framing the question of what to do for children nor in finding effective answers. Paradoxically, concern for the fall in fertility seems to spur more interest in encouraging prospective parents to have children than in helping them raise those already born. There is little recognition that the high costs of child-rearing may have reduced the propensity to have children among younger adults, particularly women.

Moreover, calls for support for children are submerged by calls for support of the family. 'Family policies' have become fertile terrain for political confrontation in the early to mid-1990s. Yet, no concrete measures—income support, family allowances, social services in deprived areas and for children most at risk—have been introduced. Even the Church, though advocating 'family values' and the need 'to support families', seems more interested in curbing abortion and contraception and in defending the virtues of the intact, traditional family than in the concrete experiences and needs of children and their families.

Current policies restrict support to social services developed in the past. For instance, local budget restrictions have led to increased user costs for child care and a reduction in the range of services offered; public debt considerations have *de facto* transformed the National Health Service into a means-tested social service, with increased costs to families. At the same time, greater labour market flexibility renders income insecure for a substantial quota of workers/parents, while discouraging development of a working-hour policy which would allow mothers and fathers to reconcile paid work and family responsibilities.

Counter-tendencies may, however, be detected at the local level, where some municipalities are developing 'child- and family-friendly' policies. Such initiatives include a rethinking of urban spaces to better meet children's needs; financial and housing support for households with young children; income support for lone mothers in need; new social services to support families under stress; the creation of a special government department for children; and new partnerships in many towns between public services and non-governmental organizations.

These new trends suggest that innovation may well come from the local level, not only from the centre, and that local experience can help change the present dominant 'policy blindness' *vis-à-vis* children (and parents). A change in outlook and policies seems particularly urgent at three levels— income support measures, social and care services for young children, and education and training—with a particular focus on children from under-privileged families and living in disadvantaged areas.

The whole system of income support needs redesigning. A universal child allowance should be introduced to cover part of the cost of raising a child. Given the current 'budget constraints' and the results of demographic research (indicating that it is increasingly problematic to have a second child and that costs rise disproportionately with the third), such a child allowance might be paid from the second child onward and only for families below a given income threshold. At the same time, it should be paid irrespective of the parents' working status, be indexed to the cost of living, and be paid in principle to the mother (or to the father when he is the main care-provider). In contrast, higher-income families could benefit from a revision of the existing tax allowances for children.

In addition, a national system in which a vital minimum amount targeted to families with insufficient income should be introduced, with clear criteria for entitlements, duration, and obligations. At present, only a few municipalities have such a measure, which however remains highly discretionary. These two measures—child allowance and income support— should be kept separate, and framed as part of a modular package aimed at supporting families. Furthermore, a system of advance payment for child support should be introduced to help single mothers in cases where separated fathers do not, or cannot, pay. These income support measures should not, however, be developed at the expense of other services for children, including child care, monitoring of child health, and development of social spaces for both children and parents.

In the area of education and training, high drop-out and failure rates, particularly but not exclusively in the South, need to be tackled aggressively. The direct link between low educational attainment and poverty (and sometimes criminality) is too evident to be ignored. A substantial investment in schools, teacher training, support activities for children at risk, including migrant children, is extremely urgent. Youth unemployment, largely deriving from lacking education and skills, also requires urgent attention. The unemployed should be able to receive assistance to complete their schooling and upgrade their skills through training opportunities. Efforts should be made to delay their entry into the labour market so that they can acquire better skills.

Initiatives aimed at improving the quality of life for children and their families require not only greater financial investment, but also an enormous cultural investment. For this to come about, new ways need to be found to effectively address the problems and to develop more constructive forms of co-operation between different levels of government and between government and citizens.

11

Advancing for Children in the Advanced Welfare State: Current Problems and Prospects in Sweden

SVEN E. OLSSON HORT

11.1. Introduction

Improving the well-being of children remains a controversial subject. While the Scandinavian experience is often cited in international discussions of welfare and poverty for its relative success in achieving equality and security, opinions vary on the welfare state approach. It is criticized by some for restricting economic growth incentives and individual freedoms. Others, fearing the unrestricted expansion of trade and commodity relationships, give their full support. But while Scandinavia is sometimes naïvely portrayed as an island of social justice in a world of injustice, the picture is more complex (Hernes, 1987; Olofsson, 1988). The European media, for instance, characterized Sweden as a 'children's gulag' in the 1980s in response to reports of high percentages of children in state care.

This chapter will present a balance sheet of the situation of children in Swedish society. In advanced nations, the cost of bringing up children outweighs their financial contribution to the family, even when public income support packages are considered. This chapter will also explore how public policies can help families raise children. It examines the following questions:

- Was the progress achieved in child welfare during the 1970–95 period as significant as that of the initial post-war period?
- Were social and economic child welfare differentials in health, education, and other important areas reduced between 1970 and 1995?
- Does social policy favour the elderly or other social groups to the detriment of children?
- Have new problems emerged for children in recent years?

The author wishes to thank Roland Spånt for his invaluable collaboration and excellent contribution to the original report for UNICEF upon which this chapter is based (Olsson and Spånt, 1991). Special thanks are also due to the editors of this volume.

11.2. Historical Background: From Poverty to Affluence

Safe from the cruelties of war since Napoleonic times, history has proved favourable to healthy child development in Sweden. Yet, 100 years ago Sweden was one of the poorest nations of Europe. During the half-century prior to World War I, one-fifth of the population emigrated to North America. Nevertheless, by the mid-nineteenth century, living conditions were, according to the infant mortality rate (Table 11.1), on a par with those in more advanced European nations.

A long-term demographic transition had already begun in the early nineteenth century. By the 1930s, Sweden had a very low level of population growth. In addition, the country experienced a swift socio-economic transformation. Industrialization began in the late nineteenth century and rapid economic growth continued until the 1970s. Because poverty was so widespread historically, the distribution of emerging resources was more egalitarian in Sweden than in most other European nations. Since the 1960s, urban affluence has replaced rural poverty as the norm.

Stability has also characterized political life and industrial relations. After World War I, the monarchy and the conservative aristocracy accepted demands for parliamentary democracy. In 1920, the first Social Democratic Labour cabinet was installed, though it was short-lived. Between 1932 and 1976, the Social Democrats were the ruling party. In 1938, an agreement between employers and employees produced peaceful industrial relations, which lasted until the 1970s when trade unions challenged this agreement. Nevertheless, private business continues to dominate the economy, and has in recent decades questioned the traditional Swedish model.

Social policy existed in Sweden before the Social Democrats discovered it (Olsson, 1993). A major impetus to family policy reform was a study by Alva and Gunnar Myrdal (see Myrdal and Myrdal, 1934; cf. also Myrdal, 1941) which led to population policy recommendations. The most impor-

Table 11.1: Infant Mortality in Selected European Countries, 1840–1990 (per 1,000 live births)

Country	1840s	1880s	1920s	Early 1950s	Early 1990s
Belgium	155	161	105	45	8
Denmark	144	137	83	28	9
Finland	—	—	94	34	6
Germany	—	228	112	48	8
Norway	119	98	52	23	8
UK	153	142	72	28	8
Sweden	154	112	60	20	6

Sources: Mitchell (1975); UN (1989); UNICEF (1991).

tant outcome was the introduction of free care for women giving birth and for other childbirth-related services, such as medical check-ups and maternity benefits. Entitlement to advance child maintenance payments was extended to single mothers. Loans were made available for newly married couples and a housing subsidy was introduced for large families. Women could no longer be fired because of marriage or pregnancy, and government employees could take paid sick leave for childbirth.

During the early 1940s, temporary state support for children with absent fathers was instituted. Following the war, favourable economic growth, the wartime accumulation of public resources and an ideological reorientation led to increased social welfare spending in education, health care, housing, and income maintenance. Between 1950 and 1970, public expenditure on family and child welfare services increased sixfold (at fixed prices); on education and general public health care expenditure quintupled, and housing allowances quadrupled; general child allowances and state loans for new housing starts doubled (Olsson, 1986, 1987). In the post-war years and until the late 1960s, the quality of housing was very poor and overcrowding was common. This finally led Parliament to approve construction of a million new apartments over a ten-year period—a goal which was achieved.

In 1962, a nine-year compulsory school system was instituted. Free school meals and health care, including dental care, initially introduced in the late 1940s, were extended to more students for longer periods. Sweden was relatively slow in introducing public preschool education. Until the mid-1960s, the care of children of preschool age was considered a private matter (Axelsson, 1992). However, because women rapidly entered the work-force, the demand for child care increased and so did state subsidies to preschools and other types of public child-minding.

A general non-means-tested and non-taxed child allowance was instituted in 1948. At the same time, tax deductions for children were abolished. Compulsory health insurance was introduced in 1955, and maternity compensation was pegged to female wages. In the 1960s, a combined study loan and educational allowance system was created to increase the educational chances of low-income children. Advance maintenance payments for lone-parent families were inflation-indexed and upgraded. In the early 1970s, individual taxation was introduced for husbands and wives, rendering the concept of 'breadwinner' more gender-neutral. By the 1960s, Sweden was the model welfare state.

Sweden had the lowest infant mortality rate in the world in the early 1970s (Cornia, 1990, table I). However, a recent study (Vågerö and Östberg, 1989), which followed a cohort of children over the 1960–79 period, shows large variations in mortality rates. The children of blue-collar families and the self-employed were at significantly higher risk than those of white-collar families. This tendency diminished with age among girls, but not for boys. Among male children of blue-collar workers, there was a 60 per cent excess risk at one year and a 30 per cent excess risk at age 19. For girls, the excess risk was around 15 per cent for all ages between one and 19. Mature children of lower-income families born before 1959 were found to be shorter than those born to higher-income parents. No height differences were found for children born in or after 1959, perhaps because they had not finished growing. A follow-up study found that a larger than expected number in the shorter-height group were in poor general health or had subsequently died (Nyström Peck, 1994), indicating a connection between social and economic conditions in childhood and morbidity and mortality.

11.3. From the Early 1970s to the Mid-1990s

11.3.1. Macroeconomic developments

Compared with the harmonious growth of the 1950s and 1960s, striking changes in the economy have occurred since the 'oil crisis' of 1973–4 (Table 11.2). Unlike other countries, unemployment remained fairly low until the early 1990s, largely due to active labour market policies. However, some industrial sectors became less competitive in world markets. In the late 1970s and early 1980s, when Sweden was governed by a non-socialist cabinet, industry underwent a rapid structural transformation. Some companies went bankrupt—on average, 1.9 per cent of industrial employees experienced company closures each year between 1970 and 1987. Capital spending dropped, no net investment took place and fixed assets fell.

In the late 1970s and early 1980s, the balance of payments on the current account deteriorated, and the deficit reached 3.6 per cent of GDP. When the Social Democrats regained power in 1982, the budget deficit was 12 per cent of GDP, while the aggregate deficit of the total public sector was

Table 11.2: Selected Macroeconomic Indicators, 1950–1993

	1950–60	1960–70	1970–80	1980–90	1990–3
Gross domestic product[a]	3.4	4.6	2.0	2.0	−1.7
Consumer price index[a]	4.8	4.0	9.1	7.6	5.4
Total government outlays[b]	29.5	38.1	57.4	63.2	66.9
Net lending[b]	0.8	4.0	1.7	−0.8	−4.5
Unemployment rate	2.3	2.6	2.3	2.6	4.5

[a] Average annual percentage changes. [b] As a percentage of GDP.
Source: SOU (1995).

over 6 per cent of GDP. The economy was characterized by weak international competitiveness, falling industrial investments and a shrinking industrial base, a large balance-of-payments deficit, a sizeable national debt, and rising unemployment. Spiralling tax deductions by individuals who had set up private pension plans, together with slow growth in the tax base due to recession and surging government subsidies to ailing industries, resulted in the once-balanced budget becoming one of dramatic deficits, which, in turn, threatened the foundations of the welfare state.

In 1982, the new government devalued the currency to enhance international competitiveness, thus enabling industries to regain lost market shares and take advantage of spare capacity. Industrial subsidies were quickly phased out. For some time, trade unions accepted the devaluation and postponed demands for compensating wage increases. Pensioners also reluctantly deferred compensatory demands. During the international boom of the 1980s, the Swedish economy grew at an annual rate of just below 3 per cent, labour force participation increased (particularly for women), unemployment fell below 2 per cent, and the balance-of-trade deficit turned into a significant surplus. By 1989, the budget deficit had been eliminated (Olsson and Spånt, 1991).

The successes of the 1980s, however, were threatened by inflation, which jumped above 6 per cent in 1989. Throughout this period, the gap between the Swedish inflation rate and the OECD average rate widened, exports suddenly declined, and a large balance-of-payments deficit reappeared. Fighting inflation became a top policy priority. To this end, the Social Democrats sought to cut welfare benefits and deprioritized the long-held goal of full employment, with the result that they lost power. In the early 1990s, during the worst recession since the 1930s, a non-socialist coalition took power (Pontusson, 1994). Open unemployment rose to almost 10 per cent, and an additional 6 per cent of the labour force were involved in public retraining programmes. Instead of unpopular austerity measures, the new government opted for deficit spending and tried to avoid raising taxes. The domestic economic crisis worsened—the real estate market crashed, major banks and insurance companies sought government aid, and interest rates shot up to record levels. A further depreciation occurred. Cuts in public expenditure were thus inevitable and, though modest, welfare benefits were especially affected. In 1994, the Social Democrats regained power. Once again they faced a huge budget deficit; this time they were also confronted with unprecedentedly high unemployment.

11.3.2. Income distribution

Of all the industrialized countries, Sweden has had one of the lowest levels of income inequality over the past fifty years. By the early 1980s, however, the steady trend towards greater income and wealth equality came to a halt (Vogel *et al.*, 1988; Persson, 1991; cf. also Vennemo, 1994). When the non-socialist cabinet first came to office in the late 1970s, programmes benefiting stockholders were instituted, even though many families were living in increasingly difficult conditions, and growing numbers were dependent on means-tested social assistance payments (see below). Because of structural changes in the economy and slow economic growth, hourly wages and disposable family incomes were at approximately the same levels in 1981 as they had been in 1974 (Figure 11.1), despite rising transfer payments (pensions benefiting the elderly). Over this period, the female labour force participation rate accelerated, with many newcomers absorbed by an expanding public sector. This explains the faster growth of disposable income relative to the wage rate after 1984. Combined with low interest rates, 100 per cent deductions on interest expenses, and full taxation of interest income, inflation redistributed wealth from savers to borrowers, especially to home-owners and companies. Sweden also followed the international tax reform trend, reducing marginal tax rates and the progressivity of the income tax.

Nevertheless, the increased inequality in Sweden was modest compared with that in other countries, including the UK and the USA (Fritzell, 1992). The top 1 per cent of all households received 3.7 per cent of total income in 1967 and 2.4 per cent in 1981, but the figure rebounded to 3.1 per cent by 1987. Between 1920 and the mid-1970s, the share of wealth held by the richest 1 per cent dropped from 50 to about 16 per cent (Spånt, 1974). During the following decade, this share wavered around 16 per

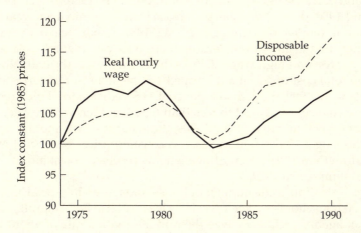

Fig. 11.1 Real Hourly Post-tax Wages and Real Disposable Household Incomes (1974–1990)

Source: SOU (1990*a*).

cent. This oscillation has been sensitive to changes on the stock market and in housing prices. Some rich Swedes have also emigrated to 'tax havens', removing their wealth from measured inequality.

While data are not yet available on the extent to which this trend towards greater inequality has affected children, one hypothesis is that it will mean larger contrasts among children of different social backgrounds. For example, differences in wealth, health, reliance on social assistance, and ethnic background are growing for different geographical areas (SOU, 1990*b*).

11.3.3. *Poverty and social assistance*

Poverty is a complex phenomenon. The Swedish welfare state aims to provide a safety net against the causes of poverty: the income losses created by unemployment, sickness, old age, and disability. Thus, means-tested transfers are minimized in favour of a full employment policy, and social assistance is a last resort.

The economic crisis of the 1980s demonstrated that holes in the safety net have remained (Tham, 1994). The receipt of social assistance has increased drastically since the early 1980s; in fact, recipiency did not decrease as expected after 1983 when the economy improved and unemployment fell. This new phenomenon ruptured the counter-cyclical relationship between unemployment and the need for social assistance that had prevailed for fifty years. Not until 1987, several years into the recovery, did the receipt of social assistance begin to decline.

Figure 11.2 illustrates annual spending on social assistance during the 1980s and early 1990s, both in current and in real (1980) prices. Between 1981 and 1986, there was a sharp increase in both nominal and real terms. The labour market deteriorated during 1981–3, but began to improve thereafter. By the end of the decade, there was low unemployment, high vacancy rates, and high wage-drift as the economy overheated. None the less, the total cost of social aid jumped 150 per cent in real terms during the decade. In 1989, more than 8 per cent of Swedish households received social assistance, compared to less than 6 per cent ten years earlier. With the unemployment crisis of the 1990s, these figures took another upward turn, showing a 19 per cent increase at constant prices between 1992 and 1993. More than 11 per cent of households received social aid in 1993, a twofold jump since 1979.

An examination of the number of households receiving social assistance per 1,000 households by age reveals a clear pattern. For example, in 1981, the peak age for recipiency was the mid-20s, with a rate of about 80 per 1,000. By 1986, this rate had leapt to about 150 per 1,000 households. The elderly are much less likely to need social assistance: only 10 per 1,000 were recipients between 1981 and 1986. Their pensions helped them avoid the economic crisis of the 1980s.

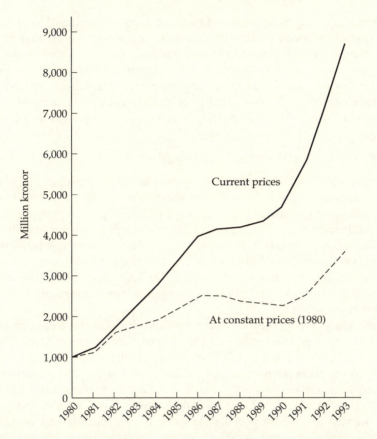

Fig. 11.2 Social Assistance Expenditure (in millions of krona, 1980–1993)
Source: SCB (1994c).

From 1980 to 1993 single men without children made up around 40 per cent of households receiving social aid. Single women without children were the second largest group, almost 25 per cent in 1993. Access to other social programmes meant that families with children were a minority. Altogether, 32 per cent of the households receiving social assistance included children, with these households divided equally between single-mother families and married couples. About 36 per cent of all mother-only families relied on aid, compared with 6 per cent of married couples with children. From a child's perspective, therefore, the family with only one wage-earner represents the highest risk to well-being.

The increased reliance on social assistance since 1980 signifies a failure of Swedish economic and social policies (Salonen, 1994). One explanation points to the influx of refugees and immigrants. Sweden welcomes a high number of immigrants, around 0.5 per cent of the population per annum. In 1993, almost 25 per cent of families obtaining social assistance were composed of foreign citizens, and they received as much as 42 per cent of total spending. Swedish families normally obtain social assistance only when they experience economic distress and, then, as a complement to regular income or transfer payments. Immigrants, however, rely on assistance for longer periods, at least until they enter the labour market. It is therefore vital that labour market policies be revised to reduce the risk of immigrants falling into chronic dependence on government assistance.

11.3.4. Demographic changes and ethical challenges

The Swedish population stands at approximately 8.6 million, and is expected to remain fairly constant in the years ahead. In 1990, children under 19 accounted for 24 per cent of the population. Roughly 17 per cent of all children were of foreign 'origin', although less than one-third of these were born outside Sweden. An exceptionally low birth-rate as late as 1983 was followed by a baby boom. In 1990, the birth-rate was 2.0, about 35 per cent higher than a decade earlier. The reproduction rate, now close to the natural replacement level (2.1), is higher than in most other Western European countries.

In the early 1980s, the low reproduction rate and the influx of immigrants led to a re-emergence of the 'population question' and general concerns about the future of the family, culture, and society. There was some apprehension that pro-natalist policies might be inadequate. Economic incentives were provided for larger families: an additional 50 per cent of the normal child allowance was given for the third child and an extra full allowance was granted for the fourth and additional children. These concerns faded as fertility increased towards the end of the decade. In the mid-1990s, as austerity measures are proposed, child welfare benefits have been debated and some marginal cut-backs have been enacted.

Sweden is unique in combining high female labour force participation and high fertility rates. This phenomenon was facilitated by the economic boom of the 1980s and by comprehensive welfare policies. While not their explicit aim, parental insurance and extensive child day-care facilities (see below) appear to have encouraged higher birth-rates. Yet, while female labour force participation rates in Denmark and Norway are almost as high, and day care, at least in Denmark, is fairly extensive, the fertility rates are much lower. This difference may be due to the less generous direct cash benefits paid to parents with newborn children in these countries (Hoem and Hoem, 1988; Leira, 1993).

In the early 1990s, the number of (free) abortions was roughly equal to 40 per cent of all births. Teenage abortions increased in recent years concurrently with reduced grants for sex education and subsidized contraceptives (Socialstyrelsen, 1990). This disturbing trend, however, led to restored funding for such programmes, and teenage abortions have once again dropped.

11.3.5. *Children and contemporary family life*

In recent decades, the structure, composition, functions, and roles of the family have changed rapidly (Näsman, 1993, 1994). Most families now conform to a modified version of the 'traditional' family model, with the husband as principal breadwinner whose earnings are supplemented by those of the female breadwinner, usually working part time. However, a diverse range of family lifestyles has appeared since the mid-1960s, provoking a tremendous impact on what is currently considered the normalcy of childhood (Qvortrup, 1994).

A low marriage rate, a large percentage of single-person households, a high rate of non-marital cohabitation, a swelling rate of family dissolution, and the extensive flow of mothers into the labour force are the five indicators used by some critics to show that Sweden has the world's lowest 'index' of family stability (Popenoe, 1988). However, this position has been challenged as unscientific, value-laden, gender- (male-) oriented, and insensitive to the unequal dependency of the traditional family (Stacey, 1994).

Over the past forty years, women's economic independence has strengthened as their employment and wages have increased. It is thus not surprising that the annual number of marriages dropped, as occurred between 1950 and 1980 (Figure 11.3), from above nine to below five per 1,000 persons. The second half of the 1980s signalled a rise in marriages, though figures were still fairly low. An exceptional peak was recorded in 1989 due to the introduction of a new pension system for widows and widowers. The average age for first marriages rose between the late 1960s and the early 1980s (23 years for women, 26 for men), as did the average age of women giving birth to their first child.

In 1990, around half of all babies were born 'out of wedlock'. There has been a long-term trend towards couples living together in circumstances resembling marriage, but without formal marriage contracts. These relationships are less stable than traditional marriages, particularly because the partners are usually younger. However, stable couples living together often marry after some years. Overall, roughly one-fifth of all couples are unmarried, with the majority under the age of 30. Out-of-wedlock children are most common among young mothers, mainly between the ages of 25 and 29.

Most children under 18 live in traditional families with both parents and perhaps with one or more siblings. However, 10 per cent of all preschool children and 17 per cent of all 13–18-year-olds live with only one parent, generally the mother. Among the younger group, the propor-

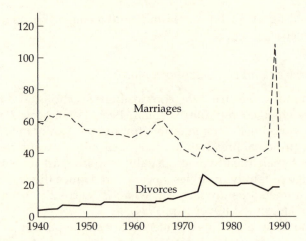

Fig. 11.3   Marriages and Divorces (1,000s, 1940–1990)
Source: SCB (1994*a*).
[a] The curves show the effects of major legislative changes in 1974 and 1989.

tion living in lone-parent families has doubled since 1960. In the late 1980s, 12 per cent of all children lived with a lone parent, generally the mother (SCB, 1989). Another 8 per cent lived with the mother and a 'stepfather', and 3 per cent with the father and a 'stepmother', although the 'new parents' were not necessarily married.

Divorce is an important factor in contemporary family life. The divorce rate peaked in the mid-1970s, with the introduction of new legislation (see Figure 11.3), and has remained at a high but fairly stable level since then. The last few years have witnessed a decline, mainly because more young couples are cohabiting without marrying. As there is no formal registration of these relationships, the number of children involved in such 'family' break-ups is unknown. The right of a child's access to both parents is recognized by law, but enforcement is another matter.

There has also been a substantial rise in the percentage of children for whom advance maintenance payments are received: from 2 per cent in 1950 to about 15 per cent since the 1980s. Expenditures jumped more than twentyfold (in constant prices) between 1950 and 1994 (RFV, 1995), with roughly one-third financed by repayments from non-custodial parents.

Growth in the number of 'recomposed' households, whether or not bound by marriage, has rendered 'step-relations' more common. This, however, has not diminished the hardship of family conflicts and the severity, especially for children, of family break-ups (Alanen, 1992). To offset some of these negative effects, local governments are obliged, as of

January 1995, to offer family counselling. Most municipal social service departments have, however, offered this service free of charge for many years.

Family contacts remain intense and there does not appear to be an increase in social isolation and loneliness. The solidarity among 'clan' members however should not be exaggerated; individuals are born into families but are free to choose their friends and partners. Loyalty is not dependent on formalized contracts among adults. The traditional parental socialization model has become somewhat obsolete. Indeed, new ideals and strategies for the well-being of children have emerged and few parents can apply the experience of their own upbringing as a model for their children's development (Dencik, 1989; Björnberg, 1992).

11.3.6. *Working parents, working life, and consumer capitalism*

With industrialization, children's contribution to the family economy through wage labour became the subject of controversy and child labour has come to be seen as a moral evil (Bolin-Hort, 1989). The legal age for factory work in Sweden rose from 12 early this century to 15 in 1949. In 1977, the law made employment conditional upon school termination, which usually occurs one or two years past the legal age for factory work (in the meantime raised to 16 and now 18). The apprenticeship system has disappeared as compulsory schooling has been extended, but new forms of transition from school to work have evolved.

An enormous change in female employment has occurred since the mid-1960s. Today, women represent 48 per cent of all workers, though they are more likely than men to work less than full time. In 1991, 0.9 million women were working part time (less than 35 hours per week) and 1.3 million were employed full time. A considerable gender gap in wages remains despite diminishing educational differences, though it is not as wide as in most other industrialized nations.

Most women work until their first child is born, and return to work within a year of the birth. Many women switch to part-time work when parental leave has elapsed. By the early 1990s over 85 per cent of all mothers of preschool children and over 90 per cent of those with children aged 11–16 were employed. There has also been a move since the mid-1980s towards longer working hours (over 20 hours per week), a trend which has continued despite increased unemployment in the 1990s. A remarkable change in the work–family relationship has taken place since the early post-war 'housewife era' when women's employment was considered detrimental for children and at odds with their family role.

Children are now subject to a dual socialization: in the family and in nurseries and schools. They now spend more time in 'public' life under the supervision of non-family members. Some critics view this as a threat to the traditional family and an invasion of the private sphere. In any case, the borders between 'public' and 'private' have become blurred, and public institutions have penetrated family life in different and distinct ways.

'Public-sector housewives' have grown in importance: between 1960 and 1990 the government share of the labour force almost doubled, from below 20 to nearly 40 per cent (Table 11.3). This expansion was mainly in the social welfare sector, where more than every second employee is female. A gender-segregated labour market emerged, and the new welfare professions, such as psychology and preschool teaching, are female dominated.

In their shift from the home to the public sector, women continue to perform domestic tasks—such as caring for the young, the old, and the sick—but they now perform this work as low-wage public employees (Boje and Drewes Nielsen, 1994). There is also a concern that because of the gender-segregated welfare sector, children in female-headed families have fewer opportunities to interact with male role models or authority figures. Thus, the role of the family and the composition of children's social networks have changed. To encourage men to spend more time with their children, legislation was passed in 1994 reserving one month of parental leave for men.

Because traditional gender roles still prevail (Dahlström and Liljeström, 1983), women's workload has mounted, and they are more prone to stress and daily fatigue. Even in cases where both spouses work full time,

Table 11.3: Public Sector Employment, 1960–1993 (1,000s)

	1960	1970	1975	1980	1985	1990	1993
Central government	316	296	406	438	424	390	362
State-subsidized activities[a]	62	117	137	173	172	170	20
County councils	—	171	257	353	411	424	405
Municipalities	—	302	396	488	525	552	731
Education	124	209	265	278	284	285	—
Health care	137	243	329	355	397	409	—
Social services	51	162	233	298	329	362	—
A. Total public sector[b]	—	886	1,196	1,457	1,580	1,700	1,500
B. Total labour force	3,244	3,913	4,098	4,248	4,367	4,500	4,195
A/B (%)	—	22.6	29.2	34.3	36.2	37.8	35.8

[a]This category mainly comprises employees, primarily teachers, in the school system administered by local councils and financed by the central government together with employees (approximately 20,000 in 1980) in social insurance offices. As of 1991, most teachers are employed by local authorities. [b]Because some categories overlap, the columns do not sum.

Source: Olsson Hort and McMurphy (1997).

women still perform the overwhelming majority of household chores (Tåhlin, 1987; Moen, 1989).

Some observers have suggested that healthy families, working parents, and government-financed child care are contradictory targets (Wolfe, 1989). To date, however, the potentially negative effects of changes in the family are being counteracted by a package of 'women-friendly' measures. Some 'father-friendly' measures have also been introduced, which might stimulate the emotional and intellectual environment of the child. But whether a 'child-friendly' society will result remains to be seen. Public policy measures in this vein are under way, but the resources to enforce them are less certain to appear.

11.3.7. *Public spending on child welfare*

The welfare state has transformed the lives of children. By the mid-1990s, real expenditure for all social welfare activities was approximately 2.5 times greater than it had been in 1970. Because of the indexing of pensions, social expenditure for the elderly grew more quickly than it did for children and adolescents. Table 11.4 illustrates the evolution of expenditure on education and on the major family and child programmes during the last two decades. Apart from education expenditure (see below), which outdistanced expenditure on all other items throughout the period, the general child allowance was the largest expenditure sub-item in 1970.

Table 11.4: Real Education and Family and Child Public Welfare Expenditures, 1970–1992 (in millions of 1980 krona)

	1970	1976	1980	1986	1988	1989	1991	1992
Parental insurance	0	2,338	3,539	4,501	6,137	6,460	7,914	8,162
General child allowance	3,874	4,833	4,995	5,168	5,827	5,595	7,217	7,191
Advance maintenance allowance	317	679	835	1,065	1,027	1,052	1,585	1,663
School meals	1,107	1,581	1,585	1,637	1,527	—	—	—
Child day-care	518	5,587	8,910	11,520	11,971	12,893	13,738	12,904
Child pensions	0	381	398	371	359	328	349	355
Assistance for education	0	973	1,200	1,592	2,309	3,996	4,102	—
Housing allowance	1,344	2,676	2,533	1,541	1,583	1,467	2,243	2,468
Individual and family allowance	2,717	1,025	2,728	4,107	4,267	4,585	5,312	6,115
Other	816	0	0	0	0	0	0	0
Education	31,719	37,170	46,177	43,477	44,351	42,247	45,770	—
Total[a]	42,400	57,245	72,901	74,978	79,358	78,623	88,230	—

[a] Some columns may not sum as indicated due to rounding.

Sources: SCB (1990) and earlier editions.

By the early 1990s, the day-care programme had become the dominant family and child sub-item, and spending on parental insurance also exceeded the general child allowance expenditure.

Real family and child public welfare expenditures, combined with those on education, have roughly doubled over the last two decades, despite the slow growth in spending in the 1980s. The GDP share of these expenditures rose from almost 10 to 13 per cent between 1970 and 1987. Due to the poor performance of the economy, real GDP barely changed between 1980 and 1982, and these social expenditures remained steady between 1980 and 1985.

Real education expenditure peaked in 1980, and accounted for 7.5 per cent of GDP during 1980–8. Education expenditure primarily benefits relatively older children; compulsory education covers children aged 7–17, while secondary school serves children up to age 20. Real education expenditure per child (10–20-year-olds) was fairly steady between 1980 and 1988 (though it has since decreased slightly). At the same time, however, the shares of the 10–15 and 15–19 age-groups increased in the total child population.

Compared to the priority given to the financing of family and child benefits, education spending was downgraded until the early 1990s. The non-socialist government of the early 1990s emphasized education more than its predecessor, but was financially constrained by the recession. The returning Social Democratic government (1994) has continued to stress education as a means of overcoming the recession and structural imbalances in the economy. Nevertheless, cut-backs in spending have occurred in the first half of this decade, and it seems likely that this expenditure will be altered in coming years.

As of 1991, the responsibility for primary and secondary education resides solely with the municipalities, which are to implement lowering of the school-entrance age from 7 to 6 (as of 1997) and to further integrate preschool with primary education. However, budgetary constraints have posed severe limits on the municipalities and state grants will most likely be reduced.

Unlike real expenditures on education, those on family and child programmes began to regain ground after 1982. From 1970 to 1992, spending in this area (at constant prices) almost quadrupled, rising from around 2.5 to about 5.7 per cent of GDP. This broad category includes parental insurance, the general child allowance, the advance maintenance allowance, school meals, child day care, child pensions, education assistance, the housing allowance, and the individual and family allowance.

Pegged to earnings and thus more sensitive to inflation, parental insurance replaced the flat-rate general child allowance in 1988 as the second largest family and child welfare expenditure. By 1976, the child day-care programme had become the most expensive sub-item (see below). The rise in spending in these two areas has been responsible for much of the growth of real expenditure per child since the mid-1970s. Some social expenditures that benefit children, including certain health care expenditures, are not reflected in these data. For instance, paediatric and other specialist services in hospitals are heavily subsidized or free of charge for children, who are also entitled to free dental care.

To offset some of the negative effects of the 1989 comprehensive tax reform on households with children, some cash benefits were raised significantly. In nominal terms, the general child allowance was doubled, though this decision was never fully implemented due to strains on the public budget in the early 1990s. The growth in real terms was less than 30 per cent between 1989 and 1991. Likewise, the advance maintenance allowance was increased to sustain the standard of living in lone-parent households. In real terms, this expenditure rose by more than 50 per cent. In addition, social costs on housing allowances grew by 53 per cent. The main problem with the tax reform was not that it increased take-home pay for most adults. Decreased income taxes were supposed to be financed by increased public revenues from indirect taxation (sales taxes, etc.). This did not eventuate, and the gap between income and outlays in the public budget was reinforced by the deep recession of the first half of the 1990s when revenues fell with increased unemployment. Thus, the more the public deficit has grown, the more the financing of public welfare programmes—including child welfare programmes—has come under critical review.

11.3.8. *The most important child welfare programmes*

To gain a more complete understanding of the situation of Swedish children, the three most important social programmes are examined below:

1. *Parental insurance.* Replacing maternity benefits in 1974, parental insurance aimed to give mothers and fathers equal standing in child-rearing (cf. Haas, 1992). Parents could thus share a total of six months of work leave at almost full pay to care for a newborn. In the late 1970s, this was increased to nine months. A further three months' leave, with a lower flat rate of pay, could be taken at any time until the child entered school. An extension of parental leave at nearly full pay to twelve months was the result of a 1988 election promise by the Social Democrats. Overall leave could also be extended (without pay, but with a guarantee of being able to return to the same job) to care for a child until the age of 18 months. In the case of multiple births, parents received six months' extra benefits for each additional child. Furthermore, parents have the right to work only 75 per cent of the full work week while their children are under 8 years of age.

The parental insurance system also includes:

• since 1980, a ten-day paid leave for fathers at the birth of a child;
• occasional leave at nearly full pay to care for a child, extended to sixty days in 1990;
• since 1980, pay for women unable to continue to work due to health problems related to pregnancy or childbirth;
• since 1986, two days' leave (at nearly full pay) per year per child aged 4–12 to participate in day care or school activities (abolished in late 1995).

2. *Child care*. With the rise in women's employment during the 1960s and 1970s, a debate was sparked over whether day care at nurseries was good for children. Because some studies found that the labour-intensive and costly day-care system had positive effects on children, the system was expanded. The debate over day care was then pursued on questions of cost and equality, as some parents received significant economic subsidies while others had to manage on their own or wait for an available place.

The overheated economy and the unexpected baby boom of the late 1980s brought attention to a 1988 election promise to provide day-care services by the end of 1991 for all children 18 months and over. This promise, however, was not respected. With the change in government in late 1991, for-profit day-care centres became eligible for public grants. Combined with increased unemployment, this has led to the disappearance of queuing.

In 1972, only 10 per cent of all 0–6-year-olds were placed in public nurseries and day-care homes. The percentage shot up in the 1970s and 1980s (Table 11.5). Nevertheless, 37 per cent of 0–6-year-old children were still cared for at home during the day in 1993. These were mainly children whose parents were on parental leave, worked flexible hours, or were 'day parents' for other children. Generally speaking, the number of places in nurseries and day-care homes is equivalent to 90 per cent of revealed demand.

3. *Education*. Considerable importance has been given to public education for over a century. Schooling is compulsory for 6–15-year-olds, and

Table 11.5: Children in Public Day-Care, 1970–1990 ('000s)

	1970	1975	1980	1985	1990	1993
Day-care nurseries	33.8	66.0	121.2	184.4	267.5	315.6
Day-care homes	36.6	49.8	93.2	113.5	155.9	135.6
'Part-time' preschools	72.0	112.0	104.7	78.0	63.1	60.9
All Swedish children 0–6 years	823	774	714	668	731	816.9

Sources: SCB (1994*a*) and earlier editions.

public financial support makes it possible for most to attend upper secondary school for three years. Municipal authorities are responsible for primary and secondary schools as well as for the transition from school to employment. While most children in the 16–19 age bracket take advantage of the education system, most children of higher-income families attend secondary schools and universities, and those of blue-collar workers typically enter vocational training courses (Erikson and Jonsson, 1993). The problem of drop-out does exist, but it is small. Indeed, several programmes designed to guarantee jobs to young people were implemented in the 1980s as a last resort for those unwilling to complete normal education. Gender differences are still apparent. Girls predominate in traditionally female areas such as nursing, while boys more commonly study sciences and technology.

11.3.9. *The health and well-being of children*

While Swedish children enjoy a favourable quality of life, class differences in the distribution of material and intellectual resources do remain. A recent study examines changes in three welfare components over the 1980s: the presence of parents; the types of care available for children; and the overall economic resources in households with children (Östberg, 1994). This discussion will focus on the first and last components.

Increased female labour force participation reduces the time mothers spend with their children. Between 1981 and 1991, the share of children aged 0–6 with dual full-time working parents increased from 14 to 24 per cent. For 7–16-year-old children, this figure rose from 27 to 38 per cent. Single mothers also increased their working hours, though flexible work times and the right to reduced hours partly offset this trend. The participation of fathers in the lives of their children, measured indirectly through the number of hours spent at the workplace, remained stable between 1981 and 1991.

This level-of-living study (cf. Erikson, 1993) also shows the distribution of material wealth among children in various social categories by means of two measures: disposable income per consumption unit and the existence of a cash margin. This study points to an improvement during the 1980s for families of all social classes. A child growing up in a skilled worker's household increased its disposable income by over 13 per cent in contrast to a rise of less than 7 per cent for a child in a household headed by a senior white-collar worker. However, it also revealed an increasingly wide gap between dual and single-headed households. The average growth for all children was almost 11 per cent, but for children living with single parents the increase was less than 2 per cent.

Cash margin, or the opportunity to raise a considerable amount of money in the event of unforeseen circumstances, provides another measure of economic security. The percentage of children without a cash margin remained stable at around 14 per cent between 1981 and 1991, most commonly in households headed by single parents or unskilled workers.

The overall picture for child health indicators is remarkable. Improvements in child mortality have been outstanding. Serious infectious diseases, deprivation, neglect, and starvation are uncommon. Growth status and nutrition are generally excellent, and deficiency diseases have been eradicated. Dental health has improved considerably, and traditionally dangerous childhood ailments have become more like minor inconveniences (Köhler and Jakobsson, 1987).

Some problems remain. Like its Nordic neighbours, Sweden stands out in a global review. Infant mortality decreased markedly until the early 1980s, and then levelled off to 5.8 per 1,000 live births in the late 1980s (Table 11.6). The neonatal mortality rate is roughly three per 1,000 live births. The child (above 1 year old) mortality rate has also declined considerably since the early post-war period and, compared to most other countries, is extremely low. However, although this decrease has favoured both sexes and has occurred in each age bracket and across the social spectrum, a recent study covering 1981–6 (Östberg, 1991) still finds differences among socio-economic groups. Among 1–4-year-olds, social class differences as reflected in mortality rates have decreased, at least among boys. In contrast, in the 5–9 age-group, this difference seems to have widened: the sons of blue-collar workers showed an excess mortality rate of 64 per cent during 1981–6 compared to about 26 per cent during 1961–6. Among girls, the excess mortality rate was 70 per cent during the more recent period compared to around 6 per cent for the earlier period. Finally, it is difficult to decipher a pattern for the older age brackets.

As in all industrialized countries, accidents, especially traffic and domestic accidents, are the single greatest cause of death among children over one year of age. While improved planning and preventive measures might further reduce the rate, Sweden nevertheless has the lowest figure among the industrialized countries, as the number of fatal accidents for children under 15 fell from roughly 400 per year in the 1950s to approximately 100 per year in the late 1980s. This was at least partly due to organized efforts initiated in the mid-1950s by a voluntary association and later by a state agency, the National Child Environment Council.

Child abuse and protection have recently become the focus of public attention (Olsson Hort, 1997). Sweden was criticized in the international media for the unusually high number of children in compulsory custody during the early 1980s. However, the number of children in compulsory care actually decreased in the 1980s (Gould, 1988), though the mid-1990s have witnessed a new increase. Sexual abuse of children has also been the subject of increased concern recently, though whether this reflects a

Table 11.6: Mortality Rates among Under-1-Year-Olds, 1980–1993 (per 1,000 live births)

	Under 1 day[a]			Under 7 days			Under 28 days			Under 6 months			Under 12 months		
	Boys	Girls	Total[b]	Boys	Girls	Total	Boys	Girls	Total	Boys	Girls	Total	Boys	Girls	Total
1980	2.3	1.2	1.8	5.3	3.1	4.2	6.0	3.8	4.9	7.7	5.3	6.5	8.1	5.7	6.9
1982	1.7	1.9	1.8	3.9	3.6	3.8	4.7	4.5	4.6	6.7	6.2	6.5	7.1	6.5	6.8
1984	1.5	1.3	1.4	3.9	2.6	3.3	4.8	3.4	4.1	6.7	5.1	5.9	7.2	5.5	6.4
1986	1.6	1.2	1.4	3.6	3.1	3.4	4.4	3.5	4.0	6.2	4.8	5.5	6.6	5.2	5.9
1988	1.5	1.0	1.3	3.7	2.4	3.1	4.3	3.0	3.7	6.3	4.5	5.4	6.6	5.0	5.8
1990	1.5	1.4	1.4	3.3	2.5	2.9	3.9	3.1	3.5	6.1	4.8	5.4	6.6	5.3	6.0
1991	1.1	1.2	1.2	3.0	2.5	2.8	3.8	3.2	3.5	6.0	5.1	5.6	6.6	5.7	6.2
1992	1.1	1.0	1.0	2.7	2.1	2.4	3.7	2.8	3.2	5.5	4.3	4.9	6.0	4.7	5.3
1993	1.0	1.0	1.0	2.7	2.0	2.4	3.6	2.7	3.1	5.6	4.4	5.0	5.9	4.7	5.3

[a]Birth and death occurred during the same calendar day. [b]Represents the overall mortality rate for the age-group.

Sources: SCB (1990) and earlier editions.

growth in magnitude of the problem or heightened awareness is not possible to know.

Drug abuse and the use of alcohol and tobacco among children is another subject of public discussion. Sweden has strong penalties for alcohol abuse, and young offenders can be held in compulsory custody for six months at a time. Though reliable statistics are difficult to obtain, use of narcotics seems to have increased in the 1960s and 1970s and then evened out. Data deriving from surveys among schoolchildren and military conscripts reveal that around 15 per cent tried illegal drugs like marijuana in the early 1970s. The figure dropped to 10 per cent towards the end of the decade and continued down to 5 per cent during the 1980s. The use of tobacco by teenagers is not illegal, but there is a strong tendency to condemn or suppress its use. Overall, smoking seems to have decreased, although it is now more common among children of lower-income families. Furthermore, children of lone parents are more likely to grow up in an environment in which the head of household is a smoker (SCB, 1981).

A new socio-medical problem is the rapid spread of allergies. While children whose parents suffer allergies are more susceptible, empirical research now assigns a larger role to environmental factors. A number of studies indicate that allergic reactions in the respiratory system have grown in importance. The medical examination undertaken by all 18-year-old Swedish boys prior to compulsory military service can be used to analyse health status trends over long periods (SOU, 1989). One study, covering the 1973–84 period for males born between 1955 and 1966, found that the frequency of asthma increased from around 2.1 per cent (20.7 cases per each 1,000 individuals) in 1973 to 3.3 per cent in 1984. Hay fever rose even more rapidly, from 5.5 to 11 per cent. There was a slower growth for atopic eczema, from 0.8 per cent to approximately 1.2 per cent, while the frequency of other forms of eczema edged up from 1.7 to 2 per cent (ibid.).

These findings ring a strong alarm. The sharp improvement in housing conditions and nutrition standards should have led to better health status among Sweden's children. The allergies of an 18-year-old can be considered the cumulative effects of heredity and the environment during childhood. Heredity cannot have changed enough in so short a time to produce these rapid increases. Thus, changes in the environment are basically responsible.

The most serious challenge to Swedish society concerns the integration of immigrant children and second-generation immigrant children. A number of specific measures, such as special language education, were introduced in the 1970s in schools and preschools. However, earmarked funds for these allocations were often the first to be dropped when cutbacks were instituted in the late 1980s. At the same time, xenophobia and anti-immigrant violence have become part of everyday life. The negative effects of urban housing segregation have especially affected these children (SOU, 1990*b*; Olsson Hort, 1993). As a result, the government in its child-rights action programme singled out refugee and immigrant children as a top priority group for social support. On the national level, new funds have been allocated (Socialdepartementet, 1993, 1994).

11.4. Conclusion: Towards an Emancipated Child Policy?

As early as the 1920s, the principle of 'the best interests of the child' became the main criterion in Sweden for all practical regulation of child–adult relationships, including custody, divorce, inheritance, and economic support during childhood. Indeed, there has been a major transformation in the juridical status of children. They now have freedom of speech, protection from corporal punishment, official recognition of both parents regardless of their marital status, the right to inherit from parents regardless of sex and birth status, as well as the legal possibility to divorce from parents and guardians.

The early 1990s, however, have been difficult years for child welfare benefits and services. The pressure on public finance has made social benefits major targets of retrenchment proposals. Commitment to the traditional universal social policy has never been at stake though, and its popularity remains (Svallfors, 1994). Most social benefits have been scrutinized and were reduced modestly in monetary terms in 1992–3. The largest child welfare programme, paternal insurance, managed to avoid cut-backs until 1994, but benefits were then reduced from 90 to 80 per cent of previous earnings. At the same time, a non-transferable month of parental insurance for fathers (at the higher level) was introduced, as was a non-transferable mother's month at the same level. Non-compensated leave of absence from work for child-minding was also extended to three years. The non-socialist government introduced a new child-care allowance for non-working parents of children up to age 3, but the incoming 1994 Social Democratic government abolished this programme on the grounds that it encouraged traditional housewifing.

As of 1 January 1995 all municipalities must offer child care to all children aged 1 to 12 within a few months of application. Public subsidies to child day-care are large and have remained so despite the economic crisis. The rationale is that child-care services generate tax revenue since they enable both parents to earn a living.

Overall, national monitoring of both children and social development has increased in recent years, and will most likely be further developed in the future (Socialstyrelsen, 1994*a*,*b*). In 1993, Parliament passed legislation for a national child ombudsman, whose task is to protect and defend the rights of children in accordance with the United Nations Convention on the Rights of the Child.

Furthermore, the incoming 1994 Social Democratic government made an unusually outspoken declaration of support for child welfare, pointing in particular to the need for high-quality, subsidized local government services such as health care, child day-care, and education (Sweden, 1995). This approach may create tensions between central and local administrations as grants will be reduced in years to come. Income tax rates may be increased for the highest income-earners. To spur economic growth and cut the public deficit, Parliament will most likely reduce cash benefits again as of 1 January 1997. Whether these measures are sufficient to sustain the viability of the welfare state remains a large question mark.

In the 1995 budget, the government proposes that replacement rates in all earnings-related cash benefits be reduced to 75 per cent. The two months of non-transferable paid parental leave will be reduced to only 85 per cent of previous earnings. For the first time since its introduction in 1948, the non-indexed flat-rate general child allowance will be reduced in nominal terms (by 100 SEK or roughly 13 dollars). The highest household income decile—ranked by the ascending order of disposable income per consumption unit—will have to shoulder almost one-third of the total budget reinforcement, i.e. the combined benefit cut-backs and tax increases. It is intended that the Gini coefficient stay virtually unchanged. Admittedly, however, this is a static analysis of changes that most experts agree would have dynamic effects on both income distribution and the overall distribution of material resources among households, with and without children.

Thus, while social justice for children will most likely stay at the top of the political agenda, considerable uncertainty remains on the question of maintaining and further developing the welfare state. The most recent review of social welfare legislation promotes a child perspective explicitly based on the provisions of the Convention on the Rights of the Child, and this will be reflected in new legislation to be introduced by a non-partisan parliament (SOU, 1994). On the one hand, children, child-related issues, and even 'child institution-building' have become more pronounced and visible in Sweden; on the other hand, recession-induced shrinking public resources have made it difficult to implement such a perspective. Nevertheless, in Sweden there is a strong commitment to a universal welfare policy, which is of utmost importance for the future of child welfare policy. In the years to come, the children of vulnerable and disadvantaged groups will receive special attention, though targeted measures will be guided by an overall policy perspective. It is thus unlikely that child welfare policy will suffer more than other welfare areas. In a longer-term perspective, a number of social and institutional barriers will need to be broken before a comprehensive social policy that recognizes children as an independent social category can fully emerge.

12

Child Well-Being in Japan: The High Cost of Economic Success

MARTHA N. OZAWA AND SHIGEMI KONO

12.1. Introduction

Rapid economic growth and demographic transformations have brought about radical changes in Japanese children's lives. On the one hand, children's economic and physical well-being has never been better, and their school attainment has surpassed that of earlier generations. Only a small percentage—about 5 to 7 per cent—of children are poor. On the other hand, Japanese children have fewer siblings, fewer relatives, and fewer friends. Changing social relations are creating a radically different social and psychological environment in which the healthy growth of children is being hindered.

This dynamic cycle of change is taking place as Japan attempts to maintain its high living standards and economic competitive edge. Ironically, the past and continuing pursuit of economic success in Japan has created an environment in which adults face increasing difficulties in raising children and in which children are placed on a treadmill of educational activities in preparation for the economic mainstream. Economic growth has not favoured children as much as it has benefited adults, especially the elderly.

This chapter describes how economic, social, and demographic changes have transformed life for Japanese children. It explains social welfare expenditures and how they affect the incomes of the vulnerable. Specific child welfare policies and programmes are described and the latest social welfare initiatives by policy-makers are highlighted.

12.2. Economic Growth

The economic growth of Japan is an envy of the world. Since the end of World War II, the Japanese economy has expanded 3.5 times as fast as the US economy (Smith, 1989). From 1966 through 1973, the Japanese economy grew at an annual rate of 9.3 per cent, considerably higher than the rates for the USA, the UK, and West Germany. Though the growth rate declined somewhat during the 1973–9 and 1979–85 periods, it increased again between 1985 and 1990. The average rate of growth during the past quarter of a century has been 5.45 per cent (Keizai Kikakucho, 1994). As a result, in 1991, Japan's per capita income ($23,210) was the third highest among industrialized countries (Sorifu, Shakai Hosho Seido Shingikai Jimukyoku, 1993).

Rapid economic growth was accompanied by low unemployment. Since 1975, the unemployment rate has always been below 3 per cent, much lower than the rate in other advanced economies (Keizai Kikakucho, 1994). Though job availability has declined somewhat in recent years, Japanese workers still find jobs easily. In 1988, 1.16 jobs were available for each job seeker, and even in 1992, after industrial restructuring, there were 1.02 jobs per worker. For certain groups, job opportunities were especially great. For each high school graduate seeking employment in 1991, 3.09 employers were offering jobs (Somucho, Seishonen Taisaku Honbu, 1993).

As the economy grew and as industries became more service-oriented and high-tech, the employment of both men and women changed markedly. The rate of labour force participation among men declined from 84.8 per cent in 1960 to 77.9 per cent in 1992, and the rate for women dropped from 54.5 per cent in 1960 to 47.6 per cent in 1980, before rising again to reach 50.7 per cent in 1992 (Somucho, Tokeikyoku, 1993).

Drastic changes have occurred in the types of jobs that women and men hold. Both men and women have moved away from family businesses or self-employment: in 1960, 41 per cent of working women were employed in non-family-business firms, whereas 75 per cent were so employed in 1992. The percentage increased for men from 62 to 82 per cent over the same period. Meanwhile, the proportion of women with professional positions increased from 5 to 12 per cent, the same percentage as men (ibid.).

Japan has been hit by a severe recession in recent years. During 1992–4, gross domestic product (GDP) growth was close to zero, unemployment rates ranged from 2.3 to 2.8 per cent, and wages did not rise (Keizai Kikakucho, 1994). However, an economic recovery is already underway.

12.3. Demographic Shifts

Japan has undergone enormous demographic changes and is becoming a country of many elderly persons and few children. To describe this phenomenon, the Japanese have coined the term, *shoshi shakai*, which literally means a society whose child population is minimized.

Shoshi shakai is mainly caused by the declining total fertility rate and the increasing life expectancy rate. As Table 12.1 indicates, Japan's total fertil-

Table 12.1: Crude Birth-Rate, Total Fertility Rate, and Net Reproduction Rate,[a] Selected years, 1925–1993

Year	Crude birth-rate	Total fertility rate	Net reproduction rate
1925	34.9	5.11	1.56
1930	32.4	4.71	1.52
1937	30.9	4.36	1.49
1940	29.4	4.11	1.44
1950	28.1	3.65	1.51
1955	19.4	2.37	1.06
1960	17.2	2.00	0.92
1965	18.6	2.14	1.01
1970	18.8	2.13	1.00
1975	17.1	1.91	0.91
1980	13.6	1.75	0.84
1985	11.9	1.76	0.85
1990	10.0	1.53	0.74
1992	9.8	1.50	0.72
1993	9.6	1.46	—

[a]Crude birth-rate is the number of live births in one year per 1,000 population. Total fertility rate is the average number of children that would be born alive to a woman if she were to bear children at each age in accordance with the prevailing age-specific fertility rates. The (female) net reproduction rate is the average number of live births of female infants that would be born to a hypothetical female birth cohort which would be subjected to a set of rates of current age-specific fertility and mortality.

Sources: Koseisho (1991*a*) (1994).

ity rate followed a persistently downward path from 5.11 in 1925 to a record low of 1.46 in 1993. Fertility rates in metropolitan areas are especially low: 1.14 in Tokyo and 1.37 in Osaka in 1992 (Koseisho, Jinko Mondai Kenkyujo, 1993). Since a total fertility rate of 2.1 implies a stable population, the 1993 figure is alarmingly low. Unlike other industrialized societies, Japan did not have a baby boom.

The net reproduction rates show that Japanese women are not recreating themselves—that is, they are having fewer than one daughter, on average. In 1992, the net reproduction rate was only 0.72, compared with 1.00 in 1970.

Shoshi shakai is compounded by population ageing. Life expectancy increased from 46.54 years for women and 44.82 years for men in 1926–30 to 82.2 years for women and 76.1 years for men in 1992. By 1975, it had surpassed the life expectancy of all other industrialized societies and has widened its lead since (Sorifu, Shakai Hosho Seido Shingikai Jimukyoku, 1993). In addition, it took only twenty-five years (from 1970 to 1995) for Japan's elderly to increase from 7 to 14 per cent of the population, while it has taken or is expected to take considerably more years for all other industrialized countries (Koseisho, Daijin Kambo Seisakuka, 1990*a*).

The proportion of children in the population is expected to decrease from 18.2 per cent in 1990 to 14.5 per cent in 2025. Over the same period, the proportion of the elderly will skyrocket from 12.1 to 25.8 per cent (Koseisho, Jinko Mondai Kenkyujo, 1992). The number of elderly people will surpass that of children (aged 0–14) in 1997. Projections by the Institute of Population Problems indicate that the total dependency ratio will increase from 43.5 per cent in 1990 to 71.3 per cent in 2090. Meanwhile, the ratio of the elderly to children is expected to increase from 0.66:1 to 1.43:1 over the same period (Koseisho, Jinko Mondai Kenkyujo, 1983, 1992, 1994).

Why are Japanese women bearing fewer children? Multiple forces seem to be at work. First, the age at first marriage has risen throughout the post-World War II years from an average of 22.9 years in 1947 to 25.9 years in 1990 for women, and for men it was 28.4 years in 1990 against 26.1 years in 1947 (Koseisho, Daijin Kanbo Tokei Johobu, 1993). Second, the proportion of men and women who intend not to marry is increasing. A survey by the Ministry of Health and Welfare found that between 1972 and 1992, 4.1 per cent versus 5.2 per cent of women and 2.3 versus 4.9 per cent of men reported that they did not intend to marry (Koseisho, 1993*a*). Another survey revealed that increasing proportions of men and women believe that marriage is not necessary: in 1987, 25 per cent of women and 16 per cent of men voiced this opinion, compared with 13 per cent and 7 per cent respectively in 1972 (Sorifu, 1972; Koseisho, Jinko Mondai Kenkyujo, 1987).

The number of children born to couples who have been married for 15–19 years steadily declined from 3.60 in 1957 to 2.21 in 1992 (Koseisho, 1993*b*). In 1992, 80 per cent of families with children had only one or two (Koseisho, 1992). The declining number of children born to couples reflects the widening gap between the ideal number of children and the intended number—this gap increased from 0.38 children in 1977 to 0.46 in 1992 (Koseisho, 1993*a*).

There is increasing resistance among men and women to rearing children. A recent survey indicated that 33.6 per cent of men and 35.3 per cent of women believed it was financially difficult to raise children. Furthermore, 21.2 per cent of men and 19.9 per cent of women thought they were too old to have the number of children they desired, and a sizeable proportion of men (18.1 per cent) and women (13.2 per cent) pointed to the shortage of adequate housing. Other reasons were concerns about educating children properly and providing for their future, as well as the lack of an adequate environment for raising children (Keikakucho, 1992).

Women's changing role in the workplace is also contributing to the fall in total fertility. Japanese corporations recruit workers under two differ-

Table 12.2: Marriage and Divorce Rates, 1947–1992
(per 1,000 population)

Year	Marriage rate	Divorce rate
1947	12.0	1.02
1950	8.6	1.01
1960	9.3	0.74
1970	10.0	0.93
1980	6.7	1.22
1985	6.1	1.39
1990	5.9	1.28
1991	6.0	1.37
1992	6.1	1.45

Source: Koseisho, Daijin Kanbo Tokei Johobu (1993).

ent terms of employment: *sogoshoku* (comprehensive employment) and *ippanshoku* (general employment) (Nakajima, 1989). *Sogoshoku* workers are expected to be upwardly mobile: corporations ensure that they follow such career paths by investing heavily through on-the-job training and frequent changes in job assignments, inevitably leading to changes of residence. In contrast, *ippanshoku* workers move horizontally among similar jobs, using similar skills and living in the same locations. Under the 1986 Law of Employment of Men and Women (*Danjo Koyo Byodo Ho*), corporations ostensibly can no longer discriminate against women in terms of *sogoshoku* and *ippanshoku*. Yet, in reality few married women work under *sogoshoku* because it is impossible to combine such employment with a family. Thus, young women in *sogoshoku* must delay or forgo marriage and child-bearing. In response to a survey on the reasons for late marriage, 73 per cent of women referred to their economic self-sufficiency, 41 per cent noted the freedom that independent living provides, and 24 per cent mentioned the obstacle that children create to career advancement (Sorifu, 1991).

Women's economic self-sufficiency is closely related to the increasing divorce rate (Ross and Sawhill, 1975; Ellwood and Crane, 1990). Table 12.2 shows the rising divorce rate and declining marriage rate, both of which contribute to diminishing numbers of children.

12.4. Living Arrangements of Children

As Japanese families have fewer children, the proportion of all households with no children has increased greatly—from 47.0 per cent in 1972 to 63.6 per cent in 1992. Although the divorce rate has risen steadily, the proportion of female-headed households with children has fluctuated

Table 12.3:   Living Arrangements of Children, 1980–1990 (percentages)

Type of household	Children under 6			Children under 18		
	1980	1985	1990	1980	1985	1990
Population of children[a]	10,426	9,042	7,920	32,405	31,511	28,333
I. In nuclear households	68.6	67.3	69.4	69.7	69.3	69.3
(1) Married couple	67.1	65.5	67.4	65.8	64.8	64.2
(2) Mother only	1.4	1.7	1.9	3.3	4.1	4.4
(3) Father only	0.1	0.1	0.1	0.6	0.7	0.7
II. In three-generation households with married couples	29.3	30.4	28.4	27.1	27.4	27.4
III. With other relatives	2.1	2.3	2.2	3.0	3.1	3.1
IV. In one-person households	—	—	—	0.3	0.2	0.2

[a] In 1,000s.

Sources: Japan Statistics Bureau, Management and Co-ordination Agency (1990); Japan Statistics Bureau (1991).

only slightly between 1.1 and 1.4 per cent of all households between 1975 and 1992 (Koseisho, Daijin Kanbo Tokei Johobu, 1986; Koseisho, 1993c).

Living arrangements are also changing. As Table 12.3 shows, the proportion of children under age 18 living only with their mother increased from 3.3 per cent to 4.4 per cent between 1980 and 1990. Among children under age 6, the proportion increased from 1.4 to 1.9 per cent during the same period. The offsetting trend is the declining proportion of children under age 18 who live in intact nuclear families, from 65.8 per cent to 64.2 per cent. The proportion living in three-generation families remained stable at about 27 per cent (Koseisho, 1993c).

12.5. Persons and Families in Need

The Japanese government has not developed official poverty thresholds. However, proxies can be used to assess the economic status of vulnerable segments of the population. We describe hereafter the economic conditions of children and families at risk of poverty by presenting data on household expenditure, household incomes, and the rate of participation in public assistance programmes.

12.5.1. Household expenditure

While rapid economic growth since World War II has lifted the economic status of all families, its impact has been uneven. Table 12.4 presents mean

Table 12.4: Mean Monthly Household Expenditures, by age,[a]
1975–1990 (in ¥1,000)

Age	1975	1980	1985	1990	Percentage change 1975–90
0–1	219.4	222.3	220.0	243.2	10.8
2–4	214.3	220.6	217.6	238.0	11.1
5–9	218.8	229.0	225.9	242.2	10.7
10–14	228.0	245.2	249.2	266.4	16.8
15–19	232.3	254.9	269.9	291.7	25.6
20–39	238.5	250.6	255.6	285.5	19.7
40–59	253.2	278.4	293.7	319.5	26.2
60–64	221.8	250.0	276.5	310.9	40.2
65–74	206.0	230.6	249.4	280.2	36.0
75–85	203.5	226.2	246.7	261.7	28.6
85+	196.8	225.2	242.7	262.4	33.3
All	233.8	251.7	262.3	289.4	23.8

[a] Figures are adjusted for inflation and values are expressed in 1990 yen; adjusted by equivalence scale based on the expenditures for a three-person household.

Source: Derived from Koseisho (1991*c*).

monthly household expenditure for persons by age. The total monthly household expenditure of each household is divided by an equivalence scale corresponding to the household size (the same scale used in the USA to calculate poverty thresholds).[1]

Table 12.4 indicates that the level of expenditure for children was higher than for the elderly in 1975, about the same in 1980, and lower by 1985. In general, from 1975 to 1990, expenditure for children (aged 1–14) increased by only 10.7 per cent to 16.8 per cent, but expenditure for the elderly (aged 65+) jumped by 28.6 per cent to 36 per cent, and for non-aged adult persons (aged 15–64) it rose by 19.7 per cent to 40.2 per cent, depending on the age brackets.

Table 12.5 presents the percentage of persons living in households with monthly expenditure below ¥150,000, which is comparable to the level of public assistance payments in 1990 for a family of three in large metropolitan areas. In contrast, in 1990, the average expenditure for a three-person family was ¥277,253. Thus ¥150,000 was about 45.1 per cent of the average expenditure.

[1] Since 1990, *Kokumin Seikatsu Doko Chosa* (Basic Survey on People's Living) has used a smaller sample than its forerunner, *Kosei Gyosei Chosa* (Basic Survey for the Health and Welfare Administration). It has thus been informally recognized that disproportionately more low-income households might have been included in the 1990 survey compared with prior ones (see Preston and Kono, 1988). Average expenditures for 1990 may be underestimated due to different sampling methods.

Table 12.5: Persons Living in Households with Monthly Expenditures below
¥150,000, by Age of Persons,[a] 1975–1990 (percentages)

Age	1975	1980	1985	1990	Percentage change 1975–90
0–1	24.5	17.1	18.7	14.3	−41.6
2–4	25.8	17.7	19.0	13.7	−46.8
5–9	24.4	14.8	16.6	12.0	−50.8
10–14	23.6	12.7	11.9	9.3	−60.6
15–19	26.2	14.2	12.4	9.0	−65.6
20–39	21.2	12.2	13.2	9.1	−57.1
40–59	21.8	10.6	10.1	6.6	−69.7
60–64	32.1	18.1	16.0	9.7	−69.8
65–74	37.7	22.9	19.3	12.3	−67.4
75–85	39.7	24.9	21.6	16.1	−59.4
85+	42.2	25.6	21.7	18.3	−56.6
All	24.3	13.6	13.6	9.3	−61.7

[a] Adjusted to value of yen in 1990; adjusted by equivalence scale based on the
expenditures for a three-person household.

Source: Derived from Koseisho (1991*c*).

The percentage of persons living with the minimum level of expenditure decreased most noticeably among middle-aged persons, followed by
the elderly. Children fared the worst. Thus, although children were traditionally less deprived than the elderly, the proportions of children and the
elderly with low-level expenditure converged greatly during the 1975–90
period. In 1990, 9.3 per cent of all persons lived in households with
monthly expenditure below ¥150,000: about 11.6 per cent of all children
and 14.1 per cent of all elderly.

12.5.2. Household income

Table 12.6 presents the average annual income of elderly households,
female-headed households with children, and other households. Average
annual income was transformed into adjusted annual income using the
equivalence scale, which sets the scale at 1 for a three-person household,
as described earlier. A quintile distribution of all households, based on
unadjusted annual incomes, is also presented, as are the size of households and the number of earners in the households.

Female-headed households with children are clearly the most economically deprived group. In 1992, their adjusted annual income was 65 per
cent of that of elderly households and 44 per cent of that of other types of
household. As many as 72 per cent of female-headed households with
children were located in the bottom 25 per cent of households, compared

Table 12.6: Household Income, by Type of Household (1992)

	Type of household		
	Elderly	Female-headed with children	Other
Annual income	¥3,053,000	¥2,490,000	¥6,837,000
Adjusted annual income	4,090,300	2,672,820	6,102,285
Household size	1.59	2.62	3.43
No. of earners	0.44	0.99	1.72
Quintile distribution of	100.0	100.0	100.0
all households by order	67.8	72.0	17.8
of unadjusted income	20.8	21.6	25.7
levels	6.5	6.0	28.1
	4.9	0.5	28.5

Source: Koseisho (1993*c*).

Table 12.7: Rate of Participation in Public Assistance, by Age, 1965–1992 (percentages)

Year	All persons	0–14 years	15–59 years	60+ years
1965	1.63	2.29	1.11	3.04
1970	1.30	1.47	0.89	3.20
1975	1.21	1.12	0.84	3.00
1980	1.22	1.19	0.89	2.52
1985	1.18	1.21	0.89	2.21
1990	0.82	0.74	0.59	1.65
1991	0.76	0.66	0.54	1.58
1992	0.72	0.63	0.49	1.52

Source: Koseisho (1993*e*).

with 67.8 per cent of the elderly households, and only 17.8 per cent of other households. Female-headed households with children had fewer than one earner in that year.

12.5.3. *Participation in the public assistance programme*

Japan's public assistance programme is non-categorical: all households, regardless of composition, can apply. Payment levels are based on the size and composition of families as well as on residential location. The rate of participation in public assistance has declined among all age-groups since the mid-1960s, with the fastest decrease among children and the slowest among over-60s (Table 12.7). Although children are less likely to be on

Table 12.8:	Rate of Participation in Public
Assistance, by Type of Household, 1965–1992
(percentages)

Year	All	Type of household		
		Elderly	Female-headed with children	Other
1965	2.32	17.35	24.82	1.55
1970	2.11	16.52	17.59	1.30
1975	2.07	14.41	17.35	1.24
1980	2.04	9.72	20.10	1.22
1985	2.04	7.95	21.68	1.20
1990	1.52	5.72	13.17	0.84
1991	1.45	5.12	11.99	0.80
1992	1.38	4.95	11.83	0.76

Source: Kosei Tokei Kyokai (1993).

public assistance than are the elderly, children who live only with their mothers are more likely to be recipients (Table 12.8). Furthermore, the participation rate among female-headed households with children declined more slowly (52 per cent) than it did among elderly households (71 per cent) between 1965 and 1992. Furthermore, the income status of female-headed households with children is considerably lower than that of elderly households. Thus, though its incidence is still low, female headship directly translates into economic hardship for children.

Children have been losing ground economically relative to the elderly and the non-aged adult populations whether average household expenditure or the minimum level of expenditure is used as a measurement.

The reader should also note an anomaly. Although, the rate of participation in public assistance is low, 0.72 per cent in 1992 (Table 12.7), a sizeable proportion (9.3 per cent in 1990) of persons live in households with low-level expenditures (Table 12.5). This discrepancy is due, in part, to the fact that household incomes are generally higher than expenditure. Some households may consume below the minimum standards, even though their incomes exceed the public assistance payment levels. Another reason is statutory. Japan's public assistance programme requires a broad range of relatives to be responsible for supporting needy families, including parents, children, siblings, grandparents, and grandchildren. Finally, the level of stigma attached to receiving public assistance is high. As a result, Japan has a low rate of participation in public assistance despite relatively high payment levels. In light of the emerging economic deprivation of children living in female-headed households, however, the current policy on public assistance needs to be scrutinized.

While bearing in mind that the lack of an official poverty line makes it difficult to estimate the percentage of children in need, on the basis of figures presented, it is safe to estimate that between 5 and 7 per cent of children are poor.

12.6. Well-Being of Children

Children's physical and material well-being has never been better, and their educational attainment has far exceeded that of earlier generations. However, new pressures are creating a world full of anxiety and difficulties for children to navigate, resulting in psychological problems unknown in earlier times.

12.6.1. *Physical well-being*

Improvement in the infant mortality rate in Japan is legendary: it literally nose-dived from 76.7 per 1,000 live births in 1947 to 4.4 in 1991, the lowest in the world (Table 12.9). The physical development of Japanese children has also been spectacular. As Table 12.10 shows, from 1960 to 1990, the heights of Japanese children increased by between 2 and 7 per cent, and their weights rose by 5 to 20 per cent, depending on the age and gender of the children.

12.6.2. *Educational attainment*

Although Japanese high school education (grades 10 to 12) is voluntary, attendance is fast becoming universal (Table 12.11). Both parents and children take college education seriously. According to a government study, 54.1 per cent of parents want their sons to attend universities, and 4.8 per cent want their sons to attend two-year colleges; the figures for

Table 12.9: Infant Mortality Rate, 1947–1991

Year	Deaths per 1,000 live births
1947	76.7
1950	60.1
1960	30.7
1970	13.1
1980	7.5
1985	5.5
1990	4.6
1991	4.4

Source: Koseisho, Daijin Kanbo Tokei Johobu (1992).

National Case-Studies

Table 12.10: Heights and Weights of Children, 1960 and 1990

	1960		1990		1960–90 change (%)	
	Heights (cm)	Weights (kg)	Heights (cm)	Weights (kg)	Heights (cm)	Weights (kg)
Age 1						
Male	79.4	10.2	81.7	10.81	3	6
Female	77.8	9.6	79.9	10.01	3	4
Age 2						
Male	85.0	11.6	87.1	12.26	2	6
Female	83.7	11.1	85.9	11.73	3	6
Age 3						
Male	91.9	13.3	95.2	14.31	4	8
Female	90.7	12.9	93.8	13.64	3	6
Age 4						
Male	98.2	15.0	102.5	16.28	4	8
Female	97.3	14.6	101.4	16.03	4	10
Age 5						
Male	104.4	16.6	108.3	18.27	4	10
Female	103.3	16.2	107.7	17.91	4	11
Age 10						
Male	131.6	28.0	138.8	33.90	5	21
Female	132.0	28.2	139.5	34.00	6	20
Age 14						
Male	155.1	45.3	164.5	54.20	7	20
Female	150.7	45.3	156.4	50.20	4	11
Age 17						
Male	165.0	56.1	170.6	62.00	3	11
Female	153.7	50.4	157.9	52.80	3	5

Sources: Koseisho (1991*d*); Monbusho (1993*a*).

Table 12.11: Enrolment in High School, University, and Two-Year College,[a] 1970–1992 (percentages)

Year	High school	University	Two-year college
1970	82.1	17.1	6.5
1975	91.9	26.7	11.0
1980	94.2	26.1	11.3
1985	93.8	26.5	11.1
1990	94.4	24.6	11.7
1992	94.8	26.4	12.4

[a]Eligible children are defined as those who are in the age-group appropriate for particular levels of education.

Source: Monbusho (1993*b*).

daughters are 24 and 24.2 per cent respectively (Sorifu, Koho Shitsu, 1992). Moreover, the percentage of fathers who believed that academic credentials are indispensable for workplace success increased from 69.8 per cent in 1982 to 73.3 per cent in 1987 (NHK Hoso Bunka Kenkyujo, Yoron Chosabu, 1989*a*). Japanese children seem to respond to their parents' high aspirations. By the time they reach fourth grade, over a quarter express the desire to go to university or college, and by ninth grade this rises to over half (Somucho, Seishonen Taisaku Honbu, 1988).

12.6.3. Material well-being

The income source of Japanese students is secure and their material well-being is high. The greatest portion (72.4 per cent) of the annual incomes of university students is provided by their parents; the remainder comes from jobs (21.3 per cent) and scholarships (5.8 per cent) (Monbusho, Kotokyoiku Kyoku 1991). High school and college graduates find jobs relatively easily and their starting salaries are comparable to those in the USA and Western Europe.

Young people's savings, expressed as a percentage of their annual income, have increased since the mid-1970s (Somucho, Tokeikyoku, 1990). Accumulated savings among men under age 30 were 46.8 per cent of their annual income in 1989, and among women in the same age-group, 54.3 per cent of their annual income.

12.6.4. Children and parents under pressure

The stress on educational achievement in Japan has adversely affected both children and their parents. Children spend too much time studying, are studying for the wrong reasons, and do not have time for other activities that are indispensable for healthy socialization.

Students study long hours outside the regular school hours—high school students spend 5.8 hours per day on their schoolwork, and those in universities or graduate schools study 3.5 hours per day (Somucho, 1988). Another survey found that children aged 10–15 typically spend 108 minutes a day studying outside the regular school hours, compared with 72 minutes for French and US children and 66 minutes for British children (Somucho, 1979).

The institution of *gakushu juku*, or simply *juku* accounts for this extensive studying. *Jukus* are for-profit after-school schools that supplement regular schoolwork. For children in higher grades, the objective of *juku* is the development of skills to pass high school and university entrance exams. Attendance in *jukus* has increased greatly over the years: for sixth- and ninth-graders respectively, it went from 26.6 and 37.4 per cent in 1975 to 41.7 and 67.1 per cent in 1993 (Monbusho, 1993*a*). Over half of all elementary schoolchildren spend at least three hours a week at *jukus* (NHK Hoso Bunka Kenkyujo, Yoron Chosabu, 1989*b*). It is not unusual to see elementary schoolchildren in subways in Tokyo at 10.30 at night returning from *jukus* (*Yomiuri Shinbun*, 31 July 1994). And of course, *juku* children study additional hours at home.

The importance of *jukus* to the Japanese stems not only from their firm belief in the inherent value of education, but also from a complex merit and employment recruitment system. This centuries-old merit system is still responsible for seeing graduates of a select, few universities chan-nelled into high-flying career paths that remain beyond the reach of other graduates.

The impact of *juku* is so profound that the role of regular schools is being undermined. Yuki *et al.* (1990) found that both children and parents consider the teaching at *jukus* more methodical and effective than at regular schools. Regular school teachers did better than *juku* teachers in this study only in broad aspects of education, such as in enhancing chil-dren's sense of right and wrong and in developing co-operation among children.

Increasingly, the mission of regular school is questioned. If children rush from school to not just one, but two or three *jukus*, what is the purpose of regular school? Is education that merely prepares children for entrance exams conducive to creating 'educated' people in the true sense of the word? (*Yomiuri Shinbun*, 31 July 1994).

With the pressure on Japanese children to study, they have little time for play. Children aged 10–15 typically spend only 96 minutes a day for play, compared with 204 minutes and 156 minutes for children in the USA and the UK respectively (Somucho, 1979). Indeed, Japanese children are more likely to meet other children in the competitive *juku* environment than in the playground.

Japanese children are frustrated, isolated, and full of self-doubt. One study found that 49.6 per cent of fifth-grade children and 74.3 per cent of ninth-graders felt anxious and had deep-seated problems; 21.5 per cent and 64.1 per cent of fifth- and ninth-graders respectively were worried about studying and passing entrance exams (Koseisho, 1991*b*). In a survey on friendship, 65.4 per cent of Japanese respondents reported that their friendships were 'discreet', compared with only 8.5 per cent of Germans (Somucho, Seishonen Taisaku Honbu, 1990). Japanese children are less likely to share their problems with their friends, take their advice, or make sacrifices for them than are American children (Nihon Seishonen Kenkyujo, 1991). Yet, paradoxically, as many as 46 per cent of senior high school students consider themselves dependent on others, mainly their parents, compared with only 23.2 per cent of their American counterparts (ibid.).

The proportion of children who refuse to go to school has increased considerably. Between 1978 and 1991, the rate of refusal, defined as absence from school for more than 30 consecutive days, more than tripled among elementary schoolchildren (from 0.03 to 0.11 per cent) and quadrupled among junior high school students (from 0.21 to 0.84 per cent) (Monbusho, 1992).

The effects of the economic, demographic, and social changes on children cast a complex, depressing image of the situation of Japanese children. At the same time, the idea of having children increasingly signals a burden for the adult population, especially in light of the changing role of women.

As attendance at *jukus* has risen, household expenditure for children's education has increased. Thus, from 1980 to 1993, the educational expenditure of households headed by persons aged 50 and over rose from 8.8 to 15.2 per cent of disposal household income. Typically, the children in these households are at or are about to enter college. Even for households headed by persons aged 40–49, educational expenditure is large and rising, going from 4.6 per cent in 1980 to 8.0 per cent in 1993 (Somucho, 1994). It is estimated that parents must spend about ¥10,000,000 ($100,000) to educate children from kindergarten to college, including *juku* expenses (Ogishima, 1990)—a heavy burden indeed, especially given that the economic standing of families with children has been declining relative to families without children.

Although all public schools in Japan are of high quality, the *jukus* create a class system in which better-off children can acquire extra knowledge and skills and poor children are excluded, giving the former even better odds of going to prestigious universities and landing the best jobs. The expenses involved make it very difficult for children who live only with their mothers to pursue a college education.

The high pressures of education for children and the economic burden created for parents has created a major public concern in Japan. It may well be that Japanese parents who decide to have few children and adults who decide to have none do not want to raise children under such pressure and hardship.

This struggle with *shoshi shakai* is having a ripple effect on people's expectations of old age. The percentage of non-aged adults who expect to depend on their children in old age declined from 51 per cent in 1952 to 15 per cent in 1990 (Mainichi Shinbunsha, 1990).

These problems may be uniquely Japanese. However, that Japanese parents—rich by international standards—feel that they cannot afford to have as many children as they desire may signify a pathology of post-industrial society. As industrialization has progressed and family businesses have been replaced by employment outside the home, as individual-based economic sufficiency has expanded, as economic security in old age has been provided through the social security programme, and as the cost of education has skyrocketed, the economic equation for having children has changed. Increasingly, the perceived direct and opportunity costs of having children outweigh the benefits. The Japanese have followed this path for many decades now, only to reach a critical point of having too few children. This, in turn, has had repercussions on the social environment, making it more and more inhospitable for children.

12.7. Social Welfare Expenditures and their Distributive Effects

Japan lags behind other industrialized societies in social welfare expenditures. It spent only 5.8 per cent of its national income on publicly supported social welfare programmes in 1970 and 14.0 per cent in 1989.

Among the six industrialized countries shown in Table 12.12, Japan spent in 1989 the lowest percentage of national income on social welfare programmes. Also, Japan spent the lowest proportion of its aggregate social expenditure on programmes in the 'other' category, which includes all social service and income support programmes for children, adults, and the elderly, except for social security benefits (Social Development Research Institute, 1992). Japan's social welfare expenditures largely finance health care and social security benefits, leaving little for other programmes.

Next, we examine the distributive effects of taxes and public income transfers on household incomes according to (1) the income level of household, (2) the age of householders, and (3) the type of household. Public income transfers include the value of health care provided by the government, as well as cash transfers. All data are for 1990.

Japan's system of taxes and transfers redistributes financial resources from households with pre-tax, pre-transfer annual incomes over

Table 12.12:   Social Welfare Expenditures as Percentages of National Income in Selected Countries, 1989

Country	Total	Health care	Social security	Other
Japan	14.0	5.4	7.1	1.4
USA	15.8	5.5	8.1	2.2
UK	22.3	6.0	9.4	6.9
West Germany	28.4	7.4	13.8	7.2
France	33.7	8.2	16.5	8.9
Sweden	44.2	11.8	16.6	15.8

Source: Social Development Research Institute (1992).

¥4,500,000 to those with annual incomes below that amount. The tax system exempts low-income persons and those on public assistance from paying social security taxes (Table 12.13).

Taxes and transfers also redistribute financial resources from the young to the old. Households headed by persons aged 60 and over are net winners, whereas those headed by under-60-year-olds are net losers. However, the degree of redistribution across generations is relatively mild. Net transfers increase the incomes of households headed by persons aged 70 and older by 45.9 per cent. Conversely, non-aged households give up 7–9 per cent of their pre-tax, pre-transfer incomes, partly because a sizeable proportion (13.1 per cent in 1992) of these are three-generation households (Kosei Tokei Kyokai, 1993) which mitigates the differential pre-tax, pre-transfer income status of the young and the old (Koseisho, Daijin Kanbo Seisakuka, 1990*b*).

Although the degree of income redistribution across household incomes

Table 12.13: Effects of Taxes and Transfers on Household Income, by Level of Household Income and Type of Household (annual figures, in ¥1,000, 1990)

Household Income	Income before taxes, before transfers	Income after taxes, after transfers	Net transfers	Net transfers (percentage)
All households	5,177	5,202	25	0.5
Less than 500	59	1,968	1,909	3,255.0
500–1,000	737	1,930	1,193	161.8
1,000–1,500	1,210	2,076	866	71.6
1,500–2,000	1,731	2,403	672	38.8
2,000–2,500	2,226	2,714	488	22.0
2,500–3,000	2,713	2,985	272	10.0
3,000–3,500	3,202	3,310	108	3.4
3,500–4,000	3,701	3,824	123	3.3
4,000–4,500	4,193	4,292	99	2.4
4,500–5,000	4,702	4,645	−57	−1.2
5,000–6,000	5,435	5,302	−133	−2.4
6,000–7,000	6,426	6,168	−258	−4.0
7,000–8,000	7,423	6,961	−462	−6.2
8,000–9,000	8,410	7,888	−522	−6.2
9,000–10,000	9,400	8,523	−877	−9.3
Over 10,000	15,313	13,000	−2,313	−15.1
Type of household				
General households	5,759	5,564	−195	−3.4
Elderly	1,298	2,861	1,563	120.4
Female-headed with children	2,203	2,761	558	25.3
On public assistance	1,445	3,749	2,304	159.4

Source: Koseisho Daijin Kanbo Seisakuka (1990*b*).

Table 12.14:   Effects of Taxes and Public Income Transfers on Distribution of Household Incomes, 1981–1990

Year	Gini Coefficients			% Reduction in Gini Coefficients		
	Before taxes, before transfers	After taxes, before transfers	After taxes, after transfers	Due to taxes	Due to transfers	Due to both
Japan						
1981	0.349	0.330	0.314	5.44	4.58	10.02
1984	0.398	0.382	0.343	4.02	9.80	13.82
1987	0.405	0.388	0.338	4.20	12.35	16.55
1990	0.433	0.421	0.364	2.77	13.16	15.93
USA						
1981	0.466	0.434	0.358	6.87	16.31	23.18
1984	0.477	0.453	0.378	5.03	15.72	20.75
1987	0.488	0.458	0.382	6.15	15.57	21.72
1990	0.490	0.461	0.382	5.92	16.12	22.04

Note: Transfers include non-cash benefits, such as medical care.

Sources: Koseisho, Daijin Kanbo Seisakuka (1990*b*); US Bureau of the Census (1992).

and across generations is relatively mild, the degree of income redistribution for particular segments of the population—elderly households, female-headed households with children, and those on public assistance—is considerably larger. In 1992, 11.8 per cent of all households were 'elderly households'—defined as households composed only of men aged 65 and over and women aged 60 and over—whereas 30 per cent of all households were headed by over-60-year-olds (Kosei Tokei Kyokai, 1993; Sorifu, Shakai Hosho Seido Shingikai Jimukyoku, 1993). The pre-tax, pre-transfer income of elderly households increased by 120.4 per cent thanks to these provisions; that of female-headed households with children, by 25.3 per cent; and that of households on public assistance, by 159.4 per cent. It is noteworthy that after taxes and transfers, households on public assistance were better off than was the general population of elderly households or female-headed households with children (see Table 12.13).

Table 12.14 presents the changes in Gini coefficients due to taxation and public transfers. Compared with the USA, Japan's distribution of pre-tax, pre-transfer income is much more equal. However, over the years, it has become more unequal at a faster rate than in the USA. Thus, between 1981 and 1990, the Gini coefficient of pre-tax, pre-transfer income increased by 24.06 per cent in Japan compared to 5.15 per cent in the USA (Table 12.14).

In Japan, the combined redistributive effect of taxes and transfers has become considerably stronger over the years, rising from 10.02 per cent in 1981 to 15.93 per cent in 1990, whereas it has remained more stable in the USA, ranging from 23.18 to 22.04 per cent. Japan's tax system has become less redistributive, while its transfer system has become more redistributive: the change in the Gini coefficient attributable to taxes decreased from 5.44 per cent in 1981 to 2.77 per cent in 1990, whereas the change attributable to transfers increased from 4.58 to 13.16 per cent over the same period.

Finally, Japan's Gini coefficient of after-tax, after-transfer income rose by 15.9 per cent between 1981 and 1990, compared with a 6.7 per cent rise in the USA over the same period.

12.8. Child Welfare Policy and Programmes[2]

Japan has established an elaborate system of child welfare programmes since the end of World War II. The Japanese Constitution guarantees a

---

[2] In this section, unless specifically noted, children are persons under age 18. Dollar figures are also shown in yen equivalents based on the exchange rate of $1 to ¥100 yen. Income ceilings applied to income tests relate to gross annual income, which includes bonuses. The terms 'social welfare', 'social security', 'social welfare services', and 'public assistance' are used here as Americans generally understand them. Key Japanese terms are translated according to the *Social Welfare and Related Services Glossary: English–Japanese Japanese–English Dictionary* (Nakamura, Kojima, and Thompson, 1981).

minimum standard of living to all people and mandates that the government promote and expand social welfare, social security, and public health services.

The Child Welfare Law of 1947 laid the philosophical foundation for public intervention in favour of children and provided the basis for subsequent legislative measures for children, including the Juvenile Law of 1948, Juvenile Institution Law of 1948, Child Support Allowance Law of 1962, Maternal and Child Health Law of 1965, Special Child Dependant's Allowance Law of 1966 (previously the Severely Mentally Retarded Child Dependant's Allowance Law of 1964), and the Children's Allowance Law of 1971 (Koseisho, Jido Katei Kyoku, 1988).

12.8.1. Income support for children

Income support for children is provided through various programmes, each targeting a specific category of children. They are co-ordinated through a unique blend of income tests, enabling some families to benefit from more than one.

1. *Children's allowances*. The Children's Allowance Law of 1971 aimed to alleviate financial burdens by providing an allowance to third and subsequent children until completion of compulsory schooling. Modifications in 1985 and 1991 led to expanded coverage and higher allowances, but a lower cut-off age. Thus, in 1994, all children under age 3 received the allowance—¥5,000 ($50) a month for first and second children and ¥10,000 ($100) a month for third and subsequent children (Kosei Tokei Kyokai, 1993; Sorifu, Shakai Hosho Seido Shingikai Jimukyoku, 1993).

These allowances are not universal as they are restricted to families with incomes below a stipulated amount, which varies according to the number of dependants. In 1993, this income level was about 52 per cent of the median income of working families (Kosei Tokei Kyokai, 1993).

2. *Child support allowances*. The Child Support Allowance Law of 1962 aids children whose fathers are deceased, absent, or incapacitated and who do not receive children's benefits under the Old-Age, Survivors, and Disability Insurance (OASDI). This programme is similar to the US Aid to Families with Dependant Children (AFDC), though it differs in its philosophy and benefit structure which are like a mothers' pension programme. There is little or no stigma attached to receiving this allowance, and families with relatively high incomes are entitled to it. Children are eligible up to age 18, or until 20 if the child is disabled.

In 1993, the first child received ¥38,860 ($388) a month, the second child, ¥5,000 ($50), the third and subsequent children, ¥2,000 ($20) each. For the first child's allowance, an automatic cost-of-living increase was introduced in 1989. Provision of allowances involves an income test. In 1992, about 1.4 per cent of all households were recipients—86 per cent were divorced, and another 5 per cent involved never-married women (Kosei Tokei Kyokai, 1993; Koseisho, 1993*d*).

3. *Special child dependant's allowances.* The Special Child Dependant's Allowance Law of 1966 recognizes that families with mentally or physically disabled children experience an added financial burden. To compensate, the programme in 1993 provided a monthly allowance of ¥47,160 ($461) for a severely disabled child and ¥31,440 ($314) for a moderately disabled child. The special child dependant's allowance is given in addition to benefits for children under OASDI (except for 18–19-year-olds), provided that families meet the income test in which OASDI benefits are included as income. An automatic cost-of-living increase was instituted in 1989.

Disabled adults whose disability originated in childhood receive flat-amount benefits under Disability Insurance, whether or not they have contributed to the system. Disability insurance and the special child dependant's allowance together guarantee a basic floor of income to virtually all disabled persons in Japan.

4. *Children's benefits under old-age, survivors, and disability insurance (OASDI).* The current Japanese social security system operates under the National Pension Law of 1985. Insured self-employed workers receive only flat-amount (first-tier) benefits; insured employed workers receive both flat-amount benefits and earnings-related (second-tier) benefits. Children under 18 years are eligible for dependant benefits, and disabled children are eligible until age 20. Flat-amount benefits are based on the number of years of employment.

Under Survivors' Insurance, effective in 1993, children receive benefits as follows: when there is a surviving spouse, the first and second children each receive a monthly benefit of ¥17,708 ($177), and subsequent children each receive ¥5,900 ($59). When there is no surviving spouse, the first child receives a monthly benefit of ¥61,411 ($614)—the amount paid to a surviving spouse. The second child receives ¥17,708; subsequent children receive ¥5,900. In both cases, the primary surviving person of the deceased worker also receives 75 per cent of the earnings-related benefits that the worker would have received if he were alive and had retired. Under Disability Insurance and Old-Age Insurance, children of disabled and retired workers receive social security benefits. First and second children receive a monthly benefit of ¥17,708 and each subsequent child receives ¥5,900 yen. All social security benefits increase according to consumer price index rises (Sorifu, Shakai Hosho Seido Shingikai Jimukyoku, 1993).

5. *Public assistance.* Provided under the Daily Life Security Law of 1950, public assistance is the non-categorical residual income maintenance programme. Three national payment standards exist, depending on the cost of living in a particular area. Standards of need are calculated on the basis of age and sex of family members; household expenses (according to

family size); housing, educational, medical, maternity, occupational, and funeral aid; and work expenses. A special one-time aid is provided when a child enrols in elementary or junior high school. An additional amount is given for this purpose to female-headed households. For families on public assistance which include a disabled person, an additional amount is provided on behalf of the person caring for the disabled person. The entire amount of children's allowances and a part of the special child dependant's allowance are excluded from the calculation of public assistance payments. Income, net of disregarded allowances and disregarded income to cover work expenses, is counted yen for yen against public assistance payments. In 1993, a typical family of three (two parents and a 4-year-old) with no income and living in a mid-level payment locale received a monthly payment of ¥152,471 ($1,524). Assuming that families on public assistance use the entire assistance payment for consumption, the consumption level of these families is about 51 per cent of that of three-person families headed by an average worker. In 1992, 0.72 per cent of the Japanese population received public assistance (Kosei Tokei Kyokai, 1993).

12.8.2. Loans for female-headed families with children

In addition to the elaborate system of income maintenance programmes involving female-headed families with children, low-interest loans are offered under the Maternal and Child Welfare Law of 1964. Such loans are granted for a variety of purposes, such as establishing or continuing a business; skills acquisition, vocational training, or job preparation; child-rearing, daily living, housing, and remarriage; and educational expenses. Education loans are interest free; 3 per cent is paid on other loans. Duration conditions for repayment range from three to ten years. In 1991 alone, 59,520 women were granted loans, amounting to a total of ¥15.7 billion ($157 million). A less comprehensive system of low-interest loans exists for other low-income families.

12.8.3. Health and social services for children

A wide range of health and social services aims to promote children's optimal development. These programmes are universal—benefits are provided, without an income test, to all children in certain categories.

1. *Health services for children and their mothers*. The Maternal and Child Health Law of 1965 provides health and related services to all children until they enter elementary school. Under this programme, expenses are paid for medical services not covered by health insurance programmes. Prenatal and postnatal care is provided and special home visits are available for premature babies.

Women must report their pregnancies to local community health centres. They are given health handbooks to record the results of health check-ups and diagnostic and treatment services until the child enters elementary school. Check-ups are provided at 3–6 months, 9–11 months, 18 months, and 36 months after birth, followed by routine, periodic check-ups until the child goes to elementary school. When necessary, more comprehensive medical examinations are performed.

In addition, counselling on nutrition, health, family planning, and parenting is provided. Workshops on childbirth, child-rearing, and parenting are open to all women before and after marriage, and after the birth of a child.

2. *Day nursery care for children.* Under the Child Welfare Law of 1947, day nursery care is provided, until school age, for children whose parents or relatives cannot provide day care and for mentally or physically disabled children. Recently, coverage was expanded to include infants under age one, extended twelve-hour care, and night care (until 10 p.m.). Fees are charged on a sliding scale. In 1992, there were 22,637 nursery care facilities—including public and privately operated facilities, serving a total of 1.6 million children (Kosei Tokei Kyokai, 1993).

The dense living conditions in Japan make it all but impossible for parents to provide play areas for children. The government has thus developed children's centres and playgrounds. A large-scale children's centre normally provides various classes, a scientific exhibit, a theatre, gallery, indoor pool, and a short-stay dormitory. A typical children's playground is 200 square metres and offers swings, a sand pit, a jungle gym, benches, and bathrooms. Neighbourhood mothers are encouraged to form mothers' clubs and children's clubs so they can use these grounds to the maximum benefit (Kosei Tokei Kyokai, 1993).

3. *Protective services for children.* Under the Child Welfare Law of 1947, child guidance centres are authorized to diagnose treatment plans for children who need protection for reasons of mental or physical retardation; undesirable environment and lack of care at home; or the child's anti-social behaviour.

Under-3-year-olds in need are placed in residential infant care facilities where they receive specialized medical and nutritional care. Older children and adolescents in such circumstances are placed in residential child-care facilities that offer a protected living environment and opportunities to pursue academic and athletic interests.

Child guidance centres take up opportunities for foster care when appropriate. Families who offer foster care are registered with the national government. In 1992, 2,159 families were actually providing foster care to 2,614 children, a mere 0.008 per cent of all children (Kosei Tokei Kyokai, 1993). The number of registered families has been declining over the years, reflecting increasing costs and the expanding participation of married women in the labour force (ibid.).

The disposition of delinquency cases by the child guidance centres depends on the age of the child and whether the delinquent act was lawful or not. Children under age 14 are sent to a residential educational facility, whether or not they committed an unlawful act. Children over 14 who commit an unlawful act are placed in a residential educational facility, a reform and training school, or a juvenile prison, depending on the severity of the offence. In addition, child guidance centres have the authority to place juveniles who are likely to commit an unlawful act either in a residential educational facility (if the child is under age 14) or in a reform and training school (if the child is aged 14 or over). Recourse to reform and training schools must always involve the family court. The total number of children (7,248) in these three types of facilities was only 0.02 per cent of the child population (Somucho Seishonen Taisaku Honbu, 1986; Kosei Tokei Kyokai, 1988).

4. *Residential facilities for mothers and children.* Under the 1947 law, female-headed families with children in need of a protected living environment are housed, at no charge, in residential facilities. The objectives of these residential facilities have changed over the years: immediately after World War II they offered housing to widows and children with no other place to live, while now they house mothers and children who are estranged from their families because of divorce or out-of-wedlock birth. Social parenting and vocational skills are taught. In 1991, 325 such facilities provided services to 11,822 persons (Tokyo-to Shakai Fukushi Kyogikai, Boshi Fukushi Bukai, 1985; Betaniya Home, 1988; Sorifu, Shakai Hosho Seido Shingikai Jimukyoku, 1993).

12.8.4. *Analysis of child welfare programmes in Japan*

Japanese policy-makers emphasize prevention, an approach which is clearly reflected, for example, in the obligatory health check-ups for all young children and in the loan system for female-headed families.

This preventive approach is possible partly because many programmes are universal in benefit provision. Other programmes, such as the Child Allowance, the Child Support Allowance, and the Special Child Dependant's Allowance, are quasi-universal, even though they are income-tested, because they have relatively high income ceilings and provide flat-amount benefits to families who meet those requirements. Programmes that take a universal or quasi-universal approach to providing benefits are effective in preventing poverty because, by design, they can reach out to the targeted groups before they become poor.

The Japanese income support programmes are effective in preventing child poverty. Even though many programmes provide relatively high levels of benefits in comparison to those of the USA, Japanese policy-makers seem unconcerned about work disincentive effects, probably because of the persistently strong economy and the social pressure to work.

Female-headed families are not looked upon with disdain. The special provisions available for them indicate that they are not considered potentially permanent social dependants. Rather, the message would appear to be that not only are they welcome to get back into the mainstream—the world of work—but that society is willing to help them do so.

The effectiveness of child welfare programmes should not be measured in isolation. These programmes can focus specifically on the problems of children because other programmes outside the child welfare sphere deal effectively with the general problems of health and income security. For example, the Japanese system of national health insurance virtually guarantees the entire population access to needed health care. Thus, health care programmes for children can target their resources to deal with disabilities and illnesses uniquely related to childhood.

The above discussion illustrates that child welfare programmes in Japan effectively provide health care services to all preschool children, income support to children in certain special categories, and social services to children who are disabled or who need protection. However, there are glaring signs that programmes do not meet the emerging needs of normal families with children. Furthermore, income transfer programmes merely provide a national minimum income to children and are therefore insufficient to abate the erosion of the relative economic status of children.

Thus, policy-makers must make a conceptual breakthrough in their thinking on the welfare state. In the future, the welfare state must focus on redistribution from families without children to families with children. On the service front, the issue will be how best to assist normal families with children so that their lives can be as fulfilling as possible.

12.9. Towards a Childs-Centred Society

Japan is obsessed with the problems that *shoshi shakai* is expected to create. In order to address them, both the general public and the government recognize that a major national commitment to building a new welfare state is needed.

There are signs that the Japanese are indeed articulating a vision of a new society. In June 1994, leaders from business, labour, academia, media, and the arts issued a report, *Visions for Social Welfare in the 21st Century* (Committee on Visions for Future Social Welfare in an Ageing Society, 1994). This report proclaimed that the costs for and the task of nurturing children should be the responsibility of the entire society; that having children should not constitute an obstacle to work or to cultural and civic activities; that families with children should not be financially disadvantaged in acquiring homes; that the educational system must be reformed; and that new employment policies should be developed which embrace the support and care of children, including flextime, shortened work hours, day-care centres at work, and guaranteed re-entry to previous jobs, together with the job training needed for re-entry. The Committee s report advocates community-based social services to assist families with children in solving their daily problems. To expand public expenditures for social services, the report recommended that the share of total social welfare expenditures devoted to programmes in the category of 'other', which includes all child welfare programmes, should be increased from the current 10 per cent to 20 per cent by 2025.

Even earlier, in June 1992, the Office of the Prime Minister created an Interministerial Committee which published a report, *Developing a Better Environment for Raising Children* (Interministerial Committee on the Development of a Better Environment for Children, 1992; Kosei Tokei Kyokai, 1993). Four goals were central to this report:

1. *Establishing a better balance between work and family.* The Committee recommended that the number of days and hours of work per week be shortened; that the Family Leave Act of 1992 be strengthened; that a comprehensive child-care system be developed and/or expanded; and that family science courses be required for both male and female students in high schools so that future generations of men can play a larger role in their children's upbringing.

2. *Improving the living conditions of families.* The Committee also recommended that a comprehensive programme be developed to enable families with children to acquire land and housing without undue financial difficulties; that special consideration be given to families with children—especially those with a large number of children—for public housing in metropolitan areas; that the government diversify the use of land to meet the needs of families; that more playgrounds and children's centres be built; and that public facilities should better meet the needs of children.

3. *Supporting children.* Recommendations were made for a more flexible and responsive educational system as well as for individual-based education, more elective courses, a limit of forty students per class, a five-day school week, and greater emphasis on extracurricular voluntary activities. The Committee also recommended that the financial burden of parents be mitigated by increasing children's allowances (introduced in 1992), by lowering co-payment for medical treatment of children under the national health insurance, and by expanding the scholarship system for kindergarten children. In addition, the Committee suggested that improvements be made in medical and social services for pregnant women as well as in

prenatal and postnatal care, child-guidance centres and child-care centres.

4. *Initiating a national public education movement.* The Committee recommended that steering committees be established across the country to create a better environment for children. In addition, a steering committee was set up by the Bureau of Children and Families of the Ministry of Health and Welfare whose aim was to foster communities in which families can be a vibrant institution and in which children can be strong and healthy.

All of these initiatives signal a deep commitment to improving public policies for families with children. No doubt, if implemented, these recommendations would significantly improve the quality of life for families with children. However, they still would not alleviate the problems faced by many women in the workplace and, as a consequence, in the family. How can women combine a career and family? Ultimately, corporate Japan must find answers to this question.

The mandate for Japan's future actions is clear. Japan needs to use its resources to equalize the quality of life between families with and without children and to guarantee a decent minimum standard of living for those on the bottom of the economic ladder. The former requires a horizontal redistribution of resources, and the latter involves a vertical redistribution of resources. The importance of maintaining a decent minimum standard of living is becoming increasingly evident as the divorce rate rises and more children live with lone parents.

Policy-makers should consider a package of income support programmes to accomplish this horizontal and vertical redistribution. First, children's allowances should be increased and made universal. Second, an earned income tax credit (EITC), similar to the one implemented in the USA should also be introduced (see Chapter 7). This combination of children's allowances and the EITC could constitute a double-decker scheme of income support for children, providing a basic floor of income to all children and redistributing income horizontally from childless families to those with children.

Of further benefit to families with children, especially families with working mothers, would be a tax credit for child care, such as the one implemented in the USA. A similar tax credit plan could help to mitigate the financial burden of the *juku*. However, this seems to be only a short-term solution. More importantly, the Japanese public and government must debate and reach consensus on the fundamental goals of education and the most effective approach to achieving those goals.

As Japan enters the world's highest level of industrialization, the traditional division of labour between men and women will no longer exist. Men will lose their relative economic advantage in the labour market because the highly developed economy will demand skills that transcend gender differences (Becker, 1981; O'Neill, 1994). The danger, however, is

PART III

Emerging Problems in the Post-Cold War Era

13

Recession, Social Policy, and Child Welfare in Post-Communist Eastern Europe: Which Way Ahead?

GIOVANNI ANDREA CORNIA

13.1. Introduction: Towards an Uncertain Future

In spite of widespread expectations of a smooth shift to the market economy and rapid improvements in standards of living, six years after the launch of market reforms, the Eastern European transition continues to face considerable obstacles. The transition has triggered a steady political disintegration in the CMEA (June 1991), followed by that of the Soviet Union, Yugoslav Federation (1991), the Czechoslovak Federal Republic (1 January 1993), and the Russian Federation and some of its components.

Not all recent developments have been negative. Some democratic institutions are being rebuilt, supply conditions have improved, market and entrepreneurial skills are being learned, and a less state-centric social policy is being developed. In several countries, over half of production already derives from the private sector. In addition, growth has recovered since 1993 in a few countries—though this was due primarily to real wage falls so large that they would have sparked a recovery in any system. In several countries, however, progress is less pronounced and a 'proto-market-economy', with strong traits of authoritarian state capitalism, is now emerging.

These relatively modest achievements, however, fall far short of expectations and have been accompanied by a disastrous decline in output, employment, and incomes, a severe worsening in child welfare, and a difficult 'social adaptation crisis'. Furthermore, it will take a long time to develop reasonable market structures. While price and trade liberalization is generally complete, it is anticipated that industrial restructuring, asset privatization, and the development of the financial sector and an 'institutional framework' (encompassing legislation on bankruptcy, anti-trust, social assistance, tax reform, banking, and so on) will take several years (EBRD, 1994).

The intensity of these processes as well as future prospects differ widely across the region. Despite the huge fiscal and social cost of the *Vereinigung* (which wiped out 45 per cent of existing jobs in only three years), growth prospects are definitely positive in the former GDR (Nauck and Joos, 1995). Central Europe and Slovenia have suffered lesser disruptions in state structures, smaller economic losses, and limited welfare deteriorations and are more likely to improve in the near future. The collapse is marked in Bulgaria, Romania, and the Baltic republics, even stronger in Russia, most other republics of the former Soviet Union (FSU), and Albania, and is extremely severe in the rest of ex-Yugoslavia and the Caucasus.

The main long-term issue is the feasibility of, and the time required for, the transition to the market economy, i.e. an economy with widespread private ownership, clear 'rules of the game', decentralized decision-making, and well-identified state functions (maintenance of law and order, regulation of market forces, enforcement of contracts, provision of public and merit goods, and guarantee of a socially acceptable income distribution; see Barr, 1994). Indeed, the model of economy and society emerging in the region remains unclear, with the possible exception of the countries of Central Europe. While the likelihood of a return to communism appears slim in most cases, there is much uncertainty about what kind of asset distribution, market structures, and state will prevail. Most likely, a 'mixed', *dirigiste*, dualistic economy will emerge, with a small national capitalist class, a significant presence of foreign investors, a still important state sector, and a growing informal economy.

The choices about 'target model' and 'long-term development path' will influence the future welfare of the population and, more particularly, of children. Whatever the direction chosen for policy reforms, endogenous trends are likely to change the conditions of families and children. Participation in the 'formal' labour force will be lower, unemployment will be higher and of greater duration. The informal sector—where smaller earnings and greater income disparity prevail—will expand. Thus, overall income distribution and poverty will reflect increasing wage disparity, income instability, and inequality. Even in countries, such as Hungary, which can boast a strong social policy, income transfers in total income will fall, while property and entrepreneurial income will increase. Recent changes in family structure and stability, fertility, and migration will also affect the survival, welfare, risks of abandonment, and socialization patterns of children. Finally, child welfare in the years ahead will depend crucially on whether the present trend towards the 'demise of the state' can be reversed. Without a clear rebuilding of a solid liberal state, it will be difficult to develop and implement a social policy and regulatory framework adequate to ensure future development.

13.2. The Reform Process: Main Thrust of Transition Reforms

With the exception of Hungary, which began adopting changes in price and ownership structures in 1968, 'systemic market reforms' were first introduced in Poland in late 1989–early 1990 with the first 'shock-therapy' programme. In most other countries of Eastern and Central Europe, similar measures were instituted in 1990 and intensified subsequently.

Except for the Baltic countries (which introduced draconian reforms immediately after their declaration of independence in mid-1991) and Russia (where the radical 'Gaidar plan' was adopted on 1 January 1992), in most of the countries of the FSU, the reforms did not generally start until the second half of 1992, were narrower in scope, and—in a few— have been characterized by sweeping policy oscillations.

With few notable exceptions (Belarus, Ukraine, and the war-affected countries of the former Yugoslavia and the Caucasus), the transition reforms have followed a similar approach in terms of priority sectors, time-frame, and main policy instruments. The former GDR is the only complete exception to this rule: apart from a few transitory norms (including in the area of privatization), no special labour market policy or social safety net was introduced as West Germany's economic and social legislation was transplanted to East Germany on 1 July 1990 and with immediate effect (Nauck and Joos, 1995). In all the other countries, the following measures were introduced, though their sequencing and sectoral emphases have varied.

13.2.1. Macroeconomic reforms

Macroeconomic measures combined fiscal and monetary stabilization with simultaneous price and trade liberalization and the unification and devaluation of the exchange rate. The last two measures were expected to generate a large, but short-lived, bout of 'corrective inflation' in order to eliminate the monetary overhang and price distortions inherited from the socialist era. A subsequent rapid decline in inflation was to be achieved through restrictive monetary and fiscal policies together with the stability of money wages and the exchange rate.

Macroeconomic conditions in some of these countries in 1989–90 necessitated stiff stabilization. In Poland, for instance, inflation in 1989 reached 680 per cent and the budget deficit and public debt stood at 7.4 and 80 per cent respectively of GDP (Bruno, 1992). Yet others, while suffering from payments crises and repressed inflation, did not initially require immediate Draconian measures. Despite sharp electoral shifts against governments which introduced shock therapies, in no case has there been a radical departure from stringent fiscal and monetary policies, though greater attention has been given to the social costs of the transition. Since then, macroeconomic policy has oscillated between an orthodox anti-inflationary stance and a pro-growth and social protection position.

The most damaging economic measures were the dismantling in 1990–1 of the CMEA trade system and the shift to international market prices for oil and raw materials for inter-CMEA trade. The economic, monetary, and political disintegration provoked by these measures imparted severe recessionary shocks to the whole area, particularly to energy-importing countries such as Bulgaria, Ukraine, and the Baltic and Caucasus countries.

13.2.2. Building the market: privatization and liberalization

'Small privatization' (of shops, restaurants, etc.) advanced rapidly, mostly through local auctions (Gelb and Grey, 1991). 'Big privatization' involving state enterprises and land proceeded along four very different lines; namely public auctions (or direct sales) to foreign and domestic investors; 'reprivatization' (entailing the return of enterprises or land to their former owners); 'spontaneous privatization' (often at convenient terms) by the management of enterprises; and shares distribution.

Despite the priority it received, 'big privatization' has met with numerous legal, accounting, and incentive problems and has often failed to transfer any sizeable amount of land (except in Albania, Romania, and the Caucasus) or capital stock to the private sector. Privatization of state enterprises is expected to continue for several years and may have negative implications for long-term asset and income distribution, efficiency, and social justice in several member nations of the FSU (Chilosi, 1994). Indeed, the predatory manner in which privatization has been carried out in most of these countries has led to considerable corruption and harmful social stratification. It has fostered inefficient markets dominated by monopolies and, in some cases, by organized crime.

Indeed, the 'proto-capitalist model' emerging in several FSU countries is closer to the 'soft-state model' typical of developing economies than to that of an efficient market economy which enjoys strong citizens' rights and well-identified state roles. In these countries, private-sector growth has been accompanied by a widespread disregard for the protection of labour and unionization as well as by mass unemployment. Entrepreneurship is confused with rent-seeking, and consumers are often at the mercy of monopolist producers and traders 'whose idea of a market is that of spot pricing in single, non-recurring, predatory transactions under monopolistic conditions' (Nuti, 1994).

A greater role for 'private decisions' and market prices in the allocation of resources has also been pursued by dismantling price controls and eliminating consumer subsidies, including those on childrens' goods. The only exceptions were for staple foods, basic drugs, some rentals, transport, and energy. Even these subsidies, however, have been (or are shortly expected to be) eliminated, indicating a preference for a 'pure market solution'.

To avoid excessive welfare losses, part of the savings gained from the abolition of consumer subsidies was to be turned into theoretically equivalent universal income subsidies. However, only in the Czech and Slovak Federal Republics has this measure proved broadly adequate. Elsewhere, subsidy removal caused a major loss of purchasing power that was not compensated by social assistance transfers. In late 1994, this approach was followed even in Georgia and Armenia, i.e. nations where an estimated 80 per cent of the population live in poverty and where the subsidy—the only 'social safety net' available—enabled families to purchase about 40 kg. of rationed bread per month with one average salary (of about $US2).

13.2.3. Institutional reforms

With hindsight, it appears that the success of the overall reform effort will depend on the creation of new 'institutions' and the preservation of the existing 'regulatory framework' for law and order, public health, social protection, and other key public functions. However, progress in establishing new 'rules of the game' for property rights, anti-trust, foreign investment, taxation, banking, wage indexation, and the safety net has been limited and slower than that required by the rapid changes provoked by 'shock therapy'. Quite clearly, a balanced approach in this area was followed only in the former GDR where the 'institutional scaffolding' was extended from West Germany.

In most countries, particularly those of the FSU, erosion of the administrative and legal systems has caused considerable welfare losses. The incidence of food poisoning and work- or traffic-related accidents has, for instance, increased. One reason for this 'de-statization' is the time-consuming nature of institution-building. The central planning system was demolished, but could not be replaced immediately. It takes time for new institutions—including those of political democracy—to become established and function normally. This 'systemic vacuum' was thus filled with makeshift solutions and spontaneous developments, which have nothing in common with the institutions of a market economy.

13.2.4. Labour market, social sector, and social 'safety nets'

Policies on employment, wages, and consumer subsidies have undergone radical changes. Artificial full employment and central determination of wages have been abandoned and, with the exception of a few FSU countries, open unemployment has increased sharply. Even in these latter countries, however, the real rate of unemployment (including people employed at zero hours and wages as well as discouraged workers) has exceeded 10 per cent (UNECE, 1994). All countries introduced some form of unemployment compensation, although the trend is towards more restrictive eligibility criteria and lower benefits (UNICEF ICDC, 1995). Despite this, public expenditure on unemployment compensation and social assistance was the most dynamic component of public social expenditures over the 1989–94 period. Early retirement and extended child-care leave for women were also used to reduce the unemployment rolls. Active labour market policies, in contrast, remained negligible (ibid.).

High inflation rates led all countries to introduce indexation of wages and benefits. However, with few exceptions (Poland and Bulgaria), indexation has been partial, carried out *ex post* and on an *ad hoc* basis. Its frequency and extent have varied substantially over time, by sector, and by type of benefit, causing large losses of income and considerable intragenerational equity problems. Child allowances and minimum wages, for instance, have been penalized more than average wages and pensions (UNICEF ICDC, 1994).

So far, child and family benefits have been broadly maintained. Though several countries have proposed targeting child and family allowances on poor families, only a few countries (such as the Czech Republic and Slovakia) have instituted a dual system with a common, low benefit for all children and a more generous means-tested one for children in poor families. In several cases, such benefits have been extended to the children of the registered unemployed (see Table 5.5). Some countries (Hungary, for instance), have introduced a child-care leave (allowing mothers to stay home on partial pay until the child reaches the age of 3). In all countries, however, these measures have been accompanied by a dramatic erosion of the real value of benefits which, in turn, reduces the efficiency of these transfer programmes (see Chapter 5). Finally, social assistance, non-existent under communist rule, has been introduced, though the scope and efficiency of this measure vary widely due to funding, institutional, and informational problems.

Policies in the fields of health, education, child care, and other social amenities have undergone gradual but significant changes. Obstacles to private provision (particularly in education) were removed. Many services provided by the government and state enterprises (in the fields of child care and kindergartens, recreation, and vocational training) were discontinued or have been decentralized to local authorities, without, however, an equivalent decentralization of resources or tax-raising powers. Substantial user fees have been instituted for kindergarten and school meals, schoolbooks, drugs, and some health services. Yet, nowhere has the state challenged the principle (but not the practice) of free and compulsory primary and secondary education.

13.3. Child Welfare Changes during the Transition

The reforms provoked a massive deterioration in human welfare throughout the region. The 1989–94 period was marked by a severe mortality crisis, though most Central European countries—such as the Czech Republic and, to a lesser degree, Slovakia and Poland—were less affected than others. While children and adolescents were not so severely struck by this crisis, it appears that they suffered more than other age-groups in other dimensions.

13.3.1. A surge in overall poverty and child poverty

Poverty and extreme poverty increased sharply over the 1989–94 period (Table 13.1). Among the eleven countries for which acceptable estimates could be obtained, the steepest increases were recorded in Bulgaria, Romania, Moldova, Lithuania, and Azerbaijan. The deterioration in Latvia and Estonia appears to have been almost as large. In 1994, between 26 and 32 per cent of the population in these countries could be considered *extremely poor*, while an additional 25 to 35 per cent were affected by less acute, but none the less debilitating, *poverty*. Scattered evidence suggests that in the urban sector of Albania, Armenia, Georgia, as well as Russia, the Ukraine, and other FSU countries affected by war, the spread of extreme poverty has been even more pronounced (Mroz and Popkin, 1994; Van Rijckeghem, 1994; Gogodze and Gogighasvili, 1995). In contrast, the phenomenon was more limited in the Czech Republic, Slovakia, Hungary, and Slovenia: inflationary explosions were avoided, drops in real wages were more modest, the existing safety nets were broadly maintained, and the surge in income inequality was contained.

The recent escalation of poverty is confirmed by other indicators of income inadequacy. In Hungary, pawning rose by one-third between 1990 and 1992 (UNICEF ICDC, 1993). Meanwhile, between 1989 and 1992 the number of recipients of social assistance spiralled in all countries. In Bulgaria, recipients of government aid jumped thirty times between 1990 and 1992 in parallel with a 40 per cent decline in household incomes. In Latvia, the number rose thirty-five times between 1992 and 1994. While helpful in avoiding acute deprivations, these benefits (which ranged between 6 and 30 per cent of the average wage) were generally unable, on their own, to lift recipients out of poverty. Finally, in most countries there

Table 13.1: Incidence of Poverty and Extreme Poverty among Households, Children, Adults, and Elderly in Selected Countries, 1989–1994

Year	Poverty[a]					Extreme Poverty[b]				
	Households	Children	Adults	Elderly	Population	Households	Children	Adults	Elderly	Population
Czech Republic										
1989	4.6	4.2	4.4	5.7	4.2	0.3	0.3	0.2	0.4	0.2
1991	23.8	43.2	26.8	12.9	29.8	0.8	0.2	0.5	0.3	0.2
1992	18.2	38.3	22.6	9.6	25.3	1.6	1.1	1.8	0.4	1.3
Hungary[c]										
1989	11.8	20.9	9.6	15.6	13.7	1.2	2.6	1.0	1.7	1.5
1991	18.5	35.0	20.5	18.7	22.0	2.1	6.3	3.0	2.2	3.4
1993	22.4	43.2	27.7	13.9	28.0	3.1	9.4	5.1	1.0	5.1
Poland[c]										
1989	26.6	36.8	22.7	34.5	28.5	5.1	8.9	5.0	5.6	6.1
1990	39.9	61.0	39.4	40.8	45.5	6.4	16.8	8.0	4.0	9.7
1992	35.5	61.6	40.5	29.0	43.8	7.2	19.9	9.2	3.4	10.9
Slovakia[c]										
1989	5.9	8.7	4.4	6.4	6.0	0.1	0.1	0.1	0.2	0.1
1991	31.6	52.1	27.4	32.1	35.0	2.5	5.8	2.3	2.5	3.3
1994	37.0	54.9	47.1	27.6	45.7	7.0	17.4	9.2	1.6	10.2
Bulgaria										
1990	13.6	17.7	11.0	18.3	13.8	2.1	2.0	1.3	3.8	2.0
1992	55.4	61.7	50.2	62.1	55.5	21.7	25.7	19.0	24.9	21.8
1994	67.1	71.9	61.4	62.3	63.5	32.1	42.5	32.1	27.5	32.7

Romania[c]										
1990	17.7	28.8	17.6	25.6	21.6	2.8	4.3	2.7	6.3	3.5
1992	47.8	66.0	50.1	54.1	55.0	17.3	29.3	18.2	21.6	21.7
1994	66.9	85.5	71.0	65.4	74.3	31.7	50.1	34.4	32.1	38.3
Estonia										
1992	40.0	52.1	37.3	67.7	43.8	18.8	26.6	16.4	47.5	21.4
1994	52.9	61.1	47.8	84.3	52.5	26.3	34.2	23.0	57.9	27.0
Lithuania[c]										
1994	70.1	79.9	66.9	85.2	74.2	44.4	56.7	40.1	60.5	47.5
Latvia										
1994	54.9	79.4	59.1	55.3	65.0	27.1	50.7	31.4	14.9	35.5
Moldova										
1989	12.8	19.6	11.8	18.5	15.3	1.9	3.1	1.7	3.4	2.4
1991	12.3	17.6	11.2	16.5	13.9	1.9	2.3	1.8	2.9	2.1
1993	—	—	—	—	70.2[d]	—	—	—	—	40.6[d]
Azerbaijan										
1994	80.9	87.7	81.7	82.3	85.1	60.5	72.5	59.1	65.4	65.2

[a] Poverty line = 40% of the 1989 average wage, except for Czech Republic (35%) and Bulgaria, Romania, Moldova, and Azerbaijan (45%). [b] Poverty line = 60% of poverty line. [c] Whenever the average income per capita derived from the household budget surveys was lower than that obtained from the national accounts, the latter was retained (together with the variance derived from the household budget surveys) to compute poverty rates. With this approach, it is possible to correct in part the growing under-reporting of income in the household budget surveys. [d] Due to lacking data on the demographic structure of income classes, it is impossible to estimate extreme poverty rates that take into account different age structures of income classes. Generally, the procedure used in these estimates permits the weighing, even by using interpolated distributions, of the net personal income per capita with the demographic composition of each income class. To do so, the following equivalence scales have been used: additional adults: 0.8; child: 0.5; elderly person: 0.7.

Source: Elaboration on UNICEF ICDC (1995).

was a fast accumulation of arrears in the payment of rent (43 per cent at the end of 1992 in Poland) and utility charges (ibid.).

The adversities of the transition have been particularly hard on both the *'old poor'* (large and single-parent families, people with severe disabilities, minority groups, and the elderly subsisting on minimum pensions) and the *'new poor'*, i.e. youth in search of first employment, uncompensated unemployed, retrenched low-skilled workers, a growing number of 'working poor' and their dependants, and a soaring number of migrants and refugees. Contrary to the widespread perception (which sees the aged as the main victims of the transition), poverty has risen faster among children, the unemployed, and the 'working poor' than among pensioners (Table 13.1; see also Mroz and Popkin, 1994; UNICEF ICDC, 1994). Three factors underlie this development: the surge in unemployment and its duration combined with diminished unemployment benefits; the increased number of people hired at very low wages or to whom wages are paid only after long delays; and better indexation of pensions relative to wages, child allowances, unemployment benefits, and social assistance. For instance, in Hungary, the proportion of poor children in relation to adults and the elderly in 1992 was about 1.5 and 2.7 times higher respectively, mainly because of increased unemployment among middle-aged heads of households (Table 13.2).

In Russia, a survey carried out in July–September 1992 shows that poverty among children below 15 years of age stood at 46 per cent, while the figure for adults in the 31–60 age bracket was 35 per cent and for male pensioners, 22 per cent. In addition, 72 per cent of families with three or more children lived in poverty. Large families suffering additional risks (single parenthood, handicap, unemployment, and so on) presented a particularly severe case (Mroz and Popkin, 1994).

In several countries, including Russia and Romania, rising child poverty is strongly related to the massive erosion of child allowances and other child-related income transfers (see also Chapter 12). Even in the Czech Republic, where the spread of low-paying jobs and the growth in unemployment were less marked than elsewhere, child poverty increased faster than for other groups.

Pensions have generally been better protected from inflation than other social transfers (UNICEF ICDC, 1994). In addition, 'working pensioners' have a double source of income, have time to tend a plot of land, are often the recipients of intrafamily income transfers, and can enjoy the fruits of accumulated assets. Furthermore, pensioners generally have better access than younger families to cheap housing, assigned to them in earlier times. Russia and Ukraine are partial exceptions in this case as elderly people depending entirely on extremely low minimum pensions fell into extreme poverty. Even in these two countries, however, the extent of the problem is comparatively modest.

Table 13.2: Incidence of Poverty by Poverty Levels and Types of Households in Hungary, 1992

	Below 70%	Between 70–80%	Between 80–100%[a]	Total	Between 100–110%	Between 110–140%	Over 140%	Total
	of the subsistence minimum				of the subsistence minimum			
In active household	3.5	2.8	10.1	16.4	7.1	24.2	52.0	83.4
In family:								
without children	1.7	1.5	6.2	9.4	5.0	20.8	64.8	90.6
with 1 child	3.3	2.2	10.0	15.5	7.6	25.8	51.1	84.5
2 children	4.5	3.9	13.0	21.4	8.8	26.9	42.9	78.6
3 children	7.5	6.6	20.8	34.9	9.9	27.4	27.8	65.1
4 and more children	15.4	10.3	23.4	49.1	10.0	23.3	17.6	50.9
In family:								
without unemployed	1.7	1.9	9.1	12.7	6.7	24.4	56.2	87.3
with 1 unemployed	10.1	6.2	14.7	31.0	8.7	24.4	35.9	69.0
2 and more unemployed	20.7	10.3	17.9	48.9	10.0	19.0	22.1	51.1
In active household	1.9	1.6	8.3	11.8	6.0	23.7	58.5	88.2
In urban area	2.8	2.6	9.6	15.0	7.1	23.3	54.6	85.0
In rural areas	3.7	2.5	10.2	16.4	6.7	25.2	51.7	83.6
Altogether	3.2	2.6	9.8	15.6	6.9	24.1	53.4	84.4

[a]The subsistence minimum is the official national poverty line, based on a basket of goods and expenditures for basic necessities, as calculated by the Central Statistical Office of Hungary.

Source: Computations by Judit Lakatos of the Hungarian Central Statistical Office.

13.3.2. Trends in overall and child mortality

Between 1989 and 1994, the crude death rate (CDR) soared in most countries of the region (Table 13.3). The largest increases were recorded in Russia, Ukraine, and the rest of the FSU (including the 'successful' Baltic countries) as well as in Romania, Bulgaria, and Hungary. Smaller and temporary upswings were registered in Poland, while the rate steadily declined in Slovakia and the Czech Republic.

The increase in mortality was greater for men than for women. In addition, the hardest hit were not children, mothers, or the elderly, but rather the working-age population. The main causes of death were cardiovascular diseases, accidents, poisoning, suicide, and homicide (Cornia with Paniccià, 1995). This mortality crisis is best explained by 'psycho-social stress' (particularly for deaths due to heart diseases, ulcers, cirrhosis, alcohol psychosis, and suicide) and the weakening of health services, rather than by impoverishment-related causes like malnutrition and infectious diseases. 'Psycho-social stress' arises when individuals must react to new and unexpected situations (divorce and family breakdown, poverty, job insecurity and unemployment, migration, and difficult emotional

Table 13.3a: Crude Death-Rate in Selected Transitional Economies (per 1,000 population)

Country	1980	1985	1989	1992	1994
Czech Republic	12.2	11.9	12.3	11.7	11.4
Slovakia	—	—	10.2	10.1	9.6
Hungary	13.6	14.0	13.7	14.4	14.4
Poland	9.8	10.3	10.0	10.2	10.0
Slovenia	9.9	10.0	9.3	9.7	9.7
Albania	6.4	5.8	5.7	5.4[a]	6.2
Bulgaria	11.1	12.0	12.0	12.6	13.2
Romania	10.4	10.9	10.7	11.6	11.7
Estonia	12.3	12.7	11.8	13.0	14.8
Latvia	12.8	13.2	12.2	13.5	16.4
Lithuania	10.5	10.9	10.3	11.1	12.5
Belarus	9.9	10.6	10.1	11.3	12.6
Moldova	10.1	10.9	8.8	9.5	11.6
Russia	11.0	11.3	10.7	12.2	15.6
Ukraine	11.4	12.1	11.7	13.5	14.7
Armenia	5.6	6.1	5.9	7.0	6.6
Azerbaijan	7.0	6.8	6.3	7.1	7.4
Georgia	8.5	8.7	8.6	9.6	8.6

[a] 1991 figure.

Source: UNICEF ICDC (1995).

Table 13.3*b*: Infant Mortality Rate in Selected Transitional Countries
(per 1,000 live births)

Country	1980	1985	1989	1992	1994
Czech Republic	18.4	14.0	10.0	9.9	7.9
Slovakia	—	—	13.5	12.6	11.2
Hungary	23.2	20.4	15.7	14.1	11.5
Poland	21.3	18.5	15.9	14.3	15.1[a]
Slovenia	15.3	13.0	8.1	8.9	6.5
Albania	50.3	30.1	30.8	30.9	43.2
Bulgaria	20.2	15.4	14.4	15.9	16.3
Romania	29.3	25.6	26.9	23.3	23.9
Estonia	17.1	14.0	14.8	15.8[b]	14.5[b]
Latvia	15.4	13.0	11.1	17.4[c]	15.5[c]
Lithuania	14.4	14.2	10.7	16.5	13.9
Belarus	16.3	14.5	11.8	12.3	13.2[d]
Moldova	35.0	30.9	18.1	15.9	22.6
Russia	22.0	20.8	17.8	18.0	18.7[e]
Ukraine	16.6	15.9	13.1	14.1	14.3
Armenia	26.2	24.8	17.5	16.5	15.1[f]
Azerbaijan	30.4	29.4	24.1	24.0	26.9
Georgia	25.4	24.0	19.6	12.4	25.2

[a] New WHO-recommended measure of live births and infant deaths was introduced in Poland in 1994. 1993 data recalculated according to the new concept show 16.1 infant deaths per 1,000 live births instead of 15.4, demonstrating that the former measure of live births excluded about 4–5% of infant deaths. [b] Estonia shifted to the WHO concept of live births, replacing the 'Soviet' concept in January 1992. According to calculations for 1992 and 1993, the change resulted in rates 16.6% higher than those based on the former concept. [c] The WHO concept of live births and infant deaths was adopted in January 1991. [d] The WHO concept of live births and infant deaths is to introduced in Belarus from 1995. [e] Russia replaced the 'Soviet' concept of live births with the WHO methodology in 1993. The increase in the IMR figure for 1993 therefore partially reflects the effect of this change, accounting for an estimated half of the 1993 increase over 1992. [f] A change in the use of the 'Soviet' concept of live births is foreseen for 1995.

Source: UNICEF ICDC (1995).

states such as anger, depression, and hopelessness) for which they lack appropriate coping behaviour (Eyer and Sterling, 1977; Beale and Nethercott, 1985, 1989, Moser *et al.*, 1986, 1987; Smith, 1992). All of these 'stressors' have intensified in recent years, even in the former GDR, where despite higher real wages and generous unemployment subsidies, considerable psycho-social stress led to a surge in the mortality rate of working-age males between 1989 and 1992. Mortality rates for infants, children, and adolescents did not worsen significantly, though moderate IMR rises occurred in South-eastern Europe and the FSU (Table 13.3). While these IMR increases may be modest and temporary, they are still disturbing, given the startling decline in fertility (see below). Elsewhere, IMR improved slowly, showing that progress can be realized even in difficult circumstances (UNICEF ICDC, 1995). In contrast, improvements in mortality for the 1–4 age-group were recorded in most countries, with the exception of a modest increment in child deaths due to cancer in Ukraine and Russia. Finally, the death-rate for the 15–19 age-group shows an imperceptible, but none the less worrisome, increase for this period, mainly due to accidents and suicide (ibid.).

With some exceptions, infant and child mortality due to infectious, parasitic, and respiratory diseases, and to accidents and poisoning either fell or stagnated at low levels (UNICEF ICDC, 1994). Despite mounting financial problems, this progress was sustained by high coverage of child immunization and basic health services.

In those countries where IMR did rise (Table 13.3), it would appear that new problems (infectious, parasitic, and digestive diseases as well as accidents) have surfaced and the old ones (congenital and perinatal factors) linger. In the last four years, congenital- and perinatal-related deaths have abruptly accelerated, due in large part to shortages of equipment, specialized staff, and adequate drug supplies.

13.3.3. Changes in the nutritional status of children

Over the 1989–94 period, low birth weight (LBW) prevalence increased sharply in Bulgaria and Romania and moderately in another five of the fourteen transitional economies for which information is regularly compiled (UNICEF ICDC, 1995). Three factors explain this increase. First, there was a rise in the share of births to mothers below 20 years of age. Secondly, deteriorating nutrition, greater stress, smoking and drinking, over-exertion, and insecurity experienced by pregnant mothers contributed. A 1993 survey in Moscow and Ekaterinburg revealed deficiencies of up to 60 per cent of the US recommended daily allowance for folic acid, iron, calcium, vitamin B1, B2, and B6, i.e. substances whose deficit can lead to growth retardation and negative pregnancy outcomes. Finally, in some countries (such as those bordering the Chernobyl area), prematurity rates increased.

The limited evidence available does not suggest any widespread or acute increase in wasting and stunting of young children (UNICEF, 1992; UNICEF Romania, 1993; Mroz and Popkin, 1994; UNICEF ICDC, 1994), though the sudden impoverishment of large sectors of the population has aggravated traditional nutritional problems (particularly, micronutrient deficiency).

13.3.4. *Widespread decline in preschool and school enrolment*

Despite shrinking child cohorts, crèche enrolment rates dropped through-out the region, including in the former GDR, in line with rises in attend-ance costs and growing female unemployment (UNICEF ICDC, 1994; Nauck and Joos, 1995). Parental leave provision did not compensate for this drop, as its coverage rate also declined (with the exception of Hungary). In addition, the proportion of children attending kinder-gartens fell, again with the exception of Hungary, Slovenia, and Azerbaijan (Table 13.4). In Lithuania, the rate fell to less than half between 1991 and 1993.

This enrolment decline may have damaging implications for child socialization, peer interaction, and preparedness for school. The drop is partly explained by the shrinking supply of kindergarten places (due to

Table 13.4:   Kindergarten Enrolment Rates and Fees

	1989	1991	1993	1994
Enrolment rates (%)				
Czech Republic	99.3	82.8	88.3	88.6[a]
Slovakia	91.5	75.7	78.0	74.9
Hungary	85.7	85.9	86.6	86.1
Poland	48.7	43.9	42.7	44.3
Bulgaria	72.8	56.1	62.6	64.6
Romania	82.9	68.7	57.8	55.2
Moldova	72.0	68.3	57.0	52.0
Russia	69.3	63.9	57.4	55.5[a]
Ukraine[b]	85.6[a]	55.0	47.0	44.0
Armenia	61.2	51.4	46.0	—
Azerbaijan	19.0	17.0	16.0	16.0
Georgia	39.6	40.2	27.7	23.3
Enrolment fees[c]				
Czech Republic	2.0	—	6.0–10.0	8.0–10.0
Slovakia	—[d]	—[e]	—[e]	—[e]
Hungary	—[d,f]	—[e]	—[e]	—[e]
Poland	25.0	36.7	18.6	—
Bulgaria	13.0[f]	9.0	15.0	9.0[f]
Romania	10.0	14.5	—	—
Russia	3.0	1.4	—	—
Ukraine	6.0	6.0	—	—

[a]Estimated. [b]Total enrolment as a percentage of all 3–5 year olds. The share of 6-year-olds in kindergartens or primary school was 55.1% in 1990, 50.2% in 1991 and 46.3% in 1992. [c]Fees are estimated and calculated as a percentage of the average wage. [d]Parents pay for meals only. [e]Parents pay for meals in public kindergartens; they may pay extra fees in private facilities. [f]Fees also depend on family income.

Source: TRANSMONEE Database.

the closure of facilities managed by government and enterprises). How-ever, demand too has fallen as the increase in unregulated user fees has inflated the private cost for these services. User fees for school meals, uniforms, heating, and bus services (let alone for tuition) now represent a sizeable share of the average wage, removing kindergartens from the reach of many families (Table 13.4).

A widespread decline in secondary enrolment rates also occurred over this period (Table 13.5). Even where rates did not dwindle, budgetary restrictions resulted in fewer facilities, lower subsidies, higher fees for non-basic activities (books, meals, and teaching materials) and a likely deterioration in the quality of education. Declines in student stipends and in the number of places available in student hostels, as well as rising costs of meals in school canteens are typical examples of changes which are jeopardizing the educational prospects of many students, particularly those living far from schools.

Table 13.5: Secondary Enrolment Rates in Selected Transitional Countries (percentage of relevant population)

Country	1980	1985	1989	1991	1994
Czech Republic[a]	89.0	84.0	89.0	79.3[b]	88.5
Slovakia[c]	—	—	88.7	88.0	90.2
Hungary[d]	69.0	72.0	74.9	74.6	81.4
Poland	77.0	78.0	78.9	78.1	82.0
Slovenia[e]	—	—	79.3	83.1	84.7
Bulgaria[f]	84.0	102.0	78.2	74.2	65.0
Romania	71.0	84.0	91.1	75.4	75.5
Estonia[g]	—	—	88.8[h]	87.8	84.6
Latvia	—	—	84.7	80.7	81.2
Lithuania[i]	—	—	93.4[h]	84.5[j]	83.4
Belarus	—	—	88.7	85.3	84.2
Moldova[k]	—	—	83.0	76.0	74.0
Russia[l]	93.0	98.0	83.6	72.4	71.7
Ukraine[m]	—	—	63.7	60.6	46.9
Azerbaijan	—	—	76.0	77.0	76.0
Georgia[n]	—	—	94.2	94.4	75.9[o]

[a]Grades 5–9. Net enrolment rate of 11–18-year-olds. [b]Estimated. [c]According to International Standard Classification of Education (ISCED). [d]Grades 9–12. [e]Ages 7–14. [f]Net enrolment rate of 15–18-year-olds. [g]Ages 12–17. Students of Russian nationality are accorded an additional year to complete grade 12. [h]1990 figure. [i]Gross enrolment rate. [j]1992 figure. [k]Ages 11–18. [l]Pupils in secondary education among the 10–16-year-old cohort. [m]Ages 16–17 (secondary education refers to grades 11–12), excluding professional schools offering secondary education (433,000 pupils in 1993). [n]Estimated for the 11–16-year-old population. [o]1993 figure.

Source: UNICEF ICDC (1995).

13.3.5. *An increasingly difficult socialization of youth*

The transition has weakened the social fabric and the institutions entrusted with the socialization of children and youth, i.e. the family, school, work, and recreation organizations. Loss of relevance and greater private costs contributed to falling school enrolments and increased drop-out rates. Even youth who complete their education, have difficulties in finding a job in a protected environment (UNICEF ICDC, 1993). Recreational and art centres, libraries, and sport associations have been reduced, thereby diminishing their socialization and social control functions. Finally, the supervisory role of the family has been further diminished by the increase in activity rates in the informal sector rendered necessary by the sharp drop in formal sector incomes.

Because of the growing cultural vacuum and pressures to seek income from any activity—whether legal, a-legal or illegal—the number of young people engaged in the informal economy or simply 'on the streets' has multiplied. This raises the chances of abuse, exploitative labour, and involvement in criminal activities. As a result, the number of reported crimes committed by youngsters and the number of youth sentenced

Table 13.6: Youth Crime Rate (number of youths aged 14–17 sentenced, per 100,000 population)

Country	1989	1991	1993	1994
Czech Republic	50.6	33.6	50.9	58.4
Slovakia	41.0	46.0	51.0	58.5
Hungary	60.1	59.9	64.2	73.5
Poland[a]	73.4	81.6	69.5	62.8
Slovenia	59.2	53.8	55.0	51.6
Bulgaria	23.9	14.7	7.7[b]	8.0[b]
Romania	12.0	16.0	31.0	40.0
Estonia[c]	38.0	50.0	63.0	78.0
Latvia	42.8	36.6	47.2	44.9
Lithuania	24.0	32.8	57.1	62.5
Belarus	32.0	43.0	57.0	59.0
Moldova	31.2	38.8	39.7	45.6
Russia	62.4	85.0	104.9	111.4
Ukraine	20.2	22.1	28.1	32.6
Armenia	3.3	5.6	10.4	10.1
Azerbaijan	5.0	4.0	9.0	9.0
Georgia	6.4	9.0	6.1[d]	—

[a] Ages 13–16. [b] Does not include administrative sanctions. [c] Ages 15–17. [d] 1992 figure.

Source: UNICEF ICDC (1995).

(Table 13.6) have risen steadily throughout the region, particularly in urban areas.

13.4. Structural Changes Affecting the Future of Child Welfare

Despite huge institutional and historical peculiarities, transition theory and policy broadly echo mainstream thinking on macroeconomic stabilization and structural adjustment. They are thus little suited to addressing the current and future policy needs of the region. Not a great deal has been written on the unique features of the economies in the region or on their long-term growth path. Yet, some distinctive trends, which are likely to affect child welfare and call for appropriate policy responses, have already been at work for some years.

13.4.1. *Changing nature of poverty and prospects for poverty*

Not only the extent, but also the nature of poverty has changed over the last few years. As in the Western countries (see Chapter 14), poverty is increasingly affecting children, the unemployed, and the working poor. However, poverty has not, as yet, given rise to an 'economic underclass' (characterized by multiple and persistent deprivations which are difficult to tackle simultaneously). For instance, the 1992–4 Hungarian data on poverty duration (TARKI, 1995) point to high exit rates from poverty: less than half of the people living in poverty in 1992 were still poor in 1994. Similarly, in Russia, there were significant movements of households between the very poor, the poor, and the non-poor over 1992–3 (Mroz and Popkin, 1994).

Three factors account for the surge in poverty. In most countries, the largest increases occurred in the initial phase of the reforms, immediately after the launch of 'big bang' price and trade liberalization, currency devaluation, and budgetary cuts, which triggered sharp recessions and large falls in average incomes per capita (Table 13.7). During this initial phase, income inequality did not increase too rapidly, nor did the anticipated erosion of the welfare state inherited from the socialist era occur. Instead, the relative share of social transfers in total household incomes often increased. During this period (1989–91/2), most of the increase in poverty was therefore explained by the fall in income per capita.

Earnings disparity widened more visibly in the second phase of the transition, particularly in Russia, Poland, Bulgaria, Lithuania, and other FSU members. This was due to a rapid rise in earnings inequality, a surge in the share of non-labour income, and the erosion of social transfers and child allowances. In other countries, particularly in Central Europe, income disparity also increased slowly during this second phase, while the

Table 13.7: Percentage Contributions to Increases in Poverty[a]

Country	Period	Percentage increase in poverty due to:	
		Fall in GDP	Greater inequality
Bulgaria	1989–94	0.59	0.41
Czech Republic	1989–92	0.73	0.27
Hungary	1989–93	0.88	0.12
Poland	1989–92	0.82	0.18
Romania	1989–94	0.64	0.36
Slovakia	1989–94	0.70	0.30

[a]Percentage changes are calculated net of demographic influences, including changes in household size, population ageing, and so on.

Source: Computations on TRANSMONEE Database.

'social transfer–GDP ratio' either increased or remained constant at high levels.

In most of the region, poverty is 'shallow', i.e. the poverty gap is equal to only 20–5 per cent of the poverty line as opposed to values of 35–40 per cent most commonly found in middle-income developing countries (Milanovic, 1995; UNICEF ICDC, 1995). Furthermore, in contrast to the situation prevailing in developing countries, the rise in 'income poverty' was not accompanied by a parallel increase in 'asset poverty' (which may have even declined as a result of the privatization at low cost of the housing stock). Also, given the high level of education prior to the transition and the continued access to subsidized social services, 'human capital poverty' has most probably not increased.

Thus, prospects for poverty reduction appear relatively positive from a growth and human capital perspective, but less so from an income inequality and social transfer perspective, at least in the countries of Southeastern Europe and the FSU. In view of the shallowness of poverty and the still considerable human capital of most of the unemployed, a continuation or acceleration of the current recovery could fairly rapidly reabsorb much existing poverty and 'economic stress'. This is particularly the case in Central Europe, where income inequality has risen slowly and where social safety nets will undergo some modification but will be broadly maintained.

In the other countries, particularly the Slavic and Caucasus countries of the FSU, rising income inequality and declining social transfers render the prospects for poverty alleviation less promising, even in the presence of a recovery of the economy. In Poland, for instance, a 4 per cent annual growth in GDP between 1992 and 1995 combined with rising social transfers did not lead to a decline in poverty because of increases in overall income and inadequate targeting of social transfers.

13.4.2. *Painful but incomplete labour market adjustments*

Registered unemployment has risen throughout Central Europe (peaking at 16 per cent in Poland in 1993), with the single exception of the Czech Republic. In the former GDR, the registered unemployment rate in 1993 stood at 16 per cent, though this doubled if people on a variety of active labour market programmes were included. Despite output losses greater than those in Central Europe, registered unemployment climbed slowly in most of the FSU (touching on 3–4 per cent, or 7–8 per cent if the ILO concept is adopted). However, high transaction costs of enrolment at labour exchanges, limited probability of job placement, and insufficient benefits explain the low level of registered unemployment in these countries. Furthermore, incentives for both employers and workers compound this tendency. Given the taxation on average salaries, companies have a strong incentive to keep workers on the books at zero-hours and zero-salary (Shapiro and Roxburgh, 1994). In turn, even if they are not being paid, workers receive some in-kind benefits (such as access to subsidized kindergartens or medical facilities) from the enterprise and hope to be first in line in case of rehiring.

In spite of a moderate but spreading recovery over the last three years, registered unemployment declined moderately over 1993–5 only in Hungary, Bulgaria, the Czech Republic, and Poland. This was mainly due to continuous 'labour shedding' in the industrial sector. 'Labour shedding' and labour reallocation towards light industry, agriculture, and private services are expected to continue for many years. Indeed, there is still a serious problem of overmanning in inefficient or ecologically unsafe industries and in socially useful but overstaffed branches of the public administration. For instance, the people per doctor ratio in Georgia and Russia is 170 and 210, respectively, against an average of 402 in the main Western market economies and about 1,200 in South American countries with similar GDP per capita (EBRD, 1994).

Three segments of the labour force were most severely affected by the rise in unemployment—women, young workers, and low-skilled workers (Table 13.8). Job losses were suffered most by mothers, especially those with many children, including in the former GDR (Nauch and Joos, 1995). Economic recession and a difficult transition from school to work caused proportionately greater difficulties for the young. Their share in total unemployment varies between 28 and 43 per cent, while their share in the working-age population is around 20–25 per cent.

After an initial boost, low inflows and even lower outflows have led to the formation of a stagnant pool of structurally unemployed, consisting mainly of middle-aged, low-skilled workers (Boeri, 1993). As a result, since 1992–3, long-term unemployment in Slovakia, Poland, and Hungary has surpassed 40 per cent of total unemployment (UNICEF ICDC, 1995).

Table 13.8:   Unemployment of 15–24-Year-Olds and Women, 1990–1994

Country	1990	1992	1994
Share of unemployed 15–24-year-olds in total unemployment			
Bulgaria (RU)	46.8	44.8	43.0[b]
Bulgaria (LS)	—	46.1	41.2
Czech Republic (RU)	—	32.3	28.3
Czech Republic (LS)	—	—	34.5
Hungary (LS)	—	27.0	27.7
Poland (RU)	—	34.6	34.6
Poland (LS)	—	28.2	30.3
Romania (LS)	—	—	45.1
Russia	—	18.6	18.6[b]
Slovakia (RU)	—	27.3	38.6
Slovakia (LS)	—	—	33.9
Slovenia (LS)	—	35.3[b]	30.6
Share of unemployed women in total unemployment			
Bulgaria (RU)	65.2	52.4	54.3
Bulgaria (LS)	—	49.9	46.4
Czech Republic (RU)	51.2	57.6	58.0
Czech Republic (LS)	—	—	54.1
Hungary (LS)	—	40.5	39.1
Poland (RU)	50.9	53.4	52.7
Poland (LS)	—	51.0	52.2
Romania (RU)	—	59.7[b]	56.9
Romania (LS)	—	—	49.7
Russia (LS)	—	72.2	35.4
Slovakia (RU)	49.7	50.6	48.2
Slovakia (LS)	—	—	46.1
Slovenia (RU)	47.9	43.9	44.9
Slovenia (LS)	—	—	42.0

[a]RU: From unemployment register. [b]1993 figure. [c]LS: Unemployment from Labour Force Surveys.

Source: TRANSMONEE Database.

This is problematic because the probability of finding a job decreases more than proportionately with increasing length of unemployment. At the same time, loss of skills increases more than proportionately. Contrary to the finding on the limited persistence of poverty, the slow emergence of a class of structurally unemployed could well lead to the formation of an 'underclass' early next century.

Even the steep rise in unemployment rates mentioned above does not provide an accurate picture of the labour market adjustments of the last six years, thus impeding the formulation of appropriate policy responses. A more comprehensive picture is offered by the declining employment rate. This measure captures not only the surge in registered unemployment but also the rising numbers of discouraged workers, early retirements, and child-care leaves. It also shows a physiological decline in 'forced employment', particularly among women (in 1985, participation rates among 40–4-year-old women ranged between 85 and 97 per cent as against 56 per cent in Western Europe). While the increase in unemployment in Poland accounts for 95 per cent of the drop in employment, it represents only a quarter in the Czech Republic and the FSU. Indeed, in Bulgaria, where early retirement was massively used as a labour market policy, it accounts for only 51 per cent. In Hungary, a considerable decline in the employment rate is explained by the increased number of women benefiting from child-care leave (which until recently provided about 70 per cent of the average salary).

Though apparently exiting the labour force, some early retirees, discouraged workers, and child-care leave beneficiaries are likely to have joined the informal sector, if on a part-time basis, not least to compensate for the fall in formal sector incomes (Rose, 1994). However, despite the development of small businesses, close to nothing is known about the size, composition, earnings, and income distribution of this sector. While the spread of the informal economy might be crucial for sustaining household livelihoods over the short term, it tends to depress tax collection and to hinder the design of support measures aiming to stimulate employment absorption and productivity in this sector. In a sense, an excessive informalization of the economy would pose considerable long-term growth, equity, and welfare problems.

Between 1989 and 1994, real wages fell by between 20 per cent (in the Czech Republic) and 40 per cent (in several countries of the FSU and Romania). Real wages dropped most where unemployment rose the least, as wage cuts provided a substitute for massive lay-offs. Three factors are reflected in this fall in real wages: the decline in output; macroeconomic influences (in the early phase of the transition, the average wage was used as an anchor of the stabilization programmes); and institutional factors (namely the progressive liberalization of wage negotiations and an unwillingness to sustain the minimum wage and civil servants' wages). Often, minimum wages and social sector wages have fallen below the subsistence minimum and are a main cause of the increased number of working poor.

Wage dispersion has risen sharply from 1991–2 (Table 13.9) as a result of the above-mentioned institutional factors. Liberalized wage negotiations have led to a closer connection between skill level and remuneration. It has also resulted in greater inter-industry variability. The latter, however, reflects not so much productivity differentials, but rather 'monopoly or political rents' favouring the military, mining, telecommunication, and financial sectors, as observed in Russia and Romania.

Table 13.9: Trends in Gini Coefficients of Earnings Distribution (×100)
during the Transition

Country	1989	1991	1993	1994	Ratio	Changes in minimum wage/av. wage ratio 1994/89 (1989 = 100)
Czech Republic	20	21	22	24	120	63.1[a]
Hungary	29[b]	—	30	—	103	108.7[c]
Slovenia	22	26	26	28	127	74.2[a]
Bulgaria	21[b]	24	28	—	133	71.8
Romania	17	21	23	—	135	56.9[c]
Poland	21	25	27	30	143	348.3
Armenia	25	—	34	—	135	28.6
Latvia	25	25	32[d]	—	128	76.2[a]
Lithuania	26	—	—	35	135	72.3
Belarus	24	—	35	—	146	30.0
Moldova	26	—	40[d]	38	146	42.9
Ukraine	24	—	35	44	183	—
Russia	27	33	46	43	160	31.2

[a] 1991 = 100. [b] 1990 figure. [c] Refers to changes over 1989–93. [d] 1992 figure.
Source: TRANSMONEE Database.

13.4.3. Recent demographic changes are likely to affect child welfare prospects

The recent radical changes in family formation, reproductive behaviour, and 'paternal mortality' are likely to have negative implications for the future of child welfare.

While the crude marriage rate was slowly drifting downwards prior to the transition, it fell by between 20 and 40 per cent between 1989 and 1994, mainly because of rising unemployment, skyrocketing housing costs, and overall uncertainty about the future (Cornia with Paniccià, 1995). In the former GDR, the decline was even more astounding, from 7.9 to 3.1 per 1,000 between 1989 and 1993 (Nauck and Joos, 1995). If sustained, this fall will reduce the reproductive potential of the region and encourage a further increase in out-of-wedlock births.

The 1989–94 period also witnessed large drops in crude birth-rates, which were accompanied by an increase in the percentage of first births in the total. The most shocking decline was observed in the prosperous former GDR, where the total fertility rate fell between 1989 and 1993 from 1.57 to 0.80, making it the lowest fertility rate worldwide and lower than that recorded during the Great Depression or during the World Wars (Nauck and Joos, 1995). Throughout the region, the slowest decline in crude birth-rates has been observed among teenagers (Table 13.10; see

Table 13.10:   Percentage Changes in Age-specific Birth-Rates, 1989–1994

Country	Age-groups						
	15–19	20–4	25–9	30–4	35–9	40–9	CBR
Belarus[a]	8.5	−18.9	−26.6	−31.3	−33.0	—	−28.7
Estonia	−10.6	−35.1	−35.6	−43.6	−42.4	−43.1	−35.4
Hungary[a]	−14.0	−16.3	−2.7	2.5	−1.9	10.0	−5.8
Lithuania[a]	1.0	−20.5	−18.9	−23.2	−13.0	−16.7	−17.8
Poland	−13.0	−17.9	−8.8	−3.4	0.0	0.0	−13.4
Romania	−21.8	−26.3	−37.2	−51.9	−57.0	−55.0	−31.3
Russia	−8.8	−26.6	−37.0	−45.8	−48.2	−48.0	−35.6

[a] 1990–3.

Source: UNICEF ICDC (1995).

also UNICEF ICDC, 1995). In Belarus and Lithuania, fertility among 15–19-year-olds actually increased.

Out-of-wedlock births (often to under-age mothers) have also risen. While this index was already slowly moving upwards in the 1980s, the last four years have shown an acceleration (Table 13.11). As in the case of births to under-age mothers, this trend does not augur well, as children of monoparental families face much higher relative risks of poverty, mortality, school drop-out, and difficult socialization.

Contributing to the drop in birth-rates were the decline in nuptiality, greater out-migration of young adults, and higher 'paternal mortality'. However, the main factor was a sharp dip in marital fertility for all age-groups. In Russia, Lithuania, and Romania, while the natality decline involved women of all reproductive ages, it appears to have been even more pronounced among women in the 30–49 age-groups than for younger women. As a 'fertility catch-up' is not possible in this group, the drop would thus appear to be permanent.

These changes in reproductive behaviour do not reflect a 'natural catching-up' with the values of Western women, who tend to attach greater importance to educational achievement, work and career, individuality, and later pregnancies (Avraamova, 1994). Rather, they are more closely associated with decline in income, inadequate housing, low child allowances, and negative expectations about the future (Haub, 1994). If these variables do not stabilize or improve, it is unlikely that the recent demographic downfall will be reversed.

Finally, with the exception of the Czech Republic and Slovakia, the transition has caused a dramatic increase in 'paternal mortality', i.e. in the death rates of the 30–49 male population. This rise, together with the widening life expectancy differential between sexes, has exacerbated the

Table 13.11: Percentage of Births to Unmarried Mothers, 1980–1994
(percentage of total births)

Country	1980	1985	1989	1991	1994
Czech Republic	5.7[a]	7.0[a]	7.7[a]	9.8	—[b]
Hungary	7.1	9.2	12.4	14.1	19.3
Poland	4.7	5.0	5.8	6.6	9.0
Slovenia	13.1	19.1	23.3	26.5	28.0[c]
Bulgaria	10.9	11.7	11.4	15.5	24.5
Romania	2.8	3.7	4.3	4.2	—
Estonia	18.3	20.7	25.3	31.1	41.0
Latvia	12.5	14.4	15.9	18.4	26.4
Lithuania[d]	6.3	6.5	6.7	7.0	10.8
Belarus[d]	6.4[e]	7.1	7.9	9.4	12.1
Moldova[d]	7.4[e]	8.8	10.4	11.8	12.3
Russia[d]	10.8	12.0	13.5	16.0	19.0
Ukraine[d]	8.8	8.3	10.8	11.9	12.8
Armenia[d]	4.3[e]	6.5	7.9	10.9	14.0[c]
Azerbaijan[d]	3.0[e]	2.6	2.5	3.7	5.2
Georgia[d]	4.7	10.5	17.7	18.7	—[f]

[a] Data refer to Czechoslovakia. [b] 10.6 (1992). [c] 1993 figure. [d] Percentage of live births.
[e] Data refer to 1979–80. [f] 21.8 (1992).
Source: UNICEF ICDC (1995).

imbalance in the sex ratio and dependency ratio, raised the number of incomplete families, increased orphanhood and widowhood, and caused considerable economic losses.

This 'population crisis' will have adverse short- and medium-term implications for child welfare as well as long-term economic and demographic trends. Among the most immediate effects are:

1. *Fewer children per family and more one-child families.* The contraction in fertility has increased the number of childless and one-child families. Because of the declining coverage of preschool education, a growing proportion of children, particularly those in younger families, risk *ceteris paribus* a 'peer socialization gap'. From this perspective, policies emphasizing child-care leave appear to be of dubious effect and may need to be reconsidered.

2. *More children in 'at risk' and monoparental families.* The increase in the proportion of births to under-age mothers and unmarried mothers, the increase in divorce rates (in Russia, Ukraine, and Belarus), and the escalation in 'paternal mortality' are pushing upwards the number of children living with only one parent. These children inevitably face a greater risk of poverty, institutionalization, disrupted educational achievement, and difficult emotional development.

3. *Undesirable long-term effects.* A major adverse effect is the natural decline in population size recorded in half of the countries of the region. In Russia, the dynamics of births and deaths is expected to reduce the 'natural population size' by 6–7 million people by the year 2000 in relation to 1991, causing a decline that will only partly be compensated by immigration. An absolute decline of the population, particularly when driven by a contraction of births, leads to a fast ageing of the population and to a deterioration of the dependency ratio. In addition, it can provide a pretext for shifting public resources away from children towards the elderly who have greater control of the political process.

Finally, higher paternal mortality and migration altered the sex ratio of cohorts of reproductive age, making the formation of new families more difficult, even when the direct negative effects of economic insecurity on marriage are excluded. In turn, these factors may *weaken the fertility potential* of a country in the short term, while the subsequent drop in birth-rates will have a similar effect in the long run.

13.5. Emerging Policy Dilemmas and Possible Solutions

This final section outlines the main elements of a realistic model of public policy which would help sustain child welfare in the countries of the region over the short and medium terms.

13.5.1. *Halt the trend towards the demise of the state*

One of the most detrimental features of the transition has been the emergence of a marked institutional vacuum caused by the dismantling of the institutions and social norms of the socialist regime without the development of satisfactory substitutes. This process inevitably resulted from the earlier interpenetration of the state and the Communist Party. In Soviet-type economies there was a nation-wide capillary dual structure of state and party organs, with the party controlling policy decisions and with key state appointments reserved for the party *nomenklatura*. The collapse of communist parties thus weakened the state and its central powers, making the pursuit of any policy other than 'pure *laissez-faire*' almost impossible.

Several mitigating factors, however, have contained this 'demise of the state': namely (i) a continued, if involuntary, large-scale state presence in the economy; (ii) the much-needed assistance or association with international institutions, which have made such involvement conditional on the adoption of conventional policies assigning an important 'provider' and 'regulator' role to the state; and (iii) the gradual filling of the systemic vacuum and a slow consolidation of non-communist institutions in Central Europe.

These positive forces need to be helped both domestically and internationally. The main long-term issue is whether, and with what timescale, a credible liberal state structure will emerge. This will require that fundamental state prerogatives be reasserted, including enforcement of law and order, tax collection, universal provision of key public goods and merit goods, promotion of extensive private ownership, and civil service reform to ensure efficient governance. In the countries of the Caucasus, for instance, civil servants' wages have fallen to $US1–2 a month, leading *de facto* to the privatization of state functions, including administration, law and order, and the military.

13.5.2. *A favourable economic policy*

As noted, the largest increases in poverty were concurrent with the massive 'price overshooting' caused by 'shock therapy'. Contrary to the image evoked by this metaphor of a short and sharp shock leading to a rapid, if painful, solution, this approach did not bring quick fixes. It overlooked the slow evolution of economic institutions, property rights, and individual behaviour, caused credibility problems, and aggravated social problems inherited from the past. Similarly, failure to maintain macroeconomic balance and to introduce structural reforms were responsible for significant social costs in the late or hesitant reformers. While lax monetary and fiscal policy and postponement of structural reforms kept unemployment at bay for a while, it inflicted huge welfare costs on the population through crippling hyperinflation.

Thus, a key ingredient in a policy package promoting the welfare of children would be the achievement of low inflation and sustainable budget deficits, while concurrently avoiding the large deflationary shocks typical of orthodox macroeconomic policy. An active tax policy is needed to ensure that government expenditures are financed by taxes and other non-inflationary methods, and not by uncontrolled money or credit emissions, as in several FSU countries. Other important components of this package include the creation of an adequate regulatory framework, widespread and equitable privatization of state assets, and broad-based, labour-intensive economic growth (see UNICEF ICDC, 1995 for details).

13.5.3. *An employment-based approach to poverty alleviation should be the main thrust of social policy*

Most of the debate on poverty alleviation in transitional economies has focused on the volume, duration, and targeting of unemployment benefits and other transfers. Past and expected labour market changes indicate, however, that a large part of the problems affecting families have to do with exit from, or non-entry into, the labour force as well as low pay and increasingly low productivity among the self-employed in a growing informal sector.

In these circumstances, a realistic poverty alleviation strategy must pay adequate attention to (i) the strong promotion of self-employment and labour productivity for an increasing number of partially employed, discouraged, and informal sector workers; (ii) active labour market policies; and (iii) better wage regulation. Measures fall into three areas.

First, it is necessary to improve the access of the poor to financial and physical assets, as has been successfully carried out in the land redistribution programmes in Albania, Romania, and Georgia. This entails further land distribution, specific credit programmes for people operating in the informal sector, and an equitable distribution of industrial assets. The employment absorption effect of these measures can be significant.

Second, in situations of radical restructuring and labour shedding, active labour market policies, rather than passive ones, are needed. Experience from middle-income developing countries shows that, at least temporarily, the government can become an 'employer of last resort'. In Chile, for instance, 13 per cent of the labour force was employed in public work schemes during the 1983 recession (Raczinsky, 1988). In addition, governments can promote employment through retraining courses and wage subsidies, i.e. measures successfully used in Western European economies.

Finally, the minimum wage should be raised to at least 25–30 per cent of the average wage. This would keep recipients of minimum incomes out of poverty and would avoid overly large increases in wage differentials that are not justified by higher productivity.

13.5.4. *Restore the overall volume of family transfers*

As noted in Section 13.2, during the first phase of the transition (1989–91), family allowance policy was characterized by an extension of coverage and an erosion of benefits. During the second phase (1991–4), most governments cut the real value of child allowances (UNICEF ICDC, 1995). The net effect of these trends has been a generalized drop in public expenditure on family allowances in relation to GDP and rising child poverty. In most of the FSU, the benefit erosion has been so marked that many transfers retain only a symbolic value. Yet, family allowances constitute a potentially powerful tool for protecting the welfare of children and families during the transition. Thus, public outlay on family allowances should not be allowed to fall below 2–2.5 per cent of GDP (depending on the share of child population in the total and the extent of child poverty). This would entail increases in child allowance expenditures ranging between 1 and 2 percentage points of GDP. The financing of this additional expenditure could be ensured by the reallocation of less useful public outlay from other budgetary lines (in Central Europe) or by improved tax collection (in the former Soviet Union).

Fiscal sustainability problems necessitate a review of transfers. Some hard choices in this area would appear to be unavoidable. Before modifying the existing system, however, it is necessary to consider the efficiency and biases of the tax and transfer system and, in particular, of its specific benefits. Data in Table 13.12 indicate that in Central Europe the transfer system has a strong poverty alleviation impact (though the same cannot be said for many FSU countries). This impact, however, is smallest for children. The problem here is not a regressive incidence of child allowances and unemployment benefits (Fajth, 1994), but rather their small volume relative to transfers targeting other groups. The reallocation of part of social expenditure to children is therefore needed.

In Central Europe some containment of social transfer expenditure might be unavoidable, given the sizeable level of tax pressure. Important savings on family allowances, child-care leave, and other benefits will be attained because of the large cohort declines (up to 35 per cent) of the last five years. This should, in principle, enable the universal character of such transfers to be maintained. However, an unfavourable political economy may shift entitlement from a citizen's-right or work-related base to a

Table 13.12: Incidence of Poverty[a] on Pre-tax, Pre-transfer Income Distribution[b] and Poverty Alleviation Rates in Selected Countries, 1991–1993

	Pre-tax, pre-transfer extreme poverty incidence		Extreme poverty alleviation rates	
	1991	1993	1991	1993
Hungary				
Households	4.3	7.0	51.6	55.4
Population	6.5	11.6	47.0	55.9
Children	11.4	19.2	44.8	51.3
Romania				
Households	15.1	36.0	44.7	32.1
Population	18.5	44.0	43.1	29.4
Children	24.5	57.4	40.8	25.9

[a] See Table 13.1 for the definition of extreme poverty line and equivalence scales and for other methodological issues faced in the computation of poverty incidence. [b] Primary income (wages, income from self-employment, co-operative incomes and pensions) before direct taxation and social transfers (excluding pensions).

Source: Author's calculations from TRANSMONEE Database.

poverty-related base. The dominant proposal is for benefits to be 'targeted on the poor' through means-testing. However, means-testing ignores the usual problems of stigma, administrative costs, and efficiency of targeting (which normally involves large 'exclusion errors') (Cornia and Stewart, 1993).

Other approaches to targeting might be more efficient. For instance, Table 13.2 and the related literature show that poverty is correlated with observable family characteristics (number of children, single parenthood, disability, and unemployment). Thus, a two-tier benefit system could provide a moderate 'first-tier' universal benefit (to avoid a benefit cancellation-induced poverty) and target the 'second tier' only on children in specific objective categories. Another approach—practicable where a large proportion of the non-poor files a tax return—is to tax a universally provided standard benefit. In this case, most benefits received by rich families would be 'clawed back' (Cornia and Stewart, 1993). Empirical analysis on Hungary, however, shows that difficulties may arise, depending on the specific tax treatment of the family (Micklewright and Jarvis, 1995).

13.5.5. *Maintain universal access to priority programmes*

In these times of deep restructuring and faltering growth, it is essential to effectively protect key programmes, including: basic maternal and child health; measures to abate the massive increase in adult male mortality; and free access to and preservation of quality standards of compulsory education and child care. The principle of universal and free access to these educational and child-care programmes has not been openly challenged, but *de facto* access has been restricted by, among others, the imposition of 'substantial user fees' (for kindergartens, school meals, schoolbooks, drugs, and some health services). In addition, supply inefficiencies inherited from the former regime have not been corrected.

Because price barriers have caused a considerable decline in the utilization of services, particularly for low-income families and their children, it is essential that they be removed for all children. If needed for efficiency reasons, small 'nominal user fees' could be introduced, but must be closely monitored. The modest additional costs deriving from the removal of these user fees should be covered by local or central taxation.

In addition, the inherited inefficiencies of public provision need to be tackled by means of new approaches alternative to the dominant 'welfarist' and 'neo-liberal' paradigms. These approaches could rely, for instance, on state financing and NGO or private provision, and would avoid the usual inefficiencies of public supply and the exclusion and fragmentation typical of the neo-liberal approach.

13.5.6. *Strengthen youth institutions and combat the splintering of the social fabric*

Adolescents have been among the main losers of the transition (due to higher mortality, increased deviant behaviour, and rising school drop-out levels, among others). Reasons for the deterioration in adolescent well-being may be traced to the weakening of the family, the collapse of youth organizations, the disintegration of the old value system, and the slow development of new values and institutions (UNICEF ICDC, 1994).

Future social policy must strengthen those 'institutions' which play an essential role in promoting the socialization of teenagers, in ameliorating their physical conditions and health status, and in containing youth crime and deviance. As the creation of alternative community-based, religious, or non-governmental structures will take time, government policy should directly support the development of these institutions of 'civil society' by means of legal, financial, and regulatory measures. Measures would include, in particular, the setting up of family support and youth centres, fostering of NGOs in areas relating to youth recreation activities, promotion of foster care, and an overall deinstitutionalization of deviant adolescents.

The new social policy should also foster a non-ideological strengthening of intra- and inter-family support and transfers. This can be an important first safety net, complemented, in turn, by the formal system. In some countries (like Japan, for instance, see Chapter 12), family members are legally obliged to financially assist other members of the family before they can approach public institutions. During the recent period of adjustment, policy-makers have often assigned private transfers an important (and probably excessive) antipoverty role, thereby exonerating the state from its obligations. Yet, it is desirable to promote the positive values and energies of family and community solidarity, while at the same time ensuring broadly universal access to a state system of income support and social security.

These policy proposals are not specific prescriptions for concrete cases and thus must obviously be adapted to the vastly different circumstances within the region. Yet, we believe that they constitute a 'minimum policy model' from which governments may draw when developing a policy package which pays adequate attention to the protection and improvement of child welfare during the difficult years ahead.

14

Child Well-Being in the West:
Towards a More Effective
Antipoverty Policy

TIMOTHY M. SMEEDING, SHELDON DANZIGER,
AND LEE RAINWATER

14.1. Introduction

The well-being of children in advanced industrialized nations is being affected by important and consistent changes in family structure, in the global economy and national labour markets, and in the political economy of the welfare state. In most countries, a greater number of children now live in one-parent families and in families in which all parents are expected to (either desire to or need to) work in the labour market. Previous studies have documented family income packaging strategies in a cross-national perspective (Rainwater *et al.*, 1987; Rainwater, 1995) and have described a range of policy regimes for families with children in the modern welfare state (Esping-Anderson, 1991; Kolberg, 1992; Wennemo, 1994).

For the most part, these analyses have described and classified the ways in which families combine earnings and property income with government-provided benefits to support their children. This chapter builds on these studies but aspires to be proscriptive rather than descriptive. That is, our review of trends in family structure, labour market outcomes, and government responses to economic and family changes provides the basis for our development of a 'generic' model of antipoverty policy for children. Although we document convergence in the causes of child poverty in advanced economies, we do not suggest that any specific set of policies will be optimal for every country. Rather, the components of the generic model serve as a standard of comparison to judge how a

The authors would like to thank the Russell Sage Foundation, the Center for Advanced Study in the Behavioral Sciences under NSF grant SBR-9022192, and UNICEF for their support for this research. Charles Ragin, Northwestern University; Andrea Cornia, UNICEF; and Koen Vleminck at LIS provided valuable comments on a prior draft and background material to improve this chapter. All errors of commission and omission are those of the authors.

nation is meeting the needs of its children, and how it might revise its family income support and child poverty policies.

We begin by describing a series of family, labour market, and public policy changes that have affected children in all advanced industrial economies. Then we review some existing mixes of these elements in various nations, and how they seem to be changing. Finally, we suggest the components of a generic system of family income support policies for children in two-parent and one-parent families.

14.2. Forces of Change in the Family, the Workplace, and the Welfare State

The case-studies in the previous section of this volume demonstrate that several forces are systematically changing both the structure and size of families and their economic well-being. These changes have occurred, though at differing speeds, in most advanced industrialized countries and in the transitional economies of Central and Eastern Europe as well. Although we describe these changes, we do not yet fully understand their causes or how to precisely separate one force from another.

14.2.1. Family changes

The most obvious trend in family structure is the rapid rise in the percentage of families headed by a single parent. This increase is driven by increases in out-of-wedlock birth-rates and divorce-rates, which have risen in most industrialized nations in the past few decades. Table 14.1 shows increases in divorce-rates, the illegitimacy ratio, and the percentage of all families headed by a single parent in selected European countries and the USA. For example, between 1960 and 1990, the percentage of all births that were out-of-wedlock increased from roughly 5 to more than 25 per cent in the USA, the UK, France, and Canada, from about 10 to about 50 per cent in Scandinavia, and from roughly 1 or 2 per cent to 10 per cent in the Netherlands and Italy. Divorce-rates doubled or more in all of these countries. By 1990, 15 to 20 per cent of families with children were headed by a single parent. A much greater percentage of children born in the 1990s will live in a single-parent family at some point during their childhood than did those born in the recent past. Bumpass (1993), for example, estimates that the *majority* of children born after 1990 in the USA will spend some time before age 18 in a single-parent family, or in a 'blended' family (i.e. with at least one adult who is not a birth parent). Antipoverty policy must confront the fact that these children have less access to parental economic and time resources than children from intact two-parent families. No matter what economic changes emerge during the next dec-

Table 14.1:	Family Structure Changes

	Divorce rate[a]		Illegitimacy ratio[b]		Single parents[c]		Employed women[d]	
	1960[e]	1990[f]	1960	1990	1960	1988	1970[g]	1988
USA	9	21	5	28	9	23	45	73
Canada	2	12	4	24	9	15	41	75
Denmark	6	13	8	46	17	20	n.a.	90
France	3	8	6	30	9	12	52	75
Germany[h]	4	8	6	11	8	14	48	62
Italy	1	2	2	6	—	—	44	61
Netherlands	2	8	1	11	9	15	24	55
Sweden	5	12	11	47	9	13	61	89
UK	2	12	5	28	6	13	43	66

[a]Divorce rate per 1,000 women. [b]Percentage of all births born to unmarried women. [c]Percentage of all family households that are single parent. 1971 and 1986 for Canada. 1976 and 1988 for Denmark. 1968 and 1988 for France. 1972 and 1988 for Germany. 1961 and 1985 for Netherlands. 1960 and 1985 for Sweden. 1961 and 1987 for the UK. Age restrictions for children differ by country. [d]Percentage of women aged 25–34 (25–39 in Italy) in the labour force. [e]1970 for Italy. [f]1989 for France; 1988 for UK. [g]1977 for Italy. [h]For former West Germany.

Source: McLanahan and Caspar (1995).

ade, all industrialized nations face pressures to provide children and custodial parents insurance against the higher risk of poverty associated with single parenthood.

14.2.2. *Labour supply changes*

A second major force is the increased labour force participation rate of women and the emergence of two- (market) earner families as the norm. Table 14.1 shows that the percentage of employed women aged 25–34 increased by about 20 percentage points in most industrialized countries between 1970 and 1988. Over these two decades, married women's employment and labour force participation also increased consistently. For example, the percentage of married women aged 15–64 in the paid labour force increased from 62 to 79 per cent in Sweden and from 50 to 69 per cent in the USA between the early 1970s and the early 1990s (OECD, 1994*a*). Although married women with children now work in greater numbers in most countries, there is a considerable diversity across countries. For example, in 1989, 38 per cent of married mothers were employed in the Netherlands, 44 per cent in Germany, and close to 60 per cent in the UK and France. The two-earner couple is now more common than the one-earner couple in most modern countries, even in those where the 'traditional family' model reigned until quite recently.

Over the same period, the labour force participation rate of married men remained fairly stable or declined slightly in most countries. In a few nations, there were even substantial declines in participation among males in late middle-age.

Women's earnings also increased relative to men's. In the USA in 1992, for example, about 20 per cent of married women earned more than their husbands (US Bureau of the Census, 1993). In 1992, 29 per cent of total husband-wife earnings were accounted for by white wives aged 25 to 44, and 36 per cent by African-American wives of the same age-group, as compared to 11 and 17 per cent respectively in 1963 (Dechter and Smock, 1994). None the less, in many families, married women still work less and more often part-time than do their husbands, especially if they have young children.

Patterns of earnings and labour force activity among lone (or single-parent) mothers in Europe and Scandinavia are similar to those in the United States. Lone mothers tend to work slightly more than married mothers: 54 per cent versus 48 per cent respectively in the European Community in 1989. But lone mothers were also more likely to be unemployed (12 versus 7 per cent). While lone mothers were more likely to work full time than were married mothers (40 versus 29 per cent), a large proportion worked only part time (16 per cent of lone mothers and 18 per cent of married mothers) (Roll, 1992, table 8). Thus, by most measures, single-parent labour market activity may exceed that of married women. However, family income remains low because the single parent is typically the only earner in such households.

Despite increased female labour force participation, there remain significant cross-country differences in the incidence of non-employment due to either unemployment or inactivity (non-participation in the formal labour market) and there is a gendered pattern to these differences. During the 1980s, for example, among those of prime work-force age (25–54 years), around an eighth of men and between a third and a half of women were non-employed, on average, in OECD countries.

Reducing labour market inactivity for parents who receive social assistance is a key goal of our antipoverty agenda. From the perspective of child well-being, recent trends in labour supply suggest that, in the absence of government intervention, the economic well-being of children in two-parent families has improved relative to that of children in single-parent families because single parents must both work and provide (or pay for) child care. It also implies that, holding family structure constant, money income inequality has increased between children whose parents have worked more and those whose parents have worked less. Given political and economic constraints which make expansion of the welfare state unlikely in most countries, raising market earnings becomes even more important if child poverty is to be reduced and the gap between children living in one- and two-parent families is to be narrowed.

14.2.3. *Wage rate changes*

The major economic problems that have emerged since the late 1970s are slow growth in wages, increased structural unemployment, and rising inequality. Skill-intensive technological change that has reduced the demand for lower-skilled workers is one of the most important contributions to these problems. A recent report, *The OECD Jobs Study* (OECD, 1994c) suggests that most nations were slow to adapt to technological changes and the rapid growth of the service sector in the 1980s.

Because fathers' earnings are the largest source of family income, growing inequality in men's wages in many nations (Gottschalk *et al.*, 1994; Gottschalk and Smeeding, 1995) affects the well-being of many children. The incidence of workers whose pay is low compared to that of the median worker has risen in many nations in recent years (for instance, UK, USA, Sweden). In some countries, such as the USA, Canada, and Australia, wages for low-skilled workers fell in real terms over the past decade. In most European nations, real wages among employed less-skilled workers were constant (or grew slowly), but unemployment remained high, particularly among youth (OECD, 1994c). In all advanced economies, employer demand shifted away from unskilled towards higher-skilled jobs.

Child poverty and inequality would therefore have increased in many countries had there not been a large increase in mothers' labour market activity and earnings. Recent studies in Australia (Saunders, 1993), Sweden (Bjorklund, 1992), the UK (Machin and Waldfogel, 1994), and the USA (Cancian and Schoeni, 1992; Cancian *et al.*, 1993b), among others, indicate that wives' earnings reduce family poverty and inequality compared to the situation in which only one parent works in the market. However, the trend is that married women's earnings have had a smaller equalizing effect in recent years (Jenkins, 1993; Blackburn and Bloom, 1994).

Taken together, the labour supply and wage rate changes reviewed here suggest that both the gross and the net (of child care) earnings of many two-earner couples may *not* be sufficient to ensure a non-poverty living standard for many children. While some two-career couples have prospered, others, particularly those who are young and with little human capital, have not fared well. We expect these labour market trends to continue throughout the 1990s.

14.2.4. *Political economy changes*

The negative effects on child well-being of these changes in family structure and labour markets have placed pressure on government policies. Rising inequality in men's earnings and growing unemployment have led some countries to propose protectionist policies and others to seek to stem the flow of international migrants. Since the late 1970s, some countries have attempted to limit labour force growth by subsidizing married women to stay at home (Netherlands), by limiting the hours that shops are open (Germany), or, most widely, by encouraging early retirement. As market forces caused unemployment to rise in some nations with high minimum wages (such as Denmark and France), there was mounting pressure on government to increase public employment (OECD, 1994c).

Together with changes in family structure, these economic changes have put extreme pressure on social budgets (OECD, 1994b). Tax revenues have risen but, in many cases, expenditure for unemployment, social assistance, and particularly old age pensions has increased more rapidly, leading to large deficits. The growing cost of health care, particularly for the elderly, and rising demand for additional education to meet the market demand for high-skilled employees, have further strained national social budgets. Although social expenditure for non-aged families in most OECD countries has fallen (or risen more slowly) since 1985, it was still greater in the mid-1990s than in 1980 (ibid.).

Because the number of retirees and survivors has continued to grow in Europe, Japan, and elsewhere, public budgets have faced pressures to meet social retirement fund commitments first. This has often required reduced spending for other social benefits, particularly those which affect children. For instance, once-free child care in Italy and the UK is now subject to user charges. Because of the political power of aged voters, demographic, political, and social changes have fostered a 'generational bias' for social spending towards the aged and away from children.

Finally, the growth of working wives has increased pressure for *all* mothers to work as a means of reducing social spending. In some economies, such as Scandinavia and France, most single mothers already combine work and social assistance benefits. In the USA, Canada, and the UK, however, there is pressure for low-income single parents receiving social assistance to 'get off the dole', even though existing welfare programmes place a high marginal tax rate on benefits.

14.2.5. *Social protection response*

Most Western European countries have maintained their extensive social welfare programmes. Social spending has adapted to changing circumstances, including population ageing, but has not withdrawn the safety net (Ploug and Kvist, 1994). The growth of long-term unemployment, disability (often disguising early retirement), single parents relying on public assistance, rising health care costs, and increased numbers of the aged have led to a near crisis in social protection. However, by the mid-1990s only small and targeted responses to the underlying forces had been implemented. In fact, Germany, France, and Belgium *expanded* means-tested benefits, particularly those for single parents. Pressure to limit long-term jobless benefits via means-testing and/or via worker-retraining pro-grammes has grown in the UK, Ireland, Belgium, Netherlands, and Germany. Proposals to raise retirement ages have been addressed in a few nations (for instance, Germany and Italy). Many countries have intro-duced 'user charges' to control the use of health care services, prescription drugs, and other social services such as child care. There is also growing pressure for more flexible and 'active' labour market policies in terms of training, education, and unemployment benefits (European Commission, 1993; OECD, 1994*c*; Gottschalk and Smeeding, 1995).

The USA has historically paid less attention to labour market and other social policies than have other industrialized nations. None the less, since the mid-1980s it has dramatically expanded the Earned Income Tax Credit (EITC) to supplement the earnings of low-income working families with children (see Chapter 7). On the other hand, pressure grows to force welfare mothers to work and to reduce social benefits to both legal and illegal immigrants. Educational expenditures and college enrolments con-tinue to grow in the USA, albeit with higher 'user charges' (tuition) in state-funded universities. The failure to provide universal health insur-ance, particularly for children, remains a serious gap in the safety net.

14.2.6. Summary

An increasingly open international market economy (with its pressures for lower wages) and family structure change (such as divorce) require more market work in economies where jobs are increasingly scarce, espe-cially for the least skilled. Will these global factors lead to a diminution of the welfare state, moving all nations towards a less generous set of pro-grammes? Or are there alternative ways to restructure income support packages for families with children so as to both restrain spending growth and reduce poverty? We now turn to a review of current approaches.

14.3. Alternative Social Policy Approaches for Families and Children

Social policies for families and children are based on a combination of three types of resources: work (earnings and non-market 'home' work); family support (care-giving) and government benefits; and taxes to pay for them. The package includes both cash and in-kind components (health, education), paid for or not (for instance, parental versus market child care). The mix of these resources varies over time and across nations. Conundrums and trade-offs among these sources of family support exist, and social policy must confront them.

14.3.1. Work

Market earnings are the primary determinant of economic well-being for all families, including single-parent families. As educational attainment and returns to investments in human capital have risen, more labour is supplied—both for prime age men and women. Typically, if wages stagnate or one parent is unemployed, the other parent will increase his/her labour supply. In low or falling wage societies, the earnings of two parents are necessary to prevent a family from sinking into poverty.

As market work has become more important, there has been a tendency to devalue non-market work. Stay-at-home mothers—in two- and one-parent families—provide services that markets and society value less now than in the past. Moreover, in some economies, particularly in the USA, only paid employment provides certain non-cash benefits, including health and life insurance and occupational pensions. In addition, labour market attachment offers a mother a form of 'divorce insurance' that may provide more than the government.

Work for single parents exemplifies the conflict between market and non-market work. The single parent must fulfil the roles of both earner/breadwinner and mother—i.e. both market and non-market work. Most single mothers cannot earn enough in the labour market to both pay for market child care *and* maintain a non-poverty standard of living. As a result, in some nations, notably Sweden, Netherlands, and France, single mothers can combine work and welfare. In others, especially the UK, USA, and Australia, they tend to either work *or* receive welfare because of the structure of welfare programmes.

Europe and America have diverged in their treatment of market versus non-market work. In Europe, the labour market provides good wages for those with jobs, but job growth has been slower and unemployment higher. In the USA, jobs are more plentiful and unemployment lower, but many jobs pay very low wages. In both Europe and America, there is need for the welfare state to supplement market outcomes, due either to unemployment or to low pay.

14.3.2. Family

Families with two working parents, or one working single parent, must balance the demands of child care and other non-market work with those of market work. The cost and availability of child care affects the net return to market work, as do the logistics of work, child care, and other necessities (physicians, shopping, etc.). Two important issues are therefore (a) the *net* return from a second parent working, including earnings net of the costs of child care, replacement home work, transportation and related work costs; and (b) workplace and work-time flexibility to meet family needs. Particularly in the case of preschool children, and low-skill mothers in low-wage economies, the *net* return from work may be very low, or even negative once child care and related costs are taken into account (Danziger and Jantii, 1995).

In single-parent households these problems are more acute. Without sufficient cash and/or in-kind support from the absent spouse, single parents typically face a low net return from working. Some societies, such as Germany and France, provide 'insurance' against loss of child support from absent spouses. But in many others, especially in the USA, the receipt of child support is erratic and adequate child support insurance is not available.

The issue of 'care-giving' extends beyond children to include care for the infirm elderly and for other adults, for sick children, and how to integrate schooling with before- and after-school provisions for care. A related issue concerns society's overall responsibility for children. Are childless couples who have never had (and never expect to have) their own children, and others whose children are not yet born (or are grown to adulthood) willing to pay taxes to improve the economic well-being of the children of other citizens? In Europe and Scandinavia, such support is often forthcoming. In the USA, despite the high social cost of child poverty, the issue remains in doubt (Palmer *et al.*, 1988; Sherman, 1994; Smeeding, 1995).

14.3.3. Government benefits and institutions

All advanced economies provide some support to families with children—directly in cash and services, and indirectly via legal institutions. Here we review some common and often controversial elements of the support package.

1. *Cash benefits.* Governments transfer cash to parents on behalf of children. Parents qualify for benefits in one of three ways: either as a right of parenthood (citizenship of children), due to previous contributions to specific funds, or because they are otherwise destitute. The social welfare literature refers to these three types as universal, social insurance, and means-tested programmes respectively. Additional 'targeting' requirements may be added (including the child's age, parental contribution status, or parent's asset position or marital status). Benefits are available to all who qualify.

The most common universal benefit is a children's (or family) allowance (which may vary according to the age of the children and/or family size). Some nations tilt benefits to favour large (France) or small (Denmark) families (Atkinson, 1993). The USA is the only advanced nation without a family allowance. Social insurance benefits are paid directly to children, primarily due to death of a parent. Unemployment compensation is family-size-adjusted in a few nations. Sickness insurance and family-leave provisions indirectly benefit children by providing their parents with the flexibility to meet both work and family needs.

Most countries also have means- or income-tested benefits. These social assistance or 'welfare' programmes differ across nations, but the essential ingredient is that all other sources of money income are taken into account in determining eligibility. The family must apply and demonstrate that it is needy. Take-up problems, the invasive nature of welfare benefits, and stigma issues are common. As a result, welfare is not very popular, even though it serves as the safety net programme of last resort for the families of poor children.

In a number of countries, the combination of the benefit reduction rate for welfare programmes and income and payroll tax rates yields high cumulative marginal tax rates—the 'welfare trap'—which discourages employment at low wages by lowering the net return to work (Atkinson, 1993; OECD, 1994c). Welfare programmes thus encourage 'off the books' work or hiding of income, and create disincentives for absent parents to make child support payments (Edin, 1994).

2. *Non-cash programmes.* Cash programmes indirectly benefit children because the money is paid to their parents or guardians. In contrast, non-cash benefits or in-kind transfers are provided directly to poor children; for example, outlay for health care and elementary and secondary education programmes typically dwarfs outlay for children under cash programmes. In education, only a few nations, including Sweden, France, and Italy, have widely available publicly subsidized preschool programmes. Mothers of young children—particularly single parents—tend to work more in these countries.

In the health care and education arenas, quality of services, differential access (by region, race, social class, etc.), and the effect of user charges on access by low-income families are key policy issues. In some countries, attempts to slow the rapid growth of health care spending have taken the form of flat user-charges which are not income tested. Thus, low-income families are more likely to forgo health care than are high-income families because of these charges.

3. *Legal institutions.* Governments also affect the economic status of children and their families via legal institutions. An important example is child support determination and enforcement of payment from the absent parent. Courts decide the amount of financial responsibility and penalties for non-payment. As divorce and out-of-wedlock births grow, these activities become all the more important. Issues of paternity determination (in the case of out-of-wedlock births) and government insurance for non-payment of child support by an absent spouse are closely related. In some countries, such as the USA and Italy (see Chapter 10), there is a large discrepancy between child support orders and child support payments.

Only a few nations, Germany, France, Netherlands among them, have government insurance for non-payment of child support.

Legal institutions also affect job status, firing practices, worker and union rights, and job interruption for child-raising (family leave). To the extent that these institutions protect jobs for parents who have other responsibilities to family, especially to children, they are an important component of social policy for children.

4. *Government as employer and work-related benefits.* The intersection between governments and labour markets involves more than job protection and family leave. Government setting of minimum wages and government's role as employer—either via permanent employment in public social services, or via its role as employer of last resort—are two important examples. In Western and Northern Europe, government's role as employer has been pervasive and has grown over the 1980s (OECD, 1994*a,b*). In Denmark, special public works programmes were begun for jobless youth (Ploug and Kvist, 1994). In Germany, particularly since unification, public works employment has increased. Several countries, in contrast, have moved to limit the role of government as employer and to 'privatize' services previously provided by the public sector. At the same time, there is an increased need for government to serve as employer of last resort and as partner to training and retraining schemes as a response to globalization and technological changes that have reduced employer demand for low-skilled workers.

One potential area where government can raise net earnings without intervening in the labour market is through the provision of work-related income transfers, such as the Earned Income Tax Credit (EITC) in the USA, or the Family Benefit in the UK. Governments provide supplements to families whose earned income is low despite high work effort. As low-wage jobs continue to grow, such supplements offer a way to target benefits to low earners.

5. *Tax systems.* Governments also affect employment through the tax structure. High employment-related taxes on employers—to fund social retirement, disability, health care, and unemployment—discourage hiring of workers. In countries such as Spain, Italy, and France, where the employer social security contribution can be 50 per cent or more of the worker's cash wage, the problem has reached epic proportions. Movements to shift the tax burden of social spending to a broader tax base (for instance, the value added tax) is growing in many nations (Metcalf, 1995).

14.4. The Antipoverty Effects of Welfare State Policies

Before we discuss an 'optimal' antipoverty policy, we evaluate how current social programmes provide for children. This section compares the economic well-being of children in the 1980s in sixteen countries: Australia, Belgium, Canada, Finland, France, Germany, Ireland, Israel, Italy, Luxembourg, Netherlands, Norway, Sweden, Switzerland, the UK, and the USA. The analysis is based on the Luxembourg Income Study (LIS) database, which provides micro-data covering various years from 1967 to the present (Smeeding *et al.*, 1990; LIS Users' Guide, 1994).

By economic well-being we refer to the material resources which families make use of in their daily lives. The concern with these resources is not with consumption *per se*, but rather with the capabilities that these resources give family members to participate in their societies (Sen, 1992). Income and other economic resources provide inputs to social activities; participation in these activities produces a given level of well-being (Rainwater, 1990).

14.4.1. *Measuring poverty and disadvantage*

Industrialized societies are highly socially stratified, though much less than most developing countries. Some individuals have more of valued resources and others less. The opportunities for social participation are vitally affected by a family's resources (Rainwater, 1974). Money income is the central resource in modern societies, but other important resources include health, family structure and stability, and parents' education and human capital. Here, we examine only money income because the surveys exclude information on other resources. For each family, we have detailed information on money income, on taxes paid, and on transfers which are cash-like—for example, housing allowances, fuel assistance, or food stamps. Unfortunately, we cannot examine the major non-cash benefits—health care, day care and preschool, general subsidies to housing, and the like. Because the level and distribution of non-cash resources varies widely across the countries, our analysis of money income must be treated with some caution (see Smeeding *et al.*, 1993 for an analysis that includes these benefits).

Families also differ in terms of their needs. We take the differing needs occasioned by family size and the head's stage in the life course into account by adjusting income for family size using an equivalence scale. While different equivalence scales yield different distributions of well-being, several studies use an equivalence scale which implies dramatic economies of scale (Buhmann *et al.*, 1988; Rainwater, 1990). Others suggest that need varies with the head of household's age.

We use an equivalence scale which defines need as the product of the cube root of family size multiplied by a factor which has need increasing roughly 1 per cent a year for head's age up to the mid-forties and then decreasing at the same rate. Hence, equivalent income is:

$$EI = Y / \left(S^{\frac{1}{3}} \times 0.99^{|A-45|} \right).$$

That is, equivalent income (*EI*) is the family's disposable income (*Y*) divided by the product of (a) the cube root of the family's size (*S*) and (b) 0.99 to the *n*th power, where *n* is defined as the absolute difference between the age of the family head and 45 years of age. We use the terms income and equivalent income interchangeably. We first determine the median equivalent income of all individuals in each country. Any child who lives in a family whose equivalent income is below 50 per cent of the median in that country in any year is defined as poor. Our calculations are weighted by the number of children in each family.

We examine results for three groups—(a) all children, (b) children in two-parent families, and (3) children in families headed by a solo mother (that is, a mother who is not currently married—there may or may not be other adults in the family).

First, child poverty rates for multiple years are found in Table 2.11 of this volume for eleven of the LIS countries for which we have more than one survey, and a single year for four countries. Concentrating on the most recent year, child poverty rates range from over 20 per cent in the USA to only about 3 per cent in Finland, Sweden, and Switzerland. The cross-country pattern of child poverty rates is quite stable over the two decades shown.

During the 1980s, child poverty rates did not improve much in any of these countries. In a few, there are hints of improvement during the 1970s (see Canada and Sweden, for instance). In the USA and the UK the situation has worsened. Over two decades, the poverty rate increased from 5 to 10 per cent in the UK and from 13 per cent to more than 20 per cent in the USA.

The contrast between the long-run trends in the USA and Canada, which have experienced similar economic and demographic changes, suggests the important role of government. The Canadian child poverty rate was 2 percentage points above the USA rate in 1970, but 8 points below it by 1991 due in large part to an activist social policy (see Hanratty and Blank, 1992; Card and Freeman, 1993).

14.4.2. Real incomes of poor children

We also compare countries according to the real income level of children at the lower end of the distribution. Because the highest relative child poverty rate was about 20 per cent in the USA, we compare the real incomes of the poorest quintile of children in each country (Table 14.2). The Penn-World tables provide for each year the ratio of real per capita income in a country to real per capita income in the USA based on Purchasing Power Parities (PPP) (Heston and Summers, 1991). We calculate from the LIS database the median equivalent income of children in the lowest quintile as a percent of the median equivalent income of all per-

Table 14.2:   Real Incomes of Children in the Lowest
Quintile as a percent of US Median Income

Nation (Year)	Real Income
Switzerland (1982)	56.7
Sweden (1992)	56.7
Finland (1991)	52.2
Belgium (1992)	50.3
Norway (1991)	50.0
Luxembourg (1985)	46.4
Germany (1984)	46.0
The Netherlands (1987)	43.8
Canada (1991)	41.2
France (1984)	39.2
Italy (1987)	37.9
UK (1986)	34.9
Australia (1989)	34.7
USA (1991)	33.0
Ireland (1987)	20.1

Note: Median income of lowest quintile of children
expressed as a percent of US median income using
Purchasing Power Parities developed by Heston and
Summers (1991).

sons. Multiplying the two ratios we have the median real income of the
children in the lowest quintile as a percentage of real US median income.

In the USA, the average child in the lowest quintile has an income one-
third of the median of all persons. The range in the low-income child's real
income in other countries is from 20 per cent in Ireland to a high of 56.7
per cent in Sweden and Switzerland. Thus, with the exception of Ireland,
the poorest fifth of children in the USA have a lower real standard of
living than the poorest fifth in the other countries.

14.4.3. The role of market income and income transfers

What are the roles of market income and transfers in producing the wide
range in child poverty? To what extent would children be poor in the
absence of transfers? How much of the variation across countries is due to
variations in market income? Market income is defined here as earnings
plus asset income, and is affected mainly by macroeconomic and employment policies. Transfer income includes all social transfers and child support payments.

Figures 14.1 and 14.2 plot the market income poverty rates of children
(that is, poverty rates based on income from earnings and assets and before
taxes and transfers—including private transfers) against child poverty

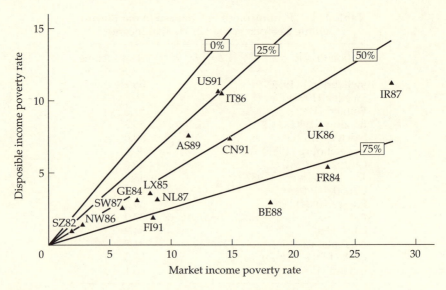

Fig. 14.1   Percentage Reduction in Two-Parent Poverty by Transfers

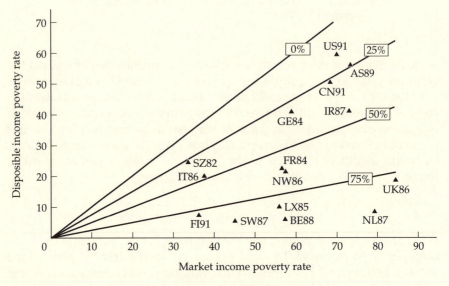

Fig. 14.2   Percentage Reduction in Solo-Mother Poverty by Transfers

rates based on total after-tax (disposable) income. Because the levels of poverty are so different for children living with two parents versus those living with a solo mother the two patterns are shown separately.

For children in two-parent families (Figure 14.1) market income poverty rates vary from below 5 per cent (Norway, Switzerland) to over 20 per cent (UK, France, and Ireland). There is also a wide range in the degree to which transfers reduce market income poverty. The lines in the figure radiating from the origin indicate the extent of poverty reduction—25 per cent, 50 per cent, and 75 per cent. In three countries—Australia, Italy, and the USA—transfers reduce child poverty in two-parent families by 24 to 33 per cent. In ten countries, the reduction ranges from a little below half to not quite two-thirds. Finally, in three countries—Finland, Belgium, and France—the reductions are three-quarters or more.

The extremely low market income rates for Norway, Switzerland, Germany, and a few others, are reduced to even lower disposable income rates. For the rest of the countries there is a great deal of movement. Belgium has a higher market income poverty rate than the other countries in group C, but its transfers produce a disposable income rate below 5 per cent. The shift for Canada is not as dramatic, but still considerable compared to the USA, Italy, or Australia. There are also differences in the disposable income poverty rates among the countries with the highest market rates (above 20 per cent). French children in two-parent families improve their situation a great deal through transfers, much more than those in the UK and Ireland.

The antipoverty effect of transfers for children in solo-mother families is quite different from that of two-parent families (Figure 14.2). The market poverty rates in all countries are very high. Only four have rates below 50 per cent (Switzerland, Italy, Finland, Sweden) and two have rates around 80 per cent (the Netherlands, UK).

The antipoverty effect of transfers varies widely. While only three countries had reductions in two-parent poverty of 75 per cent or more, we find that much reduction for solo-mothers' children in six countries. However, more countries have rates of poverty reduction around 25 per cent or less for mother-only than for two-parent families.

The result of this diversity in the proportion of children moved out of poverty by transfers is a wide range in disposable income poverty rates. The five countries with rates under 10 per cent range across all levels of market income poverty rates—from Finland (35 per cent) to Sweden (45 per cent) to Luxembourg and Belgium (55 to 56 per cent), to the Netherlands (80 per cent).

Child poverty rates are below 10 per cent in twelve of our fifteen countries for two-parent families, and in only five countries for solo-mother families. Overall the correlation between market income and disposable income poverty rates is 0.73 for children in two-parent families, but only 0.40 in solo-mother families.

On average, government income transfers to two-parent families amount to more than 25 per cent of median income (50 per cent of the poverty line) in Sweden and Ireland, and to more than 20 per cent in the

UK, Belgium, Finland, and France. At the other extreme, transfers amount to around 10 per cent or less in Australia, Luxembourg, Norway, the USA, Italy, and Switzerland.

Average transfers to solo-mother families comprise a greater share of disposable income in every country than is the case for two-parent families. In four countries they amount to 40 per cent or more of median equivalent income (or 80 per cent of the poverty line)—the Netherlands, UK, Sweden, and Luxembourg—and are almost that high in Ireland and Belgium. At the low end we find Switzerland, the USA, Italy, Finland, Germany, and Canada at less than 25 per cent.

There is a wide variation in level and trend of child poverty across the industrialized nations for which we have data, and a wide variety of approaches to addressing market income poverty. Macroeconomic policies affect unemployment, wages, and joblessness, and therefore also market-income-based child poverty. In addition, the effectiveness of the safety net in removing children from poverty is an important determinant of disposable-income poverty. The welfare states in some countries are more effective than in others. In all countries, children living with single parents fare less well than those living with both parents.

14.5. Towards a More Effective Antipoverty Policy for Children

Changes in the roles of family, work, and government policies have placed more children at risk of poverty, even in those countries with low poverty rates. The high budgetary cost of advanced welfare states has led some policy-makers to conclude that they can no longer afford the social cost of high income transfer benefits and the high taxes required to finance them. Globalization and technological changes have contributed to slow economic growth and slow growth in tax revenues. Macroeconomic policies have failed in many countries to reduce unemployment. In addition, work disincentives of the transfer system must be reduced in several countries, and employer disincentives to hire new workers must be reduced in others. At the same time, efforts to make work pay and to provide more protection against poverty are needed in the larger Anglophone nations with the highest child poverty rates (USA, Canada, Australia).

Although different nations face a similar convergence in the causes of child poverty, they use different instruments to deal with 'packaging' work, family support, and government support. In some low-to-medium poverty nations, work was the key to preventing child poverty; in others, the generosity of welfare state programmes produced low poverty rates, even where many mothers did not work. Even 'small differences' in government outlays and labour market institutions have produced more beneficial child outcomes in Canada as compared to the USA (Hanratty and Blank, 1992; Card and Freeman, 1993). Thus, while the causes of child poverty have converged, the specific public policies used to address them vary widely. There is no one single comprehensive antipoverty policy for children which is applicable to all advanced economies. Every country has different traditions, values, and culture which would prohibit wholesale importation of a set of effective antipoverty activities from country A to country B. Our review, however, does suggest that there are several lessons that hold across a range of circumstances and might comprise an optimal antipoverty strategy.

Our prototypical policy package reflects the changes in labour markets, family structure, and government policies that are common. Our policies could yield a child poverty rate of about 5 to 9 per cent in most nations. Given continuing trends in family structure and persisting gender differences in the labour market, this would reflect a poverty rate of about 20 per cent for children living in single-parent families and a rate of about 5 per cent for children in two-parent families. For some nations—for instance, USA, Canada, Italy, Australia—this requires a net reduction from their current child poverty rate and an increase in public spending. For others, including the Netherlands, Scandinavia, Belgium, this might even mean a *slightly higher* child poverty rate, but reduced public spending. Our notion is that these countries might adjust their safety net so as to better promote labour market flexibility and job growth and to lower the overall tax burden without causing an unduly large rise in poverty.

14.5.1. Work

The growing acceptance of market work for all parents suggests that the key antipoverty component is increased employment and earnings. The issue is more complex for mothers with very young children, particularly for single parents. Given high infant care costs, mothers' earnings might not comprise the major source of family support, especially in one-parent families. The French programme for single parents, *Allocation Parent Isole*, recognizes this dilemma by offering single mothers the alternative of work with smaller benefits, or non-work with larger benefits until the child is 3 (Hanratty, 1994). As the educational attainment of women, the returns to human capital, and the risk of divorce have all increased, most mothers *want* to work in the market. Thus, labour market and/or government institutions must be flexible enough for them to carry out their family and labour market responsibilities.

Increased labour market flexibility does not require the abandonment of minimum wages or other labour protections. However, the costs of employment must be lowered for employers and workers. Employer taxes which discourage new hiring, especially of low-wage workers, should be redirected to other revenue sources. Active labour market policies of the sort outlined in the recent *OECD Jobs Study* (1994c) can encourage market work among otherwise poor parents by emphasizing full employment (even at the cost of slightly higher price levels) at the macro-level, and at the micro-level by better matching of employers and potential employees, the provision of child care and other assistance to single parents, and the provision of work-related benefits to low-income/low-wage workers (for example, parental leave to care for sick children).

14.5.2. Family

Parents should support their children and, together with government assistance, provide a nurturing environment for their growth. For absent parents, this means regular payment of child support and frequent contact with children. However, the means to provide child support (a job for unemployed absent parents) and the incentive to provide child support (lowered benefit reductions in welfare programmes when child support is received by the custodial parent) must also be present.

Parents of very young children should have the economic flexibility to *not* work until the children are old enough to be placed in affordable day-care settings. Many activist 'labour market policies' are also 'family policies'. These require co-operation and co-ordination with the public sector, to which we now turn.

14.5.3. Government policy

Most democratic societies support universal programmes because *all* individuals, including those who are too young to vote, are entitled to certain rights and privileges—family allowances, refundable tax credits, other public subsidies for health and education. If parents cannot provide a minimum standard of living, government should ensure financial support on grounds of equal opportunity and treat children as 'public investment' goods.

Governments also must ensure 'social capital'—a safe and healthy environment for children, free of crime and public health risk and conducive to child development. While such public goods and services are not often considered components of antipoverty policy, it is not possible to guarantee equal opportunity to children who do *not* live in safe or healthy environments.

Governments must support workplace flexibility, via employment policy, family leave, and flexible job rules, as well as enforce workplace standards, minimum wages, and collective bargaining agreements. If work is to be valued over dependence on income transfer payments, government must make work more remunerative than welfare and ensure the availability and affordability of child care for working parents. This requires a reasonable level for the minimum wage and policies to supplement low wages or family income, such as the Earned Income Tax Credit in the USA, the UK Family Credit, or Ireland's Family Income Supplement.

Finally, government must provide basic cash or near cash assistance to those who cannot maintain steady employment. If government limits receipt of welfare assistance and requires all parents to work, then it must provide either job placement in the private sector or a minimum wage job of last resort to those who seek employment but cannot obtain a job.

14.5.4. Regional implications

Governments should provide a mix of cash, near cash assistance, and/or employment assistance, but excessive means-testing (poverty trap) should be avoided. The extent of targeting and the design of the entire system *should* vary across and sometimes within nations. Here we sketch out the implications of our generic policies for two groups of nations: Europe and Scandinavia, and the USA, suggesting how the policies in these countries might change to reflect the issues discussed above.

1. *European and Scandinavian nations.* In most European countries, despite high unemployment rates, child poverty has remained low because of the extensive welfare state. Economic and family change pressures have not yet produced a drastic retrenchment in social programmes for children. The high and rising costs of these programmes and the negative effects of taxation and regulation on employment growth, however, have led many countries to consider ways to restrain social spending growth and to better target it. This has been reflected in proposals to raise the retirement age (Germany, Italy), to control eligibility for disability benefits (Netherlands), and to control eligibility for unemployment benefits (Belgium, UK). Several governments are trying to reduce long-term unemployment by monitoring the availability of the unemployed for work, by limiting time for receipt of unemployment insurance, and by tying these benefits to retraining efforts.

There is also a need to foster job growth by increasing employer flexibility to hire and fire workers, and through other job creation strategies, even if they would reduce job security or lower minimum wages somewhat. This can be accomplished, in part by reducing high employer costs of hiring, in part by shifting from reliance on payroll taxes to general revenues (for example, value added taxes, income taxes), and perhaps by shortening the work week.

2. *US policies.* While many European nations have high unemployment rates and low child poverty rates due to their extensive welfare state and labour market regulations, the American situation is quite the reverse.

America has a relatively low unemployment rate, but the highest child poverty rate among advanced economies, due to weak labour market regulations and a smaller welfare state that limits cash outlays, child care, health care, and early school services. Compared to European countries, minimum wages are low, health insurance is not guaranteed, unemployment insurance is of limited duration, and welfare eligibility and benefits are low.

A detailed discussion of an antipoverty strategy for the USA appears in Chapter 7 of this volume and in Smeeding (1995, ch. 6). With regard to our generic model, the USA would have to adopt a number of initiatives, such as a child allowance, universal health insurance, expanded child care, and child support guarantees, if it is to cut its child poverty rate in half. Simulations suggest such a set of policies could be both feasible and affordable (Yim *et al.*, 1994).

While the European welfare state is probably 'too expensive', the USA is clearly 'too cheap'. Those countries which have universal health insurance and universal child care can reduce spending by increased reliance on income-tested co-payments for non-basic services or by pricing services so that high-income families pay more than low-income families. Better targeting of welfare state spending is much easier to accomplish than putting programmes into place for the first time.

14.6. Summary and Conclusions

As the economic and social realities of the 1990s become more uniform in industrialized Western economies, families and governments must co-operate more closely to ensure the economic viability of one- and two-parent families. The generic components of this package include:

1. *Families* that are willing and able to work in the market to support their children, and to maintain this support even when marriage and living arrangements change.

2. *Employers* that are willing to assume some of the costs of training and to support flexible labour markets and family benefits.

3. *Governments* that are willing to provide basic health care, education, and preschool services to all children; employment-related services such as job training and retraining, and job search; and family leave for parents.

4. *Transfer programmes* which provide some support via universal child allowances; child support insurance for single parents whose absent spouse cannot or will not provide child support; and subsidies for unemployment or low wages to help working families make ends meet. There also needs to be a safety net programme of limited duration to assist families with children who have otherwise fallen through the cracks and have no alternative means of emergency support.

5. *Tax programmes* that are broad based, that do not discourage employment, and which, when combined with safety net programmes, do not provide cumulative tax rates that unduly reduce incentives for beneficiaries to work.

Even though most advanced economies have experienced similar changes in family structure and in the structure of their labour markets during the past two decades, their child poverty rates vary dramatically, from less than 3 per cent to more than 20 per cent. Differences in public policies account for a significant portion of this variation. Our analysis suggests that these differences reflect differing social and political values and choices, not technical economic constraints. There is enough flexibility in the choices that can be made so that all modern advanced countries and eventually the transition economies of Eastern Europe can achieve both a dynamic, growing economy and a low child poverty rate.

BIBLIOGRAPHY

Abburrà, L. (1989), (IRES Piemonte), *L'occupazione femminile dal declino alla crescita* (Turin, Rosenberg & Sellier).

Abecassis, M. (1979), 'Planeamento Familiar', *A Criança Portuguesa*.

Accornero, A., and F. Carmignani (1986), *I paradossi della disoccupazione* (Bologna, Il Mulino).

Adam, J. (ed.) (1991), *Economic Reforms and Welfare Systems in the USSR, Poland and Hungary. Social Contract in Transformation* (New York, St Martin's Press).

Adamchak, D. (1979), 'Emerging Trends in the Relationship between Infant Mortality and Socio-economic Status', *Social Biology*, 26/1: 16–29.

Alanen, L. (1992), 'Childhood in One-Parent Families', in U. Björnberg (ed.), *One-Parent Families: Lifestyles and Values* (Amsterdam, SISWO).

Alton, T. P. (1981), 'Production and Resource Allocation in Eastern Europe: Performance, Problems, and Prospects', in Joint Economic Committee, Congress of the United States, *East European Economic Assessment* (Washington, DC).

—— (1989), 'East European GNP's, Domestic Final Uses of Gross Product, Rates of Growth, and International Comparisons', in Joint Economic Committee, Congress of the United States, *Pressures for Reform in the East European Economies* (Washington, DC).

Amaro, J. (1986), *Crianças Maltratadas, Negligenciadas ou Praticando a Mendicidade* (Lisbon, Centro de Estudos Judiciários).

Anda, R., D. Williamson, D. Jones, C. Macera, E. Eaker, A. Glassman, and J. Marks (1993), 'Depressed Effect, Hopelessness, and the Risk of Ischemic Heart Disease in a Cohort of US Adults', *Epidemiology*, 4/4.

Anderson, B. A., and B. D. Silver (1986), 'Infant Mortality in the Soviet Union: Regional Differences and Measurement Issues', *Population and Development Review*, 12/4: 705–38.

Anderson, H. R., J. D. Ramsey, and K. Bloor (1990), 'Trends in Deaths Associated with Abuse of Volatile Substances 1971–88', *St George's Hospital Medical School Report*, 3.

Andorka, R., and Z. Spéder (1994), 'Szegénység alakulása 1992 és 1994 között 90-es évek elején', in I. G. Tóth, *Társadalmi átalakulás 1992–1994: Jelenté a Magyar Háztartás Panel III. hullámának eredményeiröl* (Social Transformation: Report on the Results of the Third Wave of the Hungarian Household Panel) (Budapest).

Antonovsky, A., and J. Bernstein (1977), 'Social Class and Infant Mortality', *Social Science and Medicine*, 2.

Anuário Demográfico (various) (Lisbon, Instituto Nacional de Estatística).

Artoni, R., and E. Ranci Ortigosa (eds.) (1989), *La spesa pubblica per l'assistenza in Italia* (Milan, F. Angeli).

Atkinson, A. B. (1993), 'On Targeting Social Security: Theory and Western Experience with Family Benefits', *Welfare State Programme*, 99 (London, London School of Economics).

——and J. Micklewright (1990), 'Economic Transformation in Eastern Europe and the Distribution of Income', Paper prepared for the Conference on 'Economics for the New Europe', Oct. 1990.

Avraamova, E. (1994), 'Social and Demographic Dimensions of the Economic Transition: Impact on Families with Children', Paper presented at the international symposium, 'Social Policies during Economic Transition: Child Health, Basic Education and Social Protection', organized by UNICEF and the UN Dept. of Development Support and Managerial Services, Beijing, 18–21 July 1994.

Axelsson, C. (1992), 'Hemmafrun som försvann', *Discussion Series*, 20 (Stockholm, Institutet för social forskning).

Badelt, C. (1991), 'Austria: Family Work, Paid Employment, and Family Policy', in S. Kamerman and A. Kahn (eds.), *Child Care, Parental Leave, and the Under 3s* (Westport, Conn., Greenwood Publishing Group).

Bagatta, G. (1994), 'Le tipologie familiari al censimento del 1991. Valenze demografiche', Paper presented at the International Conference on Changes in Family Patterns in Western Countries, Bologna, 6–8 Oct. 1994.

Baglivo, A. (1980), *Il mercato dei bambini* (Milan, Feltrinelli).

Balcerzak-Paradowska, B., and B. Kolaczek (1994), 'State Policy on Family, Children and Youth', in ILSS, 'Social Policy and Social Conditions in Poland, 1989–1993', *Occasional Papers*, 4. (Warsaw, Institute of Labour and Social Studies), 43–68.

Baldwin, S. (1985), *The Costs of Caring* (New York, Routledge & Kegan Paul).

Ballestrero, V. (1979), *Dalla tutela alla parità* (Bologna, Il Mulino).

Barba Navaretti, G., and C. d'Agliano Galleani (1992), 'A Preliminary Survey of the Empirical Information on Adolescent Deviance in Industrialised Countries, 1970–90', Florence, UNICEF International Child Development Centre, Mimeo.

Barbagli, M., and C. Saraceno (1993), 'Padri e figli dopo la separazione', Paper presented at the Giornate di Demografia, Bologna, Dec. 1993.

Barbier, J. C. (1990), 'Comment Comparer les Politiques Familiales en Europe: Quelques Problemes de Methode', mimeo.

Barnett, W. (1993), 'Benefit-Cost Analysis of Preschool Education: Findings from a 25-Year Follow-Up', *American Journal of Orthopsychiatry*, 63/4: 500–8.

Barr, N. (1993), *The Economics of the Welfare State* (London, Weidenfeld & Nicolson).

——(ed.) (1994), *Labor Markets and Social Policy in Central and Eastern Europe. The Transition and Beyond* (New York, Oxford University Press).

Beale and Nethercott (1985), 'Job-loss and Family Morbidity: A Study of a Factory Closure', *Journal of the Royal College of General Practitioners*, 35: 510–14.

——(1989), 'The Nature of Unemployment Morbidity', *Journal of the Royal College of General Practitioners*, 38: 200–2.

Becker, G. S. (1981), *A Treatise on the Family* (Cambridge, Mass., Harvard University Press).

Beckerman, W., and T. Jenkinson (1986), 'What Stopped the Inflation? Unemployment or Commodity Prices?', *Economic Journal*, 96/381: 39–54.

Bee, H., M. Hammond, and S. Etres (1986), 'The Impact of Parental Life Changes on the Early Development of Children', *Research in Nursing Health*, 9.

Benini, R. (1990), 'The Soviet Union Facing Economic Crisis: The Search for a Policy of Economic and Financial Recovery', *Moct-Most*, 1: 11–37.

Bentivegna, S. (1988), 'Il sistema educativo-formativo', in Consiglio Nazionale dei Minori, *I minori in Italia* (Milan, Fr. Angeli), 176–225.

Bergson, A. (1984), 'Income Inequality under Soviet Socialism', *Journal of Economic Literature*, 22/3: 1052–99.

Berlinguer, G., L. Cecchini, and F. Terranova (1978), *Gli infortuni dei minori sul lavoro* (Rome, Il Pensiero Scientifico).

Bernabé, F. (1982), 'The Labour Market and Unemployment', in A. Boltho (ed.), *The European Economy: Growth and Crisis* (Oxford, Oxford University Press).

Besozzi, E. (1983), *Differenziazione culturale e socializzazione scolastica* (Milan, Vita e pensiero).

Betaniya Home (1988), *Shogaikoku ni okeru Hitori Oya Katei no Doko to Fukushi* (Trends in Social Welfare for Single-Parent Families in Selected Countries) (Tokyo, Betaniya Home).

Bialer, S. (1980), *Stalin's Successors: Leadership, Stability and Change in the Soviet Union* (Cambridge, Cambridge University Press).

Birth Statistics (various), Office of Population Censuses and Surveys (London, HMSO).

Bjorklund, A. (1992), 'Rising Female Labour Force Participation and the Distribution of Family Income: The Swedish Experience', *Acta Sociologica*, 35: 299–309.

Björnberg, U. (ed.) (1992), *European Parents in the 1990s: Contradictions and Comparisons* (New Brunswick, Transaction).

Blackburn, M., and D. Bloom (1994), 'Changes in the Structure of Family Income Inequality in the United States and Other Industrialized Nations During the 1980s', *Luxembourg Income Study Working Paper* 118, LIS at CEPS/INSTEAD (Nov. 1994).

Blank, R., and M. Hanratty (1993), 'Responding to Need: A Comparison of the Social Safety Net in Canada and the United States', in D. Card and R. Freeman (eds.), *Small Differences That Matter: Labor Markets and Income Maintenance in Canada and the United States* (Chicago, University of Chicago Press), 191–232.

Boeri, T. (1993), 'Labour Flows and the Persistence of Unemployment in CEE', in *Unemployment in Transition Countries: Transient or Persistent?* (Paris, Organisation for Economic Co-operation and Development).

——(1994), in OECD-CCET, *Unemployment in Transition Countries: Transient or Persistent?* (Paris, Centre for Cooperation with the Economies in Transition, Organisation for Economic Cooperation and Development).

Boje, T. P., and L. Drewes Nielsen (1994), 'Flexible Production, Employment and Gender', in T. P. Boje and S. E. Olsson Hort (eds.), *Scandinavia in a New Europe* (Oslo, Scandinavian University Press).

Bolin-Hort, P. (1989), *Work, Family and the State* (Lund, Sweden, Lund University Press).

Boltho, A. (1982a), 'Course and Causes of Collective Consumption Trends in the West', in R. C. O. Matthews and G. B. Stafford (eds.), *The Grants Economy and Collective Consumption* (London, Macmillan).

——(1982b), 'Growth', in A. Boltho (ed.), *The European Economy: Growth and Crisis* (Oxford, Oxford University Press).

——(1984), 'Economic Policy and Performance in Europe since the Second Oil Shock', in M. Emerson (ed.), *Europe's Stagflation* (Oxford, Clarendon Press).

——(1993), 'Western Europe's Economic Stagnation', *New Left Review*, 201: 60–75.

Bone, M., and H. Meltzer (1989), *The Prevalence of Disability Among Children* (London, HMSO).

Bradshaw, J. (1990), 'Child Poverty and Deprivation in the UK', *Innocenti Occasional Papers, Economic Policy Series*, 8 (Florence, UNICEF International Child Development Centre).

——(ed.) (1993), *Budget Standards for the UK* (Avebury, Gower).

——Ditch, J., H. Holmes, and P. Whiteford (1993), 'Support for Children: A Comparison of Arrangements in Fifteen Countries', *Dept. of Social Security, Research Report*, 21 (London HMSO).

——and H. Holmes (1989), *Living on the Edge: A Study of the Living Standards of Families on Benefit in Tyne and Wear* (Tyneside, Child Poverty Action Group).

——and J. Millar (1991), *Lone Parent Families in the UK* (London, HMSO).

——and J. Morgan (1987), *Budgeting on Benefit* (London, Family Policy Studies Centre).

Braithwaite, J. D., and T. E. Heleniak (1989), 'Social Welfare in the USSR: The Income Recipient Distribution', *CIR Staff Papers* (Washington, DC, Centre for International Research, Bureau of the Census, US Department of Commerce).

Brooks, K., J. L. Guasch, A. Braverman, and C. Csaki (1991), 'Agriculture and the Transition to the Market', *Journal of Economic Perspectives*, 5/4: 149–61.

Brooks-Gunn, J., P. Klebanov, and F. Liaw (1995), 'The Learning, Physical, and Emotional Environment of the Home in the Context of Poverty: The Infant Health and Development Program', *Children and Youth Services Review*, 17/1–2: 251–76.

Brown, J. (1994), *Children on Income Support* (London, Board for Social Responsibility).

Bruce, J. (ed.) (1995), *Families in Focus* (New York, Population Council).

Bruno, M. (1984), 'Stagflation in the EC Countries 1973–1981: A Cross-Sectional View', in M. Emerson (ed.), *Europe's Stagflation* (Oxford, Clarendon Press).

——(1986), 'Aggregate Supply and Demand Factors in OECD Unemployment: An Update', *Economica*, 53/10: S35–52.

——(1992), 'Stabilization and Reform in Eastern Europe: A Preliminary Evaluation', *IMF Staff Papers*, 39/3.

——and Sachs, J. (1985) *Economics of Worldwide Stagflation* (Cambridge, Mass., Harvard University Press).

Buhmann, B., L. Rainwater, G. Schmaus, and T. Smeeding (1988), 'Equivalence Scales, Well-Being Inequality and Poverty: Sensitivity Estimates Across Ten Countries Using the LIS Database', *Review of Income and Wealth*, 34: 115–42.

Bumpass, L. (1993), 'What's Happening to the Family? Interactions Between Demographers and Institutional Change', *Demography*, 27/4: 483–98.

Burghes, L. (1994), *Lone Parenthood and Family Disruption: The Outcomes for Children* (London, Family Policy Studies Centre).

Caldwell, J. (1979), 'Education as a Factor in Mortality Decline: An Examination of Nigerian Data', *Population Studies*, 33: 395–413.

Callan, T., B. Nolan, B. J. Whelan, D. F. Hannan, and S. Creighton (1989), *Poverty, Income and Welfare in Ireland* (Dublin, The Economic and Social Research Institute).

Campbell, F., and C. Ramey (1994), 'Effects of Early Intervention on Intellectual and Academic Achievement: A Follow-up Study of Children from Low-Income Families', *Child Development*, 65/2: 684–98.

Canceill, G., and A. Villeneuve (1990), 'Les inegalités de revenus: quasi status quo entre 1979 et 1984 pour les salariés et les inactifs', *Economie et statistique*, 230: 65–75.

Cancian, M., S. Danziger, and P. Gottschalk (1993a), 'The Changing Contributions of Men and Women to the Level and Distribution of Family Income, 1968–88', in D. B. Papadimitriou and E. N. Wolff (eds.), *Poverty and Prosperity in the USA in the Late Twentieth Century* (New York and London, Macmillan).

———————(1993b), 'Working Wives and Family Income Inequality Among Married Couples', in S. Danziger and P. Gottschalk (eds.), *Uneven Tides: Rising Inequality in America* (New York, Russell Sage).

——and R. Schoeni (1992), 'Wives' Earnings and the Level and Distribution of Household Income in Developed Countries', *Luxembourg Income Study Working Paper*, 84 (Luxembourg, Walferdange).

Card, D., and R. Freeman (eds.) (1993), *Small Differences that Matter* (Chicago, University of Chicago Press).

CARE-USA (1993), 'Pregnant Women's Nutrition in Moscow and Ekaterinburg Cities', Institute of Nutrition, Russia, mimeo.

Carmichael, C. L., A. J. Rugg-Gunn, and R. S. Ferrell (1989), 'The Relationship between Fluoridation, Social Class and Caries Experience in 5-Year-Old Children in Newcastle and Northumberland in 1987', *British Dental Journal*, 167/2.

Carnegie Corporation (1994), *Starting Points: Meeting the Needs of Our Youngest Children* (New York, Carnegie Corporation).

Carr Hill, R. (1986), 'Trends in Health', mimeo.

——(1988), 'Time Trends in Inequality in Health', *Journal of Biosocial Science*, 20: 265–73.

Carrilho, M. J., and J. Peixoto (1993), 'A Evoluçao Demografica em Portugal entre 1981 e 1992', *Estudios Demograficos*, 31.

Caselli, G., and V. Egidi (1989), 'La mortalità in Italia: evoluzione e problemi', in E. Sonnino (ed.), *Demografia e società in Italia* (Milan, Laterza), 149–88.

Cazzola, G. (1994), *Lo stato sociale tra crisi e riforme: il caso Italia* (Bologna, Il Mulino).

Censis (1985), *Il mercato del lavoro giovanile in provincia di Trento* (Rome, Censis).

——(1993), *Rapporto sulla situazione sociale del paese* (Milan, F. Angeli).

Central Statistical Office (1990), *Social Trends*, 20 (London, HMSO).

——(1994a), 'The Effects of Taxes and Benefits upon Household Income 1992', *Economic Trends*, 483: 101–430 (London, HMSO).

——(1994b), *Annual Abstract of Statistics* (London, HMSO).

——(1994c), *Social Focus on Children* (London, HMSO).

Chelimsky, E. (1984), 'Evaluation of the Special Supplemental Program for Women, Infants, and Children's (WIC'S) Effectiveness', *Children and Youth Services Review*, 61.

Cherlin, A. (ed.) (1988), *The Changing American Family and Public Policy* (Washington, DC, Urban Institute Press).

——Furstenberg Jr., F., and P. Chase-Lansdale (1991), 'Longitudinal Studies of Effects of Divorce on Children in Great Britain and the United States', *Science*, 252: 1386–9.

Children's Defense Fund (1989), *A Children's Defense Budget* (Washington, DC, Children's Defense Fund).

——(1994), *Wasting America's Future: Report on the Costs of Child Poverty* (Boston, Beacon Press).

Chilosi, A. (1994), 'Property and Management Privatization in Eastern European Transition: Economic Consequences of Alternative Privatization Processes', *EUI Working Paper*, RSC, 94/12 (Florence, European University Institute).

Chu, K., and G. Schwartz (1994), 'Output Decline and Government Expenditures in European Transition Countries' (Washington, DC, International Monetary Fund), mimeo.

CISEP (1994), *Social Exclusion in Portugal, Situations, Processes and Policies* (Lisbon, CISEP).

CNAF (1993), *Prestations Familiales: Recettes—Depenses—Beneficiaries* (Paris, Caisse Nationale des Allocations Familiales).

——(1994), *Recherches et Prévisions*, 36 (Paris, Caisse Nationale des Allocations Familiales).

CNR/IRP (1988), *Secondo Rapporto sulla situazione demografica italiana* (Rome, CNR/IRP).

Cochrane, J., and J. Brassard (1979), 'Child Development and Personal Social Networks', *Child Development*, 50: 601–16.

Cochrane, S. (1980), 'The Effects of Education on Health', *World Bank Staff Working Paper*, 405 (Washington, DC., World Bank).

Collins, J. (1989), 'Perinatal Epidemiology', *The Child's Doctor*, 7/1.

Colombino, U. 'Incomes, Prices and Households' Welfare in Italy, 1970–90', Unpublished paper prepared for UNICEF International Child Development Centre's project on child poverty, mimeo.

Commission on Social Justice (1994), *Social Justice: Strategies for Reversal* (London, Vintage Books).

Commissione di indagine sulla povertà e l'emarginazione (1996a), *La povertà in Italia. 1980–1994* (Rome, Presidenza del Consiglio dei Ministri).

—— (1996b), *La povertà in Italia. 1995* (Rome, Presidenza del Consiglio dei Ministri).

Commissione di Studio istituita presso la Presidenza del Consiglio dei Ministri (1985), *La Povertà in Italia* (Rome, Istituto Poligrafico dello Stato).

Committee on Visions for Future Social Welfare in an Aging Society (1994), 'Vision for Social Welfare in the 21st Century', (Tokyo, Committee on Visions for Future Social Welfare in an Ageing Society), mimeo.

Cónim, C., and M. J. Carrilho (1989), *Situação Demográfica e Perspectivas de Evolução: Portugal, 1960–2000* (Lisbon, Instituto de Estudos de Desenvolvimento).

Consiglio Nazionale dei Minori (1988), *I minori in Italia* (Milan, F. Angeli).

Consiglio Sanitario Nazionale (1993), *Relazione sullo stato nazionale del paese, 1990–91* (Rome, Consiglio Sanitario Nazionale).

Corrado, S. (1989), 'Alcune considerazioni sugli indici in campo scolastico', *Scuola Democratica*, Year 12.

Cook, J., and K. Martin (1995). 'Differences in Nutrient Adequacy Among Poor and Non-Poor Children' (Boston, Tufts University School of Nutrition).

Corcoran, M. (1995), 'Rags to Rags: Poverty and Mobility in the US', *Annual Review of Sociology*, 21.

Cornia, G. A. (1990), 'Child Poverty and Deprivation in Industrialized Countries: Recent Trends and Policy Options', *Innocenti Occasional Papers, Economic Policy Series*, 2 (Florence, UNICEF International Child Development Centre).

Cornia, G. A. (1994), 'Poverty in Latin America in the Eighties: Extent, Causes and Possible Remedies', *Giornale degli Economisti e Annali di Economia*, July-September 1994.

——with R. Paniccià (1995), 'The Demographic Impact of Sudden Impoverishment: Eastern Europe during the 1989–94 Transition', *Innocenti Occasional Papers, Economic Policy Series*, 49 (Florence, UNICEF International Child Development Centre).

——and S. Sipos (eds.) (1991), *Children and the Transition to the Market Economy: Safety Nets and Social Policies in Central and Eastern Europe* (Aldershot, Avebury).

——and F. Stewart (1993), 'Two Errors of Targeting', *Innocenti Occasional Papers, Economic Policy Series*, 36 (Florence, UNICEF International Child Development Centre).

Costa, A. B. da (1992), 'The Paradox of Poverty: Portugal 1980–89'. Ph.D. thesis, University of Bath.

——and M. Pimenta (eds.) (1991), *Minorias etnicas pobres em Lisboa* (Lisbon, CRC DEPS).

——M. Silva, J. Pereirinha, and M. Matos (1985), 'A Pobreza em Portugal', *Colecção Cáritas*, 6 (Lisbon, Cáritas Portuguesa).

Council of Europe (1993), *Recent Demographic Developments in Europe and North America 1992* (Strasbourg, Council of Europe).

CPAG (1989), 'Facts and Figures', *Poverty 74* (London, Child Poverty Action Group).

Craig, G., and C. Glendinning (1990), 'The Impact of Social Security Changes: The Views of Young People', Barnardo's Research and Development Section, mimeo.

Creighton, S. J. (1988), 'The Incidence of Child Abuse and Neglect', in K. Browne, C. Davies, and P. Stratton (eds.), *Early Prediction and Prevention of Child Abuse* (New York, Wiley).

CREL (1980), 'Cause, caratteristiche e conseguenze del lavoro minorile in alcune aree del Lazio e della Puglia', Mimeo.

Currie, J., and D. Thomas (1994), 'Does Head Start Make a Difference?', *Rand Corporation Working Paper* (Los Angeles, Rand Corporation, February).

D'Apice, C. (1981), *L'arcipelago dei consumi* (Bari, De Donato).

Dahlström, E., and R. Liljeström (1983), 'The Patriarchal Heritage and the Working-Class Women', *Acta Sociologica*, vol. 26, no. 1.

Damião, E. (1988), 'O Trabalho Infantil em Portugal', *Novos Desafios*, no. 2 (May-August).

Danziger, S. and P. Gottschalk (1985), 'The Poverty of Losing Ground', *Challenge*, pp. 32–8.

——— (1988/9), 'Increasing Inequality in the United States: What We Know and What We Don't', *Journal of Post-Keynesian Economics*, 2/2.

——— (eds.) (1993), *Uneven Tides: Rising Inequality in America* (New York, Russell Sage Foundation).

——— (1995), *America Unequal* (Cambridge, Mass., Harvard University Press).

——and M. Jantii (1995), 'The Market Economy, Welfare State, and the Economic Well-Being of Children: Evidence from Four Countries' (Michigan, University of Michigan), mimeo.

Danziger, S. K. (1995), 'Family Life and Teenage Pregnancy in the Inner-City: Experiences of African-American Youth', *Children and Youth Services Review*, 17/1–2: 183–202.

——and S. Danziger (1993), 'Child Poverty and Public Policy: Toward a Comprehensive Antipoverty Agenda', *Daedalus: America's Childhood*, 122/1: 57–84.

Davey-Smith, G., M. Bartley, and D. Blane (1990), 'The Black Report on Socioeconomic Inequalities in Health 10 Years On', *British Medical Journal*, 301: 373–7.

Davies, C. (1993), 'The Pharmaceutical Industry and Market in the USSR and its Successor States: From Reform to Fragmentation to Transition', *Scrip Reports* (United Kingdom, PJP Publications Ltd.).

Davis, C., and M. Feshbach (1980), 'Rising Infant Mortality in the USSR in the 1970's', *International Population Reports*, Series P-95, 74 (Washington, DC, Foreign Demographic Analysis Division, US Bureau of the Census).

Deacon, B. (ed.) (1992), *The New Eastern Europe: Social Policy Past, Present and Future* (Newbury Par, Calif., Sage Publications).

Dechter, A., and D. Smock (1994), 'The Fading Breadwinner's Role and the Economic Implications for Young Couples', Institute for Research on Poverty, DP 1051–94 (Madison, University of Wisconsin).

Dei, M. (1988), 'Lo sviluppo della scolarità femminile in Italia', *Polis*, 1: 143–60.

Dencik, L. (1989), 'Growing up in the Post-Modern Age: On the Child's Situation in the Modern Family and on the Position of the Family in the Welfare State', *Acta Sociologica*, 32/2.

Dept. of Employment (1989), 'Labour Force Outlook in the Year 2000', *Employment Gazette* (Apr.), 159–72.

D.o.H. (1989*a*), *Diets of British School Children* (London, HMSO).

——(1989*b*), *Personal Social Service Statistics* (London, HMSO).

——(1990), 'An Epidemiological Overview of Child Health' (Dept. of Health, London), mimeo.

DSS (1994), *Households Below Average Income: A Statistical Analysis 1979–1991/92* (London, HMSO).

DSS (various, annual), *Social Security Statistics* (London, HMSO).

Duch, R. M. (1993), 'Tolerating Economic Reform: Popular Support for Transition to a Free Market in the Former Soviet Union', *American Political Science Review*, 87/3.

Duncan, G. J., and W. Rodgers (1990), 'Lone-Parent Families and their Economic Problems: Transitory or Persistent', in OECD, 'Lone-Parent Families: The Economic Challenge', *OECD Social Policy Studies*, 8: 43–68 (Paris, Organisation for Economic Co-operation and Development).

——J. Brooks-Gunn, and P. Klebanov (1994), 'Economic Deprivation and Early Childhood Development', *Child Development*, 65/2: 296–318.

Eberstadt, N. (1989), 'Health and Mortality in Eastern Europe, 1965 to 1985', in Joint Economic Committee, Congress of the United States, *Pressures for Reform in the East European Economies* (Washington, DC).

EBRD (1994), *Transition Report* (London, European Bank for Reconstruction and Development).

Edgar, D., D. Keane, and P. Mcdonald (eds.) (1989), *Child Poverty* (Sydney, Allen & Unwin).

Edin, K. (1994), 'The Myths of Dependence and Self-Sufficiency: Women, Welfare and Low Wage Work', *WP* 67 (Rutgers, Center for Urban Policy Research).

Ekblad, S. (1993), 'Urban Stress and its Effects on Children's Lifestyles and Health in Industrialized Countries', *Innocenti Occasional Papers, Urban Children in Distress Series*, 6 (Florence, UNICEF International Child Development Centre).

Ellman, M. (1990), 'A Note on the Distribution of Income in the USSR under Gorbachev', *Soviet Studies*, 42.

——(1994), 'The Increase in Death and Disease under Katastroika', *Cambridge Journal of Economics*, 18/4.

Ellwood, D., and J. Crane (1990), 'Family Change Among Black Americans: What Do We Know?', *Journal of Economic Perspectives*, 4/4: 65–84.

——and L. Summers (1986), 'Poverty in America: Is Welfare the Answer or the Problem?', in S. Danziger and D. Weinberg (eds.), *Fighting Poverty: What Works and What Doesn't* (Cambridge, Mass., Harvard University Press), 79–105.

Equipo de Investigacion Sociologica (1984), 'Pobreza y Marginacion', *Revista de Estudios Sociales y de Sociologia Aplicada*.

Erikson, R. (1993), 'Descriptions of Inequality: The Swedish Approach to Welfare Research', in M. Nussbaum and A. Sen (eds.), *The Quality of Life* (Oxford, Clarendon Press).

——and J. Fritzell (1988), 'The Effects of the Social Welfare System in Sweden on the Well-being of Children and the Elderly', in J. Palmer, T. Smeeding, and B. B. Torrey, *The Vulnerable* (Washington, DC, Urban Institute Press).

——and J. O. Jonsson (1993), *Ursprung och utbildning—social snedrekrytering till högre studier* (Stockholm, Utbildningsdepartementet).

Esping-Anderson, G. (1991), *The Three Worlds of Welfare Capitalism* (Princeton, NJ, Princeton University Press).

Euler, M. (1988), 'Anmerkungen zur Einkommensverteilung und schicthung privater Haushalte', *Wirtschaft und Statistik*, 7: 488–98.

European Commission (1993), 'Recent Reforms in Social Protection Systems in the Community', in *Social Protection in Europe* (Brussels, Directorate General for Employment, Industrial Relations, and Social Affairs, 1993), 31–40.

European Statistical Office (1994), 'Labor Force Statistics, 1992' (Luxembourg, European Statistical Office).

European Union (1990), *Basic Statistics of the Community*, 29th edn. (Luxembourg).

——(1994), *EUROSTAT Social Protection Expenditure and Reports*, 1985–1988, 1980–1992 (Luxembourg).

Eurosocial Report, 36/4 (Vienna, European Centre for Social Welfare Policy and Research, 1990).

Eurosocial Report, 36/6 (Vienna, European Centre for Social Welfare Policy and Research, 1990).

EUROSTAT (1987), *Basic Statistics of the Community*, 24th edn. (Luxembourg, Office for Official Publications of the European Communities).

Eyer, J., and P. Sterling (1977), 'Stress-Related Mortality and Social Organization', *Review of Radical Political Economics*, 9/4.

Faccioli, F. (1988), 'Devianza e controllo istituzionale', in Consiglio Nazionale dei Minori, *I minori in Italia* (Milan, F. Angeli), 402–447.

Fajth, G. (1994), 'Family Support Policies in Transitional Economies: Challenges and Constraints', *Innocenti Occasional Papers, Economic Policy Series*, 43 (Florence, UNICEF International Child Development Centre).

Fallenbuchl, Z. M. (1981), 'The Polish Economy at the Beginning of the 1980's', in

Joint Economic Committee, Congress of the United States, *East European Economic Assessment* (Washington, DC).

Ferge, Zs. (1991), 'The Mechanisms of Social Integration: The Role of the Market', in K. J. Arrow (ed.), *Issues in Contemporary Economics*, 1 (London, Macmillan).

Feshbach, M. (1989), 'Demographic Trends in the Soviet Union: Serious Implications for the Soviet Military', *NATO Review*, 37/5: 11–15.

——and A. Friendly (1991), *Ecocide in the USSR* (New York, Basic Books).

Fiorini, F. (1981), *I sistemi educativi, problemi e metodi di analisi* (Turin, Loescher).

FiS (1989), *Narodnoe obrasovanie i kultura* (Moscow, Finansy i Statistika).

Franchi, G., B. Mapelli, and G. Librando (1987), *Donne e scuola* (Milan, F. Angeli).

Freguja, C. (1994), 'Consumi e ciclo di vita della famiglia', in Comitato Nazionale per l'anno internazionale della famiglia, *Per una politica familiare in Italia* (Rome, Presidenza del Consiglio dei Ministri, Ministero degli Affari Sociali).

Fritzell, J. (1992), 'Ojämlikhets- och fattigdomsutvecklingen under 1990-talet: Sverige i internationell belysning', in A. Björklund and J. Fritzell, *Inkomst-fördelningens utveckling. Bilaga 8 till 1992 års Långtidsutredning* (Stockholm, Finansdepartementet).

Furstenberg, F., Jr. (1995), 'Teenage Childbearing Reconsidered', Mimeo (Philadelphia, University of Pennsylvania).

——J. Brooks-Gunn and J. Morgan (1987), *Adolescent Mothers in Later Life* (New York, Cambridge University Press).

Garfinkel, I. (1988), 'The Evolution of Child Support Policy', *Focus*, 11/1 (Madison, Wis., Institute for Research on Poverty).

——(1992), *Assuring Child Support: An Extension of Social Security* (New York, Russell Sage Foundation).

——(1995), 'Economic Security for Children', in J. Hochschild, S. McLanahan, and I. Garfinkel (eds.), *Social Policies for Children* (Washington, DC: Brookings Institution).

Garfinkel, I., and S. McLanahan (1986), *Single Mothers and Their Children: A New American Dilemma* (Washington, DC, Urban Institute Press).

Gattullo, M. (1976), 'L'andamento della selezione scolastica in Italia', *Inchiesta*, 23.

——(1989), 'Scolarizzazione, selezione e classi sociali tra scuola secondaria superiore e università: le indagini speciali ISTAT', *Scuola e Città*, 1.

Gelb, A., and C. Gray (1991), *The Transformation of Economics in Central and Eastern Europe* (Washington, DC, World Bank).

General Household Survey (Office of Population Censuses and Surveys, London, HMSO).

Gerbeev, J. V. (1989), 'Profilaktika prestupnosti mezhdu molodyozhami', *Sovietskaya Pedagogika*, 7.

Ghiolla Phadraig, M. N. (1990), 'Childhood as a Social Phenomenon National Report Ireland', *Eurosocial Report* (Vienna, European Centre for Social Welfare Policy and Research).

GIOC (1986), *Tra lavoro e non lavoro* (Turin, Ed. Gruppo Abele).

GOA and UNICEF (1993), 'Children and Women of Albania: A Situation Analysis, 1993', Draft (Tirana, Government of Albania and UNICEF Tirana).

Gogodze, J., and T. Gogighsvili (1995), 'Public Policies and Social Conditions in Georgia', Paper presented at the third meeting of the MONEE Monitoring Project (Florence, UNICEF International Child Development Centre).

Gold, S. (1987), *State Tax Relief for the Poor* (Denver, National Conference of State Legislatures).

Goodman, A., and S. Webb (1994), *For Richer, For Poorer. The Changing Distribution of Income in the United Kingdom, 1961–91* (London, Institute for Fiscal Studies).

Gordon, M. S. (1988), *Social Security Policies in Industrial Countries: A Comparative Analysis* (Cambridge, Cambridge University Press).

Goskomstat (1990*a*), *Narodnoe khozyastvo SSSR v 1990* (Moscow, Finansy i Statistika).

——(1990*b*), *Molodezh SSSR* (Moscow, Finansy i Statistika, Goskomstat).

Gottschalk, P., and S. Danziger (1993), 'Family Structure, Family Size and Family Income: Accounting for Changes in the Economic Well-being of Children, 1968–1986', in S. Danziger and P. Gottschalk (eds.), *Uneven Tides: Rising Inequality in America* (New York, Russell Sage Foundation).

——B. Gustaffson, and E. Palmer (1994), 'What's Behind the Increase in Inequality?' (Boston College), mimeo.

——and T. Smeeding (1995), 'Cross-national Comparisons of Levels and Trends in Inequality' (Center for Advanced Study in the Behavioral Sciences and Boston College), mimeo.

Gould, A. (1988), *Conflict and Control in Welfare Policy: The Swedish Experience* (London and New York, Longman).

Graham, J. (1989), 'Families, Parenting Skills and Delinquency', *Home Office Research Bulletin*, 26.

Gueron, J., and E. Pauly (1991), *From Welfare to Work* (New York, Russell Sage Foundation).

Gukova, E. G. (1988), 'Vliyanyiye zhilishnih i materialnih faktorov na stabilnost molodih semey', *Sbornik 'Problemi populyacii'*.

Haas, L. (1992), *Equal Parenthood and Social Policy: A Study of Parental Leave in Sweden* (Albany, NY, State University of New York Press).

Halsey, A. H. (ed.) (1988), *British Social Trends since 1900: A Guide to the Changing Social Structure of Britain* (Cambridge, Macmillan Press).

Hanratty, M. (1994), 'Social Welfare Programs for Women and Children: The US versus France', in R. Blank (ed.), *Social Protection vs. Economic Flexibility* (Chicago, University of Chicago Press).

——and R. Blank (1992), 'Down and Out in North America: Recent Trends in Poverty Rates in the US and Canada', *Quarterly Journal of Economics*, 107: 233–254.

Hansard (1989) (London, HMSO, 8 May).

——(1990) (London, HMSO, 20 March).

Haskey, J. (1994), 'Stepfamilies and Stepchildren in Great Britain', *Population Trends*, 76 (London, HMSO).

Haub, C. (1994), 'Population Change in the Former Soviet Republics', *Population Bulletin*, 19/4 (Washington, DC, Population Reference Bureau, Inc.).

Hauser, R., and P. Semerau (1989), 'Trends in Poverty and Low Income with Federal Republic of Germany', Paper presented to the seminar on 'Poverty Statistics in the European Community', Nordwijk, the Netherlands.

Hausloher, P. (1987), 'Gorbachev's Social Contract', *Soviet Economy*, 3/1: 54–89.

Heinen, J. (1991), 'Da donne muratori a casalinghe: Politiche dell'occupazione e politiche sociali nella Polonia degli anni 1940–1960, in A. Del Re (ed.), *I rapporti sociali di sesso in Europa (1930–1960): l'impatto delle politiche sociali* (Padua, CEDAM), 91–112.

Hernes, H. M. (1987), *Welfare State and Women Power* (Oslo, Norwegian University Press).

Hertel, J. (1992), 'Einnahmen und Ausgaben privater Haushalte im Jahr 1988', *Wirtschaft und Statistik*, 9: 653–667.

Heston, A., and R. Summers (1991), 'The Penn World Table (March 5): An Expanded Set of International Comparisons, 1950–1988', *Quarterly Journal of Economics*, 106: 327–368 (May).

Hill, M. S., S. Augustyniak, G. Duncan, G. Gurin, P. Gurin, J. K. Liker, J. N. Morgan, and M. Ponza (1985), 'Motivation and Economic Mobility', *Research Report Series* of the Institute of Social Research (Ann Arbor, University of Michigan).

——and J. Sandfort (1995), 'Effects of Childhood Poverty on Productivity Later in Life: Implications for Public Policy', *Children and Youth Services Review*, 17/1–2: 91–126.

Hill, T. P. (1979), *Profits and Rates of Return* (Paris, Organisation for Economic Co-operation and Development).

Hirsl, M., J. Rusnok, and M. Fassmann (1995), 'Market Reforms and Social Welfare in the Czech Republic: A True Success Story?', *Innocenti Occasional Papers, Economic Policy Series*, 50 (Florence, UNICEF International Child Development Centre).

Hoem, B., and J. Hoem (1988), 'The Swedish Family: Aspects of Contemporary Development', *Journal of Family Issues*, 9.

Holtermann, S., and K. Clarke (1992), 'Parents, Employment Rights and Childcare', *EOC Research Discussion Series*, 4 (Manchester, EOC).

Hughes, D., *et al.* (1989), *The Health of America's Children* (Washington, DC, Children's Defense Fund).

Hultén, A., and D. Wasserman (1992), 'Suicide among Young People aged 10–29 in Sweden', *Scandinavian Journal of Social Medicine*, 2: 65–72.

Huston, A. (ed.) (1991), *Children in Poverty: Child Development and Public Policy* (New York, Cambridge University Press).

IASE (1989), *Acção Social Escolar em Números, 1980–1988* (Lisbon, Instituto de Apoio Sócio-Educativo).

ILEA (1990), 'Differences in Examination Performance'. Report of the Strategic Policy Sub-committee of the Education Committee, 19086 (London, Inner London Education Authority).

Illsley, R., and J. Le Grand (1987), 'The Measurement of Inequality in Health', in A. Williams (ed.), *Health and Economics* (Cambridge, Macmillan Press).

ILO (1988), The Cost of Social Security. Twelfth International Inquiry, 1981–1983. Comparative Tables (Geneva, International Labour Organisation).

INE (1990), *Censo* (Lisbon, Instituto Nacional de Estatística).

——(1992), *Statistical Yearbook of Portugal* (Lisbon, Instituto Nacional de Estatística).

Institute of Fiscal Studies (1990), 'Low Income Families 1979–1987', mimeo.

Institute of Medicine (1988), *Prenatal Care: Reaching Mothers, Reaching Infants* (Washington, DC, National Academy Press).

Interministerial Committee on the Development of a Better Environment for Children (1992), *Developing a Better Environment for Raising Children* (Tokyo).

International Criminal Police Organization (1990), *International Crime Statistics* (Saint-Cloud, France, International Criminal Police Organization).

ISTAT (1993), *Rapporto Annuale* (Rome, ISTAT).

——(1994), *Indagine Multiscopo sulle famiglie, 9: Il Mondo dei Bambini* (Rome, ISTAT).

Jallinoja, R. (1989), 'Women between the Family and Employment', in K. Boh, M. Bak, and C. Clason (eds.), *Changing Patterns of European Family Life: A Comparative Analysis of 14 European Countries* (London, Routledge), 95–112.

Japan Institute of Population Problems (1986), '1985 Population Projections for Japan' (Tokyo, Japan Institute of Population Problems), mimeo.

Japan Statistics Bureau (1990), *Final Report of the 1985 Population Census* (Tokyo, Management and Co-ordination Agency, Japan Statistics Bureau).

——(1991), *1990 Population Census of Japan*, 2 (Tokyo, Japan Statistics Bureau).

Jencks, C. (1992), *Rethinking Social Policy: Race, Poverty and the Underclass* (Cambridge, Mass., Harvard University Press).

Jenkins, S. (1995), 'Accounting for Inequality Trends: Decomposition Analyses for the United Kingdom, 1971–1986', *Economica*, 62: 29–63.

——and Cowell, F. (1994), 'Dwarfs and Giants in the 1980s: Trends in the UK Income Distribution', *Fiscal Studies*, 15/1: 99–118.

Jolly, R., and G. A. Cornia (eds.) (1984), *The Impact of World Recession on Children: A Study Prepared for UNICEF* (Oxford, Pergamon Press).

Jowell, R., L. Brook, G. Prior, and B. Taylor (1992), *The British Social Attitudes. The Ninth Report. Social and Community Planning Research* (Aldershot, Dartmouth).

Kahn, A., and S. Kamerman (1983), *Income Transfers for Families with Children: An Eight-Country Study* (Philadelphia, Temple University Press).

————(eds.) (1988), *Child Support: From Debt Collection to Social Policy* (Beverly Hills, Calif., Sage Publications).

Kalecki, M. (1971), *Selected Essays on the Dynamics of the Capitalist Economy* (Cambridge, Cambridge University Press).

Kalimo, R., and J. Vuori (1993), 'Unemployment and Health: Women's Resources and Coping', in K. Kauppinen Toropainen (ed.), *OECD Panel Group on Women, Work and Health, National Report: Finland* (Helsinki, Ministry of Social Affairs).

Kamerman, S., and A. Kahn (eds.) (1978), *Family Policy: Government and Families in Fourteen Countries* (New York, Columbia University Press).

————(1988), 'Social Policy and Children in the United States and Europe', in J. L. Palmer, T. Smeeding, and B. Boyle Torrey (eds.), *The Vulnerable* (Washington, DC., Urban Institute Press).

————(1989), 'Single-Parent, Female-Headed Families with Children in Western Europe: Social Change and Response', *International Social Security Review*, 1 (Geneva, International Social Security Association).

————(eds.) (1991), *Child Care, Parental Leave, and the Under 3s* (Westport, Conn., Greenwood Publishing Group).

————(1995), *Starting Right: How America Neglects Its Youngest Children and What Can We Do About It* (New York, Oxford University Press).

Keikakucho (1992), *Kokumin Seikatsu Senkodo Chosa* (Survey on People's Choices in Their Lives) (Tokyo).

Keizai Kikakucho (1994), *Keizai Hakusho* (White Paper on Economics) (Tokyo).

Kiernan, K., and V. Estaugh (1993), 'Cohabitation. Extra-marital Childbearing and Social Policy', *Occasional Paper*, 17 (London, Family Policy Studies Centre).

Kiernan, K., and M. Wicks (1990), *Family Change and Future Policy* (London, Family Policy Studies Centre, Joseph Rowntree Memorial Trust).

Klerman, L. (1991), *Alive and Well? A Research Review of Policies and Programs for Poor Young Children* (New York, National Center for Children in Poverty).

Knudsen, R. (1990), *Familieydelster i Norden 1989* (Stockholm, Norstedts Tryckeni).

Köhler, L., and G. Jakobsson (1987), *Children's Health and Well-being in the Nordic Countries* (Oxford, MacKeith).

Kolberg, J. E. (1992), *The Study of Welfare State Regimes* (New York, Sharpe).

Korenman, S., J. Miller, and J. Sjaastad (1995), 'Long-term Poverty and Child Development in the United States: Results from the NLSY', *Children and Youth Services Review*, 17/1–2: 127–155.

Kornai, J. (1986), *Contradictions and Dilemmas: Studies on the Socialist Economy and Society* (Cambridge, Mass., MIT Press).

Kornyak, V. (1994), 'Child Protection in Russia: UNICEF Report Material' (Florence: UNICEF International Child Development Centre. Ministry for Social Protection, Moscow), mimeo.

Kosei Tokei Kyokai (1988), *Kokumin no Fukushi no Doko 1988* (Trends in Social Welfare of the Japanese 1988) (Tokyo).

——(1993), *Kokumin no Fukushi no Doko 1993* (Trends in Social Welfare of the Japanese 1993) (Tokyo).

Koseisho (1991*a*), *Heisei 2-nen Jinko Dotai Kakuteisu* (Vital Statistics for the Year 1990) (Tokyo).

——(1991*b*), *Jido Kankyo Chosa* (Survey on Children's Environment) (Tokyo).

——(1991*c*), *Kokumin Seikatsu Doko Chosa* (Basic Survey on People's Living) (Tokyo).

——(1991*d*), *Nyuyoji Shintai Hatsuiku Chosa* (Survey on Physical Development of Pre-School Children) (Tokyo).

——(1992), *Kokumin Seikatsu Kiso Chosa* (Basic Survey on Living Conditions) (Tokyo).

——(1993*a*), *Dai Jukkai Shussei Doko Kihon Chose* (The 10th Survey on Trends in Child Births) (Tokyo).

——(1993*b*), *Kosei Hakusho 1993* (White Paper on Social Welfare) (Tokyo).

——(1993*c*), *Kokumin Seikatsu Kiso Chosa* (Basic Survey on Living Conditions) (Tokyo).

——(1993*d*), *Jinko Dotai Tokei 1992* (Trends in Demographic Shifts) (Tokyo).

——(1993*e*), *Shakai Fukushi Gyosei Gyomu Hokoku* (Administrative Report on Public Assistance) (Tokyo).

——(1994), *Heisei 5-nen Jinko Dotai Tokei* (Vital Statistics for the Year 1993), 1 (Tokyo).

——Daijin Kanbo Seisakuka (1990*a*), *Shakai Hosho Nyumon* (Introduction to Social Security) (Tokyo).

——Daijin Kanbo Seisakuka (1990*b*), *Shotoku Saibun Chosa* (Study on Income Redistribution) (Tokyo).

——Daijin Kanbo Tokei Johobu (1986), *Koseisho Gyosei Kiso Chosa* (Basic Survey on the Operation of the Ministry of Health and Welfare) (Tokyo).

Koseisho Daijin Kanbo Tokei Johobu (1993), *Jinko Dotai Tokei 1992* (Trends in Demographic Statistics 1992) (Tokyo).
——Jido Katei Kyoku (1988), *Jido Fukushi Ho* (The Child Welfare Law) (Tokyo, Jiji Tsushin Sha).
——Jinko Mondai Kenkyujo (1983), *Latest Demographic Statistics, 1989* (Tokyo).
——Jinko Mondai Kenkyujo (1987), *Shussei Doko Kihon Chosa* (Survey on Trends in Births) (Tokyo).
——Jinko Mondai Kenkyujo (1992), *Population Projections for Japan: 1991–2090* (Tokyo).
——Jinko Mondai Kenkyujo (1993), *Jinko Tokei Shiryoshu* (Statistical Abstracts of Demography) (Tokyo).
——Jinko Mondai Kenkyujo (1994), *Latest Demographic Statistics, 1994* (Tokyo).
Kovarik, J. (1988), 'Analytic Study of the Child Population in Czechoslovakia' (Prague), mimeo.
Kroupová, A. (1988), 'Perspectives of Czechoslovakia's Family Formation', in European Centre for Social Welfare Training and Research, *Seminar Report* (Gananoque, Ontario, European Centre for Social Welfare Training and Research), 137–142.
KSH (1991), *Magyar Statisztikai Évkönyv 1990* (Hungarian Statistical Yearbook 1990) (Budapest, Central Statistical Office).
Kumar, V. (1993), *Poverty and Inequality in the UK. The Effects on Children* (London, National Children's Bureau).
Kupa, M., and G. Fajth (1990), 'Incidence Study '90: The Hungarian Social Policy Systems and Distribution of Incomes of Households' (Budapest, Central Statistical Office and Ministry of Finance), mimeo.
La Fontaine, J. (1990), *Child Sexual Abuse* (Oxford, Polity Press).
Lampman, R. (1971), *Ends and Means of Reducing Income Poverty* (Chicago, Markham).
Landau and Nathan (1983), 'Discrimination in the Criminal Justice System', *British Journal of Criminology*, 23 (April).
Lane, D. (1990), *Soviet Society Under Perestroika* (New York, Routledge, Chapman & Hall).
Lapidus, G. (1983), 'Social Trends', in R. F. Byrnes (ed.), *After Brezhnev* (Bloomington, Ind., Indiana University Press), 186–249.
Lazutka, R., and Z. Sniukstiene (1995), 'Economic Transition in the Baltics: Independence, Market Reforms and Child Well-being in Lithuania', *Innocenti Occasional Papers, Economic Policy Series*, 53 (Florence, UNICEF International Child Development Centre).
Leather, S. (1992), 'Less Money, Less Choice: Poverty and Diet in the UK Today', in National Consumer Council, *Your Food: Whose Choice* (London, HMSO).
Leira, A. (1993), *Welfare State and Working Mothers* (Cambridge, Cambridge University Press).
Levine, H. (1982), 'Possible Causes of the Deterioration of Soviet Productivity Growth in the Period 1976–80', in Joint Economic Committee, Congress of the United States, *Soviet Economy in the 1980's: Problems and Prospects* (Washington, DC).
Libanova, E., and H. Paliy (1995), 'Public Policy and Social Conditions: Ukraine 1995' (Florence, UNICEF International Child Development Centre), mimeo.

Likhavov, A. (1987), *We Are All Responsible for Our Children* (Moscow, Novosti Press Agency).

Lindbeck, A. (1983), 'The Recent Slowdown of Productivity Growth', *Economic Journal*, 93/369: 13–14.

LIS Users Guide (1994), *Luxembourg Income Study Working Paper 7* (Luxembourg, Walferdange).

Lobstein, T. (1988), 'Poor Children and Cheap Calories', *Community Paediatric Group Newsletter*.

Lori, A., and F. Pagnanelli (1988), 'Mortalità generale e mortalità differenziale', in CNR/IRP, *Secondo Rapporto sulla situazione demografica italiana* (Rome, CNR/IRP).

Low Pay Unit (1994), 'Poor Britain', in *The New Review of the Low Pay Unit*, 29.

Lowy, A., P. Burton, and A. Briggs (1900), 'Increasing Suicide Rates in Young Adults', *British Medical Journal*, 300 (March).

Machin, S., and J. Waldfogel (1994), 'The Decline of the Male Breadwinner: Evidence on the Changing Shares of the Earnings of Husbands and Wives in Family Income in the United Kingdom' (London, University College), mimeo.

MacLean, M. (1990), 'Lone-Parent Families: Family Law and Income Transfers', in 'Lone-Parent Families: The Economic Challenge', *OECD Social Policy Studies*, 8 (Paris, Organisation for Economic Co-operation and Development).

MacLennan, E., J. Fitz, and J. Sullivan (1985), 'Working Children', *Low Pay Pamphlet*, 34 (London, Low Pay Unit).

McClure, G. M. G. (1988), 'Suicide in England and Wales', *Journal of Child Psychology and Psychiatry*, 29/3: 345–349.

McFate, K., R. Lawson, and W. J. Wilson (eds.) (1995), *Poverty, Inequality and the Future of Social Policy* (New York, Russell Sage Foundation).

——Smeeding, T., and L. Rainwater (1995), 'Markets and States: Poverty Trends and Transfer System Effectiveness in the 1980s', in K. McFate, R. Lawson, and W. J. Wilson (eds.), *Poverty, Inequality and the Future of Social Policy* (New York, Russell Sage Foundation), 29–66.

McLanahan, S., and L. Casper (1995), 'Growing Diversity and Inequality in the American Family', in R. Fanley (ed.), *State of the Union: America in the 1990's*, 2 (New York, Russell Sage Foundation), 1–45.

——and G. Sandefur (1994), *Growing Up with a Single Parent: What Hurts, What Helps* (Cambridge, Mass., Harvard University Press).

McLoyd, V. (1990), 'The Impact of Economic Hardship on Black Families and Children: Psychological Distress, Parenting, and Socioemotional Development', *Child Development*, 16: 311–346.

——Jayaratne, T., R. Ceballo, and J. Borquez (1994), 'Unemployment and Work Interruption among African American Single Mothers: Effects on Parenting and Adolescent Socioemotional Functioning', *Child Development*, 65/2: 562–589.

Maddison, A. (1989), *The World Economy in the 20th Century* (Paris, Organisation for Economic Co-operation and Development).

Mainichi Shinbunsha (1990), *Kazoku Keikaku Yoron Chosa* (Opinion Survey on Family Planning) (Tokyo).

Mare, R. (1995), 'Changes in Educational Attainment and School Enrollment', in R. Farley (ed.), *State of the Union: America in the 1990's*, 1 (New York, Russell Sage Foundation), 155–213.

Marer, P. (1981), 'Economic Performance and Prospects in Eastern Europe: Ana-
lytical Summary and Interpretation of Findings', in Joint Economic Committee,
Congress of the United States, *East European Economic Assessment* (Washington,
DC).

Mattioli, F. (1988a), 'Prevenzione e educazione nella tutela della salute', in
Consiglio Nazionale dei Minori, *I minori in Italia* (Milan, F. Angeli), 364–401.

——(1988b), 'Quale lavoro', in Consiglio Nazionale dei Minori, *I minori in Italia*
(Milan, F. Angeli), 315–363.

Maynard, R. (1995), 'Teenage Childbearing and Welfare Reform: Lessons from a
Decade of Demonstration and Evaluation Research', *Children and Youth Services
Review*, 17/1–2: 309–322.

Mazier, J., M. Basle, and V. -F. Vidal (1984), *Quand les crises durent . . .* (Paris,
Economica).

Mead, L. (1988), 'The Hidden Jobs Debate', *The Public Interest*, pp. 40–58.

——(1992), *The New Politics of Poverty: The Working Poor in America* (New York,
Basic Books).

Merkov, A. M. (1965), *Demograficheskaya statistika* (Moscow, Meditsina).

Metcalf, G. (1995), 'Value Added Taxation: An Idea Whose Time Has Come',
Journal of Economic Perspectives, 9/1: 121–140.

Meyer, C. (1994), 'Nordic State Feminism in the 1990s: Whose Ally?', in T. P. Boje
and S. E. Olsson Hort (eds.), *Scandinavia in a New Europe* (Oslo, Scandinavian
University Press).

Micklewright, J., and S. J. Jarvis (1995), 'Targeting of Family Allowance in
Hungary', in D. van de Walle and K. Nead (eds.), *Public Spending and the
Poor* (Baltimore and London, Johns Hopkins University Press for the World
Bank).

Milanovic, B. (1991), 'Poverty in Eastern Europe in the Years of Crisis, 1978 to 1987:
Poland, Hungary and Yugoslavia', *World Bank Economic Review*, 5/2: 187–202.

——(1992), 'Distributional Impact of Cash and In-Kind Transfers in Eastern
Europe and Russia. Research Project 'Social Expenditures and their Distribu-
tion Impact in Eastern Europe', Paper no. 9, Socialist Economic Reform Unit
(Washington, DC, World Bank).

Millar, J. (1989), *Poverty and the Lone-Parent Family: The Challenge to Social Policy*
(Avebury, Gower).

Mitchell, J. (1975), *European Historical Statistics* (London, Macmillan).

Moen, P. (1989), *Working Parents: Transformation in Gender Roles and Public Policies
in Sweden* (Madison, Wis., University of Wisconsin Press).

Monbusho (1992), *Gakko Kihon Chosa 1991* (Basic Survey on Schools 1991) (Tokyo).

——(1993a), *Juku Chosa* (Survey on Juku) (Tokyo).

——(1993b), *Gakko Hoken Tokei Chosa Hokokusho* (Health Statistics of School Children) (Tokyo).

——(1993c), *Gakko Kihon Chosa 1992* (Basic Survey on Schools 1992) (Tokyo).

——(1991), Kotokyoiku Kyoku, *Gakusei Seikatsu Chosa* (Survey on College Students' Life) (Tokyo).

Moriani, C. (1988), 'Redditi e consumi delle famiglie', in AIS/ISTAT, *Immagini
della società italiana* (Rome, AIS/ISTAT), 533–550.

Mortality Statistics (various) (Office of Population Censuses and Surveys, London,
HMSO).

Moser, Goldblatt, Fox, and Jones (1986), 'Unemployment and Mortality: Further Evidence from the OPCS Longitudinal Study 1971–1981', *Lancet*.

————————'Unemployment and Mortality: Comparison of the 1971 and 1981 Longitudinal Study Census Samples', *British Medical Journal*, 294, (Jan.): 86–90.

Moss, P., and E. Melhuish (1991), *Current Issues in Daycare for Young Children* (Thomas Coram Research Unit, London, HMSO).

Mroz, T. A., and B. M. Popkin (1994), 'Poverty and the Economic Transition in the Russian Federation', Carolina Population Center, University of North Carolina.

Murnane, R. (1988), 'Education and the Productivity of the Work Force: Looking Ahead', in R. Litan *et al.* (eds.), *American Living Standards: Threats and Challenges* (Washington, DC, Brookings Institution).

——(1994), 'Education and the Well-Being of the Next Generation', in S. Danziger, G. Sandefur, and D. Weinberg (eds.), *Confronting Poverty: Prescriptions for Change* (Cambridge, Mass., Harvard University Press), 289–307.

Murray, C. (1984), *Losing Ground* (New York, Basic Books).

Myrdal, A. (1941), *Nation and Family* (New York, Harper).

——and G. Myrdal (1934), *Kris i befolkningsfrågan* (Stockholm, Tiden).

MZO (1990), *Ochranyenyiye matyerskoy i zdarovi* (Moscow, Ministerstvo zdarovoochranyenyiye (Ministry of Health Care)).

NACRO (1989), 'Some Facts and Findings about Black People in the Criminal Justice System' *NACRO Briefing*.

Nakajima, M. (1989), 'Josei no Rodo to Chingin' (Women's Work and Wages), in M. N. Ozawa, Shozaburo Kimura, and Hideo Ibe (eds.), *Josei no Life cycle: Shotoku Hosho no Nichibei Hikaku* (Tokyo, University of Tokyo Press).

Nakamura, Y., Y. Kojima, and L. H. Thompson (1981), *Social Welfare and Related Services Glossary: English–Japanese Japanese–English* (Tokyo, Seishinsho Bo).

Näsman, E. (1993), 'Childhood as a Social Phenomenon. National Report. Sweden', *Eurosocial*, 36/15 (Vienna, European Centre for Social Welfare Policy and Research).

——(1994), 'Individualization and Institutionalization of Childhood in Today's Europe', in J. Qvortrup (ed.), *Childhood Matters—Social Theory, Practice and Politics* (Aldershot, Avebury).

National Committee on Children (1991), *Beyond Rhetoric: A New American Agenda for Children* (Washington, DC, National Committee on Children).

Nauck, B., and M. Joos (1995), 'East Joins West: Child Welfare and Market Reforms in the 'Special Case' of the Former GDR, *Innocenti Occasional Papers, Economic Policy Series*, 48 (Florence, UNICEF International Child Development Centre).

NCB (1987), *Investing in the Future: Child Health Ten Years after the Court Report* (London, National Children's Bureau).

NCH (1988), *Children in Danger: NCH Factfile about Children Today* (London, National Children's Home).

——(1990), *Children in Danger: NCH Factfile about Children Today* (London, National Children's Home).

Negri, N., G. Ortona, and W. Santagata (1986), 'Inflazione a misura di famiglia', *Politica e economia*, 17:5.

Nell, J., and K. Stewart (1994), 'Death in Transition: The Rise in the Death Rate in Russia since 1992', *Innocenti Occasional Papers, Economic Policy Series*, 45 (Florence, UNICEF International Child Development Centre).

Neményi, M. (1990), 'Family Policy and Early Child Care in Hungary' (Budapest, Institute of Sociology, Hungarian Academy of Sciences), mimeo.

NHK Hoso Bunka Kenkyujo, Yoron Chosabu (1989a), *Chugakusei/Kokosei no Seikatsu to Ishiki Chosa* (Survey on Living Conditions and Thoughts of Students in Junior and Senior High Schools) (Tokyo).

——(1989b), *Gendai Shogakusei no Seikatsu to Ninshiki* (Attitudes and Living Conditions of Elementary School Children) (Tokyo).

Nichols, M., and I. Shapiro (1995), *Unemployment Insurance Protection in 1994* (Washington, DC, Center on Budget and Policy Priorities).

Nihon Seishonen Kenkyujo (1991), *Kokosei Yuujin/Koibito Chosa* (Survey on High School Students' Relationships with Their Friends and Lovers) (Tokyo).

Novak, M. (1987), *The New Consensus on Family and Welfare* (Washington, DC, American Enterprise Institute for Public Policy Research).

Nuti, D. M. (1994), 'The Restoration of Proto-Capitalism in the Former Socialist Economies of Eastern and Central Europe' Paper presented at the seminar 'The World Economy in Transition', Rome, 6–8 Oct. 1994.

Nyström Peck, M. (1994), 'Childhood Class, Body Heights and Adult Health. Studies on the Relationship between Childhood, Social Class, Adult Height and Mortality in Adulthood', *Discussion Series*, 23 (Stockholm, Swedish Institute for Social Research).

Oda, M., K. Taniguchi, Wen Mei-Ling, and M. Higurashi (1989), 'Effects of High-rise Living on Physical and Mental Development of Children', *Journal of Human Ecology*, 18.

OECD (1976a), *Public Expenditure on Education* (Paris, Organisation for Economic Co-operation and Development).

——(1976b), *Public Expenditure on Income Maintenance Programmes* (Paris, Organisation for Economic Co-operation and Development).

——(1977), *Public Expenditure on Health* (Paris, Organisation for Economic Co-operation and Development).

——(1978), *The Tax/Benefit Position of Production Workers in OECD Member Countries* (Paris, Organisation for Economic Co-operation and Development).

——(1979), *Child and Family Demographic Developments in the OECD Countries* (Paris, Organisation for Economic Co-operation and Development).

——(1985), *Social Expenditures, 1960–1990* (Paris, Organisation for Economic Co-operation and Development).

——(1986), *The Tax/Benefit Position of Production Workers in OECD Member Countries, 1979–1984* (Paris, Organisation for Economic Co-operation and Development).

——(1988a), *The Future of Social Protection* (Paris, Organisation for Economic Co-operation and Development).

——(1988b), *OECD in Figures: Statistics on the Member Countries* (Paris, Organisation for Economic Co-operation and Development).

——(1989), *Economies in Transition* (Paris, Organisation for Economic Co-operation and Development).

——(1990), 'Lone-Parent Families: The Economic Challenge', *OECD Social Policy Studies*, 8 (Paris, Organisation for Economic Co-operation and Development).

——(1993), *The Tax/Benefit Position of Production Workers in OECD Member Countries, 1989–1992* (Paris, Organisation for Economic Co-operation and Development).

——(1994a), *Labor Force Statistics* (Paris, Organisation for Economic Co-operation and Development).

——(1994b), *New Orientations for Social Policy* (Paris, Organisation for Economic Co-operation and Development).

——(1994c), *The Jobs Study: Facts, Analysis and Strategy* (Paris, Organisation for Economic Co-operation and Development).

——(1995), *The OECD Jobs Study* (Paris, Organisation for Economic Co-operation and Development).

OECD Observer, various issues, including January 1984 (no. 126), 'The Future of Social Expenditures'; March 1985 (no. 133), Jeffrey Owens, 'Direct Tax Burdens: An International Comparison'; and inserts on 'The OECD Member Countries', annually.

Office of Population and Censuses. *Birth Statistics* (London, HMSO).

Ogishima, K. (1990), 'Kodomo to Shakai Hosho' (Children and Social Security), *Kodomo Katei Fukushi Joho*, pp. 35–38.

O'Higgins, M., and S. Jenkins (1989), 'Poverty in Europe Estimates for 1975, 1980 and 1988', Paper presented at the seminar on 'Poverty Statistics in the European Community', Nordwijk, The Netherlands.

O'Neill, J. E. (1994), 'The Shrinking Pay Gap', *Wall Street Journal*, A10.

Oldfield, N., and A. Yu (1993), *The Cost of a Child* (London, CPAG).

Olofsson, G. (1988), '"Den stränge fadern och den goda modern": sociologiska perspektiv på den moderna svenska staten', in U. Himmelstrand and L. Svensson (eds.), *Sverige: vardag och struktur* (Stockholm, Norstedts).

Olsson, S. E. (1986), 'Sweden', in P. Flora (ed.), *Growth to Limits: The Western European Welfare States since World War II*, iv (Berlin and New York, Aldine de Gruyter).

——(1993), *Social Policy and the Welfare State in Sweden*, 2nd edn. (Lund, Sweden, Arkiv).

——and Spånt, R. (1991), 'Children in the Welfare State: Current Problems and Prospects in Sweden', *Innocenti Occasional Papers, Economic Policies Series*, 22 (Florence, UNICEF International Child Development Centre).

Olsson Hort, S. E. (1993), 'What is Segregation, and Why is it Still an Issue in Sweden?', Paper presented at the OECD Conference on the City and Urban Renewal, European Foundation (Dublin), mimeo.

——(1997), 'Towards a Deresidualization of Swedish Child Welfare Policy and Practice', in N. Gilbert (ed.), *Combating Child Abuse: International Perspectives on Response Systems and Reporting* (Oxford, Oxford University Press), forthcoming.

——and McMurphy, S. (1997), 'Social Work in the Institutional Welfare State', in D. Elliott *et al.* (eds.), *International Handbook in Social Work Theory and Practice* (Greenwood Press, Westport, Conn.).

OPCS (1988), 'Occupational Mortality 1979–1980 and 1982–1983', *Childhood Supplement Series*, D5, 8. Office of Population Censuses and Surveys, vide Social Services Committee (1988*b*), para. 43 (London, HMSO).

Orosz, E. (1990), 'The Hungarian Country Profile: Inequalities in Health and Health Care in Hungary', *Social Science and Medicine*, 31/8: 847–57.

Östberg, V. (1991), 'Social Class Differences in Child Mortality: Sweden 1981–86', *Meddelande*, 3 (Stockholm, Swedish Institute for Social Research).

——(1994), 'Barns levnadsvillkor', in J. Fritzell and O. Lundberg (eds.), *Vardagens villkor* (Stockholm, Brombergs).

Paci, M. (ed.) (1981), *Famiglia e mercato del lavoro in una economia periferica* (Milan, F. Angeli).

Palmer, J., T. Smeeding, and B. B. Torrey (1988), *The Vulnerable* (Washington, DC, Urban Institute Press).

Palomba, F. (1984), 'Devianza minorile e risposta istituzionale', *A.A.V.V., Protagonista il minore: Adozione, devianza, lavoro* (Rome, Adn. Kronos).

Parker, S., S. Greer, and B. Zuckerman (1988), 'Double Jeopardy: The Impact of Poverty on Early Child Development', *Pediatric Clinics of North America*, 35/6: 1–14.

Pechman, J. A. (1990), 'Why We Should Stick With the Income Tax', *Brookings Review* (Washington, DC).

Pereirinha, J. (1988), 'Inequalities in Household Income Distribution and Development in Portugal', Ph.D thesis, The Hague, Institute of Social Studies.

Persson, I. (ed.) (1991), *Equality and the Welfare State* (Oslo, Scandinavian University Press).

Phillimore, P., A. Beattie, and P. Townsend (1994), 'The Widening Gap. Inequality of Health in Northern England, 1981–1991', *British Medical Journal*, 308: 1125–8.

Pinnelli, A. (1989), 'La sopravvivenza infantile', in E. Sonnino (ed.), *Demografia e società in Italia* (Rome, Editori Riuniti), 129–48.

Plano a Médio Prazo: 1977–80 (Lisbon, Imprensa Nacional-Casa de Moeda, 1977).

Platt, D., J. C. Martin, S. M. Hunt, and C. W. Lewis (1988), 'Damp Housing, Mould Growth and Symptomatic Health States', *British Medical Journal*, 298: 1673.

Ploug, N., and J. Kvist (eds.) (1994*a*), *Recent Trends in Cash Benefits in Europe* (Copenhagen, Danish National Institute of Social Research).

————(1994*b*), 'Recent Trends in Cash Benefits in Europe', *Social Security in Europe Report*, 4 (Copenhagen, Danish Institute of Social Research).

Pontusson, J. (1994), 'Sweden: After the Golden Age', in P. Anderson and P. Camiller (eds.), *Mapping the West European Left* (London, Verso).

Popenoe, D. (1988), *Disturbing the Nest* (New York, Aldine de Gruyter).

Population Trends (various) (London, HMSO).

Portes, R. (1980), 'Effects of the World Economic Crisis on the East European Economies', *World Economy*, 3/1: 13–52.

Preston, S. H., and S. Kono (1988), 'Trends in Well-being of Children and the Elderly in Japan', in J. L. Palmer, T. Smeeding, and B. Boyle Torrey (eds.), *The Vulnerable* (Washington, DC, Urban Institute Press), 277–307.

Pugliese, E. (1989), 'Jeunes et marchés du travail', in M. Maruani, E. Reynaud, and C. Romani (eds.), *La flexibilité en Italie* (Paris, MIRE, Syros).

——(1993), *Sociologia della disoccupazione* (Bologna, il Mulino).

Qvortrup, J. (ed.) (1994), *Childhood Matters—Social Theory, Practice and Politics* (Aldershot, Avebury).

Raczynski, D. (1988), 'Social Policy, Poverty, and Vulnerable Groups: Children in Chile', in G. A. Cornia, R. Jolly, and F. Stewart (eds.), *Adjustment with a Human Face: Ten Country Case Studies* (Oxford, Oxford University Press).

Rainwater, L. (1974), *What Money Buys* (New York, Basic Books).

——(1990), 'Poverty and Equivalence as Social Construction', Luxembourg Income Study Working Papers, 55 (Walferdange, Luxembourg).

——(1995), 'Poverty and the Income Package of Working Parents: The United States in Comparative Perspective', *Children and Youth Services Review*, 17/1–2: 11–41.

——M. Rein, and J. Schwartz (1987), *Income Packaging in the Welfare State* (Cambridge, Oxford University Press).

——and T. Smeeding (1995), 'Doing Poorly: The Real Income of American Children in a Comparative Perspective', Luxembourg Income Study Working Papers, 127 (Maxwell School of Citizenship and Public Affairs, Syracuse, New York).

Remenets, O. (1995), 'Annual Report by the Russian Goskomstat on the Eastern European Monitoring Report' (Florence, UNICEF International Child Development Centre), mimeo.

RFV (1995), *Socialförsäkringsfakta* (Stockholm, National Social Insurance Board).

Riazantsev, A., S. Sipos, and O. Labetsky (1992), 'Child Welfare and the Socialist Experiment: Social and Economic Trends in the USSR, 1960–90', *Innocenti Occasional Papers, Economic Policy Series*, 24 (Florence, UNICEF International Child Development Centre).

Ricolfi, L., and L. Sciolla (1980), *Senza padri né maestri* (Bari, De Donato).

Rodrigues, L., and B. Botting (1989), 'Recent Trends in Postneonatal Mortality in England', *Population Trends*, 55: 7–15.

Roll, J. (1992), *Lone Parent Families in the European Community*. A Report to the European Commission.

Rollet, C., and P. Bourdelais (1993), 'Infant Mortality in France, 1750–1950: Evaluation and Perspectives', in C. A. Corsini and P. P. Viazzo (eds.), *The Decline of Infant Mortality in Europe—1800–1950—Four National Case Studies* (Florence, UNICEF International Child Development Centre), 51–71.

Rose, R. (1994), 'Adaptation, Resilience and Destitution: Alternatives in the Ukraine', *Studies in Public Policy*, 204 (Glasgow, University of Strathclyde).

Rosenbaum, S. (1989), 'Recent Developments in Infant and Child Health: Health Status, Insurance Coverage, and Trends in Public Health Policy', in G. Miller (ed.), *Giving Children a Chance* (Washington, DC, Center for National Policy Press).

Ross, H. L., and I. V. Sawhill (1975), *Time of Transition: The Growth of Families Headed by Women* (Washington, DC, Urban Institute Press).

Rossi, N. (ed.) (1992), *La crescita ineguale: 1989–91. Primo rapporto CNEL sulla distribuzione e redistribuzione del reddito in Italia* (Bologna, Il Mulino).

——(ed.) (1994), *La transizione equa: 1992–1993. Secondo rapporto CNEL sulla distribuzione e redistribuzione del reddito in Italia* (Bologna, Il Mulino).

Roxborough, I. W., and J. C. Shapiro (1994), 'Employment Incentives of Taxes Based on the Average Wage', mimeo.

Rowe, J., M. Hundleby, and L. Garnett (1989), *Child Care Now* (London, Batsford).

Russian Economic Trends (1993), 'Sotsialnoe-Ekonomicheskoe Poloshenie Rossiiskou Federatsii' ('Socio-economic Report on the Russian Federation').

'The Russian Longitudinal Monitoring Survey Report on Economic Conditions in the Russian Federation, Round 1, July–Oct. 1992, and Round 3, July–Sept. 1993', (University of North Carolina at Chapel Hill, Goskomstat of Russia, Russian National Scientific Research Center of Preventive Medicine, World Bank, 1993), mimeo.

Rutkowska, I. (1991), 'Public Transfers in Socialist and Market Economies', *Research Paper Series*, 7 (Washington, DC, Socialist Economies Reform Unit, Country Economics Department, World Bank).

Sachs, J. (1983), 'Real Wages and Unemployment in the OECD Countries', *Brookings Papers on Economic Activity*, 1: 255–304.

Safilios-Rothschild, C. (1980), 'The Role of the Family: A Neglected Aspect of Poverty', *World Bank Staff Working Paper*, 403 (Washington, DC, World Bank).

Salonen, T. (1994), *Margins of Welfare* (Lund, Torna Hällestad Press).

Saraceno, C. (1988), *Sociologia della famiglia* (Bologna, Il Mulino).

——(1990), Child Poverty and Deprivation in Italy: 1950 to the Present', *Innocenti Occasional Papers, Economic Policy Series*, 6 (Florence, UNICEF International Child Development Centre).

——(1992), 'Trends in the Structure and Stability of the Family from 1950 to the Present: The Impact on Child Welfare', *Innocenti Occasional Papers, Economic Policy Series*, 27 (Florence, UNICEF International Child Development Centre).

——and N. Negri (1993), 'Updated National Report'. Report prepared for the EC Observatory on Policies to Combat Social Exclusion (Turin, 1993).

————(1994a), 'The Changing Italian Welfare State', *Journal of European Social Policy*, 4/1.

————(1994b), 'Locating Social Exclusion. National Report: Italy', Report prepared for the EC Observatory on Policies to Combat Social Exclusion (Turin).

Saunders, P. (1993), 'Married Women's Earnings and Family Income Inequality in the Eighties', *Australian Bulletin of Labour*, 19: 199–217.

Sawhill, I. (1988), 'Poverty and the Underclass', in I. Sawhill (ed.), *Challenge to Leadership* (Washington, DC, Urban Institute Press), 215–52.

Sawyer, M. (1976), 'Income Distribution in OECD Countries', *OECD Economic Outlook—Occasional Papers*, pp. 3–36 (Paris, Organisation for Economic Cooperation and Development).

——(1982), 'Income Distribution and the Welfare State', in A. Boltho (ed.), *The European Economy: Growth and Crisis* (Oxford, Oxford University Press).

SCB (1981), 'Om Barns Villkor', *Levnadsförhållanden Report*, 21 (Stockholm, Statistiska Centralbyrån).

——(1989), 'Barns levnadsvillkor', *Levnadsförhållanden Report*, 62 (Stockholm, Statistiska Centralbyrån).

——(1990), *Statistisk Årsbok 1991* (Stockholm, Statistisk Centralbyrån).

——(1994a), *Statistisk Årsbok 1995* (Stockholm, Statistiska Centralbyrån).

——(1994b), 'Socialbidrag under 1993', *Statistiska meddelanden*, S 33 SM 9402 (Stockholm, Statistiska centralbyrån).

Schizzerotto, A. (1975), 'I fenomeni selettivi nella scuola dell'obbligo', *Scuola e professione*, 3–4.

——(1988), 'Il ruolo dell'istruzione nei processi di mobilità sociale', *Polis*, 1: 83–124.

——(1989), 'Dinamiche temporali e territoriali nella scuola materna', *Polis*, 3: 533–58.

——(1990), 'Stabilità e mutamento nelle disuguaglianze educative collegate alla classe d'origine, al genere e all'appartenenza territoriale', *Scuola democratica*, 1.

Schorr, L. B. (1988), *Within Our Reach: Breaking the Cycle of Disadvantage* (New York, Doubleday).

SDF (Sovietsky Detsky Fond Imeni Lenina) (1990), *Polozheniye detey v SSSR 1990 god* (Moscow, Izdatelstvo Dom).

Segalen, M. (1981), *Sociologie de la famille* (Paris, Colin).

Seitz, V., and N. Apfel (1994), 'Effects of a School for Pregnant Students on the Incidence of Low-Birthweight Deliveries', *Child Development*, 65/2: 666–76.

Sen, A. (1985), *Commodities and Capabilities* (Amsterdam, North-Holland).

——(1992), *Inequality Reexamined* (Cambridge, Mass., Harvard University Press).

SEV (1981), *Statistitshesky ezhegodnik stran SEV 1981* (Statistical Yearbook of CMEA Countries, 1981) (Moscow, Finansy i Statistika).

——(1989), *Statistitshesky ezhegodnik stran SEV 1989* (Statistical Yearbook of CMEA Countries, 1989) (Moscow, Finansy i Statistika).

Sgritta, G. (1988), *La condizione dell'infanzia* (Milan, F. Angeli).

——(ed.) (1992), *La città dimenticata* (Rome, Istituto Poligrafico dello Stato).

Shapiro, J., and I. Roxburgh (1994), 'Employment-Retention Incentive Effect of the Russian Excess Wages Tax'.

Shatalin, S. S., *et al.* (1990), *Perehod k rinku. Koncepciya i Programma* (Moscow, Arhnngelskoye).

Sherman, A. (1994), *Wasting America's Future* (Boston, Beacon Press, for the Children's Defense Fund).

Silva, M. (1981), 'Emploi, besoins essentiels et industrialisation au Portugal', *World Employment Programme 2-32/Working Paper*, 29 (Geneva, International Labour Office).

——(1982), 'Crescimento Económico e Pobreza em Portugal (1950–74)', *Análise Social*, 18/72–74.

——(1984), 'Uma Estimativa da Pobreza em Portugal em Abril de 1974', *Revista de Ciências Sociais*, 1.

——(ed.) (1993), 'Crianças pobres em Lisboa: implicaçoes para a intervencao social' (Lisbon, DPS), mimeo.

——and A. B. da Costa (eds.) (1989), 'Pobreza Urbana em Portugal', *Colecção Cáritas*, 13 (Lisbon, Centro de Reflexão Cristã, Departamento de Pesquisa Social, Cáritas Portuguesa).

Sipos, S. (1991), 'Current and Structural Problems Affecting Children in Central and Eastern Europe', in G. A. Cornia and S. Sipos, *Children and the Transition to the Market Economy*: Safety Nets and Social Policies in Central and Eastern Europe (Aldershot, Avebury).

——(1992), 'Poverty Measurement in Central and Eastern Europe before the Transition to the Market Economy', *Innocenti Occasional Papers, Economic Policy Series*, 29 (Florence, UNICEF International Child Development Centre).

Smeeding, T. (1992), 'Why the U.S. Antipoverty System Doesn't Work Very Well', *Challenge*, 35: 30–35.

Smeeding, T. (ed.) (1995), 'Poor Children in Rich Countries', Mimeo (Center for Advanced Study in the Behavioral Sciences and Russell Sage Foundation).

——Boyle Torrey, B. and M. Rein (1988), 'Pattern of Income and Poverty: The Economic Status of Children and the Elderly in Eight Countries', in J. Palmer, T. Smeeding, and B. B. Torrey, *The Vulnerable* (Washington, DC, Urban Institute Press).

——O'Higgins, M., and L. Rainwater (1990), *Poverty, Inequality and the Distribution of Income in An International Context* (London, Wheatsheaf Books).

——Saunders, P., S. Jenkins, M. Wolfson, R. Hauser, J. Fritzell, and A. Hagenaars (1993), 'Poverty, Inequality and Family Living Standards Impacts Across Seven Nations. The Effect of Noncash Subsidies', *Review of Income and Wealth*, 39: 229–256.

Smith, J. P. (1989), 'Women, Mothers, and Work', in M. N. Ozawa (ed.), *Women's Life Cycle and Economic Insecurity: Problems and Proposals* (Westport, Conn., Greenwood Press), 42–70.

Smith, R. (1992), 'Without Work, All Life Goes Rotten', *British Medical Journal*, 305: 972.

Smolensky, E., S. Danziger, and P. Gottschalk (1988), 'The Declining Significance of Age in the United States: Trends in the Well-Being of Children and the Elderly since 1939', in J. Palmer, T. Smeeding, and B. Torrey (eds.), *The Vulnerable* (Washington, DC, Urban Institute Press), 24–54.

Social Services Committee (1988*a*), *Families on Low Income: Low Income Statistics*, Fourth Report, Session 1987–1988, HC 565 (London, HMSO).

——(1988*b*), *Perinatal, Neonatal and Infant Mortality*, First Report, Session 1988–1989, HC 54 (London, HMSO).

——(1989), *Social Security: Changes Implemented in April 1988*, Ninth Report, HC 437 (London, HMSO).

Social Development Research Institute (1992), *The Cost of Social Security in Japan, 1990* (Tokyo, Social Development Research Institute).

Socialdepartementet (1993), *Initial Report by Sweden on the Convention on the Rights of the Child* (Stockholm, Ministry of Health and Social Affairs).

——(1994), *National Program of Action for the Survival, Protection and Development of the Child* (Stockholm, Ministry of Health and Social Affairs).

Socialstyrelsen (1990), 'Abortförebyggande Program', Mimeo (Stockholm, Socialstyrelsen).

——(1994*a*), 'Barns villkor i förändringstider' (Stockholm, National Board of Health and Welfare).

——(1994*b*), 'Social Rapport 1994' (Stockholm, National Board of Health and Welfare).

Somucho (1979), *Jido no Jittai to ni Kansuru Kokusai Hikaku Chosa* (Survey on International Comparison in Living Conditions of Children) (Tokyo).

——(1988), *Shakai Seisaku Kihon Chosa* (Basic Survey on Social Conditions of the Population) (Tokyo).

——(1994), *Katei Chosa Hokoku* (Report of the Survey on Family Living) (Tokyo).

——(1986), Seishonen Taisaku Honbu, *Seishonen Hakusho 1986* (White Paper on Youth and Adolescents 1986) (Tokyo).

————(1988), *Shonen no Seikatsu Ishiki to Jittai ni Kansuru Chosa* (Survey on Children's Attitudes Toward Their Lives) (Tokyo).

————(1993), *Seishonen Hakusho 1992* (White Paper on Children and Adolescents) (Tokyo).

————(1990), *Seishonen no Yuujin Kankei ni Kansuru Kokusai Hikaku Chosa* (Survey on Peer Relationships among Adolescents: International Comparison) (Tokyo).

————(1990), Tokeikyoku, *Zenkoku Shohi Jittai Chosa, 1989* (The National Expenditure Survey, 1989) (Tokyo).

————(1993), *Rodokyoku Chosa Nenpo* (Annual Statistics on the Labor Force) (Tokyo).

Sonnino, E. (ed.) (1989), *Demografia e società in Italia* (Rome, Editori Riuniti).

Sorifu (1972), *Fujin ni Kansuru Yoron Chosa* (Opinion Survey on Women) (Tokyo).

——(1991), *Josei no Kurashi to Shigoto ni Kansuru Chosa* (Survey on Women and Work) (Tokyo).

——(1992), Koho Shitsu, *Chichioya no Ishiki ni Kansuru Yoron Chosa* (Survey on Parents' Thoughts about, and Plans for, Their Children) (Tokyo).

——(1993), Shakai Hosho Seido Shingikai Jimukyoku, *Shakai Hosho Tokei Nenpo 1993* (Statistical Abstracts of Social Security 1993) (Tokyo, Hoken).

Sorrentino, C. (1990), 'The Changing Family in International Perspective', *Monthly Labor Review* (Washington, DC, US Dept. of Labor).

SOU (1989), 'Statistikbilaga: omfattning av allegieröverkänslighet' *Report*, 78 (Stockholm, Socialdepartementet).

——(1990*a*), 'Långtidsutredningen', *Report*, 14 (Engl. ed. Medium Term Survey) (Stockholm, Finansdepartementet).

——(1990*b*), 'Välfärd och segregation i storstadsregionerna', *Report*, 20 (Stockholm, Storstadsutredningen).

——(1994), 'Förslag till ny socialtjänstlag', *Report*, 139 (Stockholm, Socialdepartementet).

——(1995), 'Långtidsutredningen', *Report*, 4 (Engl. ed. Medium Term Survey) (Stockholm, Finansdepartementet).

Sozialbericht (1990), (Bonn, Der Bundesminster für Arbeit und Sozialordnung).

Spånt, R. (1974), *Den svenska förmögenhetsfördelningen* (Stockholm, Prisma).

Stacey, J. (1994), 'Scents, Scholars and Stigma: The Revisionist Campaign for Family Values', *Social Text*.

Starfield, B. (1985), 'Motherhood and Apple Pie: The Effectiveness of Medical Care for Children', *Milbank Memorial Fund Quarterly*, 63/3.

——(1988), 'Child Health and Public Policy' Paper prepared for the Fae Gold Kass Lecture, Harvard University, Cambridge, Mass.

——(1994), 'Health Indicators for Preadolescent Children' (Baltimore, Johns Hopkins University School of Hygiene and Public Health).

Stein, A., E. Cambell, A. Day, K. McPhewrson, and P. J. Cooper (1987), 'Social Adversity, Low Birthweight, and Preterm Delivery', *British Medical Journal*, 295: 291–292.

Struk, P. (1990), 'On the Turn: The Current Situation of Czechoslovak Children' (Florence, UNICEF International Child Development Centre), mimeo.

Svallfors, S. (1994), 'Policy Regimes and Attitudes to Inequality: A Comparison of

Three European Nations', in T. P. Boje and S. E. Olsson Hort (eds.), *Scandinavia in a New Europe* (Oslo, Scandinavian University Press).

Sweden (1995), *The Swedish Budget 1995/96* (Stockholm, Ministry of Finance).

Szalai, J. (1989), 'Poverty in Hungary during the Period of Economic Crisis' (Budapest), mimeo.

——(1992), 'Social Policy and Child Poverty: Hungary since 1945', *Innocenti Occasional Papers, Economic Policy Series*, 32 (Florence, UNICEF International Child Development Centre).

Tagliaferri, T., S. Albertini, and M. Guiducci (1980), 'Il lavoro minorile in Italia', *Quaderni di Economia e lavoro.*

Tåhlin, M. (1987), 'Leisure time and Recreation', in R. Erikson and R. Åberg (eds.), *Welfare in Transition* (Oxford, Clarendon Press).

TARKI (1995), *A családi pótlék jövedelemtöl függö kiegészitészítésének tapasztalatai 1994-ben, elörejelzés 1995-re* (Budapest, Társadalomkutatási Informatikai Egyesülés).

Tarling, R. (1982), 'Unemployment and Crime', *Home Office Research Bulletin*, 14 (London).

Tarschys, D. (1993), 'The Success of a Failure: Gorbachev's Alcohol Policy, 1985–88', *Europe-Asia Studies*, 45/1.

Teekens, R. (1989), 'Inequality and Poverty: Portugal Compared with Greece, Ireland and Spain', *Estudos de Economia*, 10/2.

Tham, H. (1994), 'Ökar marginaliseringen i Sverige?', in J. Fritzell and O. Lundberg (eds.), *Vardagens villkor* (Stockholm, Brombergs).

Tokyo-to Shakai Fukushi Kyogikai, Boshi Fukushi Bukai (1985), *Kazoku Katei Kino no Henka ni Taigo suru tame no Boshiryo Kino ni Kansuru Kenkyu* (Research on Functions of Residential Facilities to Meet the Changing Needs of Families in Selected Countries) (Tokyo, Tokyo-to Shakai Fukushi Kyogikai, Boshi Fukushibu).

Townsend, P., and M. Davidson (1982), *Inequalities in Health: The Black Report* (Harmondsworth, Penguin).

——Phillimore, P., and A. Beattie (1988) *Health and Deprivation: Inequality in the North* (Dover, NH, Croom Helm Ltd).

Trigilia, C. (1992), *Sviluppo senza autonomia* (Bologna, Il Mulino).

Trost, J. (1985), 'Cohabitation in the Nordic Countries', in B. C. Miller and D. H. Olson (eds.), *Family Studies Review Yearbook*, 3 (Beverly Hills, Sage Publications), 590–615.

United Nations (1980), *The Economic Role of Women in the ECE Region* (New York, United Nations).

——(1982), *Levels and Trends of Mortality since 1950* (New York, United Nations).

——(1988), *National Accounts Statistics: Analysis of Main Aggregates*, 1985 (New York, United Nations).

——(1989), 'World Population Prospects, 1988', *Population Studies*, 106 (New York, Department of International Economic and Social Affairs, United Nations).

——(1991), 'World Population Prospects 1990', *Population Studies*, 120 (New York, Department of International Economic and Social Affairs, United Nations).

——(1992), *UN World Statistics in Brief* (New York, United Nations).

——(1993), *World Population Prospects: The 1992 Revision* (New York, Department of Economic and Social Information and Policy Analysis, United Nations).

——(1995), *Demographic Yearbook 1993* (New York, United Nations).

UNECE (1967), *Incomes in Postwar Europe: A Study of Policies, Growth and Distribution* (Geneva, UN Economic Commission for Europe).

——(1990), *Economic Survey of Europe in 1989–1990* (New York, United Nations Economic Commission for Europe).

——(1994), *Economic Bulletin for Europe*, 46 (New York, United Nations Economic Commission for Europe).

Unemployment Unit (various), *Unemployment Unit Review*.

UNESCO (1982), *Statistical Yearbook 1982* (Paris, UNESCO).

——(1987), *Statistical Yearbook 1987* (Paris, UNESCO).

——(1990), *Statistical Yearbook 1990* (Paris, UNESCO).

UNICEF, (1991), *The State of the World's Children, 1992* (New York, Oxford University Press).

——(1992), *Bulgaria's Children and Families: A Nationwide Situation Analysis* (Sofia, UNICEF).

——(1993), *The Situation of Child and Family in Romania* (Bucharest, UNICEF Romania and the National Committee for Child Protection, Romanian Government).

UNICEF ICDC (1993), 'Public Policy and Social Conditions', Economies in Transition Studies, *Regional Monitoring Report*, 1 (Florence, UNICEF International Child Development Centre).

——(1994), 'Crisis in Mortality, Health and Nutrition', Economies in Transition Studies, *Regional Monitoring Report*, 2 (Florence, UNICEF International Child Development Centre).

——(1995), 'Poverty, Children and Social Policy: Responses for a Brighter Future', Economies in Transition Studies, *Regional Monitoring Report*, 3 (Florence, UNICEF International Child Development Centre).

US Bureau of the Census (1990a), *Statistical Abstract of the United States* (Washington, DC, US Dept. of Commerce, Bureau of the Census).

——(1990b), 'Children's Well-being: An International Comparison', *International Population Reports Series*, P-95, 80 (Washington, DC, US Dept. of Commerce, Bureau of the Census).

——(1992a), *Statistical Abstract of the United States* (Washington, DC, US Dept. of Commerce, Bureau of the Census).

——(1992b), 'Measuring the Effects of Benefits and Taxes on Income and Poverty: 1979 to 1991', *Current Population Reports*, Series P-60, 182-RD (Washington, DC, US Government Printing Office).

——(1993), 'Money Income of Households and Persons in the United States: 1992', *Current Population Reports*, Series B-60, 184 (Washington, US Government Printing Office).

US Congress (1981), *East European Economic Assessment* (Joint Economic Cttee., Washington, DC).

——(1989), *Pressures for Reform in the East European Economies* (Joint Economic Cttee., Washington, DC).

US Council of Economic Advisers (1995), *Economic Report of the President, 1995* (Washington, DC, US Government Printing Office).

US House of Representatives, Committee on Ways and Means (1985), *Children in Poverty* (Washington, DC, US Government Printing Office).

——(1990a), Committee on Ways and Means, *Background Material and Data on Programs Within the Jurisdiction of the Committee on Ways and Means* (Washington, DC, US Government Printing Office).

US House of Representatives, (1990b), Committee on Ways and Means, *Tax Progressivity and Income Distribution* (Washington, DC, US Government Printing Office).

——(1993), Committee on Ways and Means, *Overview of Entitlement Programs: 1993 Green Book* (Washington, DC, US Government Printing Office).

——(1994), Committee on Ways and Means, *Overview of Entitlement Programs: 1994 Green Book* (Washington, DC, US Government Printing Office).

Vågerö, D., and V. Östberg (1989), 'Mortality among Children and Young Persons in Sweden in Relation to Childhood Socioeconomic Group', *Journal of Epidemiology and Community Health*, 43/3.

Van Rijckeghem, C. (1994), 'Price Liberalization, the Social Safety Nets and Income Distribution and Poverty, 1990–93: Appendix I' (Washington, DC, International Monetary Fund), mimeo.

Varley, R. (1986), 'The Government Household Transfer Data Base, 1960–1984', *OECD Department of Economics and Statistics Working Papers*, 36.

Vaughan-Whitehead, D. (1993), 'Minimum Wage in Central and Eastern Europe: Slippage of the Anchor', *ILO-CEET Reports*, 7 (Budapest, Central and Eastern European Team, International Labour Organisation).

Vennemo, I. (1994), 'Sharing the Costs of Children. Studies in the Development of Family Support in OECD Countries', *Discussion Series*, 25 (Stockholm, Swedish Institute for Social Research).

Vittori, G., A. Piazzi, and R. Jovine (1987), *Mortalità neonatale in Italia: studio sul peso alla nascita e nell'età gestazionale* (Rome, Istituto Italiano di medicina sociale).

Vogel, J., L. G. Andersson, U. Davidsson, and L. Häll (1988), 'Inequality in Sweden: Trends and the Current Situation. Living Conditions 1975–1985', *Report*, 58 (Stockholm, Statistics Sweden).

Wallich, C. (1992), 'Fiscal Decentralization: Intergovernmental Relations in Russia', *Studies of Economies in Transformation*, 6 (Washington, DC, World Bank).

Wegren, S. K. (1991), 'The Social Contract Reconsidered: Peasant-State Relations in the USSR', *Soviet Geography*, 32: 653–682.

Wennemo, I. (1994), 'Sharing the Costs of Children', *Studies on the Development of Family Support in the OECD Countries*, 25 (Stockholm, Swedish Institute for Social Research, University of Stockholm).

Whitehead, M. (1988), *The Health Divide* (Harmondsworth, Penguin).

Wilkinson, R. (1994), *Unfair Shares. The Effects of Widening Income Differences on the Welfare of the Young* (Essex, Barnardos).

Willis, C. F. (1983), *The Use Effectiveness and Impact of Police Stop and Search Powers* (London, Home Office Research Unit).

Wilson, W. J. (1987), *The Truly Disadvantaged* (Chicago, University of Chicago Press).

——(1995), *Jobless Ghettos: The Disappearance of Work and its Effect on Urban Life* (New York, Knopf).

Wise, P., and A. Meyers (1988), 'Poverty and Child Health', *The Pediatric Clinics of North America*, 35/6.

——Kotelchuck, M., M. Wilson, and M. Mills (1985), 'Racial and Socioeconomic Disparities in Childhood Mortality in Boston', *New England Journal of Medicine*, 313: 360–366.

Wolekowa, H. (1995), 'Public Policy and Social Conditions. Monitoring the Transition: Policy Changes in the Slovak Republic' (Florence, UNICEF International Child Development Centre), mimeo.

Wolfe, A. (1989), *Whose Keeper? Social Science and Moral Obligations* (Berkeley and Los Angeles, University of California Press).

Wolfe, B. (1990), 'Is There Economic Discrimination Against Children?', *Discussion Paper*, 904–900 (Madison, Wisc., Institute for Research on Poverty).

——(1994), 'Reform of Health Care for the Nonelderly Poor', pp. 253–88 in S. Danziger, G. Sandefur, and D. Weinberg (eds.), *Confronting Poverty: Prescriptions for Change* (Cambridge, Mass, Harvard University Press).

Wolfson, M. (1989), 'Canada's Low Income Cut-offs (LICOs) Problems and Prospects', Paper presented to the seminar on 'Poverty Statistics in the European Community, Nordwijk, The Netherlands.

Wood, A. (1994), *North South Trade, Employment and Inequality: Changing Fortunes in a Skill-driven World* (Oxford, Clarendon).

Woodroffe, C., M. Glickman, M. Barker, and C. Power (1993), *Children, Teenagers and Health. The Key Data* (Buckingham, Oxford University Press).

World Bank (1994), *World Tables 1994* (Washington, DC, World Bank).

World Health Organization (1993), 'Towards a Healthy Russia. Policy for Health Promotion and Disease Prevention. Focus on Noncommunicable Diseases', Draft Report, provided by WHO Regional. Office, Copenhagen.

Wynnyczuk, I. V. (1986), 'Recent Changes of the Population Development in Europe, (Prague), mimeo.

Yim, R., I. Garfinkel, and D. Meyer (1994), 'Interaction Effects of a Child Tax Credit, National Health Insurance, and Assured Child Support', Institute for Research on Parenting, DP 1047–194 (Madison, Wisc., University of Wisconsin).

Yomiuri Shinbun, 31 July 1994.

Yuki, T., Z. Sato, and K. Hashiseko (1990), *Gakushu Juku: Kodomo, Oya, Kyoshi wa Do Miteiruka* (Juku: How Are Children, Parents, and Teachers Looking At It?) (Tokyo, Gyosei).

Zafír, M. (ed.) (1991), *Létminimum 1989–1991* (The Subsistence Minimum, 1989–1991) (Budapest, Központi Statisztikai Hivatal).

ZG TPD (1990), 'Evaluation of the Current Situation of Children in Poland I', (Florence, UNICEF International Child Development Centre), mimeo.

Zimakova, T. (1991), 'Social Policy in Central and Eastern Europe from the 1950s to the Mid-1970s' (Ann Arbor, Mich., Population Studies Centre, University of Michigan), mimeo.

——(1993), 'Social Policy in Central and Eastern Europe: From Socialism to Market, 1960–92, Part II, 1990–92', Unpublished report (Florence, UNICEF International Child Development Centre).

——(1994), 'A Fragile Inheritance: Family Policy in a Changing Eastern Europe', *Research Report*, 94–311 (Ann Arbor, Mich., Population Studies Centre, University of Michigan).

Zoteev, G. N. (1991), 'The National Product and Income in the Soviet Economic System', *Moct-Most*, 1: 61–76.

INDEX